STUDIO AND CAMCORDER TELEVISION PRODUCTION

Peter Utz

Prentice Hall PTR
Upper Saddle River, New Jersey 07458
http://www.phptr.com

ISBN 0-13-632753-2

90000

9 780136 327530

39981917

Library of Congress Cataloging-in-Publication Data

Utz, Peter.
    Studio and camcorder television production / Peter Utz.
       p.   cm.
    Includes index.
    ISBN 0–13–632753–2
     1. Television--Handbooks, manuals, etc.   2. Video recording-
-Handbooks, manuals, etc.   3. Television--Production and direction-
-Handbooks, manuals, etc.   4. Camcorders--Handbooks, manuals, etc.
I. Title.
TK6642.U87   1999
778.59—dc21
                                         98–46574
                                           CIP

Acquisitions editor: Bernard M. Goodwin
Cover designer: Anthony Gemmellaro
Cover design director: Jerry Votta
Manufacturing manager: Alan Fischer
Marketing manager: Lisa Kanzelmann
Compositor/Production services: Pine Tree Composition, Inc.

Prentice Hall books are widely used by corporations and
government agencies for training, marketing, and resale.

The publisher offers discounts on this book when ordered in
bulk quantities. For more information contact:

     Corporate Sales Department
     Phone: 800-382-3419
     Fax: 201-236-7141
     E-mail: corpsales@prenhall.com

     Or write:

     Prentice Hall PTR
     Corp. Sales Dept.
     One Lake Street
     Upper Saddle River, New Jersey 07458

Printed in the United States of America
10 9 8 7 6 5 4 3 2 1

ISBN: 0-13-632753-2

PRENTICE-HALL INTERNATIONAL (UK) LIMITED, *LONDON*
PRENTICE-HALL OF AUSTRALIA PTY. LIMITED, *SYDNEY*
PRENTICE-HALL CANADA INC., *TORONTO*
PRENTICE-HALL HISPANOAMERICANA, S.A., *MEXICO*
PRENTICE-HALL OF INDIA PRIVATE LIMITED, *NEW DELHI*
PRENTICE-HALL OF JAPAN, INC., *TOKYO*
PEARSON EDUCATION ASIA PTE. LTD., *SINGAPORE*
EDITORA PRENTICE-HALL DO BRASIL, LTDA., *RIO DE JANEIRO*

CONTENTS

PREFACE

Studio and Camcorder Television Production is designed to teach the fundamentals of how to

- Operate studio and portable television equipment.
- Apply aesthetic principles to create effective and appealing imagery and sound.
- Planm, script, and organize a TV production.
- Function as a valuable TV production team member.
- Lead others as you direct the production of a TV program.

In the process, you'll get to play with some neat toys (the secret reason why most people are attracted to this field).

WHO SHOULD READ THIS BOOK

This book is designed specifically for students taking their first courses in TV production, either on a college or high school level. It assumes that students will have access to a TV studio and some portable TV equipment on which to hone their skills.

KINDS OF TV PRODUCTION

There is broadcast TV production, performed by the networks in big studios with big budgets and lots of staff. At the other end of the spectrum, there are independent videographers, individuals using $10,000 worth of equipment, who make their living shooting weddings, cable TV ads, and other events. In between, there are industrial video production shops with a staff of maybe four, using $300,000 worth of equipment and running a small studio. Most colleges are equipped this way.

As different as these three categories may seem, they share the same *fundamentals*. Creative approach, attention to preproduction planning, attractive camera angles, clear, crisp sound, and mastery of the technical devices are the foundation of all three kinds of enterprises.

This book attempts to cover all three areas, but it mostly focuses on the middle industrial area for these reasons:

- That area has the kind of equipment and setting most schools have to offer their students.
- That area offers most of the job opportunities.

Still, since we're dealing with *fundamentals,* anything you learn can be applied directly to all situations, from desktop video destined for the Internet up to commercial network broadcasting.

APPROACH

A course in TV production generally works this way: The class stampedes into the TV studio, and each member is assigned a duty as the class produces a simple TV show. Afterward, everyone rotates duties and another TV show is undertaken. And so it goes until everyone has tried everything. The tapes are then played back to demonstrate that

1. TV production is a complex and difficult endeavor.
2. Everyone starts out being dreadful at it.
3. Laughter and camaraderie are an inevitable and essential by-product of TV production.

As the course progresses, each device and technique is studied in more detail. The shows get better. More complex shows are attempted. Additional skills such as field production and scripting are introduced. Eventually, each student is given his/her own show to produce, using the other students as the crew.

This book aims to prepare the reader for this moment of truth, when creativity, planning, organization, teamwork, leadership, and technical skill all come together to spawn an engaging, well produced show.

HOW THIS BOOK WILL HELP YOU LEARN

The author is an educator first and a TV producer second. I'll be using every trick in the book to help you remember what you've learned. Some tricks:

- *We start simply and build slowly.* You exult in the triumph of simple successes before you dive headlong into the complexities and nuances of a subject. You need no previous knowledge of TV to understand this book. You don't need to be mechanically inclined. You need only a moderate reading level (I won't snow you with long words).
- As you progress through a chapter, minireviews of the key points will help you remember what's most important.
- *Technical words* that are commonly used in the profession and should be learned *will appear in* SMALL CAPITALS so that they'll stand out.
- *Small, manageable groups of technical words* to be learned will appear amid chapters, near where they are used. Some words are more important than others. Those of crucial importance that should especially be learned will be preceded by an asterisk (*) in these miniglossaries.
- In case you need to look up something, the *index is very complete.* The **bold** page numbers there will direct you to the miniglossaries, should you need to look up the meaning of a word.
- I use a *lighthearted approach.* Just when I think you're falling asleep, I'll crack a joke (or at least *I'll* think it's funny). There's no reason why video must be serious.

ADDITIONAL FEATURES OF THIS BOOK

- *Home video is included.* Nrly all educational and industrial TV producers (and many broadcasters) are using VHS and 8mm VCRs for some program distribution. Because it's so popular, it is important to know how to set up and use home video gear.
- *Studio and portable TV are both covered.* Some TV production occurs with crews, lights, several cameras, and control rooms, and in studios having everything including kitchen sinks. ENG (electronic news gathering), EFP (electronic field production), and other portable video operations are performed on the run. The well-rounded TV person needs to know both styles.

TEACHER'S MANUAL AVAILABLE

Instructors are invited to contact Prentice Hall to get a copy of the teacher's manual containing course outlines, lab setups, and study questions and answers.

ABOUT THE AUTHOR

Dr. Peter Utz received his bachelor's degree in physics and his doctorate in instructional technology from the University of Massachusetts. He has produced and directed more than 500 instructional TV productions for the City University of New York. He has also published *Video User's Handbook,* an industrial TV reference guide; *Today's Video,* a comprehensive survival guide covering all aspects of TV equipment setup and production (recommended for those who intend to make TV production or audiovisual supervision their careers); *Manual Moderno de Equipos de Video,* the Spanish version of *Today's Video; The Complete Home Video Book,* a comprehensive handbook on the setup and operation of home video equipment; *Do-It-Yourself Video, A Beginner's Guide to Home Video; Create Excellent Video;* and *Making Great Video,* handbooks for camcorder enthusiasts; and *Making Great Audio,* a manual for recording and reproducing sound. He has published over 250 articles in media and television journals, such as *AV Video* and *Camcorder* magazines. After supervising the Instructional Media Department at the County College of Morris in Randolph, New Jersey, for 17 years, he has moved into private consulting.

THE STUDIO PRODUCTION TEAM

Visit a TV studio during a production, and what will you see? For a crew that has worked together for some time on a familiar type of program, you'll see focused, disciplined activity by a variety of people, each responsible for one component of the entire show. Those pieces fit together seamlessly if each team member

- Is intimately familiar with the operation of his/her equipment.
- Understands the objectives and sequence of events in the show.
- Has prepared his/her contribution to the show—and has double-checked those elements before the show begins.
- Knows what the other team members' jobs are and, whenever their activities have to mesh, works out the details; effective communication is important here.
- Is aware of the production schedule and sticks to it.

Despite the ideal scenario above, there may be periods of sheer boredom for some team members as they wait for others to carry out their roles. And for the less practiced, the calm is occasionally punctuated by pandemonium when something goes wrong, . . . goes wrong, . . . goes wrong . . .

Often there are team members you don't even see. The PREPRODUCTION team develops the ideas for the show, arranges for its financing, develops scripts, and scouts out locations for FIELD recordings to be produced. Sets and lighting arrangements are made while titles and graphics are electronically generated.

---

*The most important terms in the miniglossaries (the ones you definitely should learn) will be preceded by an asterisk.

*Preproduction The planning that precedes the production, such as writing scripts or building sets.

*Field Anything outside the TV studio. Electronic Field Production (EFP) is performed with camcorders on location.

*Postproduction Video editing and other activities that come after the studio production.

*Freelancer or stringer Someone who works temporarily on a TV production, such as a camera operator.

Lighting director Person who carries out the creative design to set the lighting mood for a show.

Lighting engineer Person who executes the lighting director's plan by making the wire connections and operating the machinery during the show.

Lighting person Combination director/engineer in smaller operations who carries out all lighting responsibilities.

Audio director, audio engineer, audio person Similar to above, but for audio functions.

Scriptwriter

Pre-production

Setbuilder

Choreographer

Executive Producer

Post Production

Editor

Production

Camera Operator

Talent

Floor Manager

The production team

TABLE 1–1 TV Production Teams

The *Preproduction Team* plans the production.

executive producer	technical director
producer*	composer
director	choreographer
writer	set builders
art director	lighting director
graphic artists	audio director

The *Production Team* executes the production.

producer	technical director
associate producer	graphics/character generator operator
production assistant	audio person
director*	makeup artist
associate director	lighting person
talent	engineers & technicians
camera operators	videotape operator
floor manager	property manager/wardrobe

The *Postproduction Team* produces a finished tape from what was recorded in the field and in the studio.

editor	audio person
director*	narrator

*In charge

Seldom is a show finished when the studio activity ends. Often the show requires editing, the addition of music and/or narration, duplication, and packaging. This is handled by the POST-PRODUCTION team.

Big productions are definitely a team sport; they may require dozens of personnel. Tables 1–1 and 1–2 list some of those production personnel. On smaller productions, the team members do multiple jobs. Many fine-looking industrial TV productions are produced with a crew of only four. Some small shops have one or two full-time producer-directors and hire FREELANCERS or STRINGERS temporarily to handle the staff-intensive parts of bigger TV productions. Colleges often maintain a full-time technician, one or two producer-directors who also do their own editing, and pull in other staff members or students to fill in the crew during a studio shoot. It has become typical for editors to create their own electronic graphic art, animations, and titles and to do their own audio mixing. The survivors in this business are jacks of many trades.

 Mini Review

- Television production is a teamwork process. Sometimes it involves many team members, each with a specific role, but sometimes a few team members take on many roles.
- The preproduction team prepares for the show; the production team produces it; the postproduction team edits and prepares it for distribution.
- The production team should be familiar with the script so that they know what will happen in the show and can prepare for it.

Job titles are quite specific in large organizations, general in small ones. The term AUDIO DIRECTOR technically means the "creative" person who selects or designs musical scores, etc. to set the

TABLE 1–2   Production and Technical Personnel and What They Do

Personnel	Function
Executive Producer	Coordinates several programs in a series. Interfaces with clients, corporate management, advertising agencies, sponsors, and agents for talent and writers. The executive producer raises money and also approves and manages budgets.
Producer	Same as executive producer, except is in charge of an individual production. May also double as writer and/or director. Arranges the production schedule so that all elements of a production flow together smoothly.
Studio and Field Producers	In large productions, the studio producer handles all studio activities, while the field producer coordinates on-location productions.
Associate Producer (AP)	Assists the producer by carrying out production tasks such as telephoning talent and tracking deadlines.
Production Assistant (PA)	During preproduction rehearsals, takes notes of comments made by the producer or director that serve as a guide to improving the show before final taping. During the actual production, assists the producer and director in miscellaneous ways.
Director	Is ultimately responsible for transforming a script into a final TV production. Is also in charge of directing talent and all aspects of the TV production.
Producer/Director	Combines the jobs of producer and director in smaller operations. Is generally responsible for all aspects of a show from beginning to end.
Associate Director (AD)	Assists the director in miscellaneous ways during the actual production. The AD may keep track of timing or will follow the script, giving "ready" cues to crew members before action is called for by the director.
Talent	Anyone who is seen or heard in the program, whether talented or not. Those who portray themselves are called performers. Those who portray someone else on camera are called actors. Those who read narration off-camera are called announcers or narrators.
Writer	Creates audio/video scripts.
Art Director	Is responsible for set design, graphics, titles, and other creative design aspects of the show. Works closely with the lighting director to create a specific mood or ambiance for the show.
Choreographer	Arranges the movements of dancers.
Music Director	Selects music for a show or leads the live band in a variety show.
Property Manager	In large productions, keeps track of props and furniture. In small productions, this is handled by the floor manager.
Wardrobe	Designs, constructs, and keeps track of costumes in large productions.
Floor Manager	Arranges equipment, and sometimes props and scenery, on the studio floor. Gets talent into place and relays director's cues to talent. Since the director may be far away or in another room, the floor manager is responsible for coordinating activities in the studio. In field productions, the floor manager prepares the location for the shoot and cues the talent.
Floor Persons	In larger productions, the floor persons (also called grips or stage hands) prepare sets, hold cue cards or operate prompting devices, operate microphone booms, and keep cables out of the way of moving cameras.
Makeup Artist	In large productions, does the makeup for the talent.

TABLE 1–2 *Continued*

Personnel	Function
Chief Engineer	Person in charge of technical personnel, equipment selection, and systems design, operation, and maintenance.
Technician	Assists the chief engineer, especially in equipment maintenance.
Technical Director (TD)	Also called switcher, does the image switching during a studio production upon command from the director. The TD is also responsible for preparing complex special effects prior to production.
Lighting Director (LD)	Often in cooperation with the set designer, designs the "look" of the stage lighting. The lighting person is responsible for selecting the lights, positioning and aiming them, and operating the dimmer during the TV production. When on location, the lighting person is in charge of lights, reflectors, and nets used to soften harsh sunlight.
Electrician	In large studios and large field productions, the electrician is responsible for providing reliable power to all the equipment and lights.
Video Engineer	Prior to shooting, calibrates and adjusts the camera controls for the best pictures. During the show, the video engineer monitors the signals to ensure that they remain within proper standards. In smaller operations, this task is handled by the technician or chief engineer.
Videotape Operator	Operates videotape recorders during a production.
Videotape Editor	Operates videotape editing equipment, often making creative editing decisions as well.
Audio Director	Designs the soundtrack of complex productions. The audio person operates the audio console during live shows, and mixes and edits audio during postproduction. May also double as videotape operator on location.
Character Generator (CG) Operator	In complex studio productions, displays text (subtitles or full pages) and sometimes graphics upon command from the director. The CG operator prepares this text before the show.

mood for the show. Meanwhile, the AUDIO ENGINEER is the person who runs the audio console, connects microphones, and mixes the sounds together for the AUDIO DIRECTOR. Similarly, a big show may have a LIGHTING DIRECTOR to design the lighting plan and create the show's mood, while the LIGHTING ENGINEER runs the wires, hangs and aims the lights, and operates the dimmer apparatus.

In smaller shops, one person does both jobs and may take either one of these titles or the generic title AUDIO PERSON or LIGHTING PERSON. The same applies for many other positions in the TV profession.

THE SIMPLE SHOOT

Imagine that your class is asked to mount a simple studio production, such as "Why Did You Take This Course?" It's a four-minute interview show in which the host asks a class member a few questions about why he/she took this TV course. It would start with a title and music, then move to the host who reads/recites some introductory comments, then introduces the guest. The two chat, and near the end of four minutes, the host closes the show with a few comments, the music rises, and the credits roll.

Since you are all beginners, certain studio preparations will have been made for you: the lights are hung and aimed, the mikes are plugged in, the signals routed to the VCR, the cameras tested, and the script prepared. All you have to do is familiarize yourself with your equipment, prepare for the show, and then, under the director's command, make it all happen.

Let's continue the exercise: When the show is over, everyone rotates to a new assignment, learns his or her role, and mounts a new show; the host may become camera operator, the lighting person may run the VCR, and so on.

Instructors and staff may be there to get you started, and they may actually perform the first show (especially the difficult role of the director). After that, you may need to teach crew positions to each other as you rotate.

That's the scenario. Here are the fundamentals of what each person does in the show.

The Host

When you receive your "start" cue from the floor manager, begin speaking your introduction into the main camera (the one with the red TALLY LIGHT lit).

Either you'll have memorized your introduction, or you'll read it from a teleprompter or cue cards.

After welcoming the guest, you can ask your first question, which you should have memorized. You might refer to notes occasionally for additional questions.

When you see the "one minute" cue from the floor manager, you ask your wrap-up question, which should be a short one, eliciting a brief answer. When you see the "half minute" cue, you thank the guest, turn to the "on" camera, and deliver your closing statement (either memorized or read from the teleprompter or cue cards). When finished, remain silent until the floor manager or director says it's okay to speak.

This all sounds so easy . . . until you actually do it. Then you see why talk show hosts get the big bucks.

Thirteen Thoughts on Being a Good Host

1. If you have the chance to dress for the show, avoid blacks and very dark colors, whites and very light colors, tiny checks, herringbones, and stripes (they drive the cameras crazy). Pastels and subdued solid colors are good. Avoid sparkling jewelry, big dangling earrings, and loud outfits. Colorful ties and scarves are fine.
2. Study the script so that the first "take" will be a smooth one.
3. Find out as much about the guest as possible, in order to ask good questions. Especially, take time to learn how to pronounce the guest's name. "Mr. Smellybuns is here to . . . oh, excuse me, it's Mr. Smel-LAY-bins."
4. Take care of your "guest"; that's what being a host is all about. Find out what the guest needs to do (enter when called, sit, shake hands, or whatever) and prep the guest accordingly. Answer the guest's questions, and make him/her comfortable.
5. Smile. Nobody likes a sourpuss, and besides, a smile helps dispel the jitters.

---

*Tally light   Light on a camera that indicates that its picture is being recorded or broadcast. The light lets the talent and camera operator know the camera is "on the air."

*Teleprompter   Electronic device that sits near the camera lens, often using a two-way mirror to reflect script for the talent to read.

*Cue card   Poster-sized card with handwritten script for the talent to read.

Cue card holder   Person who holds up the cue cards for the talent to read.

*Lapel or tie-clip microphone   Tiny microphone that clips to the talent's lapel, tie, blouse, or somewhere on the chest.

Lavalier microphone   Older style microphone that hangs around the talent's neck on a string.

6. Respond immediately to the "start" cue, and wrap up the show quickly when signaled (the show ends with or without you).

   Your "stand by—be quiet" cue may come verbally from the floor manager or from the director, over the studio loudspeaker system. Take a relaxing breath. A few moments before you're "on," the floor manager may either count backward a few seconds to prepare you for your cue or raise his/her hand, pointing toward the ceiling. When you're on, he/she will point at you. Start immediately, speaking to *that* camera (its tally light will be on, another clue to which camera to address).

   Near the end of the show, the floor manager may hold up two fingers (two minutes left), and later one finger (one minute left), your signals to begin wrapping up the show. Don't acknowledge or stare at the cue; the floor manager will hold the finger up long enough to assure that you see it. If you see a fist held in the air, it means that half a minute is left. If the floor manager slices his/her throat with his/her finger, it means finish *immediately*.

7. Exude confidence. Who wants to watch a wishy-washy, wimpy mumblemouth?

8. Speak in a normal tone of voice during the sound check, and use that same volume during the show. Also, avoid loud laughing, shouting, or other piercing outbursts during the show (the volume will overwhelm the equipment and probably blast the headphones off the hapless audio person).

9. During the intro and wrap-up, maintain eye contact with the camera. *That's* your audience, not the studio crew or floor manager, not the floor, not the studio TV monitor. See Figure 1–1.

10. During the interview, focus your attention entirely on the guest. Don't look around the room; you never know when a camera may be taking a shot of you. Tune out all distractions. It's okay to glance at your notes briefly. Also, listen intently and react to your question's answer; an interview should seem like a discussion, which means reflecting, restating, and reacting to the guest's responses.

11. Sit up straight in your chair, lean forward, and look interested, even if you aren't.

12. Don't ask questions that require only a yes or no answer, because that's the kind of answer you'll get, followed by a pregnant silence while you think up what to say next. Ask open-ended questions. Replace "Were you the first . . ." with "How did you become the first . . ." or "What got you interested in . . ." or "When did you first discover you could . . ." Also, good eye contact, a reassuring smile, and an occasional nod of agreement will do wonders for keeping the guest talking.

13. Do not acknowledge *cues* with a nod or "uh huh." Just do whatever you were cued to do.

 Mini Review

- The host should address the camera or the guest with direct eye contact yet respond quickly to cues without visibly acknowledging them.

The Guest

Your job is the easiest; just do what you're told. In a way, *you* are the point of the show; so if you have something to say, say it, and say it with some pizzazz.

The Nine Requirements of a Guest

1. If you have a chance to dress for the show, avoid blacks and very dark colors, whites and very light colors, tiny checks, herringbones, and stripes. Pastels and subdued solid colors are good. Avoid glittering jewelry, dangling earrings, and loud outfits. Colorful ties and scarves are fine.

Direct eye contact engages the viewer.

No eye contact. Viewer observes the action of others.

Slightly off-camera look loses impact, implies insincerity.

FIGURE 1–1   Avoid slightly off-camera looks.

2. Look alert and alive. Sit upright and lean forward slightly in your chair. Don't be a slouch. Notice the "body language" in Figure 1–2.
3. Answer questions with complete sentences.
4. Be brief (maybe 1–3 sentences). Long-winded answers usually get edited out or interrupted by the host.
5. Speak distinctly and confidently. Smile.
6. Focus your attention on the *interviewer only*; nothing else in the room exists.
7. To be comfortable while seated, cross your legs at the ankles if you wish. Don't sit with your legs splayed out or with one foot on your knee, showing worn shoe leather to the audience.
8. Know what the show is going to be about and come prepared. If you know what the questions will be, try to dream up one or two great lines to answer the questions. People tend to remember colorful answers.
9. Be quiet when you hear the "Stand by" signal at the show's start. Remain quiet when the interview is over, until the floor manager or director gives the "All clear" signal.

 Mini Review

- The guest should disregard all activity in the studio, focusing his/her attention on the host.

FIGURE 1–2   "Body language" is apparent in the way the guest chooses to sit before the cameras.

The Floor Manager

Assuming the studio is already set up, the floor manager's job will be to carry out requests from the director (usually sealed in the control room). You might connect microphones to the host and guest (and disconnect them at the end of the show—before they forget they're wearing them and try to walk off while still tethered). You would also relay the director's cues to the host and guest.

Fourteen Fundamentals of Floor Management

1. Study the script to see what the show is about and what is likely to happen.
2. Seat the host and guest close together; television makes things look farther apart than they really are, as you see in Figure 1–3. Also, angle the chairs toward each other as shown in Figure 1–4.

Talent may look fine in the studio, but ...

... are too far apart for a good CAMERA SHOT

FIGURE 1–3   Seat the talent close together.

Nose-to-nose implies adversary relationship

Line-up gives no relationship between guests

Angled is comfortable

FIGURE 1–4   Angle the guests.

3. Unless the audio person wishes to do it, attach the LAVALIER, TIE-CLIP, or LAPEL MICROPHONE to the host and guest (or help them attach it). The LAPEL mike should be clipped to the person's neck-tie, lapel, or blouse near the sternum, about four inches below the chin, as shown in Figure 1–5. If the person will be speaking mostly to one side, attach the mike on that side.

   Try to hide the mike wires. They can be run under a jacket, exiting behind the performer. Acting with some discretion, you could have the performer thread the mike beneath his/her clothes, exiting between buttons on a shirt. Bring the wire around to the rear of the performer, then clip it or loop it around the performer's belt; this will keep the wires from tugging directly on the mike in the front. To keep people from tripping on the mike wires, route them behind the chairs if the performers are seated or behind them if they walk.

   If the mikes use power, make sure they are switched "on." Often, the switch is part of the power supply at the end of the eight-foot thin wire connecting the mike to the studio's regular audio cable.

   Avoid positioning the mike near jewelry or buttons to prevent recording clankety-clank as the mike moves.

4. Have the host and guest practice their moves (if any) to make sure mike cords and furniture don't get in the way.

5. Slip on your intercom headset so you can hear the director's commands.

6. The director may give a standby cue (or you can infer one from the chatter you hear over the headset) which you relate verbally to the studio members, such as "Stand by, we'll begin shortly."

7. Find out from the director which camera will shoot the host. Stand to the side of that camera to give your cue to the host. The director will say, "Ready to cue host," and you will raise one arm,

FIGURE 1–5   Placement of LAPEL or TIE CLIP microphone.

pointing your finger to the ceiling while looking at the host. If the director gives a countdown, "10, 9, 8 . . . ," you parrot the countdown as far as the number 3, just mouthing the "2, 1" so you don't make any sounds at the last moments when the mikes are "live." As a precaution, speak softly, anyway, when giving cues.

8. When you hear "Cue host" (or "Cue talent," or "Cue 'em," or whatever) point at the host. You can see this and other cues in Chapter 11.

9. If you hear a "Two minutes left" cue over your intercom, hold two fingers out where the host can easily see them, perhaps offstage behind the guest. Hold them up long enough so that you feel sure the host has seen your cue. Do the same with one finger for the one-minute cue. Use a fist (fingernails facing the host) to indicate half a minute. If the show runs long, you may hear a "Wrap it up" signal. Slit your throat with your finger to relay this cue.

10. If camera 2 has the closing shot of the host and the final statements are on a cue card or teleprompter near camera 2, point to that camera to lead the host's eyes to the right camera.

11. If you have to move around during the show, do so quietly and out of range of the cameras (behind them or to their sides).

12. You can communicate with the director before the show, but during the show you can only listen on your headset; if you speak, your voice might be recorded.

13. When the show is over, help the talent remove their microphones. Make sure no one will trip over the wires. Switch off the microphones' battery power, if they are so equipped.

14. Tidy up the set area if it became disheveled.

 Mini Review

• The floor manager acts as an extension of the director, managing all activities in the studio.

The Teleprompter Operator or Cue Card Holder

At Poverty Productions, Inc., they are still using CUE CARDS. Most other studios have graduated to electronic TELEPROMPTERS to help the talent with their lines.

FIGURE 1–6   CUE CARD held to the side, near camera lens.

Caveats of Cue Card Clasping.   If you land the prestigious job of CUE CARD HOLDER:

1. Put the cards in order so that you don't have to hunt for them during the show.
2. Wear intercom headphones so that you know what's going on.
3. Kneel, if necessary, to the side of the "taking" camera and hold the cards so that
   a. They are close to the camera lens.
   b. They are to your side so you can read them too (then you'll know when to change a card). See Figure 1–6.
4. Change cards quickly by slipping the front one away, setting it on the floor, and revealing the next card in the stack.
5. If the talent must address a different camera at another part in the show, hold the cards next to that camera.

Creating Cue Cards.   In the basic production, your script may already be loaded onto the cue cards or computer memory for you. If not, here are a few tips about cue card calligraphy:

1. Write with broad black felt markers.
2. Print big, using uppercase and lowercase lettering, to make the text easy to read.
3. Each line should be a short phrase. Break lines at natural pauses in speech. Don't write

"Hi, I'm your
host, Linda
Lisp, welcoming
you to another
edition of "Why
Did You Take This
Course?"

Instead, write:

"Hi,
I'm your host,
Linda Lisp,
welcoming you to
another edition of
"Why Did You
Take This Course?"

Teleprompter Operator Basics.　If you are the TELEPROMPTER operator, you'll be working some kind of electronic device that displays the text on two-way mirrors in front of the cameras. See Figures 1–7 and 1–8.

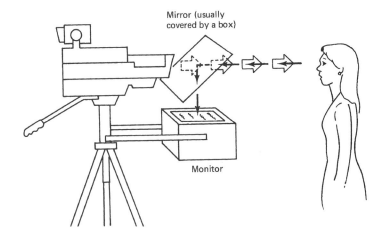

FIGURE 1–7　TELEPROMPTER using two-way mirror and a TV monitor.

FIGURE 1–8　TELEPROMPTER (Courtesy of Listec TV Equipment Corp.).

One older system uses text typed on narrow strips of paper. The strips are loaded into a contraption that moves the paper like a conveyer belt. A small TV camera on the device transfers the image of the text to the teleprompter viewers on the studio cameras. You move the text by turning a knob on a remote control. Turn the knob one way, and the text slides up the screen, ready for reading. Turn it further in that direction, and the text moves faster. Turn it less, and the text moves slower or stops. Turn the knob in the opposite direction, and the text moves backwards (making it very hard to read, I might add). This position is good for rewinding the script if you have to start a show over.

Newer systems work more like word processors. The script is typed into a computer and appears on a computer screen and on the studio cameras' teleprompters at the same time. The operator, using a mouse, keyboard buttons, or a remote control as before, makes the text scroll up the screen at a rate that matches the talent's speech.

The trick to teleprompting is to adapt to the talents' rate of speech. How fast they read the script tells you how fast to move the words.

Teleprompter Tips

1. Get a copy of the script and make sure it matches the teleprompter text. Also, make yourself comfortable with the order of events in the show so that you'll know when to do your thing.
2. Place the words the talent is speaking *now*, about a third of the way down the screen. Scroll the screen fast enough to keep the words being read at this spot. This means you will have to speed up or slow down at times, and maybe even stop.
3. Before the show, practice a little with the talent so you can get used to each other (and the talent learns to trust you).

Typing Text into a Teleprompter

1. You'll probably select the TELEPROMPTER program icon from a menu. Then you'll probably select FILE/NEW to get started.
2. As in step 3 under "Creating Cue Cards," type a phrase for each line so that the text is easy to read.
3. Leave some blank lines between the intro script and the wrap-up script so that the talent doesn't accidentally read through into the wrap-up (which leads to a very brief show).
4. You'll probably select FILE/SAVE to store your text. Select a name for the script, if prompted. When you want to use the text you've prepared, you'll probably select FILE/OPEN and type (or select from a menu) the name of your script to bring it onto the screen. Another menu item will probably take you from the "edit" mode (where you type stuff) to the "play" mode (where you display the script on the TELEPROMPTERS and control its motion).

The reason for the "probablys" in the statements above is that TELEPROMPTER programs differ in the ways they work. Look for additional instructions, usually pasted to the wall near the keyboard.

 Mini Review

- Make the teleprompter text follow the pace of the reader, not the other way around.

The Camera Operator

The camera operator's job is to aim the camera, using a mixture of logic and obedience to the director.

Since the camera is an electronic device, and its tripod is a mechanical device, it behooves you to learn something about both so you can work them smoothly during the show.

Practice.

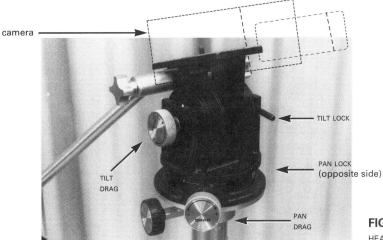

camera

TILT LOCK

PAN LOCK
(opposite side)

TILT
DRAG

PAN
DRAG

FIGURE 1–9   Controls on a tripod
HEAD.

Basic Camera Controls

1. If the camera has a cap on its lens, remove it so the camera can "see." At the end of the show, replace the cap to protect the lens.
2. Just below the camera is the TRIPOD HEAD (see Figure 1–9). It allows the camera to be aimed up and down (TILT) and from left to right (PAN). The HEAD has four important controls:

TILT LOCK—which locks the camera head so it doesn't tilt.
TILT DRAG—which makes the camera tilt loosely or with some stiffness.
PAN LOCK—which keeps the camera from aiming left to right.
PAN DRAG—which makes the camera aim either loosely or stiffly from left to right.

To work the controls:
a. Grab the camera's aiming handle and loosen the TILT LOCK and PAN LOCK controls. You'll notice the camera can now be aimed hither and thither.

Do not let go of the handle or leave the camera without first tightening the pan and tilt locks. Some cameras are poorly balanced, and without your guiding hand, can nose-dive (TILT forward abruptly), smashing their lenses or toppling over.

Tripod head   Top part of a camera tripod that holds the camera.
*Tripod or pedestal   The support that holds up the camera. The head is at the top and attaches to the camera. The dolly is underneath and has the wheels.
Head   Top part of a camera tripod that holds the camera.
*Dolly   Bottom part of a camera tripod that has wheels. Also the act of moving the camera toward or away from a subject.
*Tilt   The up-and-down motion of a camera, like nodding your head "yes."
*Tilt lock   Camera head control to lock the camera in place so it can't tilt.
Tilt drag   Tripod head control that adjusts resistance to the up-and-down motion of the camera.
*Pan   The left-right motion of a camera, like nodding your head "no."

*Pan lock   Tripod head control that freezes the position of the camera so it doesn't aim left or right.
Pan drag   Tripod head control that adjusts resistance to the left-right motion of the camera.
Drag controls   Controls that resist free motion of the camera head in various directions.
*Viewfinder   The part of a TV camera you look through to see where the camera is aimed.
*Focus   Lens adjustment to make a camera's picture sharp.
*Zoom lens   A lens that can "zoom in" or "zoom out" to give either a closer-looking picture or a wider angle of view.
*Zoom in/out   The act of adjusting the camera's lens to make the picture appear to come toward you or go away from you.
Rocker switch   A two-way switch that rocks back and forth. If pressed one way, it zooms a lens in; if pressed the other way, it zooms it out.

Tighten the HEAD controls when you leave the camera.

b. Aim the camera around to get a feel for its balance and stiffness. If the aiming feels too stiff, loosen the appropriate DRAG CONTROLS and notice the difference. With the DRAG CONTROLS too loose, the camera bobs and jiggles easily. Too tight, the DRAG CONTROLS make the camera's movement sluggish and cumbersome.

3. The camera's VIEWFINDER is usually aimable; you can tilt it so that it is comfortable to see.

4. The aiming handles of your camera usually hold your FOCUS and ZOOM controls. FOCUS makes your picture sharp, while ZOOM makes it look closer or farther away. These controls are usually mounted so that you can work them while still holding the camera's aiming handles.

You FOCUS with your fingertips. While the palm of your left hand and thumb steady the left handle, you stretch out your fingertips to rotate the FOCUS knob. Watch your viewfinder to monitor the results.

You ZOOM with the electric ROCKER SWITCH attached to the other handle. While you grasp the handle to steady the camera, slip your thumb into the ROCKER SWITCH's notch and press to the left or right. Push it one way, and the lens ZOOMS IN, magnifying the image. Pushed slightly, the ZOOM moves slowly. Pushed all the way, the ZOOM happens quickly. Pushed in the other direction, the lens ZOOMS OUT making the picture smaller. See Figure 1–10.

The Proper Way to Focus.   You can FOCUS a lens anytime, but the best time to FOCUS is before the show, when there's time to do it right.

If your camera moves toward or away from a subject, or the subject moves toward or away from you, or you change subjects, you'll probably need to refocus. If, however, your subject is sitting, dead, or tied down, you can FOCUS once and have it stay in focus for the rest of the show.

There are two ways to FOCUS:

1. Quick.
2. Good.

If your camera were "on" and your subject moved, making the image blurry, you would FOCUS as quickly and unobtrusively as possible. This would mean rotating the FOCUS knob one way or the other (you'll quickly see which way is wrong if the picture gets blurrier) until the picture becomes sharp.

If your camera is "off," you have the time to do a better FOCUSING job, which is a three-step process:

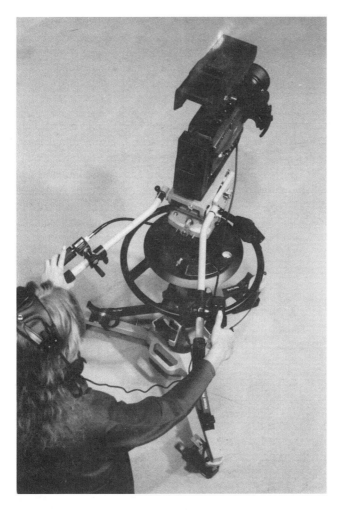

FIGURE 1–10   Rotating knob for focusing is on the left handle, ROCKER SWITCH for zooming on the right.

1. ZOOM IN all the way on the subject.
2. FOCUS for a sharp picture.
3. ZOOM OUT to the shot you want.

If you have to change shots (maybe to shoot an object or a person's hands), when you're in the clear to set up that shot, aim your camera at the object, ZOOM IN, FOCUS, then ZOOM OUT to the desired shot of the object; then wait for the shot to be used. You may be asked to ZOOM further, but this will not change your FOCUS—assuming you followed the three-step procedure above.

Basic Director's Commands and Shots.   In general, you want to shoot what's important, miss what's superfluous, and keep the action from slipping off the screen, following it as it moves. You also want to keep your picture in focus all the time.

The director may ask you to TILT UP or DOWN to make the shot more appealing, or maybe PAN LEFT or RIGHT. Follow the command right away. (In other words, be alert.) If your camera is "on," make the move smooth and graceful without bobbing, jerking, or overshooting your target.

You may be asked to make a LONG SHOT (also called a WIDE SHOT), in which case you'd ZOOM OUT. Maybe the director will ask for a MEDIUM SHOT or a CLOSE-UP. Or you may be called upon for a

TWO-SHOT (host and guest), or a ONE-SHOT (host *or* guest alone). Refer to Figure 1–11 to review the kinds of shots you might take.

The director will not call you by name (i.e., "Zelda, ZOOM IN," or "Tommy, TILT UP"), but will call you by camera number (i.e., "Camera 2, TILT UP"). Learn your camera number.

Ten Tiny Tips

1. Before the show, practice your camera moves. Know which way to press the ROCKER SWITCH to ZOOM IN. Know which way to rotate the FOCUS knob to FOCUS on something closer to you.
2. Familiarize yourself with the script if you can; it doesn't hurt to know what's coming next.
3. Put on your intercom headset so that the control room crew can communicate with you; also, you'll know what's happening in the show (the conversation is usually entertaining).
4. Up until show time, you can talk to the director and others on the intercom. After the "Stand by" cue, hush up. When the "All clear" is given at the show's end, you can speak again.
5. Don't jiggle the camera when it's "on"; the picture magnifies every shake.
6. Try to anticipate what's coming next, in case your director doesn't. If the host rises at the end of the show and your camera is "on," you don't want a close-up of his crotch. Ready yourself to TILT UP and/or ZOOM OUT to catch the entire motion. If you're sure of the motion (and it's okay with the director), it looks best if you precede the host's movement with a gradual ZOOM OUT a couple of seconds before the host rises. Even leave a little headroom for the host to "move into."
7. Keep people's heads near the top of the screen; avoid empty headroom.
8. If a person is looking to the right, *don't* center his/her head; leave a little extra "breathing room" in front of the person's face. If he/she is looking to the left, leave some extra space at the left of the screen.
9. Do what the director tells you to do, even if you disagree.
10. Cap your lens after the show.

 Mini Review

- The camera operator should anticipate what happens next and be prepared to keep a good shot when it happens.
- The right way to focus a zoom lens when your camera isn't on: Zoom in on the subject, focus the subject, zoom out to the shot you want.

The Lighting Person

The lights have been hung from the LIGHTING GRID with care (in hopes that St. Nicholas soon will be there?). Often, a studio has a slew of lights strung along the GRID, pointed every which way so that all one needs to do is select which lights to use and switch them on.

Each light can be dimmed with the DIMMER, which is connected to a DIMMER REMOTE CONTROL in the control room or the studio. Your job as lighting person is to select which lights will illuminate the talent best, then adjust their brightness.

Lighting Lessons.   Lighting has three main purposes:

1. Make enough light for the camera to "see."
2. Create dimension and texture through shadows and highlights.
3. Create a mood.

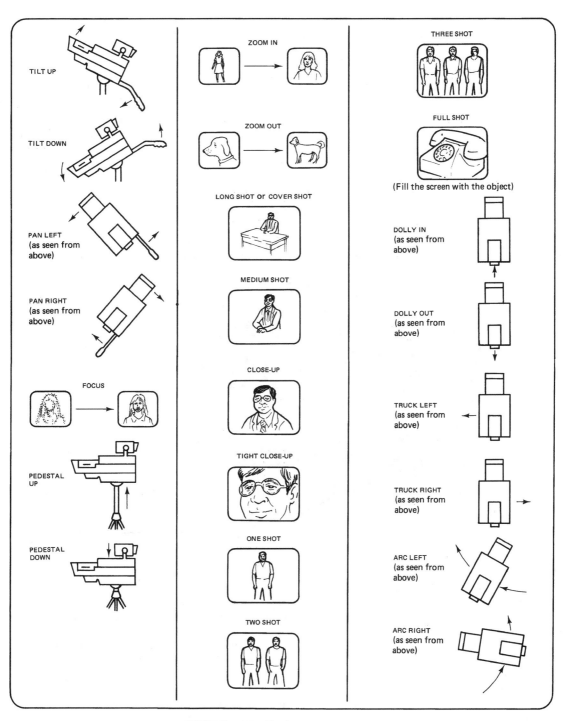

FIGURE 1–11 Basic camera moves.

We achieve the above objectives, not by turning on every light in the studio (which would toast your talent and simmer your studio), but by selecting certain lights to illuminate the subject from certain angles. We do this using a method called FOUR-POINT LIGHTING. It uses four lights, the KEY, the FILL, the BACK, and the SET light to create the desired effects.

The KEY is the main light for illuminating the subject; it comes from one side and above the subject, somewhat like the sun at 3 p.m. Figure 1–12 shows a typical KEY light along with the flaps, called BARN DOORS, that help direct the light. Figure 1–13 diagrams the positions of the KEY and other lights. This light casts shadows on the far side of the subject. Depending on the size of the light's reflector, these shadows could be HARD (sharp) or SOFT. A SCOOP light—a light with a big reflector—makes a SOFT light with fuzzy shadows. You can get a similar effect by teaming up two KEY lights side by side

BARN DOORS

FIGURE 1–12   Instrument generally used as a KEY light.

---

*Lighting grid   Framework of pipes connected to the studio ceiling from which lights are hung.

Dimmer   Electronic device to vary the brightness of lamps connected to its circuits.

*Dimmer remote control   Control panel with sliders to vary each dimmer circuit's power. The small panel connects via a multiwire cable to the actual large and heavy dimmer circuits. Those circuits feed power to the lighting grid.

*Four-point lighting   The use of four lights to provide primary illumination, controlled shadows, and a rim of highlight for dimension.

*Key light   Brightest and main source of lighting for a subject, creating the primary shadows.

*Scrim   Glass fiber or metal screen mesh that clips to the front of the lighting instrument to diffuse and soften light.

Diffusion material   White, lacy, fiberglass fabric that can be draped in front of a light to soften harsh shadows.

*Set   The background of the studio shot. A curtain, fake walls, and furniture are all part of the set.

*Set light   Lighting instrument used to illuminate the background or set.

*Barn doors   Metal flaps on a lighting instrument that can be closed or opened to direct the light and to shade areas where light is undesirable.

*Fill light   Soft, broad light whose main purpose is to fill in (reduce the blackness of) shadows created by the key light.

*Back light   Lighting instrument that illuminates the subject from behind, creating a rim of light around the edges of the subject. The back light usually has barn doors for precise control of the light's direction.

Scoop light   Funnel-shaped fill light.

*Soft light   Large lighting instrument with a built-in reflector for soft, shadow-free lighting. Also the kind of light that has soft shadows or no shadows.

*Hard light   Light that makes sharp shadows, like those from a bare bulb.

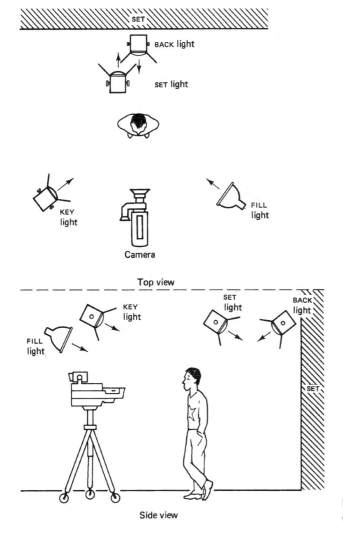

Top view

Side view

FIGURE 1–13   Typical lighting layout.

(as if they were one wide light with two bulbs) and beaming them at your subject. Although two instruments are used, you can think of this as one light in the FOUR-POINT LIGHTING scheme. Another trick to soften light is to place white fiberglass fabric (called DIFFUSION material) or a metal screen (called a SCRIM) in front of the light fixture. Figure 1–14 shows a SCRIM ON A SCOOP.

The shadows from the KEY light give the image texture and dimensionality, but the shadows may be too pronounced, making the picture too contrasty. We reduce this contrast by filling those shadows with light *from the opposite side*. This is called, appropriately, FILL light. Usually the FILL light has a big reflector to create SOFT, diffuse light. It's also weaker than the KEY light so that it doesn't overpower the KEY and make visible shadows of its own. Again, if one instrument doesn't do the trick, you can team up two, side by side, to create a softer yet brighter effect. Usually, because FILL lights spread their light over a wide area, their light is pretty weak anyway (compared to the more focused KEY light), and two FILLS may be needed to counteract one KEY. Again, you can think of the twin FILLS as one light in the scheme. As before, you can soften the FILL light even further by placing a SCRIM or DIFFUSION material in front of it.

Now that you have enough light so the camera can see, plus some shadows for dimension, we'll add some more dimensionality to really make the subject stand out from the background. We do this

FIGURE 1–14 Fiberglass SCRIM used on a SCOOP to soften the light.

with the BACK light, which hits the subject from above and behind. The light is high enough not to be "seen" by the camera, but it isn't directly over the subject. Its light creates a white rim around the subject, outlining it and separating it from the background. Figure 1–15 shows the effect as these lights team up together.

The last light in the FOUR-POINT LIGHTING scheme is the SET light. Aimed at the background, or SET, it brightens it, keeping it from looking dark or shadowy. The SET should be illuminated a little less brightly than the talent; thus, your attention is drawn to them and not to the background. In small studios, so much KEY and FILL light spills onto the SET, there's no need to bathe it with additional SET light. Most often, the SET (or lack of it) is used to create a mood. This will be discussed further in the lighting chapter.

Step-by-Step Lighting Procedure

1. Find the DIMMER REMOTE CONTROL and turn down all its sliders. Then turn its power on.
2. Go to the studio and select the lights you think you'll want to use. Ideally, they will have numbers on them, or the wires from each light will plug into a numbered outlet above the GRID. Take note of these numbers.
3. Go to the DIMMER REMOTE CONTROL and, observing that the sliders are also numbered, turn these sliders one-quarter of the way on.
4. Notice that the lighting console also has a slider called MASTER. Turn it up all the way.
5. Check in the studio to see if the lights you selected came on. If not, perhaps some wires have been plugged into the wrong sockets, and you'll have to experiment to see which lights go to which DIMMER sliders.
6. Aim a camera at the subject (or a stand-in) so that you can monitor your work on a TV screen. (Things look different to the camera than they do to your eye, so you need to use a TV monitor to judge the "real" look of the lighting setup.
7. Turn off the studio work lights or fluorescent HOUSE LIGHTS (assuming the rest of the crew doesn't need them). They are convenient for illuminating the studio during setup, but they will confuse the issue when you're trying to see the effect of just the professional lights.

---

*Master   A dimmer control that turns up or down all the other dimmer controls whose sliders are "up." When the master is down, all the lights are off. When the master is up, all the individual dimmers that are up become activated and are "on."

*House lights   General overhead work lights used in the studio during rehearsals and between productions.

Dimmer master   Dimmer control that dims all lights at once.

*Credits   The listing, usually at the show's end, of the people who participated in making it.

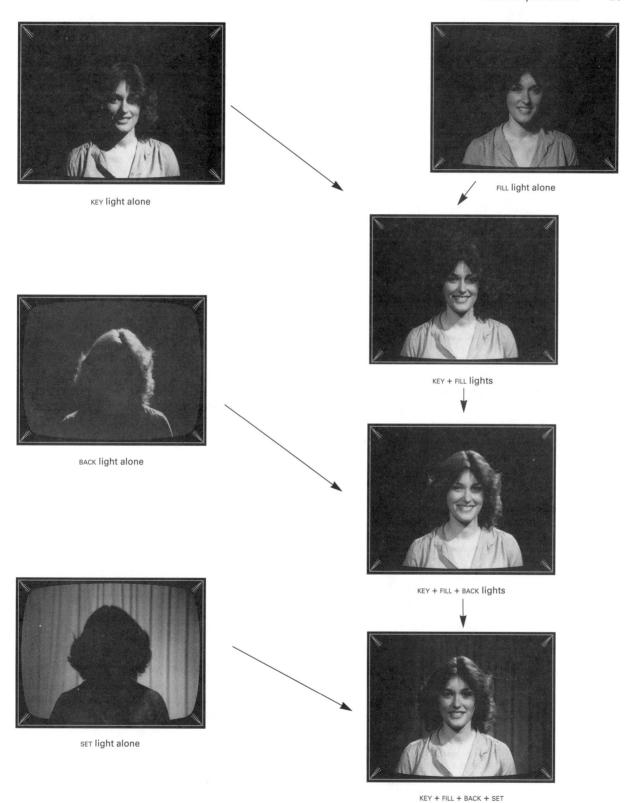

KEY light alone

FILL light alone

BACK light alone

KEY + FILL lights

KEY + FILL + BACK lights

SET light alone

KEY + FILL + BACK + SET

FIGURE 1–15 Various lighting effects in a darkened studio.

8. Turn the KEY (or KEYS) all the way up. Does the light bathe the subject? If not, move the subject, reaim the light, or choose another KEY light. Does it cast pleasing shadows? Now dim the KEY down to one quarter.

9. Turn the FILL (or FILLS) all the way up. Does the light bathe the subject? If not, move the subject or the light, or use another light. Dim the FILL to one quarter.

10. Turn the BACK light up all the way. Does it rim the subject as it should? If not, move the subject or the light, or use another light. If you move the subject, you may have to repeat steps 8 and 9 above.

11. Now turn the KEY, FILL, and BACK lights to full brightness. Look at the result in the monitor. If the shadows are too weak, dim the FILL (or use just one FILL). If the shadows are too pronounced, reduce the KEY light (dim it or use just one instrument). If the rim of BACK light glows obtrusively, dim it.

12. Last of all, add SET light. Brighten it until the SET is a little darker than the performers and portrays the mood you desire (darker is more dramatic; brighter is more cheerful or businesslike).

    Essentially, you fiddle with the DIMMER controls to achieve a pleasing balance of shadows and dimensionality.

13. When the show is over, turn on the HOUSE LIGHTS and turn the DIMMER'S MASTER down. This saves electricity, keeps the place cool, and saves the light bulbs from burning out prematurely. Switch the DIMMER REMOTE's power off if you're through using it.

Lighting Mood.   Bright lighting with few shadows looks happy, newsroom-like, and unemotional—appropriate for an interview. Dim lighting, deep shadows, and dark areas in the picture portray a dramatic mood—appropriate for suspense or a play.

You may be called upon by the director to change lighting during the show. One common move is to dim the KEY and FILL at the show's end, leaving the talent bathed in SET and BACK light as they hold after-show conversations. This also makes the image darker so that CREDITS show up better when scrolled over the picture.

 Mini Review

- Use four-point lighting: key light from one side for main illumination and to create shadows; fill light from the opposite side to diminish the shadows; back light to rim the subject, adding dimensionality; and set light to brighten the background.

The Audio Person

The audio person selects the music (in concert with the director), selects the microphones to be used, connects all the necessary items together, tests them, and then runs the audio console, or MIXER, during the show. The MIXER selects how much of each different sound will be recorded and at what volume. The audio person is responsible for the "sound mood" of the program as well as the technical quality of the sound (no hum, buzz, or distortion from loud sound). During the show, the audio person will RIDE AUDIO, making small adjustments to the sound volume to compensate for a host becoming louder with excitement or a guest becoming shy and soft-spoken, mid-show. The audio person fades up or down certain microphones when they are used or not used, and starts the music on cue from the director, perhaps fading down its volume when the talent begins to speak.

The Basic Controls on a Mixer.　　The audio MIXER is the heart of the entire sound system. Its many knobs and buttons determine which sounds will be recorded (or broadcast) and at what volume. Other knobs play a role in shaping the tone of the sound (i.e., bassy or shrill), adding effects such as echo, or manipulating whether STEREO sound is sent to the left and right speakers.

The MIXER also has meters to show how loud the sound is. The trick is to make the sound loud enough to wiggle the indicators, sometimes dipping them into the red area, but not lingering there.

Older mixers have knobs for volume controls; newer ones have sliders. With knobs, you turn to the right for more sound. With sliders, you push them up (away from you) for more sound. Figure 1–16 shows a couple of small MIXERS, and Figure 1–17 diagrams the basic controls.

Managing the Modern Mixer.　　Here are step-by-step instructions for operating the basic controls on a MIXER:

1. Turn the MIXER's power on. Its meters will light up.
2. At the right of the MIXER will be one or two (for STEREO) sliders called MASTER. When these sliders are down, *all* sound is "off." Sliding them up turns up the volume of the sources that have been selected with the individual sliders to the left. You use the MASTER to fade all selected sound up or down.
3. The individual sliders control the audio level (sound volume) of individual sources, such as microphones or CD players. Each slider is numbered so that microphone 1, plugged into socket 1 in the studio, wired to input 1 in the back of the MIXER, can be associated with slider 1 on the MIXER.

    Sometimes the wires get mixed up and mike 1 ends up on slider 4. No problem; once you know this, just make a note to yourself or stick a Post-it note or masking tape label on slider 4 telling what source it controls. Audio people often label each source they are using with the name of the person using the mike, or simply "host" or "guest." Other sources, such as the CD player, for example,

---

*Audio mixer　Electronic device that mixes audio (sound) signals from several sound sources, such as microphones, and combines them into one audio signal.

Pan or Pan pot　Pot (short for *potentiometer,* a volume control) that adjusts whether a signal will go to the left channel or the right, or be shared between the two channels by selected amounts.

Ride audio　Make constant delicate adjustments to the sound volume during a show to ensure that all sounds are loud enough but not too loud.

*Monaural　Single-channel audio. Opposite of stereo.

*Stereo　Two separate audio channels are used at the same time. One represents what the left ear would hear, and the other, the right.

*Master audio control or master fader　Mixer knob that adjusts, up or down in volume, all mixer inputs at once. Useful for fading out all mikes and sounds together.

CD (compact disc)　Small, shiny disc imbedded with microscopic pits representing digital data that can be read by a laser and converted into sound.

*Mute　A control that cuts out the sound but leaves everything else going.

LED　Light-emitting diode, a tiny lamp that can blink very quickly, uses little power, and lasts a long time. Often used as an indicator on equipment.

Cut　A segment of music on a CD, tape, or record.

Scan　Play a CD or other device forward or backward at a fast pace to quickly locate a certain spot in the music, narration, movie, or whatever.

*Music under　Music volume is reduced into the background so that narration or something else gets the audience's attention.

*Cue up　In audio, to "set up" a sound effect, music, or narration so that it will start immediately when a button is pushed.

Back-time　Figure out where to start a piece of music so that it ends at exactly a certain moment, such as the end of the show.

Index counter　A CD's time readout telling the cut number being played and how long a time it has played (or time remaining, or total time for the cut).

Fade up/down/out sound　Move the mixer's slider to smoothly increase/decrease sound or to gradually reduce it to silence.

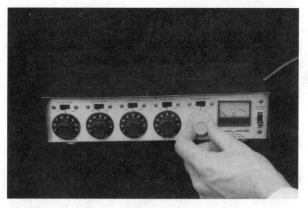

Shure portable audio MIXER. The fingers are on the MASTER volume knob.

Fostex medium-sized MIXER

FIGURE 1–16   MIXERS.

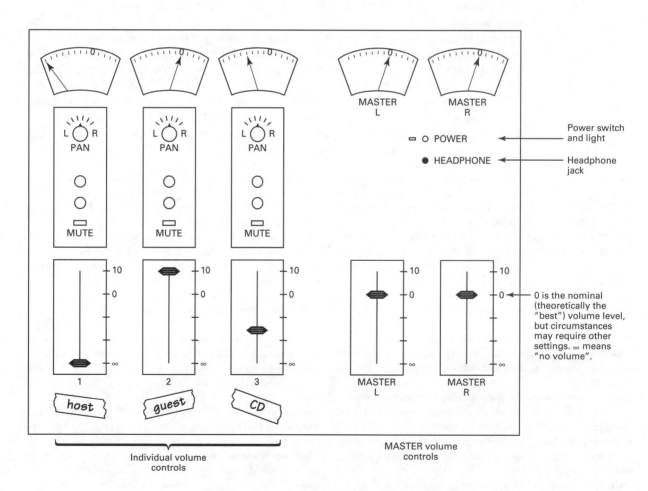

FIGURE 1–17   Simplified stereo MIXER layout.

also need to be labeled so you can find the right slider quickly. Before the show, you may want to experiment with the sliders to see which ones serve which sound sources.

4. Each slider may have a column of other controls associated with it. You'll learn about them in the audio chapter. One important button is the MUTE switch, usually at the top of the column. If you're *not* using a sound source, (a cassette tape player for instance), click its MUTE button "on" (usually pushing the button to the "down" or "in" position). This will silence that input. To activate an input (the CD player that you'll be using for music, for instance), switch the MUTE for that column "off" (usually "up" or "out"). Pressing the button toggles it on, then off, then on again.

   Another important control above each individual slider is the PAN control, or PAN POT. Turned to L, it sends the signal to the left (L) STEREO output controlled by the left (L) MASTER FADER. Turned to R, the signal goes to the right output. In the middle, it goes to both equally. For the purposes of this exercise, turn all PAN POTS to the middle for MONAURAL sound (left and right channels sound the same).

5. The meters tell you how loud your sound is. Some MIXERS have a meter for every source, some have a meter for a group of sources, and some just have a meter for the final mix of sound, the MASTER meter. Figure 1–18 shows a meter displaying a 0dB volume level, theoretically the "perfect" loudness for an audio signal.

   Some meters are made of LEDs (light-emitting diodes), shaped to form a graph. Figure 1–19 diagrams one. Again, you shoot for 0dB on the scale.

   While your performers are speaking normally, the meters should register just below 0dB on the scale, sometimes leaping into the red area above 0dB. If the meter lingers in the red, turn its volume down a bit; it's too loud.

6. The audio console will probably have a headphone output so that you can listen to the audio without distractions. The audio may also be sent to a control room amplifier so that everyone there can hear the sound. It too may have a volume control, allowing you to turn it up if the room is noisy or down if your sound is driving everybody crazy.

7. Your music will probably come from a CD player, although some shops still use audiocassettes, reel-to-reel tape players, audio cartridges, or vinyl records. (If your control room comes with a crank-up Victrola, consider studying at a more up-to-date school).

   The CD player works much like yours at home:
   a. Select a CD.
   b. Turn on the CD player's power.
   c. Press eject to open the drawer.
   d. Insert the CD, label side up.
   e. Close the drawer.
   f. Press PLAY.
   g. Adjust the MIXER's CD volume control for satisfactory sound.

FIGURE 1–18 Mixer's meter at 0dB.

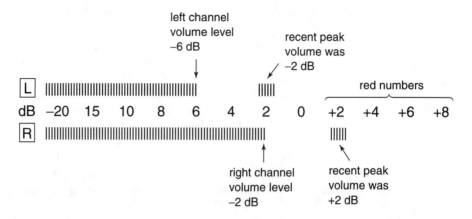

FIGURE 1–19   LED meter.

h. Select the particular CUT or song you want to use. Do this either by pressing the desired CUT number into a keypad and pressing PLAY, or by pressing an "advance" button that skips the CD to the next song.

i. Once you find the desired music, SCAN the music backwards by pressing another button on the CD player. This will get you to the silent spot just before the music begins. Press PAUSE to park the player there.

j. When you're ready to start the music, make sure the MIXER's volume is up and press PLAY (or PAUSE to UNPAUSE) on the CD player. The selected music will play.

The above method starts the music at full volume. Another alternative is to find the CUT you want, PAUSE the CD, turn down the CD volume on the MIXER, and when music is desired: Press PLAY on the CD player, then slowly FADE UP the volume on the MIXER. You can just as easily FADE OUT the volume when you're finished with the music, and then press PAUSE to stop the player (with its sound now unheard).

Some Philosophy of Sound Mixing.   For the cleanest, crispest, non-echoey sound, you want to have the volumes turned up for *only* the sources that are in use. This means that during the music segment, *only* the music control on the MIXER is up. This way you don't hear breathing or throat-clearing from the performers. Just before the host speaks, his/her volume gets turned up (maybe music *and* host are both heard together for a moment). Naturally, you'd turn down the music volume (to "off") when the show is totally underway. You turn up the guest's mike just as he/she is being introduced so that you don't hear offstage rustling or breathing from the guest. To anticipate these adjustments, the audio person needs to be familiar with the sequence of events in the show.

When music is mixed with someone speaking (a technique called MUSIC UNDER), the volume of the music is lowered so that it doesn't drown out the person's voice. Experiment to find the right music level for the occasion. Some types of music interfere with speech more than others and should be set at a lower volume.

Don't diddle with the sound controls more than absolutely necessary during the show, and diddle delicately. Big moves of the slider will make noticeable changes in the volume level and will be obtrusive. Quick outbursts of sound come and are quickly gone, requiring no adjustments. If an excited host, however, slowly gets louder during the show, edge his/her slider down a bit and see what happens. Finesse is the key.

Feel free to use both hands. You may find yourself doing several things at once.

Preparing to Mix Audio for the Simple Interview Show.   Let's assume someone has connected up the microphones and CD player and has adjusted the fancier controls on the MIXER so that it works normally.

The show will start with music, the host will speak and introduce the guest, the two will speak, the host will wrap up the show, and music will rise to finish the show. And you make this all happen.

1. Study the script so you know what will occur.
2. Put on your intercom headset to communicate with the floor manager.
3. Prepare the MIXER:
    a. Turn it on, if necessary.
    b. Turn the MASTER to full volume or maybe three-quarter volume (often 0 on its slider scale).
    c. Turn all the PAN POTS to their center position for MONAURAL sound.
    d. Find out which individual volume sliders go with which sources you'll be using. This takes some experimentation. You may have someone speak into the host's mike (turn the mike's power on if necessary) while you try different sliders, looking for the "host" slider. Remember: if the slider's MUTE is engaged, there will be so sound. Check also which slider goes with the CD player.
    e. Plug in headphones or listen to the control room speaker to evaluate the sound quality.
4. Do a sound check for all microphone sources.
    a. Have someone attach the host's and guest's microphones.
    b. Have the host speak normally into his/her mike. Perhaps have him/her recite part of the script or say his ABC's so you have a long stretch of natural sound (instead of the ubiquitous "Testing 1, 2, 3 . . ." that never gets spoken at a "normal" volume). As the host speaks, adjust his/her volume so that the meter bobs just around 0dB on the scale. Make a note of the volume level for that slider. Some audio people stick a little scrap of masking tape next to the slider's position, to mark the "proper" volume. If the volume control has to be all the way up or is barely up at all, something is misadjusted elsewhere. You'll learn how to make these adjustments in the audio chapter.
    c. Turn down the host's volume and repeat the process with the guest. Note the guest's best volume level, then turn it down to "off."
5. Select the music and test it out.
    a. Load a CD into the player as described earlier. Play some music.
    b. Adjust the music volume with the mixer's individual slider so that the meter bobs around 0dB. Mark this spot on the slider. If you have time, have the host speak and perform a MUSIC UNDER, noting the proper CD volume for this part of the show.
    c. CUE UP the music so it starts at the beginning of the CUT. As described earlier, play some music, SCAN it backwards to the silence before it begins, and PAUSE the music to park it there, ready for it to begin immediately when you push the PLAY (or UNPAUSE) button. Depending on the machine, there may also be other ways to CUE UP your music.
6. If music will be used at the end of the show, figure out how. Perhaps you will simply hit PLAY on the CD player and FADE the sound up mid-song and FADE it out at the end. Or you might CUE UP the music to end at the show's end. The former is easy but inelegant; the latter sounds cool but takes extra work. Here's how to CUE UP music for the end of the show:

    Find out how much music you'll need for the show's ending. Perhaps you can select a CUT exactly that length and follow the process in 5c above. Or, you can BACK-TIME some music to the length needed. To BACK-TIME a CD:
    a. Check the length of the CUT, or play the end of the CUT while watching the CD player's INDEX COUNTER. Note this number.

    b. Subtract the length of time you want the wrap-up music to run. If, for instance, the song runs 3:54 (3 minutes 54 seconds), and you wish to have 20 seconds of music at the show's end, you would subtract :20 from 3:54, getting 3:34.

    c. Park the CD player at 3:34 on the desired CUT and it will be ready to play from there to the end in 20 seconds.

Typically, you will CUE UP the ending music while the show is underway. The CD volume has to be down, so that the audience doesn't hear you experimenting. Using the numbers as shown above, you merely jump to the desired CUT, SCAN or PLAY (silently) to the calculated point, then PAUSE the player. When the time comes to use the music, you'd press PLAY, fade it up gently (so it doesn't start abruptly mid-song) and let it play to the end. Other ways to CUE UP music will be described later in the audio chapter.

During the Show.   Table 1–3 shows a sample script for the brief interview show "Why Did You Take This Course?" Use it as a guide to the steps that follow (filling in different names and music as appropriate). Technically, this is a *semiscripted* show because no one knows what is going to be said once the show is underway. Only the known parts of the show are written out.

TABLE 1–3   Sample Script: Why Did You Take This Course?

SHOW FORMAT: INTERVIEW
PRODUCTION DATE: 10/16/99
DIRECTOR: T. TUBERHONKER
VTR NO: 1
TOTAL TIME: 4:00

Video	*Audio*
FADE UP to CG. TITLE: "Why Did You Take This Course?"	CD MUSIC BAKERY #5 CUT 6 "Upbeat Office"
TITLE: "Host: Lisa Lisp. Guest: William Wannabe"	
TITLE: "Director: Tess Tuberhonker"	
HOST, SEATED	MUSIC UNDER *HOST*: Hi, I'm Lisa Lisp, your host for this segment of "Why Did You Take This Course?" MUSIC OUT
HOST STANDS	*HOST*: Our guest today is William Wannabe from Goshen, Massachusetts.
GUEST ENTERS. HOST & GUEST SHAKE HANDS. BOTH SIT.	*HOST*: Welcome to our show, William.

TABLE 1–3 *Continued*

	HOST INTERVIEWS GUEST
HOST & GUEST	*HOST*: Thank you, William, for coming on our show today.
	MUSIC UNDER HOST CD MUSIC BAKERY #5 CUT 6 starting at 1:06 running 20 sec.
HOST	*HOST*: I'm Lisa Lisp, your host for this segment of "Why Did You Take This Course?" Perhaps you'll take this course, too.
HOST & GUEST STAND, SHAKE HANDS, CONVERSE	MUSIC FULL
KEY & FILL LIGHTS DOWN	
DISSOLVE TO CREDITS ON CG	
CREDIT:	
"Cameras: Joanne Jitters Shakey Smith	
Technical director: Sven Svitcher	
Sound: Vera Louden	
Floor manager: Mel Adroit"	
CREDIT:	
"Lighting: Bonnie Beamer	
Titles: Missey Speller	
Associate director: Larry Lost	
Teleprompter: Reed Foster	
VTR operator: Red Buttons"	
CREDIT:	
"Directed by Tess Tuberhonker"	
FADE OUT	MUSIC ENDS

1. Make sure the host and guest volumes are off, the CD volume is up, the MASTER volume is up, and the CD is parked, ready to go.
2. On the director's cue, "Start music," hit PLAY on the CD.
3. Place one hand on the host's volume control, ready to bring it up. Place another hand on the CD volume control, ready to FADE it down.
4. Upon the director's command (when you hear "Ready to cue host" from the director), FADE up the host's mike volume.
5. FADE DOWN the music for the MUSIC UNDER either upon the director's command or after the host begins speaking (in case the director forgets to signal the MUSIC UNDER).
6. FADE OUT the music when the director commands.
7. Put one hand on the guest's volume control.
8. FADE UP the guest's mike volume when the host introduces him/her *or* when the director calls, "Bring up guest's mike."
9. As the show progresses, keep an eye on the meters and adjust both volume controls accordingly. It is common for performers to speak louder or softer during the show.
10. Get the CD player CUED UP for the show's end.
11. Near the end of the show, be ready to hit PLAY; then FADE UP the CD volume to halfway in anticipation for the MUSIC UNDER.
12. When the host thanks the guest, the director should say "Start music." Hit PLAY on the CD. FADE it up halfway (or so) for the MUSIC UNDER.
13. FADE OUT the guest's mike.
14. Put your hands on the host and CD volume controls in preparation.
15. When the host finishes speaking (or upon command from the director, "Music full"), FADE the music to full volume (the level you marked near the slider when the meter showed the music level at 0dB).
16. FADE OUT the host's mike.
17. When the music finishes, FADE OUT the MASTER volume. If the music runs longer than planned, the director may call "FADE OUT MUSIC" before it ends, so be ready to do this early.
18. After the show, return the CD to its storage area. Turn off power to the MIXER, if appropriate. Remind the floor manager to switch off battery power to the microphones and to remove the talent's mikes.

Notice that in the above procedure you carry out commands issued by the director *but also* think for yourself. Some directors don't want you to think for yourself (or you don't have a script and can't anticipate what comes next). Find out what your director wants from you and do that. Since most shows are produced with teams that have worked together before, those directors come to trust their audio people to learn the script and make decisions on their own.

There is always a dangerous fine line between *which* decisions you should make and which you should wait for the director to make. Good judgment and good luck will have you filling in for each step the director "forgets," yet waiting for crucial go-aheads from the director that keep everyone working in sync.

 Mini Review

- Adjust volumes so that the meters bob around the 0dB mark and don't linger in the red.
- Set up your sound volumes, test the mikes, cue up your music, and label your mixer sliders before the show.

The Technical Director

The technical director (also called the TD or switcher) pushes the buttons on the video console to display chosen camera shots or perform special effects. Since the PRODUCTION SWITCHER is festooned with more buttons than the Starship Enterprise, it takes an extra person just to keep track of them, especially in big shows.

It is good for the TD to have reviewed the script before show time to see if there are shots that have to be set up on the switcher. SPECIAL EFFECTS, especially, take some time to perfect so that they can be executed quickly.

In our simple talk show, there will be just two kinds of SPECIAL EFFECTS, the FADE and the DISSOLVE (where one picture slowly melts into another). The other shot changes will be CUTS (where the picture snaps from one shot to the next).

The Switcher Console. All PRODUCTION SWITCHERS are different, but all have some similarities. I will describe a fairly generic type of PRODUCTION SWITCHER for our purposes, like the one shown in Figure 1–20.

Some switchers have a MASTER FADE handle. It turns the picture black no matter what else is happening. Think of it as an "emergency exit" if you can't figure out how to get rid of your picture. We will FADE it up ("on") and leave it there for our show, FADING to black with other controls when the time comes.

Somewhere there is a row of buttons called PROGRAM. Push the CAM 1 button here, and camera 1's picture will be recorded or broadcast. Push CAM 2, and camera 2's picture is recorded. Push CG, and the CHARACTER GENERATOR's signal (generally a typed title) will be recorded. Push BLACK, and the screen will go to black. These simple button-presses are called cuts. The picture snaps from one shot to the next.

You view the results of your button-presses on the PROGRAM monitor, a TV monitor showing the final output of your switcher.

In your interview show, you will need to FADE UP from black and DISSOLVE between several shots. These simple SPECIAL EFFECTS will require you to use the PRODUCTION SWITCHER'S MIX EFFECTS BUS. Follow along in Figure 1–21, a simplified diagram of a PRODUCTION SWITCHER.

Technical director (TD) The person who pushes the buttons on the switcher during the show.

*Special effect A visual transition from one shot to another. Fancier than the simple "cut," special effects could be fades, wipes, page turns, or whatever gets you from one shot to another with some fanfare.

*Dissolve TV effect that melts one picture slowly into another. One picture fades to black, while another simultaneously fades up from black.

*Cut Switch from one picture to another directly, in the blink of an eye.

*Production switcher Push-button device that selects one or another camera's picture to be viewed or recorded.

Program The final output from a switcher that is broadcast or recorded.

*Master fade A fade lever that always fades the picture out to black or a chosen color.

*Fade Make a TV picture smoothly turn black (fade-out) or make black smoothly turn into a TV picture (fade-in or fade-up).

*Character generator (CG) Electronic device with a typewriter keyboard that electronically displays letters, numbers, and symbols on a TV screen.

Bus A group of related buttons on a switcher, often one or two rows of buttons.

*Program (PGM) bus The group of buttons on a switcher that directly selects (when pressed) which picture or special effect is broadcast or recorded.

SEG or special effects generator The part of a studio switcher that makes special effects, such as wipes.

Wipe Special effect that starts with one TV picture on the screen; then a boundary line moves across the screen (vertically, diagonally, or whatever), and where it passes, the first picture changes into a second picture.

*Effects bus Group of related buttons on video SEG/switchers to create special effects. A channel on the switcher that you can dissolve to and from, bringing a special effect onto the screen or taking it away.

M/E (mix effects) bus Group of switcher buttons that control special effects.

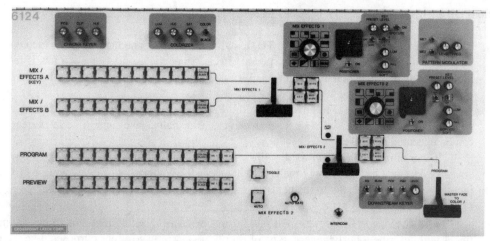

FIGURE 1–20   Simple STUDIO PRODUCTION switcher.

No, a BUS isn't a smelly vehicle that takes an hour to get you across town. It is a row of buttons on the switcher. A moment ago we described the PROGRAM BUS, the row of buttons that selects what will be shown. An EFFECTS BUS is a group of buttons that will take part in making a SPECIAL EFFECT, such as a DISSOLVE, WIPE, KEY, or whatever.

To use the EFFECTS BUS, first we have to activate it. We do this by finding the button marked M/E (for MIX/EFFECTS) on our old friend the PROGRAM BUS. Pressing M/E on the PROGRAM BUS selects the output from the M/E BUS, whatever that image turns out to be. Now, whatever you do on the M/E buttons determines what gets recorded.

The M/E BUS has to be told what kind of EFFECT to do—MIX (another name for DISSOLVE), WIPE, KEY, or whatever. A button near the M/E BUS will do that. Punch the MIX button near the M/E BUS to tell it to DISSOLVE /FADE from picture to picture.

We'll want our picture to DISSOLVE from one shot to another shot. You tell it where to start by punching one button, say CAM 1 on the A row (also called the A CHANNEL) of the M/E BUS, and another button, say CAM 2 on the B row. Now you can DISSOLVE between CAM 1 and CAM 2. You're actually DISSOLVING between whatever's punched up on CHANNEL A and whatever's punched up on CHANNEL B.

How do you activate the DISSOLVE? With the FADER BAR next to the two rows of buttons. Push it toward the A CHANNEL to DISSOLVE to what you've selected there. Pull it down to the B CHANNEL to DISSOLVE to what is selected there.

If on CHANNEL A you've selected BLK (black) and on CHANNEL B you've selected CAM 1 and your FADER BAR is *up*, then the picture will be black. Pull the bar down to B, and you'll DISSOLVE to CAM 1. (Just a technicality here, but FADE means going *to* or *from black* to something and DISSOLVE means going between two images. Many people simply use the word FADE in both situations).

---

*Mix   One of the ways of going from one TV picture to another (as opposed to wipe and key). Mix is often the name on the button that tells the fader levers to dissolve rather than wipe or key from one picture to the next.

Key (or luminance key)   Special effect that replaces the dark parts of one camera's picture with parts from another camera's picture.

Channel   A row of buttons on a switcher.

*Fader bar   A slider or handle on a switcher that allows you to fade-in or fade-out a picture or dissolve from one picture to another.

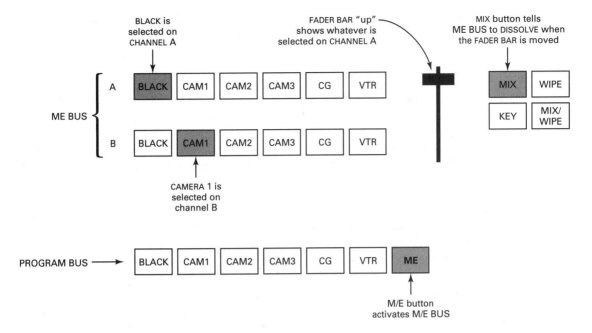

FIGURE 1–21   Simplified PRODUCTION SWITCHER layout.

If, with the FADER BAR down, you switch CHANNEL A to CAM 2, the picture won't change; CHANNEL B is still showing. Push the FADER BAR *up* and you'll DISSOLVE from CAM 1 to CAM 2.

Wanna DISSOLVE to the CG? Hit CG on the B CHANNEL. Nothing changes, *yet*. When you pull the FADER BAR *down*, you'll DISSOLVE from CAM 2 to the CG.

Wanna FADE OUT (FADE to black)? Punch BLK on the A CHANNEL and push the FADER BAR *up*.

You can CUT from shot to shot while using the M/E BUS. Say CAM 1 is on CHANNEL A, CAM 2 is on B, and the FADER is *down*. What's showing? CAM 2 shows. Now press the CAM 1 button on the B CHANNEL. The picture snaps from CAM 2 to CAM 1. Since the B CHANNEL is "on," whatever you press there will show, just like using the PROGRAM BUS.

The experts say to use the word "dissolve" between cameras, but the word "fade" is faster.

Play with the PRODUCTION SWITCHER for a while to get a "feel" for it. It will start to make sense as you experiment. You can't hurt anything by pushing buttons, so explore.

Switching for the "Why Did You Take This Course?" Show

1. Study a copy of the script. Discuss it with your director. You'll learn that there will be CUTS and DISSOLVES, a FADE UP from black, and a FADE OUT to black.
2. Set up your switching console to do the EFFECTS.
   a. Press M/E on the PROGRAM BUS to activate the M/E BUS. (Some switchers have several M/E BUSES, so select one, say M/E 1, on the PROGRAM BUS and do the rest of your business on the M/E 1 BUS).
   b. Select MIX on the M/E BUS.
   c. Move the FADER BAR *up*.
   d. Press BLK on M/E CHANNEL A. The picture will now be black.
   e. Press CG on M/E CHANNEL B. You're now ready to DISSOLVE to the CG.
3. When the show begins, here's what you'll be doing upon command from the director:

Director command	You do
a. Start with black.	Start with the FADER *up* where CHANNEL A has BLACK selected.
b. FADE to CG.	With CG already punched into CHANNEL B, simply pull the FADER *down*. The title shows.
c. Next title.	The CG changes title; you do nothing.
d. Ready to DISSOLVE to camera 1.	Press CAM 1 on the "A" CHANNEL of the M/E BUS (nothing visibly changes on screen).
e. DISSOLVE to 1.	Push the FADER *up*. CHANNEL A is now "on."
f. Ready to take 2.	Poise your finger over CAM 2 on the A CHANNEL.
g. Take 2.	Press CAM 2 on the A CHANNEL.
h. Ready to take 1.	Poise your finger over CAM 1 on the A CHANNEL.
i. Take 1.	Press CAM 1 on the A CHANNEL.

And so it goes through the show. Near the end, you may be on CAM 2 and will hear

j. Ready to DISSOLVE to CG.	Press CG on CHANNEL B of the M/E BUS.
k. DISSOLVE to CG.	Pull the FADER down to B.
l. Next credit.	You do nothing; the CG changes the title on screen.
m. Next credit.	Do nothing.
n. Ready to FADE OUT.	Press BLACK on the A CHANNEL.
o. FADE OUT.	Push the FADER BAR *up*.

You're done. Treat yourself to an Alka-Seltzer.

 Mini Review

- Learn the logic of the switcher's bus structure so that you can set up the next shot while the first is showing so that you can go to the new shot in one stroke.

The Character Generator Operator

The CHARACTER GENERATOR, or CG, is much like a word processor. You type titles and credits onto the screen using a keyboard. When you finish a screen, you save it, usually giving it a name and/or a number for later reference. Then you type in another screen of data. When done, you've stored several screens of text.

Along the way, you may have been given choices (via menu or through special buttons on the keyboard) for

a. Type style
b. Type size
c. Type color
d. Background color
e. Borders or shadows

As you make your decisions, you can see your results on a PREVIEW MONITOR or CURSOR MONITOR. Often, a second STATUS MONITOR displays file names and other data so that you can choose what to show next. Figure 1–22 shows a professional CHARACTER GENERATOR.

Once you've entered (and checked, and edited, if necessary) your text, you SAVE it, telling the machine what name or number to assign this screen of text. Do this with all your screens of text.

Next, you decide how to transition from one screen of text to the next and in what order. You can

a. Snap from page to page
b. Scroll from page to page (as in rolling credits)
c. DISSOLVE, WIPE, or transition in some other fancy way from page to page

Enter this detail, along with the order of the pages. This is done through menu items on the STATUS monitor. (Step-by-step instructions for all of this are probably pasted on the wall next to the CG. The chapter on graphics has a detailed section on operating a Dubner CHARACTER GENERATOR).

By pressing a "show" button (or making a "show" selection from the menu), you can display the first title in the series. By pressing a "change" button (perhaps an arrow key), the pages will advance. If you select a fancy transition, the text will change from page to page using that transition.

The most common mistake in TV production is displaying misspelled text on the screen. Proof your work. Have someone else proof it again. Double-check people's names against the script or a list.

During the Show

1. You'll probably start with the show title already on screen (although you could start with a blank screen and transition to your first title upon command by the director).
2. When the director calls "Change title," press the button on the CG that advances to the next title in the series.

---

*Preview monitor   A TV screen showing a view of something before it is actually recorded or broadcast.
Cursor monitor   A TV screen showing where the next character from the CG (character generator) will be typed, what has been typed so far, and how the text will look when actually recorded or broadcast (the cursor, however, won't show then).
Status monitor   A computer screen allowing you to browse files or select menu items on a character generator.

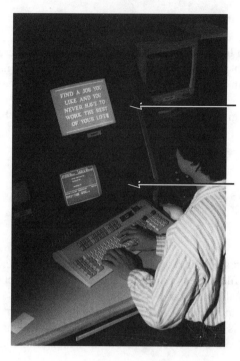

CURSOR MONITOR
shows where the
next letter will go
and shows what
the text and back-
ground may look
like.

STATUS MONITOR
shows menus,
lists of text,
and computer
commands

FIGURE 1–22   CHARACTER GENERATOR or TITLER.

 Mini Review

- Misspelling words is the most common error when making titles and credits on a character generator.

The Director

The director is in charge of the whole shebang. The director calls the shots. The director takes the blame when the show crashes and burns, even though the fault may be someone else's. Accordingly, it behooves the director to see that everybody is prepared for the show and knows what's going on (has a script, etc.). Furthermore, it's in the director's best interest to create a climate of teamwork and good spirit among the crew.

The Dozen Duties of a Deft Director

1. Learn the script so that you don't have to read it during the show. If you do all the other steps listed here, you'll learn the script effortlessly. Mark the script with additional notes and details, such as camera numbers. Table 1–3 showed a sample script, and Table 1–4 shows the same script with director's marks. There is no set of "rules" for director's marks. Just be consistent and clear.

   Circling words already on the script saves cluttering it with extra notations. Some directors don't include audio cues, leaving it to the audio people to mark their own scripts.

2. Think about what each camera will show. Try out a few shots. Avoid MATCHED SHOTS, in which both cameras give you nearly the same picture; that's a waste. Figure 1–23 shows such an example. One camera should be showing a ONE-SHOT or a MEDIUM CLOSE-UP, while the other shows

TABLE 1–4 Sample Script with Director's Marks: Why Did You Take This Course?

SHOW FORMAT: INTERVIEW
PRODUCTION DATE: 10/16/99
DIRECTOR: T. TUBERHONKER
VTR NO: 1
TOTAL TIME: 4:00

What the marks mean	*Video*	*Audio*
Fade up on CG first title. Start music full volume.	FADE UP to CG. TITLE: "Why Did You Take This Course?" *↑CG1*	CD MUSIC BAKERY #5 CUT 6 "Upbeat Office" *music full*
Take second CG title. Turn on host's mike.	TITLE: "Host: *CG2* Lisa Lisp. Guest: William Wannabe" TITLE: "Director: Tess Tuberhonker" *CG3*	*↑host*
Dissolve to medium shot of host on camera 1.	HOST, SEATED. *↑MS1*	MUSIC UNDER *HOST*: Hi, I'm Lisa Lisp, your host for this segment of "Why Did You Take This Course?" MUSIC OUT
Turn on guest's mike. Take camera 2. It's a two-shot of host and guest.	HOST STANDS.	*HOST*: Our guest today is William Wannabe from Goshen, Massachusetts. *↑guest*
	GUEST ENTERS. *2* HOST & GUEST SHAKE HANDS. BOTH SIT.	*HOST*: Welcome to our show, William.
Take 1, medium shot of guest. Take 2, medium shot of host.	*1 MS guest* *2 MS host*	HOST INTERVIEWS GUEST **3:30**
Take 1, zoom to host & guest two-shot.	HOST & GUEST. *1 MS guest zoom to host + guest*	*HOST*: Thank you, William, for coming on our show today. MUSIC UNDER HOST CD MUSIC BAKERY #5 CUT 6 starting at 1:06 running 20 sec. *(continued)* *↓guest*

TABLE 1–4   *Continued*

What the marks mean	Video	Audio
Take 2, medium shot of host.	**(2 MS)** HOST.	*HOST:* I'm Lisa Lisp, your host for this segment of "Why Did You Take This Course?" Perhaps you'll take this course, too.
Take 1, long shot of host & guest.	**(1 LS)** HOST & GUEST STAND, SHAKE HANDS, CONVERSE. KEY & FILL LIGHTS DOWN.	**(MUSIC FULL)** **(↓ host)**
Dissolve to third title on CG.	DISSOLVE TO CREDITS ON CG. **(↑ CG-3)** CREDIT: "Cameras: Joanne Jitters Shakey Smith Technical director: Sven Svitcher Sound: Vera Louden Floor manager: Mel Adroit"	
Take 4th title on CG.	CREDIT: **(CG-4)** "Lighting: Bonnie Beamer Titles: Missey Speller Associate director: Larry Lost Teleprompter: Reed Foster VTR operator: Red Buttons"	
Take 5th title on CG.	CREDIT: **(CG-5)** ——— 3:55 "Directed by Tess Tuberhonker" **(FADE OUT)** ———	**(MUSIC ENDS ↓)** ——— 4:00

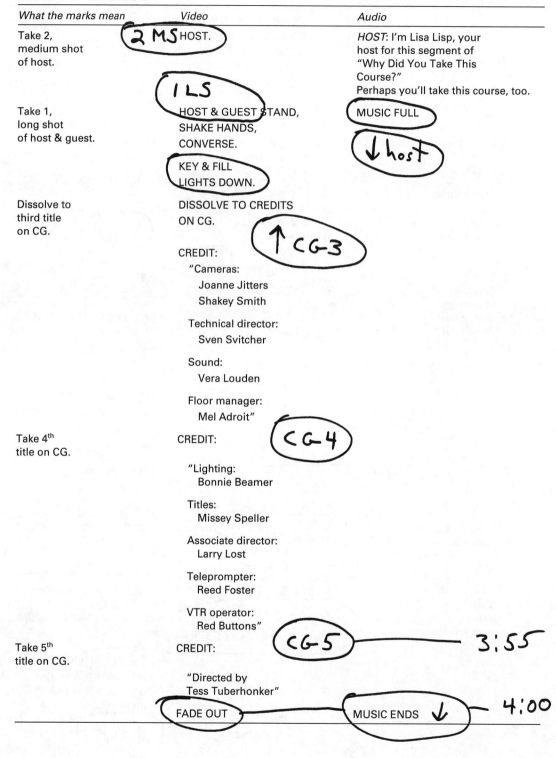

TWO-SHOT

Another TWO-SHOT. Shot changes but reveals nothing new. Change of camera position jarringly calls attention to itself.

FIGURE 1–23 Matched shots.

a TWO-SHOT or a MEDIUM or LONG SHOT, more like Figure 1–24. As you plan this out, add these notes to your script.

3. Discuss the marked script with the associate director, audio person, camera operators, technical director, and anyone else who needs to know the sequence of events.
4. Make sure someone is assigned to each task that needs to be done in the show.
5. Stay aware of your production schedule so you don't run out of time. Is there time for a practice run of the show before you record it?
6. Double-check everyone's work before show time. Is the lighting satisfactory? Are the credits spelled right? Was appropriate music selected for the show?
7. Before the show, the director (or any control room member) can use the TALKBACK system (a push-button microphone in the control room leading to speakers in the studio) to give any final comments or to alert everyone that the show is about to start.
8. When the show begins, give "ready" cues before each action, so the person who has to carry out the action is prepared to execute it.
9. Stay calm and reassuring during the shoot, even if something goes wrong. If *you* fall apart, *everything* falls apart.
10. Avoid excessive chatter. Be brief to avoid diluting people's attention.

---

*Matched shots Similar-looking views of a subject from two cameras at the same time.

One-shot Shot of a single performer or subject.

Two-shot Shot of two performers or subjects.

*Close-up Close, or zoomed-in shot of a performer, perhaps showing just the face, or a shot that fills the screen with an object.

Medium close-up Halfway between a medium and a close-up shot, perhaps showing a person's face and shoulders.

*Medium shot A shot of a person from the waist up, or the shot of an object showing some of its surroundings.

*Long shot A far away or zoomed-out shot showing the whole performance area and its inhabitants.

*Camera monitors TV monitors in the control room showing each camera's image.

CG monitor TV monitor in the control room showing the title selected on the character generator.

Leader Unrecorded space (from ten seconds to three minutes) at the beginning of a tape, often used to protect the actual program from threading damage. Also, unrecordable plastic tape attached to the beginning of a cassette roll.

*Talkback system A loudspeaker system to allow the control-room crew to speak directly to studio personnel.

ONE-SHOT

TWO-SHOT from a different camera angle.

FIGURE 1–24   Make the camera angles different to avoid MATCHED SHOTS.

11. Keep an eye on the CAMERA MONITORS in the control room so that you know what each is doing. You don't want to switch to a shot that's "bad." Nor do you want to stick with one that's going sour.

12. Don't forget to thank the crew and talent when the show's over.

What the Director Might Say During the Show.   The show is ready to start. The studio will use two cameras. The sound, titles, effects, camera angles, and VCR have all been checked. Everyone's intercom headset is on. The lights are up. The first CG title has been selected and appears on the CG MONITOR. Here's what the director is likely to say as our little interview show takes place:

Over intercom:	*Camera 1, can you hear me?*
	Camera 2, can you hear me?
	Floor manager, can you hear me?
	Teleprompter, can you hear me?
	(All respond affirmatively. The rest of the crew are in the control room with the director.)
To camera 1:	*One, give me a medium close-up of the host. Follow her up when she stands.*
To camera 2:	*Two, give me a two-shot of the host and leave empty space for the guest to step into from off-stage. Follow them as they sit.*
	(The above has been discussed with the camera operators; this is just reconfirmation.)
To TD:	*Give me black; then we'll fade to CG.*
To VCR operator:	*Ready to begin recording.*
To all, over studio talk-back system:	*Stand by, about one minute.*
	(Floor manager shushes chatty guest.)
To camera 1:	*One, tilt down a bit on Lisa.*
	(There was too much headroom in the shot.)
	Good. Hold it.

To VCR operator:	*Begin recording.* (Operator says "Recording." Director waits 10 seconds to record a black LEADER before the show begins.)
To TD:	*Ready to fade to CG.*
To audio person:	*Ready to start music.*
To both:	*Start music. Fade to CG.*
To CG operator:	*Ready next title.* (Director pauses to read title to himself.) *Change.* (The title changes.)
To floor manager:	*Ready to cue host.*
To TD:	*Ready to dissolve to 1.*
To audio person:	*Open host mike.* *Ready to music under.*
Director to crew:	*Dissolve to 1; cue host; music under.* (The host speaks.)
To audio person:	*Ready to lose music.* *Open guest mike.* *Kill music.*
To TD:	*Ready to take 2.* *Take 2.* (The guest enters.)
To camera 1:	*One, give me medium close-up of guest.*
To TD:	*Ready to take 1.* (Waits for guest to speak and for 1 to get a good shot.) *Take 1.*
To camera 2:	*Two, give me medium shot of host.* (Waits for host to ask next question and for camera 2 to get a good shot.)
To TD:	*Ready to take 2.* *Take 2.*

(Back and forth it goes between host and guest—cameras 2 and 1, with an occasional change to a two-shot as the interview progresses).

Sometime during a lull, the director asks the audio person to cue up the ending music. The audio person, having read the script has already done so and responds, "all cued up."

The associate director (or a timer, if started at the show's beginning) signals that one minute is left to the show. At this moment camera 2 has a shot of the host, and camera 1 is "on" with a shot of the guest. The director continues:

To floor manager:	*One minute left.*
To CG operator:	*Ready to start credit sequence.*
	Give me first credit.
To audio person:	*Ready to start wrap-up music under.*
	Ready to kill guest mike.
To camera 1:	*One, slowly zoom out to a two-shot of them both.*
To lighting person:	*Get ready to dim key and fill at the end of the show.*

The half-minute signal is announced.

To floor manager:	*Half minute. We'll finish on camera 2.*
	(Host thanks guest.)
To TD:	*Ready to take 2.*
	Take 2.
	(The host begins reading the wrap-up from the camera 2 teleprompter.)
To audio person:	*Fade up music under.*
	Kill guest mike.
To TD:	*Ready to take 1.*
To camera 1:	*One, zoom out a little more.*
	Good.
To TD:	*Take 1.*
	(Host and guest shake hands.)
To lighting person:	*Dim lights.*
	(From prior discussions, the lighting person knows this means dim the KEY and FILL lights, illuminating the talent with BACK and SET lights only.)
To audio person:	*Music up.*
	Kill host mike.
To TD:	*Ready to dissolve to CG.*
	Dissolve to CG.
	(First credit appears.)
To CG:	*Ready to change credits.*
	(Director reads credit from screen.)
	Change.
	(Director reads next credit.)
	Change.
To audio person:	*Fade out the music after it ends.*
	(So the *next* song on the CD won't start playing.)

To TD:	*Ready to fade to black.*
	(Director awaits last note of song.)
	Fade to black.
To VCR operator:	*Record 15 more seconds, then stop.*
	(This makes a leader for the end of the tape.)
To all, over the studio talkback system:	*Thank you, everybody. Good work. Hang on a moment while we check the tape.*
	(VCR operator says, "VCR stopped.")
To VCR operator:	*Rewind a bit and check the tape, please.*
	(The VCR operator runs the tape back one minute to sample some of the program. If for some reason it were bad, the show could be done over while everybody's present at their stations. "It's okay," he says).
	Thanks. Rewind and label it, please.
To all, over the studio PA system:	*The tape is good. Thanks again. Nice job, everybody.*

The director staggers off and swallows half a package of Tums, wrapper and all.
Some final notes:

1. The procedure above is not the only way to do or say things. Studio crews develop their own jargon over time, often abbreviating whole commands into single syllables.
2. The associate director may play a greater or lesser role in giving "ready" cues, relaying cues and timing to the floor manager, as well as telling the director how much time is left to the show.
3. Experienced crews know to perform many steps themselves without being told, saving the director from mentioning routine things like "Fade out the music after it ends," or "Record fifteen more seconds, then stop."
4. When all crew members have studied their copies of the script (and probably written their own cues on it), the show almost runs itself. Everybody knows what's coming next and automatically does his or her thing. The director "directs" much less, mostly giving cues to keep everyone synchronized.

 Mini Review

- The director must be intimately familiar with the script and make sure the other crew members know what will happen during the show.
- The director needs to give "ready" cues before calling for action.
- The director sets the team's attitude; be firm but friendly. Keep your cool.
- Thank the team when the show's over.

The Associate Director

This position exists only for big shows, "live" shows, tightly timed shows, or shows when extra personnel abound. The AD can pick up as much or as little of the load as the director allows. Where timing is critical, the AD keeps track of when things are supposed to happen and keeps the events of the show on track.

Be firm but friendly.

For fully scripted shows, the AD may concentrate on the script, while the director concentrates on the monitors and selects shots. It's hard for anyone to watch both at once. The AD, listening to the show, follows the script and tells the director and others what is scheduled to come next with words such as these:

"Thirty seconds left."
"Have Lisa read from camera 2."
"When they shake hands, fade down lights and fade up music."
Ready to kill Lisa's mike and bring music to full."

The AD needs to be quite familiar with the script and would make notations on the script to highlight actions to call out.

The AD would also time the show, warning everyone as the end approached.

The VCR Operator

The VCR (videocassette recorder) operator is responsible for recording the show. This includes checking the VCR for proper operation before the show, running the VCR during the show, checking the tape after the show, and affixing a label to the cassette and cassette box (so the show doesn't get lost or erased).

Operating a VCR. Most VCRs work about the same, although industrial models may have more buttons. Here are some generic instructions, in case you can't find the instruction manual or a five-year-old to help you. Let's assume the VCR is already wired to the TV system and any of the unusual switches on the machine have been set to the proper positions.

1. Get a blank tape. Make sure it hasn't been ERASE PROTECTED. If someone has removed the erase protection tab along the spine of the cassette (or thrown a little switch on some other kinds of cassettes), the tape can't be erased or recorded over. Blank tapes, out of the box, are always ready to be recorded. Tapes that are important to somebody usually have their tabs removed as a safety precaution.

   Also make sure the cassette is the right kind for the VCR you're using.
2. Turn the VCR's POWER *on.*
3. Press EJECT (to open the VCR's mouth or to remove a cassette that's already in the machine).
4. Insert your cassette, trapdoor first, window side up.
5. Press REWIND if the tape isn't at its beginning, unless there's already something recorded on the tape that precedes your show.
6. If this is a multispeed VCR, like VHS or SVHS, switch it to SP (Standard Play, the two-hour mode on T120 tapes). The faster SP speed makes a better recording than the slow EP (extra play) or LP (long play) or SLP (super long play) modes.
7. Make a sample recording; then play it back to make sure the machine is functioning correctly.
   a. Have the TD send you a good TV picture. (Perhaps press CAM 1 on the PROGRAM BUS of the switcher while the camera aims at something). Meanwhile, have the audio person send you sound (i.e., play a CD of music through the MIXER *at proper volume*). You should see a picture on the SWITCHER'S PROGRAM monitor and hear the CD's sound in the control room.
   b. Press RECORD/PLAY (pressing RECORD and while holding it down, pressing PLAY) and observe the VCR MONITOR, the one that shows the VCR's output (it shows what the VCR is seeing). You should see the picture from CAM 1. If you don't, seek help from a technician (or that five-year-old).
   c. Plug headphones into the VCR's headphone output and listen for the CD music. If you hear it, go on to the next step. If not, seek technical help.
   d. Adjust the AUDIO RECORD VOLUME CONTROL (if the VCR has one—or two for STEREO) so that the VCR's audio meters are wiggling just below 0dB on their scales). This indicates that proper audio volume will be recorded.
   e. After recording for a minute, press STOP; then rewind the tape. Then hit PLAY. Have the TD switch to black and the audio person stop the CD player (you want to know your VCR monitor is showing you what you're *playing*, not the signal from the SWITCHER. Similarly, you want to check the sound from the tape and not be confused with the sound coming from the audio MIXER).

---

*VCR Videocassette recorder, a device to record audio and video on tape housed in a cassette.

*Erase protected A videocassette that cannot be recorded because a plastic tab along the edge of the cassette has been removed or switched to the "protected" position.

*VCR monitor TV monitor connected to a VCR's output that displays what the VCR is recording or playing.

VHS Video home system. The most popular consumer half-inch videocassette format.

Audio record volume control Knob on an industrial VCR that sets the loudness of the audio recording. Most consumer VCRs adjust record volumes automatically and have no knobs for this.

S-VHS Super VHS, a much improved version of VHS, downwardly compatible with VHS.

*SP Standard play—the two-hour speed of a VHS VCR.

EP or ELP or SLP Extra play or extra-long play or super-long play—the six-hour speed of a VHS VCR.

LP Long play—The four-hour speed of a VHS VCR.

f. If the sound and picture are okay, press STOP; then REWIND. You're ready to record for real next time.

Recording the Show

1. The director will tell you to start the VCR recording. Press RECORD/PLAY and if the REC (record) light comes on and the VCR monitor shows an image that matches the SWITCHER'S PROGRAM monitor, all is well; say "Recording" to acknowledge that his/her command has been executed.
2. The director should allow ten seconds of black LEADER to be recorded before the show starts.
3. As the show progresses, observe the VCR monitor. Is the picture okay? If not, inform the director; there's no point in recording a defective signal. Similarly, observe the audio meters. To be extra sure the sound is good, check it on the VCR's headphones.
4. At the end of the show, let the tape run an extra fifteen seconds with black and silence. This provides a LEADER and also guarantees that viewers see sedate black after the show, not remnants of some previously recorded *Beavis and Butt-head* cartoons that hadn't been erased.
5. After stopping the recording, rewind the tape a ways and play a sample to assure yourself that the recording came out okay.
6. Label the tape along its spine. Also label the box with:
Name of show
Date of recording
Director's name

If this tape must be protected against accidental erasure, pop out the ERASE PROTECT TAB along its spine.

 Mini Review

- The associate director watches the script for events coming up and helps the director by giving "ready" cues and "time remaining" cues.
- The VCR operator should make a test recording to ensure that the equipment is functioning correctly.
- Label your tapes.

PRACTICE MAKES POLISHED

When your class has finished a series of shows, your instructor will probably play them back to you. They're usually quite a howl. The mistakes you'll see will teach you more than any list of "do's and don'ts" can. Television is definitely a learn-by-doing enterprise. The pressure of *performance* will energize your curiosity, inspiring you to discover how to improve.

Doing something *once*, however, doesn't make you much of an expert. If class time permits students only one rotation through each duty, you'll never have the opportunity to hammer the bugs out of your style. This is why it is good to rotate several times through each position. You'll see the shows getting better with each round.

The typical TV course will include lectures on the various equipment and skill, while the "lab" part of the course will immerse you in actual TV production. As your skills increase, you'll learn to write your own scripts, use fancy camera angles, create moods with your lighting, include tape shot outside the studio, and explore SPECIAL EFFECTS. The real fun is just beginning.

HOW TV WORKS

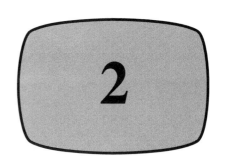

Many students take this course to escape studying engineering or science. Learning how TV works may sound complicated, but it isn't going to be. This chapter aims to satisfy your curiosity while at the same time showing you how this electronic chain of machinery all fits together. Also, the language you learn in this chapter will help you make sense of the knobs, plugs, and gadgets you will study later.

TV SETS

A TV set is a box of electronics and a big, empty glass bottle called a PICTURE TUBE. Inside the bottle is an electronic gun, sort of a machine gun that shoots electricity. This gun shoots a beam of electrons at the inside face of the TV screen, which is covered with phosphor dust. Where the electrons hit the phosphor, it glows. If you were zapped with 30,000 volts, you'd glow too (one reason for keeping your paws outside the box when the TV is operating).

To make a picture, the electron gun sweeps across the screen from side to side, much as your eyes sweep across each line of this page and eventually cover the entire page. Special SYNC circuits tell the gun how fast to sweep and when to sweep as well as when to stop shooting at the end of a line

---

Picture tube   A vacuum tube with an electron gun at one end and a phosphor screen at the other, which glows when struck by electrons from the gun.

*Sync   A circuit or a signal that directs the electron gun in a camera or TV picture tube to create a TV picture steadily on a screen. Sync also synchronizes the electronics of other TV equipment.

*Video   The picture portion of a broadcast TV signal; an electronic signal making a TV picture.

*Field   The TV picture created in one-sixtieth of a second by scanning an electron gun over *every other* line in the picture. In the United States there are 262½ odd-numbered lines in a field, followed by 262½ more even-numbered lines, making the next field one-sixtieth of a second later. The two fields together make a frame, a complete TV picture.

Odd field   A TV field made with odd-numbered sweeps of the electron gun.

Even field   A TV field made with even-numbered sweeps of the electron gun.

*Frame   A complete TV picture lasting one-thirtieth of a second, composed of two fields, or 525 scanning lines (in the United States).

*Interlace scan   Method of making a TV picture by drawing the odd numbered lines on the screen with one sweep, then filling in between with the next sweep of even numbered lines. The process is repeated approximately every one-thirtieth of a second.

Bandwidth   Electromagnetic "room" for TV channels or computer data on a wire, cable, fiber, or airwave.

Progressive scan   Method of making a computer picture by drawing all the scan lines sequentially from top to bottom.

*Pickup chip   The light-sensitive part of a TV camera that "sees" the picture and turns it into video signals.

CCD   Charge-coupled device, a popular type of image-sensing pickup chip in TV cameras.

(just as you stop reading at the end of a line and zip your eyes back to the beginning of the next line). SYNC also tells the gun to stop shooting when it reaches the bottom of a TV screen and then reaims the gun at the top and starts it shooting again. As the beam zigzags across the screen, another signal (VIDEO) tells the gun to shoot harder or weaker depending on whether it is tracing a lighter or darker part of the picture. By turning up the BRIGHTNESS control on your TV, you tell the gun to shoot harder at the screen, thus lighting up the phosphors more brightly. When SYNC gets fouled up for some reason, your picture rolls or collapses into a spaghetti of diagonal lines.

The electron gun zips its beam across the screen 15,735 times each second, and it starts at the top of the screen nearly 60 times each second. The phosphors keep glowing until the next time the beam comes around and zaps them again. Thus the screen appears smooth and flicker-free. European TVs, incidentally, retrace themselves only 50 times per second rather than 60, and, as a result, European TV flickers more noticeably than U.S. TV. Also, the signals are incompatible with U.S. TV sets. Figure 2–1 diagrams the process.

Actually, when the electron gun sweeps its lines across the screen, it doesn't do all the lines at once. First it does the odd-numbered lines, leaving empty spaces for the even-numbered lines. Then it goes back and fills in the even-numbered lines. In the first sixtieth of a second, it will sweep lines 1, 3, 5, 7, etc., making a total of 262½ lines on the screen. This is called the ODD FIELD. In the next one-sixtieth of a second, it draws lines 2, 4, 6, 8, etc., making another 262½ lines on the screen. This is called the EVEN FIELD. Therefore, it really takes one-thirtieth of a second to draw each complete picture. The complete picture is called a FRAME. Each of these frames is motionless, but because they go by so quickly (30 per second), they make the picture appear to be moving. The process is much like that of a movie projector.

This technique of sweeping half the lines onto the screen and then sweeping the other half in between them is called INTERLACE SCANNING. Why all this bother? By zapping 60 half-pictures onto the

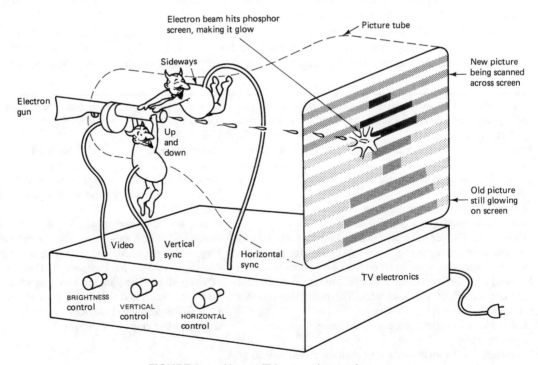

FIGURE 2–1   How a TV set makes a picture.

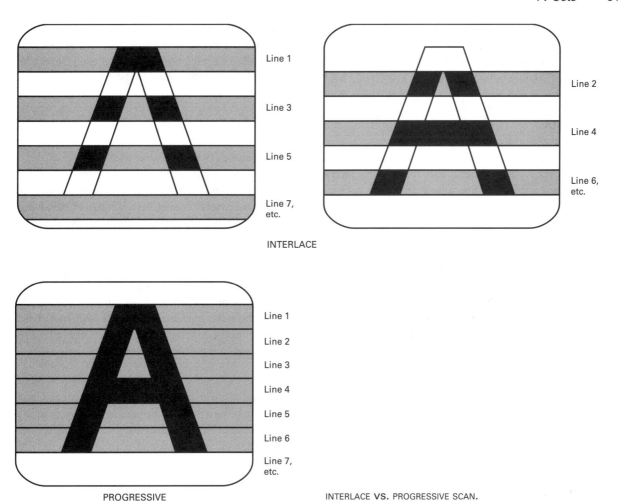

Line 1
Line 3
Line 5
Line 7, etc.

Line 2
Line 4
Line 6, etc.

INTERLACE

Line 1
Line 2
Line 3
Line 4
Line 5
Line 6
Line 7, etc.

PROGRESSIVE

INTERLACE **VS.** PROGRESSIVE SCAN.

screen each second, the image flickers less than if you zapped 30 whole pictures onto the screen each second. Why not zap 60 whole pictures onto the screen per second? Actually, computers do it this way, but 60 *whole* pictures consume too much BANDWIDTH, or space for the electrical vibrations to fit in the air without interfering with each other when broadcast. Computers send their signals a short distance over a wire, so they don't suffer these limitations.

 Mini Review

- In the United States, television signals consist of about 30 pictures or frames per second. Each picture is made of two half-pictures, called fields. There are about 60 fields per second. The above technique is called interlace scan. Computers, on the other hand, sweep the entire image onto the screen at once, a technique called progressive scan.
- Sync is an invisible part of the TV picture that holds the picture steady on the screen.

Using a technique called PROGRESSIVE SCAN, computers sweep all the lines onto their screens at once, starting from top to bottom, much like the way you read this page. They make 60 or so *complete* pictures every second. Naturally, one system is incompatible with the other. There are gadgets to convert computer images into video and vice versa; you'll read about them later in the book.

TV CAMERAS

A TV camera works like a TV set in reverse. Instead of *making* light, it *senses* light.

The camera lens focuses the image of a scene onto a light-sensitive PICKUP CHIP, sometimes called a CCD because many of these chips are CCDs (charge-coupled devices). The chip is a postage stamp–sized circuit covered with about 400,000 microscopic light sensing "eyes" made of transistor-like material. These "eyes" are lined up like pockets in a giant egg crate, and when light strikes a pocket, it generates electrons. The brighter the light, the more electrons are amassed. Thus, the light creates a tiny image made of electrons.

Another circuit in the camera measures the electric charge in the pockets, and reads the data out as a varying electric signal. SYNC circuits assure that the electric charges stream out at exactly the right speed so that one row of pockets makes the video signal for one sweep of the electron gun in the TV set. Next, SYNC reads out the next row of pockets, and the next, until the 262½ odd rows have been read. SYNC then clocks out the 262½ even rows of data, making a complete FRAME, 525 lines of video picture. Before the process starts over again, another circuit empties the chip's pockets, ready to measure more light.

So, following the process from camera to TV: The lens focuses an image on the camera's PICKUP CHIP. The chip converts the thousands of dots of light into electrical charges. A SYNC signal reads out these charges one row at a time as a varying voltage, a VIDEO signal. Thus, bright and dark parts of the picture become strong and weak voltages in the VIDEO signal. This VIDEO signal goes to your TV set and tells its electron gun to "shoot hard, shoot soft," thus creating light and dark areas on the TV screen. Figure 2–2 diagrams the process.

COLOR

In a darkened room, aim a red flashlight at a white wall, and you'll see red; turn it off, and you'll see black. Shine a blue light on the wall, and you'll see blue. Shine green, and you'll see green. Shine red and blue together, and the colors will mix to create a new color, magenta. Shine red and green, and you'll see yellow. Shine all three, and you'll get white, as illustrated in Figure 2–3. (The backcover has a color version of this figure.) All the other colors can be made from shining various proportions of these three PRIMARY COLORS.

---

*Primary colors   Three colors that can be combined to create all the other colors. TVs in the United States use red, green, and blue as primary colors.
*Monochrome   Black-and-white (not color).
*Three-chip camera   A TV camera with three pickup chips inside, one sensitive to the red parts of the picture, another sensitive to green, and the third sensitive to blue.
*NTSC video   National Television Standards Committee method used in the United States for electronically creating a

color TV signal. The color and brightness aspects of the image travel together on the same wire.
*RGB video   Video signals traveling on three separate wires. Red parts of a colored picture go on one wire; green, on the second; and blue, on the third.
*One-chip camera   A camera with one-image pickup chip that senses all the colors plus black-and-white aspects of a TV picture.

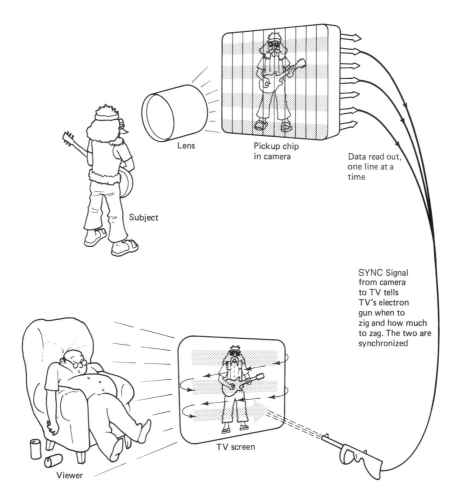

FIGURE 2–2 How the camera and TV make the picture.

A MONOCHROME (black-and-white) TV set makes its picture by electronically creating black (which is really just the absence of white) and white onto a screen in various proportions. A colored TV makes its color picture by overlapping three pictures on its screen: one red-and-black, another green-and-black, and the third blue-and-black. Where only red is projected, you see only red. Where red and green pictures overlap on the screen, you see yellow. Where all three pictures are black, you see black. Where all three colors converge with proper strength, you see white.

The picture tubes in color TV sets have three electron guns, one for each color. (The electron beams themselves don't have any color—where the beam hits the phosphor is where the color is made). The face of the color TV screen is made of dots or bars of phosphor, which glow red, blue, or green when hit by electrons. Look really closely at your TV screen while it's displaying a white picture, and you'll be able to see the tiny colored dots or stripes which make up the whole colored picture. The electron gun for the blue color is arranged so that it can hit only the blue phosphors on the screen. The red gun can hit only red, and the green gun, only green. Each of the three guns scans its own picture onto the screen, and the three pictures overlap to create dazzling views of sea rescues and loose dentures alike.

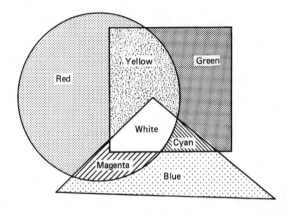

When you shine colors on a wall or light up color phosphors near each other, their colors add, making new colors.

The red circle + the green box = yellow.

The green box + the blue triangle = cyan.

The blue triangle + the red circle = magenta.

Red + green + blue = white. Different proportions of red, green, and blue make up all the other colors.

When mixing paint (rather than projecting light), the colors *subtract*, resulting in colors completely different from the above when they mix.

FIGURE 2–3   Additive color mixing (see also color version on back cover).

Color TV cameras work much like color TV sets in reverse. Somehow the camera has to make a red, a green, and a blue picture and combine them into a single VIDEO signal.

One way to do this would be to have three black-and-white TV cameras, side by side, all take a picture of the same subject. One camera would look through a red lens and see only the red parts of the picture. Another camera would look through a blue lens and would see only the blue parts of the picture. The third camera, looking through a green lens, would see only green. Thus the three black-and-white cameras could make VIDEO signals representing the red, the blue, and the green versions of the picture. To simplify matters, manufacturers have put the three cameras into the same box where they can share some of the same electronics. They also share the same lens and are called THREE-CHIP CAMERAS. So that each PICKUP CHIP can "see" a particular color, the lens image is split into three images using either two-way mirrors or glass prisms. The two methods are diagrammed in Figure 2–4. (See also color version.) Each image passes through a colored filter so that one PICKUP CHIP sees red; another, blue; and another, green. These three, single-color VIDEO signals are called RGB (red, green, blue) VIDEO and are used by computers, TV projectors, and other devices where super-sharp colored pictures are necessary. But RGB VIDEO requires three wires to carry the three colored signals. (Again, *signals*, which are a stream of electrons, don't have color; they just represent a color.) To make things simpler, most cameras have a circuit that combines the three color signals into a single VIDEO signal that requires only one wire. In the United States, this VIDEO signal is called NTSC (National Television Standards Committee) VIDEO. The TV set at the other end of the wire separates this signal back out into its red, green, and blue components, which it sends to the red, green, and blue guns in its picture tube. Because the three picture signals had to be combined to run down a single wire and then had to be separated again, some of the picture sharpness was lost in the process. For this reason, NTSC colored pictures are not as sharp as RGB or black-and-white TV pictures.

Less expensive TV color cameras use only one PICKUP CHIP to "see" all three colors. The chip has colored stripes on it much like the stripes of a color TV screen. Red parts of a picture would activate the red stripes on the camera chip. Blue parts would activate the blue stripes, and green parts would activate the green stripes. The electronics in the camera then senses which stripes were activated and turns this information into a color VIDEO signal. Because of the space taken up by the stripes on the face of the PICKUP CHIP, SINGLE-CHIP color cameras don't give as sharp a picture as THREE-CHIP color cameras.

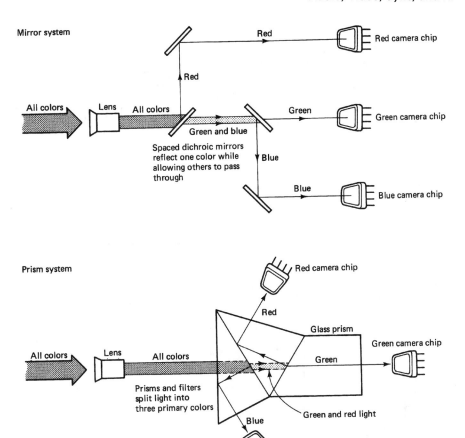

FIGURE 2–4 Three-chip color cameras break colored light into its primary colors (see also color figure).

 **Mini Review**

- Pickup chips (often CCDs) in the camera sense the light, turning it into the electrical vibrations we call video.
- All the colors on TV are made from a mixture of three primary colors—red, green, and blue.
- RGB video, where the color signals are separate, yields sharper color pictures than NTSC video, where the color signals have been combined to run down one wire.

AUDIO, VIDEO, SYNC, AND RF

When a television program is produced, whether "live" or by videotape recording, a camera takes the picture, changing it into an electrical signal called VIDEO. A microphone takes the sound and makes another electrical signal called AUDIO. And a special device called a SYNC GENERATOR creates a third

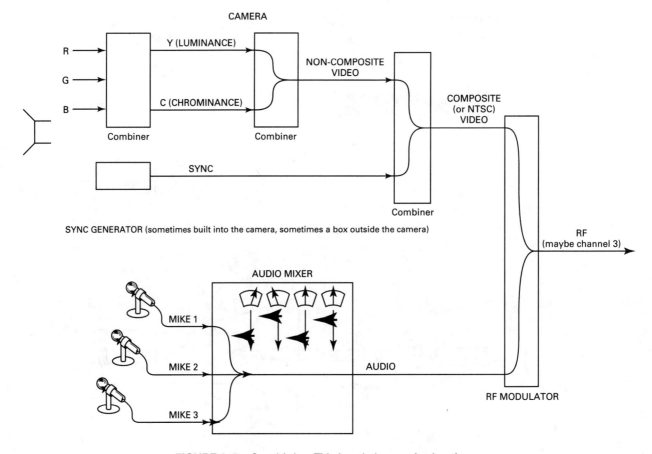

FIGURE 2–5   Combining TV signals into a single wire.

electrical signal called SYNC that keeps the picture stable. When SYNC and VIDEO are electronically combined, the signal is called COMPOSITE VIDEO, but most TV people refer to this simply as "VIDEO." The TV broadcaster then combines the AUDIO and VIDEO/ SYNC using a device called a MODULATOR, which codes the three into another signal called RF (which stands for radio frequency). The RF is transmitted, travels through the air, is picked up by your antenna, and goes into your TV receiver. By tuning your TV receiver to a particular channel (the same one that was broadcasted), the tuner circuit in the TV set decodes the RF Signal and separates it back into AUDIO and VIDEO/SYNC, as shown in Figure 2–5. The VIDEO goes to the TV screen, the AUDIO goes to the speaker, and the SYNC goes to special circuits that hold the picture steady. By adjusting your TV's BRIGHTNESS, CONTRAST, HUE, and COLOR INTEN-

---

*Modulator or RF generator   Electronic device that combines audio and video signals, coding them into RF, a TV channel number.

*Composite video   Video (picture) signal with the sync (timing) signal combined. Also means color video carried on one wire with the colors combined (encoded) with the brightness constituents of the picture.

Sync generator   An electrical device which makes sync (tim-

ing) signals which synchronize TV equipment and keep TV pictures stable.

*RF or radio frequency   The kind of signal that is broadcast through the air and comes from a TV antenna. RF is a combination of audio and video signals coded as a channel number.

Brightness   The overall lightness of a picture. The control on a TV that lightens the picture.

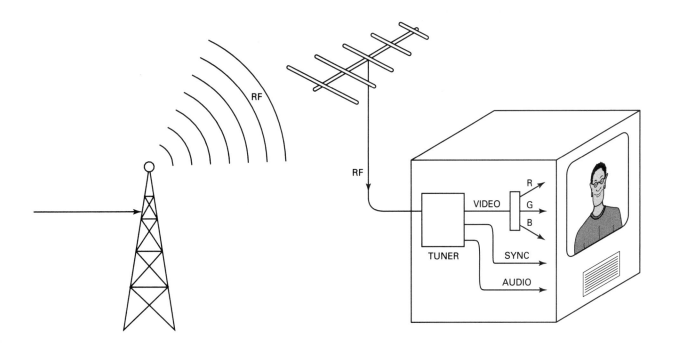

FIGURE 2–5   *Continued*

SITY knobs, you adjust the TV's VIDEO circuits. By manipulating the VOLUME control, you adjust the AUDIO circuits. By turning the VERTICAL or HORIZONTAL controls, you adjust the SYNC circuits in your TV.

Television signals may sound confusing until you realize that all you have are just a few basic signals and that the rest are merely combinations of these basic signals.

The color camera's signal, you'll remember, was really three signals, one red, one green, and one blue. To make them fit on one wire, they were combined to make one NTSC VIDEO signal. Coded into that one signal are two kinds of information. The color information is called CHROMINANCE. The black-and-white part of the information is called LUMINANCE. The CHROMINANCE part of the signal tells your TV set

---

Contrast   The lightness of the bright parts of a picture relative to the dark parts (the brights get brighter while the darks stay dark). Also the control on a TV that adjusts the contrast of the picture.

Hue   Identity or name of a color. Blue is a hue.

Color intensity   The saturation or vividness or paleness of a color. Also the control on a TV that adjusts color saturation.

Volume   Loudness.

Vertical   TV set control that keeps the image from rolling up or down on the screen.

Horizontal   TV set control that keeps the image from collapsing sideways into diagonal lines.

*Audio   The sound part of a TV broadcast. Sound, turned into an electrical signal.

what colors to paint on its screen. The LUMINANCE part of the signal actually creates the light and dark parts of the picture. A black-and-white TV senses only the LUMINANCE parts of the TV signal.

As mentioned before, the VIDEO and the SYNC signals are usually combined to form what we commonly call VIDEO. All this can fit on just one wire.

Compared to VIDEO, AUDIO sounds simple. A microphone or some other audio device makes an electrical signal that can pass down a wire and perhaps be tape-recorded. When several microphones are used at once, their signals can be mixed together (using—what else?—an AUDIO MIXER) to travel down a single wire.

The next trick is to find a way to combine the AUDIO and VIDEO signals so that the sound and picture can share the same wire. This is where RF comes in. An RF GENERATOR or MODULATOR can combine the AUDIO and VIDEO signals and change them into a TV channel number. All home videotape recorders have one of these MODULATORS built in and generally change the VIDEO and AUDIO signals into a channel 3 signal, which now can be fed to the antenna terminals of any TV set and be tuned in by switching the set to channel 3.

One of the great features of RF is that more than one channel can be transmitted on a wire at the same time. You're already familiar with how one antenna wire going to your TV set at home can give you channels 2, 4, 5, 7, etc., with no problem.

 Mini Review

- The sync signal holds the picture steady on the TV screen. It is typically part of the video signal.
- An RF generator, or modulator, can mix audio and video signals together and send them along one wire as a TV channel. Your TV tuner separates the signals back into audio and video.
- RF is fuzzier than video.
- RF allows several audio/video signals to travel on one wire; with video, only one image travels on a single wire.

The bad thing about RF is that in the process of MODULATING the AUDIO and VIDEO signals together, a little of the picture sharpness is lost. When your TV tuner separates an RF signal back into

---

Demodulator or tuner   Electronic device which changes channel numbers (RF) into video and audio signals.

*Luminance   The black-and-white (brightness only) part of a video signal.

*Chrominance or chroma   The color part of video signal.

*Y   The luminance or black-and-white part of a video signal.

*C   The chrominance or color part of a video signal.

Y/(R-Y)/(B-Y)   Pronounced Y, R minus Y, B minus Y, this is one way component video is transported; also the type of video equipment or circuits that handle such signals. The letters represent luminance with sync, red minus the luminance, blue minus the luminance.

*Component video   Video signals carrying separate colors on separate wires. RGB, Y/I/Q, Y/(R–Y)/(B–Y) are component video signals.

Y/I/Q   Another form of Y/(R–Y)/(B–Y) making component color video using luminance and two color difference signals.

*Y/C   Video signal separated into two parts: brightness (Y) and color (C). Such signals yield sharper, cleaner color than composite video signals. Also another name for S connector.

Hi8   Much-improved version of 8mm videotape, downwardly compatible with it.

*Coax or coaxial wire   Stiff, round wire about one-quarter inch in diameter, used to carry video, sync, or RF (antenna) signals.

Transcode   Change one video signal into another, such as changing Y/(R–Y)/(B–Y) into Y/C or Y/C into composite video.

*S connector   Small multipin connector carrying Y/C video signals from or to SVHS or Hi8 VCRs.

*BNC connector   The most popular industrial connector used for video or sync, sometimes used for RF.

F connector   A small socket or plug used for RF or TV signals.

VIDEO and AUDIO again, the picture sharpness decreases further still. About 10 percent of your picture sharpness is lost by MODULATING and DEMODULATING it.

RGB, YIQ, Y/C, AND OTHER ALPHABET SOUP

Back to VIDEO for a moment. Just to make things more complicated, there are a number of ways to combine the R, G, and B color signals. Just as MODULATING a VIDEO signal blurs it a little, combining the R, G, and B signals onto one wire also damages it. The highest quality VIDEO equipment and nearly all computer equipment transport the R, G, and B signals totally independently without changing them or processing them.

So why don't we run the R, G, and B wires separately from device to device without trying to combine the signals to their detriment? Cost and simplicity. The more wires and connections you have, the more circuits you need, and the more cables there are to kink, break, or get mixed up. Living in a society of people who can't set the clocks on their VCRs teaches us to seek simplicity.

Where color quality is paramount, such as in graphics computers, studio special effects switchers, and broadcast TV situations where pictures will be manipulated, layered, or where text is involved, RGB is the way to go, despite the costs. RGB, however, is quite expensive to record, so shortcuts have been developed. All involve a basic fact about TV pictures: Our eyes can see black-and-white (LUMINANCE) things sharply, but they see color (CHROMINANCE) less sharply. When a picture's LUMINANCE is sharp, we can appreciate the detail, but color sharpness is wasted on our eyes. Video engineers take this into consideration when designing high-quality color TV systems by throwing most of their electronic horsepower into making sharp LUMINANCE while scaling back the color. There are a bunch of ways they do this, but all have one thing in common: LUMINANCE (designated as the Y signal) becomes one high-quality signal on one wire, while the colors are transformed into two lesser-quality signals on two other wires, or are combined to make an even lower-quality CHROMA (designated as C) signal.

What does all this boil down to? TV signals come in different varieties with different qualities. RGB is very high quality, but it is expensive and cumbersome to use. Y/(R–Y)/(B–Y) (pronounced "Y, R minus Y, B minus Y") is another three-wire system that is cheaper than RGB and almost as good. It is used on professional VCRs and cameras. Another very similar (yet incompatible) three-wire system is Y/I/Q. All of the above describe COMPONENT video, where three wires are used to carry super-sharp LUMINANCE on one wire and two medium-sharp color signals on two other wires.

Another system, much cheaper than the above but still having pretty good quality is Y/C. Here, the VIDEO travels over two wires: one wire carries high-quality LUMINANCE (where our eyes can see the sharpness), and the other wire carries *all* the colors *combined*. The CHROMINANCE signal is somewhat degraded, but it looks okay to our eyes. Y/C is sometimes called COMPONENT (after all, there are two components to the signal), but technically it isn't *true* COMPONENT—that requires three wires. SVHS and Hi8 VCRs use Y/C, as do other semiprofessional video gadgets.

At the bottom of the quality scale is regular old one-wire COMPOSITE VIDEO with its CHROMA and LUMINANCE combined. Table 2–1 reviews these signals and their uses.

Many video devices have inputs or outputs for several types of signals. It is important to use the highest-quality signals your machine will allow. If, for instance, you're copying a tape and have the choice of using either a Y/C cable (actually several wires inside one umbilical with multipin connectors on the ends) or a regular COAX cable that carries COMPOSITE VIDEO, choose the Y/C. And if Y/(R–Y)/(B–Y) is available, use that in preference to Y/C.

Also note, RGB signals are incompatible with Y/(R–Y)/(B–Y) and Y/I/Q and Y/C, etc. Two devices can share signals only if their inputs and outputs are the same (i.e., both COMPOSITE, or both Y/C, etc.). There are devices that will TRANSCODE one kind of signal into another.

TABLE 2–1 Kinds of Video Signals

Quality	Signal	Composite/Component	Number of Wires	Connectors typically used
Best	RGB	Component	3	3 BNC
Excellent	Y/(R–Y)/(B–Y)	Component	3	3 BNC
Excellent	Y/I/Q	Component	3	3 BNC
Good	Y/C	Quasi component	2	1 Y/C or S
Average	Composite video (also called NTSC video or encoded video or just video)	Composite	1	1 BNC
Below average	RF	Video and audio combined	1	1 F

 Mini Review

- The more signals are combined, the worse they look. RGB, Y/(R–Y)/(B–Y), and Y/I/Q are the ways professionals transport the highest quality video signals using three wires. Y/C uses two wires and yields good quality. Composite video uses one wire and offers average quality. RF, where the audio and video are combined, offers below-average picture quality.
- Some TV signals are not compatible; for instance, you can't send a Y signal to a R–Y input.
- Our eyes are sensitive to luminance (black-and-white) sharpness in a picture but are not very sensitive to chrominance (color) sharpness. Therefore, a lot of effort goes into making an excellent Y (luminance) signal while economizing on the C (color) signal's quality.

DIGITAL VIDEO

The steering wheel on your car is ANALOG: you can turn it any amount in almost any direction. Your headlights are DIGITAL: they are either on or off. The good thing about DIGITAL devices is that they can be very precise. Drive to your home while a friend watches you steer (your friend doesn't look out the window), and then ask your friend to drive the same route, steering just as you did (still not looking out the window) and you'll find yourselves in a meadow somewhere. Even if your friend has a good memory, he/she won't be able to move the wheel to precisely the same positions you used, and the errors will accumulate.

On the other hand, turn on your headlights and turn them off in some sequence, as if sending Morse Code. Your friend, if he/she paid attention or took notes, would be able to precisely duplicate the sequence.

The same thing happens with video signals. The camera makes an ANALOG signal. As the signal passes through wires and other devices, it degrades; it gets distorted, weak, or noisy, like a distant TV or radio station. A DIGITIZED video signal is made of ones and zeros, like the ons and offs of the car headlights. Even if they become fuzzy as they pass through wires and devices, the numbers are still

---

*Analog Something that varies in infinite gradations. A light dimmer is analog. Analog circuits suffer noise and distortion.
*Digital Something that is either "on" or "off." A light switch is digital. On and off can be represented by the digits 1 and 0. Digital equipment copies signals without introducing noise and distortion.

ones and zeros, and represent an exact duplicate of the original signal. DIGITAL signals are more immune to degradation than ANALOG. And even if the ones and zeros do get fuzzy, there are circuits that will generate new, "sharp" ones and zeros from the old fuzzy digits.

VIDEO signals from most cameras start out ANALOG, as electrical vibrations. They can be sliced up and sampled and DIGITIZED—converted into a stream of numbers—and the numbers can be recorded as data, either on a DIGITAL VCR or by a computer.

Upon playback, those numbers can be sent to another VCR or to a computer and be rerecorded precisely, just as your friend could repeat your headlight sequence. When it's time to view the image, the data can be converted back to ANALOG and the signal sent to a TV.

Just as with COMPONENT versus COMPOSITE color signal quality, DIGITAL VIDEO signals can be acquired and recorded with various qualities. You could take many samples per second and get a very accurate rendition of each vibration of a VIDEO signal, or you could take fewer samples per second and get a looser approximation of the wave. It's like taking snapshots of a football game once per second versus making a movie of it. The snapshots will give you an idea of how the game went but will miss a lot of the action.

 Mini Review

- Analog signals can vary by any amount. Digital signals are either on or off (described by ones and zeros). Analog signals easily become distorted and inaccurate, whereas digital signals remain more precise.

CABLE AND CONNECTORS

If you go around calling connectors "widgets" and "whoosies," nobody in the profession will take you seriously. You'll never learn the names of all of them, but at least become familiar with the ones asterisked in the miniglossaries.

Video and RF

VIDEO and RF signals, because they have high frequencies, need special wire to travel through efficiently. VIDEO signals require 75Ω COAXIAL, or COAX, wire, which is round, has a single conductor in the center, and has a braided shield around the outside that helps keep the signal in and keep interference out. Like most wire, COAX is covered with a rubber-like insulation to protect it from moisture.

VIDEO signals are almost always carried through COAX. RF signals are usually carried through COAX but are sometimes carried through flat, ribbon-like antenna wire like that you see connected to some older TVs. Figures 2–6, 2–7, and 2–8 show some TV cables and connectors.

Like Mother Nature's other creatures, connectors come in two varieties, MALE and FEMALE. The plugs are MALE and the sockets are FEMALE. It doesn't take much study to detect the sexual connotation.

*75Ω   Seventy-five ohm, a way of technically describing wires, inputs, and outputs used by video equipment.

*Male   A connector with pins that stick out; a plug.

*Female   A connector with holes; a socket or jack.

Audio patch cord   Wire with audio plugs on each end for feeding signals between two audio devices.

Monitor   A TV set that has no tuner and usually has no speaker (as opposed to a TV receiver, which has both). Such a TV displays video signals but not RF signals. Any device used to observe or hear the quality of a signal (i.e., audio monitor).

*Adapter   A connector that allows one type of plug to fit into another type of socket.

To make connection, push the plug in and twist the collar ¼ turn to the right. To remove, twist to the left and withdraw.

FIGURE 2–6   BNC plug and sockets generally transport VIDEO, (COMPOSITE, RGB, Y/I/Q, Y/R-Y/B-Y), or SYNC in professional and industrial equipment.

There are three popular kinds of VIDEO plugs and sockets. Home video equipment almost always uses the PHONO, or RCA, plug shown in Figure 2–7. What is confusing about this plug is that it is also used for AUDIO. If you are not familiar with the "feel" of the cable, you can accidentally pick up an AUDIO PATCH CORD, which is used to connect CD players and audio cassette decks and *also* has RCA plugs on the end. VIDEO cables are stiffer and thicker than AUDIO cables, and that should be the tip-off as to which kind you have in your hand. Incidentally, you can use VIDEO cables with RCA plugs for AUDIO with no problem. You just shouldn't use AUDIO cables to carry VIDEO signals.

The most popular professional video connector is the BNC (bayonet nut connector), shown in Figure 2–6. You plug in a BNC by pushing the plug into the socket and rotating the collar one-quarter turn to the right until it "clicks." To remove it, turn the collar to the left and pull on the plug. Incidentally, the following is true for *all* electronic cables: When unplugging them, *always pull by the plug— never pull by the cord*. The cord is weak, and the plug is strong.

To connect, just push in with a slight twist. To remove, just pull (by the plug, not the wire) with a slight twist.

FIGURE 2–7   PHONO (or RCA) plug and socket. Normally used for AUDIO, most home and semiprofessional video equipment use these connectors for VIDEO.

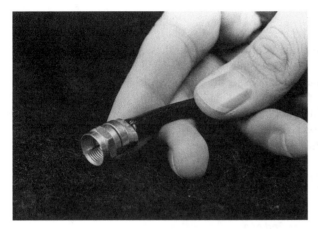

Screw-on male, used mostly on antennas.

Push-on male used mostly between VCRs and TVs.

FIGURE 2–8 F connector on the end of COAX wire.

Video Adapters

What if the cable has an RCA plug, but the socket in the back of the MONITOR is a BNC type? Such incompatibility occurs all the time because different manufacturers use different kinds of sockets. Anyone who does serious TV work stocks a bunch of ADAPTERS like those shown in Figure 2–9. These ADAPTERS permit you to convert from one kind of connector to another.

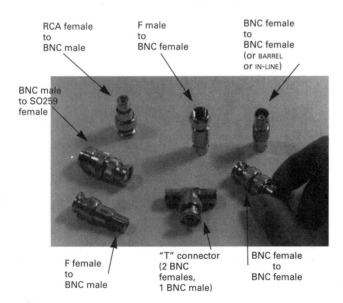

RCA female to BNC male

F male to BNC female

BNC female to BNC female (or BARREL or IN-LINE)

BNC male to SO259 female

F female to BNC male

"T" connector (2 BNC females, 1 BNC male)

BNC female to BNC female

FIGURE 2–9 VIDEO adapters.

Mini plug A small plug with one 1/8″ diameter prong, typically used on portable audio equipment.

Phone plug or 1/4″ phone plug A plug with one 1/4″ shaft, typically used on electric guitars or on large headphones.

XLR or cannon plug A three-prong plug, typically found on professional microphones, audio mixers, and other high-quality audio gear.

Phono, or RCA, plug Small connector used to carry audio signals and, in home video equipment, video signals and sometimes RF signals.

Audio Plugs and Adapters

Figure 2–10 shows the most common audio plugs. Learn the names of these plugs. You will use them frequently. The MINI, PHONE, and PHONO plugs are used mostly on home and semiprofessional equipment. The XLR plug is used on professional equipment. If the plug on your microphone doesn't fit the socket on your VCR, you'll need an ADAPTER. Figure 2–11 shows a sampling of common audio ADAPTERS. You describe an ADAPTER by telling what kind of socket and plug are on the ADAPTER. Thus, the second ADAPTER in Figure 2–11 is a "MINI PLUG TO PHONO JACK" (jack is another name for socket). People who like to talk about sex describe these ADAPTERS by gender, like "RCA female to MINI male."

	Name	Found on the End of a BALANCED or UNBALANCED Line	Used with a HI Z or LO Z Mike	Component That It Is Used With
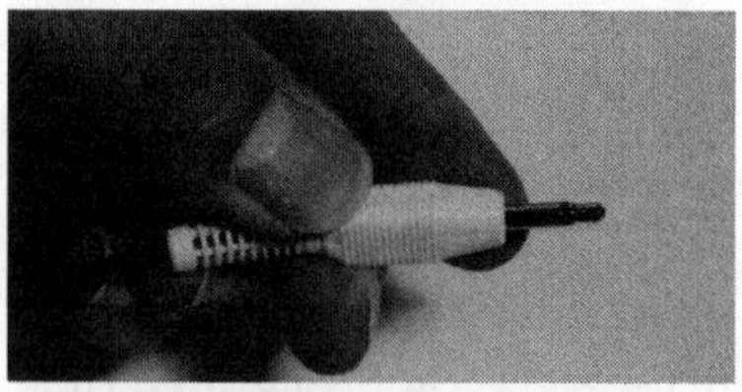	MINI PLUG	UNBALANCED	Usually HI Z	Audiocassette tape recorders, amateur camcorders, small portable equipment
	PHONE PLUG	UNBALANCED	Usually HI Z	Industrial VCRs, reel-to-reel audio-tape recorders, most school AV equipment
	RCA or PHONO PLUG	UNBALANCED	Usually HI Z	Some camcorders, some reel-to-reel audiotape recorders, CD and audiocassette players, phono turntables
	XLR or CANNON PLUG	BALANCED	Usually LO Z	Professional camcorders and VCRs; most mike mixers and other audio equipment of high quality; nearly all good microphones

FIGURE 2–10   Various audio plugs.

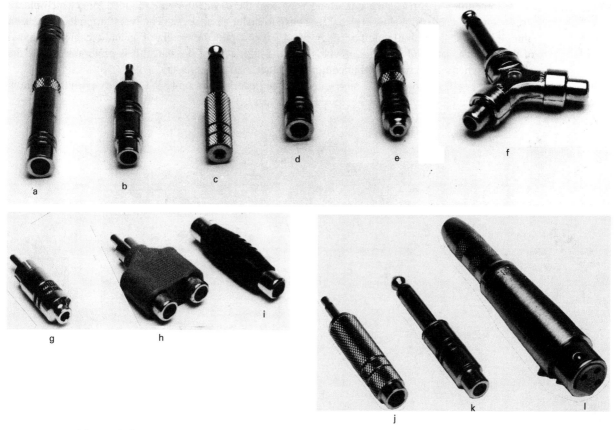

(a) PHONE jack to PHONE jack
(b) MINI plug to PHONO (RCA) jack
(c) PHONE plug to MINI jack
(d) PHONO (RCA) plug to PHONE jack
(e) MINI jack to MINI jack
(f) Y ADAPTER, two RCA jacks to PHONE plug

(g) PHONO (RCA) plug to MINI jack
(h) Y ADAPTER, two RCA jacks to an RCA plug
(i) RCA jack to RCA jack (sometimes called a BARREL CONNECTOR)
(j) MINI plug to PHONE jack
(k) PHONE plug to PHONO (RCA) jack
(l) PHONE jack to XLR jack

FIGURE 2–11 Audio ADAPTERS (Courtesy of Quality/Universal).

Although ADAPTERS make things easy for us, they have the potential for being a weak link in our audio system. They sometimes wiggle loose and make poor contact, which results in no audio or crackly sound.

 Mini Review

- Video and RF signals need to travel over specially shielded coaxial wire.
- The main professional video connector is the BNC, but there are adapters to mate other types of connectors together.
- Professional audio uses XLR connectors, but there are adapters to mate other types of connectors together.
- Avoid using adapters whenever possible; they come loose and make bad connections.

Sometimes ADAPTERS stick out a long way from the device they are plugged into, which places stress on the socket and makes the ADAPTERS easy to dislodge or break. The worst offender is the MINI plug. It is so small and frail that the weight of an ADAPTER plus the weight of an audio cable on the end of the ADAPTER can bend or break off the shaft (the male part of the plug). It is preferable to use the *right* plug when connecting together equipment rather than use ADAPTERS.

This is a big enough dose of science and engineering for now. We'll study more about how audio works and how computers get into the act in later chapters.

TV CAMERAS AND LENSES

3

KINDS OF CAMERAS

The first television cameras were as big as a St. Bernard's doghouse and took two strong men to aim and operate them. The St. Bernard hasn't changed over the years, but today you can fit the camera *and* VCR into a birdhouse.

Some cameras are configured for use only in the studio. Many of their controls are operated remotely in the control room. The cameras are tethered to the control room by a thick umbilical containing many wires. These cameras are often heavy and big, but it doesn't matter since they only have to be wheeled around the studio floor. Studio cameras often sport many knobs and special features and allow the attachment of large lenses, teleprompters, and special pedestals.

Portable cameras, on the other hand, need to be as lightweight as possible. They often have fewer features and fewer external controls. Some portable home video cameras are so automated that they have almost no visible controls at all. You simply point and shoot.

Some cameras are DOCKABLE to VCRs; they can stand alone, or they can have a VCR connected directly to them, turning them into CAMCORDERS. Other CAMCORDERS are permanently docked; the camera sends its signal *only* to the built-in VCR. Most CAMCORDERS have video inputs and outputs that allow the camera to send its signal elsewhere or to receive other video signals sent to its VCR. Figure 3–1 shows an example.

Color cameras range in price from $300 to $50,000. Naturally, the $50,000 camera gives a sharper, purer, and more stable picture than its bargain-basement home video cousin. The quality of the picture depends on many factors in the camera's makeup. Where a home video camera would use a single 1/4-inch or 1/3-inch CCD CHIP to create a full-color picture, an industrial camera would use three pickup CHIPS, one for each primary color, and each CHIP would be 2/3 of an inch wide to produce sharper pictures. The professional camera CHIPS would have more PIXELS, photosensitive transistors,

---

*Pixels   Picture elements, tiny dots that make up the picture. In a camera, pixels represent the tiny, light-sensitive transistors that store the image.
*Resolution   Picture sharpness.
*Dockable   Refers to a camera/VCR feature whereby the two can work independently or can be joined into a single unit, thus becoming a camcorder.
Smear   A temporary white vertical streak passing through bright objects in a CCD camera's picture.
*Camcorder   A VCR and camera in one unit, or as two devices joined together.

High-speed shutter   An electronic circuit in a video camera that allows the CCD chip to "see" for a very brief amount of time during each 1/60 of a second. Like in a film camera, the fast shutter speed reduces motion blur.
*Depth of field   The span of distance from a lens that appears in focus at one time. Broad depth of field occurs when both far and near objects in the picture appear sharp.
Electronic image stabilization (EIS)   Electronic mechanism used in cameras to reduce shakiness in the picture.

Color TV cameras in 1951, required two strong men to move and aim (Courtesy David Sarnoff Research Center).

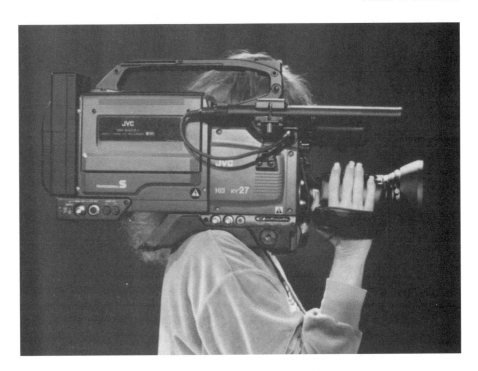

Dockable professional camcorder.

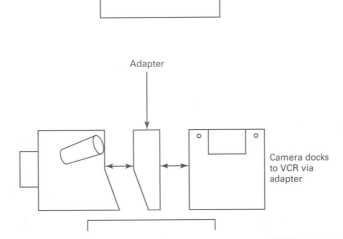

FIGURE 3–1   One-piece camcorders vs. cameras and VCRs that dock.

CCD (charge-coupled device) circuit chip is image sensor in most TV cameras.

able to "see" the picture in more detail. Figure 3–2 shows how the PIXELS in a picture affect its sharpness, or RESOLUTION.

PICKUP CHIPS manufactured for professional use have extra circuitry to make them impervious to bright lights. Common cameras and older professional cameras make a nasty streak through the picture (called SMEAR) when bright objects appear in the shot, especially a night shot. Figure 3–3 shows an example of SMEAR.

In any case, never aim a TV camera directly at the sun. The lens will focus too much heat on the CHIP and damage it. Rule of thumb: If you can't stare at it with your eyes, don't make the camera stare at it.

You may have heard of video cameras with HIGH-SPEED SHUTTERS that can take pictures at video's usual 1/60 of a second, but also at 1/100, 1/125, 1/250, 1/1000, and up to 1/10,000 of a second. The video camera doesn't have a physical shutter like a film camera, so how does it do it?

Even though the CCD pumps out a picture every 1/60 of a second (NTSC video requires this timing standard), the CCD can be told to "see" for a brief portion of this time. The CCD would sense the light for only, say, 1/2000 of a second, then stop sensing light. The CCD would still send out its image data at the normal speed of 60 FIELDS per second.

FIGURE 3–2 Compare the detail in the two pictures. One is made of 14,632 PIXELS, the other 3,658.

FIGURE 3–3   SMEAR, the result of aiming a CCD camera at a bright light.

Using a HIGH-SPEED SHUTTER does a couple of things: As any camera buff knows, if you snap a photo of Grandpa hitting a golf ball at 1/60-second shutter speed, you'll get a blur (even for Grandpa)! To "freeze" Grandpa's golf swing, you'll need to use shutter speeds at 1/250, 1/500, or 1/1000 of a second. In order to appreciate this "frozen" motion, you have to PAUSE your videotape to look at a single picture. High SHUTTER SPEEDS also darken your picture. Usually, not enough light is a bad thing, resulting in a dark, grainy picture with poor color. But sometimes when the light is too bright, such as outdoors in the snow, the high SHUTTER SPEED helps dim it. It also allows you to reduce your DEPTH OF FIELD, a shooting technique described later in this chapter.

Another thing CCD chips can do: EIS, or ELECTRONIC IMAGE STABILIZATION. The camera can hold the picture steady even though you jiggle the camera (up to a point).

 **Mini Review**

- The camera's "eye" is its light-sensitive CCD chip (or chips).

VIEWFINDERS

The VIEWFINDER is what you look through to see where your camera is aimed. Not all TV cameras have VIEWFINDERS. Many security and industrial cameras do not. Most CAMCORDERS have a VIEWFINDER that fits up against your eye. Studio cameras have larger VIEWFINDERS that are easy to see at some distance. Some VIEWFINDERS are detachable, handy for tight spaces.

CRT (cathode ray tube)   A vacuum tube with an electron gun at one end and a phosphor screen at the other that glows when struck by electrons from the gun. Computer screens and TV picture tubes are CRTs having the familiar TV screen at one end.

LCD (liquid crystal display) viewfinder   A color TV monitor made of a flat panel rather than a CRT. Usually folds out from a camcorder or is imbedded in it.

Palmcorder   Tiny camcorder that fits in the palm of your hand.

FIGURE 3–4   LCD VIEWFINDER on the left of the CAMCORDER, CRT VIEWFINDER on the right (Courtesy of Panasonic).

Nearly all TV cameras have electronic VIEWFINDERS, small TV monitors that display the picture exactly the way it is being sent to the VCR or switcher. Focus, framing, iris, and zoom all manifest themselves in the picture you see.

Two types of electronic VIEWFINDERS are the CRT type and the LCD panel. The CRT is a TV tube the size of a short cigar, with a magnifying lens in front of it. The LCD is a flat panel. The tiny CAMCORDER in Figure 3–4 has both.

Color is the one thing you don't see on most CRT VIEWFINDERS. With rare exceptions, all VIEWFINDERS are black-and-white, even on color TV cameras. That's not a mistake. Black-and-white VIEWFINDERS give a much sharper picture than color ones (of prime importance when focusing). They are smaller, lighter, and cheaper, and they adequately perform their basic mission—to display what you are viewing. VIEWFINDERS may also display messages such as battery power, pause, light level, time, and other functions of the camera or camcorder.

The tiniest camcorders have the VIEWFINDER built into the camera, streamlining the package. Industrial camcorders and cameras have detachable VIEWFINDERS. Here are some things you can do with a separate VIEWFINDER:

1. Once the VIEWFINDER is removed, the camera and VIEWFINDER are more easily packed and transported.
2. Detachable VIEWFINDERS are handy when in a pinch you need to conserve battery power—simply disconnect to save-a-watt when shooting.
3. Many VIEWFINDERS hitch up to either side of a portable camera (for left-eyed or right-eyed people), and some can be adjusted in many directions, freeing the camera operators to hold the camera above or below themselves. Some finders can be removed from the camera and attached to an extension cable for remote viewing—handy if your camera needs to be up in a tree or in the middle of a cattle drive.

The heavier, higher-quality camcorders are designed to sit on the shoulder. They have their VIEWFINDERS attached to the front of the camera, improving its balance and steadiness. Tiny PALM-

---

Return   A switch on some studio TV cameras that temporarily displays the final program image or some other video image (as opposed to the camera's own image) on the camera's viewfinder to help the camera operator position objects in the viewfinder. Useful for coordinating with other camera shots.

*MIC   Short for microphone input, a highly sensitive, low-level audio input.

*Shotgun mike   Microphone shaped like a gun barrel, which "listens" only in the direction it is aimed.

Accessory mount   Threaded hole on top of camera or camcorder for attaching a light, microphone, or other accessory.

FIGURE 3–5   Adjustable, detachable camcorder VIEWFINDER.

CORDERS are light enough to hold up to your eye and use the built-in VIEWFINDERS. Figure 3–5 shows a camcorder with a detachable VIEWFINDER.

One great advantage of the ELECTRONIC VIEWFINDER on a portable camera or camcorder is that it can display the image *played back* from your VCR. Thus, after recording a sequence, you can rewind the tape and play it through your VIEWFINDER to see how you are doing.

VIEWFINDER eyepieces sometimes have focusing adjustments of their own. The eyepieces, like binoculars, often have to be adjusted to your eye (otherwise you may think your camera's picture is blurry when really your VIEWFINDER is out of focus). To use this adjustment, aim the camera at a distant object, focus the lens at infinity (∞), and zoom out all the way. That will make a picture that *should* be sharp in the VIEWFINDER. Now adjust the eyepiece to make the VIEWFINDER picture sharp (and comfortable) for your eye. Done.

Studio TV cameras, unrestrained by size and weight, use larger, more easy-to-see VIEWFINDERS. Most sit atop the camera and can be tilted and turned in various directions. They usually have a visor around the screen to block out reflections from studio lights. They have the usual TV set controls for brightness, contrast, horizontal, and vertical, and some have switches to allow the camera operator to view another camera's picture or the picture the director has selected. This feature, called RETURN, is handy when a camera operator must keep his part of the picture in the left half of the screen while another camera operator is keeping her picture in the right part of the screen, while the director splits the screen in half. Professional TV cameras have VIEWFINDERS that can also display test signals, electronic waveforms, and messages about camera circuit operation.

Remember that the camera VIEWFINDER only *displays* the picture, it doesn't *make* it. Adjusting the VIEWFINDER's brightness, contrast, or any other controls will have no effect on the camera's recorded picture.

Some TV cameras are designed for both studio and portable use. In the studio, the camera with its full-sized VIEWFINDER is placed on a tripod and connected to a multiwire umbilical cable that remotely controls the camera's electronics. To use the camera in portable situations, the large VIEWFINDER is detached and replaced with a miniature one. The multiwire umbilical is replaced with a battery pack and a cable leading to the VCR (or the camera DOCKS to the VCR). The tripod is replaced with a cushioned shoulder mount. Figure 3–6 shows such a camera.

Portable configuration

Studio configuration

FIGURE 3–6 Industrial color camera designed for portable or studio use.

 Mini Review

- Adjusting the viewfinder's controls affects only what the camera person sees; it doesn't affect the recording.

BUILT-IN MICROPHONES

ALL CAMCORDERS and DOCKABLE industrial cameras have microphones built into them or have a mount to attach an external mike. The built-in ones are very sensitive and give good sound quality, especially for conversation.

They do have one fault. Since your camera is likely to be six feet or more away from your subject, that means that your built-in mike is also six feet away. This results in echoey speech and a distracting amount of background noise, such as doors slamming, dogs barking, traffic, wind, and even the camera operator snorting and sniffing.

You could solve all these problems by recording in a soundproof tomb and using a corpse for a camera operator (no breathing sounds). This wouldn't work if your show had to be "live," would it? When really good sound is necessary, it is possible to override the built-in mike and use a separate microphone such as a lavalier, which you hang around your talent's neck or attach to his or her lapel. The plug goes into the MIC input of the CAMCORDER. Because the subject speaks directly into the mike (a foot away), the sound is clear. If the talent moves around too much for an attached mike, you could use a SHOTGUN MIKE.

No, SHOTGUN MIKE isn't the name of a trigger-happy bootlegger. A SHOTGUN MIKE, so named because of its long shotgunlike barrel, "listens" in one direction only. Someone standing nearby could aim the SHOTGUN MIKE at the talent as he or she moved around.

Some microphones can attach to the ACCESSORY MOUNT atop the camera.

Some cameras have SHOTGUN MIKES built into them. This is handy because the microphone automatically aims wherever the camera aims.

What if you don't want your SHOTGUN mike to "listen" in only one direction? Use a *switchable* SHOTGUN mike, which works either as a SHOTGUN or as a normal mike. Some camcorders come with switchable SHOTGUNS, but separate switchable SHOTGUN mikes can be attached to the ACCESSORY MOUNT atop many cameras.

The more professional cameras allow different microphones with different characteristics to be plugged into their VCRs as needed.

 Mini Review

- The built-in mikes on camcorders tend to pick up echoes; use a lapel or shotgun mike when possible.

OPERATING CAMERAS

The simplest camera consists of a lens, a box of electronics with built-in automatic controls to give you a good picture, an electric cord for power, and a socket called VIDEO OUT. You need a cable to connect the VIDEO OUT to the VIDEO IN of the TV monitor or a VCR, as shown in Figure 3–7.

There is not much to using this camera other than connecting it, plugging it in, turning it on, letting it warm up, uncovering the lens, aiming the camera, and then focusing the lens. How can you tell if you are focused? One way is to look at a TV monitor somewhere. You could have one connected either directly to the camera or to a VCR that is connected to the camera. When the VCR is in the

---

*Video out   Socket where a video signal exits a device.
*Video in   Socket where a video signal enters a device.
Videoconferencing, or teleconferencing   A technology that allows participants in remote locations to communicate with images and sound.

*Focus   To change an image from blurry to sharp; the part of a lens that adjusts the focus.
*Iris   The part of a lens that governs how much light passes through the lens.

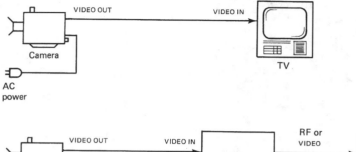

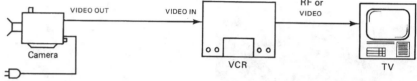

FIGURE 3–7 Connecting up a simple TV camera.

RECORD mode, its monitor will display your camera's picture. If the monitor is connected directly to the camera, it should display a picture whenever the camera is on and the lens is uncovered.

The tiny cameras that attach to computers for VIDEOCONFERENCING may have no adjustments. They are focused at maybe 5 feet, and anything closer or farther will look a little blurry.

The simplest industrial cameras will have a ZOOM lens, like the one shown in Figure 3–8.

The Lens.   Although you'll hear more about lenses later in this chapter, here are a few basics to get you started. There are three moving parts that can be adjusted on a simple ZOOM lens. When using such a lens, you reach around to the front of the camera and make your adjustments by rotating parts of the lens. Always check what you are doing by watching the VIEWFINDER or a TV monitor. The three adjustments are

1. FOCUS. Turning this part of the lens makes the picture sharp or blurry.
2. ZOOM. Turning this part of the lens makes the picture look closer or farther away.

FIGURE 3–8   ZOOM lens.

3. IRIS. Turning this part of the lens in one direction allows lots of light to pass through the lens and increases the contrast in your picture. Turning it in the other direction restricts the amount of light allowed through the lens and decreases the contrast, making the picture look grayer or darker. In general, you adjust the IRIS so that the picture looks good.

You will be using focus and zoom all the time. Usually you set the IRIS at the beginning of the show and don't touch it thereafter.

Correct Focusing. There is only one way to correctly focus a zoom lens. The method takes about five seconds and should be done before the show actually starts. During the show, you may not have time to use this proper method and will have to focus as best you can. Proper method of focusing:

1. Zoom in all the way on your central subject, making it look as close as you can.
2. Focus the lens.
3. Zoom back out to the kind of shot you want.

If you use this method, you can zoom in and out, and your subject will stay in focus. If you don't use this method, your picture will go out of focus as you zoom in, and you will have to keep refocusing repeatedly. In any case, if the distance between your subject and your camera changes—the subject moves or you move the camera or you pick another subject at a different distance from the camera—you will have to refocus if you want the picture to stay sharp throughout the entire zoom range of the lens.

Camera Controls and Connectors. You may discover extra knobs, buttons, and sockets on your TV camera. These add to the flexibility of the camera's use by allowing it to do special tasks.

Sync: The SYNC switch has positions marked IN (for INternal) and EXT (for EXTernal). In the IN position, the camera generates its own sync (INside itself), mixes it with the video, and sends both to the VIDEO OUT. You would connect the VIDEO OUT via coax cable to a TV monitor or VCR. Use INternal SYNC when using just one camera alone, perhaps feeding a VCR or TV monitor.

When the SYNC switch is set at EXT, the camera does *not* generate its own sync signal—something else, usually an external SYNC GENERATOR, must make the signal for it. Use EXTERNAL SYNC when you have *several* cameras, a switcher, and an external SYNC GENERATOR (the typical studio setup).

Why does anyone bother with EXTERNAL SYNC? Here are some reasons: If you're using several cameras at the same time and are switching from one to another, all the cameras must have their elec-

---

*Internal sync A switch on a camera that makes it generate its own sync signal, which it adds to its composite video signal.

*External sync Electronic pulses, coming from outside the TV camera, which synchronize the camera's picture with other cameras in the studio so the pictures can be mixed or switched.

Sync generator Electronic device that makes a sync signal used to synchronize the electronics of several cameras so their pictures can be mixed together.

Genlock Ability of a camera or other TV device to receive an external video signal and synchronize its own video signal to it, so that the two videos can be neatly switched or mixed.

Gain Camera adjustment which controls the strength of the camera's video signal, altering contrast and brightness of the picture.

*Boost Camera control that makes the camera extra sensitive in dim light.

Intercom An earphone/microphone headset that allows the director in the control room to speak with the camera operators in the TV studio.

Camera adapter Box of electronics that a portable camera can plug into (instead of directly into a VCR) that powers the camera and distributes the camera's video and other signals via standardized outputs.

tronics synchronized (the CCD chips must be sending their images in unison). EXTERNAL SYNC does this.

Genlock.   GENLOCK is very similar to EXTERNAL SYNC. It allows your camera to synchronize its electronics with another camera so the pictures are mixable and cleanly switchable.

With EXTERNAL SYNC, the camera requires an EXTERNAL SYNC signal to drive its electronics. With GENLOCK, the camera requires any *video* signal to drive its electronics. The GENLOCK circuit "locks onto" the video signal and synchronizes its electronics with it.

Studio cameras usually use EXTERNAL SYNC inputs because SYNC is readily available around the studio. Consumer camcorders often have no SYNC or GENLOCK inputs because they usually work alone. Portable cameras designed to *sometimes* work with other cameras have GENLOCK inputs, making them easily synchronizable with other cameras in the field (where video may be handy but SYNC is not).

Gain.   GAIN adjusts the strength of the video signal from the camera. If your picture seems a little too dark or faded, you should first throw more light on the subject. Second, you should open the lens IRIS. Third, if all else failed, you would turn up the video GAIN from the camera to boost brightness and contrast. Another name for GAIN is BOOST, and you'll see more on that shortly.

Intercom.   The INTERCOM is a headset that the camera operator wears in a studio, making it possible to listen to and speak with the director in the control room. The INTERCOM generally plugs into a socket in the TV camera, and the signals travel through the camera's multiwire umbilical cable. If the camera is working alone (without the umbilical), the INTERCOM circuit will not work.

Tally Light.   The TALLY LIGHT is a red light in the front of the camera that goes on when the TV director selects your camera's picture to be recorded. Your TALLY LIGHT will go out and another camera's TALLY LIGHT will go on when the director switches from your camera to the other camera. If the director is creating a special effect, such as a split screen that uses two cameras at once, both their TALLY LIGHTS will be on at the same time.

When a studio camera is used alone (away from the studio and switcher), the TALLY LIGHT does not operate, but some camcorders have TALLY LIGHTS that go on while recording.

A second TALLY LIGHT is usually built into the studio camera's VIEWFINDER to let the camera operator know his or her camera is "on."

A message to fledgling camera operators: Don't goof off when your TALLY LIGHT is "on."

Camera Adapter.   Portable TV cameras and camcorders do not *have* to be used portably. They can be placed on a tripod and used in the studio just like any other camera with the help of a CAMERA ADAPTER or AC ADAPTER. The CAMERA ADAPTER is a box that gets its power from a wall outlet and makes all the signals the camera needs to operate. The CAMERA ADAPTER connects to the camera with a multiwire umbilical that sends power to the camera and takes audio and video back from the camera. The box has a standard VIDEO and AUDIO output and may have a cable that sends a REMOTE PAUSE signal to a console VCR.

Controls on a Portable Color Camera

Although many portable cameras and camcorders come festooned with automatic controls, the more professional models have automatic controls with manual overrides allowing you to second-guess the built-in computers. The two most important and universal controls on a color camera are COLOR TEMPERATURE and WHITE BALANCE. These adjust how the camera "sees" colors.

Color Temperature. COLOR TEMPERATURE describes the warmth (redness) or chill (blueness) of a scene. For example, have you ever noticed how cold and sterile offices lit with fluorescent lights look? On the other hand, have you noticed the warmth in a home lit by incandescent lamps, or the warmth of a supper lit by candlelight, or the richness of the whole outdoors during an August sunset? These differences are caused by the COLOR TEMPERATURE of the light.

Under different lighting conditions, the color of things changes drastically even though you may not be aware of it with your naked eye. The eye of the camera, however, sees these differences and makes them even more pronounced. A face that looked red and rosy when lit by a sunset will look deathly pale when photographed on a foggy day. Somehow the color camera must be adjusted to compensate for these differences in lighting so that colors will look familiar and proper.

Some color cameras have a built-in set of colored glass lenses that counteract the "coldness" of the light and bring it into proper balance. The COLOR TEMPERATURE control on professional cameras is a four-position thumbwheel like the one shown in Figure 3–9. Next to the wheel is usually a chart listing which positions to set the wheel for various lighting conditions. Sometimes these conditions are described by icons (little pictures), and sometimes they are described in more technical terms. The precise measurement of COLOR TEMPERATURE will be discussed in detail in the lighting chapter, but for now Table 3–1 will tell where to turn the wheel for various lighting situations.

AUTO IRIS with manual override

COLOR TEMPERATURE wheel, set for studio 3200° K lighting

COLOR BARS (When ON, camera sends out only COLOR BARS, a test signal)

0dB, 6dB, 12dB sensitivity BOOST

FIGURE 3–9 Some controls on a color TV camera.

---

*Color temperature The redness or blueness of a scene, the result of the kind of light used to illuminate the scene. Also, the name given to the color TV camera control that adapts it to these varied lighting conditions.

*White balance The mix of primary colors that results in pure white light. On color cameras, the controls that strengthen the blue or red colors so that one doesn't overpower the other, allowing white objects to appear pure white, not tinted. Pressing one button and holding a white card in front of the camera will automatically adjust the camera's circuits to make pure white.

*Continuous white balance Camera mode that makes moment-by-moment adjustments to the white balance, using what the camera sees in its picture as a guide.

*Auto white balance Same as continuous white balance.

*Automatic iris Camera circuit that senses the amount of light in a scene and opens or closes the lens iris to adapt to it.

Backlight control A control on a TV camera that improves a backlit picture (keeps the subject from looking like a silhouette when a lot of light comes from behind the subject).

TABLE 3–1   Color Temperature Settings

Position	°K	Lighting Situation
1	3200	For shooting scenes under studio lamps or outside during a sunrise or sunset—all "warm" light conditions
2	4500	For fluorescent lamp lighting
3	6000	For bright or hazy sunshine
4	8000	For shooting outdoors in cloudy or rainy weather or with a clear blue sky without direct sunshine

Not all cameras will use the same filters or numbers for their COLOR TEMPERATURE controls. Some may simply have a two-position switch marked INDOORS/OUTDOORS. Whatever the situation, it is important to adjust your camera for the correct COLOR TEMPERATURE *first*, before making any other camera adjustments.

White Balance.   Every time you use your camera or change lighting conditions (such as moving from indoors to outdoors or even from scene to scene sometimes), you have to "teach" your camera what color *white* is.

You remember how a color picture is the composite of three pictures, one green-and-black, one red-and-black, and one blue-and-black. A certain mix of these three primary colors is needed to make pure white. If the mix is off, you get tinted white. Sometimes things that are supposed to be white (a white piece of paper on a desk) turn out not to be white at all (the desk is in an orange room, casting orange light on the paper). Still you'd like the paper to look white on camera, so by adjusting WHITE BALANCE, you adjust that mix of primary colors to *make* it white. WHITE BALANCE, or WHITE LEVEL SET, or WHITE SET is often adjusted as follows:

1. Always adjust your COLOR TEMPERATURE filter *first*. Next:
2. In the area where you plan to shoot (and in its light), place a white card in front of the color camera close enough to fill the camera's VIEWFINDER screen. If you don't have a white card, then aim the camera close-up at a white T-shirt or some other white surface. Some cameras come equipped with a milky white camera lens cap that you can place over the lens and use that as your white surface as you shoot through it.
3. Adjust your IRIS to its proper setting.
4. Press the camera's WHITE BALANCE button (it's on there somewhere).

Some cameras don't even require a WHITE BALANCE button to be pressed. Using a feature called CONTINUOUS WHITE BALANCE, or AUTO WHITE BALANCE, they adjust themselves totally automatically; but they don't do as good a job of it as you can do with a white card.

Automatic Iris.   The lens IRIS controls how much light the camera "sees." On simple cameras you manually adjust a collar on the lens to adapt to bright or dim lighting conditions. Cameras with AUTOMATIC IRIS will perform this adjustment for you, sensing the amount of light admitted through the lens and opening or closing the lens accordingly.

There are times when AUTO IRIS can get fooled. For such cases, most cameras will allow you to manually override this control. A typical situation occurs when someone is standing against a light background or in front of a window washed with daylight. The AUTO IRIS will adjust the lens to give an excellent rendition of the background, while the subject comes out dark and murky. By manually "opening" the lens further, you can get the subject (the important part of the picture) to look good while overexposing and sacrificing the unimportant background. Another name for this manual override is BACKLIGHT.

 Mini Review

- Correct focusing procedure: Zoom in, focus, then zoom out to the shot you want.
- When cameras work together in a studio, they need to have their electronics synchronized with external sync or genlock.
- To have a camera display accurate whites in its picture: Adjust its color temperature filter and its white balance settings.

Gain Boost, or Hi Sens, or + 6dB, + 12dB Boost. Cameras are designed to work with a certain amount of light. When the light gets too dim, the image from the camera gets dim and murky. The colors will look especially dingy. The BOOST control will make the camera more sensitive in dim light. This is handy when you get into situations where you have no choice but to use the existing light or one small portable light to shoot with.

You never get something for nothing. When you boost the sensitivity of the camera, you also boost the NOISE or graininess in the picture. The BOOST control should always be left *off* unless it is absolutely needed.

Usually, the switch is labeled with a number (like + 6dB) to tell you how much BOOST you are getting. The bigger the number, the bigger the BOOST.

Some cameras BOOST their sensitivity by slowing their SHUTTERS from the usual 1/60 of a second per picture to maybe 1/30 or 1/15 of a second. This allows light to strike the CCD chip from two to four times as long, improving the camera's low-light sensitivity without increasing graininess as GAIN does. Caveat: Anything in motion will look blurry.

Auto Fade. AUTO FADE is a control found on some camcorders allowing you to fade the picture out by pressing a button. This is often a neat way to end a scene, fading to black or white. AUTO FADE can also be used the other way to open a scene fading up from black to the full picture.

Electric Zoom. It is difficult to reach around in front of a portable TV camera and grasp the lens to zoom it. To simplify matters, manufacturers have built ELECTRIC ZOOM controls into their cameras, usually in the form of a ROCKER SWITCH (Figure 3–10). Press one end of the ROCKER SWITCH, and a miniature motor will zoom the lens in for a close-up. Press the other end of the switch, and the lens

---

Hi sens Same as boost.

+6dB boost A moderate boosting of a cameras' low-light sensitivity. A +12dB boost would bring a greater increase in sensitivity.

*Noise Unwanted interference that creeps into your signal. Audio noise could be hum or hiss. Video noise could be snow, graininess, or streaks in the picture.

Shutter TV camera circuit that allows the chip to "see" for a limited amount of time every 1/60 of a second. Has the same effect as a film camera's shutter but is totally electronic.

Auto fade Control on some cameras that fades the picture to black at the end of a scene or fades up from black at the beginning.

Electric zoom Electric motor on a lens or camera that zooms the lens at the touch of a button.

Digital zoom An electronic way of blowing up a picture, making it look zoomed-in. Used to any degree, it shows blockiness: parts of the image turn into little squares.

Automatic focus Electronic system in some cameras that senses whether the picture is sharp and electrically focuses the lens to correct blurry pictures.

Rocker Switch

FIGURE 3–10   ROCKER SWITCH to control ELECTRIC ZOOM on a CAMCORDER.

zooms out. On the better cameras, a gentle press of the ROCKER SWITCH zooms the lens slowly, while a firm press of the button zooms you quickly.

On professional camcorders, you hold the camera and zoom the lens with your right hand, while focusing the lens manually (by twisting the lens barrel) with your left. That leaves nothing left if you have an itch.

Digital Zoom.   This is a feature found on amateur camcorders but not professional cameras—and for a good reason: it's gauche and cheesy. DIGITAL ZOOM allows one to magnify the image electronically without actually zooming in the lens. When you zoom in a real lens, the image presented to the CCD chip gets bigger; more detail is there to be sensed. When DIGITAL ZOOM is used, no detail is added. The picture gets bigger and fuzzier at the same time. It's kind of like moving closer to the TV to read fine print; it looks bigger, but it's still fuzzy.

Automatic Focus.   Some cameras take all the guesswork out of focusing by doing it for you. These cameras are handy when novices or children and some grandmothers will be using the camera. The feature is also handy when you will be too busy to focus your shots (like getting ready to jump out of an airplane for a skydive).

AUTO FOCUS cameras are not 100% accurate. They cannot tell whether it is the flowers in the foreground that you want sharp or the bride and groom in the background that you want sharp. Some will focus on whatever is in the center of the picture. Others will focus on whatever makes up most of the picture. One type even tracks your eyeball in the viewfinder and focuses the part of the picture you're looking at. Although each system can sometimes be fooled, all systems have a manual override allowing you to switch off the AUTO FOCUS control and focus manually. Sometimes it's handy just to press the AUTO FOCUS button for a moment to focus the picture and then let the camera stay at that setting until you are ready to change the focus again.

No AUTO FOCUS system is as accurate as the human brain. Only *you* would know that Fester Jr. is the main subject that belongs in focus, not Barbecue Bill in the next yard or Hog-the-Show Hilda waving in the foreground. Switch the lens to MANUAL to override the automatic controls when shooting groups of people or scenery. Both shots require that *you* decide whether the people or the scenery is more important. MANUAL is also a good way to guarantee sharp shots of recitals, speeches, and other static images; once you get the shot focused right, you don't need to change it, and you don't want some computer circuit diddling with it. And remember that sky dive we took a few paragraphs back? Unless you need to shoot your pals as they plummet with you, all your shots will be at infinity (∞)—until you land. Might as well manually focus for ∞ and be done with it.

Studio Color Cameras

Studio color TV cameras start at about $3,000 and go out of sight at $80,000. Many good ones can be purchased for $10,000, without lens. The lens could add another $3,000–$5,000.

What is it that the "good" cameras do that the cheaper ones don't?

1. They make a sharper picture. The sharpness may achieve 400 to 700 HORIZONTAL LINES OF RESO-LUTION as opposed to 240 to 440 for home-type SINGLE-CHIP cameras.
2. They give a smoother picture with less graininess. Graininess is technically measured as so many dB SIGNAL-TO-NOISE RATIO. The bigger the dB number, the better. 62dB is appropriate for professional cameras, while 46dB is common for home cameras.
3. The professional cameras use broadcast-grade chips, circuit chips with few, if any, flaws, such as dark pixels. Cheaper cameras display more blemishes. Also, the professional chips are more immune to SMEARING in bright light.
4. Finer color adjustment is possible. SINGLE-CHIP cameras make color only one way. If two similar SINGLE-CHIP cameras are looking at the same subject and one is a little off, then you will see a difference in the color as you switch from one to the other. There's not much you can do to correct the color in these cameras. THREE-CHIP color cameras, however, allow a wider range of correction so that cameras can be more perfectly matched together.
5. They are more easily synchronized. Studio cameras are designed to work together. Their SYNC circuits must all be driven by a single source so that all paint their pictures in unison. Some cameras designed for both studio and portable use can be GENLOCKED. GENLOCK is a circuit in the camera that will "listen" to the video from another camera, VTR, or some other source and will lock its SYNC circuits to it. This makes it possible for the camera to work in harmony with other cameras.
6. They include test-signal generators. The better cameras will create COLOR BARS and other test signals that assist technicians in adjusting their circuits and adjusting their colors so that they match other cameras in the studio. Even the better portable cameras have this feature, as you could see in Figure 3–9.
7. They come with remote CAMERA CONTROL UNITS (see Figure 3–11). A CAMERA CONTROL UNIT (CCU) is a box of electronics that can adjust the camera's operation from the control room. This allows engineers to adjust the many controls on the cameras from one place without running into the studio. This also allows the camera controls to be adjusted during a show.

Horizontal lines of resolution Picture sharpness, usually measured in "lines." The greater the number of lines, the sharper the picture.

*Single-chip camera A black-and-white camera or a color camera with a pickup chip sensitive to all colors at once.

*Signal-to-noise ratio (S/N ratio) A number describing how much desired signal there is compared to undesirable background noise. The higher the S/N ratio, the "cleaner" the signal.

*Three-chip camera A TV camera with three pickup chips inside, one sensitive to the red parts of the picture, another sensitive to green, and the third sensitive to blue.

*Color bars Vertical bars of color used to test cameras and other video equipment.

*CCU or camera control unit Box of electronic circuits

that can remotely adjust the operation of a camera as well as provide power and signals to it.

Pedestal Electronic control on a camera that adjusts the brightness of the picture. Proper adjustment yields blacks that are the right darkness.

Black balance Color camera adjustment that makes blacks pure black (not tinted one color or another).

Video reverse Camera switch that makes blacks white, makes whites black, and changes colors into their complementary (opposite) colors.

Sweep reverse Button on a camera that switches the camera's picture left to right or flips it upside down.

Switcher Push-button device that selects one or another camera's picture to be viewed or recorded.

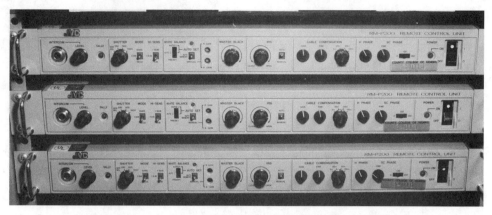

FIGURE 3–11   TV camera CCUs (Camera Control Units).

8. They have numerous specialized features such as:

   a. PEDESTAL: a control that adjusts how black the blacks are.

   b. BLACK BALANCE: a control that makes sure that blacks are not tinted (similar to what WHITE BALANCE does). Again, the pro portable cameras also have this feature.

   c. VIDEO REVERSE: makes the camera's pictures negative (blacks will be white, etc.), a handy feature for turning photographic negatives straight into positive video pictures.

   d. SWEEP REVERSE: makes the picture swap its left and right sides, giving a mirror image. This corrects the picture if the camera is shooting an image in a mirror.

   e. VERTICAL SWEEP REVERSE: flips the picture upside down. This is handy when you aim the camera up at an overhead mirror to look straight down on something. Everything ends up upside down until you throw this switch, which makes it rightside up again.

 Mini Review

- When shooting in reduced light, you can boost a camera's gain to make the image brighter and contrastier, but it may also make the image grainy or smeary.
- Compared to consumer cameras, the higher-priced professional cameras yield sharper, smoother pictures with more accurate colors.

Connecting Studio Cameras.   A portable TV camera would connect directly to a VCR. Studio cameras, on the other hand, are designed to work together and connect to a SWITCHER that can select which camera's picture is used and may even create some special effect between those pictures such as a FADE or WIPE.

Portable TV cameras have all of their electronics built into them. Studio cameras have much of their electronics built into their CAMERA CONTROL UNITS housed in the control room. Studio/portable cameras may have all of their electronics in them, but they will disregard the built-in circuits and listen only to the CCU circuits when used in the studio.

The camera and the CCU are connected by the multiwire umbilical cable that sends signals back and forth between the two. The CCU also gets a SYNC signal from the studio's master SYNC GENERATOR.

Since all the cameras' CCUs receive the SYNC signal, they all paint their pictures in unison. Each CCU sends its video to the SWITCHER.

CAMERA CARE

1. Lock your camera pedestal controls when your camera is idle. A camera with a heavy lens might suddenly tilt down, slamming its lens against the tripod.
2. Cap your lens when the camera is idle. This protects the lens glass.
3. Don't knock the camera around. It is fragile and easily misaligned.
4. Avoid extremes in temperature. CCD cameras make grainier pictures above 115°F. The heat in the trunk of a parked car on a sunny day can also damage a camera's circuits. In superfrigid weather, the zoom lens may get "sticky" and may fail to rotate smoothly.
5. Avoid dampness.

CAMERA MOUNTING EQUIPMENT

Really smooth camera movements require a tripod. A tripod also alleviates arm fatigue during long shooting sessions. During "trick" shots, it holds the camera still enough for edits to be unobtrusive (more on this in the editing chapter).

Figure 3–12 shows a tripod with a HEAD and DOLLY. The HEAD part at the top (not to be confused with the heads on a VCR, which are something else altogether) connects to your camera and allows you to aim it, using a long handle. The tripod part usually has an adjustable PEDESTAL, raised and lowered by a crank to allow for high and low shots. (And PEDESTAL is another word with two meanings. The camera height PEDESTAL has nothing to do with the camera's PEDESTAL control, a knob that electrically adjusts the camera's brightness.) The tripod legs often telescope so that the camera can be raised an additional three feet overhead. On the bottom is the DOLLY, a set of wheels that allows the tripod to glide smoothly over the floor.

Make sure you tighten the elevator lock when finished cranking it so that gravity doesn't wind it down with a "zwoop!" When you *do* decide to elevate the camera, be sure to *loosen the controls first*; otherwise the crank mechanism will strip its gears and wear out quickly.

Lighter, more portable, and cheaper than the tripod is the MONOPOD, a one-legged tripod (Figure 3–13). Although it can't stand up by itself, it takes a lot of weight off your arms and steadies your shots quite well as you hold it upright. It moves with you quickly with a minimum of setup (for when you are shooting wild scenes of that tornado ripping the town apart a block behind you).

And then there's the CENTIPOD, a furry little worm with a hundred legs. Although capable of holding only tiny cameras, the CENTIPOD is the only model that turns into a butterfly.

The PNEUMATIC STUDIO PEDESTAL is a heavy-duty monster used in professional television studios where the cameras are massive. Often there is a TELEPROMPTER attached to the camera, adding even more weight. Naturally it wouldn't be feasible for a camera operator to crank this whole shebang up and down manually. Instead, the PEDESTAL uses pneumatic pressure to help raise and lower the camera.

---

*Head   Top part of a camera tripod that holds the camera.

*Dolly   Bottom part of a camera tripod that has wheels. Also, the act of moving the camera toward or away from a subject.

Monopod   One-legged tripod.

*Pedestal   The elevation control on a camera tripod. "Pedestal up" means to raise the camera higher.

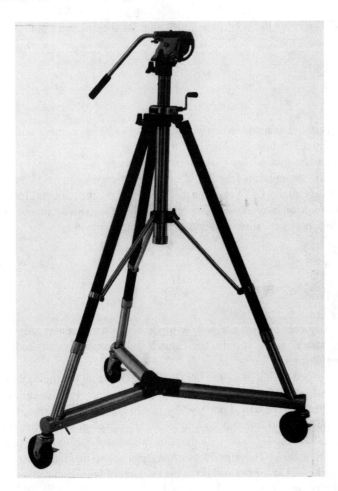

FIGURE 3–12 Simple tripod with HEAD and DOLLY (Courtesy of Comprehensive Video Supply Corp.).

The movement is so smooth that it can be done while the camera is shooting, unlike the industrial tripods that wobble as they are cranked. Professional camera PEDESTALS cost $7,000 to $30,000, which is more than some cameras. The PEDESTALS have to be pumped up before the show to ensure that they will rise to the occasion at the touch of a finger.

Heads

Figure 3–14 shows a basic FRICTION HEAD appropriate for small studios and schools.

To TILT and/or PAN your camera, first loosen the controls on the head while holding onto the handle you use to aim the camera. When PANNING or TILTING, you may want to keep these controls

---

*Friction head Inexpensive tripod head with locks to impede unwanted camera movement.

*Tilt The up-and-down motion of the camera, like nodding your head "yes."

*Pan The left-and-right motion of the camera, like nodding your head "no."

*Drag control Camera head control that resists free motion of the head in a direction.

Fluid head Camera support that dampens the tilting and panning movement of the camera, smoothing out jerky movements.

FIGURE 3–13   MONOPOD (Courtesy of Video Corp. of America).

slightly taut so they provide a little drag and thus mask some of your jars and shakes. Professionals consider anything but smooth-flowing camera movements to be very ungainly.

If you leave the camera, *tighten the HEAD controls*. The weight of the camera often makes it want to TILT. If it squirms loose while unattended, it could TILT down abruptly and smash its lens against the tripod.

The FRICTION HEAD in Figure 3–14 has a spring built into it to help hold the camera upright, making it easier to aim. Amateur and portable HEADS sold in camera stores have no way of counterbalancing the camera, making camera moves awkward and unstable.

Larger professional heavy-duty tripod HEADS are designed to be very stable and are good at smoothing out jiggles as you tilt. If the camera is balanced correctly on the HEAD, you should be able to let go of the camera handle and have the camera settle to a safe horizontal position rather than nose-diving or falling backward.

These heavy-duty HEADS often have two TILT adjustments and two PAN adjustments. The first TILT adjustment locks the head so that won't TILT. The second adjustment is called DRAG, and it has nothing to do with guys dressing in women's clothes. DRAG creates a resistance as you TILT the head. This reduces little camera jiggles, especially while you are trying to hold the camera still. If you try to TILT the camera quickly, however, the DRAG control will slow you down. (What a drag!) If you anticipate such a move, it is best to loosen the DRAG control. Similarly, the PAN lock control stops the head from PANNING, and the PAN DRAG control adds resistance to this camera movement. Inexperienced camera operators who don't realize that there are two controls for both PAN and TILT often find themselves struggling with their cameras while trying to aim them.

The better HEADS also allow you to adjust the position of the camera handles. If the camera is to be very low, then you will want the handles to come straight back so that you don't have to stoop over to aim the camera. If the camera is PEDESTALED up high, you may want to bring the handles nearly

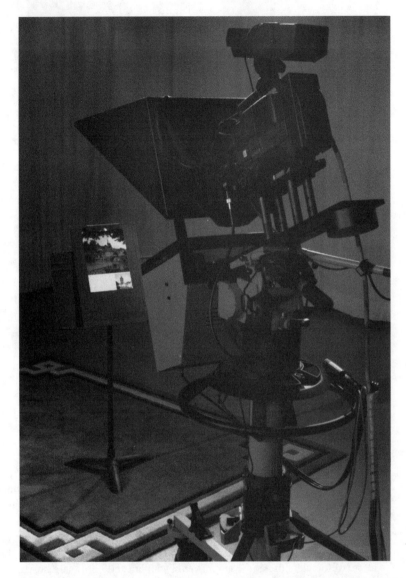

PNEUMATIC STUDIO PEDESTAL allows a heavy camera and teleprompter to be raised and lowered smoothly while on the air.

straight down so that your arms aren't waving overhead to aim the camera. And while you're at it, you might as well aim your VIEWFINDER so you see easily, as shown in Figure 3–15.

    The studio HEADS are too heavy for portable use. Professional film- and videomakers will spend several hundred dollars on a sturdy tripod and a FLUID HEAD (look back at Figure 1–9). The HEAD has oil-damped components inside it, making its movements smooth and precise.

---

*Quick release   A plate attached to the base of the camera by a bolt. The plate can then clip quickly onto the tripod head.
Wedge mount   A type of quick-release camera mount that slides into a wedge-shaped groove in the tripod head.

*Cable guards   Metal shields that sweep cables out of the way so the camera dolly doesn't roll over them.

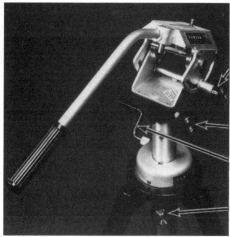

tilt lock

pan lock

elevator crank to
pedestal up
or down

elevator lock

FIGURE 3–14 Simple FRICTION HEAD for tripod.

 Mini Review

- The tripod, head, and dolly hold the camera steady and also smooth out camera moves.
- Unlock the camera head controls before aiming the camera; lock them before leaving the camera.

Before using a FLUID HEAD, loosen its controls and move the camera up and down and back and forth about ten times. The fluid gets "stiff," and it needs to be "worked" a little to allow smooth movement.

Attaching the Camera to the Head. Attaching the camera to the HEAD is sometimes tricky. There is a threaded hole in the base of the camera. In the HEAD is a captive bolt which shouldn't fall out (if you can't find the bolt, it probably fell out). Somehow that bolt has to screw into the hole in the camera's base. It's not easy to get the bolt started straight. Starting it crooked will strip the threads, so be patient.

FIGURE 3–15 Handle adjustment for comfort.

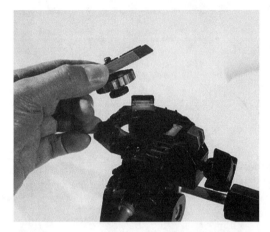

Metal plate attaches to bottom of camera (not shown) via threaded bolt. Note large tightener ring which gets tightened once the bolt is screwed into the camera as far as it will go.

Metal plate slides into grooved top of tripod head (with camera attached, of course) and the clamp is tightened.

FIGURE 3–16   QUICK RELEASE for a small camera.

Because this method of attaching cameras to HEADS is so awkward, some manufacturers have simplified the process. Some HEADS come with a removable plate that slides firmly into a groove in the HEAD and locks in place. This is called a QUICK RELEASE or a WEDGE MOUNT. The WEDGE plate can be attached to the base of the camera by using a bolt or screw. Once the plate is attached to the camera, the pair can be slid easily onto the camera head and locked in place. Figure 3–16 shows such a QUICK RELEASE mount. Figure 3–17 shows a bigger one.

Dollies

DOLLIES (except for the Cabbage Patch variety) are the casters that hold up the tripod. Almost all DOLLIES will glide smoothly over a smooth floor. For an uneven floor or a carpeted floor, bigger wheels are necessary to smooth the bumps. The simplest DOLLIES have casters that rotate in all directions, and

Press safety button, then pull lever to release camera from base. Remember to hang on to the camera.

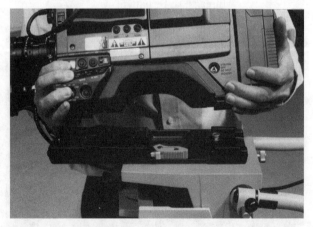

The camera comes free. To reattach, slip into groove in base and slide toward lens until the release lever clicks.

FIGURE 3–17   QUICK RELEASE for a larger camera.

FIGURE 3–18 Pulling this pin (and a twist locks it up) frees the castor to swivel in all directions.

usually the wheels will lock so that the camera doesn't roll (handy if you're shooting on the sidewalks of San Francisco). The DOLLY in Figure 3–18 has CABLE GUARDS for each caster to sweep cables out of the way as the camera traverses the floor. Another whoojit locks the casters, aiming them in a specific direction. This is handy when you want to DOLLY IN and don't want to be bothered aiming the wheels around before you can DOLLY back out. When this dingus is unlocked, the casters will rotate freely in whatever direction you pull the camera.

BASIC TRIPOD CONTROLS AND MOVEMENTS

TILT: To aim the camera up and down on a vertical axis, like nodding your head "yes." *Tilt up* means to shoot higher, toward the ceiling. *Tilt down* means to aim lower, toward the floor.

PAN: To aim the camera back and forth on a horizontal axis, like shaking your head "no." *Pan left* means to turn the camera to your left. *Pan right*, of course, means to turn it to the right (although your picture appears to move to the left).

To *DOLLY*: To travel forward or backward across the floor with the camera. *Dolly in* means to move the camera forward, tripod and all, closer to the subject. *Dolly out* means to pull back.

To *TRUCK* or *CRAB*: To travel from side to side across the floor with the camera, tripod and all. *Truck right* means to travel to your right, and *truck left* tells you to go in the other direction.

To *ARC:* To travel in an arc or circle about the subject. *Arc left* means move to the left, keeping the subject in the picture and a steady distance from the camera. *Arc right* means the opposite.

To *PEDESTAL*: To adjust the elevation of the camera above floor level. *Pedestal up* means to make the elevation greater. *Pedestal down* means to decrease the height of the camera.

DOLLY, TRUCK, PEDESTAL: When used as nouns, these words refer to parts of the camera tripod mechanism. The dolly or truck is the base with wheels that supports the actual tripod. The pedestal is the vertical shaft that raises or lowers the camera.

EFP (Electronic Field Production)   Shooting video outside the studio.

Body mount   Any device that affixes a camera to your body.

*Shoulder mount   Cushioned device connected to the base of a camera, allowing it to rest on the operator's shoulder.

Studio crane   Large studio device able to smoothly lift camera and operator high into the air.

Crane arm   Device for lifting cameras high into the air and aiming them while the camera operator remains on the ground.

Tai Chi stance   Body position for hand-holding a camera steady.

Before you DOLLY or TRUCK, make sure the wheels of the DOLLY are unlocked so they can turn. You'll be able to move the camera more easily if you anticipate and prepare by:

1. Orienting the wheels in the direction you want to go
2. Getting cable and other obstacles out of your path
3. Preparing your camera cables so that they can follow you easily

Moving cameras smoothly from place to place is difficult enough without having to wrestle with tangled and twisted cables or sticking casters as you go. One of the floor manager's roles is to help you with your cables during fancy camera moves.

Body Mounts

Docking ENG (electronic news gathering) and EFP (electronic field production) cameras are pretty heavy, especially when you have to carry them around all day. It's especially difficult to walk and run with them. Special BODY MOUNTS are sometimes used to distribute the camera's weight and stabilize the picture. Almost all ENG camcorders come with a SHOULDER MOUNT that holds the camera balanced on the shoulder of the operator. Some also serve as a stand when the camcorder is set down. Figure 3–6 showed one.

Professional Mounts

Larger, professional studios employ fancier ways to hold the camera.

The STUDIO CRANE is usually a motor-driven device with three or four wheels and a movable boom that can raise the camera from close to the studio floor (about one foot) to about ten feet high. Hydraulic pistons allow the camera to move smoothly from one position to another, carrying the camera operator along for a fun carnival ride.

The CRANE ARM is a smaller, lighter version of the heavy-duty STUDIO CRANE but without the carnival ride. It doesn't carry the camera operator with the camera. Most versions allow the camera to be operated at one end of a counterbalanced boom arm, perhaps ten feet up in the air, while the camera operator stands at the other end viewing a TV monitor and aiming the camera remotely from the floor.

Improvised Mounts

When shooting on location, you usually don't have room to carry much mounting equipment. Most camera mounting equipment is quite bulky. Here are a few shortcuts.

Wobbly camera shots will make your scenes look amateurish. Steady your camcorder by leaning it against the hood of a car, a fence, or a notch in a tree. If that's too hard, then hold the camcorder and brace yourself against something solid. Perhaps you can set your elbows on a desk or lean your shoulder against a doorway.

A pillow or bean bag (dried soup peas also work) is indispensable when doing a lot of on-location shooting. It does wonders for cradling a camera for steady shots. You can lie prone on the ground and use it to steady your low-angle shots. It's great for sinking your elbows into when you've propped yourself over the hood of a car. If you're shooting children (with a camera of course), you'll find yourself taking many medium-low-angle shots, probably while you're on your knees. A pillow or bean bag saves many a bruised kneecap.

There are a lot of ways to move without a DOLLY. Wheelchairs glide smoothly, even over irregular surfaces. One person pushes while the other sits and holds the camera.

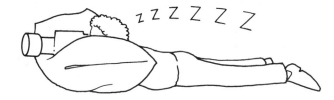

A pillow or bean bag will help you steady your shots.

If you're shooting near shopping centers, the ubiquitous shopping cart gives a smooth ride over indoor floors (find one with casters that aren't square).

How would you shoot a bowling ball as it rolled down the alley? Try lying on an upside-down carpet remnant while two helpers push you with brooms.

You can shoot from the window of a moving car, from the tailgate of a pickup truck, from an electric company cherry picker (a bucket on a long mast capable of lifting a person high into the air), or from a fire truck ladder. Speedboats, rollercoasters, and hot-air balloons are all possible sources of creative camera angles. If the bumpiness of the ride makes your picture jiggle too much, try to zoom the lens out as far as you can, hiding most of the wobbles.

CAUTION: Use common sense when shooting from any kind of vehicle. One bump could catapult you off a tailgate and onto your tailbone. Be especially wary of climbing onto the front of vehicles like bucket-loaders. Here, when you fall out, you get run over (great action footage, though).

Tai Chi Stance

If tripods are too cumbersome for you or you are moving a lot, there are several methods for steadying a hand-held camera. Figure 3–19 shows the Tai Chi stance (from Oriental martial arts), which minimizes natural body sway while putting you in excellent position for smooth moves in most any direction. Stand with your feet eighteen inches apart, slightly pigeon-toed, with weight distributed equally on both legs, knees slightly bent (not locked). Keep your neck and the camera in close to your body. From the Tai Chi position, you can PAN by turning at the waist, you can TILT using your whole torso, you can PEDESTAL DOWN by further bending your knees, and you can DOLLY in or out by proceeding to walk, bent over in the Groucho Marx style, sliding your feet along, letting your knees absorb all the ups and downs while your torso glides smoothly through the air. Perhaps it sounds more like Oriental torture than good camera posture, and indeed it gets uncomfortable over time. But with a little practice, this silly-looking stance will deliver nice-looking pictures.

 Mini Review

- When shooting without a tripod, steady yourself against something for jiggle-free shots. Use the Tai Chi stance to move the camera gracefully.

And while we are on the subject of walking with the camera, here's a good habit to get into, one practiced by professional microscope and telescope users: Stick one eye to the eyepiece but *keep both eyes open.* It may be awkward at first, but a half-hour of practice will teach your "unused" eye not to see. Thereafter, you don't have to tire your face squinting one eye closed, *and* you reap an unexpected benefit when you try to walk. Your unused eye starts keeping track of curb sides, low limbs, trip cables, and horse droppings as you march hither, thither, and yon.

Feet 18 inches apart, knees bent   To travel, walk like Groucho

FIGURE 3–19   Tai Chi position for holding a camera.

A camcorder that rests on your shoulder will give a more stable picture than a palmcorder. With the shoulder cameras, the camera gains stability by being pressed against you at several points: the eyecup (or forehead), the side of the face, the shoulder, the trigger grip, and the lens. The palmcorder, on the other hand, is held at the end of your bobbing arm. If using a palmcorder, stabilize your arms by pressing your elbows against your chest. Press the eyecup against your brow and hold onto the lens. Again, uncomfortable but stable.

As mentioned before, it will be more restful and more stable if you can brace yourself or your camera against something while shooting. Sit down, lean against a wall, brace the camera against a pole, or hold it against a car hood or a rock for rock-solid shots.

For really low shots, the movable ELECTRONIC VIEWFINDER will make it easy to look straight down into the finder while cradling the camera beneath you, perhaps at knee height. If you can connect up to a TV set to view your shots, you may not need the VIEWFINDER at all, freeing you to hold the camera anywhere. Low shots are also easily done by hugging the camera to your waist and aiming it while viewing the TV screen.

Element   Each glass part of the entire lens.
*Focal length   A numerical description of the apparent magnification or angle of view of a lens.
*Iris   An adjustable opening in a lens that governs the amount of light allowed to pass through it.

*F-stop   A numerical measure of the size of the iris opening, that indicates the amount of light that can pass through the lens. F2.8, for instance, lets through twice as much light as f4.

MORE ABOUT TV CAMERA LENSES

Anybody who wears glasses knows how important lenses are. The lens is the camera's window to the world.

How Lenses Work

Light enters the lens, becomes concentrated or magnified by the optical elements in the lens, passes through an IRIS, which reduces the light, and is then focused onto the chip, as shown in Figure 3–20.

The glass parts of the lens are called ELEMENTS, and their shape and position determine how much a picture will be magnified. The amount of magnification a lens gives you is called FOCAL LENGTH.

The positioning of the outermost ELEMENT of a lens generally determines whether far or near parts of a scene will appear sharpest. This is called FOCUS.

The third thing a lens can do is reduce the amount of light permitted through it. The IRIS or F-STOP handles this job.

All three factors are quantifiable and are used in describing the lens and its application. Let's look at each in more detail.

The Iris, or F-Stop.   The F-STOPS measure the ability of a lens to allow light through it. The IRIS ring, a rotatable collar somewhere on the lens, has numbers etched on it—typically these are 1.4, 2.0, 2.8, 4, 5.6, 8, 11, 16, and 22. The lower the F-STOP number, the more efficient the lens—or the more light it allows through for a bright, contrasty picture. In general, you'd keep the lens "wide open" (set at the lowest f-number) if you're shooting inside with minimal light. Outdoors, in bright sunshine, you'd "stop down" to a small lens opening (a high f-number) to allow limited light.

An F-STOP of 1.4 allows in twice as much light as f2. In fact, each time you "click off" an F-STOP on the IRIS—1.4, 2, 2.8, 4, 5.6—you double the amount of light to the camera. Thus, f2 admits eight times as much light as f5.6.

So where does IRIS come into the story? The IRIS is the mechanism inside the lens that cuts out the light. It performs much like the automatic IRIS in your eye, the part that makes your eyes blue or brown. Tiny flaps in the IRIS intersect to create a larger or smaller hole, permitting more or less light to pass through the lens. See Figure 3–21.

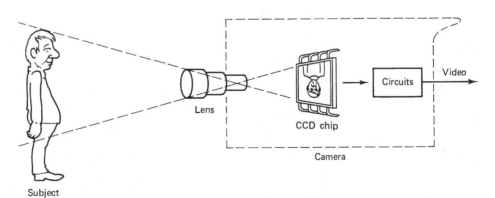

FIGURE 3–20   Lens focuses image onto CCD chip.

IRIS ring adjusts lens opening.

inside the lens

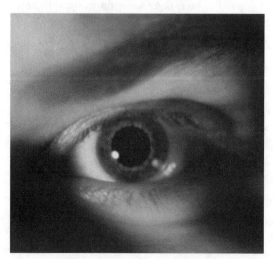
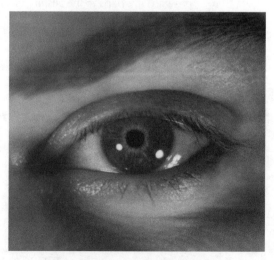

EYE

large opening needed in dim light

small opening to reduce bright light

FIGURE 3–21   IRIS.

In summary, the IRIS is adjusted to the f-number that allows in *enough light* for your camera to "see" to make a good picture but *not too much light*, which will result in too contrasty a picture or poor DEPTH OF FIELD. So what's DEPTH OF FIELD? Hint: It has nothing to do with the dimensions of farmland.

Depth of Field.   DEPTH OF FIELD is the range of distance over which a picture will remain in focus. Broad DEPTH OF FIELD occurs when something near you and something far from you can both be sharply in focus at the same time. Narrow DEPTH OF FIELD is the opposite. Things go badly out of focus when their distance from you is changed. Figure 3–22 diagrams this relationship.

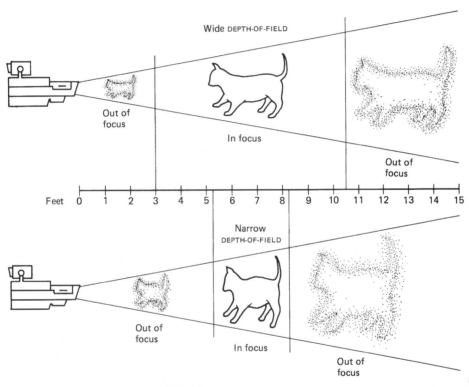

FIGURE 3–22   DEPTH OF FIELD.

Fixed focal length lens   A lens that cannot zoom.

Video level   How strong a video signal is. On VTRs, the video level control will adjust the contrast of your video recording.

*Wide-angle   The opposite of telephoto, a wide-angle lens takes in a broad panoramic view. The lens "gets everything in," but everything may appear small in the picture.

*Long shot   A wide-angle shot, making the image look far away, as if it were taken from a long distance.

*Medium shot   A shot of something that includes some of its surroundings. A medium shot of a person would include the head and chest.

*Telephoto   The opposite of wide-angle, a telephoto lens magnifies the view like binoculars. It also has a narrow field of view, concentrating on one part of a picture and cutting out the rest.

*Close-up   A shot of something taken close to it or zoomed in on it so that it fills the screen. A close-up of a person would show the face, hair, and part of the neck.

Generally, one wants to maintain broad DEPTH OF FIELD so that all aspects of the picture are sharp. There are times, however, when for artistic reasons, one would prefer to have the foreground picture (the part of the picture which is up close) sharp and the background blurry. Such a condition focuses the viewer's attention on the central attraction in the foreground or middleground while making the fuzzy background unobtrusive. And it's especially handy for hiding the inevitable scratches and smudges on your TV scenery. In such cases, poor DEPTH OF FIELD is an advantage.

The mechanism for adjusting the DEPTH OF FIELD is our old friend the IRIS. As you see in Figure 3–23, low f-numbers give poor DEPTH OF FIELD, while high f-numbers give excellent DEPTH OF FIELD.

Notice how you never get something for nothing. As you improve your DEPTH OF FIELD by increasing your f-number, you simultaneously reduce the amount of light permitted through the lens. A film photographer would make up for this loss of light by slowing down the shutter speed of his camera. This would expose the film to the light longer. But in TV cameras, you can't easily do this. TV cameras electronically take their pictures at 1/60 of a second, *almost always*. So while f22 may give you excellent DEPTH OF FIELD, it will let in very little light, giving you a gray, dull picture. f2.8 would let in plenty of light for a brilliant contrasty picture, but your DEPTH OF FIELD would be very limited. What can one do to get the best of both worlds?

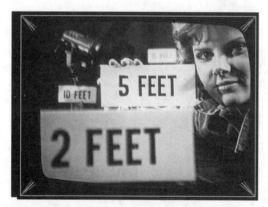

F2.8: Contrast to spare but poor DEPTH OF FIELD

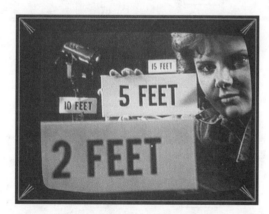

F4: A good compromise

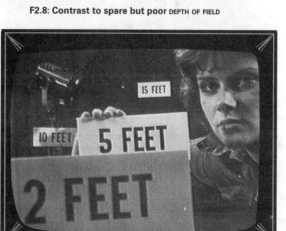

F8: Sometimes okay

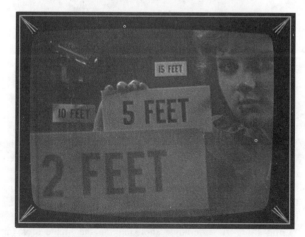

F16: Excellent DEPTH OF FIELD but picture is too faded

FIGURE 3–23   How a TV camera responds to different IRIS settings. The camera is focused at 5 feet.

THINGS THAT AFFECT A CAMERA'S SENSITIVITY		
Image Darker	*Feature*	*Image Brighter*
Higher	<—F-stop—>	Lower
Faster	<—Shutter speed—>	Slower
Off	<—Gain boost—>	+6, +12, +18dB
Telephoto	<—Zoom lens—>	Wide-angle

1. Try to get as much light on the subject as possible. This will make up for some of the light that the high f-numbers cut out.
2. Decide where to compromise. Usually, people go for the bright-enough picture and sacrifice DEPTH OF FIELD.
3. One can make the camera work harder to compensate for the insufficient light associated with the high f-number. On most cameras you can increase GAIN or use the +6dB, +12dB BOOST switch.
4. Use slower camera shutter speeds, if your camera has them. All these adjustments will enhance the contrast of your picture. Some cameras with automatic controls will make these adjustments for you. While these GAIN and BOOST adjustments will give you a brighter, more contrasty picture, the picture will become more grainy with the increase in these levels.
5. One can make the VCR work harder and increase the contrast of its recorded picture by turning up its VIDEO LEVEL control. Most home VCRs will do this automatically. As with the camera, increasing these levels also increases the graininess of the picture.

You still never get something for nothing. Broad DEPTH OF FIELD gives you poor contrast. Boosting the contrast electronically makes your picture grainier. The only way to get excellent DEPTH OF FIELD *and* a smooth and contrasty picture is to pour lots of light onto the subject. The subject had better not be a dish of ice cream.

A good compromise in the outdoor setting is to provide plenty of light and set the lens at f4 for moderate DEPTH OF FIELD and moderate contrast. Indoor shooting may generally require f2.0 to f2.8. Bright daytime shooting outdoors may permit f11 to be used.

 Mini Review

- The iris controls the amount of light allowed through the lens.
- To admit the most light through a lens, use its lowest f-stop number.
- High f-stop numbers cause the lens to yield broad depth of field, but may reduce contrast in the image.
- Narrow depth of field allows you to focus on the main subject, while foreground or background objects remain fuzzy. This makes the main subject stand out from its surroundings.

Focal Length and Zoom Lenses.   The FOCAL LENGTH of any lens is measured in inches or millimeters (mm) and describes two attributes of the lens:

1. How far from the optical center of the lens the image is focused. Most video users don't give a hoot about this measurement unless they're changing lenses.
2. How wide an angle the lens will cover. This factor gets plenty of hoots.

FIGURE 3–24   WIDE-ANGLE lens (low FOCAL LENGTH number) gives a LONG SHOT.

A lens that doesn't zoom is called a FIXED FOCAL LENGTH lens. (A lens that has been run over by a truck is called a *broken* focal length lens.) You see them on cheapie computer cameras and surveillance cameras. All the rest of today's video cameras have ZOOM lenses, lenses that can change from one FOCAL LENGTH to another.

ZOOM a lens to a FOCAL LENGTH of 9mm or less and it's called WIDE ANGLE. It will display a wide field of view like the LONG SHOT shown in Figure 3–24. It is useful for surveillance of large areas or for shooting in cramped quarters where you can't easily back up far enough to "get it all in."

A FOCAL LENGTH of about 20mm will display a medium field of view like the MEDIUM SHOT shown in Figure 3–25.

Zoom a lens to its TELEPHOTO position (a FOCAL LENGTH of 50mm or more), and it will display a narrow field of view like the CLOSE-UP shown in Figure 3–26. The TELEPHOTO lens gives close-ups of objects far from the camera. These are handy when you want to shoot action shots of a raging bull without actually climbing into the bull ring.

A zoom lens has a variable FOCAL LENGTH (as opposed to a FIXED FOCAL LENGTH) and may range from WIDE-ANGLE to TELEPHOTO. One example of how a zoom lens's range of FOCAL LENGTH can be expressed is as follows: 12–120mm. The lens can give a WIDE-ANGLE shot like a 12mm lens and can be zoomed in to give a shot like a 120mm lens. This lens has a ZOOM RATIO of 10:1 (10 to 1). You can zoom it in to ten times its lowest FOCAL LENGTH and make something look ten times closer. This ratio can also be expressed as 10×.

Such lenses cost around $300 and are typically found on home camcorders and industrial cameras. A 20:1 zoom lens would be found on the better cameras and has a broad enough zoom range to

Zoom ratio   The mathematical ratio between a zoom lens's most telephoto setting and its widest angle. A 20mm–100mm zoom lens has a zoom ratio of 1:5, or 5×.

Optical zoom ratio   The actual zoom ratio (smallest focal length divided into the largest focal length of the lens) of the physical lens without any digital enhancement from the camera, such as digital zoom.

FIGURE 3–25   A FOCAL LENGTH of about 20mm gives a MEDIUM SHOT.

permit the camera to be used in a variety of situations. It can take WIDE-ANGLE shots in a cramped Land Rover as well as TELEPHOTO shots of hungry lions in the jungle. Generally, the greater the range of the zoom, the higher the cost will zoom (like $500 to $12,000).

Zoom lenses with broad 20× or 40× ZOOM RATIOS tend to be long and heavy, making them a little hard to work with when portability is paramount. Lenses with a 10× ZOOM RATIO are relatively small and light.

Don't be fooled by some consumer camcorders sporting a 20:1 or 50:1 DIGITAL ZOOM. This zoom is accomplished by doubling or tripling the CCD pixel readout, making the picture fuzzy. Only the OPTICAL ZOOM RATIO is germane when discussing lenses.

Changing the FOCAL LENGTH of a lens does more than simply change the magnification of the picture. Other subtle changes occur. *The greater the FOCAL LENGTH, the greater the magnification of the picture, the narrower the field of view, the flatter the scene looks, and the narrower the DEPTH OF FIELD becomes.*

Baseball fans are probably familiar with the telephoto shots of games where the players in the outfield look like they are standing on top of the pitcher, who himself looks inches away from the batter (Figure 3–27). If you want to compress distance so that faraway things look closer to nearby

FIGURE 3–26   ZOOM a lens to TELEPHOTO (50mm or higher FOCAL LENGTH) and you get a CLOSE-UP picture.

FIGURE 3–27   TELEPHOTO lens flattens scene; the players look close to each other.

things, use a TELEPHOTO LENS. If you'd like to stress the difference between nearby and faraway things, use a WIDE-ANGLE shot. If a vehicle or person is coming toward you and you wish to make their motion appear slower or wish to hold them in the scene longer, then have them start from far away and use a TELEPHOTO lens. If however, you wish to exaggerate their speed or progress, use a WIDE-ANGLE lens. Once near you, the subject will appear to whip by.

WIDE-ANGLE shots have excellent DEPTH OF FIELD, and TELEPHOTO shots have poor DEPTH OF FIELD (see Figure 3–28). This sometimes makes it hard to shoot moving objects with a TELEPHOTO lens; they are constantly shifting out of focus on you. A WIDE-ANGLE lens, on the other hand, hides the focusing errors. WIDE-ANGLE shots are useful when you have to run with the camera or shoot without taking time to focus.

 Mini Review

- When you zoom a lens from wide to telephoto, the focal length increases and the picture looks nearer and flatter, and depth of field is reduced.

FOCUSING

You have learned that focusing is done by rotating part of the lens. This process always involved looking through the viewfinder (or a TV monitor) to see your results. If you have no viewfinder or are forced to guess when things are properly focused, do the following:

Observe the focus ring on the lens. You'll see numbers etched in it representing the distance in feet or in meters at which the object will be in focus. Estimate the distance to your subject and turn this ring to the appropriate number, and you will be roughly focused.

As you think back to the relationship between DEPTH OF FIELD and FOCAL LENGTH, you appreciate the fact that it is much harder to get something into focus if the DEPTH OF FIELD is very narrow. But there are times when this narrow DEPTH OF FIELD can *help* you focus.

---

*Selective focus   Adjusting the focus of a lens so that one part of the picture is sharp and other parts fuzzy, useful for directing attention.

Pull focus   Adjusting the focus of a lens, often to keep a moving subject sharp, while the camera is "on."

TELEPHOTO shot gives narrow DEPTH OF FIELD

WIDE-ANGLE shot gives broad DEPTH OF FIELD

FIGURE 3–28   How FOCAL LENGTH affects DEPTH OF FIELD.

Take the example in which you have good DEPTH OF FIELD and are trying to focus. You turn the focus ring, and the blurry picture becomes less blurry, less blurry, pretty good, fairly sharp, sharp, maybe sharper, maybe not sharper, still fairly sharp, a little blurry—so you start turning back in the other direction. There is a range where the picture doesn't change much while you turn the focus ring. Which position is right?

Now take the example of narrow DEPTH OF FIELD. You turn the focus ring, and the blurry picture becomes blurry, blurry, less blurry, good, perfect, good, blurry again—so you start turning back. Here the picture zaps into focus and out again. There is no guesswork as to where the right focus position is; there is just one narrow range where the picture is good.

The moral of the story is: *For accurate focusing, zoom in first, focus, then zoom out to the shot you want.*

What do you do when you have a subject who moves around a lot? How do you stay in focus? Here are some possibilities:

1. If you are a good focuser, just stay alert and adjust for every movement. Most of us are not good focusers, however.
2. Flood the subject with light so that you can use high f-numbers for broad DEPTH OF FIELD.
3. Stay zoomed out. Focusing inaccuracies are most noticeable in close-ups. When you are zoomed out, nearly everything appears sharp.

4. Try to get the subject to move *laterally* to you, not toward or away from you. Since the subject stays roughly the same distance from the camera, you will not have to refocus, just aim.

5. Try to use big subjects so that you can zoom out or can stay farther away from them. Why are big, zoomed-out subjects easier to focus? To fill a TV screen, little objects must be magnified. You do this by zooming in or by moving the camera closer to them. A zoomed-in lens blows up all the little focusing inaccuracies, especially if an object is itself deep or is moving toward or away from the camera. A camera close to an object also exaggerates the focusing problems. When an object three feet away from a camera moves one foot, you get a very noticeable 33 percent focusing error. When an object thirty feet away moves one foot, the error is a minor 3 percent. Combining both the zooming and the nearness concepts, we find that zooming in on a postage stamp held in somebody's hand three feet away will display formidable focusing problems as the hand moves. But zooming out on a giant poster of a postage stamp held thirty feet away poses no focusing problems even if the poster moves a foot.

6. Use your camcorder's automatic focus. This sounds like an awful cop-out, but there are times when you're just too busy with other things to pay attention to focusing.

7. If you're careening down rapids in a raft, hanging on for dear life, focusing may be the last thing on your mind. In these cases, zoom out and focus manually for infinity (∞) and leave it there—most of the action will be at some distance anyway, so ∞ will catch most of it.

8. Last and least, try to confine your subjects by seating them, tranquilizing them, encumbering them with microphone cables, or marking a spot on the floor where they must stand.

WIDE-ANGLE shots may ease your focusing efforts, but it doesn't make very interesting television—everything looks too small. Some of you may think you can use WIDE-ANGLES to dodge the drudgery of focusing without having objects look small by simply stepping closer to the objects. The trick works, but packs a surprise: *close objects become distorted,* as you see in Figure 3–29. People's noses look big, objects look warped. This is great if you're looking for a comedic, scary, or exaggerated effect. Otherwise, it's distracting.

Selective Focusing.   A tricky way to move the viewer's attention from one object to another is by SELECTIVE FOCUS. First you focus on an object in, say, the foreground, leaving the background blurry. Next you refocus for the background, blurring the foreground. Your viewer's eyes will stay riveted to whichever part of the picture is in focus at the time. Figure 3–30 shows how your attention can be moved from the time on the clock to the person asleep in bed. Another SELECTIVE FOCUS technique is used with long rows of objects (soldiers, flowers, toys on an assembly line). Focus first on the closest items and slowly refocus to the farthest ones. One by one, each will pull into focus and then retreat into a blur as your eye follows down the line to the end. This is a technique called PULL FOCUS, focusing from one object to another while the camera is "on."

To intensify the SELECTIVE FOCUS effect, it is good to have a narrow DEPTH OF FIELD. Use a long FOCAL LENGTH lens and a low F-STOP (if possible) and try to keep the nearby objects as near as possible and the far ones as far as possible.

Cable drive   Cranks or knobs, mounted on or near the tripod handles, that are connected to the lens via cables and remotely control the lens's zoom and/or focus.

*****Electric zoom**   Electric motor on a lens or camera that zooms the lens at the touch of a button.

*****ENG (electronic news gathering)**   Portable video production for the news. Often, quick-and-dirty techniques are used with a minimum of equipment and crew.

MOD (minimum operating distance)   The closest a lens can focus normally.

*****Macro lens**   A lens that can be focused on a very close object, sometimes touching it.

Lens close to face

Face distortion

Car distortion

FIGURE 3–29 WIDE-ANGLE lens distorts image when objects get close.

Lens Control Systems

Figure 3–8 showed a manual zoom lens. To focus one, you rotate the outside ring. To zoom, you rotate the middle ring. To change F-STOPS, you rotate the ring nearest the camera.

The IRIS ring is seldom adjusted manually while you are shooting. The focus and zoom rings need almost constant adjustment. It's not easy to do this with one hand. Only practice will teach your fingers which ring does what so that focusing and zooming become automatic for you.

No one ever has trouble telling amateur camera work from professional camera work. Amateurs invariably wiggle the camera while zooming, make jerky zooms, change zoom or focus too late, or zoom a little in the wrong direction before discovering their error and then have to zoom in the right direction. All of these bad moves are very obvious on the screen and make a TV production look unprofessional. There is only one way to wipe out all of these lens control problems at once, and it's summarized in one word—*practice*.

Learn which ring is focus and which is zoom. *Learn* which way to turn the zoom ring to zoom in or zoom out (it is inexcusable to "try" one direction of the ring and then the other to find out which

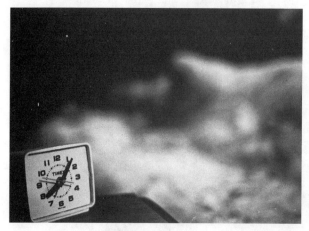

Your attention is drawn to the alarm clock.

Your attention is drawn to the sleeper.

FIGURE 3–30   SELECTIVE FOCUS.

way zooms you in; you should *know* this; it should be automatic). *Learn* which way to turn the focus ring when your subject is coming toward you.

None of this is easy, especially if you have to do it with one hand. If the camera is on a tripod and one hand is aiming the camera, then you only have one hand left for focusing and zooming. To make camera handling easier, the manufacturers have devised some ingenious ways to zoom and focus lenses.

Cable Drive.   The most typical studio setup involves a CABLE DRIVE for focusing and a ROCKER SWITCH for zooming (review Figure 1–10). The CABLE DRIVE consists of a rotating handle attached to one of the camera's aiming handles (usually the left). The rotating handle connects to a flexible cable that rotates inside a sheath, the other end of which attaches to the lens. Thus, when you turn the handle, a gear rotates the lens focus.

With a little practice, you can learn to focus at the same time you're aiming the camera by placing the camera handle in the palm of your hand and running the tips of your fingers over the rotating focus knob nearby, as shown in Figure 3–31.

FOCUSING TIPS REVIEWED

1. Practice, practice, practice, practice, practice!—or you'll be no darned good!
2. Remember, if time permits, that you focus on a subject by
   a. zooming in all the way first,
   b. focusing for a sharp picture, and then
   c. zooming out to the shot you want.
3. When you're trying to focus in step 2, use this method:
   a. Turn the focus knob until the picture changes from blurry to sharp to a *little* blurry again.
   b. Since you've gone too far, turn the knob back again slightly. Once you're used to it, this technique becomes fast and accurate.
4. If your camera is on (its tally light is lit) or if time doesn't permit proper focusing, you omit steps 2a and 2c and just focus as best you can without extra zooming.
5. Objects closer than five feet (or the closest distance etched on the lens barrel) probably cannot be focused clearly, so keep your distance.
6. Did I mention practice, practice, practice? Step 2 should take three seconds, and you will have a picture that is crystal perfect.

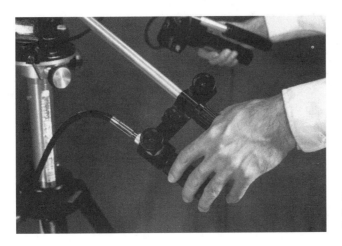

FIGURE 3–31 Focusing a handle-mounted CABLE DRIVE with your fingertips.

It takes some time to get the hang of focusing and aiming the camera in one smooth move, but with practice you can achieve very professional-looking results.

Electric Zoom.   There are still some cameras around that use a crank, attached to the right camera handle, connected to a CABLE DRIVE, attached to the lens for zooming. The camera operator would aim and focus with his/her left hand while zooming with the right. The cranking action was very smooth and precise, once you got the hang of it—until the mechanism got old and "sticky," making zooms jerky.

Most of today's studio cameras use an ELECTRIC ZOOM control. Figure 3–32 shows one mounted on the camera handle. It is a ROCKER SWITCH. You operate it by placing your thumb in the groove on the switch as shown in the figure and moving your thumb to the right to zoom in and to the left to zoom out. Pushing your thumb farther makes the camera zoom faster. Meanwhile, the rest of your right hand firmly grips the camera handle, allowing you to maintain steady aim. As before, the left hand grasps the left handle (further steadying the aim) while the fingertips focus the lens.

Manipulating all the camera controls at once takes some practice.

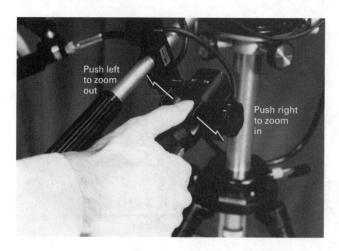

Push left to zoom out

Push right to zoom in

FIGURE 3–32   ELECTRIC ZOOM on a studio camera.

As mentioned earlier, camcorders also may have an electric zoom with a ROCKER SWITCH. As was shown in Figure 3–10, one hand slides under a strap (to help you hold the camera), and two fingers press the ROCKER SWITCH, one way to zoom in and the other way to zoom out. The other hand grasps the lens barrel to manually focus the lens. This two-handed operation allows you to focus and zoom at the same time. This is the most popular setup for industrial and ENG portable cameras.

Macro.   The typical lens can focus objects no closer than about four feet. Some of the more expensive lenses have a MOD (minimum operating distance) of a foot or two. Some consumer camcorders will focus continuously right down to ¼ of an inch from the glass lens. Others will do the same but require the lens to be zoomed out or switched to the MACRO mode first.

No, MACRO doesn't describe a type of fish (as in "Holy Macro!"). It's the ability of a lens to focus on very near objects. MACRO makes your lens nearsighted; things far away will be blurry no matter how you focus.

In their "normal" (non-MACRO) mode, most of these lenses work like any other lens, focusing down to four feet or so. They also zoom normally. To change them to MACRO, you generally throw a "safety catch" (which prevents the lens from going into this mode accidentally) and then refocus on a very near object. Sometimes the zoom control becomes the MACRO *focus* control. Many MACRO lenses can be refocused easily from a super-close-up back out to normal distances, opening the possibility of "arty" or creative transitional effects.

 Mini Review

- Telephoto shots are harder to focus than wide-angle shots.
- Learn which way to adjust the controls on the lens so you don't have to experiment "on the air."
- A macro lens can focus on close objects.

---

*Close-up lens attachment   A lens element that screws onto your existing lens, allowing it to focus closer than normal.
Diopter   The measure of a close-up lens attachment's strength. The larger the diopter number (+1, +2, +3), the closer the lens can focus.

Telephoto converter   Lens attachment to increase the focal length (magnification) of a lens for a narrower angle of view.
Wide-angle converter   Lens attachment to decrease a lens's focal length, giving the image a wider angle of view.

When the MACRO is activated, normal zoom functions are usually inoperable.

FIGURE 3–33 Lens MACRO control is usually activated by pressing a release button and rotating a collar near the base of the lens.

Unfortunately, while in the MACRO mode, most zoom lenses cannot zoom. Also, many MACRO zoom lenses have a "dead area" where they cannot focus. The MACRO mode may work from one inch to three inches and the non-MACRO mode may work from four feet to infinity, but you can't focus anywhere between three inches and four feet.

Figure 3–33 shows a professional lens MACRO being activated.

Close-up Shooting

Normally, if you try to shoot something closer than four or five feet from your camera, the picture will be blurry. If you must get closer to your work, you're already familiar with the magic of the MACRO lens. But what if your lens doesn't have this feature? Enter the CLOSE-UP LENS ATTACHMENT.

Close-up Lens Attachments. Your regular lens can be made to focus on closer subjects by the mere addition of a CLOSE-UP LENS ATTACHMENT, shown in Figure 3–34. Attach it by unscrewing the lens shade and screwing on the CLOSE-UP LENS ATTACHMENT in its place. The curved surface of the attachment should face *away* from the camera. *Do not* screw a close-up lens attachment down tight; it can easily seize up and become hard to remove. The lens shade may now be screwed onto the close-up attachment. Leave this slightly loose too.

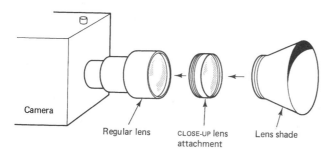

Camera   Regular lens   CLOSE-UP lens attachment   Lens shade

FIGURE 3–34 CLOSE-UP LENS ATTACHMENT.

CLOSE-UP shooting.

With a close-up lens attachment on your zoom lens, you can zoom the full range without going out of focus, assuming that you are the right distance from your subject and that you followed proper focusing procedure to start with. This is the greatest advantage of a close-up lens attachment over a MACRO lens that won't let you zoom.

A CLOSE-UP LENS ATTACHMENT doesn't appreciably magnify an image per se. It merely permits you to bring your camera closer to your subject without going out of focus. Like reading glasses, it makes your camera nearsighted.

The power of a CLOSE-UP LENS ATTACHMENT is measured in DIOPTERS. The bigger the DIOPTER number, the stronger the lens, and the closer your camera can "see" with it on. The weaker ones are +1 and +2; the stronger ones are +5 and higher. Where normally we could shoot from infinity up to 4 feet, a +1 DIOPTER CLOSE-UP LENS ATTACHMENT lets us shoot ranges from about 3 feet to 1½ feet. A +2 DIOPTER attachment gets us from 1½ feet to 1 foot, and +3 gets us from 1 foot to 3/4 foot.

Telephoto and Wide-Angle Converters

Close relatives to the CLOSE-UP LENS ATTACHMENT are the TELEPHOTO and WIDE-ANGLE CONVERTER. Whatever focal length your STANDARD or zoom lens is, these attachments will make it greater or smaller, thus yielding a wider view or a more magnified view of your subject. Figure 3–35 shows a WIDE-ANGLE and TELEPHOTO CONVERTER and the image you get when using them.

Some CONVERTERS are reversible; they're threaded at both ends. Attach the CONVERTER one way, and it multiplies your FOCAL LENGTH 1.5×, making your lens more TELEPHOTO. Attach it the opposite way, and it multiplies your FOCAL LENGTH .6×, making it more WIDE-ANGLE. If, for instance, your 6:1 zoom lens had a range of 20mm to 120mm, the 1.5× CONVERTER could make your lens act as if it were 30mm to 180mm (better for bird-watching and crocodile safaris). The other way around, the .6× CONVERTER makes your lens 12mm to 72mm (better for spelunking and indoor shots).

Normal view

TELEPHOTO and WIDE-ANGLE converters (Courtesy Recoton)

View with TELEPHOTO converter

View with WIDE-ANGLE converter

FIGURE 3–35 TELEPHOTO and WIDE-ANGLE converters.

Lens Filters

A FILTER blocks something unwanted and lets through something wanted. Lens FILTERS attach to the outside of your lens and block out unwanted colors, brightness, or glare.

Sometimes, lens attachments that are not really FILTERS are called FILTERS simply because they look like FILTERS and attach to the outside of the lens like FILTERS. They don't filter out anything; they may distort or add some special effect to the image from the lens such as star patterns, a multiple image, a halo effect, a fog effect, etc.

There are two ways to buy FILTERS. One is to buy round glass LENS ATTACHMENTS, threaded and ready to screw onto your lens. These are convenient but expensive. The other is to buy a FILTER HOLDER, which attaches to the outside of your lens, and a kit of FILTERS, which drop into the holder. This method is cheaper in the long run but more cumbersome.

 **Mini Review**

- A close-up lens attachment will make your camera "nearsighted."
- A telephoto or wide-angle converter will change the focal length range of your zoom lens.

Take a closer look at car commercials nowadays. Most will show a shiny automobile speeding down a dusty road with clear sky and buttes in the background. Take another look at that sky. Does it seem unusually blue? In almost every ad they do the same thing: throw in a GRADUATED FILTER that darkens or colors the sky while leaving the bottom half of the picture normal. If you look closely, you may even see that the tops of the mountains are also darkened by the filter.

The effect is attractive and also performs an important technical function: In the real world, the sky is often brighter than the ground. Cameras with automatic exposure will split the difference between the sky that's too bright and the ground that's too dark, leaving your car and roadway in murky shadows. The solution is to open the lens iris and overexpose the sky. Now the car and foreground look great but the light blue sky has turned to chalky white. Enter the GRADUATED FILTER, a piece of glass that is colored at the top and clear at the bottom. By positioning the camera and glass correctly, the sky will be darkened by the filter while hubcaps and road dust still glisten in the sun.

A neutral gray GRADUATED FILTER will simply darken the sky, while a blue filter will artificially make the sky blue or bluer. It's popular nowadays, especially in desert shots, to use a reddish or coral GRADUATED FILTER, making the scene look as if it had been shot at sunrise or sunset, or in the searing heat, or in the glow of a nuclear bomb blast.

This is just one example of how a filter can solve a technical problem while adding some flavor to a scene.

Must-Have Filters

1. **UV (ultraviolet) or SKYLIGHT FILTER:** These two slightly pink filters are similar enough to be considered interchangeable, so you only need one or the other. Both make hardly any difference at all in your picture, although they slightly reduce blue atmospheric haze in seaside shots and in long panoramic shots at high altitudes. Their main job is to protect your expensive coated lens from water spray, sand, fingerprints, dust, and nearby sneezes. When the SKYLIGHT FILTER gets smudged or fogged, just remove and wash it, something you cannot do with your $2,000 camera lens. And if the SKYLIGHT FILTER gets scratched, pitted, or hopelessly dirty, just throw it away and install a new one. They are not expensive.

---

*Filter   A lens attachment that eliminates glare or certain colors or modifies the image in some way.

Lens attachments   Filters, magnifiers, and other devices that fit over the camera lens.

Filter holder   Small carrier that clips onto a lens and accepts slide-in filters. Also called matte box.

*Graduated filter   Lens filter that's partly clear and partly colored or dark, making perhaps half of the picture dark.

UV filter   Similar to the skylight filter.

*Skylight filter   Slightly pink lens filter that reduces blue atmospheric haze, used mostly to protect the camera lens from dirt or scratches.

*Polarizing filter   Like Polaroid sunglasses, these lens attachments cut out glare and reflections.

*Neutral density filter   A gray glass lens attachment that diminishes light coming through the lens, thus reducing picture brightness.

Neutral density graduated filter   Lens attachment that darkens part of the image without changing its color.

*Special effect filter   Lens filter that creates star bursts, fog, multiple images, or other "arty" effects.

2. **POLARIZING FILTER:** This filter reduces shine and glare. It can darken a sky while leaving the clouds just as white as before (unlike a GRADUATED FILTER), thus exaggerating the brightness of the clouds. POLARIZING FILTERS reduce the shine in water, making it easier to see through the water to reveal fish, flora, and deep blue colors below the surface. POLARIZING FILTERS erase the shine from windows, making you better able to see through the glass. POLARIZING FILTERS change the white shine of hot pavement back to the original black tar. In car commercials, POLARIZING FILTERS reduce the glare from chrome and shiny paint, accentuating the deeper colors.

A POLARIZING FILTER, in order to work correctly, must be rotated to a certain position. Make this adjustment before you start the shoot. The affect of a POLARIZING FILTER on the sky depends on where the sun is. If you are aiming toward or away from the sun, the POLARIZER will make no difference. If the sun is to your left, right, or directly overhead, the effect will be most pronounced (clouds will look white, sky will look blue, haze will be diminished).

Remember that some lenses rotate as you focus, and the filter, if screwed onto the outside of your lens, may rotate with the lens, changing its orientation. By not screwing the filter on tightly, you can grasp it between your thumb and forefinger, holding it steady while the camera lens rotates. Some POLARIZING FILTERS rotate separately from their screw threads, allowing them to move freely even though the mechanism has been threaded tightly onto your lens. There is another solution to this rotating lens dilemma that I'll get to shortly.

3. **NEUTRAL DENSITY FILTERS:** These filters are lens attachments that are like dark glasses for your camera. They reduce the amount of light through the lens much like the IRIS or high-speed shutter do. They don't change color rendition and are very handy if you do a lot of beach or ski slope shooting where the light might be too bright for your camera even with the F-STOP at its highest number.

What would you do if you had a very bright scene but you wanted to have a narrow DEPTH OF FIELD (perhaps to emphasize something of importance)? Using low f-numbers would give you a narrow DEPTH OF FIELD but would let in too much light. Here is where a NEUTRAL DENSITY FILTER or high-speed shutter is helpful. They reduce the light so you can shoot with a narrow DEPTH OF FIELD.

One advantage of the NEUTRAL DENSITY FILTER over high shutter speeds is that the filter adds *no* artifacts to the picture; it looks 100 percent normal. The high-speed shutter, on the other hand, makes fast-moving objects look strange. Fan blades, propellers, and wagon wheels that *should* be a blur, remain sharp and flicker oddly from position to position. So although it may be quicker and more convenient to decrease your DEPTH OF FIELD using a higher shutter speed, the stroboscopic affect is sometimes distracting, making the NEUTRAL DENSITY FILTER a better solution.

4. **GRADUATED FILTER:** As mentioned earlier, TV cameras don't like high-contrast ratios. Bright things and dark things cannot both look good in the same picture. One solution is to aim some extra light at the darker parts of your picture, a process that requires extra lights or reflectors. A second solution is to use a GRADUATED FILTER so that the bright part of the picture gets dimmed by the dark part of the filter. The NEUTRAL DENSITY GRADUATED FILTER is usually used to darken a bright sky, but it can be rotated 90° and used to darken a brightly lit street on the left side of the picture to reveal someone lurking around a shadowy corner on the right side of the picture. BLUE GRADUATED FILTERS do a nice job of turning overcast days into blue skies. Just be careful how you aim the camera, or your performer's blue forehead will betray your secret.

Special Effect Filters. Figure 3–36 shows a few SPECIAL EFFECT FILTERS and their resulting images. See also Figure 3–36 among the color pages. These FILTERS can make the center of the image sharp and the outside blurry for a dreamy effect, or can make glistening parts of the picture have star

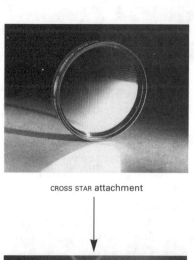

CROSS STAR attachment

MULTI-IMAGE PRISM and GRADUATED FILTERS

Before using GRADUATED FILTER (see also color figure)

Resulting STAR PATTERN image (Courtesy Spiratone)

MULTI-IMAGE (Courtesy Cokin)

After using GRADUATED FILTER Sky is darkened and no longer looks washed out (see also color figures. Courtesy Cokin).

Before using REFLECTION FILTER unsightly foreground is visible.

Before FOG filter (Courtesy Cokin)

Filter replaces foreground with etherial reflection. (Courtesy Cokin)

After FOG filter (Courtesy Cokin)

FIGURE 3–36 Camera lens effects (see also color pages).

twinkles, or can create multiple images. Another attachment can give you a foggy effect, handy for doing portraits, or saving a bundle on dry ice or fog-generating machines.

Although the TV image can be manipulated 1001 ways using computer graphics computers and programs like Adobe After Effects or Adobe Photoshop, these alterations take time, and the equipment and software costs a rising heap of dough. Many camera effects can be performed *on the spot* in just as few seconds, using FILTERS that cost just a few dollars. Think about it.

FOG FILTERS soften sharpness and reduce contrast, while causing bright parts of the picture to glow as if surrounded by a vaporous mist, cloud, or smoke. While Steven Speilberg makes mist the hard way by blowing fake smoke onto the set and shining lights through it (he loves this shot, which you'll find in nearly every one of his movies), it's easier (albeit less dramatic) to slap a FOG FILTER onto your lens and dress your actors in damp slickers. Light streaming through windows or emanating from headlights exaggerate the fog effect with a visible flare. Normally lit scenes with subdued highlights will show very little effect. DOUBLE FOG FILTERS approach the consistency of wax paper and achieve pea soup fog. For this effect to look most natural, employ overcast soft lighting.

STAR FILTERS make points of light look like stars. Their effect is hardly noticeable in normally lit scenes. Dark shots with bright lights in them, especially sharp points of light, will display a number of spokes coming from the light. This filter is manufactured by finely etching lines in the glass to diffract the light to form the stars. If parallel grooves are etched in one direction, you would get a two-point star which looks like a streak, great for enhancing the appearance of movement. Etching lines in several directions create more points to the stars, making varieties with four, six, eight, and twelve points. When the lines are etched closer together, the stars appear fatter, appropriate for accentuating the flare of flamboyant stage lighting. Wider spacing produces finer, more delicate stars.

A CENTER SPOT FILTER will create an image that is sharp in the center and blurry around the periphery. A center spot combined with a FOG FILTER will create a dreamy halo around someone's face. The outside of the picture could be fuzzy, diffused, out-of-focus, or colored, depending on the second filter. Wedding videographers use these filters when shooting maudlin, romantic kiss shots with the bride and groom smooching in the center while the rest of the picture goes dreamy.

Through Rose-Colored Glasses.

Colored filters create the obvious effect of changing the color of the scene. A cool, blue, mid-morning shot of a ship at sea with the sun in the background can be turned to a glowing, warm sunset shot with the addition of a sunset or orange filter. A blue filter will make the shot colder, almost arctic. Yellow, red, emerald, tobacco, mauve, pink, and coral are all popular colors for spicing up a dull shot.

Matte Box.

You could buy glass filters separately, each mounted in its own threaded ring, but that becomes expensive. Serious filter users buy a filter holder or MATTE BOX that attaches to the outside of their camera lens. The holder has slots that allow you to drop unmounted glass filter squares into the holder. The holder accommodates several squares at once so that they may be teamed up for a cumulative effect. The unmounted squares are cheaper than the round, mounted lenses, but their big advantage is that they don't rotate with the lens. The holder stays in the same position while

---

Fog filter   Lens filter that makes the image look foggy.
Double fog filter   Lens filter that makes the picture look very foggy.
Center spot filter   Lens filter that makes the periphery of the picture fuzzy while keeping the center sharp.

Matte box   Container that holds lens filters in slots and attaches to the front of the camera lens.

the camera lens rotates, allowing POLARIZERS to remain properly aligned and GRADUATED FILTERS to keep their orientation.

 Mini Review

- A filter is a lens attachment that can change part or all of the image's color, or can perform a special effect.
- Use a UV filter to protect the camera lens from scratches or dirt.
- A polarizing filter reduces shine, glare, or reflections in the scene.

Now that you know some of the *mechanics* of lenses, we can flex our creative muscles in the next chapter to explore the aesthetics of picture composition.

CAMERA ANGLES AND PICTURE COMPOSITION

4

So far, we've studied only how to operate the equipment. Now that we can work our machinery, let's focus on how to use it to make professional-looking pictures.

Many people may share in the production of a TV program, but the buck stops with the camera operator. What *you* get is what everyone will see. (Unfortunately, the spendable bucks don't stop anywhere near the camera operator.)

Sometimes the cameraperson is but one cog in the giant wheel of teleproduction. There are other times when the camera operator writes the script and directs the show. It is hard to tell where straightforward camera aiming ends and creative production planning begins. A good cameraperson is part scriptwriter, part director, part acting coach, and part technician all at once. For this reason, you will see more than just camera angles and cute effects covered in this chapter. The best shots don't just happen, they are planned; so you will learn how to plan them. The camera operator is not a mindless robot, a remote control responding to the verbal commands of the director. The cameraperson needs to appreciate how his or her image is to be woven into the fabric of the entire production. Having said this, it's important to stress that the director is still boss; let the director direct, even if you think he or she is wrong. In a perfect world, every camera operator has the eye and judgment of a director, but the official director still calls the shots.

In short, as you become more expert at camera work, you will be developing skills in lighting, audio, directing, and stage management. These crafts are all related, and proficiency in one adds to your competency in the others.

Our stairway to expertise will have three steps:

1. Mechanics of skillful camera handling
2. Aesthetics of picture composition
3. Camera "tricks" that add visual interest or create a mood

It is the nature of art that sometimes you will balance on several steps at once, using a camera "trick" to compose an appealing shot or using raw mechanical skill to create a desired illusion.

TV is all illusion anyway; making your audience see something that really isn't there is part of the magic of television. *A bigger part of the magic, however, is making something took like it really is. It doesn't just happen.*

You'll be shown a lot of "rules" on the aesthetics of picture composition and camera movement. These "rules" are meant to be broken at times—but *only after they've been learned.* You'll be master of your tools if you can "do it right" whenever you *need* to and then "do it your way" whenever you *want* to.

Much of TV is illusion.

Once you become aware of these "rules," "tricks," and techniques, a funny thing will happen to you: You will never be able to watch TV again without becoming conscious of the camera angles and shot composition. You'll see the "rules" being followed and sometimes broken. You'll have become a gourmet of visual craftsmanship. You'll be "video literate."

 Mini Review

- Things sometimes look different to the camera than they do to your eye. Often the camera operator must manipulate the scene through camera angles and picture composition in order to make a scene look "right."

CAMERA MOVES

First, let's review the lingo. Figure 1–11 showed the fundamental moves the camera can make. They apply whether you are using a tripod or holding the camera by hand.

If you are operating the camera in a studio, there are probably other cameras in use besides yours. To help the director keep track of them all, the cameras are numbered. Learn your camera number.

A good director will generally give you a "ready" command before asking you to do something. He or she will probably say something like "Get ready to zoom in—zoom in." This will give you time to place your hands on the proper controls and psych yourself for action.

Many actions require no commands from the director but just common sense. For instance, unless there is a special reason for not doing so, *your pictures should always be in focus and relatively centered.* You generally should follow the motion on the screen and zoom appropriately to keep the important action in the picture.

In more complicated shots where your camera would be taking only part of the final picture, you may have to consciously break these "rules." For instance, you may have to keep the performer in the right-hand half of your screen so that another camera can place something else in the left-hand part of the viewer's screen. Put another way, your viewfinder picture looks strange, but the final picture from both cameras looks fine.

Keep the tops of people's heads near the top of your viewfinder. Don't leave an airy space above them when they sit down or decapitate them when they stand up.

When performers wiggle around, they may jump out of your picture for a moment. That's okay; they'll be back. Correct *slowly* for minor compositional changes rather than trying to catch up to their every bob and weave.

When two people are on your screen (a TWO SHOT), zoom out enough to keep them both in the picture most of the time. However, if two people are in the picture and one is leaving, let the person walk out of the picture. Don't try to zoom way out and keep them both visible. It is very natural for a person to leave someone and walk out of the picture. To the viewer, it's as if the person simply left the room.

The Steady Camera

Every move you make during taping will be seen and perhaps unconsciously become part of your message. A picture that bobs around, even a little, betrays amateurism or implies that you are looking through somebody else's eyes. The camera, for instance, would follow someone down a flight of stairs, becoming the pursuer. Jumpy, hand-held camera work can also imply peril, reality (as in newsreels), and frenzy. Unless you intend to portray these moods, you'll want to keep the camera rock-solid while taping. For this reason, studio cameras spend most of their time sitting on tripods. Here are some tips on using them.

Tilt and Pan

If you're using a tripod, think ahead to loosen the controls so that your camera will move effortlessly. If you expect frequent, fast moves, such as in sports, loosen the pan and tilt locks all the way. If you're doing slow, gentle moves, leave a little drag on the controls to dampen some of the jiggles.

If, however, you find yourself shooting a motionless scene for a long time, your arms will get awfully tired holding the camera steady. It will be much easier to lock the controls and let the camera hold itself. You must remain alert for an upcoming pan or tilt so that you can get your controls unlocked in time to carry out the move.

If working with your camera hand-held, use the Tai Chi position (Figure 3–19) and move your whole torso when you tilt or pan.

If you expect to move the camera somewhere while recording, figure out where you want to go first. This avoids zigzagging and "searching" kinds of shots. If you can, PAUSE the VCR first and try out the move to practice it, and also decide on the picture composition. Then UNPAUSE and carry out your practiced move.

I recall, as an amateur, filming panoramic scenes of the Grand Canyon. I started at the ridge, moved down the wall of the canyon to the base, panned right for a ways, tilted back up to the rim, panned right some more across the rim, and then panned left for a long sweep. I was so awed by the scenery that I constantly felt as if I were missing something. I therefore crisscrossed and zigzagged my poor viewers' eyeballs into a state of dizziness. The proper technique would have been to *select* the part of the canyon I was going to show first. Next, plan a strategy for moving from one part of the panorama to the other. Next, carry out the plan in one smooth, leisurely sweep.

Be patient. Don't ruin the shot you are taking now in order to "get it all in." Strangely, your audience will never miss the shots you don't take, but they will abhor the hasty pans and the plummeting tilts you take as you try to photograph every weed and boulder.

It sometimes helps to pick an interesting beginning and an end to a sweeping panoramic shot. Try starting with a view of one canyon ridge, framed by some nearby tree limbs. In fact you could start with the limbs in focus and the background blurry and PULL FOCUS, bringing the canyon into focus. The out-of-focus tree nearby will actually add depth and dimensionality to your picture (another case where something out of focus *adds* attractiveness to the picture). Next, carry out a slow pan across the ridge, ending with a shot of tourists by your side, their children leaning over the guardrail, tempting the laws of gravity. Such a scene provides an ending to the shot, and you may happen to catch the ending to somebody's kid. At least this is a good place to "jump" to another shot.

Dolly, Truck, and Arc

If you are using a tripod on a dolly over a smooth floor, the process of traveling is easy. Do think ahead to unlock your wheels and to sweep cables and obstructions out of the way so that you don't drive bumpity-bump over them.

If time permits, aim the wheel casters in the right direction so a gentle push is all that is needed to get the camera moving. A single wayward caster will do wonders at swaying you off course during a DOLLY or TRUCK maneuver.

To further guarantee a smooth move, lay out your camera cable behind you so that it trails you easily. In professional studios, the FLOOR MANAGER would assist you in this cable-handling process. When you are working alone, it sometimes helps to throw the cable over your shoulder to keep it out of the way of the tripod. This also makes it easier to kick the cable out of the way when you're backing up.

When your camera is "on" (your tally light is lit), camera travel should be smooth and slow to give a gliding effect. When your camera is "off" and the director asks you to "truck right," then you should do it with haste. Your object is to move from here to there and get reframed and focused as fast as possible. In many cases, the director may have only two cameras taking pictures at a time. If one camera fouls up the shot, the director can quickly switch to the second camera's picture. But if the second camera is in motion or focusing or otherwise not ready, the director is stranded with the first camera with no escape. So you can see how popular you can become with your director if you are able to reset your camera quickly.

Tip: Don't jump the tally light. Make sure it has gone out before you swing your camera to the next shot.

If you are traveling with your camera hand-held, it is best to first zoom out to a wide-angle or medium-wide shot. A telephoto shot greatly magnifies camera wiggles, while wide-angle shots hide them. Use the Tai Chi posture to start from, and then glide like Groucho.

Everyone likes to take a journey. Travel gives pictures motion and reveals new things to see as we move. The dolly and truck are excellent vehicles for such excursions. Camera motion can seem very natural and does not wear thin too quickly. The camera could, for instance, dolly in and then arc around a desk as the person behind the desk speaks. This move not only presents us with a new view but also moves us from the formal across-the-desk position to a more casual face-to-face (desk to the side) position.

An arcing shot is handy for showing two people talking together. By slowly circling the two, you can start with one's face (and the back of the other's head) and arc around to the other's face, gently swinging the audience's attention from one performer to the other.

Moving the camera behind props, through bushes, or through windows or doors gives a strong three-dimensional feel to the picture.

A shot taken over a steep cliff may not convince the viewer of the canyon's depth. Trucking a camera up to the cliff's edge while looking down (and seeing the edge of the cliff disappear underfoot) can take the audience's breath away. (Take triple precautions so that *you* don't go over the edge with your camera and end up taking *really* spectacular shots.)

A wheelchair, a shopping cart, or any kind of wheeled or sliding vehicle can serve nicely as a temporary dolly. Be creative. Skis, toboggans, ice skates, mechanic's creepers, rubber rafts, parachutes, and construction cranes make fascinating (though sometimes dangerous) camera mounts.

Despite all the advertisements that you may have seen showing a smiling 115-pound model shooting a scene with a 12-pound Betacam perched comfortably on her shoulder, it just ain't so. Not only does that camcorder seem to double in weight every fifteen minutes that you carry it, but it unbalances you and hampers your moves. At least have someone serve as a "guide dog" for you while you're walking with your eyes glued to the viewfinder. The helper can also keep your mike or power cords from dragging or tangling.

Focus and Zoom

If you finish this book without learning how to properly focus a zoom lens, we both deserve an *F*. Let's review the basics one more time:

1. If your tally light is off or if your VCR is PAUSED, focus by
   a. Zooming in all the way
   b. Focusing for a sharp picture
   c. Zooming out to the shot you want
   During a studio production, do this quickly to minimize the time that your camera is "out of service."
2. If your tally light is *on* or if you're recording the camera's picture, don't use the preceding method; just keep a sharp eye on the viewfinder and focus as best you can.
3. Objects closer than four or five feet probably cannot be focused clearly, so keep your distance.
4. If your camera is on, zoom gently and smoothly. If zooming in, be constantly ready to correct your focus as you go (just in case something moves).
5. Practice, practice, practice, practice, *practice*—or you'll be no darn good!

Know your lens controls. Know by "feel" which part of the lens does what. Know instinctively which way to turn the lens to zoom in. A typical amateurish shot is the "false zoom," a slight in-then-out move made because the camera operator didn't immediately know which way to twist the zoom lens to zoom out. *Know* which way to turn the lens; don't experiment while recording. The same goes for focus; if something comes toward you, *know* whether to turn the lens clockwise or counterclockwise to FOLLOW FOCUS.

Truck   To roll a camera sideways across the floor.
Floor manager   Studio crew member who assists by handling cables or relaying the director's cues and commands.
Follow focus   Continually adjusting a lens's focus to maintain a sharp picture of a subject that is moving closer to or away from the camera.
Shot sheet   Brief list of the kinds of shots a camera operator will need to take during a show.

Mini Review

- Out-of-focus foreground objects and/or a moving camera enhance the dimensionality of a shot.
- Camera moves should be smooth and flowing. Stationary shots shouldn't jiggle.

What's FOLLOW FOCUS? That's a technique used by professional camera operators as they shoot moving objects. With a little practice, you can do it too. Zoom in on someone and have them walk toward you from thirty feet away. Try to keep their image sharp as they move. It isn't easy. With practice, you can develop the skill of following a moving target, keeping it centered, keeping it focused, and even keeping it the right size on the screen (by zooming) as it moves around.

But if you can't get the hang of it, stay zoomed out on fast-moving objects. That way your focusing errors won't be as noticeable, and you'll have less trouble keeping your moving target on the screen.

Assuming you've mastered keeping your zoomed-in shots sharp and centered, *use them; television is a close-up medium.*

Long shots, although easy to shoot, turn into monotonous mush on the TV screen. Close-ups capture the expressions, the detail, the excitement of a scene. Check out Figure 4–1 and notice how the close-up is more interesting than the long shot.

And now a word about that zoom lens of yours. Everyone who gets his/her hands on one loves playing with it. In and out, in and out, your audience's eyeballs feel like Duncan yo-yos. Zoom to your heart's content while practicing. *Then go out and force yourself to shoot without zooming.* If you

Television is a close-up medium.
Get in close.

Zoomed out, the viewer observes the action   Zoomed in, the viewer participates in it

FIGURE 4–1   CLOSE-UPS capture the excitement of a scene.

want a close-up of something, then PAUSE, zoom in to a close-up, and then UNPAUSE your recording. Do you want to create a sense of travel, motion, or exploration? Then move the whole camera. That will create a *real* sense of travel, not the overworn zoom. Although a zoom and a dolly both can make things look closer or farther away, only the dolly changes perspective as it happens. Can you sense this difference from the two examples in Figure 4–2? If not, then perhaps you have to see the picture in motion to be fully convinced.

One handy use for the zoom lens is to fill the TV screen with action when you can't move the camera. Picture a youngster up at bat. Pitcher and batter are both on screen. The wind up, the throw— it's a hit. You follow the ball into the outfield, *zooming in* as you go. When the fielder fumbles, you'll be zoomed in close to *see* the fumble rather than seeing a dot surrounded by a whole outfield. Here the zoom lens helps you fill the screen with action. To get that nice shot, however, you had to zoom *and* aim *and* refocus simultaneously, no easy task for the unpracticed.

Think Ahead

> ### DOLLY VERSUS ZOOM, TRUCK VERSUS PAN, CRANE VERSUS TILT
>
> ZOOM, PAN, and TILT are easy moves; DOLLY, TRUCK, and CRANE/PEDESTAL (move the camera vertically) are harder to set up and execute. DOLLY, TRUCK, and CRANE are more visually interesting, however, because objects actually flow relative to each other, adding parallax and dimensionality to the shot. ZOOM, PAN, and TILT only enlarge or change the angle of a shot, without changing perspective, and without offering a sense of travel.
>
> ZOOM, PAN, and TILT lack "engagement"; the viewer passively looks in from outside the scene. DOLLY, TRUCK, and CRANE involve the viewer in the scene, taking part in the action, rolling right through it or keeping pace with a performer who is going somewhere.
>
> ZOOM, PAN, and TILT create a calm, objective, cool mood, drawing no attention to the camera move. DOLLY, TRUCK, and CRANE add drama and emotion to the scene.
>
> Choose your weapon. There is a time and place for each.

The following advice may seem too obvious to deserve attention, but it deserves attention. It separates the masters from the mediocre.

Zooming in makes everything bigger but is no substitute for motion.

Traveling with the camera makes the foreground larger, moving it by you while the background stays relatively unchanged. The result is visually more involving.

FIGURE 4–2   Dolly versus zoom. Notice the background.

As a camera operator, try to anticipate every move. Be ready to tilt up if somebody is about to stand up. Be ready to zoom out if someone is about to move from one place to another. Being zoomed out makes it easier to follow unpredictable or quick movements. If someone is about to move to the left, start moving a little before your subject does. This will make a "space" for the subject to move into. Such a camera move also creates an unconscious anticipation in your viewers. They will expect the performer to move when the camera moves.

 Mini Review

- Practice using the camera controls so that they are second nature to you.
- Television is a close-up medium; use close-up shots frequently.
- Moving the camera makes a far more interesting shot than zooming the camera.
- Try to predict what is going to happen in the scene so that you are prepared for a camera move.

STUDIO PROCEDURES

In Hollywood or broadcast TV studios, procedures are very regimented. For every job there is a person who does only that job. In fact, union regulations often preclude staff members from doing each other's jobs. There are network stories of how an entire studio crew had to sit around for an hour waiting for the set director to arrive to hang a picture. No one else was allowed to. Only electricians can plug power cords in, and only lighting technicians can change burnt-out bulbs. Only the cue card person can hold cue cards for the performers to read.

Smaller studios are usually nonunion and have fewer crew handling more jobs. In a small studio, the camera operator may need to assist with lights, audio, stage management, and makeup as well as operating the camera and oiling the casters. Here is what you can expect to do as a camera operator in a mid-size studio.

Before the Shoot

Let's assume that the set and props are ready, the lights are aimed and turned on, and the performers are ready.

Hopefully, the camera operator will have some idea of what the production is about and how it is to be performed. In complex productions, the camera operator may receive a SHOT SHEET listing the kinds of shots the director will be requesting and their order. This list should be studied and the more difficult shots perhaps practiced before the shoot actually begins. The cameras should be moved to their initial positions and the camera cables laid out in such a way that nobody trips over them, yet moves can be made easily.

Unlock your pan and tilt controls and adjust your drag controls for easy motion. How well is the camera balanced on the tripod head? If it tries to nose-dive or tilt up, perhaps it needs to be slid backward or forward on the head. If you leave your camera to do something else before the show begins, relock your pan and tilt controls.

Put your intercom headset on and plug it into the camera. The director or video technician may ask you to uncap your lens and will begin the camera tweaking procedure. Here you'll probably aim your camera at a "typical" scene so that the technician (or somebody) can adjust iris, gain, pedestal, color, etc. Take this opportunity to adjust your viewfinder to give you good pictures. Try to pick a shot which has something pure black and something pure white in it. The technician will use these extreme colors to calibrate the blackest-black and whitest-white signal from the camera.

The camera setup procedure may take as much as five minutes per camera, so be patient. Each camera, one by one, may have to be white balanced, black balanced, and adjusted in a dozen ways to match the images from the other cameras.

If no floor manager is available, the director may select one of the camera operators to cue the talent and wave other instructions to them.

In many cases, the director may select one camera to follow the action and take mostly close-ups. The other camera takes COVER SHOTS, mostly medium shots and long shots. It is hard to keep close-ups in focus, especially when you have to follow hands manipulating objects. For this reason, the camera taking the COVER SHOTS must *always* keep an acceptable picture on the screen. This is the director's "safety net" for when the close-up camera loses its good shot (which it will frequently).

If shooting a talk show or interview, the director may select one camera to follow one person and another camera to follow the other. Or the director may select one camera to follow whoever is

---

Cover shot   A "safe" camera shot that is likely to be useable right away if the director's other shot or shots go sour.

speaking *except* for the interviewer or the master of ceremonies. The other camera stays with the interviewer all the time.

Sometimes a camera has to shoot a small object or mounted photograph during the show. The director has to decide which camera does what so that the camera that is "off" has time to move from the graphic to the studio scene and back again. If you happen to be that camera, you may have to set up the object and make sure it is level, well lit, not reflecting any shine, and not in a place that will be obscured or bumped during the show. Make sure the object is a workable distance from the camera and photographs are oriented perpendicularly to the camera (more on this in the graphics chapter).

Test your intercom headset just prior to the show. Make sure you and the director and the other camera operators can hear each other.

You may have learned the lingo of television, but your performers may understand none of it. If you will be giving them cues, explain what the cues mean and what they will look like. Also consider that the performers are probably nervous, and that you, the only other human contact in the studio, are their only source of confidence and consolation. So be warm and friendly.

If certain camera positions will be critical, try them out before the show. Once perfected, mark the camera position on the floor with masking tape so you can relocate it quickly during the show.

As "show time" approaches, restrict your chatter over the intercom. Don't add to the confusion. Things should become increasingly quiet as the "important" messages become the only audible communications.

During the Shoot

About fifteen seconds before the program starts, the director will probably announce over the public address system (or through your intercom system, in which case you have to relay the announcement to the performers) "Stand by." "Stand by" means be ready to start shooting and remain silent. This goes for everybody. You may be asked to relay the countdown and cue to the talent. Listening to the director over the headphones, you will probably do this: You'll say, "Stand by," and point your finger toward the ceiling. You'll then count aloud "Ten, nine, eight, seven, six, five, four, three, (pause), (pause)" and then point your finger toward the talent, who begins speaking. The purpose of not calling out the last two numbers is so that the sound of your voice doesn't get picked up by the talents' microphones if the mikes get turned up too soon. Also, this avoids having the echo of your last words bouncing around the walls when the production begins. Make sure that the performers have been forewarned that they should count the last two numbers to themselves and not expect to hear them from you. Some studios use another technique of holding up five fingers and taking one down at a time to show the countdown. This is fine if you have a floor manager whose fingers aren't busy holding the camera at the time.

During the production, the director can speak to the camera operators, but the camera folks mustn't speak back to the director—their voices might be picked up by the talents' microphones. One way to communicate with the director is to blow gently into the headset's mouthpiece. This helps to get the director's attention if you think he or she is missing something. The director may also ask you questions to which you respond yes with one blow and no with two blows into your mouthpiece. You could set up your own system where three blows means something else, like "I've got to visit the restroom" and four blows could mean . . .

If you know what shots will be taken and your shot is now finished, immediately move your camera to your next assigned shot. Do not wait until the last minute. Directors like knowing that they can cut to your shot early if necessary.

Note what kinds of shots the other camera operators are taking so that you coordinate well and don't get in the way of each other's shots.

At the end of the show, no one should begin speaking until the director gives the "all clear." Sometimes you may think the tape is finished because they have faded the picture out, but the tape may still be running and the sound may still be on. Make sure that the performers know this too.

After the Shoot

Wait a moment until the director checks the end of the tape to make sure the video heads didn't clog and that the show was actually recorded. Sometimes a part of the show needs to be done over again, so you don't want to be too hasty at packing things away.

Once the show is definitely over, cap your lens, lock your controls, and pull your camera to the side of the studio and out of the way. Coil your camera cable, making everything neat. Camera cable, being thick, is hard to coil. It seems to want to tangle and curl around on itself. Coil it in large loops which you lay onto one hand, while twisting the cable a little with the other hand to get it to circle in the right direction. For really thick cable, lay it in figure-eight shapes on the floor. Some studios use garden-hose hangers to drape camera cables over, as shown in Figure 4–3.

Next, run like heck before the director gives you something else to do, such as dismantling the 29-part set and sweeping the studio floor.

Safety Tips

1. Never park the camera aimed at a bright light.
2. Lock your camera controls when the camera is idle.
3. Cap your lens when the camera is idle.

 Mini Review

- When your camera is "off," try to move from shot to shot quickly, minimizing the length of time the director can't use your camera's shot.
- In small studios, the camera operator typically takes on several roles, such as the lighting person before the show or the cue giver during the show.
- Become familiar with the show's content and your role in the shoot. Know what kinds of shots you'll be taking.

CAMERA ANGLES AND PICTURE COMPOSITION

Basic Camera Angles and the Moods They Portray

You have already seen the results of dollying, zooming, and selective focusing. Figure 4–4 shows examples of some more basic camera angles and describes their impact.

When the camera is low, the performer looks domineering, strong, forceful, and authoritative. Political advertisers use this camera angle to strengthen the image of politicians. Nazi propagandists often shot Hitler from this angle. In the courtroom scene of *A Few Good Men,* the camera angle showed who was getting the upper hand.

Backlight control   Light coming from behind a subject. Also a control on a TV camera that improves a backlit picture (keeps it from looking like a silhouette).

Large loops over hand

Figure eight

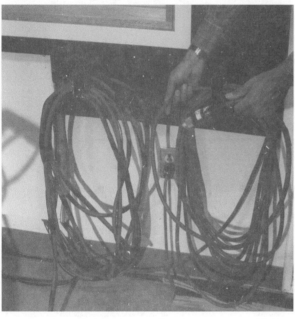

Use water hose hangers

FIGURE 4–3   Cable coiling.

When the camera is higher than eye level, the performer looks submissive, docile, unassertive, obedient, weak, or frightened. These camera angles do not have to be obvious. Slight camera height adjustments will leave a subconscious message with the viewer.

To avoid tainting the image with any special meaning, keep the camera at eye level. This is appropriate for newscasts, interviews, panel discussions, videotape depositions, and instructional presentations. Sometimes you will find it necessary to elevate the performers on risers so that when they sit down they won't be lower than the camera can go. If this isn't possible, then keep the camera far from the performers so that the angle of view is not steep.

Dominance is also implied by screen position and size. If you have two shots, one of the host and one of the guest, use a slightly larger close-up of the host to portray the host as the more influen-

Camera low. Subject looks domineering.

Camera high. Subject looks weak or subservient.

Camera at eye level. Viewer feels neutral, person-to-person relationship with performer.

People walking or running need space to move into.

People speaking need space to speak into.

Tilted shots give an aura of danger, frenzy, threat. Combined with moving hand-held camera, shows a panicked subject's viewpoint; the viewer is running, the viewer is searching, etc.

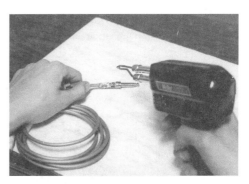

If trying to teach something, favor the doer's point of view.

FIGURE 4–4   Camera angles.

tial of the two. If during an argument between two actors, one is winning, frame your TWO SHOTS with that actor closer to the camera. It is also said that the upper right quadrant of the TV screen is more "powerful" than the lower left. To symbolically shift power from one TV character to another, frame the dominant one in the upper right-hand part of the screen where his or her presence is stronger.

People walking or running need space to move into; don't center them on your screen. People speaking need space to speak into. If you know someone is going to begin walking, zoom out far enough and start panning to give them a space to walk into before they even begin. This mentally prepares the viewer for the action and makes the shot look very natural. If a person is about to turn to the side and start speaking, you would similarly pan to the side just a moment before he or she started.

Tilted shots (also called "Dutch angles") imply danger or threat. You could use a tilted shot of someone being chased.

There are two ways to show someone how to do something. One is from the viewpoint of an onlooker; the other is from the viewpoint of the "doer." Educational studies have shown that over-the-shoulder shots from the doer's viewpoint are more instructive.

Long, wide shots make the performer look insignificant and weak, as in Figure 4–5.

Assorted camera angles can add variety to presentations and make them more enjoyable to watch as long as they *do not distract the viewer from the show*. Strive to balance creativity with singleness of purpose.

 Mini Review

- The height of your camera relative to the subject will determine whether the subject looks powerful, neutral, or weak.
- Leave space in the shot for the performers to look into or move into.

Camera Placement and Backgrounds

Two questions should come first to mind as you set up a camera shot:

1. Where is the light?
2. What's in the background?

FIGURE 4–5   Zoomed way out, subject looks insignificant and dominated by surroundings.

Lighting.   When you are driving into the sunset, it is hard to see the road. The sun glares into your eyes and makes you squint, and it creates reflections on your windshield. For cameras, the same is true, only worse. Bright lights near or behind your subject force your camera's automatic circuits to "squint," creating a very dark picture, as shown in Figure 4–6. Light also reflects off the lens ELE-MENTS, creating white dots and geometric shapes.

In general, try to keep all the light behind the camera—none behind the subject (with the exception of carefully controlled backlighting, which will be discussed in the lighting chapter). In situations where you *must* shoot toward (not at) the light, the following steps might minimize the problem:

1. Use a bigger lens shade. The lens shade (shown in Figure 3–8) is the funnel-like scoop on the outside of the lens that shields the lens from ambient light. Or you could make a giant shade with some paper and adhesive tape.
2. Zoom in some in order to avoid as much of the extraneous light as possible. A tight close-up of the face in Figure 4–6, for instance, would eliminate much of the glare from the window (but it may be easier to close the window shade than it is to maintain a good close-up of a moving face).
3. Using extra lights, throw more light on the foreground (the face in Figure 4–6) to offset the background light.
4. The bright lights are fooling the automatic iris controls into "squinting." So turn the controls to MANUAL and adjust the camera to make the subject look good even though the window behind the subject may appear overexposed or look washed out. Some cameras have a BACKLIGHT button which does just this; it overexposes a light background so that the darker main subject looks best.

Note that if the light from behind is too bright, such as the sun or an arc welder's torch (lit, of course), you may damage your camera's CCD chip, or at least overload its circuits, causing a SMEAR as in Figure 3–3.

Window shade closed

Window shade open

FIGURE 4–6   Excessive lighting from behind the subject.

Background.   The good camera operator should also take into account what is behind the subject. With just the wrong camera placement, the bush in the background could appear to grow out of the subject's ear, or a desk lamp could sprout from your performer's head, as in Figure 4–7. Avoid busy or distracting backgrounds unless they serve a purpose in your program. Clocks are especially distracting because the viewer automatically notes what time it is and chuckles at the fact that the time is wrong.

Watch for window reflections that betray the fact that a camera and lights are present. Also, make sure that cameras and microphones don't cast shadows, especially moving ones, on the set or performers.

When shooting outdoors, be especially aware of the line of the horizon. You may get so involved in shooting your subject that you forget to notice that your camera is cockeyed. A level hori-

Lamp in background looks as if it were growing out of subject's head

Give this lady a big hand

Hey, what time is it, boys and girls? (Courtesy of Imer Fiorentino Associates)

FIGURE 4–7 Distracting backgrounds.

zon is stable and unobtrusive. Unless you're looking for a special effect, the horizon should always be level. A slightly nonlevel horizon gives heightened energy to the picture. The same applies for vertical objects like tall buildings. If they are tilted, they lend urgency or excitement to the picture. Figure 4–8 shows some examples.

There are times when you want to hide the horizon. Imagine taking pictures in a rocking boat. Your tripod is firmly planted on the deck. You thought your pictures would be stable, but when you view them later, you see the ocean tilting back and forth. A few minutes of this are enough to make viewers seasick. Instead of handing out Dramamine tablets to your audience, simply zoom your camera in on the subject and avoid the rocking background.

Sometimes the background is the subject of your picture. Backgrounds could be scenes of raging oceans, peaceful valleys, or majestic mountains, or they could be giant machines, thundering waterfalls, towering pyramids, or sprawling shopping centers. In each case, the actual size of the background subject is too large to appreciate, especially on a tiny TV screen. To give your screen depth, include something in the foreground of your shot like a tree, a wagon wheel, a person, something of recognizable size. Better yet, try to include something in the foreground and middleground of the shot

Level, stable, unobtrusive horizon

Angled horizon attracts attention, heightens energy

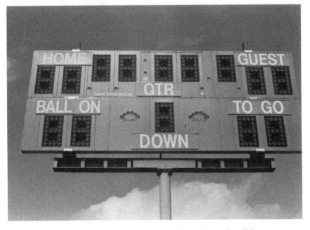

Vertical tall structure appears stable and solid

Angled tall structure implies danger and action

FIGURE 4–8 Beware of your horizon line.

to show even more dimensionality. It doesn't really matter a lot if the foreground object is a little blurry (as may be the case if you have focused on the distant background). The blurriness will further emphasize the farness of the background, and *because* the object is blurry, it won't distract attention from the background. The best photographers find a way to frame nearly every shot with a little foreground. Try to build this technique into your modus operandi. Figure 4–9 shows some examples.

 Mini Review

- Check two things when setting up a camera shot:
  1. Where is the light?
  2. What's in the background?
- Excessive light and bright backgrounds behind the subject will make the subject look dark. Darken the background, add light to the subject, or overexpose the background—whichever technique makes the subject look good.
- Try to frame nearly every shot with a little foreground to create dimensionality to the scene.

Background alone

Foreground object

Middleground and foreground object

FIGURE 4–9   Using a foreground object to emphasize the size or distance of the background.

Don'ts and Do's of Camera Angles

Now we get deeper into the aesthetics of picture composition. Before, we merely concerned ourselves with keeping subjects sharp, close, centered, and level without wiggling. If you can do that, you score 75 percent, but Francis Ford Coppola you're not. To score 100 percent, your TV screen must portray precisely the message you want it to. The image must embrace the subconscious nuances you desire yet eliminate unwanted distractions. Figure 4–10 shows some more "rules" of picture composition. Can you see why the "don'ts" should be avoided?

You shouldn't cut a person off at a natural body division such as the ankles, the bust, or the chin. It makes the body look as if there is something missing. If, however, you leave in part of the body leading to the next part, the mind will complete the rest of the body by using a psychological quirk called CLOSURE. Similarly, if talent is sitting on or leaning against something, a part of that something should be showing. Again, the mind, by seeing part of the object, will complete the rest of it.

Earlier, you were told that a good camera operator keeps the actor centered on the screen. This is still true, but a *better* camera operator adds some finesse from the RULE OF THIRDS. The RULE OF THIRDS suggests that your center of attention should not be in the dead center of the TV screen. The picture looks best when your eye is attracted to areas just off the center of the screen such as one third down from the top, one third up from the bottom, or one third in from either side.

Performers should be taught how to hold items they are displaying to the camera. The talent shouldn't be looking into a monitor and trying to center a picture for the camera operator. Centering and focusing is the cameraperson's job. Instead, the talent should place an object near his or her face and hold it as still as possible. Here the performer can easily see the detail he or she wishes to point to. Another technique is to place the object on a table (which holds it very still for close-up shooting) and to point out details without moving the object.

 Mini Review

- Don't cut a person off at a natural body division, such as the chin. Instead, leave part of the body leading to the next part, allowing the viewer's mind to complete the rest of the body.
- Follow the rule of thirds, whereby the most important part of the picture is *not* dead center on the screen but is one-third in from one edge of the screen.

More Do's of Camera Angles

Seat People Close Together.   One of the oddities of television is how it distorts space. A five-foot-wide SET becomes the entire universe for your TV show. Your audience never sees the mess of lights, cables, and clutter just a foot "off screen." To them, what they see is all that exists. Visit a TV newsroom that you've grown accustomed to viewing only on TV, and you'll be shocked at how little there is to it.

Closure   Describes how the TV viewer mentally fills in the parts of an incomplete picture.
Rule of thirds   The center of attention should not be dead center on the screen but one-third of the way down from the top, or up from the bottom, or in from one side of the screen.

Set   The props, furniture, walls, curtains, and backdrop in a scene.

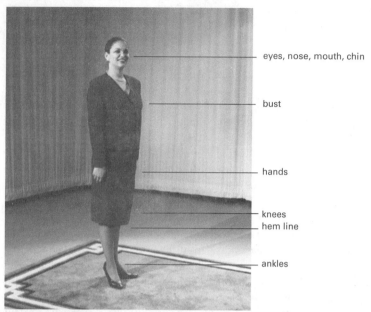

eyes, nose, mouth, chin

bust

hands

knees
hem line

ankles

Cut off a person at any of these natural divisions

Cut off feet

Include feet

cut off neck

Leave in part of the body leading to the next part.
The mind will complete the rest of the body.

FIGURE 4–10 Don'ts and do's of camera angles.

DON'T

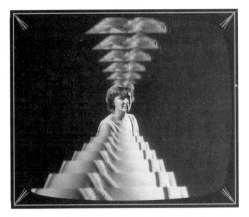

Get zoom happy using your fancy zoom lens to make yo-yos out of your viewer's eyeballs.

DON'T

Allow talent to wiggle object while looking at a TV monitor, trying to center it for the camera. Also, here the talent cannot see the object well enough to point to detail.

DO

If possible, cut from shot to shot when necessary.

Hold the object to the side of face, steadily. Let the camera operator do the centering. Detail is easy to see and point to.

Set the object on something stationary and hold it there.

FIGURE 4–10 *Continued*

DON'T

DO

Cut off a person where she contacts her surroundings. Here, the talent looks like she is leaning on the side of the TV screen.

Provide enough surroundings for a shot to explain itself: The talent is in a chair.

Provide insufficient headroom

Leave just a little space so talent doesn't "bump her head."

Use too many LONG SHOTS

Television is a CLOSE-UP medium

FIGURE 4–10   *Continued*

Change angle without changing shot size.

Change shot size when you change angle to add variety and interest.

JUMP CUT between long shots and close-ups without changing angle. With a CUT, the viewer expects a substantial change in visual information, but doesn't get it.

Change angle about 30° when cutting. Adds variety and smooth transition. Builds a fuller perception of subject.

FIGURE 4–10   *Continued*

DON'T

DO

Place most important picture element in the center of the screen.

Use the so-called RULE OF THIRDS placing important picture elements 1/3 down or 1/3 up the screen.

Centered

1/3 up from bottom

Place the eyes in the middle of the screen

Place eyes 1/3 down the screen

FIGURE 4–10   *Continued*

DON'T

Place the face in the middle of the screen. Too much headroom.

DO

Place face 1/3 down the screen

The mouth and eyes are important. Here they follow the RULE OF THIRDS, where the eyes are 1/3 down the screen and the mouth 1/3 up. Here the missing top of the head will be mentally filled in by a psychological process called CLOSURE.

FIGURE 4–10   *Continued*

One aspect of this distortion of space involves people in conversation. Normal Americans converse at about three or four feet from each other and sit even farther from each other. Not on TV. Three or four feet seems like across the room on TV (review Figure 1–3). Squeeze your people in tight to look "normal." Note that it may take some practice before your performers feel comfortable conversing from less than two feet apart.

Seat Host to One Side of Guests.   This way you avoid giving the host "tennis neck" as he ping-pongs his attention first to the guest on his left and then to the guest on his right. Cameras and viewers alike go bouncing back and forth to follow the discussion.

Placing the host between the guests has another disadvantage. If you later edit together the TWO SHOTS, which include the host and one guest (as in Figure 4–11) and then the host and the other guest, the host snaps from the left side of the frame to the right side. First he's looking to the right, and then suddenly he's aimed to the left. The setup in Figure 4–12 is more comfortable.

Raw footage   Recordings made directly from the camera, intended for editing later into a final program.

First, the host is on the left . . .   . . . then the host is suddenly on the right

FIGURE 4–11   Panel discussion with host between guests.

Angle the Guests.   This maxim applies to any shot with two or more persons in it. People facing each other nose to nose suggest an adversary relationship. It is a great way to portray an argument. But in a panel discussion, the shots imply disagreement or debate. Conversely, people lined up facing the camera look like a team of contestants. They appear ready to perform individually for the camera but not ready to react with each other. The most comfortable seating arrangement has people angled toward each other as you saw in Figure 1–4.

Reverse-Angle Shots.   No one wants to look at the back of somebody's head. But people usually face each other when speaking, and unless you like profiles, you're always going to be shooting somebody's behind.

There are lots of ways to get a dialogue with two people facing the camera, like people on a park bench, sitting in a car, or watching TV or a fireplace, or with one in front of a mirror. In fact, you'd be surprised at how many natural-looking soap-opera scenes there are that show someone facing *away* from the person they are talking with. Nevertheless, at some point, you're going to have to face the problem of how to shoot faces facing faces.

One way is the over-the-shoulder shot shown in Figure 4–13. Shooting over one person's shoulder, we get a close-up of the second person's face as he or she speaks. When the first person speaks, we swap everything around, making a medium shot of the first person over the shoulder of the second.

If you are using a single camera and editing as you go, you'll find yourself getting a lot of exercise traveling back and forth to get a face shot for each actor's lines. If shooting RAW FOOTAGE for later

TWO-SHOT

THREE-SHOT

FIGURE 4–12   Panel discussion with host to one side of guests.

Angle 1

Angle 2. Note, size of each person changes to avoid MATCHED SHOTS.

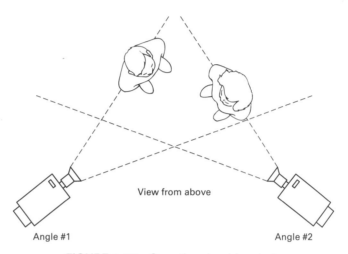

View from above

Angle #1   Angle #2

FIGURE 4–13   Over-the-shoulder shots.

editing, you could save steps by shooting the entire sequence twice, once facing one actor (or actress) and once facing the other. In fact, each sequence could be recorded on a separate cassette. When editing later, all you do is change tapes to change camera angle and get a face shot of the person speaking.

Over-the-shoulder shots are not always easy to do. Performers seem to have a way of stepping to the side and blocking your shot. To counteract this, you must always be ready to arc your camera to the left or right to unblock the shot.

Reverse-angle shots may be great for two people talking but not for cuts between hands or props and the person holding them. If a performer is angled to the right in a medium shot, his or her *hands* should be angled to the right when you cut to a close-up. To have the hands or prop suddenly change direction would be jarring to the audience. The same is true for the general flow of motion in a scene. If the action is moving to the right in one shot, it should be moving to the right in the next, at least for the start of the shot. If panning left in one shot, the following shot should continue the motion. These are examples of why the camera operator should know *how* the shots are going to be used, so that they may be recorded with later edits in mind.

Use a Familiar Object to Create a Sense of Scale.   Extreme close-ups and majestic landscape shots suffer one problem in common. The viewer cannot appreciate the smallness or largeness of the subject without a "visual yardstick" to gauge it by. Figures 2–6 and 2–9 used a hand to de-

FIGURE 4–14   Foreground figure to give scale to a landscape shot.

fine the size of a plug. Figure 4–14 uses a familiar object in the foreground to add dimension and meaning to the landscape in the background. Often a bush, a tree, a person, or an old wagon wheel serves nicely to create scale, balance, and visual variety in a scenic view.

If your picture is drab, like the colorless ash flows of Mount St. Helens, add a bystander (for size) dressed in a bright color (for pizzazz). This plan enhances the beauty of the picture *if* the person doesn't distract from the scene. Note that this is one of those rules that don't always apply.

Shooting Children.   . . . And I don't mean with a firearm. Photographing little people requires getting low. If you shoot them from the same height as you do adults, you inadvertently introduce the domination/weakness impression (look back at the example in Figure 4–4). To keep your shots neutral and unbiased, get down and shoot children at their own eye level.

The same goes when adults interview children. The adult should bend down to the same height as the child so that the camera sees both their heads at about the same level. Otherwise, you get a shot of

1. The child's body and the adult's crotch
2. The adult's torso and the child's head
3. An uninteresting long shot of both of them

 Mini Review

- Seat people close together.
- Seat the host to one side of the guests.
- How guests are angled toward each other determines how their relationships are perceived.
- An over-the-shoulder shot is a common way to show people who are speaking to each other.
- Include a familiar object in a landscape or close-up to create a sense of scale.
- Shoot children at their own eye level. Also, have adults bend down to the children's level when speaking with them.

Focus shift, or pull focus, or rack focus   The act of changing focus to sharpen objects at different distances from the camera to center attention on them.

Oblique angle   Camera angle that shows the front and a side, or maybe two sides, of an object. Oblique-angle shots convey more dimensionality than face-on shots.

Camera high

Adult interviewing from above

Eye level

Adult at child's level

FIGURE 4–15 Shooting children.

When the adult gets down to the level of the child, there is better eye contact, and a warmer relationship is implied. See Figure 4–15.

As mentioned before, some of these tasks, like positioning the performers, may not seem to be the cameraperson's job. Strictly speaking, it isn't, but in most industrial settings, the camera operator is responsible for taking a shot that is *technically* good and *also* for assuring that the shot portrays the desired mood. In small TV operations, this means being several things at once: camera operator, technician, acting coach, scenic designer, and lighting expert. Then again, this is why many people feel that educational and industrial television is more fun than commercial broadcast television.

CREATIVE CAMERA ANGLES

Popular Alternatives to the Simple Shot

There are lots of ways to show the same thing. The real skill comes in knowing when fancy shots will add spice to the scene and when they will distract the viewer and ruin the scene. Your decision will be a delicate balance between two forces. One is the pressure to "show off" as many tricks and skills as you can perform. I have seen students contrive ways to ring and blow every bell and whistle they can find on their equipment. The opposite force is the "let's-get-it-done-quick-and-dirty" approach. You get so involved in cranking out the required shots on your list that you forget to make your program visually interesting. Knowing when to be fancy and when to be straightforward makes you a master of this trade. May the force be with you.

Focus Shift.   Something (or someone) is in the foreground. Something else (or someone else) is in the background. Usually, one of these two has to be out of focus for the other to be sharp. Okay, use this to your advantage. As two people talk, focus back and forth on whichever person is speaking. It's better than panning back and forth and better than a long shot trying to get both performers sharp in the picture at once. Perhaps the foreground person's expression is paramount (i.e., tears welling in the eyes) while the background person is secondary, even distracting. So focus on the foreground, making the background blurry. Then when the background person's action becomes important (staggering to the cupboard and pouring another drink), *that* is pulled into focus, diverting attention from the face. Yet both characters can be seen at once as you shoot past the tearful face four feet from the camera and in the other half of the screen get a long shot of the drinker twelve feet away. Attention can be focused on one or the other performer, yet the viewer can *keep track of* both.

FOCUS SHIFT (or RACK FOCUS) is also a popular way to display a long line of something—soldiers, flowers, gravestones, fence posts, etc. Position yourself next to one member of the lineup and shoot toward the farthest member. Focus on the closest (or farthest) at first, and as you change focus, different members will, in turn, become sharp and then blurry as other members become sharp.

Low f-numbers and longer focal length lenses make this focus/defocus effect more pronounced.

Mirror Shots.   This is another way to slip twice as much into your picture without resorting to dull long shots. Imagine this—a close-up of a woman putting on lipstick. The camera slowly zooms (or dollies) out, revealing that her face is a reflection in a mirror. You see the side of her head in the foreground. As the camera pulls back farther, you see someone else reflected in the mirror. It's a man getting dressed across the room. As he speaks, she turns, now facing toward the camera. He steps closer, tying his tie as he walks. Now your camera has two people talking *to* each other, *facing* each other, yet you see *both faces at once*. Nice trick. How else can you get two full face shots at once?

Mirrors are useful any time you want to show both sides of something like an engine, a statue, or some complex device. They're useful for dramatic effects (an actor looks up and in the mirror sees someone climbing through the window). Occasionally, they serve as just another way of formulating a shot.

A mirror hung at an angle over the kitchen stove allows you to get straight-down-into-the-pan shots without the risk of having your camera fall into your tomato sauce. Conversely, a mirror slipped under the car allows you to document defective ball joints on autos awaiting recall.

Mirrors are a handy way to get a bird's-eye view of medical operations without risk of your camera operator fainting onto someone's intestines.

Mirrors are not the only things that reflect images. Imagine a CLOSE-UP of a man's face slowly turning toward the camera. He is wearing those mirrorlike sunglasses. You know what he's looking at when the twin likenesses of a sexy sunbather appear in the lenses.

Windows and water reflect too. Windows have an added advantage of being able to mix two pictures together for you, the figure behind the glass and the one reflected by it.

Mirrors don't even have to be flat to work. Nice effects can be had by shooting a CLOSE-UP of someone's face reflected in a shiny Christmas tree decoration, teapot, or chrome bumper. Remember all those serving dishes your folks got as wedding presents but never had occasion to use in the thirty-one years that they've been married! Hallelujah, the time has come! Use them now for twisting the

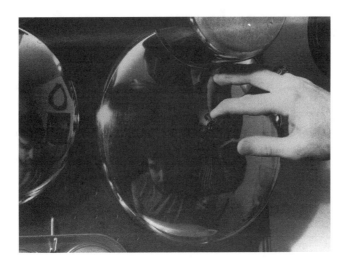

Reflection in a shiny object.

world into funhouse contortions. It is a good way to start a scene before zooming out and panning to the real world.

Parallel Movement.   Joggers, bicyclists, water-skiers, snowmobilers, and horseback riders all pose the same problem for the camera. They are fun to watch, but they're gone an instant later. To really catch the action, move with them. Videotape that jogger from your car (preferably with some-one else driving). Shoot that water-skier from the back of the tow boat or in a boat moving along next to the action; the skier stays with you while the background slips by.

In a tamer vein, if your performer takes just a few steps to the side, move with him/her. To accentuate the appearance of motion, truck the camera past some foreground object, such as a plant, windows, chemistry paraphernalia, other people, bookshelves—anything native to the environment.

Adding Movement to Still Objects.   Photos and model ships don't move. That doesn't mean that the camera can't make them come alive. Imagine a close-up of a photo of a parade. By panning across the picture to the sound of a marching band, the people will *seem* to be marching.

Imagine a slow *zoom in* on a painting, starting first with the whole town but ending with a "stroll" down the main street.

Picture the museum's dinosaur display filling the screen. Cut to a close-up of one of the models. Take the shot from slightly below the creature so that it looks domineering and dangerous. Arc the camera around the model, making it seem to turn its head. Add some tension by tilting the camera a little as you go.

Zoom in on a still photo of a horse race with the sound of crowds cheering in the background. Shake the camera as you zero in on the lead horse. You can almost see the mud flying from the hooves.

To the beat of rock music, quickly zoom in-and-out, in-and-out, on the singer's face from the record jacket. Angle your shots of the performer at the microphone, first left and then right, and cut from the first shot to the second. This will heighten energy in the scene, and if the shots are quick enough, the viewer will never notice that the performer isn't moving.

Pan across photos of antique cars. Move the camera so that the cars appear to be traveling for-ward. You won't fool anybody into thinking that the cars are really moving, but viewers are often inattentive. Leaving them with the *impression* that the cars are moving is all that is necessary.

The same trick works with photographs of birds. Pan across a photo of a bird in flight; it will appear to be gliding through the sky.

Wall Shadow.   In the movie *Goodbye Girl*, the young lady is forced to accept a male room-mate in her apartment. She's had it with his guitar playing and barges into his bedroom to complain. Seems he strums in the nude. How would you show such a scene without going R-rated?

You could use the tried-and-true guitar-in-front-of-the-genitals shot. That's okay, but what do you do for your next shot? In the movie they aimed the camera at the flustered lady standing by the door with this shadow of a man projected on the wall. It all seemed very natural, and the scene was creative and novel.

You can use this technique to show sinister shadows, lantern-cast shadows, or just a stylistic view of something before you actually see it (like a shot of the bicycle shadow on the pavement followed by a tilt up to the bicycle).

Shadows make nice surprise revelations. Consider a lady's shadow cast upon a doorway. Then into view comes the shadow's owner, a fellow dressed ridiculously in woman's clothing in order to sneak past a detective.

Low-Angle Cleanup.   If you have a busy background of unwanted cars, bushes, or signs, crouch down and shoot *up* at your subject. The cluttered horizon disappears, leaving sky, clouds, mountaintops, or the orderly tops of buildings in your shot. Low-angle shots will clean up a cluttered floor, replacing it with a sumptuous or simple ceiling.

Such angles can intensify a landscape shot by exaggerating converging lines of perspective. Roads, fences, pipelines, or sandy beaches seem to go *through* you rather than by you.

Not only do low-angle shots make people look more threatening and powerful, they seem to accelerate action. Runners, skaters, and racehorses all appear to be moving faster if shot from ankle height. A wide-angle lens intensifies the effect even more.

Just the opposite, a high-angle shot (like one from a stepladder or a rooftop) will slow down motion. With this angle and a telephoto lens, even a speeding train can be made to crawl.

Low-angle shots can simply be used as eye-candy, a way to spice up a shot. Watch a few documentaries or TV news magazines, and you'll be surprised at how many times you're treated to a shot of feet walking, or a view of a shopping cart from caster level, or a dog's-eye view of a cash register transaction. These shots don't *mean* anything, they're just visual variety.

Oblique or Three-Quarter Angle Shots.   TV is a two-dimensional medium; we manipulate the image with lighting, shadow, foreground, motion, and camera angle to create the impression of a third dimension.

For instance, take a shot of a house, face-on. You see just the front surface. The flat angle makes the house look like a set piece, a fake. Now move to the side a bit to expose an extra wall. Suddenly, the house has depth. It looks real. Crane up to show a third surface (the roof) and you'll add even more dimension. The same trick works for automobiles or sugar cubes; shoot at an angle to show depth.

The depth can be further intensified by using a shorter focal length.

Combine a low angle with an OBLIQUE ANGLE of an object, and you get a shot conveying power, weight, peril, or instability. Conversely, shot from a high angle, the same object looks nonthreatening and stable.

The Alluring Diagonal.   This isn't so much camera angle as it is picture aesthetics, but it's important anyway. Take any course in photography or art, and you'll quickly learn that diagonal lines are more attractive than horizontal or vertical lines. Crooked things are pretty. The masters of film and

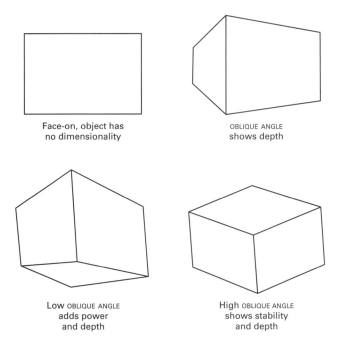

Face-on, object has
no dimensionality

OBLIQUE ANGLE
shows depth

Low OBLIQUE ANGLE
adds power
and depth

High OBLIQUE ANGLE
shows stability
and depth

OBLIQUE ANGLE confers dimensionality.

photography take great pains to place angles in their pictures, whether it's a stairway in the background or a person partially reclined in the foreground.

Similarly, objects or faces in a picture should flow in a sloping line, or several sloping lines, but not a flat one. Check out *any* episode of the *Golden Girls* and watch how they gather around the kitchen table. Two ladies are sitting at the table. The third is always on a stool, above the others. Another visitor is usually standing, higher than the rest. If you can't catch a *Golden Girl* rerun, visit any portrait studio; their family portraits will reveal the same composition, the ubiquitous diagonal.

 Mini Review

- It is a balancing act to entertain the viewer with interesting camera angles while not overdoing it which would call attention to the camera angles.
- It is a constant struggle to make the two-dimensional TV screen portray an image that looks three-dimensional. Lighting, motion, foreground, and camera angle are some techniques to enhance the dimensionality of a scene.

Lens Effects.   Back in Figure 3–36 we saw some of the effects available with lens attachments.

CENTER FOCUS creates a dream-like image where the outside edges of the picture are blurry but the center is sharp.

STAR PATTERNS, also done with lens attachments, create straight lines going through each sharp point of light in the scene. Stylistic views of rippling water in the sun or stage lights above a rock

---

Center focus   Mood-creating lens effect whereby the outside edges of a picture are blurry and the center is sharp.

Star pattern   Lens effect creating shafts of light gleaming from any bright points of light in a picture.

Dull   More interesting composition

Objects or faces placed on a diagonal look more appealing than a horizontal or vertical line-up.

group are the most common applications. The pattern can emphasize the twinkle in an eye or a glint of a tiger's tooth.

Either effect can be used to portray the point of view of a drugged, crazy, crying, frenzied, or dreaming character, showing their distorted view of the world.

For moving examples of the above plus scores of other creative shots, get the videotape *Advanced Broadcast Camera Techniques* by John Cooksey (Elite Video, 501-321-0440).

CREATING MOODS AND IMPRESSIONS WITH THE CAMERA

How you show something tells as much of your story as *what* you show. You've learned that by changing camera height you can make a performer look strong or weak. You've seen how tilted shots create suspense and how soft focus and foggy lenses create a dreamy effect. Close-ups, as you've seen, involve the viewer directly with the action. Here are some more mood-creating shots.

Progress versus Frustration

A jackrabbit is racing to the right. The camera pans along with it but slowly falls behind so that the bunny moves forward in the frame. That's progress. A mountain lion pursues to the right. Here the camera pans slightly faster than the lion can run, leaving more space in front of it. That's frustration. Score: jackrabbit, l; lion, 0.

A runner in a telephoto shot approaches and approaches and approaches in a vain attempt to reach the camera. Frustration. Shot at a wide angle, the mild-mannered accountant strolls by the camera and appears to loom forward as she nears the camera lens. The look is one of decisive action. Progress.

Suspense

Our hero creeps backwards, and the audience cringes, waiting for him to back into something awful. He looks up slowly; something terrible is bound to drop on him. He pokes his head into an air duct; what's going to grab his sweet face? He draws open the curtains; what monster will leap from behind them? As he sleeps, a large shadow slips across the bedroom wall; what is it? He washes his hands, he looks up, and through the sink window, inches from his face, there is a. . . . He sits at the dressing table and looks up into the mirror; what unholy creature will he see behind him? He casually shaves while we dolly in from behind him, stopping a breath's distance from his neck; what unwelcome hand will grasp his shoulder?

In each case, your attention is drawn to what you *don't* see, out of the camera's view, behind the curtain, in the mirror, or behind the camera as it moves closer. For a crash course in suspense shots, rent the movie *Alien*. It uses every trick in the handbook.

Anger, Secrets

Pose your performers almost nose to nose and have them shout. Voilà, anger. As they move about, keep their heads very close together.

This closeness *without* the shouting implies intimacy or secretiveness.

Speed

Keep the camera low to the ground (so you can see the ground rushing toward you) and use a wide-angle lens to portray speed. A camera on a skateboard moving at one mile per hour looks as if it's moving at sixty. A camera shooting from the roof of a tall truck at sixty miles an hour looks as if it's only traveling at twenty.

Night

Naturally, if you shoot in the dark, you don't get a picture. The object is to make the scene *look like night* but with plenty of light for the camera.

Use a neutral density filter or stop down your lens to darken the scene. One way to darken the sky without messing up your colors is to use a polarizing filter.

Keep performers in shadows or "puddles" of light as they move from place to place. Shoot with the sun halfway or three-quarters behind the performer, creating frequent silhouettes. The sun will appear to "moonlight" the scene. Turn on some streetlights, headlights, window lights, or use flashlights to complete the deception.

If shooting a "night scene" at night outdoors, use one or two harsh lights, creating distinct shadows. Try to backlight the performers to form a white ridge that outlines them.

If shooting a night scene indoors, create harsh shadows and puddles of light by using one or two bare light bulbs hidden from the camera by props. BACKLIGHT the performers to create silhouettes. If you give your actors lanterns or candles, you have an excuse to beam some light on their faces to catch their expressions. The face light doesn't *really* have to come from their lanterns; you could carefully beam some light on their faces from off camera.

TRICKS OF PERSPECTIVE

Four laws of the video world:

1. There is no depth, only width and height.
2. Anything outside the picture's frame *does not exist*; anything merely suggested in the picture *does exist*.
3. Objects have no fixed scale; they are the size that you make them.
4. It doesn't matter where things really are; they are where you make them appear to be.

For example:

1. Two boys are having a fist fight. One swings, the other's head flies back. Then a jab to the stomach (with accompanying sounds), and the vanquished folds into a mound on the ground.

   Sounds rough on the performers, but each is out of arms' way from the other when you stage them as shown in Figure 4–16. The camera can't see in 3D, so from ground level the two boys look as if they are mixing it up with each other, but actually one is maybe three feet closer to the camera and standing across from (and growling at and swinging at and kicking into) . . . empty space. Good acting and sound effects make the maneuver convincing.
2. Harry Hapless has locked himself outside a window twenty stories up. He clambers precariously along the ledge, freezing in a winter gale, until discovered by police.

   A shot up at the tall building and down at the streets from above set the stage for a close shot of the intrepid climber inching from window to window. Just outside the frame is a lawn twenty inches below, a doorway and stairs a few feet to the left and someone with a fan and confetti (snow) just off screen to the right. Also off screen is a crowd of giggling onlookers. And for police searchlights, someone is lying on the grass with a spotlight aimed up at brave Harry.

Camera

FIGURE 4–16 Punching air.

3. The helicopter succumbs to ground fire and explodes in the air. Utz Studios can't afford to destroy a chopper, and doesn't know a pilot with asbestos pants. So Utz Studios builds a two-foot model helicopter, gets the blades to rotate, hangs it in the air, fills it with incendiary, then *blam!*

4. The space shuttle lands. Darth Vader steps out and is escorted to the debriefing room.

   Start with stock footage of the shuttle landing. Follow with a close-up of a metal airline door (part of a scrap DC-10). Out pops Darth, cape and all. Follow with a long shot of Vader and company opening the door of an airfieldlike building. Cut to your studio debriefing set with them coming through any same-shaped door. These shots could have been taken weeks apart, in three different cities. It doesn't matter.

Perhaps this is a large enough dose of camera angles and techniques for one sitting. We'll be coming back for another taste of camera and shooting strategies when we discuss switchers and special effects and again when we cover editing techniques and how to get one shot to flow smoothly into another.

 Mini Review

- Varying your camera angles can create moods such as excitement, frustration, suspense, or speed.
- The four laws of television imagery are:
  1. There is no depth, only width and height.
  2. Things outside the pictures frame *do not exist;* things suggested in the picture *do exist*.
  3. Objects have no fixed scale; they are the size that you make them.
  4. It doesn't matter where things really are; they are where you make them appear to be.

---

5 LIGHTING

The human eye is an amazing thing. Even under the worst conditions, it can make wide-angle, crystal-sharp images in color. The eye is sensitive enough to see by candlelight and tough enough to perform in the desert at high noon where the sunlight is twenty thousand times brighter than a candle's light.

The television camera is frail in comparison. It needs plenty of light for good color rendition, but too much light makes things look pasty and contrasty. The TV camera can display only a two-dimensional image, which looks flat and dull compared with the 3-D panorama that our eyes give us with each glance. The eye can discern a thousand different levels of brightness in the same picture, and film about a hundred, but the best TV cameras under the best conditions can distinguish only thirty or fewer gradations of brightness at once.

Lighting serves three purposes:

1. It illuminates the scene so that the camera can at least "see" it.
2. It enhances the scene to make up for television's lack of three-dimensional imagery.
3. It sets a mood.

THE KIND OF LIGHT THE CAMERA NEEDS

Giant airport snowblowers can chew through five-foot drifts with ease. Meanwhile, your handy-dandy electric snow shovel gets flooded flinging forty flakes at a time. Having the right equipment makes a difference. The same is true for cameras. When the networks pay $20,000 or more for a TV camera, they get a machine that is hardly bothered by bright lights and dark shadows. *They'll work better* with the proper lighting, but they can also handle the rigors of a five-foot snowdrift. Industrial and home cameras, on the other hand, need all the help they can get.

This chapter will list a lot of "rules" of lighting. Some of them matter a lot, and some not very much. It all depends on how tolerant your camera and your audience are. No matter what camera you are using, the picture will always look better if you follow the "rules."

Enough Light

For consumer cameras, normal home lighting is barely sufficient to yield a picture. Although faces and objects will be recognizable, the image will be rough, grainy, or very gray and flat-looking.

Office and classroom lighting is generally sufficient for shooting. Depending on the circumstances, you may even be able to "stop down" your lens from its lowest f-number to its next lowest

Scene lit with regular incandescent home lighting

Scene lit by regular office fluorescent lamps

Scene lit by just one extra 250-watt lamp added near the camera

Scene with three well placed extra lamps

FIGURE 5–1   Ambient lighting versus extra lighting.

f-number, realizing a little better depth of field in the process. Office lighting, though it provides sufficient light to create a picture, doesn't create the shadows and contrast to yield a vivid picture; it will still look somewhat flat and lifeless. The colors may also look drab. Notice in Figure 5–1 how adding extra light changes the picture.

On a cloudy day outdoors, the light is adequate for shooting. You may be able to use f4 to f5.6 for broad depth of field.

A slightly hazy day is perfect for shooting outdoors. There will be plenty of contrast at f8, yet shadows won't be too pronounced.

Fully sunny days are pretty good for shooting. Use f11 or so. Scenery will be bright and vivid, but faces and close-ups will appear *too* contrasty. Shadows especially may look too dark, and anything lurking in them may be obliterated.

Lighting Ratio

Place something very bright next to something very, very bright, next to something very dark, next to something very, very dark, and you will be able to distinguish one from another readily. A TV camera, on the other hand, will see only two white objects and two black objects. Although your eye can handle something a thousand times brighter than something else in the same scene, and although photographic film can distinguish between an object a hundred times brighter than another in the same scene, most TV cameras can accept a LIGHT RATIO of only thirty. With home video equipment, this number may be as low as fifteen.

The brightest thing in the picture should not be more than thirty times brighter than the darkest object in the same scene. Here's what this means in practice. You wish to tape a person standing in front of an open window during the day. What your camera will see was shown in Figure 4–6. Since the light from the window is very bright, everything else looks black and silhouetted by comparison. The gradations of gray in the clothing and face are all lost. If you close the shade (see the figure again), now the whitest thing in the picture is the wall and some of the clothing. They are only about ten times brighter than the hair and other dark parts of the picture. As a result, everything between the blacks of the hair and the whites of the wall gets a chance to be seen as some gradation of brightness rather than end up black as they did before. In short, things that are super-bright must be avoided. The brightest part of the scene should be less than thirty times brighter than the darkest part of the scene. Shafts of light coming in the windows, shiny buttons, and chrome hardware (like mike stands) should be avoided or subdued.

Lighting Placement

You want most of the light to come from behind you (the camera). Avoid light coming from behind the subject (bright windows, etc.), as that will silhouette your performer as was shown back in Figure 4–6. On the other hand, try not to have all your light coming from *too near* the camera, or you'll lose your shadows, making everything look flat and dull, as in Figure 5–2.

FIGURE 5–2 One light placed near the camera yields a flat picture with almost no shadows on the subject.

---

*Lighting ratio   A comparison between the brightest part of a subject and the darkest. If the brightest white in a performer's shirt measured 60 FC (footcandles) and his black hair measured 2 FC, then the lighting ratio would be $60 \div 2 = 30$.

*Color temperature   The redness or blueness of a scene, the result of the kind of light used to illuminate the scene. Also, the name given to the color TV camera control that adapts it to these varied lighting conditions.

Lighting Color

Unless you are after special effects, you'll be using white light. But white light isn't always white. Fluorescent lights are greenish. The incandescent lights in your home are reddish. You don't see this difference with your naked eye, but your camera does. The COLOR TEMPERATURE and WHITE BALANCE controls on your color camera can make up for much of this variation. But your controls can't salvage a scene that's lit on one side with fluorescent light and on the other side with incandescent light. (See color Figure 5–3 in color tip-in). The majority of the light in your scene has to be of the same COLOR TEMPERATURE, or else you'll confuse your poor camera into giving you faces that are half pink and half magenta.

Mini Review

- The three objectives of lighting are to
  1. Illuminate the scene so the camera can "see" it.
  2. Create shadows to make the TV screen's two-dimensional image look three-dimensional.
  3. Create a mood.
- Increasing the light in a scene
  1. Generally improves the contrast and color of the scene.
  2. Permits a broader depth of field.
- Cameras prefer images that are not too contrasty; very bright objects and very dark objects do not coexist well in the same picture. For best results, reduce the light ratio to less than thirty.
- For the best color (especially on faces), illuminate the scene with lights that are all the same color temperature.

PRIMITIVE LIGHTING TECHNIQUES

Let's start with the simplest situations and the least equipment, then work our way up to artistic, professional techniques with expensive gear.

Existing Indoor Light Only

You're shooting on location and didn't bring lights (maybe you're traveling light, if I may abuse a pun). How do you illuminate your subject?

1. Place your subject where the existing illumination is best, such as outdoors (in the daytime, of course) or under office lighting.
2. If the camera with its lens wide open (lowest f-setting) still shows a poor picture because of insufficient light, seek out other light sources, such as desk lamps. Turn on every lamp in the room. Move lamps closer to the scene if possible. Replace the light bulbs in lamps with the

---

*Scrim Glass fiber or metal screen mesh that clips to the front of a lighting instrument to diffuse and soften light.
*Spot Narrowly focused light that concentrates its intensity over a limited area.

*Flood Broadly focused light that covers a large area evenly.
Bounce light Light bounced off another (usually white) surface.

highest wattage rated for the lamp. Every light that you include will add punch and contrast to your picture.

3. Avoid bright windows or lights in the background of the shot. If you wish to use light from a window, get between it and the subject so that the subject, not the camera, is facing the window light.

Most of the preceding ideas pose COLOR TEMPERATURE problems, but at least you'll have enough light to take your pictures.

Outdoor Lighting

The big challenge with outdoor shooting is shadow control. Picture a bright sunny day. The baby chases the family puss across the green lawn and under a tree. Suddenly the baby's rosy pink cheeks turn muddy gray. Your orange cat turns muddy gray. The green lawn turns muddy gray. Every once in a while you can see a white flash as the kid's outfit is caught in a stray beam of sunlight piercing the leaves.

The trick here is to fill in the shadows:

1. Shoot on hazy days when shadows are soft.
2. Shoot with the sun mostly to your back so shadows are partially hidden.
3. Glue some tinfoil to a sheet of posterboard and "fill in" the shadows with reflected light. (See Figure 5–4.)
4. Shoot with a bright light a little ways from the camera, even in broad daylight. Place the light in such a way as to "fill in" the shadows caused by the sun. To avoid COLOR TEMPERATURE problems, use a "daylight" photoflood, or use an HMI light (described later), or use a colored filter over the bulb to convert the light to 5600°K.

Bright sunlight has a way of driving a camera's AUTO IRIS crazy. The automatic control may "lock onto" the brightest part of the scene, making everything else look dark relative to it. Whenever possible, size up the lighting situation and switch to MANUAL IRIS. Let your eye and viewfinder be the

FIGURE 5–4 Outdoor light reflector of aluminum foil over posterboard helps fill in shadows without causing COLOR TEMPERATURE problems. Notice how the performer's face is easily seen, compared to the dark silhouettes of the crewmembers without the reflected light.

KINDS OF LIGHTING	
Types of Illumination	*Color Temperature*
TUNGSTEN bulb for home use	2,800°K
TUNGSTEN bulb for photographic use	3,200°K
QUARTZ-HALOGEN or TUNGSTEN IODIDE bulb	3,200°K
Daylight, early or late	3,200°K
FLUORESCENT lamp, warm white bulb	3,500°K
FLUORESCENT lamp, white bulb	4,500°K
Photoflood bulb for photographic use	5,000°K
Daylight, midday	5,500°K
HMI (HALOGEN METAL IODIDE) professional lamp	5,500°K
FLUORESCENT lamp, daylight bulb typically found in offices	6,500°K
Daylight, hazy or foggy day	7,000°K

INCANDESCENT: A light with a TUNGSTEN (metal with a high melting point) filament that glows when electricity passes through it. Common home lamps are INCANDESCENT and have a low COLOR TEMPERATURE. When INCANDESCENT lamps are dimmed, the light becomes redder, but the bulbs will last much longer. Bulbs darken with time (some of the filament boils away and coats the glass), decreasing the light's brightness and lowering the COLOR TEMPERATURE of the light.

FLUORESCENT: A light with a gas inside that glows when electricity passes through it. The COLOR TEMPERATURE is usually high. It is possible, with professional hardware, to dim FLUORESCENT lights. FLUORESCENT lights give off more light per watt than INCANDESCENT lamps, making them more efficient and cooler running. They're not easily aimed or focused. A powdered coating inside the bulb is formulated to glow a specific color; thus, FLUORESCENT lights can come in various COLOR TEMPERATURES.

QUARTZ-HALOGEN or TUNGSTEN IODIDE: Both mean the same thing. Both are INCANDESCENT lamps having a TUNGSTEN filament. The glass bulb is QUARTZ. A gas inside the bulb is IODINE (also called a HALOGEN gas). The gas helps keep the bulb from darkening with age, so that the COLOR TEMPERATURE changes very little. Unlike regular INCANDESCENT lamps, QUARTZ lights run very hot and bright, and the bulbs are quite small.

PHOTOFLOOD: A light bulb sold by photography shops that looks like a normal household lamp but burns with a bright blue-white light, much like daylight. The bulb darkens with age and usually lasts 10 hours.

DAYLIGHT: That stuff you see outdoors at noon when you're not cooped up inside reading this book.

judge of what is most important in the scene and make *that* look good, even if something else gets a little over- or underexposed.

This is the technique you use when shooting *toward* the sun: In this case, the sun acts as a strong BACK light, rimming the performer, while you use a separate lamp or a reflector to illuminate the talent's face. The background or rim may be too white, darkening the talent's face. Here you would manually open the IRIS a little (or press a BACKLIGHT button on the camera, which does the same thing) to overexpose the background while properly exposing the face. You can only "cheat" like this by one or two f-stops before you overburden the camera's electronics with excessive light. Sometimes it helps to zoom in on the face a bit to decrease the amount of bright background visible.

If you're shooting early in the morning or late in the afternoon, WHITE-BALANCE your camera often. As the sun nears the horizon, its COLOR TEMPERATURE drops rapidly toward the red. This change can sneak up on you if you're too preoccupied with your shoot to notice the changing sun.

One Light Only

You're shooting on location and you brought only one light (perhaps that's all that would fit in your saddlebags). Where do you place it?

Don't place it next to the camera, because that will give a flat picture without shadows as in Figure 5–2. In most cases, shadows are desirable because they create a sense of depth and texture to the image. Place the lamp at an angle 20° to 45° to the right and 30° to 45° above the subject. The KEY light used in Figure 1–15 is in that position.

Some cameras come with (or have as an attachable option) an on-board camera light. Since the illumination comes from close to the camera, it doesn't make beautiful light, but it does save you from having to shoot in the dark, a situation often faced by news and documentary videographers. When there *is* adequate light, the additional punch offered by the little on-board light is likely to improve the color in a person's face, add twinkle to their eyes, and make them stand out from their background just a tad.

Whenever possible, use an on-board light with its *own* battery; they suck up juice faster than a roll of Bounty paper towels, leaving little to sustain your camcorder. Some have two power settings so that you get the amount of light you want and avoid the "searchlight-in-the-face" look you get in darker venues.

Shooting with only one light has its liabilities. It is possible that the light could be so bright, compared with other light in the scene, that it "washes out" light-colored parts of the scene and creates harsh shadows. This is called EXCESSIVE LIGHTING RATIO and typically occurs when a very bright light is placed too near the subject. Figure 5–5 shows an example.

The cure for EXCESSIVE LIGHTING RATIO is to find some way to dim or diffuse the light and to create or reflect some light into the shadow areas. Try moving the light farther from your subject. Or place a metal screen, called a SCRIM, in front of the light to diffuse it. Figure 5–6 shows a SCRIM that clips onto the front of a light fixture. Maybe refocus the light from SPOT to FLOOD (described shortly).

Another alternative is to aim the light at a white ceiling or white wall and illuminate your subject with the fairly shadowless BOUNCE light.

FIGURE 5–5   Excessive LIGHTING RATIO. Too bright a lamp, too close, causes excessive contrast and deep shadows.

*Key light   Brightest and main source of lighting for a subject, creating the primary shadows.

*Fill light   Soft, broad light whose main purpose is to fill in (reduce the blackness of) shadows created by the key light.

*Back light   Lighting instrument that illuminates the subject from behind, creating a rim of light around the edges of the subject. The back light usually has barn doors for precise control of the light's direction.

*Set light   Lighting instrument used to illuminate the background or set.

*Barn doors   Metal flaps on a lighting instrument that can be closed or opened to direct the light and to shade areas where light is undesirable.

Variable focus light   A lighting fixture that can be adjusted from spot to flood or vice versa to direct the light's intensity.

Fresnel   Lighting instrument with a circularly ribbed glass lens to focus the light.

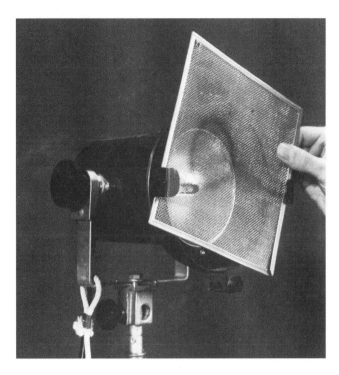

FIGURE 5–6 SCRIM clips onto light fixture to reduce and diffuse light intensity.

If the room's natural lighting seems to illuminate the left side of the face the most, you should place your professional light on the right side of the face. In this way the existing room lighting has a job to do; it fills in the shadows created by your professional light.

Two Lights Only

The professional solution to dark shadows is to use two lights. One light makes the shadows, and the other one decreases their intensity, bringing the LIGHTING RATIO back to where the camera can handle it.

Where should you place your two lights? The first light should go 20° to 45° to the side and 30° to 45° up as described earlier. You place the second light similarly up and to the *other* side of the camera as shown in Figure 5–7. The result looks like the KEY + FILL example back in Figure 1–15.

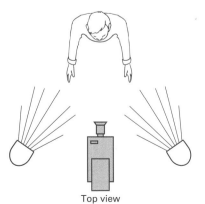

Top view

FIGURE 5–7 Using two lights.

The brighter of the two lights acts as the KEY light, providing most of the illumination of the subject, while the weaker lamp becomes the FILL light, filling in the shadows somewhat and softening the picture.

If both lights are of equal brightness, one can be made into a FILL light by

1. Moving it farther away from the subject.
2. Placing a SCRIM in front of it to diffuse the light.
3. Aiming the light at something reflective nearby. The diffused reflected light will then fill in the shadows.
4. Refocusing it from SPOT to FLOOD.

Individual taste and circumstances play a large role in setting up lights. Congress passed no law saying a light must be 20° up and 30° over. No commandment requires one lamp to be brighter than the other so that one is the KEY and the other is the FILL; they could be equal. The ideas set forth here are generalities and are flexible.

 Mini Review

- Try to make most of the light come from behind the camera.
- Avoid bright backgrounds, as they make the subject look dark.
- If you have only one light, place it to the side and above the camera so that the light hits the subject at an angle.
- If you have two lights, use the second to fill in the shadows created by the first light. Place the fill light above the camera and to the side opposite the key light.

STUDIO LIGHTING

Well-placed, carefully aimed lights of just the right color and intensity are superb for fulfilling lighting's main purposes:

1. To provide enough light so that the camera can "see"
2. To enhance the scene to overcome TV's inherent shortcomings, making the image appear sharp, vivid, and three-dimensional
3. To create a mood

Such precise lighting adjustments are possible only in a studio where you have total control over all the lighting. Ideally, there should be no windows or fluorescent office lights to contend with.

Figure 1–13 displayed a generally "typical" TV lighting layout. TV (and film) lighting consists of four basic building blocks: the KEY light, the FILL light, the BACK light, and the SET light. Let's look at each in detail.

Key Light

The KEY light is like the sun. It illuminates the subject, creating the main shadows, as was shown in Figure 1–15. These shadows help give depth and dimension to the scene.

The term KEY light does not refer to a particular type of fixture but describes the role the light plays. Almost any lighting instrument can act as a KEY light; however, some are better suited than others.

The KEY light generally has BARN DOORS (Figure 1–12), metal flaps used to direct the light or to shade certain areas of the scene. Like the SCRIM, the BARN DOORS may be clipped onto the front of the fixture.

KEY lights are usually instruments with a VARIABLE FOCUS control that can be adjusted either to FLOOD the area evenly with light or to concentrate the light in a small SPOT (Figure 5–8). Generally, if intense light is needed, adjust the instrument to SPOT. If the subject is large or moves around, SPOT may be unsatisfactory because the area illuminated is so small. The solution is either to adjust the instrument—partially or all the way—to FLOOD (sacrificing some of the brightness as the light covers a larger area) or to obtain more instruments to cover the area.

Some studio lighting instruments vary their focus by moving the lamp bulb closer to or farther from the reflector, thus spreading or concentrating the light. Others, such as the FRESNEL lamp shown in Figure 5–9, focus the light by moving the bulb closer to or farther from a lens.

Generally, when lamps are used on a stand, a knob on the instrument may be moved to adjust the lamp's focus. If the lamp is the type that hangs from the ceiling, on the bottom of the lamp there may be a loop that is easily turned by using a pole with a hook on it. See Figure 5–10.

Fill Light

Any light can be a FILL light if it fills in the shadows created by the KEY light. Professional instruments typically have a 1,000 to 2,000-watt (1 to 2 kw) bulb surrounded by a large reflective surface. The larger the surface, the more diffuse the light will be, and the softer the shadows will look. The hanging light in Figure 5–10 is called a SCOOP light (because of its shape) and is often used as a FILL light.

Light focused for SPOT

Light focused for FLOOD

FIGURE 5–8   SPOT versus FLOOD.

Scoop light   Funnel-shaped fill light.

FIGURE 5–9   FRESNEL lamp, generally used as a KEY light (Photo courtesy of Berkey Colortran, Inc.).

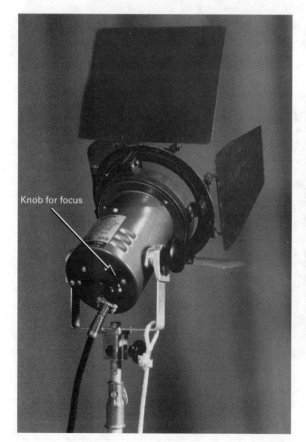

Knob for focus

Floor stand fixture

loop to adjust lamp's focus

Hanging SCOOP light

FIGURE 5–10   Focus controls.

Figure 1–15 showed the results of using a KEY light without FILL. The image is harsh and contrasty. Figure 1–15 also shows the result of using a FILL light alone and in combination with a KEY light. The relative brightness of these two lights determines the depth of the shadows created.

While setting up lighting, some people use light meters and measure the LIGHTING RATIO between KEY and FILL and the other lights. If you are not so inclined (and most industrial users are not), a pretty good lighting job can be done by "eye" if you let the camera do some of the work for you:

1. Set up your lighting the way you think it should be.
2. Aim the camera at the subject to be recorded, and look at a TV monitor to examine the image.
3. Readjust the lighting so that the image looks best *on the TV screen.*

Placement of the FILL light is generally 20° to 45° to the side of and 30° to 45° above the camera-to-subject axis, just like the KEY light, only on the opposite side of the camera from the KEY light. This placement is flexible, however, and occasionally FILL lights may be found nearer to the floor or the camera.

Since the KEY light is often thought of as the sun, it is appropriate for this light to come from fairly high up (like the sun), casting shadows downward. Since the FILL light's job is to temper those shadows, the FILL can be lower (if it were high, it too would be casting shadows downward).

The light from a FILL light can be made harder or softer. Some instruments have a FOCUS control and may also have a holder for a SCRIM, which can further soften the light.

If you don't have a proper FILL light, try softening the light from one of your unused KEY lights to do the job. Adjust its focus to FLOOD and add a SCRIM or two, or aim the light through some fiberglass DIFFUSION material. Figure 5–11 shows some of this white, translucent fabric that can be cut to size and then clipped to the BARN DOORS of a light.

The softer and more diffuse the light, the sexier and more informal your picture will look. To get the effect shown in Figure 5–12, you will need to use lots of DIFFUSION material or will have to bounce your light off a large white surface.

Note: Lighting professionals almost never light a person with a direct open face light; the light is too HARD and severe. Instead, they SCRIM the KEY instrument with DIFFUSION material to soften the light, then soften the FILL light even more than the KEY.

When you are shooting outdoors, the sun usually acts as your KEY light, and you have to dream up something for your FILL. You could bring along an electric light and position it to fill in shadows. Or you could hold up a square of white or tinfoil-covered posterboard and position it to reflect some of the sun's light onto the shaded side of your subject.

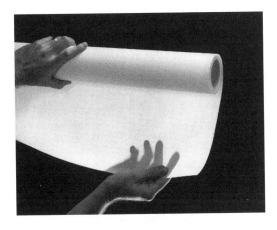

FIGURE 5–11 Diffusion material comes on a roll and can be cut to fit most lights (Courtesy Porter's Camera Store).

FIGURE 5–12   Soft indirect lighting (Courtesy of Colortran, Inc.).

Back Light

The BACK light is the third most important of your studio lights (KEY and FILL being the first and second). Its position and effect were shown in Figures 1–13 and 1–15. The BACK light is responsible for most of the dimensionality of the TV picture. Without it, the image blends into its background; with it, the image stands out and has punch.

The BACK light's job is to rim foreground subjects, separating them from the background. But don't make the BACK light *too* bright, or it will add a glow to the tops of actors' heads and shoulders, distracting the viewer from the actors' faces. Would you rim da Vinci's *The Last Supper* with a frame of blinking neon lights?

Brunettes need more BACK light, and blondes need less. Bald people need even less; in fact, a little powder would help cut the shine, allowing you to increase the BACK light to make the shoulders look better.

The light should strike from above and behind at an angle 20° to 75° up from the horizontal. The higher and farther back the lamp, the better, because the light being aimed *toward* the cameras has a tendency to shine into the lenses. This causes undesired lens reflections or maybe SMEAR when careless camera operators tilt too far up. Often the BARN DOORS are a help in shading the cameras from the lights while directing the light only on the performers. Figure 5–13 shows a couple of BACK lights with BARN DOORS.

Instead of burning your talent's eyeballs under the photon assault of the blazing sun, try using the sun as a BACK light, using reflectors to create the KEY and FILL. This technique also has a hidden ad-

---

Pattern   An aluminum cutout that fits into a pattern spotlight to create the shapes projected by the light.

Pattern spotlight (or framing spotlight)   Lighting instrument that accepts aluminum cutouts to project patterns such as venetian blinds, leaves, or other figures on the background.

Cookie   Cucolorus.

Cucoloris   A cutout pattern used in a studio light fixture to project a design (such as the shadow of a venetian blind) on a wall or floor.

Honeycomb grid   A matrix of louvers placed in front of a fluorescent light fixture to control the spread and direction of the light.

Egg crate   Honeycomb grid.

Gobo   Patterned cutout used to cast a shadow of a design, such as tree branches or venetian blinds, onto a surface. Works like a cookie, but without a special projector.

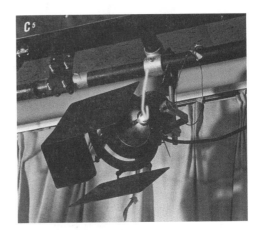

Studio setup.

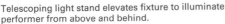

Telescoping light stand elevates fixture to illuminate performer from above and behind.

FIGURE 5–13 BACK LIGHTS with BARN DOORS.

vantage: The sun will move during a long shooting event, creating a discontinuity in the lighting angles from shot to shot. The COLOR TEMPERATURE may change, too. By using reflectors for your KEY and FILL, you can move them to correct for the sun's movement, restoring the original angle of the light (within limits). By using tinted reflectors, you can counteract the change in COLOR TEMPERATURE that results as the sun gets lower in the sky. Even though your BACK light will change as the sun moves, the differences in angle and color are not very noticeable.

Note: The above scenario doesn't break the "rule" of avoiding light behind the subject. The sun shouldn't be *in* the picture, nor should it make the background bright. Coming from *above* and behind, it rims the subject. Reflected or electrical light illuminates the subject's face, making it brighter than the background and obeying the "rules."

Set Light

The SET light illuminates the set or background. Again, Figure 1–13 showed its position, and Figure 1–15 showed its effect. Depending on the brightness of this light, a gray background can be made to look white, neutral, or black relative to the performer. It is best (usually) to have the background a tad darker than the performers so that they stand out from the background, directing your attention to them. Figure 5–14 shows one result of having too light a background. And if the background is *really* too bright, as in Figure 4–6, you may see only a silhouette of your performers, or their faces may appear very dark.

Not any light can do this job well. The set should be lit fairly evenly. A regular light aimed downward near the set will create a bright spot at the top of the set and will fade off to nothing at the bottom. Placing a lamp farther from the set will light it more evenly, but unless the subject is standing *far* in front of the set, much of the SET light will spill onto the performer. For good control, you want each of your lights to illuminate one area only so that adjusting one lamp doesn't affect anything else (it will anyway to some extent, but why make things worse?).

The woman in white fails to stand out from the white background. It is usually best to have the background darker than the subject (Courtesy of Imero Fiorentino Associates)

FIGURE 5–14   Too bright a background.

Some studios use rows of lights to illuminate the set. One tier is above the performer (but not illuminating him or her), and another group may be on the floor aimed up at the set. An easier method of illuminating the set is to use a specially designed SET light. This instrument concentrates the light and throws it *down* to illuminate the bottom of the set while throwing a diminished supply of light at the top of the set near the lamp (where, because of the nearness, the set will get more light anyway). Figure 5–15 shows such a SET light.

If you built your set to look like a room or an office, keep in mind that most room light comes from the ceiling and is aimed down. SET lights, in order to duplicate this effect, should not illuminate the tops of your set pieces too brightly. Walls should look darker at the top. When a camera looks at a wall and the top is slightly darker than the rest of the wall, the viewer mentally assumes that there is a ceiling. We all know, however, that sets are constructed without a ceiling (so that the studio lights can shine down on the set), but your viewers shouldn't deduce this.

Avoid bare white walls in the background; the solid white surface looks unnatural. To give texture to barren walls and ceilings, light them unevenly. Use soft shadows to add character and dimension.

Perhaps a PATTERN projected on the wall will imply a setting or neighborhood. Use harder shadows to create drama, softer ones to remain neutral.

The SET light spilling onto the performers is a problem. The KEY and FILL lights spilling onto the set create another problem. If room is available, try to move the set back far enough behind the performers so that this spillage is minimized. Doing so, you'll also reap the benefits of not having to con-

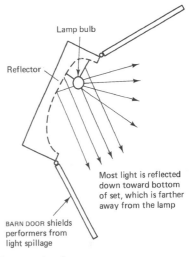

Lamp bulb

Reflector

Most light is reflected down toward bottom of set, which is farther away from the lamp

BARN DOOR shields performers from light spillage

FIGURE 5–15   SET LIGHT (Courtesy of Colortran, Inc.).

tend with so many shadows from the performers being projected onto the set from the KEY and FILL lights.

 Mini Review

- The basic studio lighting setup is:
  1. Key light: Provides the main shadows and illumination.
  2. Fill light: Coming from the side of the camera opposite the key light, the fill light reduces the darkness of the shadows created by the key light and reduces the lighting ratio.
  3. Back light: Coming from behind the subject, it creates a rim of light around the subject and makes it stand out from its background.
  4. Set light: Illuminates the background.
- Scrims and diffusion material will soften the light, making shadows less intense.
- Reflectors are often used outdoors to fill in shadows from the sun.

Pattern Spotlight

Another instrument used to illuminate sets and backgrounds is the PATTERN SPOTLIGHT, or FRAMING SPOTLIGHT, like the one in Figure 5–16. The instrument accepts aluminum cutouts and, like a projector, focuses the *pattern* from the cutouts onto the studio background. These cutouts could be of shutters,

PATTERNS

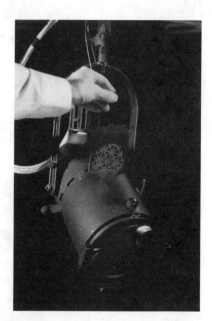

PATTERN goes in holder that slips in here

PATTERN projected on floor

FIGURE 5–16   PATTERN SPOTLIGHT.

venetian blinds, windows, clouds, church windows, leaves, or stars or even could be custom-made designs and serve to create an illusion or mood. Venetian blinds, for instance, projected onto a paneled studio set, may imply that the room is an office. A cross projected on a curtain behind a singer would give a religious mood to the set. Often you can avoid the expense and trouble of building complex windows and other set pieces if you simply project the pattern of them on the wall.

The technical term for this metal PATTERN is a COOKIE, short for CUCOLORIS, named after its inventor. Nobody seems to agree on how to spell CUCOLORIS, making the term COOKIE popular.

If you don't have a PATTERN SPOTLIGHT, you can achieve nearly the same effect by using any hard-light source and placing a GOBO (a fairly large cutout or object meant to cast a recognizable shadow) in its light path. The GOBO will project a design on the set or performers. Don't position it too close to the lamp, or your GOBO may go up in smoke.

Fluorescent Lighting

Normal fluorescent lights, the kind found in offices and supermarkets, are unflattering for video. First, the light is soft and featureless, yielding pictures that lack dimension. Second, household fluorescent lamps make an odd mixture of colors—they look white to our eyes, but cameras perceive the light differently.

Professional fluorescent lights, made for TV and film, are designed to correct these problems. Here are the advantages of professional fluorescent lights over incandescent ones:

1. Fluorescent lights are very efficient, producing more light per watt than incandescent lamps.
   A 200-watt fluorescent light can often replace a 2,000-watt tungsten soft light. This saves power and cuts down on air conditioning needs (especially important in portable situations).
2. Fluorescent tubes last longer than incandescent bulbs, generally 10,000 hours versus about 300.
3. Fluorescent lights, because the light emanates from a tube rather than a point, make excellent FILL lights, softly filling in shadows.

To better aim and control the light, fluorescent fixtures are usually equipped with HONEYCOMB GRIDS, EGG CRATES, and BARN DOORS. No, these aren't farm implements; they are louvers and slats to help direct the light.

Fluorescent light arrays cost about $1,300 each, about five to ten times the cost of a tungsten fixture of the same brightness. Figure 5–17 shows one.

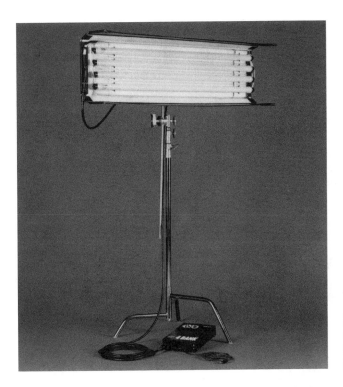

FIGURE 5–17 Fluorescent television lighting instrument requires less power than equivalent tungsten lamps (Courtesy of Kino Flo, Inc.).

Flag   Easily movable flap used with lights for casting shadows and controlling light.

*HMI light   Halogen metal iodide lighting instrument. Very efficient and uses minimal power, but requires a heavy ballast. Gives off light with 5,500°K color temperature.

Umbrella   A light reflector made like an umbrella with a silvery underside, used to soften light from portable lighting instruments.

PORTABLE LIGHTING

Name three lights you would take with you on location. Heineken Lite, Michelob Lite, and portable light, right?

Portable lights can be purchased as kits, which may include three or four small-sized 500-watt fixtures with BARN DOORS and adjustable mounts by which they can be attached to portable telescoping lighting stands like those shown in Figure 5–18. Some lighting instruments attach to a heavy-duty clamp that can be clipped about anywhere. Some special clamps will hitch to a drop ceiling like those found in offices and schools. Many kits contain SCRIMS, extension cords, and other handy gadgets, like FLAGS (easily movable flaps for casting shadows and controlling light spillage).

These lights are commonly used indoors and in temporary or quasi-"studios." They are quite popular in schools. Even in larger studios, stand-mounted lights are useful, especially when you want light to come from a low angle. They are a nuisance, however, when you trip over the power cord or when the floor stands get in your way.

Portable lighting kits may also be used outdoors, but they pose three problems:

1. *Color temperature*. Sunlight usually has a COLOR TEMPERATURE of 5,000° to 7,000°K. Incandescent studio lamps usually have a COLOR TEMPERATURE of 3,200°K. This means that if the sun were the KEY and a portable light were your FILL, your KEY would look bluish, and your FILL would look reddish.
2. *Electric consumption*. Normal studio lights and their portable counterparts typically use 500 to 1,000 watts each. This is a lot of power! Often, no more than one or two such lights can be connected to a household wall outlet at once without tripping a circuit breaker. Even the extension cords for such lights must be heavy duty.
3. *Instability*. When lights with big reflectors catch the wind, they set sail for the ground.

For every complex problem, there is always an equally expensive solution. To raise the COLOR TEMPERATURE of an incandescent lamp, special filters, the shape and size of SCRIMS, can be inserted into the instrument to cut out some of the redness of the light. These filters also cut light output significantly, requiring about twice the number of lights to get the same effect.

FIGURE 5–18 Portable lighting kit (Courtesy of Colortran, Inc.).

Fluorescent lights, as mentioned earlier, can provide plenty of FILL light for a reasonably low number of watts, and tubes can be found to match the daylight COLOR TEMPERATURE. Fluorescent lamps have to be used quite near a subject because their diffuse light diminishes quickly with distance; their light can't be "beamed" like a spotlight.

COLOR TEMPERATURE, beam distance, and power problems are all solved elegantly and expensively with the HMI light (Figure 5–19).

HMI Lights

HMI stands for halogen metal iodide, which describes the materials which make up the light bulb. It is a special instrument that creates 5,500°K "daylight" and puts out about three times as much light as a tungsten bulb of the same wattage rating. It also generates about half as much heat.

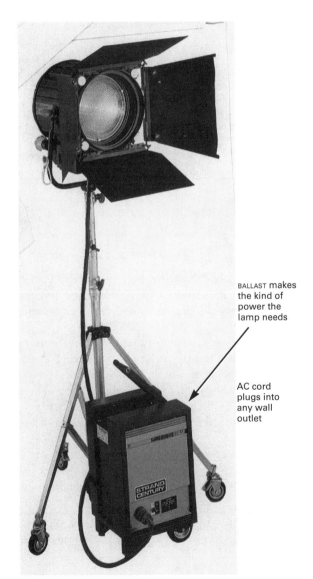

BALLAST makes the kind of power the lamp needs

AC cord plugs into any wall outlet

FIGURE 5–19   HMI light (Courtesy of Strand Century).

Because the instrument makes the right daylight COLOR TEMPERATURE to start with, it doesn't need a brightness-robbing filter to correct its COLOR TEMPERATURE. Because of its correct COLOR TEMPERATURE and high efficiency, a 1,200-watt HMI light produces just about as much light as a 10-kilowatt tungsten lamp that's been filtered to daylight COLOR TEMPERATURE. The HMI can plug into any standard wall socket without blowing a fuse, whereas the 10-kilowatt unit would require special wiring to be installed by a licensed electrician.

Umbrellas

SOFT lights generally have big reflectors, making them hard to carry. UMBRELLAS with silvery undersides unfold to do a nice job of focusing soft light from a small lamp. Essentially, the lamp faces the umbrella, which reflects the light onto the subject. By changing the lamp-to-umbrella position, you can change the intensity and spread of the light beam. Many portable lights have built-in brackets to hold umbrellas. Mary Poppins could have used one.

 Mini Review

- By projecting a pattern of light on the wall or floor, you can imply objects in the shot (such as a window) that don't exist, thus creating a mood.
- Common fluorescent lights make unattractive colors, but professional fluorescent lights make soft light with excellent color while using relatively little electric power.
- HMI lights make outdoor color temperatures and use relatively little power.

LIGHTING TECHNIQUES

Lighting Several Areas at Once

The lighting plan for one camera angle may not necessarily work for another camera far from that angle. So guess what you have to do? Check the camera angles before show time to see if lighting problems exist for these various angles. If they do, use the same techniques as before to KEY, FILL, BACK, and SET light for each camera angle.

Sometimes the performers will be moving around. So that they don't walk out of the light, lamps have to be provided to illuminate the paths that the performers will take. It could take dozens of lamps to illuminate an entire set. In professional studios it is common to see rows of KEY lights flanked by dozens of FILL lights lined up, crowding the rafters. BACK lights seem to be aiming in every direction. These setups were made one step at a time using the techniques described in this chapter: KEY, FILL, BACK, and SET. The process was repeated for every angle and for every stage position until the entire area was lit.

Sometimes the lighting strategy gets so complex that you need to sketch out your plans on a piece of paper before you try to execute them. This plan is called a LIGHTING PLOT, it shows what types of instruments are used and where they are aimed and gives each light a number so that it's easier to

---

*Lighting plot   A drawing to show where the lights are to be aimed. May also include fixture numbers and circuit numbers and show prop and performer positions.

*Gel   Colored material that looks like cellophane and can be placed in front of a lamp to color the light. Usually the flimsy gel material is held in a frame that fits the fixture's scrim holder.

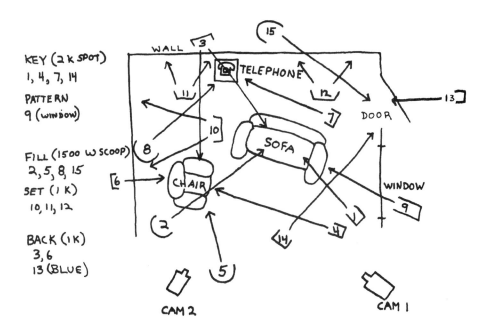

FIGURE 5–20 LIGHTING PLOT.

refer to later. The LIGHTING PLOT may also include details such as props and furniture and may even show where the talent will be standing or moving. Figure 5–20 is a LIGHTING PLOT for a small studio production. Notice that the PLOT doesn't have to be a work of art, just functional.

The LIGHTING PLOT not only serves to organize your plans (before you start climbing ladders and lugging hardware from position to position) but also allows you to give the plan to another person to execute.

Many studios don't have a great number of lighting instruments to work with. In such cases, one tries to get a single instrument to do two jobs at once. For instance, in the interview setting shown in Figure 5–21, one person's KEY light is the other person's FILL.

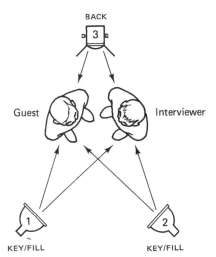

FIGURE 5–21 Let one person's KEY be another's FILL.

If your performer must move from one area to another and you don't have enough instruments to light the entire path, then light the beginning and end points of his or her journey and use low FILL lighting for in between. Check out PBS's *Wall Street Week in Review* for a good example of this kind of lighting.

Lighting for Color

The basic principles of black-and-white lighting generally hold true for color. Color, however, permits new lighting possibilities while exacting new constraints. With insufficient light, color cameras will produce grainy pictures with muddy color.

With color we can get creative, illuminating our sets and performers with colored lights. Actually, the lightbulbs themselves are always white. The lighting instruments have slots in them to hold colored panes of glass or plastic or to hold GELS, a popular theatrical supply that looks like colored cellophane. (Most are actually made from colored gelatin, hence the name GEL). The light that shines through the gels ends up colored. The GELS slip into the instruments much like a SCRIM does (Figure 5–22).

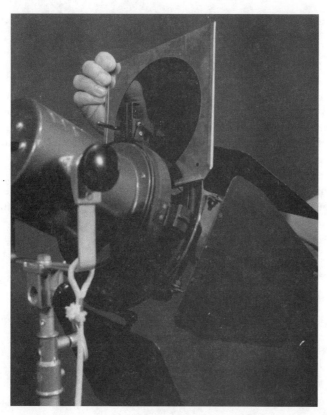

FIGURE 5–22   Colored GEL.

Tungsten-halogen   Common TV lamp with a tungsten filament (glowing wire inside) and a quartz bulb filled with iodine (a halogen) gas. It's small, generally operates at 3,200K° color temperature, and runs very hot.

*Chroma key   Video effect whereby blue (or other selected color) parts of a TV picture are replaced with another picture.

Be aware that colored GELS intercept a lot of light. A solid red, green, or blue GEL will trap about 92 percent of the light, letting through about 8 percent. Thus, your 1,000-watt fixture may yield only 80 watts of red (or whatever) light. Pastel GELS transmit more light.

If you are using diffusion materials *and* a colored GEL over a light, put the GEL on the outside, *over* the diffusion. In this way the GEL will deliver its proper color, undiluted by the white of the diffusion material.

Blue lights can give the impression of nighttime, darkness, or cold (this characteristic explains why instrument 13 in Figure 5–20 was blue). Red lighting may convey warmth and happiness or fire. Lighting an object with different-colored lights from different angles offers dimensionality and visual appeal. We pay for this new creative freedom with new headaches. The camera doesn't "see" things exactly the way we do, so something that looks pleasant to the naked eye may look abominable on the TV screen. Lighting adjustments must be made with both eyes on a color monitor. As the talent moves from one area of the stage to another, the relative brightness of various lamps will change, thus changing substantially the vividness, the highlights, the darkness of the shadows, the overall contrast, and even the color of the subject. To accommodate these problems, the lighting person must be familiar with all the moves likely to be made on the set, and he or she must illuminate each performer for each area.

Background color can be used to add dimensionality to a scene. The complementary coloration of the background can help to emphasize the subject.

Faces are perhaps the hardest things to illuminate correctly. No one may notice if a shirt, table, or backdrop appears more bluish or greenish than it's supposed to. But flesh tones that appear pale, greenish, or reddish brown will not be tolerated (unless you are shooting Dracula, the Creature from the Black Lagoon, or the Jolly Green Giant). Not only are skin tones sensitive to outright color changes under various lighting and backgrounds, but these tones are also sensitive to changes in COLOR TEMPERATURE.

COLOR TEMPERATURE made its debut in Chapter 3, where we adjusted the various doohickies on color cameras. Look out, 'cause here comes another dose of COLOR TEMPERATURE. COLOR TEMPERATURE is measured in degrees Kelvin. 3,200°K (3,200 degrees Kelvin) describes a lamp with a COLOR TEMPERATURE appropriate for color TV cameras. As this number goes up to about 6,000°K, the light gets bluer and "colder" (this seems backwards, but as the COLOR TEMPERATURE increases, the scene looks "colder"). Fluorescent lights and foggy days exhibit such COLOR TEMPERATURES. As the number drops down to about 2,000°K, the light gets redder and "warmer." Incandescent lamps in the home create such COLOR TEMPERATURES. A face, not to look too red or too pallid, should be illuminated by 3,200°K lamps. This COLOR TEMPERATURE is available from studio QUARTZ-IODINE or TUNGSTEN-HALOGEN lamps, or from the sun early or late on a clear day, or from a properly chosen professional fluorescent TV light.

Rules of Color

Much of what has been written about TV color relates more to artistic taste than to objective principles. Here are some of the more widely held "rules" of TV color:

1. Avoid pure whites. They will be too bright for most color cameras. Avoid pale yellow and light off-whites as these may be too bright for the cameras. White embroidery on a white shirt will certainly disappear. Light colors and light gray will probably all reproduce on TV as just "white." Medium-tone colors reproduce best. Dark colors such as maroon, black, and purple may all appear as "black" on TV. The preceding information assumes that other things (such as people) will appear in the picture too. If not, you can sometimes cheat; for instance, to show white embroidery on a white shirt, have the shirt (and maybe a slightly darker background) fill the screen. Light the shirt from the side so the embroidery has shadows.

2. Do not mix common fluorescent lamps with TUNGSTEN or QUARTZ lamps on your set. In other words, turn off the studio's overhead "house lights" before adjusting your studio lights, and certainly before shooting. The mixture creates COLOR TEMPERATURE problems. If your TV lights are very bright, however, they will overpower the fluorescent lamps, making their effect on the color negligible. Similarly, if shooting outdoors, avoid using 3,200°K tungsten lights to augment the scene or to fill in shadows. The light will appear reddish. Use HMI or 6,300°K fluorescent lights if you have them, or employ a blue GEL to "get the red out" of your tungsten light. If the GEL trick knocks the light brightness down too much, then it's time to break rules: Use the 3,200°K light "bare" and hope the sun will overpower it so much no one will notice the red.

3. The background for a colored object should be either gray or a complementary color. For instance, red looks best before a blue-green background; yellow, in front of blue; green, in front of magenta; orange, in front of green; and flesh tones look best with a cyan background.

4. Bright, multicolored subjects look best before a smooth, neutral background. Especially avoid "busy" backgrounds, as they distract the eye from the main subject.

5. Attention is attracted to items with saturated (pure or solid) color. Pastels attract less attention and are good for backgrounds.

6. Use as few colors in a scene as possible—perhaps two or three complementary colors are sufficient for covering large areas.

7. Some colors become indistinguishable when shown on a color TV screen. The colors between red-orange and magenta end up looking about the same. Similarly, blue and violet look about the same on the screen. In fact lavender and blue-green all look blue on TV. Your graphic artist should therefore *avoid* highlighting a red apple with red-orange or trimming a blue robe with violet. These nuances in hue will not reproduce.

8. Let the TV screen be your guide. The TV screen will never look exactly the same as the live image. Using a calibrated TV monitor and properly adjusted cameras, study the screen image. If it's not right, forget what the scene looks like to your naked eye, forget the "rules," and start adjusting lights to make everything look right on the TV monitor.

 Mini Review

- Use a lighting plot to diagram where your lights will be aimed.
- A gel placed in front of the light fixture allows you to color the light.
- Color temperature is measured in degrees Kelvin. The higher the number of degrees, the bluer the light. 3,200°K is commonly used in studios. Lights with lower color temperature look reddish.
- For clothing and sets, avoid pure white, pure black, very dark colors, and very light colors.

Lighting for Chroma Key

CHROMA KEY, a video effect whereby blue (or some other selected color) parts of a picture can be replaced by another picture, will be discussed in Chapter 11. A weathercaster, standing in front of a blue curtain, can have the blue replaced with a weather map and appear to be standing in front of the giant map. The actual map may be a picture on another camera or be an electronic graphic.

How do you light for this? Let's assume we are CHROMA KEYING with blue (although other colors are possible, green being popular).

Basically,

1. Make sure the curtain (or background surface) is *evenly* lit—equal brightness everywhere. It should be a constant color blue all over, and the curtain should be lit bright enough to match foreground elements of the picture (i.e., the talent).
2. Make sure no blue appears on the performer.

Now for the fine points:

1. Match the performer's lighting to the background lighting. If the background is an image of Mt. Rainier in the afternoon sun, the KEY light on the performer needs to come from the same angle and be the same hardness and COLOR TEMPERATURE as the afternoon sun on the mountain.
2. Keep the blue of the backdrop from reflecting on the performer. Blue glow from the background, for instance, may tint edges of the talent's white skin or light-colored shirt. Solution: Stand the talent far away from the backdrop, or GEL the talent's BACK light with a color complimentary to the backdrop, in this case light amber, straw, or yellow. If you are using a green backdrop, the complimentary BACK light color would be red. The amber counteracts the blue tinge and keeps the talent's shoulders and shirt folds from disappearing into the background picture or looking grainy, semitransparent, or showing a border around the talent.
3. Avoid shiny objects like badges, jewelry, shiny buttons, watch crystals, etc. They are sometimes interpreted by the CHROMA KEY circuits as blue.
4. If the background has texture (i.e., a blue rectangle within a frame), avoid shadows on the background; they will appear as "not-blue" and will look like a black "ghost" in your picture. Lower or soften your set light so that shadows are eliminated, or redesign the set to remove the shadow.

The best backdrops for CHROMA KEYING would be smooth and featureless.

Lighting Motivation

So far we've aimed the lights from where we wanted them to make a presentable TV picture. But does the light make sense? If MODELING light comes from the side, place a table lamp somewhere in the right side of the picture (turned on with a low-wattage bulb), maybe in the background and out of focus. If the lamp is turned on, it had better not be casting a shadow on the wall behind it from the KEY light. Very gauche and highly unbelievable. And how about people supposedly lit by desk lamps? Where should their shadows be? Cast downward from an elevated KEY light, or high on the walls from a waist-height KEY light?

Someone seen near a day-lit window will need most of their light coming from the window side; have your KEY come from that side.

Outdoors in this solar system, the sun casts but one shadow. Don't let your artificial lights or reflectors make two.

People viewing computer screens, TV sets, or electronic instruments usually get some "instrument glow" on their faces.

Candles on a table give you the excuse to beam light straight down from above, illuminating the tabletop and floral arrangement. You can also beam some soft, reddish light on the actors' faces.

Actors carrying lanterns also have an excuse to have their faces lit.

Wave a tree branch in front of a blue light beamed through a window-shaped GOBO, and you have stormy moonlight from outdoors. A few flashes of white light make lightning. Dribble water over a sheet of glass, then shine hard light through it to project rain on the actors' faces or a back wall. All you need now is a scary knock at the door.

Mood Lighting and Special Effects

Now for some lighting trickery.

For the evil look, aim the lamp up from under the chin as shown in Figure 5–23. A weaker, low-angle light will give a more subtle effect. Lighting from below builds an unconscious suspense to the shot, perhaps making the performer look untrustworthy or devious.

For the soft, sexy, bedroom look, use reflected light only, either by aiming the instruments at white posterboards or white foamcore or by using lots of DIFFUSION material. Figure 5–12 showed the intimacy of soft, indirect lighting.

A large, soft KEY light near the camera lens erases wrinkles, making actors look younger. It also makes them look flat, like cardboard cutouts.

Hard, direct light accentuates textures and flaws in smooth surfaces. A hard KEY from a side angle will show lines in a face and promote the appearance of age. To get hard lighting, like that in Figure 5–24, avoid lamps with big reflectors or use the lamps at some distance from the subject. Use a typical KEY light as your FILL light. Have the lights hit the subject more from the side than from straight on in order to accent the shadows. The texture of a surface becomes more pronounced as the light skims along it from the edge.

FIGURE 5–23   Evil look with lamp from below.

Foam core   Stiff mounting board made of plastic foam sandwiched between paper.

Posterboard   Stiff cardboard sheet, usually white on one side.

Modeling light   Light aimed at the subject from the side, creating a white ridge of light to add dimension.

Dulling spray   Aerosol spray used by film and video professionals to reduce shine on objects.

*Lighting grid   Framework of pipes connected to the studio ceiling from which lights are hung.

*Dimmer remote control   Control panel with sliders to vary each dimmer circuit's power. The small panel connects via a multiwire cable to the actual large and heavy dimmer circuits. Those circuits feed power to the lighting grid.

Two-channel dimmer   Lighting dimmer with two sets of dimmer slider controls that allow you to set up one lighting arrangement on one set of sliders and another lighting arrangement on another.

*Preset   On multichannel dimmers, the dimmers can be set up (preset) for one lighting arrangement on one channel, and then the channel is turned off, essentially "storing" the lighting setup for use later when the channel is reactivated.

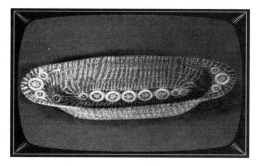
Soft, diffused lighting

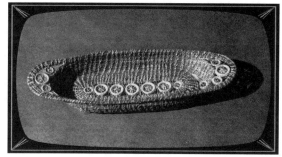
Hard, direct lighting from the side

FIGURE 5–24   Hard, direct lighting emphasizes texture.

With all the other lights in their normal positions, adding a MODELING light aimed from the side of the subject can further accent the dimensionality and texture of the subject. It is especially handy when something, such as a large hat or a prop, blocks the BACK light from doing its job.

Comedies demand upbeat, happy lighting. This is generally done by providing plenty of brightness and FILL lighting. Shadows are minimized, and backgrounds are fairly bright.

Mysteries and dramas are the opposite. Backgrounds are darker, shadows deeper, and overall illumination is lower. The scene may have dark areas and "puddles" of light through which the performers pass. Don't be afraid to allow your performers to pass into and out of the light, to move through shadows, or to be totally backlit, obscuring their features. A drama isn't a newscast; the viewer doesn't expect a perfectly lit view of a cat burglar. The shadows and vagaries improve the scene.

Lighting can sometimes provide a quick-and-dirty way to create the illusion that something is there when it really isn't. Are people supposed to be driving in a car in the evening? Park the car somewhere with a blank background (such as in an open area) and have somebody wave a light across the car (from front to back) once in a while to imply passing headlights.

Are folks chatting next to a fire? Wave some strips of fabric around in front of red or yellow lights so "flames" dance across their faces.

With imagination you can project plants, rain effects, explosions, rocket takeoffs, police car flashers, lighthouse beacons, colored spacecraft control panel reflections, green radar scope reflections, all kinds of things, on your performers and their backgrounds.

 Mini Review

- The best backgrounds for chroma key are smooth and evenly lit.
- When lamps are seen in the picture, consider whether the light is logical: Is it coming from a believable direction? Does it go with other things in the scene?
- Hard light from the side enhances texture and wrinkles. Soft light from nearer the camera smooths texture.
- News and comedies call for bright, evenly distributed lighting, while drama and mysteries need darker, uneven lighting with more pronounced shadows.

Are you trying to fake night? Darken the image by manually closing your camera's iris or adding a neutral density filter. Use lots of BACK light, deep shadows, and "puddles" of light for actors to move through. Turn on street lights, porch and window lights, and car headlights. Use blue lights (except for the BACK light, which can stay white) or attach a blue filter to your camera to change sunlight to blue "moonlight." If you don't have a blue lens filter, try shooting through a clean piece of blue GEL. Manually deactivate the camera's AUTO WHITE BALANCE so it doesn't try to correct for what you've done. Dress your actors in muted colors—your eyes sense colors poorly in "real" diminished light. Use hard KEY lights, GELLED blue if necessary, but remember the motivation of the light; if it's from a nearby lantern, the light needs to be reddish.

SPECIAL LIGHTING PROBLEMS

Shine

Glass, metal, or wet objects pose special lighting problems for television because of the reflection of the studio lights off shiny surfaces on the objects. To minimize these harsh, shiny spots, use soft indirect lighting. Perhaps a SCOOP light can act as the KEY light while another instrument aimed away from the subject and toward a white reflector can act as a FILL. If you have a white ceiling, try aiming all the lights at it for glare-free indirect lighting. Where appropriate, use SCRIMS or other semitransparent items to diffuse the light from the lamps. Make sure, however, that your diffusers don't melt or catch fire from the heat of the lamp.

Although this technique solves the shine problem and is appropriate for shooting mechanical objects up close, it is not likely to flatter performers. If both must occupy the same screen, compromises must be made. Can any of the shiny objects like watches or bracelets or shiny buttons be removed? Can the bows of a performer's glasses be raised half an inch to reflect studio lights downward? Can chrome mike stands be traded for ones with a dull finish? Can an actor's face or bald pate be powdered to reduce shine? If a shiny object plays an essential part in the scene, it may be dulled with DULLING SPRAY, a professionally made spray designed specifically to deshine reflective surfaces. Cornstarch, stale beer, milk, or even cloth tape can also be used to make shiny things dull. Unbuffed furniture polish works well on paneling, desks, and other flat reflective surfaces. And when you're done shooting, just buff everything back to a sparkle. Soap works well on small chrome surfaces; rub a little on and smear it around with a dampened finger.

Close-up shots of super-shiny items like silverware may call for extraordinary dulling efforts. Here, one may erect a tent made of a white sheet over the objects. Lights aimed at the tent from the outside will softly illuminate the area inside the tent. The TV camera can poke its lens in through a hole somewhere to shoot the results.

Eyeglass Shadows

Eyeglass shadows sometimes dance across your performer's cheeks like horizontal windshield wipers. If your performers can't switch to contact lenses or manage without their spectacles, then soften the KEY light (to soften the shadow) and/or lower its position as shown in Figure 5–25.

LIGHTING PROCEDURE

Where do you start?

1. First, figure out where the action will take place.
2. Figure out the desired camera angles.

KEY light is positioned too high, casting a shadow of eyeglasses across eyes.

KEY light lowered to six feet from floor hides eyeglass shadow.

FIGURE 5–25   Shadows caused by glasses.

3. Plan which lights you wish to use for KEY, FILL, BACK, and SET lighting. Place and aim these lights approximately.
4. Turn off the HOUSE LIGHTS (general room lights), darkening the room. These lights complicate matters, interfering with the next step.
5. One at a time, test out each light for proper placement, aiming, and focusing.
6. Now, switch on all four lights (KEY, FILL, BACK, and SET if used) for *one of your camera positions*. With your camera at the angle it will be shooting, display the results of your lighting arrangement. Watching a video monitor, adjust the four levels for the proper balance *on the TV.*
7. Find the next camera angle or stage position and start the process over.
8. Once all positions are lit, try them all at once and make final adjustments.

Most professionals, when lighting people, will light the faces first, starting with close-ups. If they can get the close-ups to look right, they figure everything else will fall into place. Also, face close-ups are scrutinized by viewers; lighting flaws will be noticed. Viewers are slightly less observant of medium and long shots—which doesn't mean you can be sloppy. It means first priority goes to the close-ups, and you make everything else work around them.

Mini Review

- Shiny objects may exceed the contrast ratio of the camera. Reduce the shine by using dulling spray or using soft, indirect light.
- When lighting a large area for several camera angles, adjust the key, fill, back, and set lights for one camera position. Turn them off and repeat the process with new lights for the next camera angle. When you have finished, turn on all the above lights and make your final adjustments.
- Light people's close-up face shots with extra care; lighting flaws are easily noticed on faces.

DIMMERS

A light DIMMER does just that, it dims lights. The DIMMER makes it very easy to adjust the relative brightness of lights and to fine-tune your LIGHTING RATIO.

You would use the DIMMER in steps 5, 6, and 8 in the preceding section as you raised or lowered the intensity of lights to get the effect you wanted in the TV monitor.

When working with color equipment, professionals avoid using DIMMERS because a dimmed tungsten light gives a reddish glow, affecting the COLOR TEMPERATURE of the scene. To *properly* change brightness in color studios, one either has to change to a lower-power lamp bulb, move the instrument farther away from the subject, place gray filters in front of the lamps, or place SCRIMS on the lamp fixtures.

Because DIMMERS are so convenient, however, most color studios use them anyway, up to a point, to vary the brightness of their lights. The lights can be dimmed about 10 percent without affecting the COLOR TEMPERATURE appreciably. From 10 percent to 30 percent, the light gets redder but is often good enough for all but your "best" productions or tightest close-ups. The redness really starts to show when you dim the light more than 30 percent. Since the color shift is most noticeable on faces, it is best to keep the face lights at nearly full brightness. The other lights can be dimmed freely.

There are little DIMMERS and big DIMMERS. The little ones are portable and plug into a heavy-duty wall outlet or are wired to a power main by an electrician. Each instrument is plugged into a socket on the DIMMER board as diagrammed in Figure 5–26. Notice that some of your lamps may have their own ON/OFF switches. When these are used with a DIMMER, they may be left in the *on* position (thus you avoid climbing a ladder to turn them on each time you use them). Next, the DIMMER's corresponding power switch is flipped *on* to activate the circuit. Then the dimming control is raised or lowered to adjust the brightness of the light.

Caution: Before plugging in a lamp, make sure the power switch for that circuit (or for all circuits if each circuit doesn't have its own power switch) is turned off. If the switch, the lamp, and the dimming controls are all on, giant sparks may jump around each socket as you plug in the lamp. Even bigger sparks may appear if you try to pull out a lamp plug while the power is still on. In short, power down the DIMMER before plugging anything in or unplugging it.

Some DIMMERS allow more than one light to be operated by a single circuit. Be sure not to exceed the power capacity of the unit by putting too many lamps on one circuit. For example, a small five-channel dimmer like the one in Figure 5–26 could be rated for 2,000 watts (abbreviated 2,000w or 2kw) per channel. That means that each DIMMER control can power no more than 2,000 watts of light, such as two 1,000-watt instruments, three 600-watt instruments, or one 2,000-watt instrument.

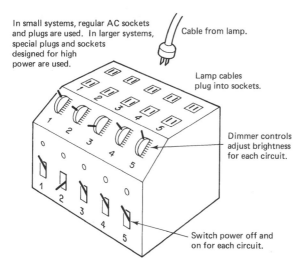

In small systems, regular AC sockets and plugs are used. In larger systems, special plugs and sockets designed for high power are used.

Cable from lamp.

Lamp cables plug into sockets.

Dimmer controls adjust brightness for each circuit.

Switch power off and on for each circuit.

FIGURE 5–26   Small DIMMER.

DIMMERS are generally designed for tungsten lights only. If you need to dim fluorescent or HMI lights, you will need special DIMMERS.

Larger DIMMERS designed for permanent studios place a DIMMER REMOTE CONTROL panel in the studio or control room where it is convenient to operate. The actual guts of the DIMMER are large, heavy, and bulky, and they sometimes buzz while in operation. This part of the mechanism is usually placed in another room, out of the way and out of earshot. This big DIMMER then feeds power to the LIGHTING GRID, which is a framework of pipes attached to the studio ceiling from which the lights are hung. The GRID contains the electrical outlets for each of the DIMMER circuits. Figure 5–27 diagrams the setup, and Figure 5–28 shows a professional DIMMER REMOTE CONTROL.

Some DIMMERS work like a mike mixer; individual dimming controls adjust brightness on individual circuits, while a MASTER dimming control adjusts all of them simultaneously.

The DIMMER in Figure 5–28 has TWO CHANNELS. The top bank of sliders controls one CHANNEL, while the middle bank controls the other. Normally, you may do all your lighting with just one CHANNEL, but sometimes you have a complicated lighting change during your show that doesn't afford you the time to diddle the DIMMERS. So what you do is set up your lighting change on one channel (this is called a PRESET) but do the rest of your show on the other channel. Here's an example:

You have a scene in which the electricity is supposed to go out in someone's living room. Naturally, you can't simply turn off the light, because then the TV cameras wouldn't be able to see. Generally, you create a darkness *effect* by aiming one hard (perhaps blue) light in from the side and using one BACK light on your performers. This will create dark shadows and the *look* of nighttime. Here's how the lighting setup would go:

1. Turn off the HOUSE LIGHTS.
2. Turn down all the DIMMERS and both SUBMASTER controls, and turn up the main MASTER.
3. On CHANNEL ONE, turn the SUBMASTER all the way up.

Submaster dimming control   Lighting control that fades up or down all the lights for a particular channel.

Patch bay   Like a telephone switchboard, a console of sockets leading to the studio lights and another set of sockets leading to the dimmer circuits. Connecting the two via patch cords allows various dimmers to activate certain lights.

*C-clamp   C-shaped clamp used to hang lighting instruments from the ceiling grid.

Patch cable   This special heavy-duty lighting cable plugs into the patch bay to carry current from the dimmer circuit to the grid circuit and studio lamp.

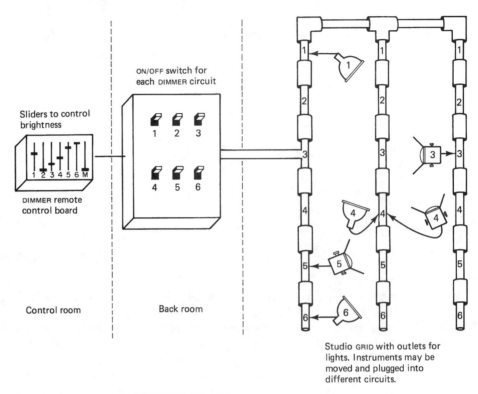

FIGURE 5–27 Permanent DIMMER setup.

4. Next, turn up the DIMMER controls for the desired side light and BACK light for the "dark room" scene. Once adjusted, fade the CHANNEL ONE SUBMASTER all the way down.
5. Turn up the CHANNEL TWO SUBMASTER all the way.
6. Adjust the remaining DIMMERs for the normal room lighting setup.
7. Start your show by fading up the CHANNEL TWO SUBMASTER, which will light the whole set normally.

REMOTE CONTROL (usually in the studio or control room)

FIGURE 5–28 DIMMER and REMOTE CONTROL.

8. When the show reaches the point where the lights go out, you quickly fade up the CHANNEL ONE SUBMASTER while simultaneously fading down the CHANNEL TWO SUBMASTER.

9. If later in the scene the lights come back on again, you reverse the process, dimming ONE while bringing up TWO.

Thus, by moving two faders, all the lights will change to the brightness you PRESET them to be. It saves you from adjusting four or five knobs all at once as the scene lighting changes. Larger DIMMERS may have three or more PRESETS, and you might be able to switch from one to another with just one press of a button. Some even have "memories" that allow you to program in dozens of lighting setups and go from one to another with just the press of one button.

Speaking of memories, unless you have a good one, take note of your DIMMER settings and lamp positions. You may need to do a similar show in a month, or may need to reshoot part of this one in a week. Any lighting changes will be seen as a *continuity* error when the new scenes are edited with the old ones.

The DIMMER in Figure 5–28 also has switches and sliders across the bottom to permit selected controls to work independently from the MASTER. Thus, you could keep selected lights *on* even while the MASTER dimmer is turned off. Here's how they might be handy:

Say you had only a ONE-CHANNEL DIMMER board (or a TWO-CHANNEL unit where the second channel was already occupied) and you wanted to create the effect described earlier. You could switch the BACK light and side light *on* independently and leave them on for the entire scene. You'd set up the rest of the lights on the DIMMERS. Before the blackout scene occurred, *all* the lights would be on, but the "nighttime" lights would be drowned out by the "normal" lights. However, when the blackout occurred, you would dim the MASTER, which would take out all the lights but the two independent ones, which would now comprise your "nighttime" scene. Thus, you did the whole job with just one CHANNEL.

Larger, more professional DIMMER systems have PATCH BAYS, which are like telephone operator switchboards. Instead of climbing a ladder to plug a fixture into this GRID outlet or that, you would plug each lighting instrument into a numbered socket in the GRID. Meanwhile, each DIMMER circuit controls a series of sockets in the PATCH BAY. By connecting a lighting patch cord between one DIMMER circuit and one GRID outlet, you connect one light to that circuit. You can do this conveniently for a large number of lights until you have filled your PATCH BAY with a spaghetti of PATCHES. Figure 5–29 diagrams the process.

 Mini Review

- Dimming a light more than 30 percent will change its color temperature noticeably.
- Before connecting or disconnecting a lamp, make sure the power for that circuit is turned off.
- Always turn out the house lights when adjusting your studio lighting.
- A dimmer with presets, multiple channels, or memories allows you to set up the lighting brightnesses on that dimmer for several scenes, making it easy for you to go from one lighting arrangement to another.
- The lighting grid and patch bays allow you to connect any light to any dimmer control.

It is handy to label the number of each GRID circuit on its corresponding PATCH cable; thus, you know what you're connecting where. It wouldn't help much to label the instrument number on each PATCH cable because the instruments move around from circuit to circuit as you connect them in dif-

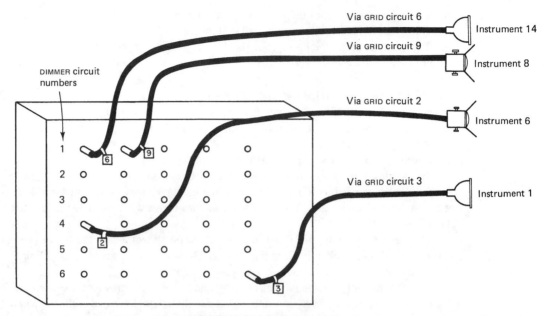

FIGURE 5–29 Lighting PATCH BAY.

ferent places on the GRID. Put another way, when standing in the studio and looking up at the lighting instruments, you don't care what the number of the lighting instrument is as much as you care what circuit it is going into. If you want to illuminate a certain light, you find out its circuit number and then trace it back to find out which DIMMER control that circuit is connected to. Then turning up that DIMMER should turn on that light.

As before, several instruments can be plugged into the same dimming circuit, but you must always be careful not to overload the circuit. It is wise to know the capacity of each circuit in your dimmer system.

LIGHTING HARDWARE

Lighting Grid

In a studio, the lights must hang from something. Often this something is a combination of criss-crossed pipes suspended from the ceiling and forming the LIGHTING GRID (Figure 5–30). The lighting instruments are connected to C-CLAMPS (Figure 5–31), which attach to the GRID pipes throughout the

---

Antigravity hangers Spring-loaded mechanisms between the lights and the grid to allow the lights to be individually lowered (and stay put at various heights) simply by pulling them down or pushing them up.

*Safety cord Loop of chain, cable, or rope that fastens loosely around the lamp and the grid pipe and stops the lamp from falling if its C-clamp becomes undone.

Amp (or ampere) A measure of the volume of electrical cur-rent. Institutional circuits are usually rated for 20A (amps). Electric wires may get hot as this number is approached.

Volt A measure of electrical pressure. In the United States, 120 V (volts) is the standard available from common electrical outlets in homes or institutions.

*Watt A measure of electrical power. Amps times volts equals watts. A studio light may use 1,000 W (watts). Institutional wiring may handle 2,400 watts per circuit.

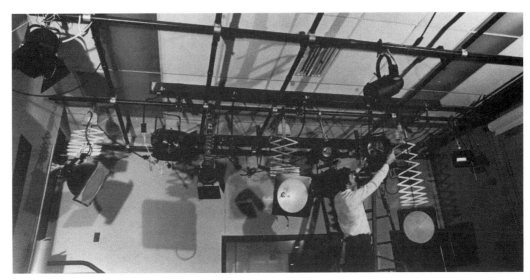

FIGURE 5–30 LIGHTING GRID.

studio. Sometimes the pipes have electric wires in them and sockets where the pipes intersect. Other systems may have separate wiring conduit, and small power sockets will hang down from it spaced every three feet or so. There are usually several sockets for every DIMMER circuit. The lamps may be plugged into these sockets, with care taken not to exceed the power rating of any one circuit by running too many lamps from it.

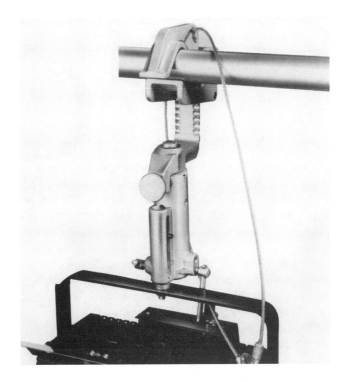

FIGURE 5–31 C-CLAMP for hanging lights from a pipe GRID (Courtesy Quality/Universal).

Make sure the power is off before connecting or disconnecting a studio light.

FIGURE 5–32   Studio lighting plugs and sockets.

Lighting Connectors

Professional lighting instruments use special heavy-duty plugs and wire like those shown in Figure 5–32. Just line up the pins and plug them in. To remove the plugs, just pull the connectors straight apart.

Antigravity Hangers

No, an ANTIGRAVITY HANGER has nothing to do with alien spacecraft hidden at an air force base in Roswell, New Mexico. It is a counterbalance to help you raise and lower lights hanging from the grid. Figure 5–33 shows examples.

CARE OF LAMPS

Fixtures Get Hot

And boy, do they! They make as much heat as a toaster and can fricassee your fingers if you don't stay clear. Keep the instrument away from anything combustible or meltable. Make sure that the power cord for the fixture isn't draped over the instrument (it could melt). Watch where the lamp is aimed. You can feel the heat of a 1,000-watt lamp from ten feet away, so you can imagine how hot it gets right in front of it. For instance, aiming the lamp at a wall or curtain one foot away or so could start a fire in a matter of minutes.

When handling instruments, let them cool before attempting to change bulbs or SCRIMS (unless you go around wearing asbestos gloves). Do not attempt to store instruments until they have cooled adequately. Don't be too surprised if the paint burns off the BARN DOORS sometimes; it doesn't look pretty, but it's common wear and tear.

Try to "warm up" large lighting instruments for a moment at reduced power before dimming up to full power. This prolongs bulb life and reduces the chance of cracking the glass on a cold FRESNEL lens.

FIGURE 5–33 ANTIGRAVITY HANGERS.

Fixtures get hot.

Moving Lamps

It's okay to aim a light while it is lit, but do not jar, shake, bump, or walk with a lamp while it is lit. The filament in the light bulb is white-hot and *extremely* fragile. When the lamp is not glowing, the filament is solid again and is fairly rugged. When you turn off a lamp, always let it cool for a few seconds before moving it. Yes, a few seconds is all that is necessary.

Whenever you attach a light to the GRID, *always connect the* SAFETY CORD (review Figure 5–31— you can see it wrapped around the light fixture and the GRID PIPE). Sometimes the frequent aiming, turning, and moving of a lighting instrument will loosen the mount so that it is hanging by only a whisker. Attaching the SAFETY CORD adds one extra measure of security, so that if the lamp *does* come loose, it doesn't bonk somebody on the head or, worse yet, smash a camera. Some SAFETY CORDS are made of rope, others of wire with a spring-loaded clip, while others might be chain. For lamps with long ANTIGRAVITY HANGERS, you should use one SAFETY CORD to connect the C-CLAMP to the GRID and another to connect the lighting instrument to the bottom of the ANTIGRAVITY HANGER.

Changing Bulbs

You can assume that a light bulb has burned out when the lamp stops working. To confirm that the bulb has expired, first *turn off the power to the instrument.* Take a close look at the bulb. If it has a big bulge, if it is blackened, if it is cloudy inside, or if the filament is clearly broken, the bulb is shot. If none of the preceding is true, perhaps the bulb is good and the instrument, switch, DIMMER, cable, or something else is misconnected or defective.

Bulbs last between ten and five hundred hours, depending on the manufacturer and type. When lamps are dimmed, they last much longer than they would at full brightness.

Never touch a good bulb with your fingers, or it won't be much good anymore. Traces of oil from your fingers can chemically change the glass when the bulb heats up. The glass devitrifies and fails right where the fingerprints were. Handle bulbs with a clean cloth, gloves, or with the packing that came with the bulb.

Replace bulbs with exactly the same type of bulb or its equivalent. Some fixtures can take bulbs of different power and brightness. *Do not exceed the power rating of the instrument.* Removing a 600-watt bulb from a fixture designed for a 600-watt bulb and putting in a 2,000-watt bulb will give you more light—until the fixture and its wiring self-cremate.

To help you find a replacement bulb, hang onto the one you just took out of the lamp. If you examine its base, it will probably have a three-letter code that designates an exact replacement for the bulb. Bulb boxes usually have this three-letter code emblazoned on them as well as other details such as wattage. Some lighting fixtures have a tag on them telling the bulb type appropriate for the fixture.

Power Requirements

AMPS times VOLTS equals WATTS. Homes and schools run on 120 VOLTS, so if a circuit is good for 15 AMPS (as is typical in homes), then you may use up to $15 \times 120 = 1,800$ WATTS of power on that circuit. If a circuit is rated at 20 AMPS (schools and businesses usually are), then you can use $20 \times 120 = 2,400$ WATTS. In short, the house current you get from the wall socket in your home is good for about 1,800 WATTS. Institutional electrical outlets can sustain about 2,400 WATTS. So how many 1,000-WATT lamps can you use at home without blowing a fuse or burning the house down?

Before turning on any light, check to see what else is on the same circuit and is also using power. Check also to make sure that you aren't running several lights off one extension cord. An extension cord rated for 15 AMPS (a label on it may say 15A at 120V, meaning that it can take 15 AMPS of electrical current) can carry only 1,800 watts of power. Even if you are working in a school whose outlets are rated for 20 amps (2,400 watts), your extension cord may safely handle only 1,800 watts.

Once you are set up for a remote production and are satisfied that you aren't overburdening the wiring, you're ready to go. Switch the lights on *one at a time* rather than all at once because they use abnormally high amounts of power at the moment when they are just lighting up. Switching all the lights on at once could cause a "surge" of power and blow a fuse. If you switch the lights on one at a time, the smaller surges are spaced out and are less likely to overburden the wiring.

Mini Review

- Let lighting fixtures cool before handling them. Do not transport a lamp while it is lit.
- When moving or attaching lights to a grid, make sure you've connected the safety cord to keep the lamp from falling on someone.
- Turn off the power to the instrument before changing bulbs or connecting or unplugging a lamp.
- Never touch a studio bulb with your fingers.
- When connecting lights, don't exceed the power rating for your extension cord or electrical outlet.

---

6 AUDIO

Half of video is audio, but it never seems to get the attention it deserves. Turn off the picture on your TV set, and the sound will give you a very good idea of what is going on. Turn off the sound, however, and the picture will leave you puzzled.

Television production uses much the same sound equipment and techniques that are used in radio and other audio enterprises. The big difference is that television audio is harder to do. Where radio people can *read* scripts into *nearby* microphones in *soundproof rooms*, television people often have to *memorize* their lines and speak them into *hidden* microphones in a neat-looking environment, on a studio set, or out in the field.

THE BASICS

The microphone picks up sound vibrations and turns them into tiny electrical signals that travel down a wire into a VCR or mixer. The AUDIO LEVEL CONTROL on the mixer or on the VCR (if it has one) allows you to adjust the volume of the sound being recorded. Portable and home VCRs have AUTOMATIC AUDIO LEVEL or AUTOMATIC GAIN CONTROLS (AGC) that adjust themselves.

What kind of microphone should you use? Any kind that has a plug that fits the VCR or mixer will probably work. Try it. You can't hurt anything by trying it. If the plug doesn't fit the device, use an ADAPTER (Figure 2–11) to make it fit. If the mike is designed to hang around the neck or clip to a lapel but the performer wants to hold it or put it on a stand, it will still work. The mike will still pick up sound. If the mike is designated for stand use but the performer wants it to hang around his or her neck, get some string and tie the mike around his or her neck. It will still work.

---

*Mixer Device used to combine audio signals and control their volume.

Audio level control A volume control. Adjusts sound recording loudness on VCRs.

Automatic gain control (AGC) Electronic circuit that automatically adjusts the loudness of a recording.

*Adapter A connector that allows one type of plug to fit into another type of socket.

Condenser A sound-sensing component of a condenser microphone.

Condenser microphone A professional type of microphone that senses sound with a condenser. It requires an external power supply for operation.

*Electret condenser microphone An industrial/professional microphone that senses sound with a condenser. It requires a battery for operation.

*Dynamic microphone A microphone that requires no power in order to operate and senses sound via a coil of wire.

*Pressure zone microphone (PZM) Microphone mounted on a flat plate. It senses sound reflected from the plate.

Stereo microphone Microphone that "hears" in two directions and sends out two separate audio signals to a stereo recorder.

Musical recording.

Camcorders have built-in microphones that automatically pick up the sound as you make a recording. Although these built-in microphones are handy, they all have one flaw. If the camera is eight feet from the performer, then your microphone is also eight feet from the performer and will pick up room echoes and noises galore. For this reason, a separate microphone is often a better way to catch the words of your performer; the mike stays near the talent's mouth and gets good sound, while the camera stays at some distance for a flexibility of shots.

These are the basic basics of audio. With them you will be successful at recording the sounds you want most of the time. Audio is somewhat forgiving. Even if not done perfectly, it is still frequently usable.

The rest of this chapter is dedicated to helping you make the sound perfectly right. If your sound is poor, it will distract the viewers from the message. If the sound is mediocre, the entire presentation

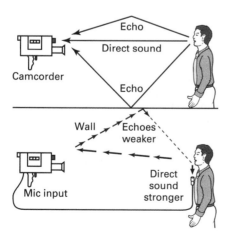

Camcorder mike vs close miking.

will appear amateurish and will leave the impression of sloppy workmanship. Professional audio is like paint on a car. The car drives okay without it, but that extra shine is what turns people's heads. How impressive do you want your show to be? Our quest is for clean, crisp, high-fidelity sound without echoes, buzz, hum, hiss, distortion, or other unwanted noises. Once we have it *technically* right, we can focus on making the sound *interesting* and creative.

THE MICROPHONE

How a Microphone Works

Sound vibrates a diaphragm inside the microphone, making a tiny electrical signal that passes down the mike cable. Many things can be done to that signal before it gets to its destination. Nearly all these things are electrical in nature.

Kinds of Microphones

The words CONDENSER and DYNAMIC refer to what's inside the microphone that makes it work. These components contribute to the microphone's characteristics: its fidelity, its sensitivity, its ruggedness, and its cost.

The words OMNIDIRECTIONAL, CARDIOID, UNIDIRECTIONAL, and BIDIRECTIONAL describe in which direction(s) the microphone is designed to "hear." You'll see later how the various kinds of microphones are selected for different situations, but first review Figure 2–10 and then browse through Tables 6–1 through 6–4 to become more familiar with audio lingo. These words are important and will be used throughout the rest of this chapter.

 Mini Review

- Keeping the mike close to the talent's mouth records the talent's voice clearly while rejecting room echo and other background noise.
- Although nearly any microphone will work in most any situation, matching the right mike to the task will yield better sound.
- Condenser and dynamic describe two technologies that microphones use to change sound into audio signals.
- Omnidirectional, cardioid, unidirectional, and bidirectional describe the directions in which the microphone "hears" best.

TABLE 6–1   How Microphones Produce their Signals

Condenser microphone A microphone that uses a condenser (a small electrical component) to create the signal. One of the standard microphones in the broadcast industry, it has good sensitivity to a wide range of sound volume and pitch. Disadvantages include fragility, expense, and the fact that this particular kind of microphone operates only with batteries or with some external power supply.

Electret condenser microphone An improved version of the condenser microphone that needs only a tiny power supply to operate. Used alone or built into portable TV cameras, this microphone gives good sensitivity to a wide range of sound volume and pitch and gives especially clear voice reproduction. Disadvantages include fragility (especially to heat and dampness) and the occasional need to replace the small battery that powers the microphone circuit.

Dynamic microphone Lacks the fidelity of the condenser microphone but is good enough for most video use. This frequently used microphone is rugged and quite trouble-free. Its name comes from the fact that its signal is generated by a moving (hence the word *dynamic*) coil of wire and a magnet.

TABLE 6–2   Pickup Patterns—the Directions in Which Microphones Hear Best

Omnidirectional microphone Can hear in all directions regardless of where it is aimed.

Cardioid microphone Can hear very well in front of it, medium well to the side of it, and hardly at all in back of it.

Directional or unidirectional microphone Can hear very well in front of it and hardly at all anywhere else.

Shotgun microphone A very unidirectional microphone that looks like a shotgun barrel.

Bidirectional microphone Can hear well in only two directions: front and back.

PZM microphone Can hear only to one side of it.

Dynamic Microphone.   Most common among the semiprofessional and professional microphones is the DYNAMIC microphone (Figure 6–1). DYNAMIC microphones are quite rugged and reliable, require no special power supply or batteries, and respond to a wide range of audio frequencies. They are usable under severe temperature and humidity conditions. They generally cost from $50 to $300, depending on their quality. DYNAMIC mikes do tend to pick up hum from nearby magnetic fields, like motors and electronic devices.

DYNAMIC microphones can be made with OMNIDIRECTIONAL, CARDIOID, or UNIDIRECTIONAL pickup patterns. They can be peanut-sized LAVALIER types, or larger hand-held types, or giant SHOTGUN types designed to be hung from microphone BOOMS.

If your mike cables have to be more than a hundred feet in length, you will probably find DYNAMIC mikes too weak to produce an adequate signal. CONDENSER mikes will usually do the job.

Condenser Microphone.   CONDENSER microphones (Figure 6–2) have an extremely wide frequency response (pick up a wide range of audio frequencies) and are excellent for voice and music. They can be used indoors or outdoors, but extremes in temperature and humidity may hurt the microphone. Treat them gently, even when turned off.

CONDENSER mikes require an external power supply to make them work and may cost $400 to $600. Some have a modular design, allowing you to attach different "heads" to the "body" of the microphone, making it CARDIOID or SHOTGUN or especially sensitive to certain frequencies.

Electret Condenser Microphone.   ELECTRET CONDENSER microphones (Figure 6–3) have good frequency response, are much cheaper than CONDENSER microphones, and can be made very tiny. Their smallness makes them excellent choices for TIE CLIP or LAPEL microphones, which should be unobtrusive or nearly invisible.

Like the CONDENSER microphone, they require a power supply, but a tiny battery may be all that is needed. ELECTRET CONDENSER mikes generally cost $35 to $250, which makes them just the right

TABLE 6–3   Microphone Cables

Unbalanced line An audio cable that has two conductors only. It has a center wire with a braided shield (the second wire) surrounding it. At the end of the cable is a two-conductor plug, such as an RCA, mini, phono, or phone plug (examples were shown in Figure 2–10). This method of carrying audio is usually found on inexpensive equipment and usually has short cables.

Balanced line An audio cable with three conductors (two center wires plus a braided shield). It terminates with a three-pin plug such as an XLR or cannon plug (also shown in Figure 2–10). This kind of wire is usually used with expensive or professional equipment. The balanced line is extremely impervious to extraneous electrical interference; or put another way, unwanted buzzes and hums don't sneak onto your recording.

TABLE 6–4   Audio Plugs and Sockets

Cannon, or XLR plug Shown in Figure 2–10, this three-pin plug is used with professional audio equipment using balanced lines.

Mini, phono, RCA, phone Popular types of audio plugs used with unbalanced lines. Phone plugs are very durable and are preferred in educational and institutional settings. Mini plugs are flimsier than their bigger brothers but are small and are used on miniature audio and video gear.

---

price for the industrial market. They can have an OMNIDIRECTIONAL, CARDIOID, or UNIDIRECTIONAL pickup pattern.

Although their sound fidelity is better than all but the most expensive DYNAMIC mikes, ELECTRET CONDENSER mikes are not quite as rugged. They should not be left in the sun, heat, or high humidity, but with a little care, they can be used freely outdoors.

Pressure Zone Microphone.   The PRESSURE ZONE MICROPHONE (or PZM, Figure 6–4) is quite different from the others. It usually sits on a desk or flat surface, which acts to reflect the sound waves into the microphone. It can also be hung with a flat plate attached to it for funneling the sound.

PZMs have a hemispheric pickup pattern (they listen to everything on the top side of them), which makes them ideal for picking up large group discussions and audience reactions. For instance, a PZM sitting in the middle of a table will pick up the voices of all the people sitting around the table. Unfortunately, the PZM also will pick up the sounds of finger tapping and paper rustling and the thumps of people knocking their knees against the table legs. Placing a thin rubber cushion or mouse pad under the mike may help.

A PZM mounted on a wall in a room will nicely pick up all the sounds in the room. Lay one on a theater stage six feet in front of a singer or speechmaker, and you'll get surprisingly good sound without having a mike appear in the picture.

Stereo Microphone.   To pick up stereophonic sound, you can use two microphones. Sometimes it's handier to use a single STEREO microphone, which is actually two microphones built onto the

Sennheiser MD 421 II professional microphone used for music and voices

FIGURE 6–1 DYNAMIC microphone (Courtesy of Sennheiser).

FIGURE 6–2 CONDENSER microphone (Courtesy of Quality/Universal).

same body so that it looks like a single microphone. Half the microphone listens in one direction and sends the signal to the left channel through a stereo plug at the other end. The other half sends its signal out through another conductor on the same plug.

STEREO microphones are very handy for amateur stereo recording but are not popular among professionals because excellent stereo sound requires careful microphone placement, where one micro-

Hand-held (Courtesy of Quality/Universal)

FIGURE 6–3 ELECTRET CONDENSER microphones.

---

*Omnidirectional Microphone that senses sound from all directions equally.

*Pickup pattern The areas in which a microphone picks up the best sound. Also, a diagram depicting a microphone's sensitivity in different directions.

*Cardioid microphone Mike that senses sound in front of it more than to the sides. It senses little sound to its rear.

Directional microphone Microphone that needs to be "aimed" because it is more sensitive in one direction than another.

Unidirectional microphone Mike that is sensitive in the direction it is pointed and insensitive in other directions.

*Shotgun microphone Microphone shaped like a gun barrel that "listens" only in the direction in which it is aimed.

Bidirectional microphone Mike that senses sound both in front of and behind it.

Proximity effect Thunderous bass boost heard when people speak or instruments are played too near the face of a directional microphone.

Hypercardioid, or supercardioid, microphone Very unidirectional and slightly cardioid microphone.

FIGURE 6–4   PRESSURE ZONE MICRO-PHONE (PZM) (Courtesy of Radio Shack).

phone goes one place while the other microphone goes another. Having them tied together on the same body is considered a compromise.

 Mini Review

- Condenser and electret condenser microphones must be treated gently, and they abhor humidity and temperature extremes.
- Electret condenser microphones require a battery and can be tiny, making them excellent choices for unobtrusive lapel microphones.
- The PZM mike excels at picking up conversations around a table or above a stage.

Pickup Patterns

No, a PICKUP PATTERN has nothing to do with how men introduce themselves to ladies in bars. Microphones are designed to listen in various directions. Sometimes you want them to work like your ears and listen in all directions equally. Sometimes you want them to be like binoculars and listen in only one direction, rejecting noises from behind and to the side. There are four basic microphone pickup patterns: OMNIDIRECTIONAL (listens in all directions), DIRECTIONAL (listens in one direction), CARDIOID (listens mostly in one direction but a little to the sides), and BIDIRECTIONAL (listens in two directions). Figure 6–5 diagrams the different microphone pickup patterns.

Omnidirectional.   OMNIDIRECTIONAL microphones are equally sensitive to sound from all directions. No microphone is perfectly OMNIDIRECTIONAL, because the body of the microphone interferes with sound reception from the rear. OMNIS are less expensive than their DIRECTIONAL brothers and therefore are the type usually built into home camcorders.

OMNIS are excellent for close work. If a speaker turns his or her face to the side or the microphone moves a little, the sound is relatively unchanged because the microphone can "listen" in all directions. This becomes a disadvantage when the microphone is used to pick up a distant sound because the microphone will hear the room echoes and offstage sounds as well as the sound of your performer.

Directional.   DIRECTIONAL is a fairly general term indicating that a microphone has greater sensitivity in one direction than it does in others. DIRECTIONAL microphones are good for picking up small groups of people where you want all of them to be heard but you don't want to hear room

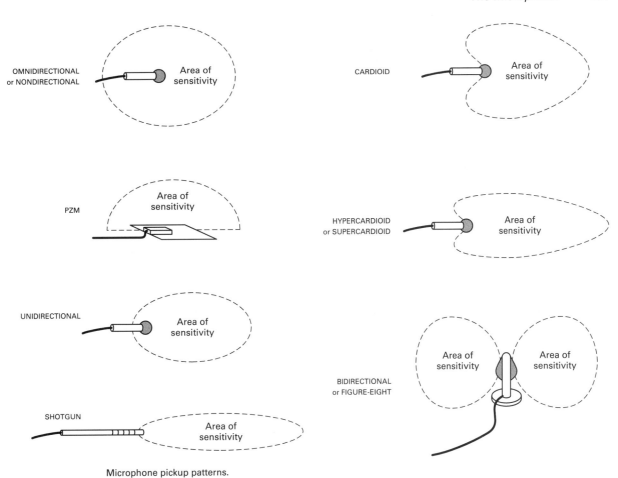

Microphone pickup patterns.

FIGURE 6–5 Microphone PICKUP PATTERNS.

echoes and other background sounds. DIRECTIONAL microphones have also been used on podiums where they pick up the sound of the person speaking but reject the sound of the audience or any loud-speakers in the audience area.

All DIRECTIONAL microphones exhibit the PROXIMITY EFFECT; if you speak too close to the microphone, it boosts the bass in your voice thunderously. It also makes the letters *b, p,* and *t* sound like bombs bursting in air. OMNIDIRECTIONAL mikes don't exhibit this problem until you are about an inch from the mike. Thus, performers need to stay a foot or so away from their DIRECTIONAL mikes to avoid consonant bombardment.

Unidirectional. UNIDIRECTIONAL microphones are very sensitive in the direction they are pointed and are insensitive to the sides and rear. They make it possible to move the microphone a little farther from the talent (perhaps getting the mike out of the picture) yet still pick up the sound of the talent loud and clear. They also reject room echoes. They are so sensitive that when used close to a person speaking, if the microphone is turned slightly away from the person, or the person moves from the center of the microphone's domain, or the person turns to the side and speaks, the volume of their voice will drop noticeably. UNIDIRECTIONAL mikes can be used up close only if your talent is tied down and has a stiff neck.

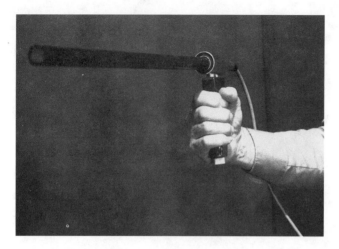

FIGURE 6–6   SHOTGUN microphone with vibration-absorbing handle.

Shotgun.   Figure 6–6 shows a SHOTGUN microphone. You can see how it gets its name. It is a very UNIDIRECTIONAL microphone, rejecting all sounds except those coming from where it's pointed. These microphones are especially useful in noisy environments and in situations where you have to pick up sound from quite some distance away.

Short ones (about a foot long) are not as directional as long ones (several feet in length). You can sometimes see a very long shotgun mike at the rear of the room during presidential press conferences.

SHOTGUN microphones are so effective at rejecting off-center sounds that accurate aiming becomes a constant hassle. If a person moves, or if two people are speaking, the SHOTGUN microphone has to be aimed precisely at the speaker's face or else he or she may not be heard at all.

Cardioid.   The CARDIOID microphone gets this name from its heart-shaped pickup pattern (review Figure 6–5). These microphones are very popular among professionals. The CARDIOID pattern allows the talent to work at a greater distance from the microphone without having the mike pick up too many room echoes. Yet the microphone allows the talent to move his or her face or the microphone a little without losing that much sound volume. Thus, microphone aiming is not as critical as with UNIDIRECTIONAL mikes.

CARDIOIDS are very insensitive out their rears, making them good for cutting out audience or crowd sounds, machine sounds, room echoes, or sounds from loudspeakers in the room.

One disadvantage of some CARDIOID mikes is that the frequency response at the center of the microphone's pattern is a little different from the frequency response at the side. Thus, if a person turns his or her head or the mike while speaking into it, some of the low frequencies may be lost.

Microphones generally don't have the words CARDIOID, OMNIDIRECTIONAL, or UNIDIRECTIONAL printed on them. CARDIOIDS physically look pretty much like OMNIS. People who work with audio generally memorize the company and model numbers of the various microphones in order to tell them apart, and they will seek an "Electro-Voice RE-16" if they want an OMNIDIRECTIONAL mike or perhaps ask for a "Sure SM58" if they want a CARDIOID. One hint to a mike's directionality: If it has vents down the neck of the mike, it's DIRECTIONAL. If it's solid, its probably OMNI. Lapel mikes, because they are always near the talent's mouth, are almost always OMNIS.

Hypercardioid or Supercardioid.   HYPERCARDIOID and SUPERCARDIOID mikes are more sensitive in one direction than their brothers the CARDIOID mikes. You might think of them as a cross between UNIDIRECTIONAL and CARDIOID. They are popular for studio BOOMS, FISHPOLES (described shortly), sports, and field production.

Bidirectional.   BIDIRECTIONAL or FIGURE-8 or BIPOLAR microphones listen in two directions. The term FIGURE-8 comes from the shape of the pickup pattern (review Figure 6–5).

BIDIRECTIONAL mikes are quite rare outside the professional studios. The BIDIRECTIONAL pattern is most useful when you have a host seated at a desk and a guest opposite the host. The same microphone can pick up both.

 **Mini Review**

- To pick up the "wanted" sounds while reducing "unwanted" sounds, match the microphone's pickup pattern to the recording situation.
- Directional microphones are good at rejecting background noise and echoes, and they are sensitive primarily in the direction they are aimed. This directionality is especially true of the shotgun mike.
- Directional microphones exaggerate bass and breath sounds when the talent gets too close to them, yet they may yield weak sound if the talent turns away from them.

Balanced and Unbalanced Lines

BALANCED and UNBALANCED LINES are two ways the mike cable can carry the signal to its destination. The higher-quality BALANCED LINE has two conductors inside a metal shield, making a total of three wires for the cable. The plug at the end of such a cable would have to have three pins, like the XLR connector shown in Figure 2–10. BALANCED LINES can carry signals a long distance (over fifty feet) yet will pick up very little stray electrical interference (called "noise"). Most professional and industrial audio equipment and the higher-quality VCRs use BALANCED LINES.

Home and semiprofessional audio equipment and home VCRs are designed for UNBALANCED LINES. These cables have only one conductor inside a woven shield, making the cables thinner than their BALANCED counterparts. Two-conductor plugs like the MINI, PHONE, and RCA plugs shown in Figure 2–10 go with UNBALANCED LINES. UNBALANCED LINES work okay between electronic devices that make strong signals, like CD players and tape decks, as long as the wires are kept short (under six feet or so).

The mikes, the plugs, and the wires for UNBALANCED systems are inexpensive and simple to maintain. Since many videographers generally work close to their VCRs, use the mediocre mikes on their camcorders, play back their sounds through the tiny speakers on portable TVs, and usually aren't very discriminating about their sound anyway, UNBALANCED LINES are often good enough for these users.

Professionals generally have made the investment in good mikes, cables, mixers, and other audio equipment, so by popular demand, the pro equipment accepts signals from BALANCED LINES.

---

*Balanced lines   An audio cable with three wires, two inside a shield. Corresponding connectors have three prongs.

*Unbalanced lines   An audio cable with two wires, one of which is a shield surrounding the other.

*Cannon, or XLR, plug   Three-prong audio plug used with balanced lines.

*Mini plug Tiny ($\frac{1}{8}$″ thick) plug used mostly on portable audio equipment having unbalanced lines.

*Phono, or RCA, plug   Plug commonly used to connect consumer audio components using unbalanced lines.

*Phone plug   Sturdy $\frac{1}{4}$″ thick plug used on school AV equipment, headphones, electric guitars, and other audio gear having unbalanced lines.

Transformer   Part of an audio adapter that changes balanced lines to unbalanced, and vice-versa.

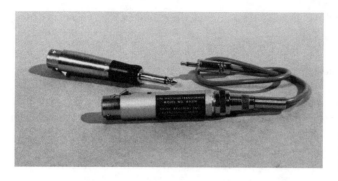

FIGURE 6–7 Audio IMPEDANCE MATCHING TRANSFORMERS may also adapt from BALANCED LINES to UNBALANCED.

So what do you do if your mike is BALANCED and your VCR is not? As I'm sure you've guessed by now, there are ADAPTERS that change BALANCED into UNBALANCED LINES and vice versa. To change a BALANCED microphone line into an UNBALANCED LINE for a small VCR, you would use an ADAPTER that had a three-pronged XLR socket at one end and perhaps a PHONE plug or MINI plug at the other. Inside the ADAPTER is a tiny TRANSFORMER that converts one system into the other. Figure 6–7 shows such an ADAPTER.

 Mini Review

- Use balanced lines (with XLR connectors) to conduct audio signals long distances with the least noise and other interference.
- Unbalanced lines are okay for carrying audio signals between machines that are close together.
- An audio transformer adapts unbalanced lines to balanced ones and vice versa.

Frequency Response

FREQUENCY RESPONSE describes the fidelity of a microphone, its ability to pick up high tones and low tones. A mike's FREQUENCY RESPONSE is described by the number of vibrations per second that the microphone can reproduce. Lower-priced industrial microphones used by school audiovisual centers generally have a FREQUENCY RESPONSE of 80–12kHz (80 to 12,000 vibrations per second). Better professional mikes will give a *wider* FREQUENCY RESPONSE of 50–15kHz. True high fidelity requires a frequency range of 20–20kHz. Only hi-fi VCRs can reproduce this FREQUENCY RESPONSE. Also, only young healthy people can hear this wide range of frequencies. Most of us hear only in the 50–15kHz range, which is what most industrial VCRs can reproduce.

A microphone should be as sensitive to one frequency as it is to another. Otherwise, when recording music, the bassoon will sound louder than it is supposed to, and the flute might hardly be

---

Frequency response   The ability of a device to pick up high tones (high audio frequencies) as well as low tones equally well. For audio, the perfect frequency response would be 20Hz to 20kHz, the full range of human hearing.

Flat frequency response   Sensitive to all sound pitches equally.

Lavalier microphone   A small mike hung by a string around the performer's neck.

Lapel, or tie clip, microphone   A tiny mike that can be attached to the performer's lapel or tie.

Low cut filter   An audio circuit, often built into mixers and mikes, that reduces low tones from a sound signal.

Sound coloration   The characteristic tone a microphone gives to the sounds it picks up.

audible. This evenhanded sound reproduction is called a FLAT FREQUENCY RESPONSE and is preferred for music recording.

Microphones used primarily for voice, such as LAVALIERS, have an uneven FREQUENCY RESPONSE. They're made that way on purpose in order to emphasize the clarity of voice sounds while reducing undesirable low tones such as the rumble of wind or the resonance of a person's chest as he or she speaks (with the LAVALIER microphone hung right next to their chest). Also, since LAPEL and LAVALIER microphones are usually close to people's mouths and bass sounds are stronger there, the LAVALIER microphone needs to have reduced bass sensitivity. When microphones are used close to the speaker's mouth, in the wind, in echoey rooms, or near the rumble of air conditioners, they pick up too much bass. A neat feature on some mikes is a switch that reduces the bass FREQUENCY RESPONSE. This switch may be called LOW CUT or BASS ROLLOFF. No, LOW CUT has nothing to do with plunging necklines; it simply means that the low frequencies are cut down, or weakened.

The FREQUENCY RESPONSE of a microphone gives it character. One microphone may sound like the inside of a tin can, while another sounds shrill, while another sounds muffled. When shooting various scenes using microphones, you should be aware that if you change microphones in the middle of a production, your sound character, called SOUND COLORATION, will change noticeably. Edits made later using another microphone may stick out like a sore ear.

Microphone Stands and Mounts

Now that we have our microphone happily plugged in, what do we hold it up with? Unless you are holding the mike in your hand, you will need a stand or something.

Desk Stands.   DESK STANDS like the ones shown in Figure 6–8 are most convenient for indoor work. The general-purpose one is thinner and less obtrusive, while the adjustable DESK STAND allows more freedom in raising or lowering the microphone's height. Because they are obtrusive, most TV people prefer LAPEL mikes, leaving the DESK STANDS to the radio people.

Floor Stands.   Standup speakers or singers will probably use a FLOOR STAND like the one in Figure 6–9. FLOOR STANDS come with an elevation adjustment for performers of different heights. The base is usually quite heavy to keep the microphone from tipping over. Some models have a small BOOM that allows the microphone to get into places where the stand would be in the way (as over pianos and drums and in front of seated people playing instruments). The FLOOR STAND puts some distance between the microphone and the sounds of heavy footsteps and scuffling feet. If floor vibrations are still picked up, you might consider placing the mike stand on something spongy, like a carpet remnant or a stale pizza pie.

Both FLOOR and DESK STANDS come in shiny chrome or charcoal gray or brown. The dark mike stands are much better for television because they don't reflect the studio lights, blinding your camera. If you are cursed with shiny mike stands, try spraying them with DULLING SPRAY to reduce their shine.

Boom Mike Stands.   A BOOM is the sound that you hear when a microphone stand falls over. It is also the name given to the long arm used to hold the microphone out in front of the talent.

Desk stand   A small microphone holder that sits on a desk.
*Floor stand   Microphone holder that stands on the floor and reaches up to shoulder height.
*Boom   An arm that sticks out, often with a mike hung on the end.

*Dulling spray   Aerosol spray used by film and video professionals to reduce shine on objects.

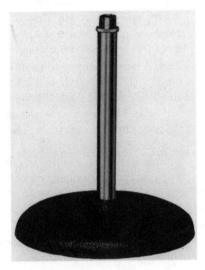

Adjustable height   General purpose

FIGURE 6–8   DESK STANDS (Courtesy of Quality/Universal).

One of the simplest, the BABY BOOM, is shown in Figure 6–10. Maybe it was invented in the post–World War II era (hence the name "Postwar Baby Boom"?). Joking aside, these are handy when you need to keep the stand out of the way so that your cameras can see the performers better. They're also good for getting a microphone up higher or down lower than a normal mike stand could do.

Another handy BOOM is the FISH POLE (Figure 6–10 top). Essentially, it is just a stick with a microphone on the end. It is lightweight and portable and allows you to catch the sound up close to a moving target. The problem is that it always takes an extra person to aim the FISH POLE, and that person's arms usually get tired very early in your production.

The portable studio BOOM often has a long telescoping rod mounted on casters so that it can be moved about the studio floor. BOOMS can be raised, lowered, and swung left and right. More complex models allow the BOOM arm to be lengthened or shortened as the performer draws nearer to it or moves farther from it.

Lavaliers and Lapel Clips.

LAVALIER microphones are OMNIDIRECTIONAL and are designed to be worn on the chest about eight inches below the talent's chin. Because of the vibration of the chest, bass sounds are very loud. Also, the treble sounds of the lips are some distance from the microphone. A properly made LAVALIER mike will have its FREQUENCY RESPONSE adjusted for this so that it cuts out

---

Baby boom   Small boom stand for holding a microphone.   **Gaffer tape**   Wide cloth tape.
Fish pole   A portable boom in the form of a pole with a mike at the end.

FIGURE 6–9 FLOOR STAND (Courtesy of Quality/Universal).

FISH POLE

Baby BOOM

Portable studio BOOM

FIGURE 6–10 FISH POLE and studio BOOMS.

the excessive bass and boosts the weak treble. Ordinary microphones don't tailor their FREQUENCY RE-SPONSE this way and will sound bassy when hung around a performer's neck. Similarly, a LAVALIER microphone sounds a bit shrill if hand-held or mounted on a mike stand.

Thanks to the ELECTRET CONDENSER, minuscule LAPEL CLIP microphones the size of a pencil eraser have replaced the LAVALIER. Clipped to a performer's tie or lapel, the mikes are unobtrusive and almost invisible. Their cables are extremely thin and pliable and run to a battery-fed power supply about the size of a cigar. Regular mike cord extends out the other end and to your VCR.

 Mini Review

- A broad, flat frequency response yields high-fidelity sound, which is appropriate for music.
- Different mikes sound different because they have different frequency responses. If you are shooting scenes that will be edited together, use mikes of the same type of mike to avoid a noticeable change in sound coloration.
- Placing a mike stand on something spongy will reduce the noise from footsteps or clunking objects on a desk.

Tip: If you're running long extension cables from cameras, mikes, or lights, slip the cables under a carpet or tape them to the floor using wide duct tape or GAFFER tape. Run wires *over* doorways, if possible. When using mikes on stands, try tying, taping, or clipping the mike cord to the stand's base. Not only will the wire be less of an obstacle resting on the floor, but if tugged, it is less likely to topple the stand.

CHOOSING AND USING THE PROPER MICROPHONE FOR A RECORDING

You want the best sound. You know that mikes with BALANCED LINES will introduce the least interference and noise into your signal, so use them if you have them.

"Watch your cables, especially when mikes are attached to clothing."

The closer the microphone is to the subject, the clearer and less echoey the sound will be. However, placing a mike too close to the performer (say three inches) often results in the mike picking up unsavory snorts and lip noises.

One Person, One Microphone

Hand and Stand Mikes. If the talent is standing on a podium or sitting at a desk, a CARDIOID or UNIDIRECTIONAL mike on a floor stand or desk stand may be best. If the talent turns to the side while speaking (while addressing a widely spaced audience), the CARDIOID mike is better. It is less sensitive to the fact that the performer may not be standing directly in front of it. An OMNIDIRECTIONAL mike would work but tends to pick up too many room noises.

The larger hand-held and stand microphones have excellent FREQUENCY RESPONSE and can handle a wide range of volume, making them excellent for singers or instrumentalists.

The *least* desirable way to mike a performer is with an OMNIDIRECTIONAL mike from any distance from the person. The OMNI will pick up echoes galore along with backstage sounds of people shuffling, camerapeople snoring, or studio crew tripping over cables.

Lavalier and Lapel Clips. If the talent is sitting, standing, or walking around, a LAVALIER or LAPEL CLIP or TIE CLIP mike may be best. They don't give terrific fidelity but are excellent for voice. Being close to the talent's mouth, they reject room noise and provide excellent "presence" (intimacy).

Center the LAV or LAPEL mike about eight inches from the performer's mouth as in Figure 1–5.

If the performer expects to move around a lot, it is good to attach the wire to the performer's body or have the person hold some wire in his or her hand so that it will trail along easily.

If the mike mustn't show, it may be hidden under a thin layer of clothing; however, the rustle of the clothing rubbing against the mike becomes a problem. You'll get clearer sound if the microphone isn't covered. Today's tiny LAPEL mikes can easily poke their heads out through buttonholes or can be camouflaged as tie clips.

Be on the alert for buttons and zippers that go clankity-clank against the microphone when your performer starts moving around. Also watch out for performers who beat their chests during dramatic scenes.

The mike cable may also need to be hidden. The wire can usually be threaded down beneath the shirt or blouse and down a pant leg to exit at the ankle. A mike cable could exit the rear of a blouse or the bottom of a skirt or could run down the back of a leg, under a shoe strap, and across the floor. It is often good to anchor the mike cable wherever it leaves the body so that small tugs on the wire do not jiggle the microphone. The cable could be anchored at a belt loop or taped to an ankle. Using an ace bandage, you can strap a TIE CLIP mike's battery power supply to your performer's ankle.

Boom Mikes. If the talent is too active, or if for aesthetic reasons the mike or cable must not show, you may wish to use a BOOM microphone. BOOM has nothing to do with the sound of the mike falling on the floor. The term BOOM microphone actually refers to the mechanism that holds the microphone rather than to the microphone itself. Various microphones can be used on a BOOM, generally CARDIOIDS and UNIDIRECTIONALS. The BOOM itself can either be a giant wheeled vehicle or a simple FISH POLE with a microphone on the end. BOOMS are expensive (except for the FISH POLE type), and someone must operate them in order to keep the mike close to the performer and yet out of the picture. You also have to worry that the mike BOOM might cast a shadow in the picture. Often the FISH POLE mike is positioned low, just out of the shot, and aimed upward toward the talent.

The larger BOOM mikes are used mostly for dramatic productions, and the FISH POLES for on-the-spot news interviews.

Wireless Mikes.   For the very active performer, the WIRELESS microphone may be the answer. Instead of sending its signal down a wire to the VCR, the WIRELESS mike changes the signal into a radio wave and broadcasts this wave to a UHF or an FM radio receiver up to four hundred feet away. The receiver then sends a regular audio signal to the VCR or mixer, as diagrammed in Figure 6–11. Good systems generally use the quieter UHF frequencies and are a bit expensive ($2000 to $5000). UHF mikes also have shorter, easier-to-hide antennas than their VHF cousins. Less expensive ($1200 to $2500) professional mikes use FM (also called VHF) radio frequencies. These devices are well made, but their frequencies are busier and more subject to interference. Inexpensive ($250 to $1500) FM WIRELESS mikes are also available for prosumers who can stay near the talent and can tolerate occasional hiss or crackles in the sound. All WIRELESS mikes are a tad more complicated to operate than a wired microphone. They are unbeatable in cases where the talent dances while singing, circulates among other people, interviews members of an audience, rides a bicycle, skydives, or climbs around machinery.

WIRELESS microphones do have their faults. When used indoors or near metal, their signals sometimes bounce off something before reaching the receiver. These "bounced" signals sometimes

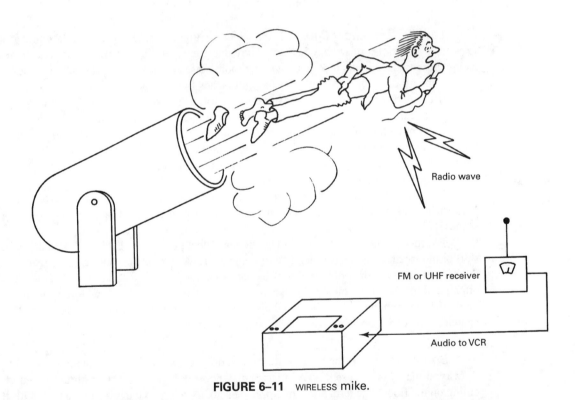

Radio wave

FM or UHF receiver

Audio to VCR

FIGURE 6–11   WIRELESS mike.

*Wireless microphone   A mike transmitting a radio (UHF or FM) signal to a receiver rather than sending the signal over a wire. It is used by performers who need freedom to move without mike cords.

UHF   Ultra high frequency; TV channels 14–69.

FM   Frequency modulation; the radio frequencies between 88MHz and 108MHz.

VHF   Very high frequency; TV channels 2–13.

Diversity receiver   Wireless microphone *receiver* using two antennas that can "listen" to a signal from the mike. The receiver picks the antenna giving the best signal, thus yielding more reliable reception (fewer audio dropouts).

A WIRELESS microphone can give you more freedom to move.

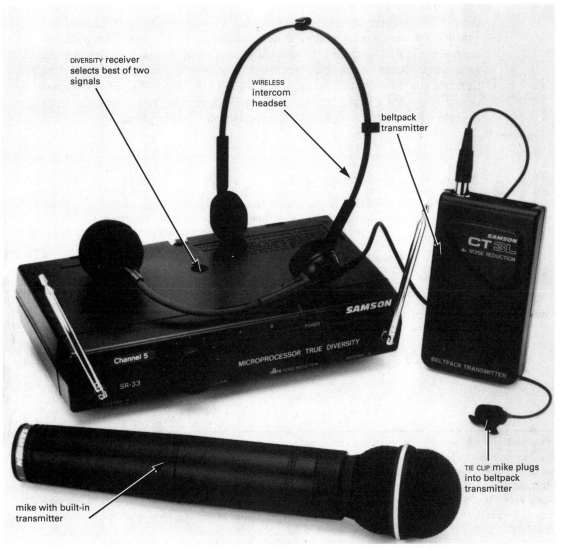

DIVERSITY receiver selects best of two signals

WIRELESS intercom headset

beltpack transmitter

mike with built-in transmitter

TIE CLIP mike plugs into beltpack transmitter

WIRELESS microphone transmitters, and DIVERSITY receiver (Courtesy of Samson).

interfere with the direct signal, weakening it or canceling it out altogether. As the performer moves and turns, you will hear short bursts of hiss or silence in place of your good sound. This interruption sounds like what you sometimes hear on a stereo FM radio in a car traveling through a city, under an overpass, or in the mountains. The sound will be great most of the time, but occasionally it fades out. This is especially true of $250 WIRELESS mikes.

The more expensive WIRELESS microphones go to great lengths to reduce these annoying dropouts. Many use two antennas on their receiver—if one antenna can't pick up the signal, the other probably can. These are called DIVERSITY RECEIVERS.

WIRELESS mikes can have the transmitter built into the mike body itself, perfect for performers who hold their mikes in their hands or pass them around. Other models allow a LAPEL or other standard mike to be plugged into a cigarette-pack-sized transmitter that is hidden elsewhere on the performer. This is best for dancing singers, dramatic actors, or undercover reporters.

Shotgun.   One problem with the STAND or DESK microphones is that they are clearly seen in the shot. If your DESK mike must remain out of view of the camera, try hiding it in a prop, perhaps among the flowers in a centerpiece or camouflaged as part of some tabletop artwork. Otherwise, you may need to use a SHOTGUN mike placed just out of view of the camera. If the performer stays in one spot, the SHOTGUN can be mounted on a stand in the same way as a regular mike. If the performer is active, then you'll need to have someone aim the mike, following the performer as he or she moves. Incidentally, anyone charged with this task should be wearing headphones and listening to the signal from the microphone. Doing this will improve attentiveness to accurate aiming.

 Mini Review

- Hand-held mikes have a broader frequency response than lapel mikes, making hand-helds more appropriate for musical recording.
- Place the lapel mike eight inches from the talent's mouth. Anchor its cable so it doesn't tug on the mike when the talent moves.
- A wireless mike permits the talent to move freely, but the signal is sometimes affected by radio interference or nearby metal.

Two People, One Microphone

It is better to have a separate mike for each person; in that way you can adjust the volume of each source independently. If this option isn't available, then we try to get one mike to hear two people and the least room noise.

*Feedback   A loud screech coming from a loudspeaker when sound enters a microphone, gets amplified, and then comes out the speaker only to be picked up again by the microphone and amplified more.

3-to-1 rule   Position mikes at least three times farther from each other than they are from the people speaking into them.

Phase   The *timing* of when electrical or sound vibrations reach a place, like an input or a microphone. When in phase, the vibrations strengthen each other, making a strong signal.

Out of phase signals cancel each other out, weakening the result. Electrical and sound signals need to be kept in phase.

Phase cancellation   The hollow sound you hear when two microphones are positioned in such a way as to pick up opposing parts of a sound wave.

Out of phase   Having electrical or sound vibrations that oppose the desired vibrations, weakening them.

Hand-held microphone   Mike designed to be held in the hand or clamped to a stand.

If the two people are sitting across from each other at a desk, the best mike might be a BIDIREC-TIONAL one placed on a desk stand between them. The mike is sensitive in two directions only and rejects much of the room echo.

A BOOM mike or a SHOTGUN mike might also work if the mike has to stay out of the picture and if you have an operator to aim it.

As is done on many game shows and news interviews, the emcee or reporter can hold a mike (preferably a CARDIOID type) in his or her hand and hold it up to each of the respondents to catch the replies.

Several People, Several Microphones

A LAV for each performer is the best situation. This way you can adjust each person's mike volume independently.

If six or more people are speaking, you'll probably run out of microphones and inputs for these microphones, so compromise. Try grouping the people into threes or so and aiming a CARDIOID microphone toward each group. If you are severely limited in the number of microphones you can use, try planting an OMNIDIRECTIONAL mike in the middle of the group with a LAV or CARDIOID delegated to the group leader or to the most important speaker.

PZM mikes are handy for group situations. They will pick up everyone speaking around a table and do a good job at rejecting room echo.

For news conferences where several individuals will be using a podium and others from the audience will be asking questions, place one mike at the podium and place another on a stand in the aisle for the audience. The intent is that the audience members will step up to the mike in the aisle when asking their questions. If a loudspeaker system is also in use for the conference, these microphones should all be CARDIOID or UNIDIRECTIONAL in order to reject as much of the loudspeaker's sound as possible, thus avoiding FEEDBACK.

No, FEEDBACK isn't the chef's position on a football team; it's the screech or whoop that results when sound is picked up by a microphone, goes through an amplifier, and comes out a speaker loud enough to get back into the microphone again. Around and around it cycles, making a raucous shriek. DIRECTIONAL mikes can reject much of this speaker sound, cutting down on FEEDBACK. An even better way to fight FEEDBACK at a news conference is to use a SHOTGUN microphone and an alert assistant to aim the microphone toward each person speaking.

If you do find yourself placing mikes on desk stands in front of several people, follow the 3-TO-1 RULE: The distance between mikes should be at least three times the distance from each microphone and the nearest talker. So if you position mikes one foot in front of each board member at a conference table, make sure the mikes are all three feet apart. This layout avoids PHASE CANCELLATION in the sound.

If you have two performers seated beside each other and wearing LAPEL MIKES, place the mikes on the lapel they will be facing as they look at each other.

Musical Recording

If the performers are singing, fidelity is paramount. TIE CLIP mikes are generally designed for speech and are therefore inappropriate. The best fidelity usually comes from the larger HAND-HELD mike (which can also be used on a DESK, a FLOOR STAND, or a BOOM). If possible, mike each singer separately for individualized volume control and keep each performer one or two feet from the mike. If you run short of mikes, group the singers.

Musical recording is a science in itself. If it is necessary to group the musicians, do it so that the lead has a separate mike from the rest, the rhythm gets a mike, the bass gets a mike, the chorus shares a mike, and related instruments share microphones. This way you have independent control of the volume coming from each *section* of the band.

Stereo Microphones

Simply plug one mike into the left MIC IN and another into the right MIC IN and shoot. Whatever is picked up by the left mike is recorded on the left channel, and what goes in the right mike is recorded on the right channel (assuming you have a stereo VCR).

Separating the mikes so they each hear something different will improve the stereo effect. Figure 6–12 diagrams the hookup.

A strange problem sometimes occurs when two microphones are spaced some distance apart. One mike will hear a sound, and another mike will hear the same sound a moment later (perhaps the second mike is farther away from the source, so that it takes the sound a while to travel to it). If you listen to the effect in stereo, you don't hear any problem. You won't consciously perceive the delay, but unconsciously the delay adds a certain "color" to the sound. The problem arises when you play this stereo signal through a *monaural* system such as a single speaker in a TV. If the sound from the second mike is delayed and OUT OF PHASE with the sound from the first mike, the signals cancel each other. You will hardly hear any sound at all, or it may sound hollow or echoey. To avoid this problem, it is good to always check out your sound on a monaural system just to make sure that it is compatible.

Figure 6–13 shows two better ways to mike for stereo. The first, called X-Y STEREO MIKING or CO-INCIDENT PAIR MIKING requires two CARDIOID mikes, crossed in an X shape, one pointed to the left of the stage area and the other to the right. Although the two mikes' PICKUP PATTERNS overlap a little, one will "listen" mostly to one side and the other will "listen" to the other. The two mike signals can go to a stereo camcorder or to some other stereo recorder.

The second method, called M-S (for MID-SIDE) STEREO MIKING requires special equipment. You need a mike with a FIGURE EIGHT PICKUP PATTERN "listening" to the left and the right. A CARDIOID mike points straight forward. The two signals go to a special ENCODER, a circuit that *adds* the signals together and sends the sum to the *left* channel output, and subtracts the signals from each other and sends the difference to the *right* channel output. Mathematically, what comes out of the ENCODER box ends up stereo.

One advantage of the preceding methods: You are unlikely to have PHASE CANCELLATION problems, because the mikes are close together.

Redundant Mikes

Your college president is to give an important speech at graduation and wants *you* to do the video recording. What happens if the microphone poops out and you record a silent movie of his flapping lips? Your graduation prospects poop out, that's what happens. It's not good to have your future hanging on the thread of a single microphone. So use two. You could just plunk two microphones onto the podium, one to the left and one to the right of the president as in Figure 6–14. They would probably

---

X-Y stereo miking Mike setup for stereo using two cardioids crossed, one aiming left, the other right, their heads almost touching.
M-S stereo miking Mike setup for stereo using a bidirectional and a cardioid mike close together and an encoder to manipulate the signals into stereo.

Encoder Electronic device to combine M-S audio signals in a way to create stereo.
Double system sound Process of recording sound with two recorders at once.

FIGURE 6–12   Recording stereo from microphones.

work, but you're taking a chance with PHASE problems. As the president moves from left to right, his voice reaches one microphone before it reaches the other. If that second microphone gets its sound one-half vibration later than the first, its signal will *subtract* from the first mike's signal rather than *add* to it. His voice will be hollow, weak, tinny, or bassy and unintelligible, or it may sound as if you're hearing it through a big water pipe. What's tricky here is that the sound problem will not occur all the time. You may test for it and not hear a problem, but the president, who's a little shorter than

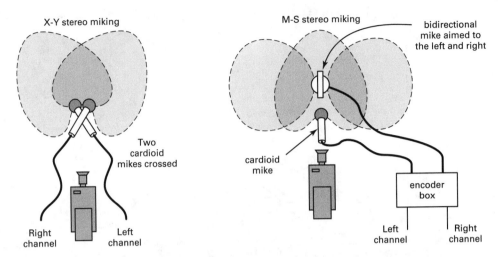

FIGURE 6–13   Two better ways to record stereo with microphones.

you and leaning a little more forward than you did, may find just the magic spots where the sound will fade out. Incidentally, you've heard this sound effect many times before. Darth Vader's voice was processed to sound this way. Some Beatles music, too. Still, I don't think your college president would be amused by the effect.

The right way to set up redundant desk, stand, or podium mikes is shown in Figure 6–15. The "heads" of the two mikes should be very close together, almost touching. The left mike should be pointing to the right to pick up the sounds in that area. The right mike would point to the left, picking up sounds in that area. If two CARDIOID mikes are used, their pickup areas will overlap nicely, covering the entire front of the podium or desk area. Because the mikes are close together, they both hear all sounds at the same time, and your signals will never be OUT OF PHASE.

TIE CLIP microphones can also be made redundant by clipping two mikes, one above the other, to the performer's tie or lapel. There are also double clips that will neatly hold two TIE CLIP mikes at once.

FIGURE 6–14   Wrong way to use two microphones for one person.

Mini Review

* Directional mikes fight feedback from nearby loudspeakers.
* Giving each individual a mike allows you maximum control over the sound. If you run low on mikes (or inputs), group the talent or instruments with one mike per group.
* To avoid phase cancellation with stereo or redundant mikes, position them so that they nearly touch each other and aim them inward at right angles to each other.

Double System Sound

What if you absolutely *have* to record the sound of an event and don't trust that your camcorder or VCR will get it? Or maybe you can't easily get the desired sound into your VCR (e.g., you're moving from place to place and you can't be disconnecting and reconnecting mike wires). DOUBLE SYSTEM SOUND is the process of recording the sound on an independent audio recorder, perhaps positioned strategically on a lectern or altar. It can be set up to record clear sound to be edited into your video later.

Banishing Unwanted Noise from a Recording

Wind.   Even a slight breeze over a microphone can cause a deep rumbling and rattling that sounds like a thunderstorm in the background of your recording.
   Solutions:

1. Stay out of the wind, and don't interview politicians.
2. Buy a WINDSCREEN, a foam boot that fits over the mike and protects it from breezes while letting other sounds through.

FIGURE 6–15   Right way to set up two mikes for a single person.

---

*Windscreen   Foam boot that fits over a microphone to shield it from wind noises.
*Audio meter   Meter that indicates the loudness of an audio signal. Could also be a string of LEDs that light up like a bar graph.

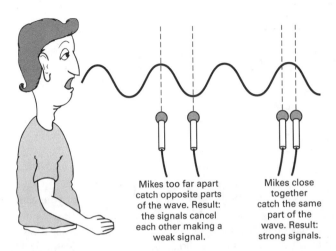

Mikes too far apart catch opposite parts of the wave. Result: the signals cancel each other making a weak signal.

Mikes close together catch the same part of the wave. Result: strong signals.   PHASE CANCELLATION.

3. In a pinch, take off your sock and put it over the mike to deflect the wind. Be prepared for wise-cracks like "Your audio stinks."
4. The following makes an excellent WINDSCREEN and also offers protection from water spray: a condom. Unroll the unlubricated condom over the head of the mike. Secure it tightly with GAFFER TAPE or string where the wire leaves the mike. You'll be practicing "safe sound."

Hand Noise.   Nervous hands holding a microphone can cause more shuffling, cracking, and creaking noises than a haunted house in a hurricane. Countermeasures: Set the mike on a stand or hang a LAV around the talent's neck with the warning "Don't touch it. Don't touch it. Don't touch it." If the performers *must* handle the mikes, tell them merely to grip the mike and not to fidget with or fondle it.

Stand Noise.   The mike is on a table stand, and every time the talent bumps the table, it sounds like a kettle drum rolling down a stairwell.

WIND or pop screen on microphone (Courtesy of Radio Shack).

Home made WINDSCREEN.

Solutions:

1. Have the talent keep their hands and knees still.
2. Insulate the base of the mike stand from the table with a piece of carpet, a mouse pad, a quiche Lorraine, or anything spongy.

Lav Noises. *Before recording anything from a LAV, first check to see that there are no buttons or tie clasps for the mike to clank against.* Murphy's 34th Law states that the clanking starts only when the show starts, not during rehearsals.

Mouth Noise. Performers love to put their lips to the mike. Perhaps they don't trust the wizardry of electronics to sense their feeble sounds from a foot away and amplify them to spellbinding proportions. As a result, two things happen. When the performer speaks loudly, the sound distorts. When the performer pronounces the letters *t, b,* and especially *p*, it sounds like bombs bursting in air.
Solutions:

1. Teach performers to trust the mike. Have them keep their distance. Cover the top of the mike with erect porcupine quills.
2. Use professional mikes designed for such abuse. They have a wire screen atop them that puts some distance between the lips and the actual microphone. They also contain built-in WIND-SCREENS and "pop" filters. Furthermore, they can withstand the excessive volume found a half-inch from a rock singer's lips.

Room Noise. The closer the mike is to the performer and the louder the performer speaks, the less room noise will be heard. So what do you do if the performer starts "popping *p's*," as described above? As shown in Figure 6–16, place the mike at *an angle to the side* rather than directly in front of the performer's mouth. The offensive consonants will fly straight forward, hurting no one, yet missing the microphone. Put another way, *the mike should "look" at the performer* (or his mouth), *but the performer should not "look" at the mike.*

As mentioned before, CARDIOID and UNIDIRECTIONAL mikes are best for rejecting extraneous room noise. They are, however, worse for "popping p's."

Try to place your performer in a quiet part of the room, away from windows, fans, loudspeakers, and—not to be forgotten—the whirring videotape recorder.

The echoes in a reverberant room can be quelled by placing a carpet on the floor, drawing the curtains, or hanging blankets on the walls. I recall taping a lesson once in a hospital room that echoed like a giant canyon. I stretched a clothesline between two opposite walls, scrounged 30 doctors' smocks from the hospital cloakroom, and hung them across the clothesline. Except for the stage area, the place looked like a dry-cleaning establishment, but the smocks succeeded in subduing the echoes . . . echoes . . . echoes.

Feedback. This loud screech or howl (sometimes called "back squeal") is very common when loudspeakers or public address systems are in use. It results when sound goes into the microphone, gets boosted by the amplifier for the loudspeaker system, and comes out the loudspeakers only to be picked up by the microphone again and amplified. It goes out through the speakers and into the mike: 'round, 'round it goes, getting louder all the time.

Solutions:

1. For immediate relief, turn down the volume on the amplifier that is causing the FEEDBACK. Disconnecting or switching off the microphone (some have ON/OFF switches) will also terminate the noise. This solution has the disadvantage of negating the whole purpose of having a loudspeaker system. What good is it if you can't turn it up loud? Solution 2 is the better answer once solution 1 has been employed in order to save eardrums in the interim.
2. Proper placement of speakers and selection of microphones will give long-range relief from FEEDBACK. The whole trick is to keep the microphone from hearing the loudspeakers:
   a. Keep the loudspeakers away from the mikes.
   b. Aim the loudspeakers away from the mikes. Note that some loudspeakers allow sound to project behind them as well as in front of them, so don't get behind the loudspeakers.
   c. Aim the mikes away from the loudspeakers.
   d. Use CARDIOID or UNIDIRECTIONAL mikes.
   e. Keep the performers as close to the mikes as is practical. If excessive movement makes standing mikes inappropriate, use TIE CLIPS so the mikes remain close to the performers.

FIGURE 6–16 Microphone placement to avoid "popping p's" at close range.

Testing a Microphone

"Clunk, clunk, blow, blow, testing—1—2—3—testing—1—2—3—testing—testing . . . " Such is the traditional prelude to every sound recording.

The ceremony of testing a microphone has two steps: The first is to find out if it is working at *all*, and the second is to make it work well. The procedure is easiest if you have a helper at the controls to adjust volumes, to monitor the sound, to check plugs, and to watch the audio meter. After you have plugged the mike into its proper receptacle (mixer, VTR, or whatever) and turned up the volume for that mike, you're ready for the tests.

Test 1.   Either tap the mike with your fingernail (while listening for the clunk, clunk over the monitoring speaker) or speak into the mike while your assistant listens for sound and notes whether the audio meter needle wiggles. If it doesn't, check your wires, mixer connections, and switches to see what's killing your sound. One popular trouble spot is ADAPTERS. They often get loose and cause crackly, intermittent sound. Try to find mikes and cables that fit directly, avoiding this weak link in the audio chain. One way *not* to test a mike is to blow into it. The ritual of blowing into a mike is like squeezing eggs in a supermarket to test for freshness. Some mikes are too fragile to withstand the "blow" test.

 Mini Review

- When shooting outdoors, use a windscreen.
- Aim the mike at the performer's mouth, but the performer should not speak directly toward the mike.
- Avoid using adapters whenever possible; they often cause the audio to crackle or cut out.
- Don't blow into a mike to test it; instead, lightly scratch or tap it with your fingernail and listen for sound.

Test 2.   Once you've established that you're getting sound, you make the *audio level* adjustments to ensure that your recording is made at the right volume. This is done by having the talent talk normally into the mike. It is difficult to make novice performers speak normally. So give them something to talk about. Tell them to count to thirty or to say their ABCs. *Do not* allow them to hold their mikes up to their mouths while you are checking the audio level—you will not get a representative sample of their normal speech volume. *Do not* allow them to stoop down to or lean into their stand mikes. This, too, will yield an unrepresentative volume level. *Do not* let them say just "testing" or "One—two—three . . ." because people tend to shout these words with unnatural loudness.

If the mike is feeding directly into a VTR with manual audio controls, observe the AUDIO METER. It should wiggle when people speak, but it should rarely dip into the red area. "Rarely" doesn't mean never; loud outbursts are expected to sweep the needle into the red for a moment. If possible, listen to the sound on headphones or a speaker in order to judge the sound quality. Is the sound distorted? Is there a buzz, a hum, or a hiss in the background? If so, something is wrong. Seek technical help.

In short, if the meter reads low, turn up the volume. If the meter points into the red area, turn the volume down. The meter should always be wiggling visibly but not be lingering in the red.

PROPER AUDIO LEVEL

Automatic Volume Control

Automatic volume control, sometimes abbreviated AVC or AGC (for automatic gain control—*gain* is another word for *volume*), is present on all camcorders and home VCRs. A few of the better models have a switch on them that allows you to select AGC or MANUAL volume control.

The advantage of AGC is obvious. Recordings are made automatically at the right volume level—no muss, no fuss. It's all done with a circuit that "listens" to the audio, and if it gets too loud, it turns the volume down. If it gets too low, it turns the volume up.

So why ever bother with manual controls? There are cases where AGC is not helpful at all. Say you were using an AGC machine to record an interview in a blacksmith's shop. The talent speaks, everything sounds fine, and then somebody's hammer strikes an anvil. The AGC reacts to the loud sound by lowering the record volume drastically and then slowly raising it again to the level appropriate for speech. The recording could sound like this:

> *Under the spreading chestnut tree,*
> *The Village Smithy sta*—WHANG!
> *. . . ty man . . . He*
> *. . . ith . . . and sinewy hands.*
> *And the muscles*—WHANG! *. . . rms*
> *. . . strong . . . iron bands.*

It would be better if the loud noise came and went in a flash, leaving most of the speech intact, like this:

> *Under the spreading chestnut tree,*
> *The Village Smithy stands.*
> *The smith, a mighty man is he*
> *With*—WHANG! *. . . and sinewy hands.*
> *And the muscles of his*—WHANG! *. . . arms*
> —WHANG! *. . . strong as iron bands.*

AGC is similarly troublesome in situations where, long, quiet pauses occur between sentences. When the talent stops speaking, the AGC circuit "hears" nothing and slowly turns up its volume. Still "hearing" nothing, it turns the volume up higher and higher. Turned way up, the machine records every little noise in the room, shuffling, sniffing, VTR motor noise, some electronically caused hum or buzzing, automobiles outdoors, and fire whistles in the next town. Then the first syllable out of the talent's mouth, after this long pause, skewers your eardrums because the volume is far too high for speech and hasn't yet turned itself down.

In short, AGC is helpful when you expect a fairly constant level of sound. AGC doesn't like long silent pauses or short loud noises. AGC tends to wreck music, which is *meant* to have quiet parts and loud parts. There are, incidentally, AGC devices made to overcome these problems. They are somewhat expensive and aren't built into the reasonably priced VTRs.

Manual Volume Control

As described before, you adjust the RECORD VOLUME LEVEL (or whatever the manufacturer calls it) to wiggle the meter without making it loiter in the red area. Also, monitor the sound coming out of the VTR (using headphones or a monitor/receiver) to see if the sound is clear and undistorted.

Once the audio level is set (during checkout while you were setting up), the circumstances of the production will dictate whether it will need to be adjusted again. If the audio is from a professionally prerecorded source or if the audio is from a speech or dictation in which the loudness was relatively even, it is possible to make the entire recording without twiddling the audio knobs and with only occasionally checking the meter. If the sound source changes its volume frequently or drastically, you may have to "ride audio," twiddling the knobs and watching the meters intently.

How much do you twiddle? Answer: the least possible to keep the audio level about right. You're twiddling too much if every shriek or cough makes you turn the volume down. Brief noises are loud, yes. They sound distorted when recorded at high volumes, yes. But they are gone in an instant and easily forgotten. Brief pauses and whispers are quiet, yes. But whispers are supposed to be quiet, and silent pauses are not unnatural for us to hear and may even be a refreshing break from the monotony of constant chatter. While playing back a tape, it is irritating for the viewer to have to rise from his comfy seat to readjust rising and falling volume because of some overzealous knob-twiddler who adjusted the record level too often. In short,

1. React quickly to sustained bursts of noise or substantial passages that would be lost if not adjusted for.
2. Don't react to momentary sounds or silences.
3. As conversations ebb and flow in volume, gradually make tiny adjustments in order to compensate. Do it in such a way that no one will notice that the volume is being changed.

 **Mini Review**

- Adjust the mixer and VCR meters to wiggle with normal sounds, but don't let the needle linger in the red area.
- Automatic gain control (AGC) is convenient, but manual control is more accurate, especially if the program will contain loud bursts of sound or long quiet passages.
- Make gradual and conservative adjustments to volume controls during a show. Don't overreact to brief outbursts or quiet stretches.

MIXERS

A mixer accepts signals from various sources, allows each signal to be individually adjusted for loudness (even adjusted all the way down to no loudness at all), and sends this combination to a VCR or some other recording device. All the VCR volume control instructions that you just read also apply to the mixer. As with all production equipment, you can have small, medium-sized, and enormous mixers that can do basic, moderate, and miraculous tasks. Figure 1–16 showed some mixers.

Inputs to the Mixer

Microphones are generally plugged into the MIC INPUT sockets in the back of the mixer, up to one mike for each volume control knob on the front of the device. On the more professional models, the inputs are the XLR types for BALANCED LINES, and they have a little pushbutton near each socket to release the plug so that it can be removed.

---

*Low-level, (lo-level) or microphone-level signal** Weak audio signal, as from a microphone.

*High-level (or hi-level) signal** Strong audio signal typically sent from an aux out or a line out of a device.

*Trim or gain control** Volume control that adjusts the mixer's input sensitivity. Turned up, the input works with mikes; turned down, it works with hi-level sources.

Phantom power Power fed from a mixer's mike input to run a condenser microphone.

All the microphone inputs are LO-LEVEL INPUTS, which means they accept tiny signals only. Microphone signals are weak and match the mixer's sensitive inputs.

The MIC INPUTS are not designed for stronger signals like those coming from an FM tuner, CD player, a VCR LINE OUT or AUDIO OUT, any earphone output, any speaker output, any preamplifier output, or just about anything that boosts the signal before sending it out. For these LINE-LEVEL or HI-LEVEL sources, one must use a different input on the mixer (if it has such): the AUX (for AUXILIARY) IN or the LINE IN.

These inputs are less sensitive than LO-LEVEL inputs and work well with stronger signals. Use AUX or LINE IN when you have some musical background or sound effects that you wish to mix with the voices on the microphones. The HI-LEVEL or LINE outputs of tape decks, FM radios, CD players, cassette players, or similar devices can be connected to the AUX IN for this purpose.

The preceding is true for one kind of mixer, but there is another kind of mixer that handles HI- and LO-LEVEL signals differently. These mixers will have switches near their mike inputs that change them from LO-LEVEL (for mikes) to HI-LEVEL (for CD players, etc.). Flip the switch to the appropriate position when plugging in a sound source.

Still other mixers have GAIN or TRIM controls to adjust the sensitivity of each input to the mixer. Usually these controls are in a cluster or a column above the mixer's actual VOLUME control for that input.

Once everything is plugged into the mixer and is working, *label each of the mixer's knobs or sliders* to tell which source is controlled by which knob. For example, near knob 1, stick a piece of masking tape with the word CASS marked on it. This way, during production, you don't have to be asking yourself, "Let's see, is knob 1 the audiocassette player, or is it the CD player?"

Phantom Power.   CONDENSER mikes need power to run. They could get this power from an auxiliary power supply connected in the line somewhere, or they might get it from the mixer (if it has this feature). Power from the mixer is called PHANTOM POWER. (Batman uses it all the time.) Throwing a switch near the mike input to the mixer sends juice to power the CONDENSER microphone.

Don't send PHANTOM POWER to DYNAMIC or ELECTRET CONDENSER mikes. They don't want outside help and will roast in remonstration.

Outputs from the Mixer

The mixer's output sends the combined signals to the VCR or other device. Just as each microphone's volume is adjustable with a knob on the mixer, the volume of the signal the mixer sends out is also adjustable with the MASTER volume control. Usually this knob is a different color, shape, or size from the rest. Turning the MASTER down turns down all the signals coming out of the mixer. This is a very convenient feature, especially at the end of a program that uses multiple mikes—you'd have to be an octopus to turn down all the individual mike volume controls simultaneously.

LO-LEVEL AND HI-LEVEL AUDIO

Lo-level signals are weak signals, like those made by microphones. Hi-level signals are strong signals, like those from CD players, audiocassette decks, and the audio output from VCRs.

Lo-level signals need to go to lo-level (sensitive) inputs on mixers and recorders. Sometimes these are labeled MIC. Hi-level signals need to go to hi-level inputs such as the AUX or LINE inputs of devices.

If you send a hi-level signal into a lo-level input, the sound will be loud or distorted, like a portable radio turned up too loud. If you send a lo-level signal to a hi-level input, the sound will be weak, tinny, and hissy.

Some inputs have switches or gain/trim controls to change their inputs from lo to hi.

The mixer may have several outputs. Although one output from a mixer is all that is needed to feed a VCR, the others are there to permit flexibility in setting up and using the audio system.

Mike Out or Mike Level Out or Lo Level Out.   This is an audio output that has a tiny signal like that of a microphone; thus, it can be plugged into the MIC IN of a VCR or other device. To this end, the audio cable and plugs are just like microphone cables and plugs. It is as if the mixer were pretending to be a microphone: It is putting out a signal just like a mike, and the signal goes to wherever a mike's signal could have gone.

Line Out or Hi Level Out or Aux Out or Audio Out.   A medium-sized signal emanates from this output and is destined to go to a VCR's LINE IN or AUX IN.

 Mini Review

- Connect microphones to the lo-level or mic inputs of a mixer; connect tape decks or CD players to the hi-level or aux inputs.
- Label the mixer to show which source goes to which volume control.
- To record sound from a mixer, connect the mixer's line or audio output to a VCR's line or aux or audio input.

Headphone.   This is another output for monitoring the audio signal over headphones. This output is a fairly strong signal, usually too strong for feeding VCRs.

Stereo and Multichannel Mixers

A stereo mixer is two mixers in one box. It can handle two independent channels of sound. Everything we've said so far is also true for stereo mixers, only doubled: there are two meters to track volume, two MASTER volume controls, twice as many inputs, and two (or more) outputs. The signals that go in any mixer input can be sent to the mixer's left or right output, or mixed between the two using the PAN POT. Turned to the left, the signal will go to the left mixer output. Turned to the right, the sound goes to the right. The POT (potentiometer, or volume control) can be adjusted anywhere in between, apportioning the sound between the channels. For MONAURAL sound, the PAN POT is turned halfway, to its "center" position, making half the sound go to each stereo channel.

The HEADPHONE output of a stereo mixer is stereo, so you hear both channels.

Audition   The act of checking on a sound signal but not recording it. Also, a mixer channel that can be listened to or adjusted but is not necessarily recorded.

Cue   To set up a sound effect or music (as in "cue up"). Also the name of the audio mixer's channel that plays sounds to the audio person while they are being cued up.

Pot   Potentiometer, or volume control.

***Pan pot**   Pot (short for potentiometer, or volume control) that adjusts whether a signal will go to the left channel or the right, or be shared between the two by selected amounts.

***Mute**   A control that cuts out the sound but leaves everything else going.

***Group**   A combination of signals from a mixer. Several inputs, assigned to a group, are all controlled together and go to that group's output in the mixer. The left channel, for instance, is a group in a stereo mixer.

***Equalize**   Filter or boost certain tones of sound.

Echo   The repetition of a sound, like "hello, hello, hello," etc.

Reverberation, or reverb   The continuance of a sound after the original sound has ceased. Also, the device that artificially adds reverberations to audio.

Mixers can have more than two channels. Four-channel mixers have four of everything inside and four outputs, usually called GROUP 1, GROUP 2, GROUP 3, and GROUP 4. An input to such a mixer is assigned (through a pushbutton) to a GROUP or pair of GROUPS, say GROUP 3–4. Now the PAN POT can be adjusted to send the signal to GROUP 3, or to GROUP 4, or to some balance between them. All inputs are eventually assigned to GROUPS, and each GROUP has its own meter, MASTER AUDIO control, and output. The outputs could go to a four-channel recorder. A mixer with four GROUPS can be used for stereo; just ignore two of the GROUPS. Send, for instance, all your signals to GROUPS 1 or 2, PAN between them as necessary, connect the GROUP 1 and 2 outputs to your stereo VCR inputs, and adjust the GROUP 1 and 2 MASTER VOLUME controls, watching meters 1 and 2.

Big stereo and multichannel mixers can look daunting at first, festooned with more knobs and buttons than Starship Enterprise. Rest assured, there is logic to it all. Every input has a column of controls and maybe a meter associated with it. Look down the column, and you'll see all the things you can do to the signal on its way through the mixer, such as MUTE it (make the signal 100% silent), TRIM it (make it weaker if it is too strong for the input and distorts), EQUALIZE it (change its tone), PAN it, send it to a particular channel or GROUP, send it temporarily out of the mixer to another device like an ECHO or REVERB unit, or do other special effects with the signal. If you can't get any sound out of one of these monsters, just be patient and follow the signal's path, checking all the knobs, switches, and sliders in its column. Then check the GROUP outputs to see where *they* are going. All the output control is likely to be clustered on the right side of the mixer. In fact each GROUP may have its own column of knobs. Trace the signal through the GROUP and out the selected output to see where the signal got lost.

Monitoring Audio

The mikes and other devices feed their signals into the mixer, where the sounds get combined. The audio signal could be fed to the VCR and monitored either on the VCR's speaker (if it has one), or on headphones plugged into the VCR, or on a monitor/ receiver connected to the VCR's audio and video outputs. What happens if you get no sound on the VCR monitor/receiver? Is it the VCR's fault? The mixer's fault? The mike's fault? If the mixer has a meter and the meter wiggles when someone speaks into the microphone, the mixer and mike are most likely working. If you can plug headphones into the HEADPHONE jack on the mixer, you can make doubly sure that the mixer and mike are working well. If the headphones and the meter are still, then the problem is probably in the microphone or in the mixer. Try another microphone: If it works where the first one didn't, the first mike (or its cable or plug) may be bad, or its ON/OFF switch is *off*, or perhaps its battery (if it uses one) is dead.

Once you've proven that your signal is playing through the mixer, you turn your investigation to the VCR. Is the mixer's output plugged into the VCR's input? Is the VCR's volume up? Is it in the

Professional audio mixer (Courtesy Yamaha Corp. of America).

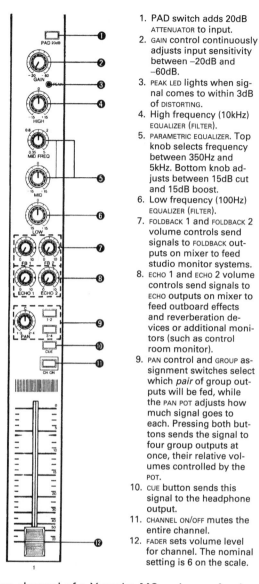

1. PAD switch adds 20dB ATTENUATOR to input.
2. GAIN control continuously adjusts input sensitivity between –20dB and –60dB.
3. PEAK LED lights when signal comes to within 3dB of DISTORTING.
4. High frequency (10kHz) EQUALIZER (FILTER).
5. PARAMETRIC EQUALIZER. Top knob selects frequency between 350Hz and 5kHz. Bottom knob adjusts between 15dB cut and 15dB boost.
6. Low frequency (100Hz) EQUALIZER (FILTER).
7. FOLDBACK 1 and FOLDBACK 2 volume controls send signals to FOLDBACK outputs on mixer to feed studio monitor systems.
8. ECHO 1 and ECHO 2 volume controls send signals to ECHO outputs on mixer to feed outboard effects and reverberation devices or additional monitors (such as control room monitor).
9. PAN control and GROUP assignment switches select which *pair* of group outputs will be fed, while the PAN POT adjusts how much signal goes to each. Pressing both buttons sends the signal to four group outputs at once, their relative volumes controlled by the POT.
10. CUE button sends this signal to the headphone output.
11. CHANNEL ON/OFF mutes the entire channel.
12. FADER sets volume level for channel. The nominal setting is 6 on the scale.

One channel of a Yamaha MC series professional mixer.

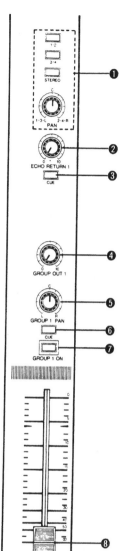

1. ECHO PAN and STEREO ASSIGN controls will take the signal coming from the outboard effects device and send it to GROUPS 1-2, and/or GROUPS 3-4, or to the left or right stereo output, depending on which button(s) are pressed. The PAN POT apportions the signal between the selected channels.
2. The ECHO RETURN control adjusts the volume of the echo signal coming into the mixer.
3. The CUE button permits the ECHO signal to go to the headphones for monitoring.
4. The mixer has a separate output for each GROUP. GROUP OUT 1 controls the volume of the GROUP 1 output (but doesn't affect the final PROGRAM out).
5. The group 1 PAN control apportions the GROUP 1 signal to the left or right stereo channels.
6. This CUE control allows the headphones to monitor GROUP 1.
7. GROUP 1 ON mutes the entire group.
8. The GROUP 1 fader adjusts the volume for the group.

Group output section of a Yamaha MC series professional mixer.

RECORD mode? (Remember that some VCRs don't allow you to monitor their signals unless they are in RECORD.) Is the VCR's audio monitoring system (or the monitor/receiver) volume turned up? Are all the cables tight?

Some studios make a big deal of monitoring their audio accurately. They use the LINE OUT from the mixer to feed the VCR. They use a second output to feed a separate loudspeaker system in the control room so that they may hear exactly what is being sent to the VCRs (not relying solely on the wiggling meter needle). Some places monitor the LINE OUT *from* the *VCR* by sending that signal to another loudspeaker system. By doing so, they know what the VCR is putting out when it is recording or playing back a tape.

Given a choice, the best place to monitor audio during a recording is the VCR's LINE OUT. Thus, if anything goes wrong with your audio signal *anywhere* in the system, you'll hear the problem there at the final output.

 Mini Review

- Each input on a large mixer has all its controls arranged in a column. The controls in that column affect the volume and other attributes of that one sound.
- Always check your audio quality before going "on the air" or starting a recording.

Professional Audio Control Boards

The professional audio control boards are mixers with extra gadgets. They are bigger, cost more, are very flexible in application, last a long time, and can pass a very high-quality signal. One of the important features on these giant mixers allows you to AUDITION or CUE a selection before use.

Audition or Cue.   Say that you wish to play the sound effect of a "boing" while someone winds his pocketwatch. How do you find the specific sound on your sound-effects CD that has the "boing" without having your audience hear you search for it? You can't have your listeners hear you play "hee haw," "meow," "cluck, cluck," and "plop" as you seek out the "boing." You would like to play these selections to yourself, find the right one, get it ready to go, and then, at the right time, play it for everybody to hear.

Near the mixer's knob that controls the audio from the CD player will be a switch that is likely to say PROGRAM/OFF/CUE. On other models, the knob itself, when turned fully counterclockwise, will click into a CUE position. One way or another, that knob will either work in the PROGRAM mode or the CUE mode, or it will be switched OFF and will not send signals anywhere.

In the PROGRAM mode, the mixer sends its signal through to the VCR after you have adjusted its volume with the individual volume control on the mixer. In the OFF position, the mixer refuses to pass the signal, and nothing gets recorded. In the CUE position, the mixer passes the audio signal but not to the VCR or to the audience. The signal goes to a separate output or to a CUE SPEAKER built into the mixer. You hear the selections on this speaker as you find the right place on the CD. Once you find it, you are CUED up and ready to play the CD at the appropriate time after you have flipped the switch back to PROGRAM.

AUDITION is much the same as CUE. Sometimes you would like to send a signal to someone else (or yourself) to hear, but not to the audience. This is easy to do if your mixer has an AUDITION channel. Putting these ideas together, we can see that each channel on the mixer (which is controlled by a slider or a POT) can send its signal to perhaps four places: OFF (no place at all), PROGRAM (to the VCR), CUE (to the audio person for setting up sound effects, etc.), and AUDITION (for the audio person or anyone else who needs to hear a signal passing through the mixer).

Here is an example of how all these controls could be used during a production: Your show is rolling along, and people are speaking into several microphones. Those POTS are turned to PROGRAM, and the sound is being recorded on the VCR. During the show you are trying to set up the music for ending the show. The music is on an audiocassette player, so you turn the audiocassette POT to CUE and wind to the right part of the tape. You (and not the audience and not the VCR) listen to the musical selections over the CUE SPEAKER on the mixer. When you've located the selection you want, you stop the audiocassette player and switch the audiocassette POT to PROGRAM (you may wish to turn the audiocassette POT down first so that you can FADE UP the music when the time comes). Meanwhile, the director may ask you if the VCR is recording everything all right. You could get up and walk over to the VCR and check its meter or turn up its monitor, but what if the VCR is in the next room or on another floor altogether, as at CBS? Here's where you use AUDITION. The VCR is probably sending its AUDIO OUT to one of the inputs on your mixer. If you could listen to that input, you could tell how the VCR was doing. You could turn that knob to CUE and listen to the sound. Generally, the CUE speaker is a cheap speaker built into the mixer and is useful only for finding the right place on CDs and other sources. It is not good for measuring fidelity. The AUDITION channel, however, is generally a high-fidelity channel and may feed a HEADPHONE output on the mixer or may feed a speaker in the control room. By switching the POT marked "VCR" to the AUDITION position, you will be able to hear the VCR's output either on headphones or the control room speaker in full fidelity.

Often the HEADPHONE output of the professional audio control board can be switched so that the audio person may listen to the PROGRAM, AUDITION, or CUE channel. This is nice because the control room crew usually suffers enough confusion without hearing a menagerie of "hee haw" and "cluck, cluck" as you CUE UP your sound effects over the control room loudspeakers.

Talkback or Studio Address.   Some professional audio consoles have a TALKBACK system that allows the audio director (or anybody else who gets his or her hands on the switch) to speak into a mike in the control room and have the sound come out of a loudspeaker in the studio. It's good for making announcements like "Stand by" or "Everybody take a break." To operate, the TALKBACK mike usually requires you to push a button somewhere and hold it down while speaking.

Foldback.   Some studios use one mixer for microphones alone and another mixer for all the sound effects, background, music, and so forth. When set up a certain way, the two mixers can permit an audio technique called FOLDBACK. Some mixers have this feature built in.

Say you want a surprised look on a performer's face as soon as his watch goes "boing." Normally, with a single mixer, the performer wouldn't hear the "boing" (and thus couldn't react to it at the exact time of the "boing") *unless* the sound was piped out to the studio for him to hear. When you send the mixer's sound out to the performer, his microphone's sound gets piped out there too. Unless the sound volume from the speaker in the studio is very low (running the risk that the performer may not hear it), the sound from the loudspeaker will go into the performer's microphone, into the mixer, and eventually out the speaker again, around and around. Instead of a "boing," you get the "wheech" of FEEDBACK.

To avoid FEEDBACK, you wish to send only the sound effects out to the studio, not the microphone sounds. This is done by having all the sound effects and music go into one of two mixers. The output of this first mixer goes to two places: to the studio and to the second mixer. The studio now gets only the output of the first mixer, that output being the sound effects or music. The second mixer also gets a taste of that output on one of its volume controls. Meanwhile, it mixes the sounds from the

---

*Talkback, or studio address   A loudspeaker system that allows the control-room crew to speak directly to studio personnel.

Foldback   Audio mixing system that allows sound effects, music, etc. to be mixed, amplified, and sent to the studio for performers to hear, as well as to be recorded, mixed with the sounds from their microphones.

Aux send   An output/input path on mixers that allow a signal to be manipulated by a device outside the mixer.

*Parametric equalizer   Audio device that adjusts to reduce or boost a selected range of frequencies.

*Segue (pronounced "SEG-way")   A smooth change from one sound, place, or subject to another.

Sting   Short sound effect or a few notes of music or just a chord used to introduce, segue between, or end scenes.

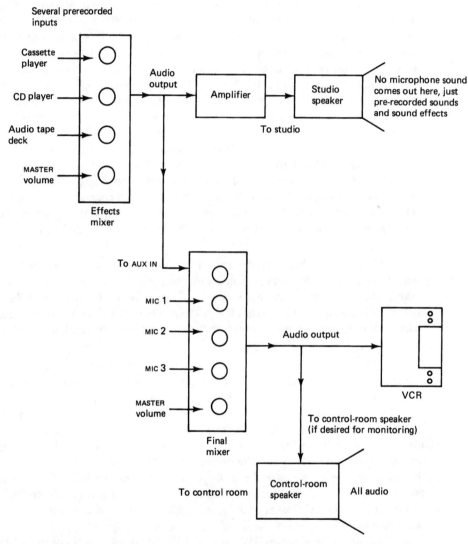

FIGURE 6–17   Two mixers permitting FOLDBACK (only a few sources are shown).

other mikes. The second mixer sends this total combination to the VCR for recording. Figure 6–17 diagrams this setup.

Some mixers can use the AUDITION channel for FOLDBACK, while others, as mentioned before, have dedicated FOLDBACK circuits built into them.

The average TV production doesn't have much call for "boings," but a common use of FOLDBACK involves music. A rock group, for instance, can perform a song wearing street clothes (or rags), reading sheet music, and standing near their carefully placed microphones. Through the magic of FOLDBACK, they can later hear their recording played back and can dance and jump in the studio, *pretending* to be performing the music. The prerecorded music would be video-recorded, along with the images of their silent shenanigans. If desired, one could also mix in the audio of their "live" screeches, howls, comments, or harmony recorded in the studio, without fear of FEEDBACK from the studio speakers.

Aux Send/Return.   The AUX SEND allows you to take a signal that has entered the mixer and send it out to an auxiliary device (REVERB UNIT, EQUALIZER, or special effects box). From that device, the signal comes back into the mixer (using the RETURN input) to continue its progress through the mixer.

Parametric Equalizer.   This knob, often found on mixers, allows you to select a narrow band of frequencies, say 50 to 70Hz, and either filter them out of your sound or boost them. Everything may be variable: the chosen frequency, the spread of frequencies around the chosen frequency, and the amount of cut or boost. PARAMETRIC EQUALIZERS are handy for reducing the recorded buzz of fluorescent lights or air conditioners or for sharpening the tinkle of a bell. Human speech, which carries much of its intelligibility at 4,000Hz, could be made to stand out from other background noise and could be more easily understood if boosted at that frequency.

 Mini Review

- Audition and cue are mixer features that allow you to select and prehear a sound before it is actually recorded or broadcast.
- Foldback allows performers to hear certain sounds (perhaps music to dance to) but does not cause feedback.

SOUND MIXING TECHNIQUES

There is no substitute for creativity. There are some basics, however, that can help. In fact, your library may have several books written solely on sound mixing; it gets that involved.

Segue

SEGUE (pronounced "SEG-way") is a fade from one sound to another. For instance, the sounds of machinery can be smoothly replaced with music. The machinery's volume control is lowered at the same time that the music volume control is raised. This procedure is also often done between two pieces of music; as one finishes, the other is being faded up.

A more sophisticated SEGUE uses an intermediate sound when changing from one audio passage to another. For instance, to go from one scene in a play to another, during the last line in scene one, there come a few bars of appropriate music. As the music begins to fade out, the first line in scene two is delivered. Briefer things like jokes or single statements may deserve a sound effect, laughter, applause, or a single note or chord of music (such a musical passage is called a STING) between them.

Some SEGUES prepare the listener for things to come, such as faint machinery noise before we open the engine room door or the sound of windshield wipers before the actors begin to speak in the car on a rainy night. A famous Hitchcock SEGUE is a woman's scream that suddenly changes to the scream of a train's whistle as the train chugs into the next scene. Another popular SEGUE is the dance

---

Music under   Music volume is reduced into the background so that narration or something else gets the audience's attention.

Voiceover   Narration added to and louder than background sounds or music.

Sound mix   The process of editing and mixing numerous sounds into the final form heard by the audience.

VU   Volume unit—a measure of loudness. A VU meter measures the strength of an audio signal. A 0VU ("zero V-U") setting is considered optimum sound volume.

troupe's rehearsing to "one, two, three, four, one, two, . . ." as we dissolve the picture and sound to the actual on-stage performance of the number with all the glitter and music.

Music Under, Sound Mix, Voiceover

Your production begins with a snappy musical selection. The title fades in and then dissolves to the opening scene. Someone is about to speak. The music fades down just before the first words are heard. This is a MUSIC UNDER. The music became subordinate to the speech and is played *under* it.

Sometimes you have to decide whether to fade the music out entirely when the action starts or to MUSIC UNDER holding it in the background throughout the scene. If the music is needed for dramatic effect, either to create a mood or just to provide continuity through long gaps in action or conversation, then keep it in. If, however, the action or conversation is very important, then don't distract your audience with background music.

So how loud should the background music be? The answer, of course, depends on the particular situation: There's no hard rule. In general, keep in mind that background music is *background* music. Keep the volume low—lower than your natural inclinations would have you set it. How many amateur productions have you sat through while straining to hear the dialogue through that "noise" in the background?

One guide to proper volume setting can be your VU meter. If your narration makes your needle huddle as it should around 0dB (the 100% mark on the scale), the background should wiggle the needle about –8dB (about 40 percent on the scale). If you have only a nonprofessional record level meter, the narration should wiggle the needle just below the red, while the background should wiggle it one-fourth to one-third of its range.

Again, these are just generalities. Some musical selections are inherently more obtrusive than others. For instance, while listening to a narration, the viewer may hardly be aware of instrumental music in the background. Conversely, a song with words competes with the narration for the viewer's attention. Because singing with words is so distracting, it's best to avoid it in favor of instrumentals.

Not all background sound is music. Street sounds, machines, sirens, motors, gunfire—all can be background to your dialogue. Some of these sounds may not be background at all but are interjected between dialogue, such as "thud," "crash," and the like. How all these sound effects and backgrounds are woven together is called the SOUND MIX, and it's the audio director's job to mix them effectively. He or she may vary engine background noise up and down to favor the actors when they speak. The audio director may drastically reduce the engine noise to coincide with a change of setting or of camera position. He or she may combine music with barnyard sounds, mix that with the dialogue of the actors, and top it off with a few specialty effects.

Sometimes you are handed a videotape or a film and are told to add narration. The original sound on the tape will be kept but only as background for the narration. Adding narration is called a VOICEOVER. The voice you're adding is imposed over and is louder than the original sounds. Although sound editing will be covered more completely in Chapter 14, here, briefly, is what happens.

Mr. Expert brings in a tape showing his foundry in action. The tape shows the busy machines while you hear them foundering away in the background. Mr. Expert also brings a script that he wishes to read through parts of the recording. To do this, you set up a VCR to copy his original tape from a VCP (videocassette player). The VCP's video goes directly to the VCR. The audio from the VCP goes to a mixer. Mr. Expert's microphone also feeds to the mixer. The mixer combines and regulates the two sources and feeds the combination to the VCR. As the VCP plays, the VCR records, copying the picture and whatever original sound the mixer lets through. Mr. Expert reads his script as he keeps one eye on the VCP's monitor screen. You adjust audio levels, sometimes favoring the background sounds (when the narrator is silent) and sometimes lowering them (when the narrator speaks). That's a VOICEOVER. If he doesn't like the way the final tape comes out, you can erase it and do it over, since his original tape was not altered in the process. You can do this over and over again until you get it exactly right. If, after repeated redoing, Mr. Expert still doesn't like it, you may choose to alter his original tape—over his head!

Sometimes the script is narrated by someone far away or long ago. You'll get a videocassette with background sounds and an audiocassette with the narrator's story. Here the process is about the same, except that an audiotape player is providing the narration rather than a live person. Instead of the narrator slowing down, speeding up, or stopping his reading to coincide with the pictures he sees from the VCP, you, the audio director, must stop and start the audiotape player to coincide with the pictures. If you have the script or memorize the narration, you will be able to choose good places to stop the audiotape from playing without catching the narrator between words.

Several Performers—Each with His or Her Own Microphone

When all the microphones are turned on at the same time, not only do you hear the sound of the one person speaking, but also you hear the breathing and shuffling of the others in the background. You also get the hollow echo of the speaker as his or her voice is picked up on everybody else's microphone.

To avoid this, turn down all the inactive mikes, allowing only the speaker's mike to be live. This is easy to do in a scripted production like a newscast or a play, but it is difficult to do in a free discussion. In such cases, you have to suffer the disturbing background sounds resulting from leaving all the mikes live, because if you turn off the unused mikes and then turn them up after a new person has started speaking, you will lose his or her first few words.

One partial solution may be to *lower* by a third or a half the unused microphone volumes, raising them after the person begins speaking. Although the person's first words may be weak, they will be audible and will soon be up to full volume. Allow the dynamics of the discussion to be your guide. If the speech is coming in a crossfire from everyone, keep all the mikes open. If someone seldom speaks, lower his or her mike. If the speakers render long monologues, take a chance on turning down the other mikes until the speech sounds finished. Good audio requires lightning-fast reactions coupled with a dose of anticipation.

 Mini Review

- Music and segues create continuity between scenes.
- Keep your background music sedate and low enough that it doesn't compete with the dialog.
- Turn down the volume of idle microphones to avoid unnecessary noise and echoes.

Cueing a CD Player

You wish to push a button and have that "boing" happen instantaneously, right in sync with the action of the performer as he winds his watch. Once you find the "boing" on the CD, you need to get it backed up to just before the "boing" so that it will play the instant the PLAY button is pressed. If you leave too much space before the "boing," when you play it during the production, you'll get "... boing." That's too late. If you don't back it up far enough, you'll get "... ing," the tail end of the sound.

Proper CUEING of a sound effect on a nonprofessional CD player goes like this:

1. Switch the mixer's CD input to the CUE mode. Adjust volume controls as needed.
2. Using the printed index that came with the CD, maybe advance the CD player to the group called "mechanical sounds," where the "boing" resides.
3. Play the "boing" to check it out.
4. Scan backwards to before the "boing" and get a sense of when it's coming. You may have to do this a couple of times.
5. Scan backwards again, this time hitting PAUSE on the CD player just before the sound.
6. Switch the mixer from CUE to PROGRAM. Turn up the CD's volume control on the mixer.
7. When you want the "boing," just hit PLAY on the CD player.
8. When the "boing" is finished, either turn down the CD volume or switch it to STOP so that you don't catch the "clunk, clunk" that follows the "boing."

Using a professional CD player and professionally made sound-effect CDs, the process is simpler and more exact. Every sound, be it a music selection or a sound effect, is separately indexed—by number—on the disc. If you punch in the number for *boing* and hit PLAY, the *boing* will play; you don't have to search for it. The other steps are the same as described earlier.

One thing to watch out for: The meters of some mixers will display a source's level in the PROGRAM mode but not in the CUE mode. So once your production starts, you can CUE UP your sound effect, but you can't tell whether it's loud enough (using the meter) until you're in the PROGRAM mode and the sound effect is already being aired—perhaps at the wrong volume until you make the adjustment as it plays, which is already too late. Solution: Prior to your actual TV production, be sure to check the proper volume level for your sound effects.

Always make a habit of marking the proper volume settings on the knobs so that you know where to turn them during the show. This preproduction planning can save guesswork, confusion, and precious time during the actual shooting.

Cueing up other devices requires a similar technique. Since some machines don't scan backwards, you may be required to play forward to the desired sound, stop, rewind a speck, play again, and by trial and error find the beginning of the desired passage.

Cueing a Reel-to-Reel Tape

People still use analog reel-to-reel tape players, so here's the (slightly antiquated) technique of cueing up a *boing* on one of these dinosaurs.

In general, you switch your mixer to CUE and play the tape, when you get to "boing," you stop the tape, back it up to just an inch or so before the sound began, and leave the tape parked there ready to play. Switch the mixer to PROGRAM. Hit PLAY when the time comes.

Mechanically, you do the following:

1. While your mixer is in the CUE mode, you play the tape until you come to the "boing."
2. Find the beginning of the "boing." Depending on the kind of reel-to-reel tape recorder you are using, you may use one of the following two procedures:
   a. Procedure 1:
      i. Press STOP to stop the tape.
      ii. Throw a CUEING lever, which physically places the tape heads against the tape. In this position, the heads will "listen" to the tape when it moves, even while the machine is on STOP (see Figure 6–18).
      iii. Place your left hand on the left reel and your right hand on the right reel and manually back the tape up, keeping it slightly taut. You will hear the "boing" playing backwards.

FIGURE 6–18 Lever places audio heads against tape so that you can hear sound when the tape is manually moved.

    iv. If you are unsure of what you are hearing, you may wish to "rock" the tape back and forth, listening to the *boing* backward and forward a few times until you are sure you've got the *b* in *boing*.

    v. Back the tape up an inch more. Good sound-effects tapes leave space between the effects so that you should not run into the *hee haw* that precedes the *boing*. Also, some reel-to-reel tape recorders start and stop on a dime. You may need only a ½ inch of tape silence before the sound effect to give the machine a running start to play the sound smoothly. Older mechanical tape machines may need a couple inches of tape to get a smooth rolling start. If your sound effects are recorded at 7½ inches per second (as they should be), then 1 inch equals about 1/7 second, a very small delay before your sound effect begins. If, however, your sound-effects tape was recorded at 3¾ inches per second, the delay for ½ inch of tape will give you a 1/7 second head start.

  b. Procedure 2:

    i. When you find your *boing*, press PAUSE on your tape player.

    ii. While in PAUSE, manually back up your tape by turning the reels.

    iii. When you reach the *b* in *boing*, move the tape just a little farther (about an inch) so that it has some "start-up" time.

3. Switch your mixer to PROGRAM. When the time comes, press PLAY on your audiotape player, and out comes *boing*. Don't forget to kill the sound afterward, or you'll catch the *cluck, cluck* that follows it.

Cueing a Phonograph Record

The process is similar to cueing a tape.

1. Switch the mixer to CUE mode.
2. Start the turntable.
3. Manually lay the tone arm onto the record grooves, picking it up and searching for the *boing*.
4. When you find the *boing*, stop the disk by either (depending on the record player)
  a. Shifting the turntable to neutral and braking its rotation with your finger.

b. Switching the turntable to STOP and braking its rotation with your finger.

c. Physically braking the motion of the disc with your fingers. You hold the disc on the edge while the felt turntable skids around underneath.

5. Physically rotate the disc backwards in search of the *b* in *boing*. Rock it backwards and forwards to get a "feel" for the sound's position, then back up a tad farther.

6. Switch the mixer to PROGRAM.

7. Start the disc playing by either

a. Shifting the turntable into gear

b. Switching the turntable to ON or PLAY

c. Letting go of the record's edge.

RECORDING STEREO

Although the following discussion will focus on stereo for video recording, the rules for stereo *audio* recording are about the same. So how *does* one record in stereo?

With Mikes

With microphones it's easy. Simply plug one mike into the left MIC IN and another into the right MIC IN and shoot. Whatever is picked up by the left mike is recorded on the left channel, and whatever goes into the right mike is recorded on the right channel. Figures 6–12 and 6–13 diagrammed the process.

Although some VCRs adjust the recording volume automatically, others have two manual controls: one for the left volume and one for the right volume. Set both controls so that the volumes are fairly equal and rarely exceed 0VU on the meter scale.

From CDs and Tapes

To record stereo sound from a CD or tape player, simply connect *two* PATCH CORDS from the player's left and right outputs to the VCR's left and right audio inputs. Play the CD or tape, hit DUB or RECORD on the VCR, and the electric genies do the rest. Figure 6–19 diagrams the hookup. Incidentally, if you hook up only one channel (use one PATCH CORD), many camcorders and VCRs will automatically switch to MONAURAL and record the same signal on both channels. If you really want channel 2 to be silent, feed that input a PATCH CORD that goes nowhere.

Stereo Connectors

You can tell that a headphone or microphone is stereo by looking at its connector. Instead of having a shaft and a tip at the end of the plug, as do some in Table 6–1 and Figure 2–11, the plug will have a tip, a ring, and a shaft (often called "tip-ring-sleeve") as shown in Figure 6–20. The shaft of the plug

---

*Patch cord   A short cable that connects the output of one device to the input of another.

Dub   To duplicate, as in "please dub this tape." Also, the name for the copy of a tape, as in "the dub is on the shelf." Dub cables assist in the process of sending signals from a VCP (video cassette player) to a VCR. *Audio* dub means to replace the present recorded sound with new sound.

*Room tone   A character, "color," or individual "personal-ity" of a sound recorded in a particular room, caused by echoes and background noises in the room.

Sound perspective   Sonic attributes of a sound that make it sound near or far from us.

Tone generator   Electronic circuit often built into mixers, which can create an even, standardized audio signal. Used for checking volume levels, it provides a handy reference tone.

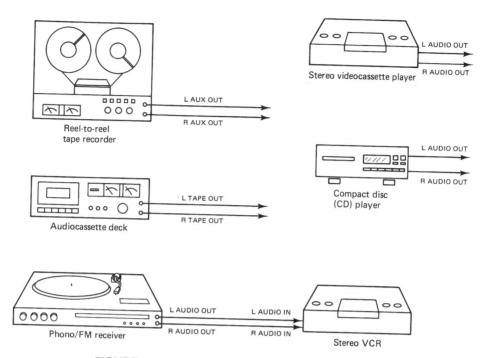

FIGURE 6–19   Recording stereo from CDs and tapes.

Audio PATCH CORD.

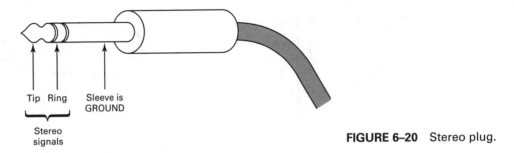

Tip Ring   Sleeve is
             GROUND

Stereo
signals

FIGURE 6–20   Stereo plug.

is "ground," and the tip and ring carry the two signals. Other stereo devices may simply have two plugs rather than one combo plug. Devices using BALANCED LINES use two plugs.

 Mini Review

- Cue up sound effects and mark their volumes on the mixer sliders so that they are ready to use during the show.
- Cueing up a sound involves finding it, listening to it, and parking the player just before the beginning of the sound. If you did this procedure by using the mixer's "audition" or "cue" channel (unheard by the audience), remember to switch the source back to "program" so that it gets heard or recorded when you press "play."
- Recording stereo requires either two microphones or a connection with two patch cords to a CD player or some other stereo device.

RECORDING AUDIO THAT IS TO BE EDITED

For close-up shots, use a close mike; for distant shots, pull the mike farther away. This will make the close shots "sound" close (the bass sounds will be stronger and have "presence") and the far shots will "sound" farther away. Thus the sound better matches the shots. This is called SOUND PERSPECTIVE. Where SOUND PERSPECTIVE is important (as in drama or realism), LAPEL mikes are unsuitable. BOOM mikes are easier to move.

When you edit videotapes, possibly manipulating audio and video separately, the two sometimes get unsyncronized. Start each recording with something visible that makes a noise, such as having someone clap their hands once on camera. Next, do your countdown, cue your talent, and start your scene for real. The sound will be a good guide for the editor later to associate with the motion, synchronizing the audio and video for the rest of the scene.

Also record some background sound (called ROOM TONE). Tell everybody to be quiet and record a minute of ambient background sound in the room, factory, party, or forest where you happen to be recording. Not only can you use this as filler between prepared audio segments (as opposed to a jarring silence) for continuity, but the sound serves as a nice background for voiceovers that you might decide to add later.

If you have a TONE GENERATOR, record a thirty-second sample of 0dB TONE at the beginning of your tape to help the editor calibrate his/her equipment. More about this in Chapter 14 (Editing a Videotape).

OTHER AUDIO DEVICES

Audio Patch Bay

Figure 6–21 shows an audio PATCH BAY. It is like a telephone operator's switchboard that allows any phone to be connected to any other phone in the building. What the operator's switchboard did for phones, the AUDIO PATCH BAY does for audio signals. Without a PATCH BAY, if you wanted the CD player to go where the cassette player now goes, you'd have to dig around the spaghetti of wires behind the equipment to make this change. If the CD player had a plug different from the cassette player's, you'd have to find an adapter to make the plug fit in the socket. You may even have to remove the equipment from the console just to *see* the plugs.

What a drag! Solution: Send all the inputs and outputs for *everything* to a place called a PATCH BAY. Here, like the telephone operator, you can connect any device to any other device externally, simply, and with a standardized plug.

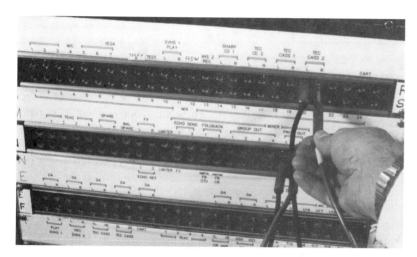

FIGURE 6–21 Audio PATCH BAY.

Patch bay In audio, several rows of sockets connected to the inputs and outputs of various audio devices. Plugging a patch cable into a pair of sockets connects them so that the signal can travel from one device to the other.

Normal-through, or normaled In a patch bay, the top socket is automatically connected to the socket directly beneath when no patch cable is plugged into either. The signal "normally" travels through from one to the other.

Synchronization clearance Permission acquired from music copyright holders to use parts of their music to go along with parts of your TV show.

Fair use Part of the copyright law that allows copyrighted music to be copied, without permission, under specific circumstances.

Buyout Method for paying to use copyrighted music. The user pays one fee to record in his/her TV productions any of a producer's music for a set length of time.

Needle drop Method for paying to use copyrighted music. The user pays separately for each piece of music used.

Music blanket Method for paying to use copyrighted music. The user pays a fee based on the length of his/her show.

Annual music license Method for paying to use copyrighted music. An institution or company pays one fee for permission to perform the music (e.g., for band recitals, plays, graduations) on site for a year.

Just because the PATCH BAY has lots of plugs and sockets, it doesn't mean that you can connect *anything* to *anything*. If you PATCHED microphone 3 to the place where the audiocassette player went, you probably got no sound. The audiocassette player was sending a HIGH-LEVEL signal to a HIGH-LEVEL input. When you plugged the LOW-LEVEL microphone into the HIGH-LEVEL input via the PATCH BAY, the mike didn't have enough oomph to register a sound. In short, only compatible outputs can be PATCHED to inputs if you want sweet sound.

Many PATCH BAYS are NORMAL-THROUGH. This feature means that if you don't plug anything into the PATCH BAY, whatever is available at the top socket automatically goes to the bottom socket. For instance, if the top socket is labeled VCR OUT and the socket directly beneath it is labeled MIXER 4 IN, then the VCR is connected to that mixer input even though nothing is plugged into the sockets. As soon as you plug a PATCH CORD into *either* of those two sockets, that connection is undone. The socket then gets/sends its signal from/to wherever the PATCH CORD goes. Disconnecting the PATCH CORD re-establishes the NORMALED circuit.

PRERECORDED MUSIC AND EFFECTS

There's nothing like a little wind and thunder to add spice to a video show. And some music is a nice way to start off a program or wrap it up. Where do these sounds come from?

Popular Music

It is possible to use commercially available prerecorded music from a CD album or music recorded from the radio. Such music is easily accessible and recognizable. There's just one problem: copyright clearance. If you're just using the music for a class exercise, you can skip the rest of this section. The copyright police aren't likely to come after you for temporarily using somebody's music in such a private and limited way. This may be considered a FAIR USE of copyrighted music. Also, many schools pay for an ANNUAL MUSIC LICENSE to use music on campus in plays and recitals, and this license is likely to cover classroom use of music as well. If, however, you're producing a tape for a client or a tape that you will distribute publicly (whether for profit or for nonprofit), then you must take this copyright thing seriously, obeying the rules that follow.

Prerecorded music is generally copyrighted. Someone else owns the right to copy, perform (play in public), and make money from it. Radio stations, record producers, sheet music distributors, and filmmakers all pay royalties to the copyright holder (and sometimes to the performers, too) for the right to distribute the work. You, too, may need permission to use someone else's music in your TV production. In most cases, this permission will cost you money—a lot of money if the music is very popular.

Before committing yourself to a popular music selection, find out who produced it (the name will be on the record label, or you could look the data up in music-listing catalogs). Send a letter telling what song you wish to use, how much of the song will be used, how it will be used in the production, who the audience will be, and how the program will be distributed. The record company (or copyright holder) will either say you may not use the music, may use it for free, or may use it for a fee.

If you are unclear as to who owns the copyright to the music you want, try this: Check the record label for the letters ASCAP, BMI, or SESAC. These are three large licensing agencies that act on behalf of many copyright holders.

Commercially available music that will be used as part of a TV production must also have a SYNCHRONIZATION CLEARANCE. This is the right to mate someone's music to your TV show, that is, as an introduction or a background. For SESAC music you can obtain SYNC rights directly from SESAC. For all the others, you contact

The Harry Fox Agency
Synchronization Licensing
110 East 59th Street
New York, NY 10022
Tel.: (212) 370–5330

EMI Music Publishing
810 7th Ave.
New York, NY 10019
Tel.: (212)-830–2000

They will send you a standardized form asking how the music will be used and will calculate the fee.

Music and Sound-Effects Libraries

Nearly all music and sound-effects heard in industrial video programs come from music and sound effects *libraries*, sets of CDs or tapes containing everything from a cuckoo clock to a steamship whistle or from a dripping roof to a raging waterfall. Music is also widely varied. It may be organized by length, instrument type, or style. Styles could befit the stately entrance of a king, the silent stalk of a slithering snake, or the gaiety of a camping trip. Thousands of albums are available from stock music and sound effects producers. The licenses work in several different ways:

BUYOUT: Here you pay one fee for the set of CDs or DAT tapes and can use the music any way you wish in your productions as long as you want.
CDs cost about $75 to $250 each.

NEEDLE DROP: This is a one-time fee you pay for a specific cut of music in a specific production. The fee could run about $60 per cut, depending on the length of the cut.

MUSIC BLANKET: This method charges you a fee based on the length of your show (maybe $250 for a ten-minute show), regardless of the number of cuts you used from the provider's album.

ANNUAL MUSIC LICENSE: Particularly useful for those who do a lot of productions, here you pay one fee (maybe $1,000) for the year and can use as much of the production music as you want for the year.

Some licensing contracts restrict you to certain kinds of productions (i.e., non-broadcast, national network TV commercials, theatrical productions) and charge rates proportionate to the expected size of your audience.

Music Selection

When you are selecting music, the most important consideration is how fast or slow it moves. Tempo will create a mood or reinforce the nature of the visuals. A fast tempo would support a montage of quick scenes previewing or reviewing a program. Something slower would go better with scenes of a thief sneaking through a building but would speed up upon the thief's hasty retreat.

If you are scoring the music behind a voice, try to match the tempo of the music to the pace of the voice. Slow, serious, reflective narration deserves slow, serious music. Excited, happy narration needs bright, up-tempo music.

Avoid recognizable music or music with rhythmic or melodic elements that draws attention to itself. It may distract the audience and interfere with their ability to concentrate on the narrator's message. This is especially true in educational or industrial TV programs.

The musical selection could be short to emphasize a point (*Ta da!* the orchestra rejoices as our hero conquers the mountain peak) or could linger in the background to set a psychological attitude. A rich string sound conveys class and luxury. Electric guitars and keyboards conjure up pop/rock visions associated with youth. Banjos and fiddles promote a "down-home" or southern country feeling.

Match your music to your audience. Do you think the board of directors will appreciate their yearly sales figures supported by a Nashville pickin' fanfare? Would your exercise class enjoy a stately and conservative orchestral sonata?

 **Mini Review**

- If the production is to be edited, record a sample of quiet "room tone" in the room where you will be recording and start each tape with a test tone.
- The audio patch bay allows you to connect nearly any audio device with any other in the studio.
- Prerecorded music and sound effects are usually copyrighted, requiring you to pay a fee if they are used in a distributed TV production.
- Match the tempo and energy of your music with that of the pictures.

DIGITAL AUDIO

Your steering wheel is ANALOG; you can steer your car slightly left, very right, or anywhere in between. Your headlights are DIGITAL; they're either "off" or "on." Where ANALOG equipment works with varying electrical voltages, DIGITAL equipment uses "on" and "off" signals, or ones and zeroes.

DIGITAL equipment has several advantages over ANALOG:

1. DIGITAL circuits are often smaller, cheaper, and easier to build than ANALOG.
2. DIGITAL signals are easily copied without degradation.

ANALOG electrical vibrations pick up noise and interference, making audio and video copies worse than originals. DIGITAL copies of a signal are simply copies of ones and zeroes; even if the ones and zeroes are fuzzy, weak, too strong, or slightly distorted, they are still ones and zeroes. Copying machines can "replace" incoming fuzzy ones and zeroes with sharp new ones, keeping the stream of numbers exactly the same and thus reproducing a signal perfectly.

So how do sound vibrations get turned into digits? The sound waves are changed to electrical vibrations by the microphone, then amplified (made bigger) in the mixer. An ANALOG-TO-DIGITAL (A/D) CONVERTER measures the strength of the wave thousands of times per second (referred to as "samples per second") and assigns a number to each sample. Thus, the vibrations become a stream of numbers. Another circuit changes the numbers mathematically into a series of ones and zeros that get

---

Analog   A signal that varies continuously, as opposed to a digital signal made of discrete levels. A device that works with analog signals.

*Digital   Something that is either "on" or "off." A light switch is digital. On and off can be represented by the digits 1 and 0. Digital equipment copies signals without introducing noise and distortion.

Analog-to-digital (A-to-D) converter   A circuit that samples an analog signal and expresses the information as digital data.

Digital-to-analog (D-to-A) converter   A circuit that changes digital data into analog signals, such as audio.

Test tone   Electronically generated audio signal, often created by the mixer, used to help set audio levels on recorders and other audio equipment.

Sampling frequency   In digital audio equipment, the number of times per second a device measures the signal; the number of times an analog wave gets "sliced up" for measurement and conversion to digits.

CD-ROM   Compact Disc—Read-Only Memory, a CD with data files on it, readable by your computer.

recorded by a computer or digital audio or video recorder. When the signal needs to be heard, the ones and zeros are converted to voltages that reconstitute a wave that simulates the original audio signal. Figure 6–22 diagrams the process.

Digitized Audio

There are three common approaches to providing audio in TV or MULTIMEDIA programs:

1. Direct playback from the audio tracks of a CD or DAT (DIGITAL AUDIOTAPE)
2. WAVE audio, a computer file holding a digital representation of the actual sound
3. MIDI, a computer file of performance instructions (not the actual sounds)

Each has its advantages and weaknesses.

Compact Disc (CD) and Digital Audiotape (DAT)

When sound is recorded DIGITALLY, its electrical vibrations are sliced up into tiny samples (44,100 samples per second in the case of a CD, 48,000 samples per second for DAT) and the samples converted into numbers. These DIGITS, expressed as binary ones and zeroes, are converted into "pits" and shiny places in a spiral on a CD. When "read" by a pinpoint of laser light in the CD player, the digital data are converted back into ANALOG sound.

Although not as delicate as phonograph records, CDs still need gentle care. Fingerprints and scratches cause data losses heard as clicks or distortions to the sound. Handle CDs by their edges and park them in their jewel cases when not in use.

CDs can't be cued up by rocking them back and forth like reel-to-reel tapes or phono records. The best you can do is to play the disc, then PAUSE it just before the desired selection. When ready, UNPAUSE the disc for your sound.

Although all CDs and CD players permit you to jump directly to particular songs or tracks, only certain CDs and professional CD players INDEX the songs into smaller segments. Industrial production music libraries often INDEX their music and sound effects, making it easier to play just one movement of a symphony, one verse of a song, or one cock-a-doodle of a rooster.

DIGITAL AUDIOTAPE machines, like CDs, store sounds digitally, permitting wide frequency response, low noise, and superb copyability. The tape looks like an 8mm videocassette (slightly larger than an audiocassette) and is recorded by a spinning video head, much as in a VCR. Besides making superb hi-fi original recordings, DAT machines can record the data directly from other CDs or DATs.

---

*DIN connector   Round, multipin plug or socket.

*Multimedia   Audio, video, text, graphics, and other information delivered by computer.

DAT   Digital audiotape, a cassette with binary data representing stereo sound. Also, the machine that converts analog audio to digital and records it, as well as plays it back converting the digital data to analog audio.

*WAVE, or .WAV file   A computer file of digitized sound.

*MIDI, or .MID file   Musical Instrument Digital Interface, a standardized way of sending digital instructions between audio devices and musical instruments, telling them, for instance, what notes to play.

Index   Subdivision of a song or track on a CD, allowing you to select and play a particular stanza or phrase.

Sound card   Computer circuit that digitizes audio or converts digital audio back to sound signals, and perhaps plays audio from MIDI instructions.

Headroom   On an audio meter, the space between the highest sound peak registering on the meter and the 0dB mark (maximum level recordable); the "safety margin" before the sound overloads the machine.

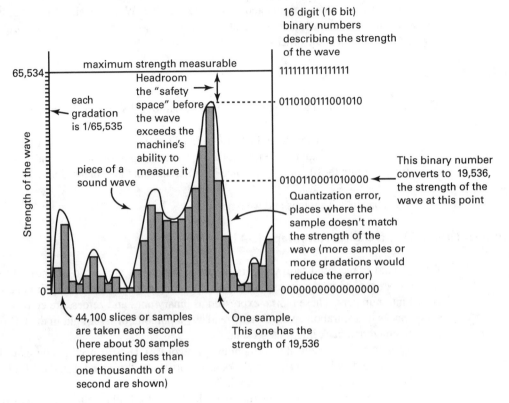

FIGURE 6–22   How an audio wave changes to numbers.

To prevent people from duping off copies and copies-of-copies of copyrighted music, the manufacturers have equipped DAT machines with copy-thwarting circuits called SCMS (Serial Copy Management System). You can, of course, copy any of your own original sounds as many times as you want.

DAT recorders cost $700 to $2,000, depending on features, and, for the technophiles among you, they can record sound at 32k, 44k, or 48k samples per second. Recordings can last up to 120 minutes per cassette.

Working with digital audio equipment is quite similar to working with analog gear. Audio goes in, audio comes out, and it doesn't matter to you what it's doing inside the box. Keep your connectors tight. Use BALANCED LINES to avoid hum, and pay attention to signal levels so that they're strong, but not too strong.

How does DAT recording differ from analog?

1. Digital recorders can not tolerate signals that are too strong. On analog recorders, the volume meter would pin itself in the red area and your sound would be distorted for a moment. On digital gear, the signal goes all to pieces if you exceed the max. It is wise to check your source carefully to make sure your maximum volumes are a shade below the maximum on the DAT meter scale. For instance, if copying from a videotape sound track, play the tape into the DAT machine, watching for the loudest audio passages. Turn the DAT record volume down enough so these passages don't reach the maximum on the DAT meter (or memorize where these loud passages are and turn the record volume control down before you get to them).

Figure 2–4 *Three–chip color camera breaks colored light into its primary colors.*

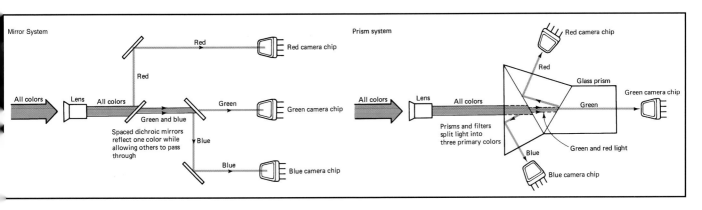

Figure 3–36 *Camera filter (Courtesy of Cokin).*

Before using GRADUATED FILTER, y is pale and washed out.

After using GRADUATED FILTER.

Figure 5–3 COLOR TEMPERATURE *mismatch*.

Common fluorescent light from our left mixes poorly with incandescent light from our right.

Figure 7–21 CHROMA KEY *using blue. (See also back cover.)*

Camera #1

Camera #2

CHROMA KEY

Camera #1

Camera #2

Camera #2 in the studio shoots a photo. A video tape or a computer generated graphic could also provide the background picture.

CHROMA KEY

Figure 8–13 *Good and bad colors for lettering and backgrounds.*

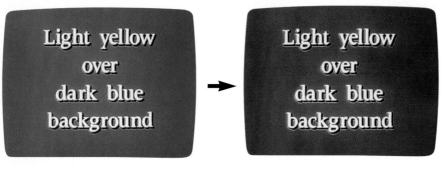

Light yellow over blue background is visually appealing …

… and also shows up well on b&w TV.

Saturated yellow letters may look okay in color but compare them with b&w Figure 8-

Green letters over a blue-green background look awful and are also hard to see. Avoid colors that are similar or are near each other on the color selector continuum of your CHARACTER GENERATOR. Also when letters are the same brightness as their background, they disappear when viewed on black-and-white TVs...

...as seen here.

Figure 8–25 *Compression ratio compared*

Close-up of screen showing high compression blockiness. Compute stores 37 minutes of audio and video per gigabyte.

Similar close-up of screen. Blockiness is barely visible. Low compression stores 11 minutes pe gigabyte.

Figure 8–26 WIREFRAME.

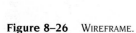

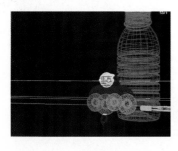

Shows the structure onto which surfaces are placed. Objects can be moved in real time (you can test your animation on the the spot).

Figure 8–27 FLATSHADE (*also called* QUICK-SHADE).

Popular, quick way to show what a final image will look like. Objects can move but require powerful computers and the motion is often a bit slow.

Figure 8–28 *Final* RENDER.

This RENDER took 3 minutes. Your mileage may vary depending on the complexity of the picture and your computer speed. One can't edit or move objects in this mode except with top-of-the-line graphics workstations.

DAT, DIGITAL AUDIO TAPE RECORDER (Courtesy of Technics).

The above process is called "leaving HEADROOM" which is a way of saying "don't let the signal bump its head on the ceiling," the zero number on the DAT meter scale (Figure 6–23).

Unlike the analog days where you tried to hit 0VU on the recording meter with your sound or TEST TONE, in the digital world you shoot for −20dB. Zero is the *danger zone.* Audio levels above 0dB FS (FS means full scale) will sound like clicks or pops.

If you're trying to calibrate your analog mixer with your DAT recorder using a TEST TONE, do this: Adjust the TONE volume on the mixer to read 0VU. Adjust the record volume on the DAT machine to

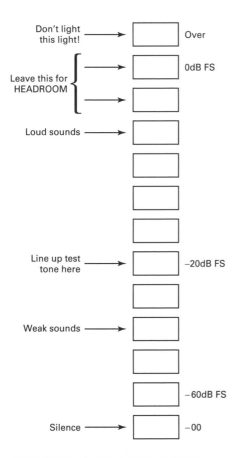

* The FS means "Full Scale," the maximum allowable signal.

FIGURE 6–23   Digital audio level meter.

read –20dB. Now you can watch the VU meter, keeping it below +3VU or watch the DAT meter, keeping it below 0 dB FS.

2. If you are feeding signals from one digital audio device to another, use their *digital inputs and outputs* directly, if possible, to copy the *digits*, not the converted audio. Each analog/digital conversion your audio takes adds some artifacts to the sound. If the two machines use different SAMPLING frequencies (e.g., one is 44.1kHz and the other is 48kHz), throw a switch on the *recorder* to have it work in the *player's* frequency.

3. Digital recording equipment can often record TIME CODE (explained in Chapter 14), useful for synchronizing the audio to the video events while editing.

CDs and DATS spew out binary digits that get converted to sound. They don't make files such as those we're used to on computers. Playing a CD from your computer's CD-ROM drive doesn't use your computer's "brain." The digits bypass your computer's memory and go directly to a DIGITAL-TO-ANALOG CONVERTER in your computer's SOUND CARD that sends audio to an output in the back of the card.

Wave Files

WAVE audio is a computer file (you can recognize these files by their file names that end in .WAV) having a digital representation of the actual sound. You could, for instance, speak into a microphone connected to your SOUND CARD and have the digitized speech saved as a file called MYVOICE.WAV on your computer's hard drive. You could record a song or copy a whole CD of music into your .WAV file, but the file would end up huge.

Unlike CDs that store data at a standard quality, you can record WAVE files at lower, more data-frugal, bit rates and sampling rates. Instead of sampling at 44.1kHz, you could (by using a menu in your sound software) choose 22kHz or 11kHz.

WAVE files can be played, copied, edited (using audio editing software), attached to word processing and e-mail documents (the recipient can read *and* hear the words), and incorporated into multimedia programs.

Wave pattern representing the phrase, *Today's Video*, digitized and ready to be edited.

MIDI

MIDI, which stands for musical instrument digital interface, is a standardized way to send instructions from one instrument, computer, sound card, or other digital audio device, to another. MIDI is digital (data made of ones and zeros), but it isn't sound; it is instructions on which note to play, how hard to play the note, how long to hold the note, and similar details. MIDI can handle large numbers of notes at once, and can assign certain notes to certain musical instruments. And since notes are, in a way, button-presses, an "instrument" could be a piano, synthesizer, or VCR playing, pausing, and rewinding on MIDI command, or stage lights switching on and off in time to music.

The actual sound comes from an electronic musical instrument or a sound generator circuit. It could be digital or analog, and could be a SOUND CARD in your computer or a stand-alone device. Like a music box or player piano, the MIDI instructions just tell the sound generator what notes to play. Since sound requires a lot of digital data but instructions on which note to play need very little data, MIDI is a compact way to store and transmit "music."

You can install a MIDI card in your computer; many SOUND CARDS have MIDI built-in. On the back of the card is a pair of DIN (multipin) sockets. Connect them to any MIDI-compatible musical keyboard or drum machine, and your computer can direct an entire symphony. There are sound generator boxes that can produce the sounds of dozens of different instruments at once. With a MIDI compatible synthesizer, you can even concoct your own sounds.

You can recognize a MIDI file by the .MID file extension at the end of the file name. Like a word processing file, a MIDI file can be created from scratch, edited, copied, or sent over the Internet. You can change the tempo of the MIDI instructions, their key, and which instruments (banjo, violin, voices, pipe organ) will play the sounds.

Rather than acquiring prepared music from a production house, you could get licensed MIDI files of songs and use them to produce your own music, changing it to fit your needs. The drums could be muted, the tempo sped up, the oboes replaced with tubas, and the ending made to repeat twelve times, for instance.

Choosing a Digital Format

If you have prerecorded music or lengthy voice-overs, use a CD or DAT; there's just too much data to handle easily as a WAVE or other type of file.

If you can make the music inside your computer, then use MIDI files. You don't have to store tons of data from the actual music, just the playing instructions, which are brief.

If the sound passage is short (a few sentences or a sound effect), then WAVE files are easy to handle and edit. If you have a long sound passage, you might break it into several shorter clips and use WAVE files.

 Mini Review

- Analog signals degrade when copied; digital signals do not.
- Digital audio recorders cannot tolerate signals that are too strong; you must not exceed 0dB on their meters.
- Wave (.WAV) files are digital representations of a sound that can be copied or edited on a computer.
- Midi (.MID) files are digital data that represent strokes on a musical instrument (not the actual sounds). The files can be copied and edited with a computer and represent very little data.

SUMMARY: GETTING THE BEST AUDIO

Room

1. Use a quiet room, one with thick walls and tight-fitting doors to seal out extraneous noise.
2. Keep the room quiet by turning off fans, noisy air conditioners, and other machines while taping. Move the VCR as far away from the microphone as possible, perhaps by placing it behind something or by moving it to another room.
3. Use an anechoic room. Reduce echoes by hanging curtains, laying carpet, or draping blankets over the walls.

Microphone

1. Use a mike with a BALANCED LINE to keep electronic "noise" from sneaking into your cable.
2. Whenever feasible, use DIRECTIONAL microphones to reject room noise, especially if the mikes cannot be kept close to the performers.
3. Keep mikes close (6 to 18 inches) to your performers.
4. When possible, keep the performers from handling mikes or cords during the recording, *or* use a specially constructed mike that insulates against hand and cord noises.
5. If the mike has a switch called LOW CUT filter, leave it *off* for music and *on* for speech.
6. Use a WINDSCREEN if miking outdoors.
7. Place carpet or foam under the mike stand to keep floor or desk vibrations from being recorded.
8. If the mike is to be hand-held, choose an OMNIDIRECTIONAL one. CARDIOIDS and DIRECTIONALS are often too sensitive to hand noises and "booming" when held too close to the performer's mouth.

Cable

1. Again, use BALANCED LINES whenever possible. Keep cable runs to three hundred feet or less.
2. If using UNBALANCED LINES, make sure you are using *shielded* cable only. Keep cable length to an absolute minimum, no more than thirty feet *maximum* for microphones.
3. Keep people from tripping by tying cables to your mike stand base or by taping cables to the floor in heavy traffic areas.
4. Loop the TIE CLIP mike cable through the performer's belt so the cable isn't tugging directly on the microphone as he or she moves.

Inputs

1. Use LINE or HIGH-LEVEL signals whenever available to feed AUX or HIGH LEVEL inputs (i.e., feed the mixer's HIGH LEVEL OUT to your VCR's LINE IN). This reduces the electronic noise that can creep into your cables.
2. Keep enough ADAPTERS handy so you can use *what's best* and not have to make do with *what fits*.

Mixers

1. To judge volume levels, trust the mixer's meter. To judge fidelity, trust your ears. Monitor everything.

2. Avoid using mixer filters when recording music. Use them primarily for speech or for adapting to poor room acoustics.

3. Attempt to record the highest-level signal possible without distorting your sound or reaching the maximum on any digital equipment. VU meters should ride consistently around 0dB with occasional spikes up to +3dB. Doing this assures that your source is much louder than background hiss and noise on your tape. Digital recorders should never hear signals above 0dB, the max on their scales.

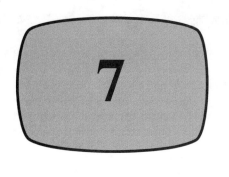

CAMERA SWITCHING AND SPECIAL EFFECTS

To select which camera gets "on the air" (or onto the tape), you need a switcher. Learning to operate a switcher from a book is much like learning origami over the telephone or learning about relationships from the soap operas. As one studies, one must have the equipment in hand in order to visualize the results of each manipulation. Experiment. See what happens. The experience of *doing* will develop skills faster than the experience of *reading*.

Some folks get along just fine without ever having a switcher or more than one camera. They may record all the MEDIUM SHOTS at one time and then move the camera and record all the CLOSE-UPS later. This raw footage is then viewed and logged, and the best scenes are selected. One by one, these scenes are edited onto a master tape. Because the scenes change from close shots to far shots, the viewer never knows that only one camera was used. It looks as if the director simply switched from one camera to another. Thus, it is possible to assemble a complete, nice-looking show with but one camera and no switcher. This is called the SINGLE CAMERA TECHNIQUE.

The problem with this technique is that it is so time consuming. The performance has to be done and redone for each camera angle recorded. Special attention must be paid to continuity of action, so that if the farmer is holding the chicken in his left hand in the long shot, the chicken had better be in his left hand again when you shoot the scene again for close-ups. The viewing, logging, and selecting of shots and the final editing of the raw footage into a master tape takes many hours.

This is where a switcher saves a heap of time. If one camera is taking medium or long shots and another is taking close-ups, an alert director, by pressing a button, can select the shot to be recorded. There are no continuity problems, no reviewing, no logging, and no editing. Unless someone makes a mistake, you end up with a final, nice-looking tape at the end of one performance. What took the SINGLE-CAMERA people half a week to produce may take you only half an hour to produce by using a switcher.

Producing a whole show "live" with a switcher requires great skill (and a pint of stomach acid). In the real world, directors and performers make mistakes. Editing may still be needed, but since most of the show has already been assembled by the switcher, the task is much quicker.

Single camera technique   Method of making a TV production by using one camera, shooting scenes from different positions, and later editing together the best shots.

Sync generator   Electronic device that makes the sync signal that synchronizes the electronics of several cameras so that their pictures can be mixed together.

Loop or bridge   Electrical connection that allows most of the signal to enter one socket and exit from an adjacent socket to be used elsewhere.

*Line, or program, monitor   TV monitor that shows the final signal that is being broadcast or sent to the VTRs.

*Camera monitor   TV monitor in the control room that shows a particular TV camera's picture.

There are different kinds of switchers, from supersimple to outrageously complex. We are going to start with a simple one and gently work our way toward those multibutton dragons seen in commercial television stations.

THE SIMPLE SWITCHER

Figure 7–1 diagrams how the simple switcher hooks up to the cameras in the studio. Mounted somewhere in the control room is a box of electronics called a SYNC GENERATOR. Rather like a pacemaker for the heart of the studio, the SYNC GENERATOR makes signals that flow *to* the cameras to synchronize their electronics so that they all are producing their pictures in unison. This allows the pictures to be mixed together later and switched cleanly by the switcher. You may never see or touch the SYNC GENERATOR, but you need to know it exists and what it does. If it fails, or doesn't get turned on with the rest of the studio gear, the camera pictures will roll, flop over, or turn into a mess of diagonal lines.

To reduce the number of wires to trip over in the studio, each camera's SYNC signals, along with the camera's video signals, intercom signals, and other TV signals, all travel through one umbilical, the camera cable. With so many wires inside, the camera cable is about as stiff and thick as a water hose.

In little studios, the cameras' video signals may first go to TV monitors (so the director can see what each camera is shooting), and then the signal is LOOPED or BRIDGED (passed along at nearly full strength) to its next destination, the switcher. By pressing a button on the switcher, you select one of the signals, which then leaves the switcher and goes to the LINE, or PROGRAM monitor that displays the chosen picture.

The video signal is LOOPED through the LINE MONITOR on the way to the VCR. The VCR, in turn, has a monitor to show what *it* "sees." Usually the VCR monitor shows the same picture as the LINE MONITOR, but not always. What happens if the VCR is *playing* rather than *recording*? You'll see the

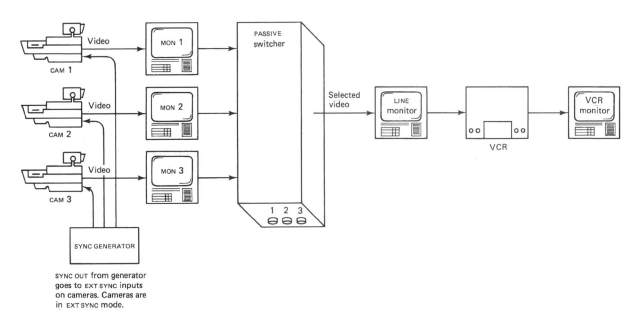

FIGURE 7–1 Simple switcher.

image that is being played, not the camera/switcher's image. And what if something went wrong with the wires to the VCR or the VCR pooped out? The LINE monitor would show that the switcher was sending out a good signal but the VCR wasn't getting it.

Similarly, the CAMERA MONITORS are a handy way to diagnose problems between the cameras and the switcher. If one CAMERA MONITOR shows a screwy image while the others look okay, something's probably wrong with that one camera. If they're all screwy, maybe the SYNC GENERATOR went haywire. And if the CAMERA MONITOR images look good, but the switcher's LINE MONITOR has a bad image, maybe something's askew with the switcher. You may not be able to fix the problem, but you'll have an idea where the cause is.

Some switchers manufacture their own SYNC and send it to the cameras. Others use one camera's video to make a SYNC signal to send to the other cameras. Still others have built in FRAME SYNCHRONIZERS, devices that synchronize the cameras' video signals *inside* the switcher, making the SYNC GENERATOR unnecessary.

Many switchers take in the camera signals directly, sending out signals for the CAMERA MONITORS.

Enough about the spaghetti of switcher connections; it's time to tinker with this tempting toy.

 Mini Review

- Compared to editing video, using a switcher expedites the process of assembling camera shots into a program.
- For camera images to be cleanly switched and mixed together, the camera signals must be synchronized. The studio sync generator generally does this task.
- Monitoring each camera's image, the switcher's image, and the VCR's image helps you diagnose problems in the TV system.

Fader

Figure 7–2 diagrams a simple FADER (no relation to Darth Vader). This FADER has two channels, A and B. By pressing (for instance) button 2 on the top row of buttons, camera 2 is now feeding into channel A. By pressing button 1 on the bottom bank, we get camera 1 to feed to channel B. Thus, camera 2 is on A and camera 1 is on B. The two FADER levers to the right control how much of each channel is selected for recording.

As shown in the figure, the A FADER is all the way *on* and the B FADER is all the way *off*, so the device is passing only the A signal, which is what? Camera 2. Now to DISSOLVE to camera 1's picture, pull both levers all the way down. This decreases A's strength while increasing B's.

Sync   Circuit or a signal that directs the electron gun in a camera or TV picture tube to create a TV picture steadily on a screen. Sync also synchronizes the electronics of other TV equipment.

Frame synchronizer   Electronic device to synchronize two independent video signals so they can be mixed.

*Superimposition, or super   Two pictures that are shown one atop the other. They may look semitransparent or "ghosty." A dissolve stopped halfway.

*Key (or luminance key)   Special effect in which the dark parts of one camera's picture are replaced with parts from another camera's picture.

*Fade   Effect in which a TV picture smoothly turns black (a fade-out) or black smoothly turns to a TV picture (a fade-in).

*Fader   Slider or handle on a switcher that allows you to fade-in or fade-out a picture or dissolve from one picture to another.

*Dissolve (or lap dissolve)   TV effect in which one picture slowly melts into another. One picture fades to black while another simultaneously fades up from black.

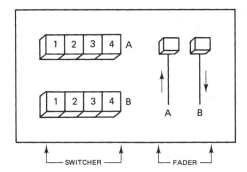

FIGURE 7–2   FADER.

From here let's DISSOLVE to camera 4. First switch the A channel (which is now *off*) from 2 to 4 by pressing the 4 button. Then slide both levers all the way up. A becomes stronger as B becomes weaker, and what is A now? Camera 4, so 4's picture is now *on*.

To FADE OUT, merely move the FADE lever, which is *on*, to *off* while not touching the other lever. The left lever (A channel) would be down while the right one (B channel) would be up; both are now *off*, and both pictures have disappeared.

Pulling both levers only halfway allows both pictures to be seen at once. This effect is called a SUPERIMPOSITION, abbreviated as SUPER. Figures 7–3 and 7–4 show SUPERS of two images. Here you get one half of A's signal and one half of B's signal, making one whole picture (made of two pictures). It is also possible to leave the A lever all the way up (*on*) and the B lever all the way down (*on*) and get a SUPER, but this method may pose a problem: If you get a whole picture signal from A and add a whole signal from B, that makes your total signal twice as strong as it is supposed to be and messes up the video levels on your VCR. So don't SUPER two pictures by moving both FADE levers all the way *on*; just move each to halfway *on*. *An exception to the rule:* If you have two white pictures with black backgrounds (as happens to be the case in Figure 7–4) and the images will not overlap when the SUPER is executed, then both FADE levers may be moved all the way to *on*. In fact, the picture will look best when made this way. This particular operation is permissible because you are not adding one signal (one picture) *over the top* of the other signal (the other picture). The two white images occupy different places on the TV screen and don't mix together to create doubly bright spots on the screen.

Incidentally, some FADERS are fused together; you can't move the bars separately. When you pull the single bar, one channel gets stronger while the other gets weaker.

You will notice in Figure 7–3 that when two pictures are SUPERIMPOSED, they have a "ghosty" effect—you can half-see through both of them. The image is confusing and not very appealing, but it can be useful for special effects. (If you created the ghost of a man, would you call him a SUPER man?)

Words can also be SUPERIMPOSED over a picture. Camera 1 may view the performer, while camera 2 views a graphic with printing on it.

For this SUPER to look its best, use black paper with white lettering. The white lettering will show up, while the black part of the graphic will disappear and not fog up the rest of your picture. Figure 7–5 shows an example.

SUPERS are an imperfect way to put words on a screen because they are so "ghosty." They seem to disappear into light parts of the picture, as shown in Figure 7–6. If you *must* SUPER words, then use the technique similar to what you saw in Figure 7–3. You place the performer in one part of the picture, leaving a dark area in another part. You position the white lettering on another camera so that it will appear over the dark part of the first picture, as shown in Figure 7–7. It is not necessary that the spot where the letters go be absolutely black; just try to make sure that it is very dark—the darker the better.

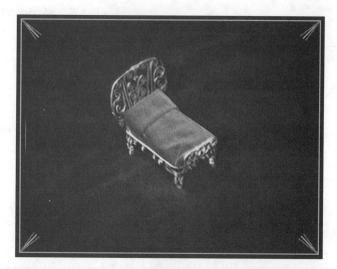

Camera 1

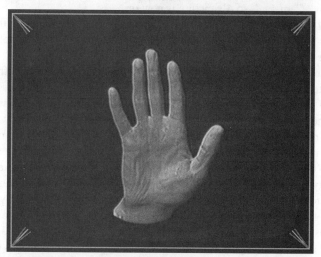

Camera 2

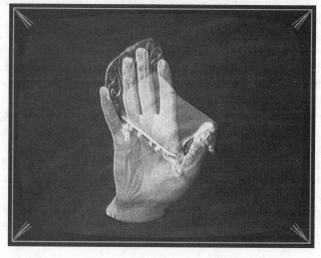

SUPER

FIGURE 7–3 SUPER two images which overlap.

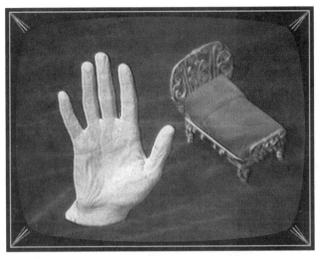

Here it's okay to fade both camera images all the way up

FIGURE 7–4   SUPER two images which do not overlap.

Titler or graphic on camera 1 with white letters over black background

Camera 2

SUPER. Notice that lettering is slightly transparent. DROP SHADOW isn't possible with SUPER. White letters over black background is the only combination that works well.

KEY. Notice that lettering is opaque and with the help of DROP SHADOW stands out clearly.

FIGURE 7–5   Compare a SUPER with a KEY.

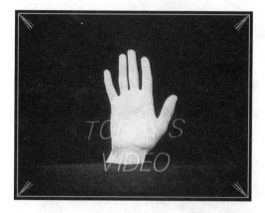

FIGURE 7–6 White words disappearing into parts of a white picture.

KEY is a better method of putting words on a screen because the letters are solid, not ghosty (review Figure 7–5). We'll unlock KEY's mysteries in a minute.

Special Effects Generator

The simplest SPECIAL EFFECTS GENERATORS (hereafter abbreviated SEGs) have the familiar switches and levers for FADING and also have a few more buttons and levers, as diagrammed in Figure 7–8. The buttons select various CORNER INSERTS, and the levers do WIPES. The buttons are labeled with little pictures to show what the effect will look like, and these pictures may also indicate which part of the final picture is from channel A and which part is from channel B. If you slide the WIPE levers to the middle position, your TV screen should show an image that looks like the little picture on the pushbutton.

FIGURE 7–7 SUPER white letters over dark part of picture.

Special effects generator (SEG) Electronic video device that creates effects such as wipes, fades, keys, etc.

*Wipe Special effect that starts with one TV picture on the screen, then a boundary line moves across the screen (vertically, diagonally, or whatever), and where it passes, the first picture changes into a second picture.

*Corner insert Wipe effect in which one corner of the TV screen shows one camera's picture while the rest of the screen shows another's.

*Split screen Wipe that stops partway across the picture, revealing a section of the original picture and a section of the new picture.

Vertical wipe Wipe in which a horizontal boundary line sweeps vertically through the screen, changing the picture as it goes.

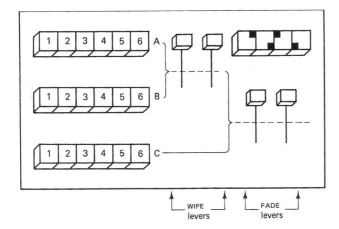

FIGURE 7–8 Simple SPECIAL EFFECTS
GENERATOR.

Moving one of these WIPE levers at this point will either *widen* or *narrow* the CORNER INSERT. Sliding the other lever will either *lengthen* or *shorten* the CORNER INSERT height. It is possible to widen the CORNER INSERT all the way across the screen, thereby creating a horizontally SPLIT SCREEN. Now, by adjusting the other lever, you can raise and lower the split in the screen. This action is called a VERTI-CAL WIPE and is shown in Figure 7–9. You can lower it enough to make it disappear or raise it enough to fill the whole screen.

Learning which lever to move to get the desired effect takes time and experience with the machine. Experiment. There is no button or lever on the SEG that can permanently harm anything if you play with it.

The simplest SEG, such as the Panasonic AVE5 shown in Figure 7–10, may have buttons to select whether the device will create FADES *or* WIPES. More complex SEGs allow you to DISSOLVE *to* a SPE-CIAL EFFECT and then DISSOLVE back *from* it to a regular camera shot. The more complex SEGs (like the one diagrammed back in Figure 7–8) do this by having three channels to work with. Figure 7–11 diagrams how they work.

Channels A and B in Figure 7–9 are called the EFFECTS channels or EFFECTS BUS, while C is just a regular channel. You DISSOLVE TO EFFECTS by sliding the FADE levers from the C channel to the EFFECTS channels, where A and B do their stuff.

Here are some examples of how to use this device:

1. *To switch (CUT) directly from one camera's picture to another:* Let's start with the FADE levers down so that the C channel is on. Simply press any C button for the desired camera shot. It doesn't matter which buttons are pressed on A or B or where the WIPE levers are.

Effects bus Group of related buttons on video SEG/switch-ers to create special effects. A channel on the switcher that you can dissolve to and from, bringing a special effect onto the screen or taking it away.

Studio production switcher Large switcher/SEG that receives all the video sources (inputs from cameras, etc.) and is used to select the pictures or effects to be shown.

Eff 1 (or effects bus 1) A video source can be selected on channel A. Another source can be selected on channel B. A combination of these two can be a special effect that is avail-

able through a circuit called the effects bus. There may be several effects set up on several effects busses. Eff 1 is the name given to just one of those effects busses.

Diagonal split screen Split screen that is divided diagonally.

Cascading or Reentry Process of creating one special effect and then using it as a source (as if the picture had come directly from the camera) that can now be mixed with another picture to create another special effect. Process allows effects to be piggybacked atop one another.

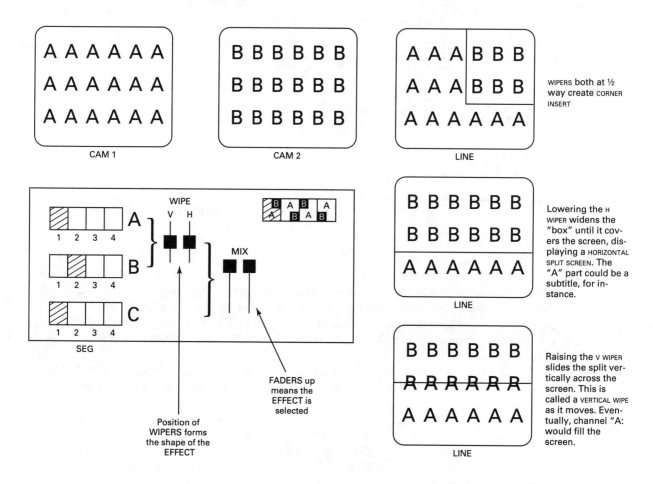

FIGURE 7–9   Making CORNER INSERTS and SPLIT SCREENS.

2. *To DISSOLVE from camera 1 to camera 2:* You might start out with the camera 1 button pressed on the C BUS and the FADE levers *down.* You will eventually push the FADE levers *up* to DISSOLVE to camera 2's picture. To have camera 2's picture waiting for us when we FADE to the EFFECTS BUS (channels A and B), we first have to manipulate those levers. If on the B BUS we press the camera 2 button and slide the WIPE levers all the way down, we will be creating a picture in which camera 2 fills the screen. Put another way, the WIPE levers create a CORNER INSERT that looks like the little picture on the pushbuttons. The B channel fills the little black box on the button, and the A channel fills the white area on the button. By moving the WIPE levers all the way to the B position, the little box will get larger until only the B channel shows. If camera 2 is what the B channel is showing, then your EFFECTS are simply a picture from camera 2.

Back to our exercise: We wanted to FADE from camera 1 to camera 2. To do this, we created an EFFECT, which was simply camera 2. We did this by punching the 2 button on channel B and pulling the WIPE levers down. FADING to camera 2 simply required sliding the FADE levers up.

Once the FADE levers are up and the WIPE levers are down, channel B is what shows. If you now wish to switch to camera 3, you may do it by punching the 3 button on the B BUS.

FIGURE 7–10   Press the MIX button on the Panasonic AVE5 SWITCHER/SEG and the slider will DISSOLVE from channel B to channel A. Press the WIPE button, and the slider will WIPE from channel B to A.

Now if you wish to DISSOLVE from camera 3 to camera 4, you would first press 4 on the C BUS and then slide the FADERS down to DISSOLVE from the B BUS (camera 3) to the C BUS (camera 4).

3. *To DISSOLVE to a CORNER INSERT and back out again:* Let's let channel A show camera 1, channel B show camera 2, and channel C show camera 3. Figure 7–11 will help you follow along.

The EFFECTS buttons are pressed so that A (camera 1) is in the upper right-hand corner of B (camera 2) when the WIPE levers are halfway down. With the FADE levers all the way down, we are displaying only camera 3 (the C channel).

To show the CORNER INSERT of cameras 1 and 2, just DISSOLVE TO EFFECTS by moving the FADE levers up. To DISSOLVE to 3 again, just move the FADE levers back down.

If you didn't want to DISSOLVE to a fancy CORNER INSERT but just wanted to DISSOLVE to camera 2 from camera 3, you would first have to move the WIPE levers to make the CORNER INSERT (which is channel A's picture) as small as possible until B (camera 2's picture) fills the screen entirely. Now that the EFFECTS channel shows camera 2's picture, you can DISSOLVE from camera 3 to camera 2 by moving the FADE levers up.

Say you wish now to CUT to camera 4, which button do you press? Button 4, right? But on which channel—A, B, or C? Well, we know C isn't the answer because a moment ago we slid the FADER to the EFFECTS mode to show camera 2 (if we were still in the C channel, the answer would have been to press 4 on channel C). What you do to C at this point won't show until you slide the FADE levers back down again. That leaves A and B channels. Although logic and time could give you the answer, there is a faster way to figure this out. Camera 2 is *on* right now, and you want camera 4. Whichever channel has the 2 button pressed is the channel you want to switch to 4. Thus, you press button 4 on channel B.

4. *To DISSOLVE to a SPLIT SCREEN:* Say you are in the C channel with camera 2, as diagrammed in Figure 7–12. You want to DISSOLVE TO A SPLIT SCREEN with some words (from camera 1) at the bottom of camera 2's picture. You want camera 2 to remain on the screen except for the bottom part, which you want to dissolve to the words. How is this procedure done?

FIGURE 7–11   DISSOLVING to a CORNER INSERT on an SEG.

Since there is no law that stops you from punching in the same camera number in more than one channel, you punch a 2 into A and a 2 into C. B would get switched to camera 1. The WIPE levers would be manipulated for the desired effect. In other words, channel C is showing camera 2. The EFFECTS BUS is showing camera 2 with the words from camera 1 under it.

You now can DISSOLVE from C (camera 2) to the EFFECTS by raising the FADE levers.

On fancier SEGS that offer diagonals, diamonds, squares, circles, and so on, the process is essentially the same. Figures 7–13 through 7–16 show some examples. First punch the button that selects the desired type of EFFECT. Next, create the desired EFFECT on the EFFECTS channels while displaying the C channel. You may then DISSOLVE *to* and *from* for the EFFECTS by moving the FADE levers.

 **Mini Review**

- Faders and wipers are switcher controls that allow you to adjust how much of a camera's picture or an effect will show.
- Pressing a button on a switcher's program bus sends that image to the switcher's output for recording or broadcasting.

FIGURE 7–12   DISSOLVING to a SPLIT SCREEN while keeping part of your picture.

Camera 1

CORNER INSERT

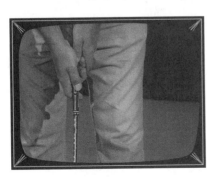

Camera 2

FIGURE 7–13   CORNER INSERT.

FIGURE 7–14   VERTICAL SPLIT SCREEN with BORDER.

STUDIO PRODUCTION SWITCHER

The STUDIO PRODUCTION SWITCHER is a complex SEG, with goodies galore. These switchers vary greatly in the features they possess. Indeed, if you visit a network control room, you'll see the most elaborate switchers in existence. Figure 7–17 shows one.

This switcher has more buttons than Napoleon's dress uniform, but don't let that throw you. Its basic operation is much like what you've already seen. Refer to Figure 7–17 as you follow these basic exercises:

1. *Switch from camera 1 to camera 2:* There are many ways to do this:
   a. Assume the bottom FADER is up and the PGM (PROGRAM) BUS (second long row from the bottom) has camera 1 punched on. The PROGRAM, or final output from the switcher, is thus camera 1. To switch to camera 2, simply press the camera 2 button on the PGM row of buttons. Done.
   b. If the PGM BUS has the EFF 1 button pressed (four buttons to the left of the bottom FADER), then the EFF 1 (EFFECTS 1 BUS) is in charge. Whatever the top two rows of buttons and their FADER do will make your final picture. To the left and right of the top FADER are buttons that make that lever act as a FADER or a WIPER or something else. Let's assume the MIX (FADE) button up there is pressed so that the FADER can DISSOLVE from channel A to B. If the lever is up and channel A has camera 1 punched *on*, then camera 1 is what will show. If you press the camera 2 button on A, you then switch (also called TAKE or CUT) to camera 2. Thus, all switching is done on the top row of buttons.
   c. If the PGM BUS has the EFF 2 button pressed, then the two EFF 2 rows of buttons (EFF 2 BUS) are in charge. If EFF 2's FADER is in the FADE mode and up and if its channel A has the camera 1 button pressed, then camera 1's picture will show. Simply press the camera 2 button on the EFF 2 channel A row to CUT to camera 2.
   d. This is similar to example c: If the PGM BUS is in the EFF 3 mode, then the third FADER does the business between its A and B channels. If that FADER says the B channel is on and camera 1 is punched in there, simply punch the camera 2 button next to it to switch to camera 2.
   e. If you press the camera 2 button on the PGM BUS, camera 2 will appear, and the EFF 1, 2, or 3 buttons will automatically switch off, and camera 2's picture will appear.

CIRCLE WIPE with a SOFT EDGE

BOX WIPE with a BORDER

MODULATED WIPE wiggles with wavy edges

FIGURE 7–15 Other EFFECTS (there are hundreds).

2. *DISSOLVE from camera 1 to camera 2:* You have a choice of carrying out this DISSOLVE effect on EFFECTS BUS 1, 2, or 3. Say you choose EFF 1. The bottom FADER will be up, its EFF 1 button is pressed, the top FADER (let's say) is up, and camera 1 is punched up on channel A. To get ready to DISSOLVE to camera 2, you press the camera 2 button on channel B. Double-check the FADER control buttons to make sure that lever will DISSOLVE (not WIPE, etc.) from channel A to B when you move it. When ready, pull the top FADER down to DISSOLVE to camera 2.

3. *DISSOLVE from one effect to another effect:* This is what all those extra buttons and EFFECTS BUSSES are all about. You can set up one effect, say a CORNER INSERT, on EFF 1. You can set up another effect, say a DIAGONAL SPLIT, on EFF 2. On EFF 3, channel A, the EFF 1 button is pressed. On EFF 3, channel B, the EFF 2 button is pressed. Moving the EFF 3 FADER down, assuming that it's in the MIX mode, will DISSOLVE the picture from the first effect (CORNER INSERT) to the second effect (DIAGONAL SPLIT). For all this to be recorded, the PGM BUS must have the EFF 3 button pressed.

Panasonic AVE5 has switcher, SEG, audio mixer, lots of EFFECTS, and digital STILL STORE (to freeze pictures)

One of several MOSAIC effects on AVE5

One of 98 adjustable WIPE patterns found on Panasonic AVE7 SEG

KEY effect allows another camera or a CHARACTER GENERATOR to put words over the image. Note, with SEGs costing under $2000, there may be some stair-steppiness to the letters.

FIGURE 7–16 Fancy effects with SWITCHER/SEGs like the Panasonic AVE5 or AVE7, MX-30 or MX-50, or the Videonics MX-1.

This process is called CASCADING or REENTRY. You use a FADER to go from one picture to another. *How* you go is determined by the buttons which tell the FADER to WIPE, DISSOLVE, etc. *Where* you go depends on what's selected on its A and B channels. You could punch up just a camera, or you could punch up *another* EFFECTS BUS. That BUS, in turn, could be showing a simple camera shot or a fancy effect determined by *its* FADER and *its* A and B channels. *And*, one of *its* channels could be displaying *another* EFFECTS bus, with another effect either happening or waiting to happen.

Although the *professional* STUDIO PRODUCTION SWITCHER is a fun-looking toy, we're going to scale our sights back a bit to a smaller model. Educational, industrial, and business users can generally af-

On these under-$2000 digital SEGs, some of the WIPE patterns are a bit stair-steppy (not smooth).

PICTURE-IN-A-PICTURE (PIP) effect where one camera's picture is squeezed and fits over another.

FIGURE 7–16 *Continued*

ford the $4000 to $10,000 variety of switcher such as the one shown earlier in Figure 1–20. Let's discuss some of the features found on one of these mini-monsters.

Inputs

Industrial STUDIO PRODUCTION SWITCHERS generally have from six to twelve inputs. The signals could come from cameras, videotape players, CHARACTER GENERATORS (electronic titlers), or any other video sources.

If the signals are coming from SYNCHRONIZED cameras or other sources where the video signals are locked in step, they are called SYNCHRONOUS, and the switcher will be able to CUT or DISSOLVE or WIPE, etc. from one to the next smoothly. If, however, the input signal is not SYNCHRONIZED to the others (such as an off-air TV broadcast or the output from a common VCR), the signal is called ASYNCHRONOUS. You could switch to that signal using your switcher, but there would be a blip in the picture. If using these sources causes a glitch, then why use them? Convenience. They allow you to plug everything you've got into this one "master control" to make original recordings through it or copy tapes through it all at the push of a button. During a live show, however, you wouldn't try to switch from one ASYNCHRONOUS source to another.

---

*Character generator   Electronic device that allows you to type titles onto the TV image.

Synchronous   Referring to a TV device that coordinates its video signal with a master sync source, thereby making an image that can be mixed with others in the studio.

Asynchronous   Referring to a device or signal that is not synchronized but is running independently without external sync circuits that hold it to the same rhythm as the rest of the studio equipment.

Preview   Channel on a switcher/SEG that sends out to your preview monitor a view of an effect so that you can adjust or perfect the effect before using it. It is like *audition* in audio.

Auto preview   Mechanism on a switcher/SEG that automatically displays on your preview monitor any effect *not* being recorded but ready to be shown once selected.

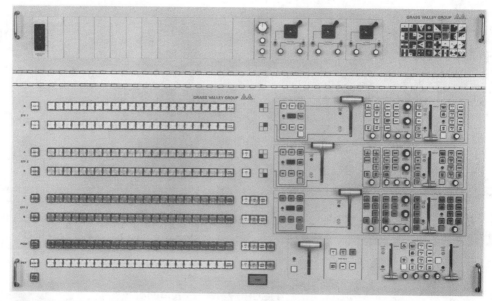

FIGURE 7–17   Professional STUDIO PRODUCTION SWITCHER (Courtesy of Grass Valley Corp.).

Preview and Program

Remember umpteen pages ago when you wanted to DISSOLVE from camera 2 to a CORNER INSERT between cameras 1 and 2? It would have been nice to have seen the INSERT before you took potluck and DISSOLVED to it. PREVIEW lets you see the EFFECT before you are committed to it. Your PREVIEW monitor will display the effect automatically, assuming that the right buttons have been pressed. On the switcher shown earlier in Figure 1–20, you can PREVIEW any source simply by pressing its button. By pressing the ME1 or ME2 buttons (they're like EFF 1 and EFF 2 discussed earlier; ME stands for MIX/EFFECTS), the switcher will PREVIEW automatically whatever scene is ready to come up next.

Once you are satisfied with the picture on the PREVIEW monitor, you can record it by moving a FADER or pressing the appropriate button on the switcher's PROGRAM BUS.

PROGRAM means whatever signal or combination of signals is to be recorded by your VCR or broadcast. PREVIEW is like AUDITION or CUE on the audio console: It is for your information only so that you can make sure the pictures are satisfactory before you use them.

Using Preview to Show What Your VCR Is Doing

Your switcher selects a signal and sends it out the PROGRAM channel to your VCR. What do you suppose would happen if you took the VIDEO OUT from that same VCR and fed it back into the switcher as shown in Figure 7–18? If you then pressed the PREVIEW button for "VCR," you could PREVIEW the output of your VCR *while* it is making its recording. So what's the advantage of PREVIEWING the VCR's output? It shows the same picture as the LINE monitor, right? Right—when the VCR is recording correctly. However, if the VCR's VIDEO LEVEL creeps up too high, the problem won't appear on the LINE monitor; it will show up on the VCR monitor or the VCR's meter. If the VCR and its monitor are in the next room or are hard to see, you may not notice the problem. If, however, the VCR is playing its signal through the PREVIEW monitor, which is generally right in front of you, any VCR problems will capture your attention.

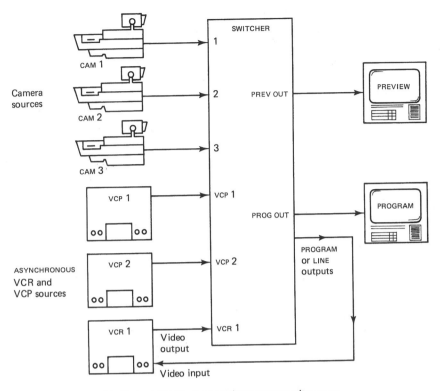

To display VCR 1's signal on the PREVIEW monitor, press the VCR 1 button on the PREVIEW BUS. To preview camera effects, press the appropriate button (could be called ME1, ME2, or AUTO, depending upon manufacturer) and the effects will automatically be displayed on the PREVIEW monitor

FIGURE 7–18   Using the PREVIEW monitor to display the output of a VCR while it is recording.

Not only can the PREVIEW monitor show you what your VCR is doing while it records, but it can also display your VCR's picture during playback. This is most useful when you need to edit out a mistake during a show. The PREVIEW monitor will allow you to watch the tape play while you're getting ready to edit in to a new live scene.

Of course the PREVIEW monitor can display only one picture at a time, so when it is showing the VCR's output, it's no longer previewing EFFECTS. To keep tabs on both, you may switch back and forth between the VCR and the EFFECTS by alternately pressing the VCR button and the AUTO PREVIEW (or ME1 or ME2, or whatever) button on the switcher's PREVIEW BUS.

In short, using the PREVIEW monitor to display VCRs, VCPs, as well as EFFECTS puts many signals at your fingertips without cluttering the console with numerous monitors. One does all the jobs.

Border

Sometimes you'd like to SPLIT a screen and not have anyone realize you did it. This would be handy if you had one performer standing still in front of one camera and a second performer dancing in front of a second camera. If you horizontally SPLIT the screen at both performers' belt lines, you could have a very silly-looking effect of someone's torso standing still while their legs are dancing like crazy.

(For this effect to work, you would also need the same background for both performers.) Using an invisible SPLIT, you are able to have props and pictures occupy part of the screen without letting the audience know that the effect is contrived.

There are other times, however, when you wish to place a border around your INSERT or WIPE to make it stand out better, as in Figure 7–14. Many switchers will allow you to adjust the width of the border as well as its color.

 Mini Review

- Wipes, keys, and other special effects are set up on the effects bus of the switcher.
- The preview monitor shows what an effect will look like before you record or broadcast it.

Key

No, KEY isn't the thing you leave in your ignition after locking and closing your car door. KEY is a special effect in which part of a camera's picture is cut out, as if with scissors, and replaced with another camera's picture. You can DISSOLVE to and from this effect in the same way as you would DISSOLVE to a SPLIT SCREEN.

There are two kinds of KEY effects. One replaces all the *black* parts of one camera's picture with parts from another camera. The other, called CHROMA KEY, replaces all the *blue* (or some other selected color) parts of one camera's picture with parts from another camera's picture. KEY can be used to create a special effect or to make something disappear or to make words appear on a screen. Let's first study the black-and-white KEY.

Black-and-White, or Luminance, Key.   Figures 7–19 and 7–20 show examples of a simple black-and-white KEY.

Going to this mode requires some forethought and a little knob twiddling. To create the effect shown in Figure 7–19,

1. Press the KEY button on the switcher.
2. On channel A of the switcher, punch in camera 1.
3. On channel B of the switcher, punch in camera 2.

---

*Key (or luminance key)   Special effect where the dark parts of one camera's picture are replaced with parts from another camera's picture.

*Chroma key   Key effect triggered by the color blue (or some other selected color) rather than black.

*Border   Split screen effect that makes a visible line (of chosen width and color) between the pictures sharing the screen.

Key sensitivity   Control on a switcher/SEG that determines *how dark* something has to be before it disappears and is replaced by another camera's picture. In chroma keys, it determines how much of a color something needs before it is replaced by another camera's picture.

*External key   Key effect in which the dark and light parts of one camera's image determine which of two other cameras' pictures will be shown. (None of the images *have* to come from cameras, but they usually do). Also, the absence or presence of a color could be used to determine which parts of two other images would be shown.

Alpha channel   Signal used in video graphics to cut a hole in an image, a hole that gets filled with another image.

*Drop shadow   Dark ridge placed on one side of letters to make them look as if they were three-dimensional because they cast shadows. The letters become easier to see because of the edging.

Camera 1 (channel A)

KEY

Camera 2 (channel B)

FIGURE 7–19 Black area replaced with another picture.

The camera on the A channel will have some parts of its picture replaced with parts from the B channel. All of A's dark parts will be replaced with B's picture. It is as if all the light parts of A were real and as if all the dark parts were transparent and through them you could see B's picture. Now the question is, how dark must parts of A's picture be before they become transparent? The answer lies with the KEY SENSITIVITY (or KEY SENS) adjustment. This knob determines the threshold at which the equipment will call something black or white. Adjusted all the way in one direction, the KEY SENS will consider *everything* in A's picture dark enough to be transparent. Turned the other way, *nothing* from A will be transparent. With the help from PREVIEW and a little experimenting, the right effect can be perfected and DISSOLVED to when needed.

4. Adjust KEY SENS so that the part you wish to have disappear disappears. Watch carefully to make sure that other dark parts of the picture (like the performer's hair or eyes) do not also disappear.

Camera 1

Camera 2

Camera 2

FIGURE 7–20   EXTERNAL KEY.

Careful adjustment of KEY SENS will keep the edges of your dark object from appearing too grainy and ragged. Smooth, shadow-free lighting is necessary to achieve a good KEY effect.

In this example, you must adjust your lighting and KEY SENS so that only the black sheet of paper disappears. Camera 2 must be carefully aimed so that the desired part of the picture shows when you go to the effect.

Keying Words.   The most frequent use for the KEY effect is for KEYING IN words on the TV screen. Here a white word on a black background would be fed to channel B of the switcher. In the KEY mode, the black background will disappear and be replaced by the picture from channel A. Thus, it will seem as if solid white paper letters were pasted over the picture from channel A.

This is a sharper, more solid effect than the SUPERIMPOSITION you saw earlier. With the SUPER, the words were ghosty. With KEY, the lettering is opaque and solid. Figure 7–5 compared the two effects.

As in the cases described earlier, if you want to DISSOLVE from, say, camera 2 to 2-with-a-word-on-the-bottom by using the switcher in Figure 1–20, you could do the following:

1. Feed camera 2's picture to the PROGRAM channel and the B channel.
2. Put the word on the A channel.
3. Switch the MIX/EFFECTS 1 BUS to KEY, using one of the four buttons clustered next to that FADER.

Camera 3   EXTERNAL KEY

Camera 3   EXTERNAL KEY

FIGURE 7–20   *Continued*

4. Adjust KEY SENS while examining it on the PREVIEW monitor.
5. Press the MIX button next to the MIX/EFFECTS 2 FADER.
6. DISSOLVE to EFFECTS by moving the FADER for MIX/EFFECTS 2.

The effect will fade in while the rest of the picture will remain the same. You can get out of the effect by DISSOLVING in the opposite direction from the EFFECT back down to the C channel.

External Key.   EXTERNAL KEY is like regular KEY, only fancier. Here an *additional* camera decides, depending on the light and dark *it* sees, which of the two *other* cameras' pictures will be shown. Figure 7–20 shows examples of an EXTERNAL KEY. There, camera 1 is the controlling camera; it decides which parts of camera 2's and camera 3's pictures will be shown. When camera 1 sees white, camera 2's picture will show. Where camera 1 sees black, camera 3's picture shows.

To make your switcher work in this mode, you need to find the INT/EXT knob near the KEY knob on the switcher. On some switchers there may not be any button for you to press to select which camera does the controlling. In such cases, the controlling camera signal must be sent into the switcher through a socket in the back of the switcher. But, normally, switching the INT/EXT knob to EXT automatically makes the external camera the controlling factor. Meanwhile, the remaining two (or more) cameras may be selected on the A and B channels as usual. You can DISSOLVE TO and FROM this effect also.

No law demands that the EXTERNAL KEY must remain still. It could be a graphic, and your camera operator could ZOOM in on the graphic, making the black-and-white parts grow larger. Imagine for a moment that the controlling camera were looking at the word *today* spelled out in big fat letters (as also shown in Figure 7–20). The camera operator could start zoomed out on the word and zoom in on it until the *o* in *today* completely filled the screen. As camera 1 zoomed in, more and more of camera 3's image would show until it completely filled the screen, a very imaginative transition.

One fancy way to change from one camera shot to another is to make an image that starts all white, and little by little gets blackened in. Little squares can fill the picture, or blobs of paint can drool until they cover the picture as in Figure 7–20. This image could come from a camera tilting up across a black-and-white handmade graphic, or it could be a videotape of the drool in motion, or it could be a computer-generated animation. If this signal is now played into the EXT KEY input, you will see an exotic transition from camera 2's picture to camera 3's picture happening wherever the black appeared on the EXT KEY input.

Using black and white paper, cutouts, paint, and other moving methods to change a white screen into a black screen, you can create inexpensive and unique wipes and special effects. Some SEGs cost thousands of dollars because of the wide array of special effects they have programmed into them. Using EXT KEY and a little time, you can recreate or surpass these effects yourself at little cost.

Another name for EXTERNAL KEY is ALPHA CHANNEL. It plays an important role in putting BORDERS and DROP SHADOWS around CHARACTER GENERATED text to make it stand out better.

 **Mini Review**

• Key is an effect in which part of an image is removed and replaced with another image. It is often used to add text to an image.

Chroma Key.   In color systems, one may use a color to trigger the KEY process. The technique is the same, only instead of all the black parts of the picture becoming transparent and being replaced with another picture, all the blue (or some other selectable color) parts are replaced with another camera's picture. The process is called CHROMA KEY and is demonstrated in Figure 7–21. (See also color Figure 7–21 on back cover.)

CHROMA KEY is easier to use than black-and-white KEY when you wish to replace part of one picture with part of another. A recurrent problem with black-and-white KEY is that the switcher can never quite decide whether something is black or not and tends to take out the wrong parts of your picture. Even with careful lighting, it is impossible not to have the insides of someone's mouth, the shadow of a lapel, or some black part of a prop disappear and be replaced with another camera's picture. This is where CHROMA KEY becomes handy. Pure blue is a relatively rare color. Except for blue eyes and serious head wounds, it is not found on the body, and you can easily take precautions to see that costumes and props don't have any blue in them. Thus, by placing a person and his props in front of a large blue

Cyclorama   Smooth studio curtain.

*Downstream keyer   Circuit in the switcher/SEG that will key an image (usually a word) over the top of a picture or special effect. This is often the last thing done to the signal before it exits the switcher to be recorded.

Matte   Special kind of key effect in which light parts of a picture are removed and replaced with a chosen color.

Background generator   SEG circuit that adds color to a black background, useful for keying words onto a colored background.

Posterization   Visual effect of reducing a picture's varied brightness levels down to just one or two, giving it a flat, posterlike or cartoonlike look.

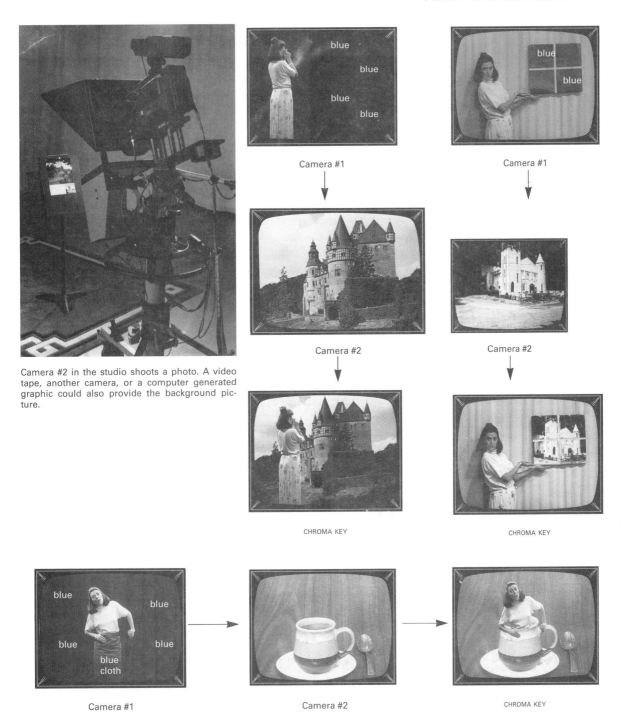

Camera #2 in the studio shoots a photo. A video tape, another camera, or a computer generated graphic could also provide the background picture.

Camera #1

Camera #1

Camera #2

Camera #2

CHROMA KEY

CHROMA KEY

Camera #1

Camera #2

CHROMA KEY

FIGURE 7–21   CHROMA KEY using blue (see also color figures on back cover).

curtain (often called a CHROMA KEY BLUE CYCLORAMA), you can replace the entire background with a picture from a postcard, slide, movie, videotape, or a computer animation or graphic. You could even make your performers disappear from the picture by dressing them *completely* in blue. If they carried props around the set, the props would mysteriously float when seen on the TV screen. It is also possible for the talent to hold something blue in his or her hand, like a blue crystal ball. A swirling, ghostly effect could then be created in the crystal ball. Zooming in on the crystal ball would make that ghostly scene grow larger and larger until it filled the screen entirely, a nice transition from the real world to the crystal ball world.

CHROMA KEY is not perfect. Care must still be taken in lighting the set. TV cameras tend to turn dark, shadowy areas into dark blue instead of pure black. If you're KEYING on blue, your CHROMA KEYER may cut those shadowy areas out of your picture. You would counteract this effect by making sure that your lighting was soft and that there were no deep shadows. Another problem that you may have seen on newscasts, especially on weathercasts, involves a performer who wears clothing *close to* blue. The TV camera sees the aqua or lavender in someone's tie and immediately slices it out, replacing it with a hurricane over the Carolinas.

Sometimes when a performer gets too close to his blue background, the reflection of the blue background on the light-colored clothing makes the clothing look bluish, especially at the edges. The camera, seeing blue-edged clothing, cuts out the shoulders or elbows of your performer, replacing them with a rough and grainy edge. One way to counteract this effect is to use AMBER GELS in your backlights. The amber light tends to counteract the blue, giving your performer sharper edges that are easier for the CHROMA KEY to "see."

You can make an EXTERNAL CHROMA KEY using the same technique as black-and-white EXTERNAL KEY. As before, the CHROMA KEY sensitivity to blue is adjusted with a KEY SENS control. Another control on the switcher adjusts *which* color the CHROMA KEYER will be sensitive to. You could CHROMA-KEY on yellow if you wanted to replace the leaves on an autumn tree with psychedelic, flashing blue-and-red candy stripes.

Downstream Keyer.   Sometimes you'd like to do several effects at once. If your switcher is busy doing a WIPE, how can you KEY a word over that WIPE? The answer is to use a DOWNSTREAM KEYER.

First you set up the WIPE, SUPER, or KEY EFFECT, or whatever else you want your picture to be. The next trick is to KEY some words or effect *over the top of* this picture. By switching on the DOWNSTREAM KEYER, you can send a graphic or title from a camera or character generator into the switcher to be added to the picture, *downstream*, after all the other effects have been done. Figure 7–22 shows a SPLIT SCREEN with a DOWNSTREAM KEY added to it.

Matte

No, MATTE isn't a nickname for a fellow named Matthew. MATTE is like KEY except that you can adjust the color and brightness of the part being KEYED IN.

On the simple fader, you would SUPER a word on the screen. It would be readable but pale; you could see through it; it would have no zip. KEY added opaqueness to the lettering, but still the zip was lacking. The word would be only as bright as the whiteness in its lettering. If perchance you were KEYING a white word onto a too-light scene, the white word would almost disappear. What you would like is the ability to turn that white word black or some other color that would show up well (without recreating a graphic again). This is an instance in which MATTE would be helpful.

MATTE allows, through the LUMINANCE adjustment on the switcher (probably near the MATTE and KEY knobs), the lettering to appear very white, gray, black, or whatever. The black matting comes in handy when you haven't any dark places on the screen to put a white word. Instead, you find a white

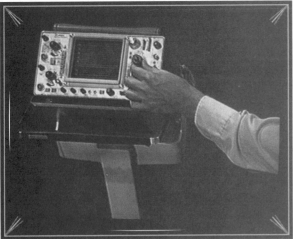

Camera 1

Camera 2

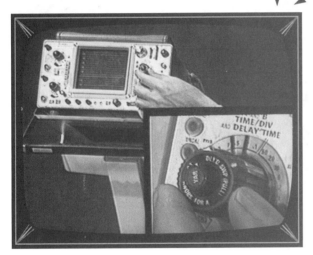

SPLIT SCREEN effect

Camera 3 or CHARACTER GENERATOR

Resulting DOWNSTREAM KEY

FIGURE 7–22 DOWNSTREAM KEY.

part of the picture and emboss a dark word. Another possibility is to make the MATTE *very* white so that the word is brighter than the rest of the picture.

Except for MATTE's adjustable coloration, it is in all other respects like KEY. It can be DISSOLVED TO, it needs a KEY SENSITIVITY adjustment to decide which grays will be considered black (or in color systems, which colors will be considered the trigger colors), and it can be auditioned on the PREVIEW monitor.

MATTE is good for more than words; it can also be used for artistic effects. Where KEY would allow you to place a person into a picture, MATTE would allow you to take the continuous gray tones out of the person before sticking him or her on the picture. The effect is cartoonlike and is called POS-TERIZATION. Figure 7–23 shows an example.

KEY

MATTE white

MATTE black

FIGURE 7–23   MATTING a person over a scene.

In color systems, not only can you MATTE various shades of black and white, but you may also COLORIZE the effect. Use caution, however, when MATTING color subtitles onto a picture—the tinted words may look pretty, but white or light yellow is usually more legible.

Here is an example to make things totally confusing: Say you had the word "WELCOME" printed in red on a green background. By using KEY, you could make the green disappear (by selecting green as your KEY color) and have a red "WELCOME" appear over a picture of someone's house. Using MATTE, you could do the same thing, but also you could replace the red letters with another color of your choosing, say yellow. Now you have a yellow "WELCOME" appearing over someone's house (you might call this a welcome matte). Instead of using someone's house, you could use an image created by a BACKGROUND GENERATOR on your SEG (one of those things where instead of fading to black, you can fade to a color). Say that you chose the BACKGROUND COLOR of chartreuse. Now you'll have a yellow "WELCOME" pasted on a chartreuse background. So you see how you can start with a sign having red letters over green and convert it to a sign with yellow letters over chartreuse, just by using MATTE and diddling with the SEG controls.

Joystick

The JOYSTICK was invented long before video games. The JOYSTICK is a lever on the switcher that can move in all directions to position various special effects on the screen. For instance, if you wanted to compose a diamond-shaped insert of somebody's face in the upper right-hand corner of the screen, you'd first select that particular pattern on the EFFECTS BUS of your switcher. Next, you'd adjust the size with the WIPE levers. Then, using the JOYSTICK, you'd position the pattern in the corner of the screen. Don't forget that the camera operator has to position the face in the upper right portion of his or her viewfinder screen as well. Figure 7–24 shows an example.

Soft Key and Soft Wipe

SOFT KEYS and WIPES have soft, fuzzy edges. Figure 7–25 shows a SOFT WIPE. A SOFT WIPE, besides being gentle on your nose when you have the flu, is useful for hiding the WIPE on the screen. If the two images are fairly similar in brightness and color, the SOFT WIPE blends discreetly from one image to the next. A SOFT KEY, besides being difficult to start your car with, also allows your effect to blend naturally with another picture. Instead of having a hard, grainy, unrealistic edge, the KEY image has a soft, natural-looking edge.

Colorizer

CHARACTER GENERATORS and monochrome cameras aimed at black-and-white titles can give you white lettering on a black background. If your switcher has a COLORIZER, it can change the color of that lettering to any color you like. This feature is much like the MATTE effect, in which you could change both the brightness and color of the MATTE. You can use this for strange POSTERIZATION effects as well as for making pretty colored words and borders for your WIPES and INSERTS.

Joystick Multiposition lever on a studio switcher that positions special effects anywhere on the TV screen.

Colorize To add color to something electronically. A matte can be white, black, gray, or colorized; so can wipe borders and backgrounds.

Soft key Key effect with a fuzzy, soft edge.

Soft wipe Split screen or wipe effect with a soft border where the two pictures join.

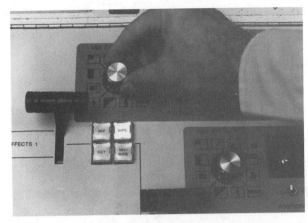

Select a pattern

Adjust its size

Adjust its position

Camera 1

Camera 2

Effect

FIGURE 7–24 Positioning an effect with the JOYSTICK.

Mini Review

- Chroma key removes a certain color from an image and replaces it with another image.
- Once a title is keyed, it can be matted or colorized to make it contrast with its background.

Spotlight

Sometimes you would like to point your viewers' attention to something on the screen. One way to do this would be to have your performer physically point to the object. Another way would be to have the desired part of the picture be brighter than the surrounding parts, as if a spotlight were aimed at it. This is the SPOTLIGHT effect shown in Figure 7–26. It is quite useful for technical and educational programs for which your viewers need to focus their attention on one small part of a larger machine or a particular line of poetry.

Master Fade to Black

It's easy to FADE TO BLACK during a TV show. It's like dissolving from one camera to another, except that the other camera happens to be capped, turned off, or just not there. Some switchers even have a button called BLACK, which you can FADE to. Still, some productions get so complex that it is difficult to figure out how to undo the effects that have been set up. MASTER FADE TO BLACK saves us from all this thinking (a welcome relief). It fades your picture to black no matter what effects or buttons you have selected on your switcher. It *always* works and therefore is handy when you are in a panic. Think

FIGURE 7–25 SOFT WIPE.

Spotlight   Special effect that highlights a portion of the picture as if a spotlight were aimed at it.

*Tally light   Lamp on the TV camera that goes on when the camera's image has been selected by the TV director. It tells both the performer and the camera operator that the camera is "on."

Master fade to black   Lever on a switcher that fades the picture either to black or up from black.

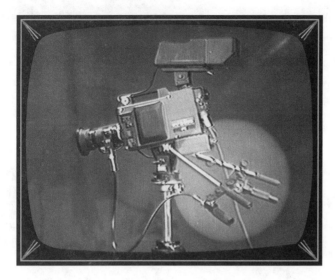

FIGURE 7-26   SPOTLIGHT.

of it the same way you think of the MASTER VOLUME on your audio mixer. It fades down all sources at once.

Sometimes when you start using the switcher at the beginning of the day, you may wonder why you can't get a picture out of it. This may be because your MASTER FADER is faded down. Before you go pulling out your transistors or your hair, check your MASTER FADER to make sure that it's faded up.

Background Generator

A BACKGROUND GENERATOR will turn a black background into the color of your choice. Say that you were going to KEY a title onto the TV screen. You'd use either a CHARACTER GENERATOR or a camera aimed at white letters on a black background to create the title. These letters could be simply KEYED over a black background, but that would be boring. You could substitute the signal from the BACKGROUND GENERATOR for the black background and make the picture more interesting. Don't forget that you can also COLORIZE the letters in your words by using another function of your SEG in order to make your letters look pretty, too. For best results, you should use a dark-colored background and light-colored letters.

Tally System

All STUDIO PRODUCTION SWITCHERS have a system that simultaneously lights the switcher buttons along with the TALLY LIGHTS on the cameras when the switcher buttons are pressed. When a camera's TALLY LIGHT is on, it tells performers and camera operators that the camera's picture is being used.

SEMIPROFESSIONAL SWITCHERS AND SEGS

Designed for the home video user but also used in shoestring television operations are other switchers that can do special effects. There are $600 gizmos that are able to fade from a camera or video player's picture to a chosen color. One can get pretty tired of seeing the picture fade or wipe to green between shots. To dissolve between two independent (nonsynchronized, i.e., home video) cameras or

VCRs, one could buy a small switcher with FRAME SYNCHRONIZERS built into it, like the one you saw in Figure 7–16. These gadgets cost from $500 to $3500 and perform dissolves, wipes, mosaics, strobes, negative colors, monochrome (changes color to black-and-white), posterization, and numerous other effects between two independent video sources (VCRs, cameras, computers with video output, or character generators). To put it another way, they don't require you to use professional SYNCHRONIZED cameras and a SYNC generator. These boxes take in the ASYNCHRONOUS signals from any video source and adjust them so that they are SYNCHRONOUS, and their images can be mixed. Some mix audio, too. Some will also colorize the title and add EDGING or DROP SHADOW to the letters.

Switchers inside Computers

It is possible to place all the "brains" of a STUDIO PRODUCTION SWITCHER on a circuit board and slip it into a computer. Instead of having a typical switcher console, you would see a picture of one on your computer screen. Instead of pulling faders and pressing switcher buttons, you would be pointing and clicking with your computer's mouse or pressing keys on the keyboard. All the video inputs and outputs would reside on the computer card, so essentially you'd be plugging your cameras, VCRs, and the like into the back of your computer.

Such is the plan behind the recently popular VIDEO TOASTER, whose computer screen is shown in Figure 7–27. Advantage: The TOASTER is a lot cheaper than a full-fledged switcher. Disadvantage: It is harder to press the buttons and move the FADER on the screen while using a mouse than it is to use a physical switcher with real buttons and FADERS at your fingertips. The TOASTER and its brothers are more appropriate for the POSTPRODUCTION switching that is done in the editing process. There, you have more time to make decisions and find the right buttons to press.

An offspring of the TOASTER, called TRINITY, includes the switcher console; and the computer also handles editing, character generation, paint, animation, and lots of effects. Trinity also has built-

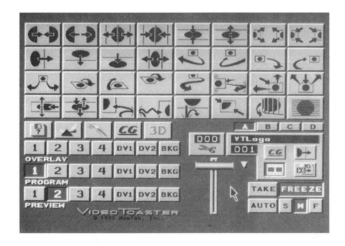

FIGURE 7–27 Video Toaster puts a video SWITCHER/ SEG/CHARACTER GENERATOR and electronic graphics into your Amiga computer.

Edging Dark (or occasionally white) ridge around letters to make them stand out.

Video toaster One brand of switcher built onto a circuit board that fits into a computer.

Postproduction switcher Switcher/SEG with automated features designed to be controlled by computer, by editor-controller, or manually, often by using menus to select functions.

Trinity Recent, improved version of the Video Toaster manufactured by Play, Inc.

in FRAME SYNCHRONIZERS, all for about $5000. It's an example of how digital circuitry is making it possible to do more while spending less.

THE TECHNICAL DIRECTOR

Now that you see what goes into pushing all those buttons on the switcher, it makes sense to have a crew member dedicated to that one task. Trying to direct and do the switching for your own show requires six eyes, five arms, three brains, and nerves of steel. In the meantime, who runs the audio, who watches the video levels, and who follows the script? In productions of any complexity, the TECHNICAL DIRECTOR (abbreviated TD) removes from the director's fingers the load of *finding* the right buttons and *perfecting* the effects on PREVIEW before using them. This leaves the director with the task of "calling the shots" (telling everyone what to do), a task requiring only four eyes, three arms, one-and-a-half brains, and ulcers of steel.

In this chapter we've concentrated on how to work the gadgets. In Chapters 10 and 11, we'll dive into the art of production planning and directing. It is the *decisions* you make that create an interesting show, not how many bells and whistles you have available to ring or blow.

 Mini Review

- Semiprofessional switchers may have built-in frame synchronizers that accept signals from asynchronous sources, such as consumer camcorders and VCRs, so that their images can be mixed.
- Switchers installed in computers are more appropriate for postproduction editing than live production because their controls are harder to activate.

---

*Technical director   Person who pushes the buttons on the switcher/SEG during the show.

TELEVISION GRAPHICS AND TITLES

The essence of TV graphics boils down to three rules:

1. Make it fit the shape of a TV screen.
2. Keep it simple.
3. Make it bold.

Whether you create your graphics with a computer or with markers and bits of paper, those three commandments remain the same.

ASPECT RATIO

A TV screen is a box that is a little wider than it is tall. If the screen were 16 inches wide, it would be 12 inches tall. If it were 4 inches wide, it would be 3 inches tall. However wide it is, it is three-quarters as tall. This is called a 4:3 (four-to-three) ASPECT RATIO and is diagrammed in Figure 8–1.

As a consequence, visuals for television should have a 4:3 ASPECT RATIO if they are to fill the screen evenly. Panoramas don't fit this ratio because they are too wide. Telephone poles don't fit because they are too tall. Strictly speaking, even a square box is too tall to fit perfectly on a TV screen.

When showing a panorama on a TV screen, you must either display a long, long shot of it, showing a lot of sky and ground, or you must sacrifice some of the width of the panorama, getting just a fraction of it. To display a square box, you must decide whether to cut off its top and bottom in the TV picture or whether to get all of it by leaving an empty space on its left and right.

Making the Picture Fit the TV Screen

Just because your TV screen is a box doesn't mean that you can only shoot box-shaped things. If your scene, or a photograph of your scene, is very tall, as in Figure 8–2, there are three ways to show it:

1. Zoom out to get all the picture in, but with wasted space on the left and right.
2. Zoom in to fill the screen with the most important part of the picture, sacrificing the remainder of the picture.
3. Zoom in on one part of the picture, perhaps near the bottom, and slowly tilt up to take in the rest of it.

---

*Aspect ratio   Shape of a TV screen expressed in width compared to height. Common TV screens have a 4:3 aspect ratio.

Logo   Symbol or trademark representing a specific company, organization, or TV station.

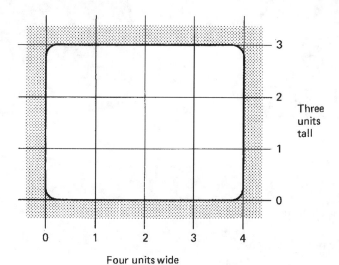

FIGURE 8–1   ASPECT RATIO of TV screen.

The first method is somewhat obtrusive and works best when the audience is prepared for it, such as viewing snapshots from an album. Solution 2 is fine if losing part of your picture doesn't hurt your message. Method 3 has the advantage of adding motion to your scene, but it is sometimes hard to find a meaningful starting and ending point for your tilt.

For wide scenes, use a similar technique:

1. Zoom out, leaving a margin at the top and bottom of the picture.
2. Zoom in on part of the picture, sacrificing the rest.
3. Zoom in on part of the picture and pan to another part.

Zoom out, showing entire picture but with wasted space at sides. Mount the photo on a neutral background so the side margins do not distract from the central picture.

Zoom in on most important part of picture, sacrificing the rest.

Zoom in on one part of picture and tilt to take in rest of picture.

FIGURE 8–2   Making a vertical picture fit TV's ASPECT RATIO.

Making Words Fit the TV Screen

The composition of words, titles, and LOGOS (a LOGO is a TV station's or program's symbol or trademark) leaves us more flexibility than pictures. One can arrange the words or whatever to fit the 4:3 dimensions of the screen. Figure 8–3 shows some good and some bad graphic compositions.

Sometimes a formula or single line of text must remain intact as a single line and cannot be shaped into a box. In this case, consider adding a supporting graphic to the empty space on the screen to add balance and help fill the screen. Figure 8–4 shows a good example of how adding graphic sym-

FIGURE 8–3   ASPECT RATIO of words on screen.

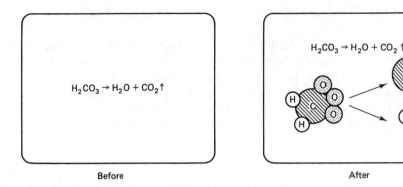

FIGURE 8–4   Adding graphics to a line of text reinforces the concept while maintaining the ASPECT RATIO.

bols to a chemical formula strengthens the instructional concept of the formula while conforming to the TV screen shape.

When accurate workmanship is necessary, it is good to measure out, in faint lines, the 4:3 shape of the TV screen on your blank art paper before you or your graphic artist begins to draw. The lines will act as a guide and can later be erased. When such care is not warranted, one may simply think boxes when planning graphic composition.

The Chalkboard Dilemma

Although the old "chalk and talk" presentation is not television at its best, such TV lessons are produced every day in high schools and colleges and at business meetings. Often the instructor, unfamiliar with television's ASPECT RATIO, writes across the chalkboard in his normal fashion. This does not televise well, because the lettering is often too small when you zoom out to get it all in. But when you zoom in, your camera views only part of the sentence at a time. TV instructors have to be taught to "think boxes." They will probably never conform to the 4:3 ASPECT RATIO you desire, but if they can be convinced to always write in short multiple lines, the results will look much better. Figure 8–5 shows an example.

 Mini Review

- These are the three rules of creating a TV graphic:
  1. Make the graphic fit the shape of a TV screen.
  2. Keep it simple.
  3. Make it bold.
- The TV screen has a 4:3 aspect ratio; that is, it is 4 units wide by 3 units tall.

SAFE TITLE AREA

Two things you *don't* want to do are to

1. Show your audience the edge of your graphic or title sign.
2. Have a piece of the title disappear behind the edge of the viewer's TV screen.

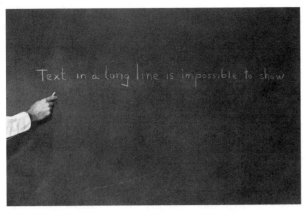

Long sentence is either too small ...

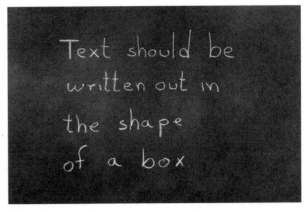

Have instructor "think boxes" when writing.

... or part of it is missed.

FIGURE 8–5 Writing on the chalkboard.

Both problems can be avoided by

1. Leaving an adequate margin around the title or drawing.
2. Shooting the graphic so as to leave a little extra space around all sides of its image on your TV monitor.

This extra space allows for the fact that the camera and the studio monitors generally show the *whole* TV picture, while the home viewer's TV cuts off the edges. Some home (and school) TV sets are poorly adjusted anyway, causing even further loss of the TV picture on the edges. To allow for this, the SAFE TITLE AREA is utilized, principally confining all important matter to the middle portion of the TV screen. See Figure 8–6.

---

*Safe title area Central portion of a graphic or a control-room monitor's TV screen that can always be seen when the picture is viewed on misadjusted TV sets; the place where it is "safe" to put a title because you know it will all show.
Dead border area Blank margin around a graphic that never shows on TV.

Scanned area Part of a graphic "seen" by the studio camera and control room monitor but not necessarily seen by viewers on their home TV sets.

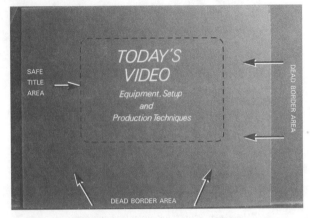

Original title card

Misadjusted TV monitor

As seen in camera viewfinder or UNDERSCANNED control room monitor.

Misadjusted TV monitor

Well adjusted normal TV monitor

FIGURE 8–6   Picture areas compared.

Use the SAFE TITLE AREA.

The SAFE TITLE AREA holds the essential information that should *always* show on the home viewer's screen. The DEAD BORDER AREA is the blank part of your title card, which *never* shows on the TV screen. In fact, along its edge you'll often find little notes or picture sequence numbers penciled in to help the studio crew arrange and position the cards. Between the DEAD BORDER AREA and the SAFE TITLE AREA is the nether world of the SCANNED AREA. The SCANNED AREA shows on your studio TV monitors and cameras, but it cannot be trusted to *always* show on home TV sets. Since this part of the picture is untrustworthy, it should not contain anything important. Figure 8–7 shows the SCANNED AREA, SAFE TITLE AREA, and DEAD BORDER AREA of a title card.

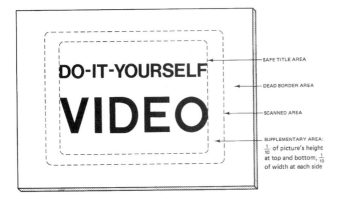

FIGURE 8–7 Areas of a title card.

---

*Underscanned Referring to a TV picture that is smaller than the screen, showing the black edges around the picture on the screen.

Underscanned monitor TV monitor that can shrink its picture to display the edges.

FIGURE 8–8   UNDERSCANNED control room monitor with SAFE TITLE AREA marked in.

The DEAD BORDER AREA is the camera operator's margin. It doesn't matter if the border is one inch or three inches in width as long as it's large enough to make it easy for the camera operator to shoot the picture without getting the edge of the title card in the shot.

Some TV control rooms use preview and program TV monitors that are UNDERSCANNED (showing the entire scanned picture plus the black sync pulse that borders the picture). To remind them of what part of the TV picture the home viewer can actually see, the control room crew often puts marker lines on their TV screens that indicate the SAFE TITLE AREA. Figure 8–8 shows what this would look like. As before, anything important belongs inside the marked-off SAFE TITLE AREA.

When you are making titles and visuals, it is sometimes convenient to make them all about the same size. Although the titles, regardless of their actual size, may all come out looking the same once the camera operator has zoomed in or out on the title, it is easier on the cameraperson not to have to make this adjustment each time—especially if the visuals come in rapid succession.

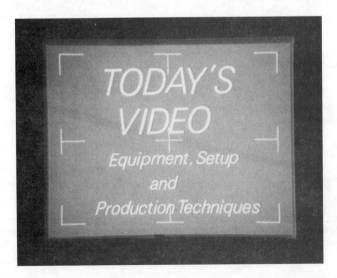

Some camera viewfinders electronically superimpose a guide to show the SCANNED AREA and SAFE TITLE AREA. This title is within the SCANNED AREA but falls outside the SAFE TITLE AREA (parts of the markers intersect with the title).

Mini Review

- Because some TV sets are misadjusted, you must avoid letting text or important elements of your graphics come too close to the edge of the TV screen.

BOLDNESS AND SIMPLICITY

Unlike cinema, slides, photographs, and the printed page, TV is a fuzzy medium. Fine detail turns into blurry grays and hazy shadows. With your eyes alone, look at a newspaper three feet away; you can probably read the entire page. Fill a TV screen with that same page, and you can read only the main headlines, and even they don't leap off the screen and grab you. Figure 8–9 shows this phenomenon.

Photo

VCR

Photo

VCR

FIGURE 8–9 Comparison of a regular photograph with the same shot played back on a VCR. Notice how TV loses a lot of detail.

Too many words, too distant

Zoom in and limit words

Zoom in on printed material.

Visuals for TV need to be bold, simple, and uncluttered. Figure 8–10 shows some examples of simple, easy-to-read, yet attractive tables and graphs.

Titling for TV needs to be brief, broad, and bold in order to have impact. Wordy subtitles that need to be small and unobtrusive should be limited to *no more than twenty-five to thirty characters per line* to remain legible. Remember, too, that something that looks pretty sharp in a dimly lit control room and that is seen through your high-resolution video monitor connected directly to your TV camera will lose a lot of oomph once it is recorded, edited, and copied, and then the copy played back on an inexpensive video player through RF into a casually adjusted TV set. It's a wonder that there is any picture left at all, much less a sharp one. Figure 8–11 shows what happens to character-generated text that has run the gauntlet from camera to editor to playback of a tape copy.

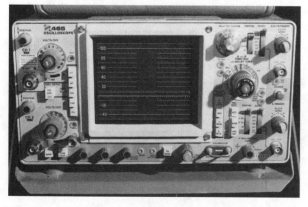

Too much detail

Zoom in on main items

Avoid clutter.

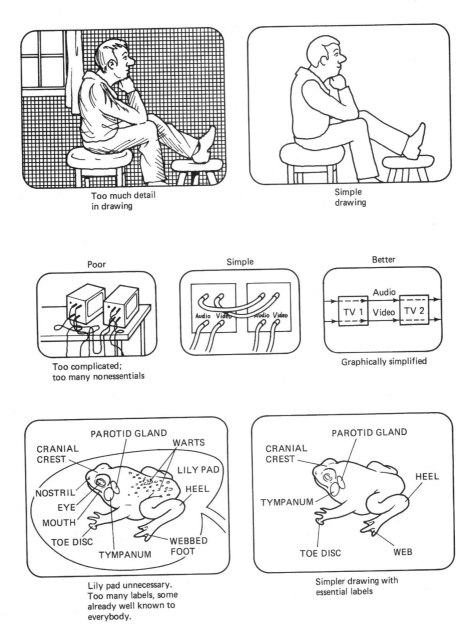

Boldness and simplicity in TV visuals.

One way to test for boldness is to step back from your proposed visual, squint your eyes, and look at it through your eyelashes. Doing this shows what the image will look like when the viewer sees it. Give every title, drawing, and photograph the old "squint test," and two things are bound to happen: Your visuals will stand up to the rigors of the TV medium, and your friends will arrange optometrist appointments for you.

One thing to avoid in graphics, photos, and your talent's wardrobe is patterns of fine lines or herringbones. On TV they may vibrate with a shimmering rainbow of colors.

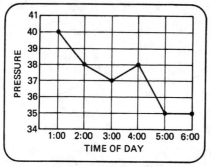

Graph too frail. Grid to graph lines confusing. "PRESSURE" printed sideways . . . hard to read. Too much labeling.

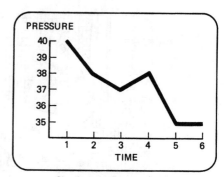

Simple, bold. Exact readings may be part of narrative.

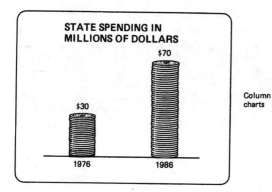

Column charts

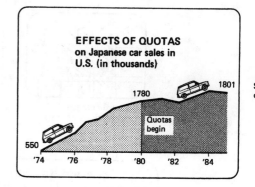

Surface chart

Pie chart

Bar chart

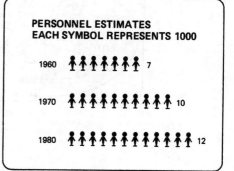

FIGURE 8–10   Simple tables and charts help your viewers remember the facts.

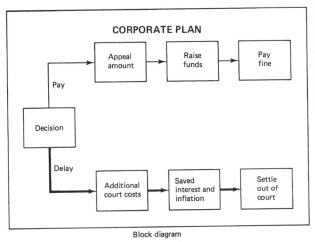

Block diagram

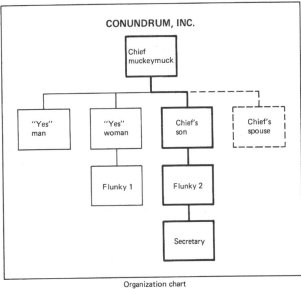

Organization chart

FIGURE 8–10 *Continued*

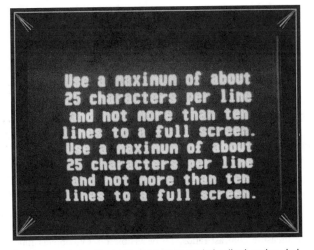

Control room TV monitor

Another example of text after it's been recorded, edited, and copied onto VHS and played over RF into a consumer TV set. Text looks pretty mushy.

FIGURE 8–11 Limit your long text passages to ten lines of 25 characters per line.

GRAY SCALE

Early in Chapter 5 you learned that a TV camera could accept a LIGHTING RATIO up to 30:1. The brightest thing in a scene couldn't be more than thirty times brighter than the darkest thing in the same scene. Once the cameras, VTRs, and TV sets are finished with your picture, you'll find that the brightest white you will ever see on your *TV screen* is only twenty times brighter than the darkest black. This brightness range can be divided into ten gradations, which is called the GRAY SCALE (Figure 8–12). Although it sounds a bit like a skin disease, it is merely a chart of bars of various brightness. For one object to *appear* brighter than another *on your TV*, it must be *at least* one step brighter on this reference chart, the GRAY SCALE; otherwise, the brightness difference is just too small to register.

What does this all mean to the graphic artist? It means that the artist should not place things that are very close together on the GRAY SCALE close together on a picture. Even though the items may have a slightly different brightness, your camera and TV may not pick up this difference, and the two items may merge together into a single mass. To make one object stand out from another, it needs to be significantly lighter or darker than its neighbor (a one- to two-step jump on the ten-step GRAY SCALE). For instance, if black were step ten and white were step one on the scale, Caucasian faces would fall between two and four on the scale. If lettering is to be seen across such a face, it should be darker than step five or as white as step one in order to stand out. Although one-step differences may show, they will fail the boldness test. A three-step difference in GRAY SCALE comes with a money-back guarantee that your object or lettering will stand out from its background.

Try to avoid using pure whites and pure blacks in your graphics. If some part of the picture is blisteringly white, it will make all the light gray, medium gray, and darker parts of the picture look too

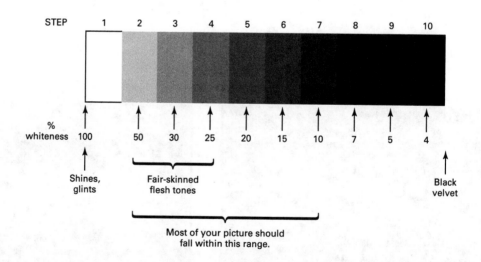

FIGURE 8–12　Ten-step GRAY SCALE.

*Gray scale　Standard of ten steps from black to white used to measure contrast ratios. To be visible on TV, objects must be at least one gray scale step different in brightness from their backgrounds.

Status, or menu, monitor　Computer screen on a character generator that helps you navigate through menus and commands.

Cursor monitor　TV monitor that shows what you've typed and where the next character will be typed.

Color compatible　Referring to an image that can be viewed easily on black-and-white TVs as well as on color ones.

dark in comparison. If, on the other hand, the whites aren't so terribly white when compared with the grays, all the tones will get a fighting chance to be seen. As a general rule, use off-white paper (yellow, light green, or buff) to allow the full range of grays to be seen by the camera. Incidentally, those off-white backgrounds, under most lighting, will still look white when seen on the TV screen.

If there are no grays in your picture (such as a black title on a white background), you can get away with using white paper and black print *or vice versa*. Go easy on the lighting, as some TV cameras will smear the letters if the contrast is too great.

Color Compatibility

If you place a light blue card next to a light green card next to a light red card and look at them, you can tell one from another easily (unless you're color-blind). Aim a color TV camera at the three colors and observe the results on a color TV monitor, and you will still be able to tell the three apart. If however, you view the result on a black-and-white TV, the three cards may look exactly the same, blending into one shade of gray. This is because, although the colors are different, the cards' relative brightness on the GRAY SCALE is the same.

Since there are over 83 million black-and-white TV sets in use in the United States, it behooves us to consider these viewers when planning our graphics. For graphics to look good both in color and black-and-white, important features of a graphic should be one or two GRAY SCALE steps different from their backgrounds. When you are in doubt, it is always good to test your graphic on a black-and-white TV to see if it maintains its punch. See color Figure 8–13 for examples of COLOR COMPATIBILITY and incompatibility.

 Mini Review

- Titling for TV needs to be brief, broad, and bold—no more than 25 to 30 characters per line.
- Avoid pure black and pure white in graphics.
- To be visible on black-and-white TVs, objects in a graphic must be significantly different in brightness from their surroundings.

Poor choice of text brightness is saved only by the DROP SHADOW edging on the letters (*see also* color Figure 8–13).

FIGURE 8–13 When text fails to be 1 or 2 GRAY SCALE steps from its background, it is hard to read on black-and-white TVs (see also color examples).

CHARACTER GENERATOR

No, a CHARACTER GENERATOR isn't an alien machine that creates those weird guys you find talking to themselves in the New York subways. A CHARACTER GENERATOR (CG), or TITLER, is a computerized typewriter that electronically places the words on a TV screen rather than on a piece of paper. Just type, and there they are. Depending on the kind of CHARACTER GENERATOR used, the device may store sentences—even pages—for later display. It may display bulletins crawling horizontally across the TV screen or columns rolling vertically from the bottom to the top of the TV screen. Some machines allow the editing and changing of prepared material in the generator's memory while other parts of the material are being displayed.

A $400 CHARACTER GENERATOR will probably display only words and numbers and have perhaps a couple of pages of memory (so that the typing doesn't have to be done "live" when you use it but can rather be prepared and previewed in advance of taping). Most CHARACTER GENERATORS will colorize the lettering and will even generate background colors. The second example in Figure 8–11 came from such a TITLER.

For about $700, a generator will form better-looking letters in several sizes with edging or drop shadows (shadows at the right and bottom of each letter to make it look three-dimensional).

By adding a $500 to $2000 board to your computer, you can make video signals from your computer (something that computers don't normally do—except for the video-friendly Amiga). Those video signals could be titles; all you need is software that makes the letters and colors. This software costs from $100 to $1000.

Depending on the model, the CHARACTER GENERATOR may be able to scroll data such as weather reports across the bottom of the screen (repeating the information when it reaches the end) while also rolling news across the top of the screen. Meanwhile, it can flip from advertisement to advertisement in the middle of the screen, as you've probably seen on some of your cable TV channels. Certain words may flash on and off to attract attention. Besides having several pages of active memory, some models allow the data to be recorded on floppy discs or computer chip memory so that hundreds of pages may be stored. Figure 1–22 showed a CHARACTER GENERATOR, and Figure 8–14 shows the type styles you can expect from this mid-priced model.

Professional CHARACTER GENERATORS, like the Dubner shown in Figure 8–14, work with two screens, a STATUS or MENU monitor that helps you select functions, features, and stored titles and backgrounds, and a color CURSOR MONITOR that lets you preview your title layout, positioning, and colors. Black-and-white Figure 8–15 shows a Dubner STATUS monitor. Turn to color Figure 8–15 on the back cover to view a Dubner CURSOR MONITOR screen.

Before your show begins, you would type in your titles, check out how they look on your CURSOR MONITOR (or even the switcher's PREVIEW MONITOR, if you wanted), and then store each title as an EVENT. With a few keystrokes you could simply activate each title as it was needed during the show. If you had a series of titles (or one where extra lines appeared as a list grew), you would need to figure out how to get from one image to the next. The pro TITLERS let you select fancy transitions that take you from one title to another. This series of EVENTS can be programmed into the CHARACTER GENERATOR and viewed on the CG's STATUS monitor, as shown in Figure 8–16. As in word processing, you can update, edit, and change the list on the screen, thus changing the sequence of titles and/or transitions.

Event   Single title or transition from one title to another.
Anti-alias   Smoothing-out of jagged or stair-steppy edges of electronic graphics or generated characters.
*Font   Style and shape of lettering.
Proportional letter spacing   Typography in which the space between letters depends on the shape and size of the letters.

Gradient background   Background that goes smoothly from light to dark or from one color to another, typically used behind titles.

FIGURE 8–14 Sample type faces from a Dubner CHARACTER GENERATOR.

Anti-Aliasing

No, this isn't my Uncle Alias's wife. It has to do with the stair-steppiness you see sometimes when computers try to make rounded shapes. TITLERS, graphics workstations, and digital SEGs, depending upon their quality, exhibit a certain amount of ALIASING like what you saw in Figure 7–15. To hide this "chunkiness," the better machines blur the edges of the image a bit, smoothing out the bumps. This blurring process is called ANTI-ALIASING. Of course, if the stair-steps are too pronounced (i.e., if the TITLER is very cheap), the image is beyond saving; ANTI-ALIASING will just make the image too blurry. Higher-quality computers and CGs make tinier stair-steps and crisper, sharper, less stair-steppy images that need very little smoothing to look good.

CHARACTER GENERATORS costing $3,000 to $6,000 have more bells and whistles than you can ever clang or toot. Here are some of their features:

- Numerous roll speeds (to run the credits quickly . . . until they come to *your* name)
- Automatic centering of a line of text, or of a whole page of text
- Several standard FONTS (type styles), upgradable with additional fonts
- Array of more colors (maybe 512 instead of 16 or 64) for text or background
- Hundreds of character sizes
- PROPORTIONAL letter spacing

Dubner STATUS MONITOR

FIGURE 8–15 CHARACTER GENERATOR MENU for selecting letter styles, edging, backgrounds, colors (see back cover to view CURSOR MONITOR screen).

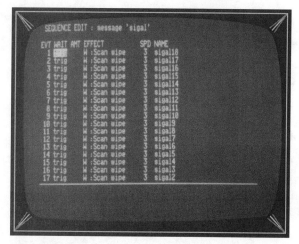

First image ready for "EVENT ONE"

Using the CHARACTER GENERATOR'S MENU screen, select the text that will be displayed. Then assign a transition, in this case "scan wipe". Each text change becomes an EVENT. By triggering the events in sequence (usually by one keystroke), the CHARACTER GENERATOR will perform the effect as it changes from one title to the next.

"Scan wipe" transition

Second image ready for "EVENT TWO"

FIGURE 8–16 Transition effects from one title to another.

- Preview channel (so that you can type on one channel while the other is being recorded or broadcast)
- User-created fonts (like drippy letters, or letters with teeth or cat whiskers)

The advanced CHARACTER GENERATORS can make animated FONTS that move about the screen, tumble and twirl in 3-D, and glow or reflect light as if they were made of glass or silver. When you're finished having fun flying your titles hither and thither, come back to earth for a moment to remember the basics of readability:

1. Make the title fit the shape of the TV screen.
2. Keep it simple.
3. Make it bold.

Busy, bright, contrasty background obscures text   Darken the background so that text stands out

FIGURE 8–17   Text competes with background.

Let's explore the catechism of character creation further.

Title Placement and Background

Without the help of EDGING or DROP SHADOW, a white title disappears when placed over a white background. Figures 7–6 and 7–7 showed how moving a white title to a darker part of the picture made the title show up better. Similarly, a dark title should be moved to a light part of the picture to show up well.

Some backgrounds, especially the busy, bright, and contrasty ones, compete with titles no matter what color they are. Figures 8–17 and 8–18 show examples.

You should avoid busy backgrounds. If you have no choice, then try darkening the background, perhaps with the camera's IRIS or GAIN controls. Another possibility might be to defocus the background. Doing this will make the foreground stand out more. If you plan carefully, you can have the

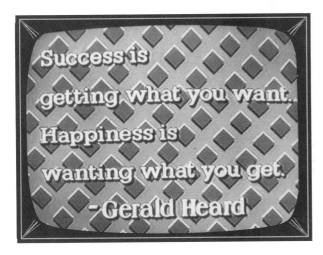

FIGURE 8–18   Pretty TITLER-generated backgrounds can also be distracting.

title disappear as the background picture comes into focus. If it is the end of a production, you can have the picture defocus as the title or credits appear.

A title should not appear like a bumper sticker wrapped across someone's face. Instead, try to find a place for the face and a place for the title so that they don't fight with each other. Across the shirt pockets or at mid-waist is often a good spot.

All these warnings should not make you afraid of adding backgrounds to your titles. A drawing or photo can add meaning and pizzazz to a title. In fact, the picture may be remembered long after the words have been forgotten, so this powerful visual tool should not be dismissed offhandedly.

A GRADIENT background that goes smoothly from light to dark (often light blue to dark blue) is more interesting than a plain background, yet it is totally nondistracting, as you can see in Figure 8–19.

Letter Edging and Color

You've already learned that to make things stand out from each other, they should be two or more steps apart on the GRAY SCALE. To make things stand out even more, they should be EDGED—that is, have a border to further accentuate their edges. This is especially true for lettering. If you can't manage to put a border all around your letters, then try for a DROP SHADOW that gives one edge a dark ridge, which also makes the letter look three-dimensional. Review Figures 8–11, 8–15, 8–16, and 8–17, and notice how the black EDGING sets the letters off and how the DROP SHADOW sets them off even further, giving them added dimension and "snap."

For letter colors, white is a guaranteed winner (except over pure white backgrounds). Yellow and pale colors are good too. Avoid saturated (pure) colors with very little white in them. They will appear fuzzy on screen. For best visibility, the letters should be pale (high LUMINANCE, low color SATURATION), and the background should be dark (dark gray or blue works fine).

Title Spacing and Legibility

Titles look best when neither crowded nor sprawled. As shown in Figure 8–20, the general rule is to leave a one-half-letter-height space between lines of text. When using both uppercase and lowercase letters, you may need a little more space between lines. The capital letters and *ascenders* (parts that

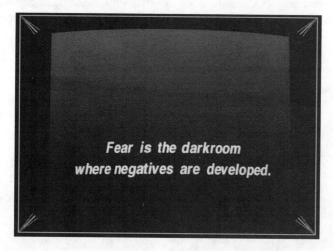

FIGURE 8–19   GRADIENT background is opulent yet sedate.

---

*Luminance   Black-and-white (brightness only) part of a video signal.

*Saturation   Purity and vividness of a color. A stop sign is saturated red. Pink, garnet, or cardinal are less saturated reds.

Too little space between lines looks crowded

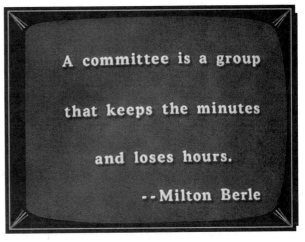

Too much space between lines is hard to read

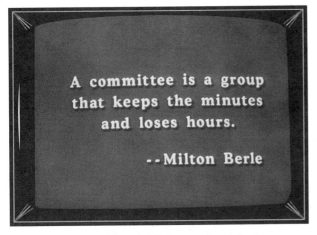

About 1/2 letter height between lines is best

FIGURE 8–20 Avoid FONTS that are frail or skinny.

stick up in letters like *b, d, l, k*) shouldn't almost touch the *descenders* (letter parts that stick down as in *g, p, q*) from the line above.

Long words, especially unfamiliar ones, should be presented in uppercase and lowercase; words printed all in capitals are hard to read.

Title Clustering

Titles, like good friends, should stick together. Words should be clustered close enough together to be read as a group, to convey a single concept. For instance, read the following program title:

The Video Club
of
Transylvania
proudly
presents
Transylvania High School's
performance of
Vladimir Dracula's
BLEEPS, BLOOPERS,
and
PRACTICAL JOKES

When these titles roll through the screen, you see only four or five lines at a time. The four or five lines you see never make sense together. Instead, the title should be condensed and regrouped and shown as three separate screens or rolled across the screen:

Vladimir Dracula's
BLEEPS, BLOOPERS,
and
PRACTICAL JOKES

Produced by
TRANSYLVANIA
HIGH SCHOOL

Sponsored by
TRANSYLVANIA
VIDEO CLUB

Now the TV screen always holds a complete concept or phrase at a time.
At the end of a show, the CREDITS can appear in one of two ways or as a combination of both.

1. Single CREDITS can flash on the screen one after another.
2. CREDITS can roll continuously up through the screen.
3. A few important CREDITS can flash individually, followed by the lesser credits rolling through the screen.

When organizing the text for rolling CREDITS, you have two choices, as shown in Figure 8–21:

1. As shown in example A, blocks of copy are separated by only a line or two of blank screen. Each block follows closely on the heels of the preceding block. This procedure may be the only way to move an immense amount of text through the screen in a short amount of time. Of course, this presentation diminishes both the importance of the text and the viewer's retention of the information.
2. Method B in the figure places a large gap between each block of copy so that as one block is leaving the screen, another is entering. Be sure to leave a large blank area before and after the

---

*Credits   List of participants in a TV production, usually scrolled at the end of the show.

*Copy stand   Device for holding a camera and graphic so that the camera can easily be focused on a graphic.

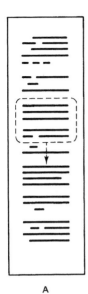 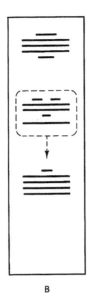

A   B   **FIGURE 8–21** Two versions of ROLLING CREDITS.

credit roll so that you have a clean place to start and a place to end with no words on the screen. Method B is best for briefer credits or for occasions when you wish to place greater emphasis on each block of information.

 Mini Review

- The character generator not only adds text to the TV screen but can often colorize it, change its background color, and add edging and drop shadow to make the titles stand out.
- Many character generators allow you to store numerous titles and make transitions between them in appealing ways.
- Avoid busy, bright, or contrasty backgrounds for titles.
- For best visibility, use white or pale yellow text over dark gray or blue backgrounds.
- Cluster the words in a title so that the TV screen always holds a complete concept or phrase at a time.

MAKING GRAPHICS COME ALIVE

Those of us blessed with creativity will have no trouble making graphics come alive. Good artists and photographers can find ways to make almost anything look real or interesting.

Then there's the rest of us. No law says that a still picture must remain stationary. A camera can pan, tilt, and zoom over a photograph or over a painting as if it were shooting something "live" in the studio. Quick cutting and active movements can make the pictures themselves seem to be moving. Still photographs become movies; battle scenes become the actual battles (with the help of sound effects); birds glide through the sky; ships roll back and forth; earthquake scenes shake up and down; amusement park rides streak by while the lights of the midway grow blurry and dissolve to the next scene.

Cutouts can be placed over visuals and moved, simulating animation. Scenes can have holes cut in them with movement behind the holes simulating running water, snow, vehicles passing by, or whatever.

In the documentary *The Story of Manhattan Beach*, the author recalls finding a black-and-white photograph of an iron gate, a landmark torn down in World War II. By enlarging the photo, gluing it to posterboard, and cutting the posterboard into a gate shape, we were able to open the program with the opening of the gate. By keying the gate over another scene, it appeared that the gate had this other scene behind it. Naturally, the cutout had to be very carefully lit and smoothly opened in order to maintain the illusion.

Detailed photographs and paintings offer an excellent opportunity to zoom in on one part of the picture and slowly pan, taking a trip from one part of the scene to another. Your audience can slowly stroll down a street in Luxembourg or be barraged with close-ups of Civil War cannon fire and soldiers diving for cover. All these shots may be taken from the same picture, just by using close-ups of different parts, panning from one area to another, and zooming in on centers of interest.

When you wish to show something complicated, or unfamiliar, it is often best to begin with a wide, establishing shot of the item and its surroundings. Then you zoom in on the specific part of the picture, detailing the concept that you wish to highlight.

LIGHTING GRAPHICS

A professional-looking graphic is generally one that leaves no hint as to how it was constructed. Curly edges on letters and grainy paper fibers in the background make graphics look gauche and amateurish.

Some of these flaws can be de-emphasized by the use of flat, shadowless lighting. Lamps can be set up to the left and right of the camera and aimed at the graphic. Each light "washes out" some of the shadow created by the other light. making the image fairly shadowless. The "softer" (more diffused) the lights, the better.

The angle of the lights is not too critical. If, however, they are too close to the camera, glossy paper, shiny paper, or lettering surfaces may reflect light into the camera lens. Placed at too great an angle from the camera, the lights begin to create shadows and may also illuminate the graphic unevenly. An angle of 45° from the camera/visual axis is a good compromise.

Sometimes, it is more convenient to mount a camera facing straight down by using a COPY STAND as shown in Figure 8–22. The camera can be raised and lowered to suit particular needs. Close-up lenses make it possible to blow up small visuals to a large size. Because the base is flat, materials tend

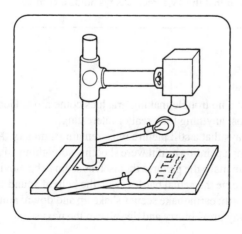

FIGURE 8–22   COPY STAND.

to lie flat and are easier to shuffle around than when graphics are placed on a vertical or angled stand. A pane of antiglare glass may be used to hold items flat. Again, the COPY STAND lights would be at 45° angles to the graphic. Make sure to turn off any overhead ceiling lights when using the COPY STAND to avoid getting unwanted reflections off the visual from these lights.

FOCUSING ON GRAPHICS

All the focusing procedures in Chapter 3 also apply to focusing on graphics; however, small things like graphics are harder to focus on than larger things. One way to minimize the focusing problem is to first ensure that the graphic is exactly perpendicular to the camera's line of sight, as shown in Figure 8–23. This way, all parts of the graphic are equidistant (almost) from the camera lens and are therefore all in focus at the same time.

Another way to minimize the focusing problem is to flood the visual with light and to "stop down" the camera lens to a higher f-number for maximum depth of field.

 Mini Review

- By moving the camera, you can add motion to still graphics.
- For the sharpest, undistorted pictures, position your camera perpendicular to the plane of the graphic.
- Angle your lights at 45° from the plane of the graphic to avoid reflections and shadows.

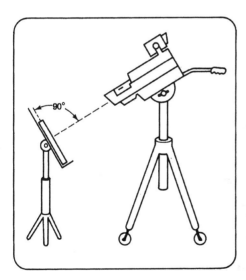

FIGURE 8–23 Graphic kept perpendicular to camera's line of sight.

---

*Telecine, or film chain Movie projector/TV camera combination designed for converting movie images to video.
Multiplexer Mirrored device that selects which one of several projectors shines its image into a TV camera for transferring film to video.

Landscape Image that is oriented so that it is wider than it is tall (as opposed to "portrait," where it is taller than it is wide).

DISPLAYING SLIDES AND MOVIES

Professional TV studios usually have a TELECINE or FILM CHAIN, a device that mates a film projector to a TV camera. Sometimes several projectors (i.e., 35mm slide, 16mm movie, 8mm movie) are hooked up to a single camera as in Figure 8–24. In this case the gadget is called a MULTIPLEXER.

To use the slide projector, you'd first load your slides into the carousels (usually there are two). The odd-numbered slides go into one, and the even-numbered slides go into the other. When you show the slides, the mechanism alternates between displaying the slide in the left carousel and displaying the slide in the right. The process is so quick, you hardly see the blink.

Make sure you photograph your original slides in LANDSCAPE orientation (wider than they are tall), or else the TV camera will cut off the tops and bottoms of your pictures while leaving black margins on the sides.

Buttons in the control room light the projector and advance the carousels.

Movie film is shown by using a special projector that is designed for use with TV equipment. Ordinary movie projectors work at the wrong speed for TV, causing a shadow to roll through the TV picture.

As you did with slides, after loading the projector, you would press a button in the control room to activate the projector.

In studios where slides and movies are seldom used, the film is usually sent out to a commercial service that produces a videotape that you can edit into your TV production.

Mirror box selects which projector shines into the camera

TV camera

Filmstrip projector

16 mm projector with 5-blade shutter

35 mm DOUBLE DRUM slide projector

FIGURE 8–24   MULTIPLEXER.

For showing the occasional slide, one might illuminate the slide from behind and focus on it with a camera that has a macro lens. Special slide-holding lens attachments are also available.

If all else fails, you can always darken the room, aim the projector at a smooth, white sheet of paper, and shoot the image with your camera.

 Mini Review

- If taking slides for video, orient the slides horizontally so they resemble the shape of the TV screen.

COMPUTER GRAPHICS

You've already seen how character generators can add words electronically to the TV image. They can also add backgrounds and perform animated transitions between pages of text. It's a small jump from there to the world of electronic graphics where you "draw" by using a mouse or light pen and can create three-dimensional images that move or bend, have shadows, and act like objects in the real world.

What you can do depends on

1. The horsepower of your computer.
2. The efficiency and flexibility of your software.
3. The extent of your creativity.

Computer horsepower is a finite commodity. A digital picture consists of hundreds of thousands of dots. Pictures with more detail may comprise millions of dots. Something has to store, retrieve, and keep track of all those dots. The computer's RAM (RANDOM ACCESS MEMORY) is one measure of its brain power. The size of its HARD DRIVE, measured in GIGABYTES (GB), describes how many pictures the computer can store. Color images demand that those millions of dots have different colors, necessitating that even more data be manipulated and stored. A realistic picture consisting of 16 million different colors will use more resources than a cartoonlike picture with just 16 colors.

Then there's motion. An animated or moving picture requires the computer to retrieve, display, or record all those dots in less than 1/60 of a second in order to be ready to handle the next video picture coming 1/60 of a second later.

And if the computer is called upon to manipulate the data (i.e., perform a RENDER or a special effect), it may need to perform millions of calculations to change the data that represents the picture.

If the image is analog, the computer has to digitize it. If the data is COMPRESSED, the computer needs to DECOMPRESS it before working with it. All this takes computer horsepower.

RAM (random access memory)   Size of a computer's "brain," measured in megabytes, describing the amount of data the computer can process and temporarily store at any moment.

*Megabyte (MB)   One million bytes, roughly enough data to store one picture or 500 typed pages.

Gigabyte (GB)   One billion bytes, or 1,000 megabytes.

*Hard drive   Spinning magnetic disk that is generally inside a computer. The hard drive stores and retrieves data and computer programs.

*Render   Electronically perform the calculations that create the surfaces, shadows, and reflections in a three-dimensional scene.

Compression   Process for storing digital data in a smaller space than it would normally take. A 2:1 compression would squeeze the data into half their original size.

The computer software and hardware you need for electronic graphics depends on how it's going to be used:

1. *Photojournalism.* Pictures may have lots of detail with millions of colors, suitable for magazines and other print media. One picture may claim 30 megabytes of data. Images are generally sent to a color printer.
2. *Video.* Less detail is necessary because TV pictures are relatively fuzzy, but the pictures must be retrieved and processed at the rate of 60 fields per second. Motion video demands a data rate of about 30 megabytes per second. Colors must be NTSC compatible (some computer-made colors look awful on TV), and lines must be bold enough not to flicker or disappear between TV's scan lines. Audio may have to be synchronized with the video, either through a sound card in your computer or a dual-purpose audio/video card.
3. *CD-ROM, Internet, and World Wide Web publishing.* Here the data must be squashed down to the least number of bytes so that it doesn't take forever to download over telephone lines at about 1/30 of a megabyte per second. Detail, colors, and motion are all compromised to make the pictures data-stingy. Data needs to be highly COMPRESSED. Audio is often part of the video presentation, requiring the playback computer to have a sound card and speakers.

Types of Computer Graphics

2-D Paint. If you're familiar with Microsoft Windows, Windows '95, or '98, you've probably played with Microsoft Paint, a simple PAINT system that allows you to draw pictures on your computer screen and save them as files.

A menu offers you "brushes" and "pens" of various shapes and sizes to "draw" with, using a mouse or a GRAPHICS TABLET and an electronic "pen." The menu may offer straight and curved lines, boxes, circles, and other shapes. You can color the lines you draw, or fill the objects you draw with color (or fill the background behind the objects with color).

As in word processing, parts of a picture can be selected and copied, moved, or deleted. Parts of a picture can be blown up, making it easier for you to make detailed changes.

Although you can create images that look three-dimensional (3-D)—like a house, for instance—the images are still two-dimensional (2-D); you can't turn them around and see their backsides. You can warp, stretch, rotate, and modify a image in numerous ways, but like a sheet of paper, the image is forever two-dimensional.

Images can consist of LAYERS, as if drawn on sheets of clear plastic. One layer may be Bart Simpson's face and nothing else. Another may be his body only. A third layer may hold his background, perhaps a classroom. You can change the expression on Bart's face without redrawing his body or the classroom, and can then combine the three layers to show a complete scene.

---

*Paint, or 2-D paint   Electronic graphics technique or software that allows you to draw flat images on the computer screen, like drawing on a piece of paper. The images can be colored, warped, rotated, resized, and manipulated in various ways, then stored electronically.

Graphics tablet   Flat surface connected to an electronic pen or sliding puck similar to a mouse, connected to a computer and allowing you to "draw" images electronically.

*Layer   Part of a computer image, separate from the other parts, which can be changed independently from them, such as changing the background behind a cartoon figure.

*3-D modeling   Electronic graphics technique or software that allows one to designate points in three-dimensional space,

connect those points, cover the resulting wireframe with a selected material, then move or rotate the object, showing it from various angles. Objects can be combined and allowed to reflect or cast shadows upon each other and/or their backgrounds.

*Wireframe   Electronic graphics image whereby selected points are connected by lines that form the "skeleton" of an object.

*Animation   Technique or result of creating a series of still images and then playing them quickly in sequence to create motion.

Scanner   Desktop device that "looks" at a document, photo, or page of a book, digitizes it and records it as a computer file. The process takes about half a minute.

GRAPHICS TABLET and electronic pen.

3-D Modeling. With the help of 3-D MODELING software, you could, for instance, designate eight dots in space, representing the corners of a cube. You could then connect the dots, forming a WIREFRAME of the cube. The WIREFRAME can be rotated, shrunk, squeezed, or moved easily.

Next, you could cover the surface of the stick-figure cube with a material selected from a menu, such as marble. You may have several types, textures, and colors of marble to choose from. Once the marble material is "wrapped" over the surface of the cube, a lighting scheme can be selected to illuminate the cube. A background surface can be chosen from another menu and placed behind the cube. Additional objects can be manufactured and placed in front of or behind the cube or each other. Some objects can be complex, consisting of thousands of WIREFRAME triangles to form space ships or faces. Shadows from one object can bend and fold as they pass over another object. Some objects can be silver with dazzling reflections, others refractive like a crystal ball.

Once the objects are positioned and RENDERED, and the image is stored as a file, you can move or change the objects and repeat the process to create a second, slightly different image, and then save it. Make a series of such images, play them back in quick succession, and you have ANIMATION.

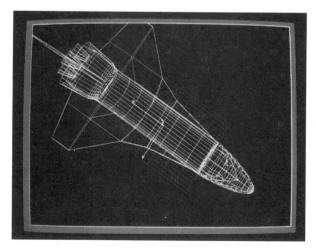

WIREFRAME

RENDERED image

WIREFRAME and RENDERED image.

Electronic pictures don't have to be drawn from scratch. You can start with a picture and add LAYERS to it, or you can modify the original picture in various ways. Here, a TV camera or SCANNER sends a digitized image to the computer, which stores it as a file. PAINT software allows the file to be read and displayed on the computer screen. The image can be warped, stretched, recolored, or modified in various ways. It is possible to add new LAYERS to the picture so that the LAYERS can be modified without disturbing the original. Often a title is added as a LAYER. When finished, you can save the result as a new file.

 Mini Review

- Computers for television graphics need large amounts of RAM and large, fast hard drives to handle the tremendous amount of data involved in moving pictures.
- 2-D paint systems allow you to create or modify flat pictures.
- 3-D modeling systems create objects by covering wire frames with various surfaces and illuminating them with artificial light. The result is a synthetic object that can be rotated and moved to various positions and that can display realistic shadows, reflections, and refractions.
- Most paint and modeling systems allow you to work in layers, changing one aspect of the picture without affecting others.

Video Capture

VIDEO CAPTURE CARDS (also called VIDEO DIGITIZERS or FRAME GRABBERS) are circuit boards that go into your computer and do the job of converting analog video into computer data. You insert the card in your computer or plug an external capture device into your PC's parallel port. You plug your camera or VCR into the CAPTURE CARD, press the CAPTURE button, and one frame of the video signal will be frozen on the screen. The digitized image can then be stored as a file.

For higher-quality images, you can use a SCANNER, a device that looks like a fax or photocopier, (which some are). The SCANNER connects to a board inserted into your computer. Software allows you to run the SCANNER from your keyboard or mouse, and offers you menus for color, resolution, and type of file to make. You place the document, picture, or book on the SCANNER, activate it, and about half a minute later you have a detailed, digitized image file ready for editing or IMPORTATION into other programs.

For moving images, there are VIDEO CAPTURE CARDS that process each video image into a file in 1/60 of a second. Thus, motion video at 30 frames per second (60 fields per second) can be digitized. The resulting files can be *viewed* from the HARD DRIVE by using an AVI PLAYER (a program that plays .AVI-type files). An AVI PLAYER is built into Windows '95 and '98. The files can also be played on-screen or edited on the HARD DRIVE using NONLINEAR EDITING software and/or hardware (described further in Chapter 14). Most VIDEO CAPTURE CARDS also work in reverse, converting digital images back to video recordable on your VCR.

---

*Video capture card   Computer circuit capable of converting a video signal into a digital computer signal that can be stored on disk or manipulated.

Import   Copy the data from another computer file into the file you're working on, translating its format along the way so that it is compatible with your software.

AVI player   Computer program that plays motion video from a certain kind of data files called .AVI files.

*Nonlinear editing (NLE)   Assembling video sequences that are randomly accessible, typically digitized onto a hard drive. The process is much like word processing in that sound/picture sequences can be moved, deleted, copied, or changed electronically before being displayed or copied to videotape.

Some VIDEO CAPTURE CARDS simultaneously capture audio and keep it synchronized with the video. Otherwise, you would use a SOUND CARD or AUDIO DIGITIZING CARD to convert the analog audio into digital audio files. Software would coordinate the playback of both so that they could be edited and/or synchronized.

Compression

Because video requires the computer to process and store a whopping 30MB per second, which only expensive professional models can presently do, compromises must be made.

COMPRESSION is one compromise by which less important data is discarded in order to get the file sizes smaller.

JPEG (Joint Photographic Experts Group) is one type of COMPRESSION used mostly on single pictures. Once COMPRESSED, the data is called a "JPEG file" (pronounced JAY-peg). The more a file's data is COMPRESSED, the worse the picture looks. Color Figure 8–25 compares an image having a small amount of COMPRESSION with one having a large amount. The higher the COMPRESSION RATIO (amount of compression), the smaller the file size, but the worse the picture looks.

When COMPRESSION ratios rise above 3:1, pictures start to appear coarse. Pictures are very blocky at 40:1. JPEG files can be quite small, perfect for sending still pictures and short sequences over the Internet. For longer video sequences, turn to MPEG (pronounced M-peg) COMPRESSION, which squeezes files 100:1 or more. Other forms of COMPRESSION are MJPEG (motion JPEG), MPEG-1 (used on home computers and CD-ROMs) and MPEG-2 (used on professional computers, DVDs, and digital VCRs).

Compression, incidentally, does not change the size of the image, only its file size (the amount of data stored in the file).

 Mini Review

- A video capture card allows you to convert video images into digital data that can be stored and manipulated by the computer.
- A scanner allows you to convert a photograph or drawing into digital data that can be stored or manipulated by the computer.
- Compression is a method of reducing the amount of data in a picture so that it is easier for the computer to handle and store. Compression, however, may degrade the quality of the picture.

Firewire (P1394)

You wouldn't need to digitize your captured video (which actually harms the image a little) if it were already digital. If, for instance, it came from a digital camcorder via a FIREWIRE connection (described in Chapter 9) it would already be digital *with* 5:1 COMPRESSION, ripe and ready for your computer.

Almost. You still need to buy a $900 board to accept the FIREWIRE signal and convert it to the right kind of files. Once recorded onto your HARD DRIVE as files, you can edit or PAINT the images as

---

JPEG   Joint Photographic Experts Group, the name given to a type of image data compression. Compression ratios are likely to be 5:1 to 10:1.

*Compression ratio   Amount of data reduction in a digital picture. A 10:1 compression shrinks the data more than a 3:1 compression.

MPEG   Motion Pictures Experts Group, the name given to a powerful type of image data compression used on moving pictures. Compression ratios of 100:1 are possible.

*Firewire, or IEEE P1394   Standard for transmitting compressed video data used by DV format digital videocassette recorders.

before. The more expensive boards have more features, such as remote VCR control, editing, and ability to also capture analog video.

When finished messing with the images, you can export them back out of your computer, through the board, and via FIREWIRE, into your digital camcorder or digital VCR.

 Mini Review

- Firewire (P1394) is a method of directly transferring data from a digital camcorder or digital VCR to a computer or to another digital camcorder or VCR.

3-D Graphics and Animation

Lightwave, Wavefront/Alias, Ray Dream Design, Real 3-D, Truespace, and others make 3-D animation *packages*. Each software package contains certain elements for building objects and moving them. Some packages are designed for specific work, such as architecture, landscapes, or people. If you're just doing landscaping, for instance, use software designed just for that. It will be cheaper and easier to use, and it will operate faster than generic 3-D art software.

The main package always consists of several environments. They may be separate windows or be seamlessly intertwined, but the different activities exist:

1. MODELER. Here is where you set dots in space and connect them with a WIREFRAME to build your 3-D object hanging in space.
2. MATERIALS EDITOR. Here is where you select surface properties for the material you use to cover the WIREFRAME. From your menus you could select
   a. The finish of the surface (i.e., shiny or dull).
   b. The overall transparency of the material (i.e., glass, paper, iron).
   c. TEXTURE MAPS, which define other surface properties, such as the roughness of a surface (i.e., the skin of an orange peel). TEXTURE MAPS also describe the print and color of the surface (i.e., red + woodgrain = redwood; maroon + woodgrain = mahogany). In addition, TEXTURE MAPS, like the KEY effect, can determine what is "cut out" of a surface and replaced with another material.

Modeler   Part of a 3-D graphics package that builds the 3-D object in space.

Material   Data that describes the underlying properties of the surface being wrapped around a wireframe. Those properties are reflectivity, refractivity, transparency, and color.

Materials editor   Part of a 3-D graphics package that makes the surfaces that cover the wireframes made in modeler.

Texture map   Data that describes a material—its color, roughness, and surface design (i.e., woodgrain)—and whether parts will be cut out and replaced by another surface. Several layered texture maps can be used together.

Preview   Channel on a switcher/SEG that sends out to your preview monitor a view of an effect so that you can adjust or perfect the effect before using it. Like *audition* in audio.

Image   Part of a 3-D graphics package that renders the final image.

Flatshade, or quickshade   Simple, flat surface applied to wireframes to give them substance and realism. Flat surfaces stretched between wireframe lines render quickly.

Try this analogy: The stud framework of a house is like a WIREFRAME. You could (if you were a real cheapskate and building codes permitted) staple wallpaper to the studs to make the walls look solid. The basic wallpaper is a MATERIAL and has underlying properties: a basic color (say slate blue), reflectivity (a shiny surface), refractivity (thick glass wallpaper might have this, but our wallpaper happens to lack this), and transparency (you can see light through it). Now add the flower pattern to the wallpaper, perforate the paper or cut designs in it, then emboss it, and you'll have the wildest abode in town.

3. PREVIEW (or LAYOUT or STAGING, depending on the software). Here is where you stage all the parts of a picture to see how they're coming together. You'd assemble the imaginary lights, camera (your eyeball view), objects, atmosphere (i.e., fog), and other attributes, such as an unseen canvas of trees or clouds *behind* the camera that can reflect off windows, water, and other shiny surfaces in the picture. PREVIEW is also where you map out the motion of objects and/or the camera.

4. IMAGE (or RENDERER, depending on system). Here is where you RENDER (compute the finished version of) your final picture.

Various 3-D packages continue with other useful features, such as light reflections and refractions, as well as programs that connect mechanical things together. (If you're animating the figure of a person holding a cup and you grab the hand to lift the cup, the rest of the body will follow naturally—the arm won't detach.)

 Mini Review

- Most 3-D graphics packages start with a wireframe and then allow you to add surfaces (defined by texture maps) to those wireframes. You can preview how the image looks along with the effects of certain lighting before you render the final picture.

Graphic artistry requires that you master both 2-D and 3-D domains. Some things are easier to do in 2-D than in 3-D, and vice versa. You can transport files from one domain to the other and enjoy the best of both virtual worlds.

Color Figures 8–26 through 8–28 show a 3-D image in various stages of completion.

Layering the Synthetic World onto the Real World

You can start with a real-world image from a TV camera or SCANNED IN from a photograph and then add an object to that picture. In Figure 8–29 you see a fountain with a giant marble sphere next to it. The globe was made using 3-D graphics, starting with a spherical WIREFRAME (they come predesigned; you just select the size and shape). The WIREFRAME was covered with the granite texture (chosen from a menu of textures) and illuminated with artificial light to give it a shadow. The globe/shadow combination were then LAYERED over the real scene.

If the ball were supposed to be rolling, the process would have to be repeated a hundred times or so. Each frame of video would have the globe rotated some, maybe positioned farther to the side, maybe a tad larger. Seen as a sequence, the 3-D ANIMATION of the globe layered upon the original moving video can look real.

PAINT systems can just as easily (after you've spent a month of frustration learning how to run the computer program) remove objects from a picture. As shown in Figure 8–30, the woman from

The sphere was created using 3D graphics and LAYERED over the real image of the fountain.

FIGURE 8–29 Adding a synthetic image to a real image.

Scan in a picture. Here we will use the picture from Figure 8–29. Let's wipe out the woman with the child in the left corner. Zoomed in, we can see our hapless victims better.

Grass and cement are selected from elsewhere in the picture and copied over the people.

After some smoothing to soften hard edge, the people have been erased . . .

FIGURE 8–30 Removing an object from a picture.

Figure 8–29 can be cut out and replaced with realistic "background." This process also must be repeated hundreds of times if the background image is moving.

Filters and Effects

A camera lens filter changes the image passing through it. An electronic graphics FILTER changes an image, too. Figure 8–31 shows what you get when you take the image from Figure 8–29 and run it through a few FILTERS.

Your graphics package may come with some FILTERS built in. Third-party vendors sell additional FILTER software that works with the more popular paint and effects programs.

Unlike the effects of glass lens filters, the amount of distortion you get through a graphics FILTER is broadly variable. You could make ripples narrow or broad, shallow or deep, angled or scattered, concentrated or spreading out. On better systems, a PREVIEW screen lets you see a sample of what an effect will look like without dragging you through a time-consuming RENDER of the whole picture.

Electronic Graphics Is Still an Art

With all this techno-talk about pixels, filters, layers, and compression, one would think electronic graphics was for engineers only. Not so. You still need a sense of art, picture composition, and color selection to work in electronic graphics. Creativity and attention to detail can't hurt either. Take a look at Figure 8–32. Do you see an artistic blunder?

And one more thought. If you saw the movie *Toy Story*, you experienced the apex of fine graphsmanship. The reflections in Buzz Lightyear's space suit and refractions through his helmet visor were superb. Every texture looked real, and every shadow followed realistically and wrapped around objects in its path, and a million little sound effects validated every action. Do you remember

"Ripple" filter in Adobe Photoshop ...

..."zigzag" filter ...

FIGURE 8–31 Additional effects performed on Figure 8–29.

*Filter Electronic graphics name for any special effect. A ripple filter adds ripples to a 2-D picture.
Desktop video Integration of several video disciplines, (i.e., titles, graphics, switcher, video editing) using one or several computers. Except for the cameras and microphones that gather the original footage, most of the production process can take place on a desktop computer.

Aw, you peeked! Answer: The shadow is in the wrong place. Also: The bottom of the sphere could use a little softening or flattening so that it doesn't look like it's floating.

FIGURE 8–32 What's wrong with this picture? Don't look at the answer until you've studied the picture.

those things about *Toy Story*? Or do you remember the story? Or the personality of the characters? Engineering without a story is just an amusement park ride, fun for a moment, but it goes nowhere.

A note about careers. There was a day when a studio hired a graphic artist, video editor, audio director, and other crew members. A few big studios still do. Today's small studios combine a lot of jobs, and the job of graphic artist is one that often gets combined. Watch out, you may be it.

On the same note, with the expanding role of computers in television, it's logical to find the box that does the titles, also to be the box that does the video editing, and also to be the box that does the graphics and animation. The chameleon computer can do it all. This, they call DESKTOP VIDEO. And if you're the person who runs the box, you're probably the person who needs to know all the jobs. The client who comes to you for editing will expect you to also put in the titles and, if not *do* the animation, at least adjust it while assembling the project. Even if you can't draw a bath, you may end up as the graphic artist for your company. Brace yourself.

 Mini Review

- Synthetic images can be created in 3-D, then layered atop real images. By repeating this process with small changes, you can create an animation.
- Paint systems can remove objects from a picture.
- Some graphics packages have software called filters that allow you to modify a picture or make special effects.
- Don't get so involved in the technology that you forget to tell a story.

VIDEOTAPE RECORDERS

9

Over 90 percent of U.S. households have videocassette recorders (VCRs). The ubiquitous VCR may be familiar to most of us, but it is still inscrutable, especially the models with lots of features. Maybe that's why so many of them are flashing "12:00."

KINDS OF VIDEOTAPE RECORDERS

Videotape recorders are like critters in the ocean; they come in all shapes and sizes. There are professional videotape recorders that cost more than a home. Some consumer models cost just a little more than dinner for four at a restaurant with tablecloths.

Everything is going digital nowadays, and so are video recorders. Since DIGITAL VIDEOCASSETTE (DVC) RECORDERS are more complicated than their analog brothers, we'll cover them later in the chapter. Besides, once you get used to the ins and outs of simple analog VCRs, the more complex models will seem less intimidating.

VCRs, VTRs, and Camcorders

A VTR is a videotape recorder. It can both record and play back videotape. Technically, "VTR" means only reel-to-reel recorders (as opposed to cassette), but people commonly use this term to mean any video recorder, even videocassette recorders.

A VCR is a videocassette recorder. It can record a videocassette or play it back. The CASSETTE, or VIDEOCASSETTE, is a small case that holds a full reel of videotape and an empty take-up reel. After the cassette has been inserted into the VCR, the machine automatically draws the tape from the cassette, threads it, plays it, and winds it back onto the take-up reel. You can remove a cassette in the middle of a program (the machine automatically unthreads the tape before it ejects the cassette to you)

---

*Digital videocassette (DVC) recorder   VCR that records and plays back digital data representing a video picture and sound.

*Videotape recorder (VTR)   Machine that can record picture and sound on a tape. Nearly all can also play back a tape. Although a videocassette recorder is also a video*tape* recorder, VTR usually implies that reel-to-reel tape is used rather than cassette.

*Videocassette recorder (VCR)   Videotape recorder that uses cassettes rather than open reels of tape.

*Videocassette   Box containing videotape connected to an internal supply reel and a take-up reel, used in VCRs.

Videotape player (VTP)   Machine that can play a videotape but cannot record one.

Videocassette player (VCP)   Machine that can play a videocassette but cannot record one.

*Camcorder   VCR and camera in one unit, or as two devices joined together.

*Dockable   Referring to the ability to join a camera with a VCR so that the pair become one unit, such as one camcorder.

He's the only one who knows how to work the remote.

and come back later to pick up where you left off. Rewinding is not required unless you want the tape to start at the beginning again. A VTP is a videotape player, and a VCP is a videocassette player. Neither record; they just play. They are handy for libraries and learning centers, where tapes are to be played and not accidentally recorded over and erased.

CAMCORDERS (if you just arrived from Mars) are VCRs too. Not only can a CAMCORDER record sound and picture from its built-in microphone and camera, but many models can also record audio and video signals sent to them over a wire. Nearly all CAMCORDERS can also play back their tapes to a TV monitor or receiver. Consumer CAMCORDERS are one-piece units; all the components are molded into one compact body. Professional CAMCORDERS are often two-piece; the camera is one part, the VCR another, and the two DOCK (join) together to make one somewhat bulky device. The advantage of DOCKABLE parts is that you can select the type of camera that you want separately from the type of VCR, then match the two into a "custom" CAMCORDER. There is more on CAMCORDERS in Chapter 13.

COMPATIBILITY

In order to play a tape, you must have the right kind of machine. The 8mm tape a friend brought you from her dream vacation in Secaucus, New Jersey, won't play in your school's VHS machine; the cassette is a different shape and the tape is a different size. The two are INCOMPATIBLE. To simplify matters, various manufacturers and video associations have agreed to standardize on several FORMATS. *So if a tape is recorded on a certain FORMAT machine, it should play back on the same FORMAT machine* regardless of manufacturer. Fortunately, most tapes are distributed in the VHS FORMAT, and VHS is the most common type of VCR.

Even if the tape and VCR are the same FORMAT, there are still some things that can go wrong . . . go wrong . . . go wrong . . .

Compatibility.

1. Some VCRs play at only one speed; the tape may have been recorded at a different speed.
2. Tapes made in some foreign countries need to be played back on VCPs designed for that foreign standard.

 Mini Review

- For a VCR to play a tape, the two must
  a. Be the same format.
  b. Run at the same speed.
  c. Share the same country standards.

---

*Compatible Referring to the ability to play a tape on any same-format machine and get good picture and sound.

*Format The way that the tapes, cassettes, and video recorders and players are designed, so that one machine can play another machine's tapes. Machines of the same format should be able to play each other's tapes.

Prosumer Professional consumer, someone halfway between a professional videographer and an amateur, often working in video as a sideline. Also refers to equipment halfway between professional and amateur grade, typically costing more and performing better than common home equipment, but not as good as true professional gear.

*8mm Eight millimeter. Nearly 1/4-inch-wide tape used in popular lightweight home camcorders. This was also the width of home movie film, which was also called 8mm.

T-120 Standard size of a VHS videocassette. Plays for two or six hours.

*Hi8 Much improved version of 8mm format. Hi8 VCRs can also record and play 8mm tapes.

*SVHS Super VHS, much improved version of VHS format. SVHS VCRs can also record and play VHS tapes.

VHS-C VHS compact format using VHS tape in a minicassette.

*DV Digital Video Format, in which images and sound are recorded as digital data onto 1/4-inch cassettes with very high quality.

*DVC PRO Panasonic professional format based on DV but using a wider track and faster tape speed to record more data with less compression than consumer DV.

*DVCAM Sony professional digital VCR format using 1/4-inch tape, able to play DV tapes.

FORMAT

No, FORMAT isn't a small rug on which to wipe your feet. FORMAT describes the size of the tape and cassette a VCR uses, along with many technical similarities that a family of VCRs share.

For the common business, industrial, and school video user, there is one primary low-budget FORMAT: VHS. It is found in most colleges, most public schools, many industrial media centers, a few commercial TV production shops, and about 90 percent of U.S. homes. VHS, which stands for Video Home System, uses 1/2-inch tape in cassettes capable of recording/playing for two to six hours on a standard T-120 cassette.

Other, popular consumer FORMATS are the following:

- *8MM:* Used mostly in consumer camcorders, this 8 millimeter (about 5/16 inch) wide tape is small, allowing the CAMCORDER to be small and lightweight.
- *HI8:* HI8 mm tape is a higher-quality version of 8MM tape that is used occasionally by professionals and PROSUMERS and is found mostly in CAMCORDERS. A HI8 CAMCORDER can record or play back either a HI8 tape *or* an 8MM tape. An 8MM machine cannot record or play HI8 tape. Although 8MM tape and HI8 *tape* are different, the cassettes look almost identical except for the 8MM or HI8 logos.
- *SVHS:* Super VHS (SVHS) is a higher-quality version of VHS, used by professionals and PROSUMERS (semiprofessionals). An SVHS machine can record or play on SVHS tape *or* a VHS tape. A VHS machine cannot play or record on SVHS tape. Although VHS tape is different from SVHS tape, the cassettes (the shells that hold the tape) look almost identical except for the logo VHS or SVHS.
- *VHS-C:* VHS Compact is VHS tape housed in a miniature cassette, the size of a deck of cards. It is used mostly in consumer camcorders. The mouth of a VHS-C camcorder is big enough only for the little tape, so it can't play a "standard" VHS cassette. Only a few VHS machines can accept the tiny cassettes directly; most require an adapter that houses the little tape in a bigger box. Once in the bigger holder, the tape can be recorded or played in any VHS VCR.
- *SVHS-C:* This is the same as the preceding, except that the tape is the higher-quality SVHS. VHS-C CAMCORDERS can't record or play SVHS-C, but SVHS-C CAMCORDERS can record or play VHS-C tapes. With an adapter, SVHS-C cassettes can be played in SVHS VCRs.
- *DV:* Digital Video is a high-quality video recording FORMAT that converts the picture and sound to data and stores it on tiny 1/4-inch cassettes. Used almost exclusively in CAMCORDERS, DV tapes can be recorded or played in professional DVCAM and DVC PRO machines, but the professional tapes won't work in the consumer DV CAMCORDERS. DV CAMCORDERS cost about $1000 to $4000, positioning them at the pricey end of the consumer scale.

For professional, educational, industrial, and PROSUMER users, the popular FORMATS are the following:

- *BETACAM:* This Sony FORMAT, using 1/2-inch tape in cassettes, was most popular among professionals and news teams several years ago. It has been supplanted by BETACAM SP and several dig-

---

Betacam   Aging popular professional camcorder format.
*Betacam SP   Improved version of Betacam, also able to play Betacam tapes, very popular among professionals.
Betacam SX   Professional digital Betacam format using 1/2-inch cassettes and also able to play Betacam SP tapes.
Digital Betacam   Professional digital format using 1/2-inch cassettes. Image quality is superior to Betacam SX.

MII   Older professional camcorder format using VHS-like cassettes.
3/4U   Aging industrial videocassette format. Uses 3/4-inch tape in cassettes.

ital FORMATS. The BETACAM decks (the VCRs that DOCK to the cameras) can often (but not always) play BETACAM SP tapes.

- *BETACAM SP:* Sony's BETACAM Superior Performance is an improved version of BETACAM, and in the mid-1990s it became the most widely used professional video FORMAT.
- *BETACAM SX:* Used mostly in news acquisition, this digital FORMAT from Sony uses 1/2-inch cassettes and yields pictures about the same quality as BETACAM SP. BETACAM SX can also play back analog BETACAM and BETACAM SP tapes.
- *DIGITAL BETACAM:* This is also a digital video FORMAT using 1/2-inch cassettes, but this Sony FORMAT is used primarily for high-quality broadcast applications (the pictures are better than BETACAM SP and SX).
- *DVC PRO:* Panasonic, Philips, and Ikegami market this professional version of the DV (digital video) FORMAT. These CAMCORDERS and DECKS can also play consumer DV tapes and DVCAM tapes.
- *DVCAM:* This is Sony's professional version of the DV FORMAT. DVCAM VCRs can also record and play consumer DV tapes.

Figure 9–1 shows some popular home and industrial videocassette recorder types and the cassettes that go into them.

Here are some less popular and older FORMATS you may come across:

- *MII:* Second most popular commercial and professional CAMCORDER FORMAT in the early 1990s, often used in news.
- *3/4U:* Also called U-Matic, this was the most popular industrial VCR in the 1970s. It was found in nearly every college and industrial media center and many public schools. Too heavy to be used for boat anchors, a few are still kicking around. The tape was 3/4 of an inch wide and came in cassettes about the size of a box of chocolates.

Later in this chapter we'll discuss the high-end professional digital VCR formats D1, D2, D3, D5, etc.

In short, if a home or school friend brings you a tape, most of the time it will be VHS. Occasionally it will be one of the other formats, 3/4U (archaic schools and industry), 8MM, or VHS-C (mostly vacationing camcordists). PROSUMERS and wealthy friends may bring you SVHS, HI8, or DV tapes.

If a professional brings you a tape, it's likely to be BETACAM SP, MII, BETACAM SX or DIGITAL BETA, DVCAM, DVCPRO, or one of the other digital FORMATS.

 Mini Review

- The common consumer formats are 8MM and VHS.
- The common prosumer formats are HI8, SVHS, and DV.
- The professional VCR formats are Betacam (SP, SX, and digital), DVCPRO, and DVCAM.
- Older formats include MII and 3/4U.

Tape Speeds

Some VCRs can record at different speeds to squeeze more out of a tape (at lower picture quality). The two popular speeds on a VHS machine are VHS-2 and VHS-6, which represent two-hour and six-hour recordings on a standard T-120 cassette. Other names for these two speeds are SP (standard

VHS (Courtesy of Philips Consumer Electronics Company)

VHS cassette

3/4U (Courtesy of Sony Corporation of America)

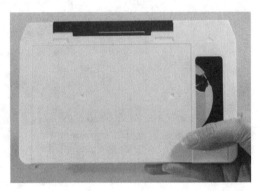

3/4U cassette

8mm CAMCORDER

8mm cassette

FIGURE 9–1 Different FORMAT VCRs and tape.

Betacam-SP VCR (Courtesy of Sony Electronics, Business, and Professional Group)

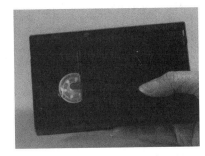

Betacam-SP cassette

FIGURE 9–1   *Continued*

play) and EP (extra long play). Another name for the VHS-6 speed is SLP (super long play). Nearly all VHS machines will play both speeds. Most will record at the two-hour (SP) or six-hour (EP) speeds. Exceptions: Some VHS editors and camcorders record/play only SP. HI8 and 8MM CAMCORDERS can usually work at two speeds, yielding two hours or four hours of recording on a standard length tape.

Super Enhancements

SVHS and HI8 are SUPER FORMATS. The SVHS and HI8 cassettes look like their normal brothers (except for the SVHS or HI8 logo on the cassette), but the tape inside is special. The tape is designed to work only with SVHS and HI8 VCRs. These VCRs make sharper pictures than regular VHS and 8MM VCRs, but to do it requires that the SUPER tape and the SUPER machines be teamed together. PROSUMERS use these two FORMATS frequently because the picture quality is so much better than VHS and 8MM.

The SUPER machines can *also* record and play back *normal* tapes. Regular VHS and 8MM VCRs can't, however, play the SUPER tapes; the cassettes fit in the VCRs, but the picture looks terrible.

SVHS and HI8 VCRs have a choice of inputs and outputs. You could use the COMPOSITE inputs/outputs for signals like those you'd get from regular VCRs, or you could use the Y/C inputs/outputs to connect with other SUPER VCRs or higher-quality equipment having these connectors.

Bottom line: Use a SUPER VCR if you can (along with the SUPER tape), and you'll get better results than with regular VHS and 8MM. Also, to transport the signals with minimal degradation, use the Y/C connectors in preference to COMPOSITE.

Hi-Fi Sound

Some VHS, and all 8MM, HI8, and SVHS VCRs can record high-fidelity sound. The sound is invisibly coded into the picture and becomes part of it. If a HI-FI recorded tape is played back on a HI-FI VCR,

---

*Super   SVHS, Hi8, ED Beta 3/4U-SP or any improvement to a VCR format that increases the picture sharpness above 400 lines of resolution. Sometimes called High Band.

*Composite video   Combination of three color video signals traveling on one wire. NTSC video is composite video.

*Y/C (or S)   Method of transmitting color video over two wires, one carrying luminance (Y) and the other carrying color (C). Also called super or S-video, as it is employed on super VHS (SVHS) VCRs and camcorders. Hi8 camcorders also use Y/C video.

*Hi-fi   Ability of some VCRs to record high-fidelity or true-to-life sound. VHS and 8mm hi-fi VCRs record stereo sound with almost "perfect" sound quality.

you will hear the extraordinary fidelity. If, however, a VHS tape is recorded on a regular "lo-fi" VCR, or if a "lo-fi" tape is played on a HI-FI VCR, then only low fidelity will be heard.

We'll come back to FORMATS later in the chapter when we discuss, in more detail, VCRs that record COMPONENT video and DIGITAL video. Meanwhile, Table 9–1 reviews some analog video FORMATS.

 Mini Review

- The super formats SVHS and HI8 yield sharper pictures than the regular formats, VHS and 8MM.
- Super format tapes will not play on regular machines, but regular tapes will play on super VCRs.
- Use the Y/C connectors in preference to composite video cables to assure the best picture quality.

Foreign Standards

A tape recorded in Europe on a VHS recorder will not play on a VHS VCR here in the United States; the electricity is different there, and European TVs make the picture in a slightly different fashion. Even though the FORMAT is the same, tapes made using different TV standards are not interchangeable. Blank tapes that are purchased overseas, however, can be used on USA equipment, and vice versa.

The United States uses the NTSC (National Television Systems Committee) standard, which broadcasts 525 interlaced scanning lines every 1/30 of a second, puts the sound at a certain frequency, and encodes the color a certain way.

In most of Europe, Australia, Italy, and Singapore, the PAL (Phase Alternate Line) system is used, with 625 scanning lines repeated every 1/25 of a second along with other differences. There are variations of PAL like PAL-M in Brazil.

Russia, France, Iran, Poland, Saudi Arabia, and Issas use SECAM (SEquential Color And Memory), which scans 625 lines (except for France, which uses 819 lines) every 1/25 of a second plus further variations from PAL.

In short, you can't play most foreign tapes on your VCR even if they're both the same FORMAT.

There are professional machines called STANDARDS CONVERTERS that will change one country's standard of TV signal into another country's standard. Also, some MULTISTANDARD VCRs will play tapes from foreign countries.

 Mini Review

- The three main television standards are NTSC (used in the USA), PAL, and SECAM.

---

*NTSC   National Television Standards Committee. Experts who developed the NTSC video standards that ensure that all TV signals in the United States are compatible.

PAL   Phase Alternate Line—a European video standard incompatible with the U.S. NTSC system.

SECAM   SEquential Color And Memory, the television standard used in France and some other countries.

Standards converter   Electronic device that changes one standard of video signal into another (e.g., NTSC into PAL) or vice versa, bridging the gap of incompatibility between standards.

Multistandard VCR   VCR that can play and sometimes record tapes in PAL or SECAM standards, as well as in NTSC.

TABLE 9–1   Popular Analog Video Recorder Formats

Format	Tape Size	Notes
VHS	1/2-inch cassette	Comprising almost all of the home VCR market, VHS (video home system) is also common among industry and schools. Actually three formats, VHS-2, VHS-4, and VHS-6 (or SP, LP, and EP, as some call it), represent three speeds yielding 2, 4, or 6 hours of playing time (depending on tape length—these playing times are for a common T-120 videocassette). When recording, *you* choose the recording speed. When a tape is played back, the *VCR* automatically switches to the right speed (if it can; a few VCRs can operate only at the SP speed).
VHS-C	1/2-inch mini-cassette	Stands for VHS compact. Ultraminiature VCR recording in the VHS format but using smaller 20- to 60-minute cassette, about the size of a deck of cards. The mouth of a VHS-C machine is too small to hold a normal VHS tape, but a VHS-C cassette can be played in a normal-sized VHS player if you stick the tiny cassette in a special adapter first. A few regular VHS and SVHS machines will take VHS-C cassettes directly without the adapter.
8MM	1/4-inch mini-cassette	This is 8mm tape in minicassettes, popular for its small size, which records 2 or 4 hours, depending on tape speed.
3/4U	3/4-inch cassette	Formerly used in schools and industry. A cassette plays up to 1 hour. Picture is about 20 percent sharper than that from 1/2-inch home VCRs.
BETACAM	1/2-inch cassette	Sony's professional analog component camcorder and studio format using 1/2-inch tape in 30-minute cassettes (camcorders) or larger, 90-minute cassettes (studio).
MII	1/2-inch cassette	Matsushita's professional analog component camcorder and studio format using 20- to 90-minute cassettes.
SVHS, HI8, BETACAM-SP, 3/4U-SP	Various	Improved versions of the preceding formats. BETACAM-SP players cost $5,000 and up; editing VCRs, $10,000 to $18,000; camcorders, $12,000 to $42,000. SVHS VCRs cost $1,200 to $6,700, depending upon features and editing capability.
C	1-inch reel-to-reel	Older, high-quality, but expensive, professional studio format. Tapes play 90 minutes.

PLAYING A TAPE

Your instructor says, "Play this tape to the class. The equipment is set up. I'll be back in half an hour." Stay cool. Here's what you do:

1. *Turn on the TV* you will use to watch this presentation. While it is warming up, *turn on the power for the tape player.* A pilot light will probably come on to tell you the machine is getting power. If it isn't, look for a TIMER switch and flip it (some timers must be OFF for the VCR to work).

2. *Put the cassette in the machine.* To make sure the VCR doesn't already have a tape in it, press the machine's EJECT button, and its mouth will open, spitting out the old cassette. Remove the

---

Output selector   Switch determining which of several signals will be fed to a VCR's output for viewing.

*Search   VCR mode that plays a tape at five to ten times normal speed, backward or forward, handy for finding scenes quickly on a tape.

Index counter   Mechanical indicator on older VCRs that is somewhat similar to the mileage meter on a car—that is, it changes numbers as the tape moves through the machine. It is handy for locating events on a tape or estimating the length of a production.

*Elapsed time counter   VCR index counter that indicates in minutes and seconds how much tape has played or been fast-forwarded.

Control track time code   Rhythmic signal recorded on a videotape's control track that guides the VCR during playback.

Time code   Way of measuring where (how far from the beginning of a tape) scenes are located. Usually, a magnetic pulse is recorded on the tape that can be converted into a listing of hours, minutes, seconds, frames.

new videocassette from its box. Holding the cassette so that its skinny spine label is right side up (readable), and its window (and the square label) face the ceiling, insert the cassette into the machine's mouth. The little trapdoor on the cassette goes in first.

3. *Give the cassette a gentle push,* and the VCR should swallow it. If the VCR is an old top loader, slide the cassette into the open hole, then press down on the cassette compartment lid (closing its mouth) until it clicks, locking it into place (gulp!). Many VCRs start to play automatically at this point. We're not ready for that yet, so press STOP, if necessary.

4. *Rewind the tape to the beginning, if necessary.* Do this by pressing the REWIND button. You do not have to hold the button down.

5. *Play the tape.* Press the PLAY (or FORWARD or FWD) button on the VCR to set things into motion.

6. *Tune in the TV set.* If the VCR is sending its signal to the *antenna* input of the TV set, then tune the set to channel 3 or 4. If the VCR is sending *video* and *audio* to the TV set, make sure the set is switched to LINE or AUX or VTR (*not AIR*). At this point you should be viewing the tape. *Hint*: A lot of the time, you can't tell if what you're seeing on the TV screen is the tape playing or some other TV show. To tell, hit STILL or PAUSE to freeze the tape. If the TV picture freezes, you know you're showing the tape. Hit PLAY again, and the picture will jump to life, further assuring you that the TV is "listening" to the VCR. If, instead, you see some other TV show playing, you know the TV isn't "listening" to the VCR. Here are some possibilities:

   a. Maybe the TV is on the wrong channel.

   b. Maybe the antenna signal instead of the VCR signal is going to your TV. Look on the VCR for an OUTPUT SELECT (or TV/VIDEO or TV/CASSETTE or TV/VTR) switch and flip it to VCR (*away from* TV). Sometimes a TV screen menu will show you an "INPUT 1" and an "INPUT 2." Maybe INPUT 1 is the antenna (or cable TV) and INPUT 2 is your VCR. Sometimes the channel number just below 2 activates the AUXILIARY INPUT (audio and video). Whatever, try the various inputs to see if anything works.

   c. If none of the preceding steps work, look at the back of the set to see if the VCR is even connected to the TV. There should be *some* connection between the two.

   d. Double-check to see that the tape is indeed in PAUSE or PLAYing. When the VCR is STOPped or OFF, *its* antenna signals are usually passed straight through to the TV, confusing everybody.

7. *Adjust the TV.* Loudness, brightness, color, and so forth are adjustments made only on the TV receiver. Stopping, playing, rewinding, and fast forwarding (winding ahead) are all functions of the VCR.

Assuming everything is working, rewind the tape to the beginning again so that it's ready for the instructor (who shows up four hours later, and two minutes before you are ready to go home).

Finding Things Quickly on a Tape

As your instructor ran out the door, he told you to show the class the part of the tape on "folding bathtubs," a new product the science department has just perfected. Here's how you'd find that section of the tape: You could play the tape straight through until you came to that part, but that would be very tedious.

You could switch the player to FAST FORWARD, let it wind for half a minute, and then switch it to PLAY to see if you were there. If not, you could hit STOP, then FAST FORWARD for another half a minute, then PLAY another sample. If you knew the sequence of events on the tape, or you knew the folding bathtub exposition ran thirty minutes or so, then this method might work okay. In most cases, however, trying to find something on a tape this way is too haphazard. You could skip past something in FAST FORWARD and not even know it.

If you have some idea of where something is on a tape, you may try this: On many machines, 1 minute of fast forwarding equals 40 to 60 minutes of regular playing time (at the SP speed. Triple the playing time if the tape was recorded at EP). So if you think the section you want is 15 minutes into the tape, let it FAST FORWARD for about 15 seconds. This process is also very haphazard because some tape machines wind faster than others or wind faster at the end of a tape than at the beginning.

Another way to gauge how far you are into a tape is to look through the window on the cassette. If something is near the middle of the tape, then the cassette take-up reel (the one on the right) should be about half full, or about equal to the one on the left.

Nearly all videotape players have FAST SCAN or PICTURE SEARCH capabilities. It's like a FAST FOR-WARD or REWIND *with the picture showing*. If you FAST-FORWARD to near where you think the segment starts, you can then switch to PLAY, and then to the FORWARD SEARCH mode and watch the tape at five or ten times the normal speed until you get to the point you want. Note that FAST FORWARD and REWIND are faster than the SEARCH speeds, so it's best to get close to your target using FAST FORWARD or REWIND.

All these methods are cumbersome. The best way to find something on a tape is to use the INDEX COUNTER, or TIME ELAPSED COUNTER.

Index Counter.   Older tape machines have an INDEX COUNTER. Working like the odometer on your car, it keeps track of how many times the tape reels went around. INDEX COUNTERS are not espe-cially accurate, but at least they give you some idea of where you are on the tape.

Had your instructor INDEXED his tape, he would have written something like the following on a sheet of paper and put it with the tape or in the tape box:

Index	Contents
000	Violin-tuning machine
225	Water hardener
340	Dandruff vacuum
405	Folding bathtub
560	Underwater bicycle
780	Shag carpet shears
900	Spiderweb remover
950	Infant repellent
1070	End

To use this index, you would

1. REWIND the tape to the beginning.
2. Locate the INDEX COUNTER or TAPE FOOTAGE COUNTER. By pressing a button or turning a dial nearby, RESET the numbers on the counter to 000.
3. To view the segment on folding bathtubs, FAST-FORWARD the machine to about 400. STOP. Then PLAY and watch for the dandruff vacuum section to finish and the folding bathtub section to begin.

The index allows you to jump ahead to 900 and examine the spiderweb remover and then go back to 225 and see the presentation on water hardeners.

Elapsed Time Counter.   Recent VCRs have accurate ELAPSED TIME COUNTERS that keep track of hours, minutes, seconds, and in the case of professional equipment, individual frames. A number like 1:24:16 would mean 1 hour, 24 minutes, and 16 seconds into the tape. A professional machine might read 1:03:49:25, meaning 1 hour, 3 minutes, 49 seconds and 25 frames into the tape, accurate indeed—if used right. If you remove the cassette, or turn off the VCR, it loses track of where it was. It will start up at 0:00:00 (or 0:00:00:00) when turned on or when a half-played tape is inserted. For the machine to keep an accurate count, you need to REWIND the tape to its beginning, RESET the counter to 0:00:00, and then FAST FORWARD the tape to wherever you're searching.

Another caveat: If part of the tape is unrecorded (has "snow" on it), then the numbers won't advance over that part. The numbers only count *recorded* tape.

The ELAPSED TIME COUNTER (also called CONTROL TRACK COUNTER) measures tape usage by counting CONTROL TRACK pulses, little blips recorded on the tape along with every picture. Since there are nearly thirty pictures in each second of video, the VCR keeps track of just how many pictures have gone by to calculate the time elapsed. Unrecorded tape has no blips, so the VCR can't keep track of that. Inserting a half-played tape into the VCR doesn't tell the VCR where it is on the tape—the blips all look alike; the VCR can tell only that blips are progressing (tape is playing forward) or regressing (tape is going backward). In fact, when the tape PAUSES or STOPS, the VCR may lose track of a blip or two.

Some VCRs will indicate TAPE REMAINING, an estimate of how much time is left on a videocassette. To do the calculation, a VHS VCR assumes that a standard T-120 cassette is used and that the tape started playing (or recording) at its beginning. It simply notes the ELAPSED TIME and subtracts it from 120 minutes (or 360 minutes for EP) to get the TAPE REMAINING figure.

Professional VCRs and some high-end consumer camcorders using TIME CODE have a superaccurate way of keeping track of tape position. Here, *each picture* on the tape has a specific number associated with it, and the VCR displays this number as hours, minutes, seconds, frames. For this system to work, the tape has to have a TIME CODE signal recorded on it, and the VCR must be equipped with a TIME CODE reader. Chuck a half-played TIME CODED tape into one of these babies, and you'll know instantly *exactly* where you are on the tape. More on this in Chapter 14 (Editing a Videotape).

There are a bunch of ways to connect these gizmos together. Figure 9–2 shows how you can use RF (antenna signals) or VIDEO/AUDIO outputs to transport your signal from the VCR to the TV. Regular home TVs may work only with RF, while industrial TVs accept video and audio directly. Remember to activate the right input on the TV so that it "listens" to your VCR's signal.

SVHS, HI8, and some professional VCRs make two kinds of video signals, COMPOSITE and Y/C. The COMPOSITE video output works fine with common TV monitors. If your TV monitor accepts a multipin S CONNECTOR, then use this wire in place of the video wire. Figure 9–3 shows some S connectors. Sending Y/C signals to the monitor will yield sharper, cleaner colors than sending COMPOSITE video

Setting up a VCR.

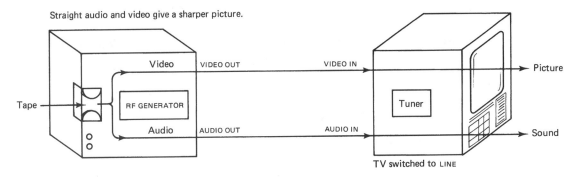

Straight audio and video give a sharper picture.

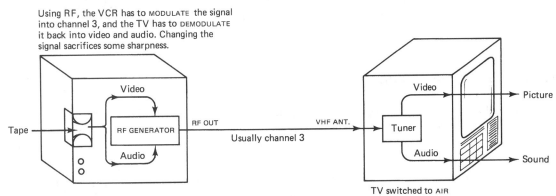

Using RF, the VCR has to MODULATE the signal into channel 3, and the TV has to DEMODULATE it back into video and audio. Changing the signal sacrifices some sharpness.

FIGURE 9–2 RF vs. video between a tape player and TV monitor/receiver.

FIGURE 9–3 Y/C (or S) connector carries color (C) signals on one wire and luminance (Y) signals on another so that the two do not interfere with each other.

through coax wire. You still connect the audio cable in the usual way (VCR AUDIO OUT to TV AUDIO IN).

 **Mini Review**

- When playing a tape, make sure the TV is "listening" to the VCR.
- Use the index counter or elapsed time counter to find scenes quickly on a tape.
- Connecting a TV to a VCR via RF yields the lowest-quality picture. Using composite video and audio cables yields a better picture. Using Y/C and audio offers the best picture.

MAKING A VIDEOTAPE RECORDING

All the procedures that you learned about playing a tape will apply to recording a tape. You load the tape cassette the same way. Also, the tape must be the same FORMAT as the machine.

Before we get to specifics, here are some generalities which apply to nearly all video recorders:

1. You have to tell them which of their inputs to "listen" to. The INPUT SELECTOR does this. Often, you may choose between a TV or tuner input, a camera input, or a general video input (good for about anything else). Sometimes the VCR's channel selector does this; you might tune to the channel below channel 2 to get "AUX INPUT." Sometimes the INPUT SELECTOR is found through an on-screen menu, using your VCR's remote control.
2. You always want to monitor (watch) your recording, and to do this you have to tell the recorder what signal to send out to the TV. This is done with the TV/VCR switch or OUTPUT SELECTOR. Home recorders can send either the antenna signal or the tape signal to the TV. Some industrial models can display the signal *going to* the tape or a signal *played off* the tape as it records.

If the VCR has automatic video and audio circuits (as most do), here's what to do after loading a tape:

1. *Check the video and audio before starting to record.*
   a. Press the big red RECORD button. If it won't stay activated after you release it, try the RECORD/PAUSE buttons together (press RECORD and while holding it down, press PAUSE).
   b. Glance at the monitor/receiver connected to the VCR and notice if it is displaying a reasonably good picture and has acceptable volume for the sound. If there is no picture or no sound, something is wrong. When it is connected to the VCR, the monitor/receiver displays

---

Input selector Switch determining which input (which source) a VCR will "listen" to.

Attenuator Small electronic device that reduces the strength of an audio signal.

Preamp Electronic device that boosts weak electrical signals (like those from a microphone) to hi-level signals (appropriate for audio inputs on VCRs).

*Leader Unrecorded space (from 10 seconds to 3 minutes) at the beginning of a tape, often used to protect the actual pro-

gram from threading damage. Also, unrecordable plastic tape attached to the beginnings of cassette rolls.

Video level Term describing how strong a video signal is. On VTRs, the video level control will adjust the contrast of your video recording.

*Still frame Frozen picture that comes from a VCR when you switch it from play to pause.

what the VCR "sees." If there is something wrong with the signal going to the VCR or if the VCR is doing something wrong, the difficulty will become evident on the monitor/receiver. Stop everything right there until the problem is located and corrected.

2. *To begin the recording, do the following:*

   a. About thirty seconds before the show actually begins, push the RECORD button down. While holding it down, switch the machine to PLAY or FORWARD. Camcorders often require you to go into the RECORD/PAUSE mode. If your VCR or camcorder puts you in the RECORD/PAUSE mode, it may want you to press PAUSE to unpause and begin recording. Others want you to hit PLAY. Try everything or read the instructions to get a feel for how your VCR operates.

   b. After the program starts, keep an eye on the monitor/receiver to make sure the picture and the sound remain okay.

3. *When the program ends, let the machine run an extra thirty seconds and then press the STOP button.* The reason for the thirty-second space at the beginning and end of the tape is to provide a LEADER. Why bother with a LEADER? (Anarchists have asked this question for years.)

   a. When VCRs thread and unthread the tape, they may scratch it a little, degrading the picture. The LEADER assures that only unimportant things get scratched.

   b. Some VCRs automatically advance the tape a bit before they begin playing it. If other people with machines different from yours borrow your tape, you don't want them to miss the first thirty seconds of your dazzling presentation. The LEADER acts as a safety margin before the beginning of the show.

   c. If the tape is to be edited later, the editing VCRs need a picture to "lock onto" as they get a running start before performing the edit.

Avoiding Feedback

Sometimes when you press the RECORD button, or when you simply connect the VCR to a microphone, you hear a loud screech coming from the monitor speaker. That's FEEDBACK. Sound goes in the mike, through the VCR, back out the monitor speaker, and then into the mike in an escalating cycle.

Solution: Turn down the monitor's volume and/or use headphones to listen to the sound. Or keep the mike far from the monitor speaker.

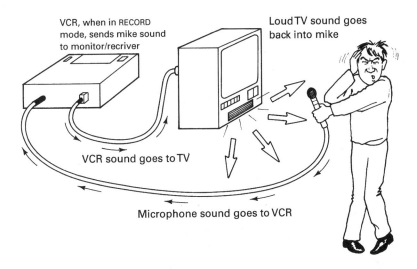

VCR, when in RECORD mode, sends mike sound to monitor/recriver

Loud TV sound goes back into mike

VCR sound goes to TV

Microphone sound goes to VCR

Audio FEEDBACK.

Industrial VCR with Manual Controls

Some VCRs can control audio and video either automatically or manually. Look for switches called VIDEO LEVEL: MAN/AUTO and AUDIO LEVEL: MAN/AUTO. Switching these to MAN will give you personal control over the video and/or audio recording circuits. Switching these to AUTO lets some circuits make the decisions for you. Often the automatic circuits yield satisfactory sound and picture levels, but sometimes they get confused and you have to take the helm manually.

If you wish to take manual control over the VCR's recording levels, you do the following:

1. *Switch the video and/or audio level control(s) to* MAN.

2. *Check the video level.* Press the VCR's red RECORD (or RECORD/PAUSE) button. This starts the recorder's "record" circuits going so that you may adjust the VIDEO LEVEL and observe the results on the VIDEO LEVEL METER.

Have your video source—the camera or whatever you are using—send you a sample picture so that your VCR can "see" a typical, normal signal. Next, look at the meter labeled VIDEO, VIDEO LEVEL, or just LEVEL. If the VCR has only one meter, that means the meter can show *either* audio *or* video levels. A nearby VIDEO/AUDIO switch will make the meter display the video *or* audio level. Switch it to VIDEO.

This meter should now be pointing in the green area. If it points below the green, turn up the VIDEO or VIDEO LEVEL control until the meter needle goes into the green. Otherwise, the picture will come out too faded. If the needle points beyond the green into the red area, turn the VIDEO control down, or else the picture will have too much contrast or may even have streaks in it. The VIDEO control actually adjusts the brightness and contrast of your recording.

Some recorders allow you to monitor (that is, examine or look at) the recorder's picture and sound in the STOP mode as well as in the RECORD mode. You can tell when you are using that kind of VTR because the TV monitor connected to the VTR will display a picture while the VTR is in the STOP mode but will lose the picture if you turn the VTR's power off.

Take a glance at the TV monitor or monitor/receiver to see how the picture looks. Note that *adjusting your TV set will not affect your recording at all*. A monitor doesn't *make* the pictures; it only *displays* them for your convenience.

3. *Check the audio level.* With the record button still down, have someone speak normally into the microphone (or play a sample of the audio source that is going to be recorded). At the same time, observe the AUDIO or AUDIO LEVEL or LEVEL meter (remember to switch it to AUDIO if it is a dual-purpose meter). The needle should wiggle around just below the red area.

It is okay if the needle occasionally dips into the red area—the audience will accept momentary loud noises. But if the needle is too low or if it barely moves, the sound is too weak. Turn up the AUDIO control. On the other hand, if the needle is in the red area too much, or "pins" (goes as far as it can go and holds there), the audio is too loud; turn it down.

Now, hear what it sounds like on the monitor/receiver. If the meter says the sound is right but the monitor/receiver is blasting you in the ear, probably the sound on the monitor/receiver is too loud and needs to be turned down.

Incidentally, some VTRs don't need a monitor/receiver for sound because they have their own speakers or a headphone output for listening to the sound.

Back to meters for a moment. Some VCRs have a TRACKING meter to show how well a VCR is *playing* a tape. By adjusting the TRACKING control and watching the meter so that you maximize the reading, you'll get the VCR to play the tape as clearly as possible. During recording, TRACKING is automatic—there is nothing to adjust. The meter is usually switchable and serves also as the AUDIO or VIDEO level meter.

Mini Review

- When making a recording, tell the VCR which input to "listen" to.
- Check the video and audio before starting to record.
- Leave a blank leader lasting thirty seconds before and after the program.
- Check video and audio levels using the VCRs meters unless those functions are automatically controlled.

Record/Play/Pause Dangers

As mentioned before, some VCRs require you to press RECORD and PLAY in order to monitor your picture. Since you don't *really* want to be recording at this time, you can press PAUSE to suspend tape motion until you are ready to begin. (On some machines you simply hit RECORD/PAUSE.)

When you do this, the video recording heads start spinning and wearing against the tape. You can usually hear them. This is okay for a couple of minutes, but most VCRs protect the tape and their heads by switching themselves to STOP after three minutes. Don't let this surprise you; the automatic shutdown is normal. In fact, if you have finished making your audio and video checks, you will save wear and tear on the machine and tape by switching it manually to STOP. Incidentally, the same is true when playing a tape: If you switch the VCR to PAUSE, the heads will be wearing against the tape. Try to avoid unnecessary PAUSES. Again, the VCR will automatically shut down if you leave it displaying a STILL FRAME for more than three minutes.

CONNECTING AN INDUSTRIAL VCR FOR A RECORDING

Home VCRs generally receive antenna or cable TV signals. Most of the connections involve RF. Industrial VCRs generally deal with audio and video signals coming from cameras and other studio and control room gadgets. Fancy editing video recorders fall into this category and will be discussed further in Chapter 14. Here are some generalizations on how to set up industrial VCRs.

1. Identify your signal sources.
2. Plug the sources into the VCR inputs.
3. Plug a monitoring device into the VCR.
4. Give all devices power (i.e., plug them in or install batteries) and turn them on.
5. Insert the videocassette.
6. Do your audio and video checks.
7. Record and play back a sample to make sure everything is working.
8. Begin recording.

Let's look at these steps in arduous detail:

1. *Identify your signal sources* (camera, microphone, or whatever) and run video and audio cables from them to your VCR. If possible, run the video sources through a monitor first so that you can confirm for yourself that there is indeed satisfactory video coming over those cables (as in Figure 9–4). The signals, whether connected directly to the VCR or connected indirectly by looping through the monitor, must go to the VCR inputs.
2. *Plug the sources into the VCR inputs.* A VCR can handle only one video and only one audio source at a time (except for two-channel or stereo VCRs, which can record two audio tracks at

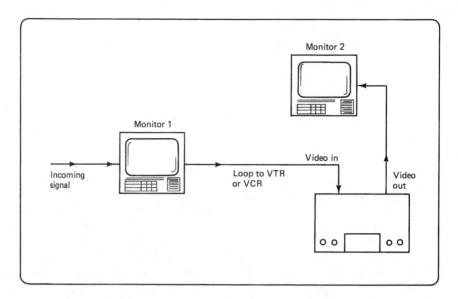

FIGURE 9–4 Setup showing the first monitor displaying the incoming signal and the second monitor displaying the VCR output.

once). If you are using two cameras or two microphones, they must be connected into some intermediate device that can select or mix the signals and send out only one video signal and only one audio signal. Figure 9–5 shows such a setup.

Audio. Most VCRs have a socket labeled MICROPHONE where an appropriate mike can be plugged in. An adapter may be necessary if the plug doesn't fit the socket. This socket is appropriate for weak audio signals, such as microphones and the MICROPHONE OUTPUT of an audio mixer.

In general, if your audio source has no power supply of its own, doesn't use batteries, and doesn't need to be plugged into the wall to work, it should be plugged into the MICROPHONE INPUT or MIKE IN of the VCR.

VCRs are likely to have another audio input labeled AUX (for AUXiliary) or LINE or LINE IN or HIGH LEVEL IN or AUDIO IN. These inputs are not so sensitive and can take the stronger audio signals you would get from a

CD player
Audio tape deck
Audiocassette player
Monitor/receiver
VTR or VCR
Mike mixer
Computer sound card

You can expect a strong audio signal from a device if its output is labeled

LINE OUT

HIGH LEVEL OUT

PROGRAM OUT

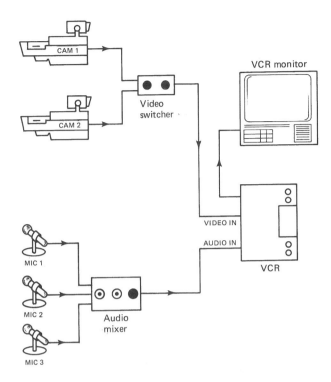

FIGURE 9–5 Multiple sources going to VCR inputs.

AUX OUT

PREAMP OUT

AUDIO OUT

PHONE

EAR

MONITOR OUT

In most cases, if the audio source needs electricity to operate, the audio signal should go in the AUX IN or LINE IN of the VTR as shown in Figure 9–6.

LO-LEVEL AND HI-LEVEL EXPLAINED

A microphone turns sound into a tiny electrical signal. A preamplifier changes the tiny signal into a medium-sized electrical signal. An amplifier turns a medium-sized signal into a big electrical signal. A speaker changes a big signal into sound. Because medium-sized signals are easiest for electronic equipment to handle, most audio devices have PREAMP or HI-LEVEL outputs for sending medium-strength signals to other devices. They also have LINE, HI-LEVEL, or AUX inputs to receive medium-strength signals from other devices. Don't let the name HI-LEVEL fool you; it is only high relative to the puny mike-level signals. HI-LEVEL really has medium strength.

Some audio devices have earphone, headphone, or speaker outputs. These are higher than so called HI-LEVEL signals. In some cases, signals from these outputs are too strong even for the AUX IN of a VTR: The recorded sound may come out raspy and distorted. The cure for this is to connect an AUDIO ATTENUATOR between the source and the input. The ATTENUATOR cuts down the strength of the signal. If you don't have an ATTENUATOR and if the source's signal is too strong, try turning its volume control down very low.

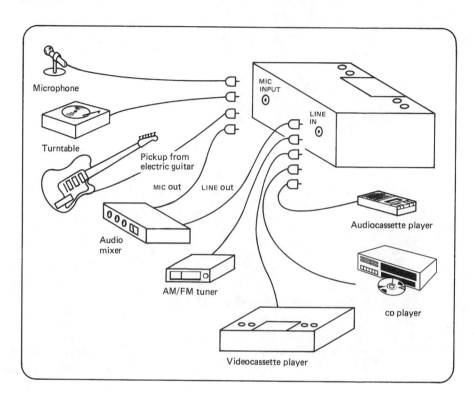

FIGURE 9–6   HIGH LEVEL and LOW LEVEL audio sources.

Video. Somewhere on the VCR you'll find a video input. It will be marked

VIDEO IN

COMPOSITE VIDEO OR COMP

Y/C

Y/R-Y/B-Y OR COMPONENT VIDEO (actually three sockets)

CAMERA

If it's a home VCR, the socket will be the RCA type and will take an RCA plug (review Figure 2–7).

If it's an industrial VCR, the video connector is most likely a BNC (review Figure 2–6). If your source offers Y/C video, use an S Connector (Figure 9–3).

If your source is component video, you'll need three cables to carry the Y, R-Y, and B-Y (or Y/U/V, etc.) signals. The VCR will have BNC sockets labeled for each of the component signals.

If you have a choice of which connectors to use, component (three separate cables) is best, Y/C second best, composite third best. If RF is available, use it as your last resort.

Some portable VCRs may have a multipin socket labeled CAMERA. This connector receives video and maybe audio from the camera, while perhaps sending power to the camera, and may even allow you to play tape from the VCR into the camera viewfinder.

Digital VCRs will have a digital video input where the signal arrives over a multipin cable from another digital VCR, a digital camera, or a computer. We'll cover digital VCRs later.

However the signal arrives at the VCR, somehow the VCR has to be told to "listen" to the appropriate input (although a few "sense" which input is in use and switch themselves).

Somewhere on the VCR will be a switch called SOURCE or INPUT SELECTOR or CAMERA/TV/LINE or COMPOSITE/YC, or COMPOSITE/COMPONENT, or some such thing that tells the machine which particular input to use for its recording. Now activate the input.

3. *Plug a monitoring device into the VCR* (as in Figure 9–7). Somehow you must be able to find out how the VCR is handling the video and audio.

Some professional VCRs, especially editors, have *two* sets of outputs, the regular AUDIO and VIDEO outputs, plus special MONITOR OUTPUTS. MONITOR OUTPUTS are supposed to feed AUDIO and VIDEO to monitors (who would have guessed?) leaving the other outputs to feed other things. MONITOR OUTPUTS on VCRs have an extra feature: They are able to display menus and tape status (i.e., TIME ELAPSED COUNTER) on the monitor screen. The regular VIDEO OUTPUTS still present a normal video signal. Thus, viewing the monitor output can tell you much more than what's on the tape; it tells you what's happening with the machine.

As mentioned earlier, it is always wise to monitor the signals *going into* the VCR as well as those *coming out* of the VCR so that if something goes wrong, you'll have some idea about where the problem is.

4. *Power everything up.*
5. *Thread the tape or insert the cassette.*
6. *Do your video and audio checks.*
7. *Record and play back something to make sure everything is working.*
8. *Now you are ready to record (Ta dah!).*

 Mini Review

- When numerous sources are connected to a VCR, they have to go through switchers or mixers so that only one video signal and one audio signal enter the VCR.
- Low-level audio sources go to the VCR's microphone input, while high-level audio sources go to its line-in or audio-in.
- Monitor your signals both before they go into the VCR and after they have passed through the VCR so that you can quickly diagnose signal problems.

OTHER FEATURES ON SOME VCRS

Some VCRs have more doodads than you'll ever have time to diddle. Here are a few.

Monitor output   Output on a VCR that connects to a TV monitor and allows you to see and hear the VCR's signal as well as view VCR status menus, such as elapsed time.

Dew indicator   Light on the VCR apprising you of the fact that the VCR's insides are damp and the machine will remain shut down until they dry.

Memory   On a VCR's index counter, this button tells the machine to stop rewinding when it reaches 000 on the counter. Helpful in noting and locating spots on a tape.

Index search, index record   System for recording a trigger pulse invisibly on the tape so that when the tape is played in fast forward or rewind, it will stop when it reaches the marked spot.

Reset   To set something back to the beginning. Resetting an index counter changes all the numbers to zero.

*Tracking   Adjustment on VTRs so that they play the video tracks from the tape, following exactly the path that the recorder took. Good tracking results in a clear, stable picture.

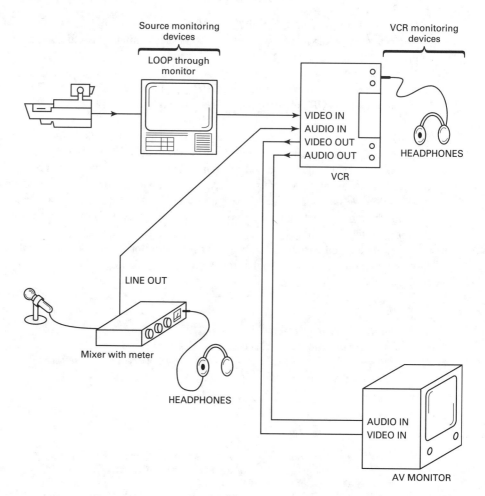

FIGURE 9–7   Monitoring both the sources and the VCR.

Dew Indicator

For the VCR to operate properly, the tape has to slide smoothly through its internal mechanism. When the machine is cold and the air is humid, the surfaces become "sticky," and the tape risks getting hung up and damaged. The DEW INDICATOR senses this dampness (illuminating a light to notify you of this) and makes you wait until it's safe. In a way, your DEW INDICATOR is a *don't* indicator. If the DEW INDICATOR brings your TV production to a standstill, just leave the machine *on* and wait an hour or so for the light to go out. Sitting and staring at the machine will not shorten this process. When the light goes out, your VCR will function normally again.

Counter/Reset/Memory/Index

You've already seen how the INDEX COUNTER can help you find things on a tape. Some counters have a MEMORY button that makes locating things even easier. The MEMORY button will stop the machine from rewinding whenever the INDEX COUNTER reaches 000. Here's how to use it.

Features galore.

Say you are playing or recording *Star Trek* and you think you'd like to come back to the exciting scene where aliens burn up all the circuits on the *Enterprise* (for the sixty-seventh time). First you set the COUNTER RESET to 000. Next, switch MEMORY on. Let the tape continue playing. Later, when you want to find that spot, simply press REWIND. When the counter reaches 000, the machine will automatically STOP. You are there.

One disadvantage of this system is that when you press RESET midtape, you are no longer keeping chronological track of elapsed time. This may or may not be a problem, depending on whether you're trying to keep a log of what's where on the tape.

INDEX SEARCH is a feature found on some VCRs. Press the INDEX or INDEX RECORD button while recording *or playing* a tape, and an invisible, inaudible trigger signal will be recorded on the tape's CONTROL TRACK. Later on, you press the INDEX SEARCH button (or whatever its called on your machine) and press FAST FORWARD (or REWIND, if you're at the end of a tape). The VCR will start winding (or rewinding) the tape, "listening" for the trigger. When the VCR senses the pulse on the tape, it stops and begins to play.

Speed Select

Industrial VCRs and camcorders are generally designed for one standard speed only, but many home and prosumer recorders are equipped with two speeds: SP (two-hour standard play), and SLP or EP (six-hour super long play or extra play). Of course, tapes of different lengths will affect how long the VCR can record at a given speed. On VHS cassettes, the number after the T (T-120, T-60, T-15) tells how long the tape can record/play at the SP speed.

You select the tape speed when recording. VCRs automatically sense and adjust themselves to the correct speed when playing back. If recording with a two-speed machine, you should select the fastest speed (the shortest recording time) for the highest-quality recording and to assure that your tape will be playable on industrial machines.

Tracking

TRACKING has nothing to do with following hoofprints in the prairie. It describes how a VCP follows the magnetic footprints along a tape. When TRACKING is well adjusted, the video player's heads follow exactly the same magnetic paths laid down by the VCR when the tape was recorded.

Generally, you shouldn't have to adjust the TRACKING control. Leave it in the FIX or center position. When you are playing a tape, if your picture shows a band of hash across it as in Figure 9–8 or jiggles a lot, it is time to adjust TRACKING. Turn it until the picture clears up.

If you're using a HI-FI VCR and you hear popping or crackling in the sound, this is also a symptom of MISTRACKING, even though the picture may look okay. If adjusting TRACKING doesn't fix the problem, then switch to the LINEAR or NORMAL (not HI-FI) sound track. (Don't forget to switch back to HI-FI later, or you'll be listening to the low-fidelity LINEAR sound track for months into the future, wondering why your tapes sound so bad).

The TRACKING control compensates for minor differences between similar FORMAT recorders and tapes. You are most likely to have to use it when playing a tape recorded on someone else's machine

FIGURE 9–8   TRACKING misadjustment.

---

*Linear (or normal) audio track**   Audio recording made in a line along the edge of a videotape (as opposed to hi-fi sound imbedded in the video tracks on the tape).

*Analog VTR**   Video recorder that records the continuously varying video signal onto the tape (as opposed to digital).

*Digital VTR**   Video recorder that converts the video signal to ones and zeroes (digits) and records the numbers. Upon playback, the numbers are converted back to video.

AFM   Audio frequency modulation, a technique used in VHS, SVHS, 8mm, and Hi8 VCRs to record/play hi-fi sound, invisibly imbedded in the picture.

Frequency response   The ability of a device to pick up high tones (high audio frequencies) and low tones equally well. For audio, the perfect frequency response would be from 20Hz to 20kHz, the full range of human hearing.

PCM   Pulse code modulation, a second method of recording hi-fi sound with 8mm and Hi8 VCRs. Unlike AFM, PCM audio can be edited without affecting the picture.

Audio dub   Feature on video recorders that allows you to record new sound (erasing the old sound) on a tape while leaving the picture untouched.

DV   Digital video. Format in which images and sound are recorded as digital data onto 1/4-inch cassettes with very high quality.

DVR   Digital video recorder. A VCR or computer disk recorder that records/plays digits representing audio and video.

or even when playing your own tapes when your machine gets worn and out-of-adjustment. This control does nothing when you are recording—only when you are playing tapes.

Some VCRs (all 8MM types), have AUTOMATIC TRACKING, making their adjustments electronically with no help from you.

Audio Dub

When you record a program, you automatically record both picture and sound. With AUDIO DUB you can go back and rerecord *new* sound, erasing the old sound as you go and leaving the picture untouched.

To activate the AUDIO DUB feature,

1. Plug a microphone into MIC IN, or plug some other audio signal source into AUDIO IN as described earlier. If using a camcorder, you can even use the microphone built into the camcorder.
2. You may wish to check your sound before you start recording by listening to it through your system. You could
   a. Plug an earphone into the EARPHONE jack if your VCR has one.
   b. Run RF to your TV and monitor your sound there.
   c. Connect your home stereo receiver to the AUDIO OUT jack on the VCR.
      On some decks, you will automatically be able to hear your audio source with the VCR on STOP. On others, you must press AUDIO DUB to send the sound through the monitoring outputs. On a few, press AUDIO DUB/PAUSE simultaneously to hear your source.
3. Find where you wish to start dubbing new sound.
4. Press AUDIO DUB and PLAY together (or just PLAY or just PAUSE after you've hit AUDIO DUB).
5. You will hear the new sound being recorded. The old sound is being erased as you go.
6. When you're done, press STOP.

The above is entirely true for low-fidelity VCRs, but HI-FI VCRs add a slight wrinkle to the above strategy. The HI-FI sound is imbedded permanently into the video signal. It can't be removed without erasing (recording over) the video. The linear audio tracks, however, *can* be erased and rerecorded. AUDIO DUB works only on the LINEAR or NORMAL tracks.

Therefore, picture the confusion when someone records a wedding in HI-FI sound, then AUDIO DUBS narration and music onto the tape. The bride, playing the tape on a HI-FI VCR (which automatically defaults to playing the HI-FI sound tracks) hears only the HI-FI sound caught on camera, not the narration, etc. To hear the "finished" sound, she has to switch her VCR to the LINEAR audio track, if she knows how to.

Similar situation: The wedding videographer edits the original tapes, selecting the best clips. The videographer then goes over the tape a second time, sprucing it up with music, sound effects, and poetry. The bride plays the tape on her HI-FI VCR and hears snippets of sound, sometimes no sound, or an incoherent jumble. Same problem: Each clip that was *edited* contained picture-and-sound joined inexorably in HI-FI matrimony. All the later improvements to the sound were done on the LINEAR track. The bride (unaware of video's complexities) automatically heard the HI FI tracks (raw sound) and never heard the finished version of the tape. Tapes with edited sound on the LINEAR tracks should be clearly labeled as such.

Stereo

Many home and professional VCRs will record and play back in stereo. There are two audio tracks, one for the left channel and one for the right channel.

There are several ways to get signals onto those two channels. One way is to send the signal to the left and right AUDIO INPUTS on the VCR. Another way is to use a stereo microphone connected to the VCR while making your recording. Stereo camcorders have stereo mikes built-in.

 Mini Review

- If a VCR gets damp, its dew sensor will shut it down.
- For the best picture and sound, record important shows at the VCR's fastest speed.
- Unless tracking is handled automatically, adjust it while playing a tape to get the smoothest picture.
- Audio dub allows you to record new sound on a videotape.
- VHS and SVHS hi-fi audio tracks are recorded as part of the picture and cannot be separated. If new sound must be added, it is added to the tape's low-fidelity linear track.

AUDIO ON VCRS

Various FORMAT VCRs handle their audio differently. Some audio can be edited, some can't. Some have high fidelity, others low. Some are stereo, some four-track, some monaural, and some are digital. Since audio for VCRs is confusing for most people, let's examine the subject in excruciating detail:

VHS AND SVHS LINEAR

Old VHS VCRs and inexpensive VHS VCRs use LINEAR audio; the sound is recorded in a long stripe along the edge of the tape, as shown in Figure 9–12. The fidelity at the SP speed sounds much like a cheap audiocassette deck. At EP the FREQUENCY RESPONSE sounds just a little better than a telephone.

Professional and editing VHS decks may handle stereo LINEAR tracks; the wide mono track is split in two, like a two-lane highway where there used to be one wide lane.

VHS LINEAR tracks can be erased and rerecorded (dubbed, or edited) independently of the video. The video can also be edited without touching the LINEAR audio. On professional decks it is possible to edit one of the stereo audio tracks independently of the other; in fact, the one track can be playing while the other is recording.

Mono and stereo LINEAR audio is compatible; a stereo tape will play in mono on a mono VCR, and a mono tape will play mono on a stereo VCR.

All of the preceding is true for SVHS as well as VHS.

VHS AND SVHS HI-FI

Some VHS VCRs and all SVHS VCRs handle hi-fi stereo audio. Here's how they do it: Each spinning video head has an audio head attached to it, a little way upstream of it. As the pair takes a diagonal swipe across the tape, the audio head records stereo sound's magnetism deeply into the tape. Immediately afterward, the video head comes along to record its vibrations over the top of the audio magnetism. It's sort of like paving a highway over a dirt road. The video vibrations are recorded along the surface of the tape without disturbing the audio magnetism buried deeply below. Upon playback, the audio head senses only the deep magnetism, ignoring the shallow vibrations, while the video head reads only the shallow vibrations, ignoring the deep ones. Thus, two signals are recorded together on the same stretch of tape.

Once the first head pair has taken a swipe across the tape, a second head pair takes a swipe, laying down more audio and video next to it. Some VCRs have four head pairs. Figure 9–12 diagrams the diagonal paths the spinning video heads take across the tape.

Once the two signals have been magnetized into the tape, it is impossible to separate them. The hi-fi audio and video are linked forever. The pair can be erased, and the pair can be copied onto another tape, and in the copying process the audio can be manipulated and edited separately from the video because the audio and video are traveling independently over separate wires. But the two signals are inexorably joined while they reside on the same tape together.

Because the audio heads move quickly across the tape, they are able to record excellent fidelity, rivaling CD quality. FREQUENCY RESPONSE is 20Hz to 20kHz, the full span of human hearing. You can even record time code (described in Chapter 14) on one hi-fi channel without bothering the other or the video.

Hi-fi VCRs generally record LINEAR audio at the same time they record hi-fi audio. The track layout is the same as the layout you saw in Figure 9–12, only the hi-fi sound is part of the diagonal video tracks in the diagram. Upon playback, you can select whether to hear the hi-fi stereo signal or the (usually monaural) LINEAR sound tracks, or a mixture of the two. There is only one stereo audio output on nonprofessional VCRs, so you can't play the hi-fi sound and send it one place while you simultaneously play the LINEAR sound tracks, sending them somewhere else.

When you make an audio edit or audio DUB on a hi-fi machine, the signal is automatically sent to the LINEAR tracks.

8MM AND HI8 HI-FI AFM SOUND

8MM and HI8 camcorders and VCRs have never had LINEAR audio tracks like VHS. Both audio and video are recorded onto the tape using just the video heads in a method called AFM. Upon playback, circuits separate the coded signal from the video and convert it back to audio.

As with VHS hi-fi, AFM audio is married to the video; it can't be separately erased, edited, or dubbed unless you play the tape, manipulate the audio and video *outside* the VCP, then rerecord the new mix onto another tape (going down a generation in quality). The FREQUENCY RESPONSE is a respectable 20Hz to 20kHz, nearly CD quality. Most VCRs and camcorders record only mono AFM.

Betacam and Betacam SP camcorders use the preceding technique for recording audio, but they can record in stereo. Also, they have two LINEAR audio tracks.

8MM AND HI8 HI-FI STEREO PCM SOUND

No, PCM has nothing to do with hormonal mood swings. PCM stands for PULSE CODE MODULATION, a method for recording *editable* stereo audio on 8MM and HI8 VCRs. It's a feature found on a few top-of-the-line camcorders and on 8MM and HI8 prosumer editors.

Audio is digitized, and the two strings of data (one for the left channel, one for the right) are recorded by the spinning video heads at the end of each sweep across the tape. When the tape is played back, the video head reads the video, and at the end of its swipe, it reads the audio data, which gets converted back to sound. VCRs without PCM record nothing at the end of their sweeps and ignore PCM data when playing back tapes.

The PCM audio has good stereo sound quality (30Hz to 15kHz FREQUENCY RESPONSE). Most importantly, the PCM tracks can be dubbed or edited separately from the video.

Like VHS hi-fi, consumer decks have but one audio output; you can play the AFM sound or the PCM sound or a mix of the two. You'll need an industrial deck to get separate outputs for the two.

3/4U VCR SOUND

All 3/4U VCRs have two linear audio tracks. You can record on channel 1 (track 1) or channel 2 (track 2). Upon playback, you have the choice of listening to channel 1, channel 2, or a mixture of both by flipping the AUDIO MONITOR selector from CH-1 to CH-2 or to MIX.

DIGITAL VIDEO RECORDERS

DIGITAL VCRs slice the video signal into tiny chunks, measure them, give each measurement a number, and record the number digitally. Thus, instead of recording vibrating video signals, DIGITAL VCRs record long streams of numbers—ones and zeroes. Upon playback, the ones and zeroes are converted back into video signals for display.

One great advantage of DIGITAL VCRs is that you can make copies of a DIGITAL video tape without losing appreciable quality. With ANALOG VCRs, every time you copy a tape, signal errors and

D1 digital VCR (Courtesy of Sony).

noise add up to cause graininess, fuzziness, and color aberrations in the picture. When DIGITAL VCRs copy tape, they are copying ones and zeroes. Even if the numbers are a little fuzzy, they are still ones and zeroes that can be accurately read by the machine. Thus, a copy of a DIGITAL video tape is *exactly* the same as the original. This has great advantages when you are editing many layers or generations.

DIGITAL VCR FORMATS

Let's start calling digital video DV, and digital videocassette recorders DVRs. Just as analog VCRs have different formats to describe their cassette size and method of recording, so do DVRs. Table 9–2 summarizes the main differences between DVR FORMATS.

Despite their differences, DVRs behave much the same as their analog brothers. Some are even compatible with analog VCRs. They rewind, play, record, and erase tapes just as in the analog world. DVRs have many of the same features as analog VCRs. Most of the buttons have the same names. Their analog inputs and outputs obey *all* the video laws you've learned already. The analog cables and connectors are the same. Tapes still need to be labeled to keep track of them. The more things change, the more they stay the same.

THE COMPUTER/DVR RELATIONSHIP

Moving regular data between computers and hard drives is a snap compared to moving video data. With video and audio, there is a *lot* of data, it has to move quickly, and it has to arrive on time or else the picture hiccups or the sound warbles. For this reason, DVRs and computers designed to work with DVRs (i.e., editing workstations) need fast inputs and outputs and betweenputs. Still, they're generally not fast enough, and the data has to be compressed to a manageable stream.

---

*Video capture card   Circuit installed in a computer to change video signals into data the computer can handle, and vice versa.

*Sound card   Circuit installed in a computer to change audio signals into data the computer can handle, and vice versa.

*Firewire or IEEE P1394   Standard for transmitting compressed video data used by DV format digital videocassette recorders.

*Safety tab   Button or tab on a videocassette that can be removed to render the tape unrecordable (thus unerasable).

TABLE 9–2 Digital Videotape Formats at a Glance

Designation	Video	Compression	Tape Size	Maker	Notes
D1	Component	Not compressed	3/4-inch	Sony	
D2	Composite	Not compressed	3/4-inch	Sony/Ampex	Same tape shell as D1 but not compatible with it.
D3	Composite	Not compressed	1/2-inch	Panasonic	
D4					Not used; unlucky number in Japanese culture.
D5	Component	Not compressed	1/2-inch	Panasonic	
D6	Component	Compressed	3/4-inch		Digital HDTV recorder using D1 tape.
D7 (DVC PRO)	Component	Compressed	1/4-inch	Panasonic, Ikegami, Philips	Compatible with DV and DVCAM.
DCT	Component	Compressed	3/4-inch	Ampex	
Betacam SX	Component	Compressed	1/2-inch	Sony	Can play Betacam SP.
Digital Betacam	Component	Compressed	1/2-inch	Sony	Some models also play Betacam and Betacam SP.
DV	Component	Compressed	1/4-inch	Several	Consumer.
Digital S	Component	Compressed	1/2-inch	JVC	Can also play SVHS.
DVCAM	Component	Compressed	1/4-inch	Sony	Compatible with DV.
Camcutter	Component	Compressed	Disk	Avid/Ikegami	Removable magnetic disk recorder.

Computers generally take video into a VIDEO CAPTURE CARD and audio into a SOUND CARD, send the data through the computer, which processes and prepares the data to be recorded on the computer's hard drive. To retrieve the data, the procedure is reversed.

Recording and playing audio/video data to/from a hard disk requires fast computers, fast VIDEO and AUDIO cards, and nimble hard drives. Computers that can smoothly handle high-quality video cost a lot. Common computers can do the job, but the picture quality is equal to VHS. One way to take some of the pressure off the computer is to predigitize and precompress the signal before giving it to the computer. It's like the way mama bird predigests worms before regurgitating them to her chicks. The method of conveying predigested data between DV camcorders and computers is called FIREWIRE, or IEEE P1394.

Firewire, IEEE P1394

IEEE P1394 (better known as FIREWIRE) aims to be a shortcut through many of the problems faced by people trying to get computers to mate with DVRs. DV camcorders (including the professional versions, DVCAM and DVCPRO) sample the picture, then compress the data 5:1 making the stream of data well within FIREWIRE's capabilities, and within the grasp of common hard drives and computers. And audio *is included*—it doesn't have to be treated separately.

Because a DV camcorder is already outputting *data* (as opposed to video/audio), we skip the audio and video CAPTURE BOARDS. Data flows from camcorder (or DVR) to computer and back directly, with no nasty conversions. No external compression circuits are needed, because the compression was already done in the DV camera. A circuit board is needed to adapt the DV data to the computer environment and vice versa, but it is nothing that damages the signal. Figure 9–9 shows a consumer DV camcorder and cassette.

FIGURE 9–9   Panasonic DV camcorder with cassette (Courtesy of Panasonic).

 Mini Review

- When you copy an analog videotape, the signal degrades; when you copy a digital videotape, there is no appreciable loss.
- The main digital VCR formats are DV, DVCPRO, DVCAM, Digital Betacam, and Digital-S.
- Video and audio comprise a huge amount of data. Most VCRs and computers must compress the data (damaging it slightly) in order to handle it affordably.
- IEEE P1394 (firewire) is a method for transferring precompressed digital data from DV camcorders to other DVRs and computers.

AVOIDING ACCIDENTAL ERASURE

Picture yourself recording the *Beavis & Butthead Do America* epic and looking down at the cassette box to discover that you're recording over priceless sequences of your college president receiving an award from Peewee Herman. Or you loan your school's only copy of "Emergency Medical Care" to your neighbor and get it back with his kids' recording of Saturday morning cartoons on it. Murphy's 108th Law of Recording states that junk recordings *never* get accidentally erased; prized ones *always* do.

Nothing short of copying all of your tapes and keeping them in a vault will completely protect them. But two easy precautions will save you a lot of disappointments:

1. *Label everything as soon as it is recorded.* Don't guess what is on your tapes. You're likely to record over your wrong guesses.
2. *Remove the SAFETY TAB from the videocassette so the tape cannot be recorded upon.* Figure 9–10 shows how.

VHS, SVHS: Break off the plastic safety tab from the label edge of the cassette (don't bother keeping the tab; covering the hole with a piece of scotch tape will restore the cassette's recordability).

VHS, SVHS:
To protect a recording from accidental erasure, break off the SAFETY TAB on the rear edge of the videocassette using a screwdriver. With the tab removed, the VCR's RECORD button won't activate and the tape is "safe" from erasure. If you change your mind and wish to record, cover the hole with a piece of adhesive tape.

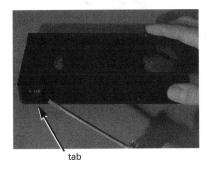

To prevent erasure

To record again

8mm, HI8:
Slide tab to the left to prevent erasure, to the right to record again

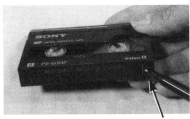

tab

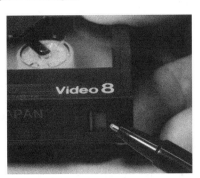

To prevent erasure

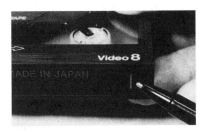

To record again

Betacam, Betacam-SP:
Slide tab up or down

3/4U, 3/4U-SP:
Turn tape over and pop out red button to protect cassette from being recorded over. Reinsert button to restore recording ability.

With red tab *up*, tape can be erased

Snap red tab down to prevent erasure/recording.

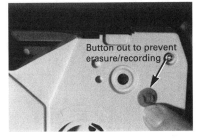

Button out to prevent erasure/recording

FIGURE 9–10 Preventing accidental erasure.

8MM, HI8: Throw the switch on the rear of the cassette.

BETACAM, BETACAM SP: Turn the cassette upside down and find the tab along one edge. Press the tab down into the cassette to prevent recording. Snap it back up to restore recordability.

3/4U, 3/4U-SP: Pop out the red button on the bottom of the cassette. Save the buttons. You will need them if you change your mind someday and wish to record over your tapes (erasing them).

DV: As with 8MM, throw the switch on the rear of the cassette.

This procedure does not affect playback or any other feature of the VCR or tape. It just defeats the VCR's RECORD function.

BULK ERASING

You automatically erase tape when you record over it. Sometimes you'd like to wipe a tape clean in one swell foop. BULK ERASING assures that when you reuse a tape, the remnants of other shows that didn't get recorded over are gone. It's as if the tape were brand new. BULK-ERASING tapes saves a lot of embarrassment when tapes used for personal or prurient purposes are then used for business or school. Ahem.

A BULK ERASER will erase a tape even if the cassette's ERASE PROTECT tab has been removed or switched to the "protect" position.

CARE OF VIDEOTAPE

Magnetic tape is not an archival medium. Although the magnetism recorded on it will last easily fifty years, the plastic ribbon itself stretches and contracts with heat and cold, and "relaxes" with age, causing the picture to bend at the top. A tape can be played between 100 and 200 times before the picture becomes noticeably degraded. PAUSING wears out the tape quickly.

Digital videotape never suffers the "bends" and its picture never looks bad . . . it's either perfect or totally unviewable, nothing in between. It's wise to make copies of DV tapes (DV copies are as good as the original) while they're still playable. DV tapes stretch and disintegrate just as do their analog brothers.

The lifetime of your recording is directly related to how carefully it is *stored* and how gently it's *used*. Here are the rules of storage:

1. *Store cassettes upright, in a vertical position.* This prevents the edges of the tape ribbon from getting roughed up against the inside of the cassette as it lies on its side.
2. *Keep the cassettes in their boxes.* This keeps out the dust and dirt that cause DROPOUTS. DROPOUTS have nothing to do with students who hang around in the student lounge rather than attending classes. DROPOUTS are speckles of snow in the TV picture, the result of dirt coming in the way of the VCR's playback head as it plays a tape, or the result of magnetic material shedding from the tape. Figure 9–11 shows a DROPOUT, and Figure 9–12 diagrams some other tape torturers.

Bulk tape eraser   Large electromagnet used for erasing (demagnetizing) an entire reel or cassette of audiotape or videotape all at once. The procedure takes about four seconds.
*Dropout   Speck or streak of snow on the TV screen seen when a videotape player hits a fleck of dirt, a scratch, or a "bare" spot when the tape is playing. Dust can also cause a dropout to be *recorded* on a tape.

FIGURE 9–11 DROPOUT as it appears on a TV screen.

3. *Store tapes at average temperature and humidity*—about 70°F (20°C) and 50 percent or less humidity. Temperatures above 140°F (60°C) will permanently damage the tape (the cassette warps). A car trunk, passenger area, or glove compartment on a hot day may easily exceed the 140°F maximum. Leaving a tape in the sun may also overheat it. Mildew will grow on damp tapes.

4. *Keep tapes away from magnetic fields*, such as hi-fi speakers, amplifiers, transformers, magnets, or big electric motors. The magnetism from these devices can partially erase your tape.

5. *Don't leave recorded tapes threaded in the VCR* for days or weeks; this creases them where they are bent around the tape guides.

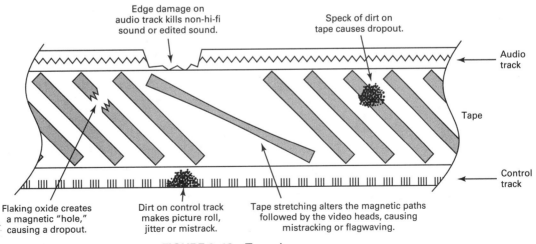

FIGURE 9–12 Tape damage.

6. *Remove or switch the* SAFETY TAB *on any tape you wish to* "erase-proof."
7. *Keep cassette labels smooth and tight.* Dog-eared, loose, wrinkled labels, or labels-over-labels tend to snag in the VCR.
8. *Treat cassettes gently.* Dropping them rubs the delicate tape edges against the cassette housings, abrading the tape. If you badly damage a cassette, don't try to play it. It may jam in your VCR. You can buy new cassette shells as kits and transfer the tape to the new housing.

 Mini Review

- By removing the safety tab or throwing a switch on a videocassette, you can render it unrecordable, thus protecting it from accidental erasure.
- For best results, keep videocassettes clean, dry, and at average temperature and humidity.

PLANNING AND SCRIPTING

10

Television production is 99 percent planning and 1 percent production. The 1 percent part gets the glamour, while the 99 percent part actually makes the show.

Nothing brings good luck like not relying on it. Every step in the production process that hasn't been planned, discussed, reviewed, and made watertight will spring a flood when the tape begins to roll.

Part of the planning process involves assembling the right equipment and creating an environment where it can do its job. Another part of the planning process involves assembling the right people and giving them an environment conducive to performing their jobs. Last, yet most important in the planning process, is assembling the good ideas that will eventually become your program. The finest equipment, people, and production techniques all go to waste if you are producing a show that nobody wants to see or that your sponsor cannot afford. All the pieces of the production puzzle—the equipment, the talent, the crew, the script, and of course the basic plan—must fit together.

In most small and mid-size productions, all the preceding responsibilities rest with the director. Then, when showtime arrives, the director does the "directing." More about this in Chapter 11, "Directing."

PREPLANNING

Planning is what we do to assure that our TV production goes smoothly. Preplanning is what we do before we decide that a production is even necessary, or appropriate, or cost effective. The amateurs in this business jump directly into the exciting TV production details without thinking about the real *reason* for producing the show. *Communications problem solvers* aspire to a higher goal, found at the preplanning stage. They focus on the following questions:

1. What problems are the client trying to solve?
2. What symptoms tell the client there is a problem?
3. What is causing the problem?
4. How serious is the problem?
5. What is the cost of not fixing the problem?
6. How much is the client (or yourself) willing to spend to fix the problem?

Who knows, maybe a couple photos, an audiocassette, or a pamphlet is what's really needed, not a video. If a video is called for, maybe a quickie cheapie will do. Or maybe the job deserves some real muscle. Or maybe a combination of media (e.g., posters and e-mail to reinforce the TV show) will communicate best. A few minutes of honest thought here may save you weeks of wasted work later.

Next, prepare a STATEMENT OF PURPOSE, a concise list of the show's objectives.

Statement of Purpose

The French Foreign Legion had a saying: "When in doubt, gallop." Doesn't work in video (didn't work for them, either). Don't start writing until you have a concrete idea of what you want to communicate. Sometimes it's a client or teacher whose fuzzy ideas have to be clarified before you proceed with the treatment. One way to track down a show's elusive purpose is to require the originator (or yourself) to *write, in one or two sentences, what the program is supposed to achieve.* This focuses your energy on a main purpose, an anchor that will keep you from rambling or getting lost in detail.

Here are some questions to ask:

1. What new thing(s) do you want the viewers to know that they don't know now?
2. What do you want the viewers to be able to do that they can't do now?
3. What do you want the viewers to believe or feel that they don't believe or feel now?

Answers to the above questions determine whether your show will be *telling, selling,* or *yelling,* three completely different approaches to presentation. If, for instance, you're producing a tape to *demonstrate* how to use the new Wonder Widget, would you include artsy low-angle shots with fog and colored lasers glinting off its sweaty surface? No; such a technique would *promote* the Widget, inspiring worship rather than understanding. Save the fog and lasers for the marketing and motivational projects.

Once your clients have undergone this exercise, they will have a better grasp of what they really wanted. They also will be more *committed* to the expectations and objectives of the project. (Now is a good time to have the key decision-maker sign and date a typed copy of your STATEMENT OF PURPOSE, clarifying for everyone the direction the project is headed).

Determine Your Audience

Before you can educate, entertain, inform, or persuade your viewers, you need to know who they are and how much they know about your subject. You will be adjusting your time, format, and level of sophistication for your audience.

Consider these questions:

1. How will people be watching this message?
2. What kind of people make up your audience (i.e., their location, age, race, gender, education)?
3. How do the viewers feel about your subject and who's communicating it?
4. What attitudes and biases do the viewers have?

---

*Statement of purpose, or treatment   Document listing in a few sentences the objective of a TV production and what the desired outcomes will be.

ECU   Extreme close-up, often framing a person's eyes one-third down from the top of the TV screen and lips one-third up from the bottom.

CU   Close-up shot, often a face-and-shoulders shot.

If multiple copies of this program will be distributed, then you need to keep a sharp master tape for making those copies. Use your best equipment and try to reduce multigeneration editing. If the program is to be broadcast, you must produce a glitch-free tape made to high technical standards.

Will you have a captive audience? If so, you have the luxury of spending a few minutes developing your topic or developing the background for your story. If your audience consists of passersby, as in a store, then you have to grab 'em by the throat with something flashy and inject them with a brief message before they wriggle away. Don't let another twenty seconds go by without reaching for their throats again.

Children are also known to have short attention spans. You must reach them with a lively, colorful presentation that covers (and repeats) only a few main topics. Adults, incidentally, aren't much different. They lose interest and daydream just as kids do (only adults are too polite to swing from the chandeliers when a production gets boring).

The only audience that will sit attentively through a detailed, straightforward teleproduction consists of individuals who are deeply interested in the subject matter and intend to use the information right away, and perhaps your girl/boyfriend during the early stages of the relationship.

 Mini Review

- The director is responsible for scheduling and preplanning all aspects of the show.
- During the preplanning stage, the director determines the purpose of the show and whether video is the most appropriate medium.
- Using the statement of purpose, the director clarifies the objectives of the show.
- The director needs to match the style and content of a show to its audience.

Consider Your Resources

If you have an editing VCR, then the world of out-of-sequence recording and complex staging is at your fingertips. If you have portable gear, that means that you are not tied to the studio.

What's your budget? How much time and personnel will you have? Usually the budget plays a large role in determining how complex a production can be.

Will you have a content expert or technical consultant there during taping to stop you from making embarrassing mistakes? ("Observe, students, as we test the patient's reflexes using this refrigerated stethoscope.")

Choose a Program Format or a Combination of Formats

If you draw a blank trying to imagine where to start, Table 10–1 lists a few possibilities.

Keep the plan simple. The secret of being tiresome is to tell everything. The two-hour treatise showing every detail about something will not be as efficient or memorable as the 10-minute presentation that repeats the main point several times.

Get Approvals

When money is involved, it is wise to make sure the sponsor is willing to pay for the work you are doing. It is wise to find *one* individual who has the authority to "sign off" on the project each step of the way. Often this approval process is tied to the payment scheme, as in the following schedule:

Activity	Percent of Total Payment
1. Prepare general treatment	10
2. Prepare rough script	20
3. Prepare finished script	20
4. Shoot raw footage and prepare rough edit for review	30
5. Complete fine edit	20

In this schedule, the client can stop you before you spend too much money pursuing the wrong angle or creating the wrong mood. At the same time, this protects you from the client willy-nilly changing his or her mind, requiring you to do a lot of the job over. Nothing stops a client from changing his or her mind after signing off; in fact this is commonly done. The client, however, pays extra for this privilege and thus may think twice before proposing wholesale changes at the last stage of production.

TABLE 10–1 Several TV Show Formats

Format	Uses
Show and tell	This is straightforward presentation of facts. You explain an activity as you show it.
Spokesperson	A recognized authority adds credibility to your message.
Interview with man-on-the-street, or victim, or groupie, etc.	Viewers identify with J. Q. Citizen. An interview adds color to facts and statistics by introducing a human element or drama.
Skit	An acted-out situation is visually more exciting and leaves a more memorable impression than a simple declaration of facts.
Animation	It's costly, but it cuts out extraneous visual material and is more entertaining.
Charts and graphics	Simplifying complex ideas makes them more memorable.

Grab the audience, be visual, and KISS (Keep It Simple, Stupid!).

Now with the preplanning behind us, we start the production planning.

 **Mini Review**

- Several types of show formats include show-and-tell, spokesperson, interview, skits, animation, charts, and graphics.
- Keep the production plan simple. Don't try to say or do too much.
- When payments are concerned, keep the client informed as the production takes shape, getting approvals and payments as you go.

SCRIPTS AND STORYBOARDS

First you learn how to write; then you learn how to write between the lines. That's poetry. Script writing gives you many more lines to write between. There's the narration or spoken channel with its statements and nuances. There's the audio channel with its mood-creating musical track or environment-establishing sound effects. There's the visual channel, not only displaying the obvious but also implying further messages through camera angles and editing.

Writing

Writing is a creative endeavor. Some are blessed with the magic; others write textbooks on video. It's hard to make "rules" on writing; the rules are like toys on Christmas: so many are broken, but still the fun is there.

Be Visual.   Words, words, words . . . is this television? Think pictures. Close your eyes. Imagine telling your story without a single word. Sure, it's not easy, but try anyway. Close your eyes (you're still reading!); what do you see? Can you visualize the story unfolding? The script you are *now* creating is the difference between radio and television. Consider this: The movies *Alien, Close Encounters of the Third Kind,* and *Space Odyssey 2001* ended with a long stretch without words. There was plenty of script, plenty of shots and planning, and finally a feast for the eyes, ears, and imagination, but no words. What a relief!

If you look down through your script and find the audio column filled with narration and the video column listing a few spare hints of what pictures will show, then you have a radio script with pictures. Rewrite the script or find somebody who knows how to write for television.

Involve People in Your Subject.   People are most important. How the characters trapped in a situation work their way out involves the audience. Here is an example without people (directly):

Rusted bolts are sometimes hard to unscrew. No amount of effort seems to break them loose. Before ruining the bolt's head, try applying some penetrating oil to the base of the . . .

But notice the difference when people are included:

"What's the matter, Harry, rusty bolt won't unscrew?" (Harry gets angry, contorting himself and his wrench into ridiculous positions. Harry gets a grip and pulls with all his might.) "Harder, Harry, I think it's coming!" (Harry's grip breaks loose, and he flies across the room.) "Oh, Harry! Before you ruin that bolt and yourself, too, why don't you try some penetrating oil. . . ."

Clutter works against you. Keep It Simple, Stupid (KISS).

Grab the Audience.   "What we want is story that starts with an earthquake and works its way up to a climax"—*Samuel Goldwyn*. All TV programs need the audience's attention to succeed. Show some action, some mystery, tragedy, beauty, or humor. Or tease them with the sounds of something just around the corner. Whatever, grab the viewer's interest right at the start.

Prose for Television.   Granted, TV can't be all pictures. Even if we try our best to make our shows visual, we often have to provide a narrative. At least if we *have* to use words, let's write them in a visual language. Table 10–2 shows some differences between regular writing and TV writing. Note that these are generalities and not unbreakable rules.

Here's an example of printed prose:

> Affix the mounting wedge to the base of the camera, screwing the mounting bolt into the camera's base plate. Finger-tighten the bolt and then rotate the tightener ring clockwise, finger-tightening the ring. Slip the wedge into the camera head and lock the wedge clamp.

Here's how it would sound if the prose were matched to the video:

> This is the camera mounting wedge, useful for quickly releasing the camera from its tripod. To attach the wedge to the camera, first locate the mounting hole in the base of the camera. Align the fastener bolt with the hole, and thread the bolt into the base, as you can see here. Notice that the narrow end of the wedge plate is pointing toward the front of the camera. Finger-tighten the bolt, and then screw down the tightener ring like this. Now the camera is ready to be placed on the tripod. Slip it into the grooves in the head, and slide it forward, like so. Once the camera is snug, find the quick release lever, and tighten it down. Now this baby is going nowhere.

Notice how redundant the TV prose is compared to printed prose. There are several reasons why this redundancy is needed:

TABLE 10–2 Regular Prose versus Prose for TV

Regular Prose	TV Style
1. Uses complete sentences.	1. Uses incomplete sentences and phrases and may resemble captions.
2. Is concentrated, compact, and compressed.	2. Is repetitive and more wordy.
3. Uses formal arguments and deductive reasoning, sometimes requiring mental consideration of an abstract thought.	3. Is descriptive. Announces, proclaims, declares.
4. Uses logical transitions between sentences, such as *thus, because, therefore.*	4. Uses adverbial transitions, such as *here, now, then.*
5. Presents a logical argument to make a point. Develops a thesis. Ideas are derived through reasoning, surmised.	5. Illustrates the point or narrates a process.
6. Explains verbally.	6. Directs attention.
7. Modifies phrases for brevity, such as "the grid lights" rather than "the lights in the grid."	7. Tends to prepositional modification, such as "on the dimmer panel" or "at the beginning of the recording."
8. Uses long, complex sentences.	8. Uses short, simple sentences. (The ear has a shorter attention span than the eye.)
9. Uses variable sentence construction.	9. Uses declarative sentences—subject to verb to object.
10. Uses formal vocabulary and infrequently used words.	10. Uses the common, frequently heard words found in everyday speech.
11. Uses synonyms. Says something only once, figuring the reader can always come back to review the point.	11. Avoids synonyms. Tends to redundantly repeat the same thing over and over again, tautologously duplicating the . . . (you get the idea).

1. A *reader* can concentrate on difficult or complex passages and skim the familiar, skipping back and forth across a sentence. Further, the subject of a sentence can apply to a very complex predicate. Once entangled in the tail of the sentence, the viewer may have forgotten the subject, but, unlike the reader, the viewer can't zip back to review. Thus, the subjects are repeated, and sentences are kept down to one single thought each.

2. Cues to direct the viewer's attention are critical in order to ensure that important visual elements are not missed.

3. Since the viewer has but one shot at getting your message, it's wise to slow down the presentation rate, especially if the content is difficult to grasp.

4. Most importantly, actions usually proceed more slowly than words. What sometimes takes one moment to describe takes three moments to show, so that the words have to be spread out to coincide with the action.

This recommendation doesn't mean that you must fill every instant of action with constant chatter (don't try to tell this to sports announcers, though). Once you've set a tone of continuously narrated action, it may be disconcerting to the viewers to get a burst of information and then have the pictures catch up in silence.

If you find it inappropriate to stretch the narration (you don't want to describe the obvious just to fill time), you can always resort to filling the audio track with the environment's sounds (contestants, machines, traffic, office noise) or with light music. The music or sound will bridge the action while letting viewers know that their hearing aids didn't go dead.

Scripting Dialog. Grunts, *ummms*, sighs, and silences are all part of the rhythm of natural speech. Without these nonverbal and semiverbal reactions, your actors will seem stilted. To assure colorful characters and believable drama, write these digressions into your script. They also help define the character to the performers.

 Mini Review

- Television is a visual medium. Script the imagery as well as the words.
- Viewers identify with people more than with things, so involve people with the subject.
- Prose written to be read silently needs to be different from prose written to be spoken aloud. Take this into consideration when writing scripts for television.

Narration. A waterfall of words have we, and not a drop of visual variety to quench our parched cerebrum. The static boredom of the "big talking head," as the industry calls it, promises to haunt us as doggedly as death and taxes. Whether our excuse is low budget, absence of visual material, or lack of imagination, we will all eventually sink to the depths of the droning voice.

Humankind faces and deals with death and taxes, so shall we bravely deal with "talkie-face." Table 10–3 shows four basic narration formats and their applications. These may be used alone or in combination such as voice-over narration followed by guest expert. Such combinations offer a change of voice, tone, and pace, thus increasing interest. Using Table 10–3 as a base, we shall now try to squeeze more visual interest out of old talkie-puss.

1. *Shoot talent in their work areas.* Have the designer talk among his drawings, the chemist talk in her laboratory, the pilot talk at the airport, the machinist talk in front of his lathe, or the executive talk at her desk. Such familiar environments relax the talent, providing some insight to their personalities, add credibility to their roles, give you a location to shoot cutaways to hide edits with later, and most of all, frames Old Talkie-Puss with an interesting background.

Shoot talent in a stress environment.

TABLE 10-3 Basic Narration Formats

Format	Description	Example	Speech	Application	Scripting
Voiceover	As video activity is shown, off-screen narrator describes.	"As oil pollutes the wet-lands, waterfowl perish."	Formal, well-enunciated, perfect lines.	No personality super-imposed on content. Narrator is the Voice of Truth, representing facts, not controversy. Direct but boring. Requires a constant stream of visual matter.	Offers maximum control of program. Easiest script to write, shoot, and edit because every-thing is planned in advance.
Guide	Talks to the camera, sometimes disappearing off screen as an event is displayed. Leads the viewer places. Sometimes interacts with subject.	"We now are entering the shaft where twelve miners died. Here we see. . . ." or "Can you tell the folks at home what it's like. . . ."	Off-camera speech is formal. When interacting with others on camera, speech is informal.	Requires less visual matter. When there's nothing to show, show the guide talking. Guide unobtrusively controls direction of investigation while viewers feel as though they are making "discoveries" on their own. Acting as an audience representative, guide may ask subjects questions. Subjects respond directly to camera.	Easy script and program control, except when guide interacts with real subjects. Their responses may not fit the precon-ceived script.
Guest expert	An official, celebrity, or expert explains what he or she does or how a task was done. Expert may later join in the action using the eavesdrop format.	"When I first noticed a deviation in the planet's orbit, I thought it was some error in our calculations or an equipment failure."	Informal, as if talking to a single person, the viewer.	Lends authority and credibility to content. Must be titled or introduced so viewers know who the expert is. Viewer perceives speaker as a human being and may associate with that relationship. Speaker becomes part of subject.	Difficult to script because you can develop only a rough outline of mater-ial. Preplanning with the expert may aid scripting, but beware of stilted, formal tone if the talent is not a professional speaker.

(continued)

361

TABLE 10–3 *Continued*

Format	Description	Example	Speech	Application	Scripting
Eavesdrop	Actions unfold as the camera looks on. We overhear conversations between the participants. Interviewing falls into this format or into guide format.	"Hi, Mrs. Pevar, how is your bladder today? Hmmm, your stitches are healing up nicely."	Very informal.	More interesting and memorable presentation. Creates some distance between speaker and viewer. Permits few full-face shots. To be unobtrusive, you must often be able to shoot in confined space using available light, a shotgun microphone, a hand-held or easily movable camera, and only two crew members. And you must usually be able to change focus or f-stop quickly. Skilled interviewer can probe and repeat unanswered questions, thus speeding the reluctant or inarticulate speaker to a brief and informative statement.	Scripted role-plays require writing finesse and good actors. Using real-life participants affords the scriptwriter little control until the raw footage comes in.

Taking this idea further, you can *shoot the talent while they perform their jobs or practice their arts*. Not only are the performers in a comfortable environment, but they have something to do with their hands while they speak. Unlike the "show-and-tell" format described earlier, the talent aren't necessarily showing or telling *what* they are doing; they are just discussing a topic related to their actions. For instance, an artist could interpret the style of another artist as he himself molds a clay bust. Or the talent could describe the physical benefits of a Swedish massage—while receiving one.

In many situations, the talent can *present their lectures in a stressful environment*, such as driving a race car, swimming, answering telephones in a busy office, or performing surgery. The surrounding action will add immediacy, naturalism, and excitement to the discourse.

2. *Shoot talent in an atypical environment.* Here we do *just the opposite* of method 1 but for *exactly the same reasons*. The executive explains management strategies while pruning roses and wearing faded overalls. The judge discusses prison reform while playing with her dog in the backyard. The school custodian describes heating systems while tuning his violin for a weekend orchestral performance. The obvious counterpoint of such scenes strengthens our respect for the speakers as human beings and adds extra dimensions to their personalities. The shock of the juxtaposition opens our tired eyes.

3. *Shoot talent while they are walking or driving.* Not only do the talent have something to do while they speak (which may also have a calming effect on them), but also the viewer senses that the characters are genuine, doing real-world things. Such shots make excellent bridges from one topic to another, like this: "So that's how the program should work in theory. I'm taking you now to our field headquarters outside Bakersfield. One reason why this system is so effective. . . ." On our way to Bakersfield, we hear introductory descriptions of what we're about to see.

4. *Shoot talent in extreme close-ups.* With the eyes one-third down from the top of the screen and the mouth one-third up, you get a very intimate and engaging face shot. If you plan to edit, remember that you don't want jump cuts from one ECU (extreme close-up) to another ECU, so provide cutaways or some medium shots. Also, if you plan to title someone, do it on a medium shot across the talent's chest, not on an ECU across the teeth (for this reason it is good to begin interviews with an introductory "shirt pockets" shot which leaves space for the person's name and title).

Audience reaction research has shown that attention level is much higher when the screen displays full-face ECUs and CUs (close-ups) and there are rapid cuts from one person to another. Many of us assume that a variety of shots, including some long shots, will maintain interest, but the research does not bear out that assumption. Another thing that the research shows is that you should never keep your camera on a three-shot (a long shot) for more than three or four seconds, especially in an interview. The audience cannot see the participants' facial reactions in a three-shot and so tends to lose interest. Watch *60 Minutes* for perfect examples of interview shots.

5. *Shoot the talent out of a cannon.* Only kidding; however, with a telephoto lens and a long mike cord, what an eye-opener you'd have!

6. *Move talent around.* For instance, have Talkie-Puss refer to models, charts, and other graphics. Instead of placing those props together, have them spread around the studio, perhaps in "puddles" of light. The talent strolls from item to item while talking, perhaps pointing, holding, uncovering, or manipulating the item at each stop. The "puddles" of illumination afford us a change of lighting as the talent walks through shadows to each well-lit area. Even with the entire set well lit, the change of scene as the talent strolls and extols will allure the viewers.

Spreading out the graphics has a side benefit too. It puts into use that old educational axiom that you should reveal material only when it becomes immediately relevant to the topic.

7. *Move the camera around.* If the talent can't move, then move the camera. Arc it around so that the background setting changes. Everyone likes to go on a journey, and moving the camera up, down, or in an arc does exactly that. The change in perspective or background could coincide with the change in topics, thus providing a visual bridge.

You could dolly in or out with the talent (like the walking in example 3). *Do not simply zoom in and out on the talent.* It is not visually exciting. Unfortunately, it is so easy, it gets overdone. It is bad enough that you are accosting your viewers with Talkie-Face; don't yo-yo the eyeballs with meaningless zooms.

8. *Contrive cutaways.* These could be

a. A close-up of an object of interest (followed by a move out to include the talent).

b. Just the opposite: Start with a medium shot, then move in on the object (or symbol of the object) just discussed, while the talent moves out of the scene. You could even go out of focus in close-up, dissolve to an out-of-focus shot of the next object, and, while focusing on that, zoom out to include your talent as he or she arrives in the next scene.

9. *Shoot two heads.* Not necessarily on the same performer. They always say two heads are better than one, don't they? Two heads offer a variety of two talkie-faces interrupting each other perhaps to underscore certain talkie-points (and if they both talk simultaneously, the show could be over in half the time!).

Like it or not, narration and talking faces are here to stay, probably because they are so cheap and easy to do. This rut of least resistance is addictive, however. Jump at any opportunity you can find to use pictures instead of words; sound effects instead of narration; and lighting, music, camera angles, or editing to make your point.

 Mini Review

- Spice up interviews by shooting talent as they work or travel, or shoot them in unusual or fascinating environments.

Script Preparation

There are four common formats for making scripts (ergo the term formats, rather than twomats or threemats):

Script preparation.

TABLE 10–4   Treatment Format

MATH LESSON 26, 5/17/99

Instructor shows how to use a sextant. Lesson is given at a chalkboard. Animation is inserted.

1. Series theme, title.
2. Instructor descends rung ladder onto set and introduces the concept of triangulation.
3. Graphic 1, math puzzle, ladder against wall. How high a wall can the ladder scale?
4. Instructor works out problem on chalkboard.
5. Graphic 2, height of tree measured by triangulation.
6. Instructor works out problem at chalkboard.
7. Instructor describes sextant. CU on sextant from camera 2.
8. Cut to animation with voice-over, "Navigation by Sextant." Cue talent after the words "You can thank your lucky stars. . . ."
9. Instructor concludes and reviews concept of triangulation. Instructor ascends ladder off the set, to the series theme.
10. Graphic end title with series theme.

Approximate length of program: 20 minutes.

1. TREATMENT
2. SCREENPLAY
3. FULL PAGE
4. SPLIT PAGE

The TREATMENT works well with testimonial, documentary, impromptu, and other hard-to-script-ahead productions. It is a general set of guidelines describing the tone of the project and general techniques you'll use to achieve it. It would contain an outline or RUNDOWN of the important events in the production. (Note: TREATMENT has two meanings in two contexts: In preproduction it is a paragraph stating objectives. In scriptwriting it is a general outline for a script.) Table 10–4 shows a sample.

The SCREENPLAY or CENTER COLUMN FORMAT (Table 10–5) works well when the dialog must be precisely followed, but the shots and creative interpretation are left up to the director and actors. Thus, the content is hard and fast, but the specific methods of presentation are flexible. Dramatic scripts, reading like a play, are often typed in the SCREENPLAY format. Typically, the characters' names are in capital letters; the stage directions are in parentheses. There is plenty of room in the margins for director's and actor's notes. In the example shown, the director has even diagrammed the staging and moves, as well as the camera shots.

The FULL PAGE format (Table 10–6) is much like the SCREENPLAY format except that it has a more detailed description of the setting, action, and dialogue. Each scene is numbered, taking you through a chronological overview of the sights and sounds of the program. This and the SCREENPLAY formats are used by the Writers Guild of America, and many writers consider these the only professional formats

---

*Treatment format, or rundown   Script format listing general description of a program's content, direction, and style.

Screenplay, or live TV format, or center column format   Script format with dialogue in the center of the page and big margins for director's notations.

Full page or feature film format   Script format with dia-logue in the center of the page and a detailed description of action and shots also in the center.

Split page or two-column format   Two-column (or more) script format with video described on the left and audio on the right.

Rundown   Outline of the important events in a TV program.

TABLE 10–5   Dramatic Script (SCREENPLAY Format) with Director's Marks

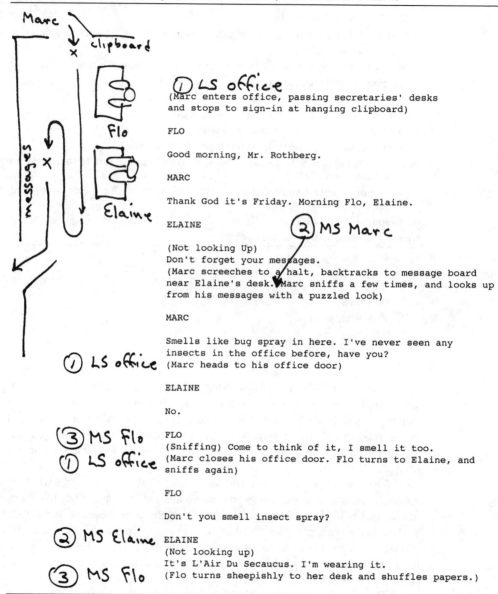

① **LS office**
(Marc enters office, passing secretaries' desks
and stops to sign-in at hanging clipboard)

FLO

Good morning, Mr. Rothberg.

MARC

Thank God it's Friday. Morning Flo, Elaine.

ELAINE   ② **MS Marc**

(Not looking Up)
Don't forget your messages.
(Marc screeches to a halt, backtracks to message board
near Elaine's desk. Marc sniffs a few times, and looks up
from his messages with a puzzled look)

MARC

Smells like bug spray in here. I've never seen any
insects in the office before, have you?
① **LS office**   (Marc heads to his office door)

ELAINE

No.

③ **MS Flo**   FLO
① **LS office** (Sniffing) Come to think of it, I smell it too.
                 (Marc closes his office door. Flo turns to Elaine, and
                 sniffs again)

FLO

Don't you smell insect spray?

② **MS Elaine** ELAINE
                 (Not looking up)
                 It's L'Air Du Secaucus. I'm wearing it.
③ **MS Flo**   (Flo turns sheepishly to her desk and shuffles papers.)

for film or video scripts. They are more often used for dramatic teleproduction than for instructional or documentary projects. One advantage of the FULL PAGE and SCREENPLAY formats is that they can be produced on any run-of-the-mill word processor, unlike the more complicated SPLIT PAGE format with its two columns.

The SPLIT PAGE or TWO-COLUMN script format is the most common approach for producers of corporate and instructional videos, news, and TV commercials. Generally, the video column is on the left and the audio column is on the right. You intuitively know what visuals go with what sounds as your eye scans down the page. Table 10–7 shows a sample TWO-COLUMN news script to which some ex-

TABLE 10–6   FULL PAGE Script Format

1. CU of Jalapeno potato chips bag being torn open.

2. MS of Jack and Jill giggling as Jack pours chips into bowl.

JACK

(To Jill) They look just like normal chips.

JILL

(To Jack, shaking her head in disapproval
and rolling her eyes) Oh, we shouldn't be
doing this. He'll burst a vessel.

SFX: Door slam

JACK

Ooo, quick! (Closing bag and foisting it on Jill, who
grabs it to her chest in surprise) Get rid of this!

3. LS with door on left, Jack and Jill behind table. Jill tosses
   bag onto top of refrigerator, and both snap to a fake casual
   stance as William enters through door.

JACK AND JILL (Together) Hi, Will.

WILLIAM

(Passing through) What are you two up to?
(In same breath, never stopping his gait)
Ah, chips. (William grabs a big sloppy handful.)

4. MS of William cramming chips into his face. He opens the
   refrigerator door and takes out a can of soda.

5. LS of William kicking the refrigerator door closed with his
   foot and exiting whence he came, popping open the can.

6. MS of Jack and Jill, puzzled.

WILLIAM

(Sound from offstage) Mm. Good.

Jack and Jill stare at the bowl. Both reach for chips
and showing their teeth, take a tiny bite of one.

7. CU of Jack's face as his eyes bulge.

JACK

Aaagh!

8. MS of both running to the sink and grasping handfuls of
   water to their mouths.

planatory notes have been added. Table 10–8 shows what it looks like once the director has marked up the script. Explanatory notes appear there too.

Some contend that TWO-COLUMN scripting tempts writers to compose all the audio first, then fill in the video, making the program's audio carry most of the load. This is okay for slide shows and speeches with visual support, but it is a blueprint for lackluster video. The SCREENPLAY formats force writers to develop the image first (location, type of shot, action), then fill in the verbiage. The disadvantage is that a lot of effort may go into the staging and shooting angles before the client has even approved the script. Adding these things later to the TWO-COLUMN script saves throwing away some of this work as the script changes.

Which format should you use? Whatever works for you. All that matters is that the intent be clear and the technique consistent. You can even invent your own format. Some directors draw STORYBOARD pictures in the *video* column. Some have video *and* storyboard columns. Some use a column

TABLE 10–7   Newscast Script with Explanatory Notes

Translation		
Shot of Walter. Slide of Capitol keyed behind Walter.	WALTER FX: SLIDE, CAPITOL	—THERE WAS NEARLY A RIOT TODAY ON CAPITOL HILL AS ANGRY SENIOR CITIZENS STORMED A CONGRESSIONAL PICNIC GIVEN ON THE FRONT LAWN.
Remove keyed slide.	OFF FX	HERE'S CINDY LISP WITH THE DETAILS.
Play videotape #2, which lasts 1 minute, 15 seconds.	VT2 1:15	
Back to Walter.	WALTER	—SPOKESMEN FOR THE GRAY PANTHERS DENY HAVING ANY INVOLVEMENT IN THE RAMPAGE.
Play news music. Key in character generator with moving words across bottom of screen.	THEME FX: CRAWL, "COMING NEXT: MARKET ANALYSIS"	—BE BACK IN A MINUTE WITH TODAY'S MARKET ANALYSIS.
Fade to black.	FADE OUT	

Table 10–8   Newscast Script with Director's Marks

Translation		
Camera #1 is on with Walter on left of screen, leaving room for slide of Capitol	① WALTER (on left) FX: SLIDE, CAPITOL	--THERE WAS NEARLY A RIOT TODAY ON CAPITOL HILL AS ANGRY SENIOR
Start VTP 2 rolling (IT'S BACKSPACED). Center Walter.	Roll VT2 OFF FX (center) SOT	CITIZENS STORMED A CONGRESSIONAL PICNIC GIVEN ON THE FRONT LAWN. HERE'S CINDY
Use sound-on-tape. Switch to VTP 2.	VT2 1:15	LISP WITH THE DETAILS.
Switch to camera #1.	① WALTER	--SPOKESMEN FOR THE GRAY PANTHERS DENY HAVING ANY INVOLVEMENT IN THE RAMPAGE.
Fade in to music.	↑ THEME	--BE BACK IN A
Key crawl over Walter, then start crawl so it moves onto the Screen. Switch to camera #2 with a long shot of Walter. Fade out audio and video.	FX: CRAWL, "COMING NEXT: MARKET ANALYSIS" 2 LS FADE OUT	MINUTE WITH TODAY'S MARKET ANALYSIS.

for narration and a column for audio effects. Sometimes all production information (audio and video) appears on the left, while only narration is on the right.

It is sometimes helpful for complicated audio and video moves to type the page sideways with narration in the middle, video in a column on the left, and audio on the right. Each audio or video cue is keyed to a particular word in a narration by drawing (marking a line) from the word to the cue.

Because of a diversity of production styles, no one set of scriptmarking symbols or methods has become universal. If you invent a system of your own, take care to

1. Make symbols that are clear and unambiguous.
2. Once you have a system, stick to it.
3. Avoid overmarking your script. The clutter will confuse you during the hubbub of production.
4. For "live" productions, place your cue marks *before* the desired action.
5. If the script is clearly marked, simply circle the script cues rather than duplicating them.
6. Feel free to draw little pictures to visualize moves or positions.

Fully scripted shows assist in planning shots, a necessity during complex productions. The director can see everything that will happen and has to contend with only a few surprises. On the other hand, a detailed script burdens the director with too many things to keep track of during the whirlwind of a performance.

Partial scripting in the form of a TREATMENT or RUNDOWN is common for interviews, instructional programs, and variety shows where a good deal of ad-libbing is expected. The script not only would contain detail about the production's beginning and end but would also include any complicated camera moves involving visuals, tapes, or sound effects. Otherwise, the director knows just the general direction that the program is taking and "wings" it, picking the best shots possible.

Since amateur performers aren't renowned for their willingness to memorize lines, the RUNDOWN is often as close to a script as you will get. More mistakes and poorer production quality may be the result of such partially ad-lib programs, but they are relatively cheap to produce and, thanks to videotape, can be done over if flubbed. Incidentally, you'd be surprised at how much preparation goes into a really good ad-lib speech!

A detailed script is especially useful when you are having someone else edit your raw footage. The script acts as an instruction sheet, telling what shots are desired and where. A person who has not been involved with your production could study the script, log the shots, create an edit decision list, and edit your program. Except for a few places where the taped action doesn't match the script exactly or where editing style plays a substantial role, the final production should come out looking 95 percent the way you intended it to.

 Mini Review

- News, dramas, and documentaries use various scripting formats. Match the format to the client or application.

---

*Storyboard Series of comic-book-like sketches showing what the TV scenes should look like. The corresponding narration and sound descriptions are typed at the bottom of each sketch.

*Production schedule, or timeline A listing of major production tasks and when they will take place.

Floor plan A sketch, showing from above where objects, walls, doors, cameras, etc. are to be positioned on the studio floor.

Storyboards

A STORYBOARD has nothing to do with telling such a dull story that your audience falls asleep. A STORY-BOARD is a series of sketches depicting the main pictorial element of a scene (Figure 10–1). The narration usually accompanies each picture. The result is quite similar to a comic strip, only the words are outside the picture. STORYBOARDS become especially worthwhile when

1. It is difficult to describe a scene with only words.
2. Others will have to carry out your plan. The STORYBOARD clearly shows what you want your audience to see.
3. A production's cost or importance warrants prior approval. The STORYBOARD is a concise way of representing what the final production *may* look like.

If you think that only sissies use STORYBOARDS and that they are amateurish and time consuming, consider this: Alfred Hitchcock drew his own STORYBOARDS—shot by shot—for every one of his movies.

 Mini Review

- Storyboards show more clearly than scripts what you want your audience to see.

Small educational productions are seldom complicated enough to require a STORYBOARD. As shows move up in complexity, simple hand-drawn STORYBOARDS like the one in Figure 10–1 are quite satisfactory. *You do not have to be an artist to get your point across, so don't let your artistic inabilities hinder you from making your own STORYBOARDS.* They do not have to be works of art.

THE FLOOR PLAN

And speaking of works of art (or lack of), prepare a FLOOR PLAN to show where the props, sets, performers, and cameras go. It doesn't have to be pretty, just instructive. If you're particularly lazy, you can combine the FLOOR PLAN with the LIGHTING PLOT (review Figure 5–20). The FLOOR PLAN helps the director visualize where things will go, and it also shows the crew what the director had in mind. Figure 10–2 shows a FLOOR PLAN.

THE PRODUCTION SCHEDULE

This is the haunting reality of the *real* TV production world: *Every second costs a dime.* Maybe more. To best marshal your resources, take time to list all the things that have to happen in order for your show to take place. Next, place this list on a TIMELINE or PRODUCTION SCHEDULE, to lay out a plan for when each part of the project will occur. An interview project might have the following PRODUCTION SCHEDULE:

May 4   Confirm that Krusty the Clown is available for the interview on May 9. Confirm that the studio and crew are available for May 9.

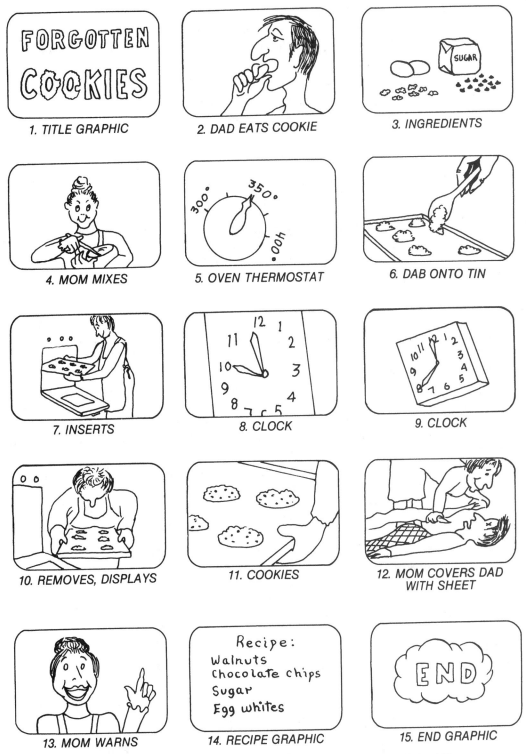

1. TITLE GRAPHIC

2. DAD EATS COOKIE

3. INGREDIENTS

4. MOM MIXES

5. OVEN THERMOSTAT

6. DAB ONTO TIN

7. INSERTS

8. CLOCK

9. CLOCK

10. REMOVES, DISPLAYS

11. COOKIES

12. MOM COVERS DAD WITH SHEET

13. MOM WARNS

14. RECIPE GRAPHIC

15. END GRAPHIC

FIGURE 10–1 Amateur STORYBOARD works fine and requires little skill.

May 5   First preproduction meeting. Prepare RUNDOWN. Begin script work and research. Begin floor plan, prop, and set lists.

May 8   Second preproduction meeting. Script ready. Floor plan ready. Make final changes. Set and prop requests confirmed.

May 9   Production. Studio 1.

May 10   Postproduction, if any (i.e., titles, music, editing).

May 12   Air date (or delivery of tape).

The PRODUCTION SCHEDULE keeps you on track, forcing you to consider each step and give it thought as you assign it a date on the page. The process helps filter out unrealistic hopes and expectations. Then, as you follow the TIMELINE, you can see your progress and adapt accordingly. If you're falling behind, you can work longer or harder or add more helpers. If you get hopelessly behind, you might consider delaying your production date (if you're not ready, you would waste everybody's time when they arrived to shoot. This would cost you credibility and perhaps a peck of pesos).

Prepare another PRODUCTION SCHEDULE for the day of shooting. Again, try to think of everything that must happen and when. A half-hour interview show might have the following PRODUCTION SCHEDULE for the shooting date:

9:00 A.M.   Crew call—Production crew, equipment operators, and setup people all arrive on site ready to work.

9:15–9:45   Technical meeting—Director describes the show to the crew. Crew confirms that all props, sets, and other materials are available.

9:45–11:30   Setup and lighting—Using the director's floor plans, scripts, and other handouts, the crew positions the sets and props, loads the titles in the character generator, cues up music, tests the microphones, aims the lights, and adjusts the cameras.

11:30 A.M.–12:30 P.M.   Meal—Don't forget that the crew are people and need to eat. Be sure everyone knows to return by 12:30 *sharp*.

12:15–12:30   Guests arrive—Brief the guests in a relaxed atmosphere. Discuss various aspects of the show, so that the guests feel comfortable.

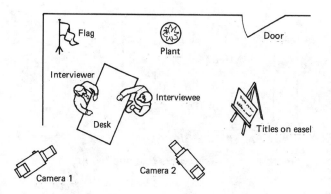

FIGURE 10–2   FLOOR PLAN shows positions of props and cameras (and sometimes lights).

To relax the performer, invite him to the studio before the actual production begins.

12:30–12:45	Brief rehearsal—It's not necessary to do the whole show (because it is an interview, which would become stale if practiced too much), but practicing the beginning and end of the show will iron out bugs such as bad camera angles, shine on a guest's head, tangled mike wires, bad shadows, etc.
12:45–1:00	Final corrections—Here's where you fix the problems discovered a moment ago.
1:00–1:45	Produce the show—Even though it's a thirty-minute show, there may be a false start or a problem mid-show that requires a reshoot.
1:45–2:15	Spill—Extra time in case things *really* go wrong.
2:15–3:15	Strike—Not related to a protest from the crew, "strike" refers to the removal of sets and props from the studio and the general cleanup of the studio and control room.

On-location shoots and productions that include outside footage are even more complicated (and subject to Murphy's Laws and other gremlins). They too need detailed production schedules and accurate predictions of what and who will be needed where and when. More on this in Chapter 13, "On-Location Shooting."

 Mini Review

- Preparing your production schedule helps you plan the events and resources you'll need to mount your production.
- The production schedule shows both you and your crew what needs to be done and when, as well as whether you're getting behind schedule.

11 DIRECTING

The director is responsible for "calling the shots" during a production. There's really much more to the job than this. The director's role begins long before the beginning of the shoot and usually ends in the wee hours after the postproduction editing. Directors may include in their production planning such things as

1. *Concept planning:* clarifying the objectives of the show and determining the best format for the production.
2. *Timing:* making the show and all its segments come out the right length.
3. *Visualization:* translating an idea or a script into screen images and mapping out the sequence of images.
4. *Lighting and floor plan preparation:* sketching the positions, angles, and types of lights to be used and also diagramming the positions of the set, props, and talent in the scene.
5. *Script preparation:* marking the script for camera shots, cues, transitions, and BLOCKING (position and movement of the talent).
6. *Rehearsal:* guiding the actors in their portrayal of the scene as well as practicing the scene in the studio to familiarize the crew with their moves.

A director's postproduction activities may include

1. *Checking the raw footage:* making sure that there is a technically acceptable "take" for each scene (*before* the studio has been cleared and the actors sent home).
2. *Editing the raw footage:* including the insertion of graphics, titles, and music.

The things a director does before and after production will most likely determine the quality of the show. That's why I've devoted so many precious pages to the subject. Now let's further explore the business the director handles immediately before and during production.

---

*Blocking   Planning out everyone's position and movement for the show.

BEFORE THE SHOOT

Preparing Yourself

1. *Learn the script.* During the show, you won't have time to look at the script for more than a second. Consequently, the script can act only as a reference for you—that is, as a list of reminders and cues. You should already know the content.

2. *Study difficult segments in detail.* The beginning and end of a show generally mix camera moves, music, graphics, and cues all at the same time. Sit down quietly and "talk through" the directions you will give during these difficult parts. Rehearse these segments until you can recite the commands without the script. Thus, when you get to these complex places, you can give your full attention to observing how well they are coming out rather than following your place in the script.

And while you're at it, *make and study a lighting plot, floor plan, prop list, and perhaps a storyboard.* Doing so will help you plan and visualize your shots. The prop list reminds you to assemble all the needed props *before* the show.

3. *While setting up and rehearsing in the studio, check your available time.* Where does the time go? Know you're starting to fall behind before you're behind. Otherwise, you won't exercise the necessary pressure to stay on schedule.

Unless you're paying an arm and a hoof for studio time, schedule it liberally. TV productions *always* take longer than estimated.

4. *Think through every move.* Every event in a production sequence should be planned out so that there are no "weak spots" or impossible moves to contend with during the actual shoot. For instance, is there time for camera 1 to break away from the prop and get focused back on the guest? If you have two sound effects on CDs and only one player, can the audio person get the second effect cued up in time? Will the camera taking tight close-ups slip into the other camera's view? Will you have boom microphone shadows? Will the dancers be able to hear the music they're dancing to?

At the end, do you want to simply fade out and roll credits over black, or do you want to turn out all the studio lights but one, have the talent exit the lit area, and then key the credits over the empty set? Are there enough hands to run the lights? Do you need to leave studio lights on to illuminate the final graphic? Can the white lab coats, cited in the props list, be exchanged for blue ones that won't exceed the camera's contrast limitations?

 **Mini Review**

- The director should be thoroughly familiar with the script.
- The director's role is not merely to "call the shots," but to plan every step of the production.

Preparing Your Crew

1. *Delegate tasks. The most frequent, most costly, most demoralizing error made by amateur directors is failure to delegate.* Time is cheap before a production; time is dear during it. Do you want your crew and talent standing around while *you* adjust the lights, *you* arrange the chairs, *you* look for props, and *you* type the credits into the character generator? No way! In commercial, professional settings, *all* tasks *must* be carried out by specialists, usually long before the shoot. The small-time operator follows a similar but less formal code.

Prepare your crew.

Whip out that floor plan you made earlier and give it to a camera operator (in small studios) or to the floor manager (in medium-sized studios). Also give that person the prop list and perhaps a copy of the storyboard as a guide in the placement of the sets, furniture, and props. Then go on to something else. Conjure up your lighting plot and pass it to the lighting director (or another camera operator assigned to the task) and then go on to something else. Provide a script to the audio director so that he or she can locate, check audio levels on, and cue up all the sound effects. The audio person can then also mike the talent and adjust those levels. With another copy of the script in hand, the technical director can set up special effects and anticipate the kinds of commands to follow. Are there titles to be fed into a character generator? Have somebody do it. Are there slides for the film chain? They should already be sequentially numbered, ready to pass on to someone. The engineer or videotape operator should be told how long a tape to load and whether it's an editing blank to be used in the VCR's insert mode or simply a blank tape. Does the tape need time code? The VTR operator will also handle the audio and video checks necessary to assure that the VTR levels are set. The storyboard you prepared comes into play as you brief the camera operators and talent on the shots that will be taken.

Here's where your preparations pay off. The studio and control room are abuzz with busy beavers, setting things up and checking them out. Assuming your beavers are somewhat experienced and your written directions are clear, you won't have to spend much time telling people what to do. They'll figure out which lamp goes to which dimmer, which volume control goes to which mike, and which buttons create which special effect. Theoretically, you should be able to leave the area for about twenty minutes and come back to find everything ready to go.

Even if things don't go this easily (they won't), the idea that *you are free to handle special problems will maximize the efficiency of your studio setup. You're free to answer questions, check other people's work, assist the talent, and even (heaven forbid) have time to think.*

2. *Develop a silent response code.* Crew members can communicate with the director over their intercom headphones before a shoot, but during the shoot this conversation will be picked up by the studio mikes. Develop some code whereby the camera operators can communicate with you (the director) silently. Try having them blow into their mouthpieces—once for "yes," twice for "no," and three times for "I've got a problem." Four blows could mean "Shooting close-ups of cat dissections is making me sick to my stomach." No telling what five blows could mean.

3. *Direct the studio rehearsal from the control room.* Don't keep running out to the studio to correct things. It wastes time while everyone's concentration lapses. Instead, make your shot judgments based on what you see in your camera monitors, and rely on your studio personnel to rectify problems.

4. *Explain what went wrong.* If you stop taping because of a mechanical problem, announce this over the studio address system. Otherwise the crew and actors get uptight, thinking they were at fault. If they did screw up, explain what was wrong and why, so that people can correct it. If, for instance, one performer is blocking another or has a hand in the way of something to be shown, don't assume the performer knows it—he or she can't see the camera monitors. Speak up. On the other hand, there are times when a good director takes the blame (making up a reason) for stopping rather than embarrassing the talent or a crew member or making them nervous.

5. *Announce return times.* Something often breaks down during setup. Perhaps it will be fifteen minutes before you are ready to go. Let your unneeded crew and performers take a break. Tell them what time it is on your clock and *exactly* what time they should be back and ready to go. Otherwise, you'll find yourself waiting and chasing. Meanwhile, since the studio is inactive, shut down those broiling lights.

6. *Do an audio check.* Unless the audio director is handling these details independently, make sure the audio person knows whose mike is on which knob. See that each performer has recited something while the audio person made volume adjustments. Sound effects and music also need to be checked for proper volume.

7. *Do an intercom check.* Call each person on the headphone intercom to make sure everyone can hear you. Chaos results when a crew member loses contact and is flying deaf.

8. *Do a video check.* Unless a video engineer and lighting person have checked this for you, do it yourself just before you start the show. Have the cameras provide long shots of the performers or views of what will be their "typical" shot for the show. Observe the apparent lighting. Are the shadows and highlights appealing? Now check the waveform monitor and, if necessary, adjust each camera's iris, gain, and pedestal one by one to make blacks black and whites white. Switch from one camera to the next to see if the pictures' overall brightness matches. Have all your cameras aim at the same thing, perhaps a performer, and, while switching between them, observe a color monitor. Is the color matched between the cameras?

Have your camera operators perform a complete and careful focus. Are their pictures sharp?

Older equipment electronics "drift," making yesterday's adjustments inapplicable today. The adjustments may drift even during an hour's rehearsal. So the fine adjustments are best made at the last moment, with the lights set the way they'll be, with the talent and props shown the way they'll be, and with the equipment warmed up and ready to go.

If you're shooting graphics or objects on easels, check to see that they are level. A temporary horizontal split across the TV screen will give you a line to use as a reference.

9. *Turn off the studio line monitor.* Unless the talent has a special need to see the shots during the show, remove this distraction from their sight. Otherwise, they will tend to look at themselves in the monitor rather than respond to the camera or to each other.

 Mini Review

- To avoid being a production's bottleneck, the director must delegate most tasks.
- The floor plan, lighting plot, and storyboard will help the production crew carry out what the director has in mind for the show.
- Check audio, video, and intercom operation before show time.

Preparing Your Talent

Rehearsing and preparing semiprofessional or novice performers is a science deserving a section of its own (coming in Chapter 12). For now, here are a few fundamentals:

1. *Banish the kibitzers.* The well-meaning entourage of friends and "experts" who follow your talent into the production area can be a disaster in the studio. They are used to giving their two-cents worth even when that is all their advice is worth. There can be only one director. Be it. With the cackling hangers-on gently removed from the area, the talent will be able to listen to *you* without distraction. You may not be used to giving people orders, but this is the one time when that's *exactly* your role. And they will listen. The trick here is to remove the competing voices and take charge as *the expert*, the director.

2. *Rehearse the words first and the* BLOCKING *(movement on camera) second.* It is difficult for beginners to master both at once. Once your talent is comfortable with their lines, move on to their motions—walking, sitting, turning from one camera to another, or handling props.

Sometimes it is hard to explain to a beginner how to speak forcefully or with excitement. You might try reciting the president's lines into an audiocassette recorder the way *you* think they should sound and then give him or her the cassette the day before shooting.

3. *Try not to overrehearse your talent.* They are likely to lose spontaneity, and you'll hear flattened modulation with less energy and more boredom.

4. *Shoot in short sections.* This gives the novice performer a "breather" and time to master the words and motions of each scene.

5. *Give your talent star treatment.* See that your guests are comfortable. Have someone attach the talents' mikes in the right place for them. This will build their self-esteem and confidence, counteracting their nervousness.

Between takes, offer encouragement, reinforcing the things they are doing well and gently suggesting *one or two* improvements, if needed. Try not to use too many "don'ts." Be positive.

When a production must be stopped, explain to the talent the reason for the "cut." They will be more comfortable knowing what is going on and being "included" as part of the team.

If your talent has been under the lights for a while, have someone bring him or her a glass of water during a break in the action. This not only soothes parched throats but makes the talent feel important and pampered.

When all is over, if you discover that some of your guests have been "edited out" and will not appear in the final program, send a thank-you letter to the participants, extending your regrets and appreciation.

 Mini Review

- The director needs to create an atmosphere that comforts and encourages the talent.

DURING THE SHOOT

1. *Be firm but friendly.* Critical observations that people might accept face-to-face create tensions when heard over the one-way communication of the studio public address system.

2. *Continually scrutinize preview monitors.* Is the shot you're taking okay? If so, *there's nothing more for you to do with that shot, so don't waste time looking at it.* Go on to the next shot. Get it set

DIRECTING NONPROFESSIONAL TALENT

In our league, most of our TV talent will be semiprofessionals or nonprofessionals, and the less they know, the more you will have to encourage, coach, and calm them. Perhaps the best first step in their education is to present them with Table 12–1 in the next chapter, "Basic Do's and Don'ts of Being the Talent." (Don't make a photocopy; just hack out the page. That way, when this page is lost, you will have to buy another copy of this book, enriching Peter Utz and Prentice Hall.) If interviews are involved, you may also wish to familiarize your talent with a later section of Chapter 12, "The Interview." Now, Mr. or Mrs. Director, here are some hints for you.

Prepping Talent. Don't make your talent work in a vacuum. Tell them about the show as a whole. Let them know how they fit into the overall story or objective. Tell them if you plan to use voice-over (narration), slow motion, or special effects. Knowing more about the final look of the program will help them "play" to that end.

Nonprofessional talents' biggest problem is usually nervousness. To dispel the "butterflies," invite the performers to the studio before the actual production begins. Talk to them as they sit in the studio getting used to the frenzy of cables, lights, headphones, and people everywhere.

Rehearsal. Chances are that the rehearsal will not take place in the studio. The TV studio is too expensive a piece of real estate (usually) for people to simply stand and practice lines together. The rehearsals usually occur in an empty room somewhere, and the final run-throughs are done in the studio.

Here's a list of more things to remember:

1. *Give a script to everybody who needs one.* Don't be parsimonious. Be prepared.
2. *Avoid excessive script revisions.* Wrong versions of actions, groupings, and lines have a way of getting remembered and new versions forgotten.
3. *Provide a pronunciation guide to technical language and the names of people.* "Welcome to our show, Mr. Smelleybuns . . . oh, excuse me, Mr. Smel-LAY-bins."
4. *Explain about editing.* Amateurs aren't known for pulling off twenty-minute scenes flawlessly. You will probably be shooting in short segments. Explain how the "magic" of editing will assemble the pieces together later.
5. *Let performers know the set floor plan.* If they know where everything is, they are less likely to rehearse their moves in a forbidden zone (as on a wall or in the sink). Provide them with reasonable substitutes for props. One actress recalls practicing a phone conversation using just her hand. On live television, the phone rang as scripted. She went to answer it, but instead of lifting the receiver, she automatically picked up her fist to her cheek and held an entire two-minute conversation with her little finger.
6. *Have the moves and identities learned along with the lines.* Executives, teachers, and nonactors will probably have to learn the lines first and the moves second. One problem at a time is all they can handle. Actors, however, even beginners, can generally learn to handle both at once. Include the moves and identities along with the lines to provide a better "feel" for the action while helping the actors learn the dialogue. Call the actors by their character names to increase their identity and their involvement with the character.
7. *Inform actors of the shots you will be taking.* They will then feel free to wave their hands in long shots, stand very still and include very subtle facial expressions during tight close-ups, and relax when they know that they are not in the shot at all. They should also know to keep still when they're in the background of someone else's shot lest they distract the viewer.
8. *Do not overrehearse.* The performers will lose spontaneity.
9. *Praise often:* Never embarrass. Acting is frustrating. Most novices and semipros desperately need feedback and encouragement. Build them up; relax them. Take their minds off their egos and self-consciousness and put them into their roles. If you must criticize, do so positively. Be constructive. Besides, if the talent is nonprofessional, you're probably not paying them enough to take *any* abuse—no matter how much they deserve it, no matter how frustrated you become. So be nice, lest they walk out, and then we'll see how frustrated you can *now* become.

Shooting.

1. *Shoot the most difficult scenes first when people are fresh.* Go back and do the easy scenes later when everyone is tired and cranky.
2. *Remind actors to listen to each other.* Otherwise, they will just recite *their* lines without reacting to other actor's lines in a realistic way.

3. *Walk an actor through a scene when using voice-over.* If a narration is going to be dubbed in anyway, you might as well enjoy the freedom of verbally coaching the actor as he performs the scene, like "Walk a little slower . . . pick up the photograph . . . hold it steady . . . steady . . . good, walk away to your right."

4. *Give actors something to do.* Unless you want the "background" actors standing with their hands in their pockets jingling their car keys and driving the sound person mad, give them a prop to hold or something to do. How about a glass of lemonade to drink, a rag to polish with, a bolt to tighten, a book to leaf through, or a dinner date to silently chat with. Anything, as long as it visually doesn't upstage the speaking talent.

5. *Kill the studio lights when not needed between takes.* Don't parboil your actors and crew. Meanwhile, save-a-kilowatt.

6. *Have a pitcher of ice water and cups in the studio.* It's a nice touch and cheaper than Harvey's Bristol Cream.

up and ready to go. When you switch to that shot and it's okay, check on the *next* shot, and so on. You end up seldom looking at what's being used but rather always preparing what's coming up next. *Looking ahead is the essence of direction.*

The director is in charge of quality. This doesn't mean giving commands like "Two, go to a close-up of Chloe's cloak," and then *automatically* taking the shot. It means watching the camera (or preview) monitor to check that camera 2's shot is steady, sharp, and centered before you take it.

The same goes for special effects. You preview an effect to make sure it's satisfactory before taking it.

3. *Give "ready" cues to switcher, audio, cameras, talent, and others.* Don't just call out "Take 2" or "Kill mike 2." There will be a delay before the crew can carry out these commands. Instead, always say "Ready to take 2—take 2," so the buttons are found and ready to be pressed instantly.

Similarly, warn the cameras of an action about to take place (after all, *you* have the script) such as, "They're going to stand in a second; get ready to follow them up."

Talent and floor manager need ready cues, too. Over your studio address system, call out, "Stand by, we roll in fifteen seconds," so they can psych up for action. Say to the floor manager, "Ready to cue talent," so he or she puts a finger in the air, ready to point at the talent when your "Cue talent" comes. Give your "Cue talent" indication a moment early because there's a lag before the manager can respond. For instance, say, "Ready to cue talent; ready to fade to 1. Cue talent, fade to 1." By the time you've faded to 1, the talent has started.

If you've given a "ready" cue and then change your mind, nullify the cue. Don't say, "Ready to take 1. Take 2." Odds are that your TD (technical director) will take 1.

4. *Give a "standby" cue to sources.* Lighting or character generators operators who have been unoccupied for some time may not be ready when you give your cue. So remind them that their parts are coming up shortly. Thus, they'll have their hands on the controls when you give your immediate cue.

5. *Avoid matched shots.* Say you're "winging it" through an unscripted or semiscripted show. Don't let both cameras give you similar shots. You remember how visually poor it is to switch from one long shot to another long shot of the same subject or from a medium to a close-up shot of a subject from the same angle. Since you can't aesthetically switch from one camera to its twin, why have the twin? It's doing you no good. Worse yet, if the shot goes bad from the camera that's on, you have no "safety shot" to fall back on, no acceptable place to go.

So delegate certain shots to certain cameras with complementary shots going to the remaining cameras. For instance, say, "Camera 1, stay with the host; camera 2, stay close on his hands." Now, while camera 2 is centering or focusing on the tough-to-get shots, camera 1 is giving an acceptable backup and establishing shot.

6. *Give your signals clearly and precisely.* Don't mumble, don't shout. Appear relaxed but alert.

7. *Keep track of which camera is on.* You don't want to call for a cut or dissolve to the camera that's already on. One way to keep track is with your fingers. Placing your thumb on your pointing finger means that you're on camera 1; placing it on the long finger means that you're on camera 2, and so on.

Some switching consoles have a tally light for each camera monitor. Instead of viewing the program and preview monitors, your eyes are always scanning the camera monitors. You know which camera is *on* by which monitor has its tally lit.

8. *Speak only when necessary.* Too much chatter over the intercom headsets dilutes people's attention.

9. *Call out the camera before giving instructions to it.* For instance, say "Camera 2, zoom in." This avoids having all the cameras start to zoom in until they hear *who* was supposed to do it.

10. *Get cutaways if you plan to do much editing.* These can be produced even after the actual show is over—simple shots of nodding host, attentive guests, audience, or props. Even if you don't expect to use them, get cutaways anyway. You never know when you may have to hide a matched shot or a jump cut or a flubbed shot during postproduction editing. Some directors do it the other way around—shoot cutaways first. These shots of the main actor's rear and the respondent's face give the actor extra rehearsal time before the more critical face shots are recorded. Also, if extras have been hired to be in the background, you can get these shots over with and let them go home.

11. *Decide whether to start again.* This is the toughest decision a director has to make. While taping a production, an error is made. Do you holler "Cut!" and start over, or do you let it ride? Some factors to consider in this decision are these:

   a. Is the program short and easily "redoable"?

   b. Is this error or a series of false starts likely to dampen the talent's performance?

   c. Are you near the beginning, where very little will be lost by starting over, or are you near the end of your show?

   d. Can you edit, resuming your recording from just prior to the error?

   e. How bad is the error, how discriminating are the viewers, and how hard is it to do the part over?

Rest assured, whatever you ultimately do, Murphy's 308th law will get you: "If you stopped, you should have kept going; if you kept going, you should have stopped."

Over-the-shoulder shot, useful as a cutaway.

12. *Above all, be positive and supportive of your staff and talent.* They *will* make mistakes. If you make them fearful, they'll freeze up and commit more mistakes. Relax and encourage them, and they'll be creative, confident, and energetic. And they'll treat each other better. The above goes *double* on the shoot where everything seems to be going wrong. An accusatory attitude will worsen your woes.

 Mini Review

- During a live shoot, keep an eye on the shot coming *next*.
- Give "ready" cues.
- Avoid matched shots.
- Shoot cutaways to edit in later, if needed.

THE DIRECTOR IN ACTION

It's zero hour. The video, audio, and intercom checks are over, the lights are up, and the show is about to begin. Figure 11–1 shows what a partially scripted, simple, five-minute, two-camera interview show might sound like as heard over Dan Director's intercom.

FIGURE 11–1 The director's commands during a show and the resulting shots.

To TD: *Ready on black.*

To Engineer: *Ready to roll VTR.*

Over studio speaker: *Stand by about one minute.*

Over intercom: *One, tilt up a bit on the castle. Good. Hold it.*

To Engineer: *Roll VTR.* Engineer says, "Rolling."

During the ten seconds it takes for the VCR to get up to speed, *Ready bars, ready tone. Take bars and tone.*

bars

During the next forty seconds of bars and test tone, *CG, get title. Ready to key title over one.* Effect appears on preview monitor.

Over studio speaker: *Thirty seconds.*

To TD: *Ready to fade to black.*

To AD: *Ready to lose tone. Fade to black, lose tone.*

To AD: *Ready countdown. Start countdown.* There are eight audio beeps, one second apart. During the beeps, *Ready to start music. Ready to fade to effects.* Two seconds after the last beep, *Start music. Fade up.*

effects

Ready to cue host. Open host mike. Ready to fade out music. Ready to dissolve to two. Dissolve to two, cue host, lose music.

camera 2

To CG: *Monfries title.*

To TD: *Ready to key title over two. Ready to dissolve to effects. Dissolve.*

effects

Ready to lose title. Lose it.

camera 2

One, get a long shot with host on left. Guest will walk in on right when introduced. Follow them with a two-shot. Open guest mike. Ready to take one. Take one.

camera 1

camera 1

Two, get a medium shot of guest after she sits. One, zoom in a little and follow them down as they sit. Good. One hold that shot.

camera 1

Waits for camera 2 to focus on guest. *Ready to take two. Take two.*

Camera 2

Stephanie title. Ready to key title over two. Ready to dissolve to effects. Dissolve.

title over camera 2

Ready to lose effects. Ready to take one. Lose effects. Take one.

camera 1

To Engineer: *Tape one coming up.*

To AD: *It's silent. They'll narrate.* Engineer has tape cued and puts it in pause mode, backspaced five seconds. The director listens for the tape to be introduced by the guest. *Roll tape one.* Engineer says, "Rolling." *Ready to dissolve to VT1.* Five seconds elapse as VTP1 reaches speed. *Dissolve to VT1.*

tape 1

The talent can see the tape playing on the studio monitor.

Anasazi title. Ready to key title over VT1. Ready to dissolve to effects. Dissolve.

effects

Ready to lose effects. Ready to dissolve to one. Ready to cue talent for end of clip. Lose effects, cue talent, dissolve to one. Floor manager, standing near TV monitor, places arm in front of the studio monitor screen, pointing toward guest.

camera 1

To Engineer: *Get second tape ready. Ready to take two. Take two.*

camera 2

To AD: *This tape has sound. Ready to lower their mikes and fade up sound on tape.* Director awaits introduction for second tape. *Roll tape.* Engineer says, "Rolling." *Ready to dissolve to VT2. Ready sound.* After five seconds, *dissolve to VT2, fade up sound on tape, fade out mikes.* Through foldback, the VT2 sound plays into the studio for the talent.

tape two

Rushmore title. Ready to key title over VT2. Ready to dissolve to effects. Dissolve.

effects

Ready to lose effects. Ready to dissolve to two. Ready to cue talent. Ready to bring up mikes and fade out sound on tape. Lose effects. Bring up mikes. Cue talent. Lose sound on tape. Dissolve to two.

camera 2

At the appropriate time; *Cue host, two minutes left.*

Ready to take one. Take one.

camera 1

There are several more switches back and forth between one and two, following the conversation. At the appropriate time, *Cue talent thirty seconds.*

Ready to roll credits. Ready music. Ready closing tape. It's silent. Engineer says, "It's on VT1." *Ready lighting change.*

One, be ready to follow them up, as they stand.

camera 1

Start music. The music folds back into the studio as a cue to the talent. *Kill mikes. Change lights.* Key and fill lights are dimmed as preprogrammed.

change lights

Key CG over one. Take effects. Roll credits.

roll credits

credits continue

Ready to roll tape. Ready to dissolve to VT3 when credits end. Engineer says, "That's VT1 it's on." *Sorry, ready to dissolve to VT1. Roll tape.* Engineer says, "Rolling." After five seconds, *Dissolve to VT1.*

end of tape

Ready to fade to black when music ends. Ready to kill all sound. When music ends, *Fade out picture and sound.* Waits ten seconds.

To Engineer: *OK, stop tape. Rewind to beginning and play. Bring up houselights and kill studio lights.*

Over studio speaker: *Very good. Thank you, everybody. Please stay put while we check the tape. You want to see it too? . . . Okay.*

To Switcher: *Take VTR four.* To Audio: *Play sound on tape four to studio.* The tape plays through.

To Studio: *Looks fine. We're done. Thank you.*

To Crew: *Good work! Thank you.*

To Engineer: *Ken, you saved my tush on VT3. Muchas gracias.*

Dan Director pulls an Alka Seltzer package from his pocket, opens it, swallows the tablet whole, and staggers from the control room.

The director's lingo in a similar show may be either more lengthy or more abbreviated than that in Figure 11–1, depending upon how long the crew and director have worked together. If you do five shows in a week with this format, by the second week everyone will know what to do, and the director's commands may be single syllables. The "ready" cues will always be there, but phrases like "fade up music on VT1" might become "up music."

The preceding example also assumed the director knew the script and the content of the tapes while the crew was vaguely familiar with what was coming. In other situations, the crew may already know whether sound is on the tape, etc.

A last note: In some studios an AD (assistant director) keeps track of timing and whether there's sound on the tape, etc., announcing these details to the director and crew when appropriate. This takes some pressure off the director.

SELECTION OF SHOTS AND EFFECTS—DECISIONS THE DIRECTOR HAS TO MAKE

Here you are in the big time, facing a bank of silent gray monitors in a chilly, darkened control room. The smell of nervous perspiration is in the air—your perspiration. Which shots do you use? Do you CUT or DISSOLVE? Do you WIPE the subtitle up from the bottom or MATTE it over the picture? The answers to these questions are subjective. Composition of shots is an artistic and creative endeavor. Here are some generalizations.

Dissolves versus Cuts versus Wipes versus Fade-outs

Cuts are easiest and quickest to do, requiring only the push of a button. CUTTING from one camera to another is the least obtrusive way of showing *different views of the same thing.* Changing from a close-up to a medium shot is best done with a CUT. Changing from a performer's face to what the performer is seeing or holding is appropriate for a CUT. Switching from a shot of a football kicker to a long shot of both teams on the field and then to a shot of the receiver is best accomplished with CUTS.

DISSOLVES, on the other hand, imply a *change in time or place.* One would DISSOLVE from an interview to a slide or tape of the subject being discussed. A DISSOLVE implies "meanwhile, back at the ranch" or "later that evening" or "see this example of what I am talking about." Like a new paragraph, a DISSOLVE brings an end to one series of thoughts and a beginning to another. DISSOLVES are generally inappropriate for merely changing shots. You wouldn't DISSOLVE from the batter who just hit the ball to the shortstop who is about to catch it. Nor would you DISSOLVE from a medium shot of a performer to a close-up shot of a performer (unless it is for dramatic effect, such as a slow DISSOLVE from a long shot of a singer to a close-up of the singer's face).

Kiss black   Fade to black followed immediately by a fade up on a new picture.

A montage of rapid-fire shots is best portrayed with CUTS, which in themselves can add tension and excitement to the scene. DISSOLVES, on the other hand, are not only difficult for the switcher to handle in rapid succession but in themselves create the opposite impression: one of calm, casual, serene, relaxing entertainment. Beauty, awe, and deep significance are often portrayed with DISSOLVES.

A FADE-OUT or FADE TO BLACK implies an ending, while a FADE-IN or FADE-UP implies a beginning. A FADE-OUT followed by a FADE-IN (which the experts call KISS BLACK) indicates a *significant* change of place or time or train of thought. Where the DISSOLVE was similar to going from one paragraph to a new paragraph, a KISS BLACK is more like ending one chapter and beginning a new chapter.

Incidentally, DISSOLVE technically means to melt from one picture to another, whereas a FADE means you are changing from a picture to black or vice versa. Many experts, however, outside their classrooms, will use these words interchangeably. Perhaps they do so because it's easier to say "FADE" than "DISSOLVE" when they're in a hurry. So don't be surprised if you hear someone say, "Fade from camera 1 to camera 2."

A WIPE, like a DISSOLVE, implies a change in time or place. It also gives the feeling that the new scene is *replacing* rather than simply following the previous scene. WIPES are spicier than DISSOLVES, and they should be used very sparingly lest their novelty wear off and they begin to distract your audience from the content of your production.

Split Screen versus Matte and Key

Say you have a title, subtitle, or label you wish to have share the screen with your performer. Do you SPLIT-SCREEN it at the bottom, or do you MATTE it somewhere? In making this decision, here are some things to consider: A SPLIT-SCREEN intrudes on your picture (taking a section of it), whereas the MATTE is less obtrusive; you can see the scene between the words in the MATTE so that you don't feel that you are sacrificing so much of your picture to the subtitle. However, with a MATTE, you have little control of the background behind the words as the scene moves and changes. What do you do if the bottom of the screen has a lot of white in it? Quickly change your MATTE to black? Shove your words to the top or to the middle of your screen? Such action would be more distracting to the viewer than simply SPLITTING the screen so that the words always have the best background for easy reading. The decision about whether to SPLIT SCREEN or MATTE depends on the kinds of scenes that are expected and how important the words are. If the words are paramount, sacrifice a section of the picture with a SPLIT SCREEN. If the words are secondary and the scenes will accommodate them, use MATTE. Whatever you decide, be consistent. Use one method or the other throughout the show lest the audience be distracted by your change in technique.

Transitions

How often should you change shots, and what kinds of shots should you change to? The main object is to follow the action, keeping it *on* the screen (unless, for dramatic effect, you are hiding the action from the audience). If keeping the action on the screen means frequently alternating shots between cameras, then do it. But if you have a good view of the action on one camera and an equal or worse shot of the same thing on another camera, then keep the first shot. Don't change shots just because the buttons are there on the switcher. As long as the viewers see what they want and need to see, they don't care how many shots were used in the process of displaying it to them.

Some directors change shots just to add variety to the show. The wisdom of this procedure depends on the creativity and savvy of the director, the objectives of the program, and the content of the particular shots. Switching to a side shot of the news anchorperson while revealing the busy newsroom in the background adds variety and style to the end of the newscast. Doing this *in the midst* of a news presentation would detract from it. Cutting to a close-up of an interviewee's nervous, wringing hands adds variety (and insight) to a *60 Minutes* exposé. Displaying this shot while the interviewee is making an important point, however, would be distracting to the audience. Showing this shot while the interviewer is asking the question might even confuse the audience—they might assume they were watching the *interviewer's* hands.

Perching a camera up in the rafters offers a great opportunity to spice up your presentation of a square dance. A shot of the action from above adds variety. Since you've gone to the trouble of hoisting the camera up there, why not also use it to view the poetry reading coming up next? This unusual shot should add plenty of variety, right? Ridiculous as it sounds, this is one of the toughest decisions facing a fledgling director—whether to get mileage out of something in one's production arsenal or to disregard the dazzling things one *can* do and instead do what is best for the total production. The production should come first. Try not to get pizzazz-happy. Skip the fancy overhead shot if it doesn't add to the drama of the poem.

To experience an example of what the author feels is excessive and intrusive shot changing, rent the popular videotape *Lord of the Dance*, a Celtic music/dance video with Michael Flatley. The music and dancing were superb, but the directing drove me nuts. Compare this to *Riverdance*. The musical and dancing styles were the same, but this production didn't intrude on the content. You got to enjoy the *show*, not the video effects.

Sometimes the shots you use imply what's coming next on the screen. The switch from a medium shot to a long shot of a performer indicates that a performer is about to move or be joined by someone. Cutting to a close-up of a performer's face readies the audience to catch his or her expression. If you now switch to a medium shot, viewers will expect a gesture; and a shot of the door prepares the viewers for an entry. Making any of these shot changes without a specific purpose will not add variety to your show—it will only confuse your viewers. Therefore, change shots for a purpose, not for idle variety.

Matched Shots.   One outgrowth of the preceding philosophy is the following general rule: Avoid going from a two-shot to another two-shot or going from a long shot to another long shot or from a close-up to another close-up. These are called MATCHED SHOTS (review Figure 1–23). Switch from one thing to *something else*—from a long shot to a medium shot, for instance. The main idea is to offer a *different* view of something when changing shots. The medium shots of the same thing reveal nothing new and are purposeless. In fact, it is often good to assign camera operators a responsibility for specific kinds of shots so that you avoid getting a duplication of shots from two or more cameras. What good is it to have essentially the same picture coming from two different cameras? One is being wasted.

A few exceptions to this rule include the case described earlier in which the medium shot of the news anchorperson was followed by another medium shot of the anchorperson from the side with the newsroom in the background. Another exception to the rule relates to the portrayal of a dialogue: Shooting over one person's shoulder, we get a close-up of the second person's face as he or she speaks. When the first person speaks, we swap everything around, taking a close-up of the first person over the shoulder of the second. In both of these cases, although we are switching from a medium shot to another medium shot or from a close-up to another close-up, the content of the shots is significantly different. The shots thus justify themselves. They have a valid purpose. They display something that needed to be shown and perhaps could not have been shown as well in some other way.

This doesn't mean that over-the-shoulder shots should always be matched in size; it just means that they *may* be matched. It is likely, just because of the camera angles, that the closer person will be

---

*Matched shots   Similar-looking views of a subject from two cameras at the same time.

*Vector line   Imaginary line dividing the set (action area) in two; all camera angles must be taken from one side of this line to maintain unambiguous transitions from shot to shot.

slightly larger and higher than the farther person, unmatching the shots a bit. You can also exaggerate this effect on purpose; having one person higher and larger than the other person in the over-the-shoulder shot will imply power, importance, assertiveness, and dominance to the larger person. Over-the-shoulder shots of a boss and an employee would generally have the boss positioned higher and shown larger than the employee.

 Mini Review

- After the shoot, thank your crew and talent.
- Use cuts to show different views of the same thing.
- Use dissolves, wipes, and other effects to call attention to a change in time or place.
- Avoid fancy camera angles and effects if they would distract the viewer from your message.

Vector Line.   With the possible exception of the over-the-shoulder shots, you almost never shoot any subject from opposite sides. Opposing shots can easily confuse the audience because what was on the left in one shot is suddenly on the right in the other. The action that a moment ago was flowing to "stage right" is suddenly moving to "stage left." Consider, for example, a shot of a race car crossing the finish line as viewed from a camera in the grandstand. It is speeding to the right. If you switch to a shot of the same car viewed from the island at the center of the track, the car will be speeding to the left. Did the driver turn around? Is this another car, and is a collision about to occur? Where am I (the viewer)? Similarly, as a performer exits through a doorway, walking to the right, when the camera outside the room picks her up, the performer must still be traveling to the right. Even though the performer may be walking mostly away from you in the first shot and mostly toward you in the second shot, still the flow of travel in both cases is essentially to the right. To have the transition appear otherwise would momentarily confuse the viewers.

One way to avoid perplexing camera viewpoints is to think in terms of angles as shown in Figure 11–2. Two cameras can shoot a subject from 60° apart, from 90° apart, or even from 120° apart. Beyond that, as the angle between cameras stretches to 180°, the risk of confounding the audience's sense of direction increases.

Another way to avoid opposing shots is to draw a mental line straight through the center of the stage or performance area. Professionals call this the VECTOR LINE. The cameras can work on one side of that line only, never on the other. Better yet, the cameras shouldn't even come near the imaginary line while shooting the performance.

What do you do in those rare cases when you *have* to shoot a subject from many different angles? First, you could move the camera while it's "on the air," arcing it (and your audience) around to the other side of the subject. Second, you could have the subject move past the camera as the camera pans, keeping the subject in sight. Third, you could use more than two camera angles to shoot the scene. For example, in Figure 11–2, if camera 1 were first shooting the scene, you could switch to camera 3 or 4. From either of those camera positions, you could later switch to position 5. From 5 you could later switch to position 6, and then from 6 switch back home to position 1. Each camera angle was within 120° of the previous one, but taken in steps, the angles totaled a full 360° sweep.

---

*Establishing shot Introductory shot showing viewers where the scene takes place.

Revelation Camera angle that hides something important and then reveals it for dramatic effect.

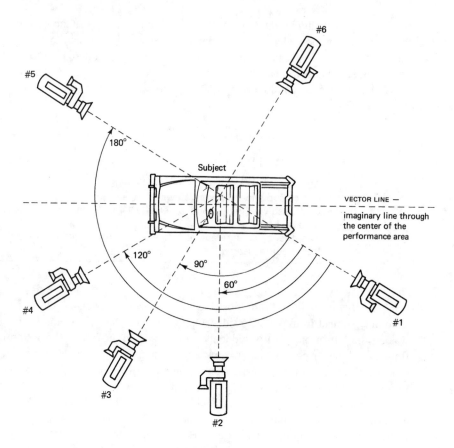

You can switch from cameras #1 to #2, #1 to #3, or #1 to #4, but switching from #1 to #5 or from #3 to #6, would confuse the viewer.

FIGURE 11–2 Camera angles and VECTOR LINE (as seen from above).

Establishing Shot.   Two more kinds of shots in the director's arsenal are ESTABLISHING SHOTS and REVELATIONS. An ESTABLISHING SHOT is usually a wide shot that introduces the viewer to the setting where the action is about to take place. It may be a shot of the village before we see the inn, or a shot of the inn before we see the lobby, or a wide shot of the lobby before we meet the innkeeper. It may be a shot of the patient on the operating table before we see the tonsillectomy. Whatever the ESTABLISHING SHOT, it sets the stage for the program so that the viewers have an idea of what to expect. Without the ESTABLISHING SHOTS of the inn or its lobby, the viewers—instead of observing the content of the opening scene—may be asking themselves, Is this a home? Is this a tavern? Is this a city hotel or a country motel? Is this today or forty years ago? In the case of the tonsillectomy, the audience of medical students may be wondering, Is this patient a child or an adult? What are the operating conditions? The answers to all these questions *may* become apparent as the show progresses, but it's more efficient to sweep them all out of the way with a moment's ESTABLISHING SHOT.

A REVELATION does just the opposite. Something is purposely omitted from the scene and is later revealed to surprise the audience. For example, we are watching the end of the guided tour at the city zoo. The camera slowly zooms out from a close-up of the tour guide's talking face to reveal that he is behind bars, and on the cage door the sign reads "Tour guide—please do not feed." Another example would be an opening close-up of a news reporter picking up a teddy bear from beneath a wooden plank. As she begins to speak, the camera draws back to a long shot, revealing earthquake desolation in the background. Here, for dramatic purposes, visual curiosity is piqued and then satisfied with a revelation.

THE SKILLFUL DIRECTOR

Although camera techniques and picture composition sound as if they're the cameraperson's business and not the director's, *everything* in a TV production is the director's business. He or she must be fully aware of the various camera angles and how they will fit together into the final production. It is poetry of cooperation to watch a TV director DISSOLVE from one camera shot to another while the first camera is defocusing its shot and the second camera is focusing on something else. To work smoothly, all things have to happen exactly at the same time and in perfect harmony. And when its done smoothly, the production elements are nearly invisible to the viewer. Invisibility is the key.

The good director focuses the viewer's attention on the story, not on production techniques. Camera angles and transitions should happen without the viewer being aware of them. The director uses these tools to communicate a message to the viewer's subconscious. This method of communication is one of the reasons that television is such a powerful medium. You can *show* the viewer something. You can let the viewer *hear* a conversation. You can add a musical background to create a mood. You can adjust the lighting to reinforce the mood. You can add sound effects to make the environment more convincing. Already you're "messaging" the viewer in five different ways, and still you have more tricks up your sleeves. Camera angles and transitions from shot to shot give the director two more doorways to the viewer's mind, or heart, or conscience.

It's no wonder that television, when skillfully executed, can make a nation riot, or laugh, or weep.

 **Mini Review**

- Keep all cameras to one side of the vector line.
- Use an establishing shot to orient the viewer to the time and place of the scene.
- The director is responsible for all aspects of the TV production.
- Television communicates to many levels of the viewer's consciousness. A combination of sounds, lighting, music, and effects can work together to create a powerful message.

12

TV TALENT

By *talent*, we mean interviewers, guests, hosts, performers, actors, instructors—anybody on the screen—and not necessarily the prodigies among them, either. As the teleproducer, your job is to help the "talent" perform at their very best. You may need to dress them, rehearse them, comfort them, educate them, and sometimes pacify them. And just when you get used to the pressure behind the scenes and are questioning the quality of your performers, *presto*, you get dragged into the production and have to perform yourself. This will keep you humble, because performing isn't easy either.

BEING THE TALENT

Whether you happen to be the talent or whether you've been given the job of transforming your college president from a blob into a smooth-talking, confident William F. Buckley, there are a number of guidelines a performer needs to know in order to "look good" on television. Table 12–1 summarizes the most important of these.

The sections that follow will go into deeper detail about clothing, mannerisms, and self-conduct during a TV interview. The last subject (interviews) is often taught in expensive workshops around the country. It is given to executives who may be cornered by television reporters and will need to present a good image for their company.

Eyes

It has been said that 40 percent of the message is verbal and that the other 60 percent is nonverbal. The audience will unconsciously be studying your eyes in search for confidence, credibility, and enthusiasm.

If you are addressing the audience, you should look directly at the camera. You're allowed to blink (after all, you're not in a trance) and occasionally glance at notes or at something you're holding. You may feel that the unbroken gaze at the lens looks strange (you wouldn't consider staring at a person that way), but on TV it looks normal and is preferred. Don't be afraid to smile, raise your eyebrows, or to change your facial expression—you're not a zombie.

If you're being interviewed, you should have 90 percent eye contact with the interviewer. This concentration will make you appear interested and attentive. Even when the interviewer is talking,

---

*Talent Performer, actor, newscaster, etc.
Interrupted feedback Intercom system that feeds the program's sound (music and voices) to the talent's ear; the program can be interrupted, however, by a private announcement—perhaps a command from the director—directly from the control room.

396

TABLE 12–1 Basic Do's and Don'ts of Being the Talent

1. *Dress right.* Avoid herringbones and small checks (they turn rainbow colors on TV). Don't wear pure white (it dazzles the camera) or pure black or navy (it disappears into a black blot on the screen). Avoid shiny jewelry and digital watches that go "beep" every half hour. Check for combed hair, straight ties, flat collars, zipped flies.

2. *Be punctual.* Time is very expensive in a TV studio.

3. *Be attentive.* Excessive background chatter while the director or others are trying to communicate is punishable by strangulation.

4. *Speak with normal volume during the voice check.* Say your ABCs or something. This lets the audio operator know how far to turn up your mike's volume.

5. *Don't acknowledge cues.* When the floor manager points to you (which means "You're on!"), don't nod or say "uh-huh" before you begin. Or when she holds up three fingers to indicate that you have three minutes left, don't interrupt yourself and look at her with a "uh, three more minutes, huh?" Simply act your role, not revealing any awareness of the behind-the-scene activity.

6. *Be aware of the camera.* If you're talking to your audience, talk to the camera lens. Not to the floor director next to the camera. Not to the studio monitor with that big close-up of your smiley kisser. Not into the great televoid of the studio. Not at the floor, your microphone, or the desk. Don't read your notes. Talk to the camera lens.

   And which camera might that be, you ask, flanked by two of the silent beasts? The one with the red tally light that's lit. What if the light goes out, indicating that another camera's on? Don't look around until you find the other and say, "Oh, there you are!" Simply shift your gaze to something else for a second (such as your notes or another guest) and then look straight at the other camera and continue without skipping a beat.

   If not talking directly to the audience (such as in a drama or interview), *do not* look at the camera or anything else behind the scenes. Ignore the camera if it moves to another position. Be oblivious to the floor manager's tripping over a stack of cue cards. Don't look up if a studio light burns out. Disregard the camera operator who starts giggling. *They don't exist.* What's happening on stage is all that exists.

7. *Restrain your movements.* There's no need to project your voice or to dramatize actions as on a stage. The mike will pick up a whisper or a sigh. The camera will reveal a flick of the eyebrow.

   Give warning cues before you move. If you jump up from your chair during a close-up, the audience will see a nice crotch shot. Rather, tentatively move as if to rise, and then rise slowly. This, the camera can follow. When holding things to be displayed, move them slowly.

8. *Respond immediately to the floor manager's cues.* If the floor manager, for instance, moves a finger across her neck in a slicing move, the show is over, with or without you. Say goodnight, Gracie.

9. *Sit slightly forward in your chair.* So that you look interested and not too casual.

10. *Speak clearly and distinctly.* Who wants to listen to a mumble-mouth?

11. *Use your hands, but only to express ideas.* The hands will help you communicate. But fussy, nervous movements (finger picking, palm rubbing, pencil tapping, smoking—yes, *smoking*) will catch the viewers' eyes and distract them from your message.

you never know whether a camera is looking at you. As soon as you look away from the interviewer, you run the risk of being caught by the camera. This advice also goes for when the interviewer opens or closes the program. Watch the interviewer, not the lighting grid, not the antics of the stagehands. Glue your eyes to the interviewer until the director calls "Cut."

Avoid slightly off-camera looks. Review Figure 1–1.

Chairs

For performers to look comfortable, they need comfortable chairs. A good TV studio will invest in several matching, soft chairs with armrests. These chairs should not rock or swivel, because that's what nervous performers will do in them, making your audience seasick. If swivel chairs are all that are available, the talent should plant one or two elbows on a table or desk in front of them to impede their natural inclination to rock or swivel.

Again, 60 percent of the message is nonverbal body language. As the guest, you should lean forward in your chair to show involvement and interest. This stance also creates an eye-to-eye appearance of equality between you and the interviewer. It also allows a tighter shot because both of your heads are closer together.

Each guest's chair should be at a 45° angle from the interviewer (review Figure 1–4). This causes you to lean slightly to one side, resting your elbow on the armrest, freeing your hands for gesturing rather than white-knuckling the chair.

It is best to sit in the front part of the chair. This stance shows involvement while avoiding the Lincoln Memorial image—or just the opposite, a slouch. Review Figure 1–2.

Hands

Except for wild waving, gestures are constructive. They look natural and illustrate your speech. More important, gestures will take your hands away from twisting your rings, tugging at your earlobes, gripping your knees, or grasping your chair arms as if you were riding a tilt-a-whirl.

Legs

Avoid splayed legs. Use the "finishing school" position, crossing your legs at the ankles.

Crossing your legs at the knees may be all right, if room permits. Generally, you are in such close quarters that if you and another person cross your legs normally with the dangling foot closest to the other person, your feet will tangle. If you cross your legs so that your foot is aimed *away* from the other person, your body language will appear to be defensive.

Voice

Your voice naturally tightens when you're tense. To relax your voice,

- Arrive at the shoot early. Hurrying and worrying about arriving in time will rattle you.
- Drink some tea, juice, or water. Don't drink milk; it clogs the nasal passages and is sticky in the mouth. (And by the way, visit the bathroom; you know what nervousness does to the bladder.)
- Chant or hum low notes on the way to the shoot. This relaxes the back of the throat.

Clothes

Suits should be medium blue, brown, green, or charcoal gray. Solids look better than pinstripes. Avoid bright, saturated colors like red, orange, or yellow. Pastels are good.

The evils of stripes are shown in Figure 12–1 (see also back cover). Avoid them along with checks and herringbones.

Don't wear a white shirt. Pale blue or tan looks good.

Colored ties with conservative patterns look nice.

Vests look a bit formal, constricting TV talent like sausage casings.

Socks should reach halfway up the calf, covering the ankle.

Women appear best in a conservative dress or a good regulation business suit with a little jewelry and a scarf for color, perhaps tucked into a jacket so as not to look too busy around the face. Avoid pants and blouse outfits unless you wish to look like a *Wheel of Fortune* contestant. Avoid stripes and loud, bold, or vibrant patterns.

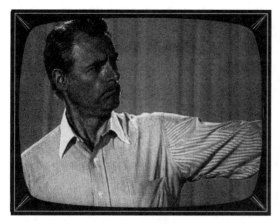

Lines of moiré dance across sleeve . . .   . . . as it moves

FIGURE 12–1 Avoid striped shirts and herringbone jackets as they cause moiré and flashing rainbow colors (see also back cover).

Avoid bow-tied blouses—they look too much like a uniform. A blouse should not be bright or white; deep or pale tones are better.

Simple pumps look more feminine than boots on camera.

Jewelry is always a problem because it flashes. Network TV cameras costing $40,000 to $100,000 can handle the glint of dazzling diamonds, but the lower-priced educational and industrial cameras cannot. So avoid diamonds and other shiny things. Pearls, gold button earrings, and small gold neck chains should work out okay. Avoid dangling earrings that waggle and distract the audience.

At all costs, avoid black and loud plaids unless you're a nun or a comedian.

 Mini Review

- If you are addressing the camera, look directly at the camera lens. If you are interacting with other talent on stage, maintain eye contact with them and *don't* look at the camera.
- Sit upright and appear alert.
- In your clothing, avoid stripes, herringbones, solid blacks or whites, and bright, saturated colors. Pastels and medium solid colors look good.
- Avoid shiny jewelry.

Getting Your Cues

The floor manager or a camera operator will probably give you your cue to start performing or to wrap up the show. Figure 12–2 shows what some of these cues look like.

Remember, don't acknowledge the cues with a nod or any other noticeable reaction; just do what the cues advise.

More opulent studios have little earphones and a system called IFB (INTERRUPTED FEEDFACK) that allows the director or someone in the control room to give you verbal cues while you're on the air. It's hard for amateurs to hold a decent conversation while someone's speaking in their ears, but with practice, the two of you (the director and the talent) can get quite good at it. The movie *Broadcast News*

Cue	[Picture]	Meaning	Hand Signal
Stand by		Show is about to start.	Point finger at the ceiling.
Cue.		Begin performing.	Point toward the talent. If the talent is to address a different camera, point to that camera.
Speed up.		Accelerate what you are doing. You are going too slowly.	Crank finger forward, much like the "cuckoo" gesture.
Stretch.		Slow down. Too much time left. Keep talking.	Pretend to stretch a rubber band.
One minute left.		Finish what you are doing. One minute 'til the end.	Hold one finger in the air for a time for the talent to notice it (but don't expect the person to acknowledge it while performing). Holding up 2 fingers means 2 minutes left, etc.

FIGURE 12–2 Floor manager cues.

Cue	[Picture]	Meaning	Hand Signal
Cut.		The show is ending now. Stop immediately.	Slice your throat with your finger.
Walk.		Move in direction shown.	Let your fingers do the walking.
Stop.		Go no further. Stay put.	Hold your hand out as a traffic cop does.
Speak up.		You're talking too softly.	Cup hand behind ear.
Get closer to mike.		The talent is too far from his or her mike.	Move palm of hand towards lips.

FIGURE 12–2 *Continued*

Cue	[Picture]	Meaning	Hand Signal
Look here.		Look into this camera.	Point toward your camera lens. To encourage the talent to speak to another camera, point to *its* lens.
Smile.		You're too serious; smile. (Many amateur performers are nervous and forget to use their charm.)	Smile broadly and point to your mouth.
Relax (not standardized).		Relax. (Many amateurs need help loosening up. Do this only before a show.)	Cock your ears, wave your fingers, cross your eyes, and stick out your tongue.

FIGURE 12–2 *Continued*

demonstrated an excellent example of IFB in use during a news program. Having been on both sides of an IFB in shows, I can personally agree with the comment in the movie that the sensation of having someone "in your head" or being "inside someone's head" during a show is incredibly intimate, even spooky.

PROMPTING METHODS

The director has four choices when it comes to putting words in your mouth:

1. Have you memorize the script
2. Have you ad-lib loosely from an outline
3. Dub in narration
4. Have you read your lines during the performance

The first option is fine if you're an actor who has the time to learn your lines and the skill to recite them with spontaneity. Option 2 works well if you're a talented subject-matter expert working with a RUNDOWN sheet. There's likely to be a lot of chaff in such a production, though. Option 3 needs a lot of visuals and may still be dull. Option 4 allows for careful scripting, little memorization, very little chaff to edit out, and a "live" performer on the screen rather than a disembodied voice. All your director has to do is find a way to put words into your mouth so that you don't "look like" you're reading.

Teleprompting Systems

Costing $3000 to $5000, these devices are generally attached to the cameras and display your script near the lens. Your script is typed on a computer. When the text is rolled on the computer screen, it can also be fed to another computer screen attached to the camera. Other systems scan-convert the computer image to video and send the text to a TV monitor attached to the camera, as was shown in Figure 1–8. Older systems have your script typed on a roll of narrow paper, and then the paper is slipped into a motorized feeder that moves the paper under a simple TV camera.

For portable shoots, there are lightweight TELEPROMPTERS that use laptop computers and LCD monitor screens attached to the camera.

The speed of the text is controlled by computer mouse or with a handheld device that can advance the text slowly, quickly, or however it is needed. You can even stop the text or run it backwards (not recommended while the talent is trying to read it).

To make it possible for you to look directly at the camera lens while simultaneously reading script, the video wizards designed a mirror system (review Figures 1–7 and 1–8).

One thing about TELEPROMPTERS—Murphy's 99th law states that the TELEPROMPTER will fail as soon as you're on the air live. The only insurance against such a disaster is to hang onto a copy of the script to refer to until the prompter catches up.

The script is handy for other purposes too. When the director switches from camera 1 to camera 2, you can simply look down at the script, read for a moment, and then look up at the second camera. It all looks natural. In newscasts, the script becomes a prop. The audience expects a news report to be *read*, not *recited*. The occasional glance down gives the news report a sense of credibility. If you don't believe this fake realism is important, think back to the last editorial reply you saw, with a non-professional who read unblinking from the TELEPROMPTER as if hypnotized.

Spoken text usually flows at the rate of about 150 words per minute, but there's a lot of variance from that number. Beginners feel pressured by the TELEPROMPTER because they think they have to keep up with it. Just the opposite should be true, for the prompter is operated by a human being somewhere, rolling it (hopefully) at just the right speed to keep the spoken lines about one-third down the screen. To dispel your fears, try out the prompter, first speaking slowly and then quickly, and watch what happens. Eureka! You'll discover that the TELEPROMPTER follows *you*, not the other way around.

 Mini Review

- Don't acknowledge cues; simply carry them out.
- Learn to trust the teleprompter; it will move at whatever speed you read it.

Cue Cards

Irreverently aliased "idiot cards," these two-foot by three-foot posterboards covered with felt-pen printing are the backbone of educational and industrial TV prompting. If you prepare your own CUE CARDS, number the cards to keep them in order. (You can imagine what happens to your show when

---

*Teleprompter Device that sits near the camera lens and allows the performer to read the text while his or her eyes appear to be looking at the camera lens (the viewer).

*Cue card Posterboard with large writing on it to prompt the talent.

Cue card holder Person who holds up the cue cards where the talent can read them.

Crib notes.

they are presented out of order.) The CUE CARD HOLDER (catchy job title) holds the cards near the taking camera's lens and to the side so he or she can read along with you and know when to change cards (review Figure 1–6). Since the cards are not *in front* of the cameras lens, you will have that familiar off-center stare during close-ups.

Crib notes

The actor opens the refrigerator door and secretly reads a little notation there, pulls out a milk carton, and reads something taped to the back while pouring the contents into a bowl. Next, he reads from the tabletop while stirring the mixture and then reads a little more of his script among the pages of his cookbook as he checks his recipe. Popping the mixture in the oven, the actor reads a hidden note tucked inside the oven door and turns and reads the final closing from his cuff. It can be done, but it's hard not to have the audience notice.

TV MAKEUP

Television is a close-up medium. It emphasizes facial characteristics, intensifies colors, and magnifies details—including blemishes.

Males tend to think makeup, even for TV, is "sissy" or false. They may prefer to "be themselves." They may not realize that the hot lights will bring shiny oils and perspiration to their faces. Remember that the camera accents natural facial shine or discolorations, making you *not* look like yourself. Makeup helps counteract the camera's infidelity. Without it, you won't look your best (unless you're making up for *Dracula* or *Night of the Living Dead* characterizations). Makeup is an important element in your metamorphosis from "average street person" to "confident professional."

Still, your attention to makeup will vary with the complexity of the operation. A professional studio will employ a makeup artist. Professional actors will usually know how to apply their own makeup and may come appropriately equipped. Tiny seat-of-the-pants TV studios may never bother with makeup—they have their hands full keeping the recorders running and their wires untangled. Between these extremes we have the situation where anyone with a bottle of talc becomes the "expert," responsible for everyone's makeup.

A woman who has been applying makeup to her own face since adolescence can probably make herself up better than anybody else can. Nevertheless, makeup that looks fine on the street may make her look like a hooker on the TV screen. So before she proceeds making up her face, she should adjust her techniques to the color TV medium:

1. Any greens and bluish tones (and dark reds are bluish) are accentuated by the camera. Avoid them. Light reds, yellows, tans, browns, and dark grays are preferred. Be careful with orange; it sometimes shows up yellow on camera.
2. Avoid heavy shading such as dark eye shadow or dark rouge.
3. Avoid brightly colored lipstick or eye shadow.
4. Avoid lip gloss. Blot lipstick to dull the shine.

To really be sure your makeup will look good on TV, get in front of a camera under the studio lights and take a look at yourself on a monitor.

The basic TV studio makeup kit would include the following:

1. A bottle of witch hazel, alcohol, or other astringent to clean your face before applying makeup
2. Cotton balls to apply the astringent
3. A small natural (or sea) sponge to apply whichever type of makeup you choose
4. A compact of translucent powder used to dull shiny noses, foreheads, and bald pates
5. Mirror, tissues, hand towels, soap, and water for the removal of makeup

Pancake, a popular type of makeup, comes in a dry form and is applied with a damp sponge; it washes off easily with water. Mehron Star Blend, Max Factor, and Steins brands are found under Theatrical Supply in your Yellow Pages. Mehron Star Blend, for instance, is a solid cake that comes in a jar. It comes in shades of TV4 (the lightest) to TV10. TV4, TV5, and TV6 will cover most situations.

More advanced makeup kits may contain moist/dry eye shadow, eyeliner, eyebrow pencil, tinted or translucent powder, puffs and brushes, blushes or rouges in assorted colors, lipstick, cleansing cream, applicator sponges, crepe wool, mascara, false eyelashes, hair whitener, spirit gum, nose wax, moisturizers, stipple sponges, and facial toners. Student kits, like the one in Figure 12–3, cost about $25.

Beards

Men appearing on camera should bring a shaving kit for "touch-ups" or in case the shooting runs late.

Even after shaving, most men have a darker tone to their beardline. The camera will perceive this as bluish. A slightly orange creme base makeup will neutralize the blue tone. Don't use too much, or you'll start to look like an orange.

A thin coat of the creme makeup applied with a stipple sponge and powdered lightly, with the excess powder removed with a damp sponge, should dispel the Homer Simpson beardline.

Television makeup kit (Courtesy of Bob Kelly Cosmetics).

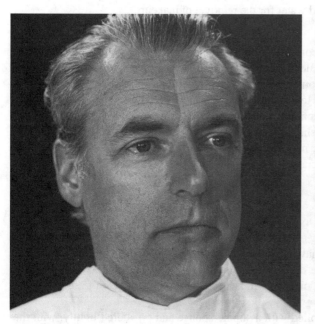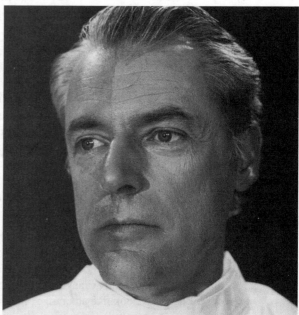

Base makeup neutralizes beardline, smooths features, and hides blemishes. A little powder reduces shine.

 **Mini Review**

- Makeup is sometimes necessary to counteract some of the shortcomings of television. Rather than making you look "fake," makeup can make you look more like your "real" self.
- Men's beards appear bluish and often need a thin coat of orange creme and/or powder to restore the natural skin color on television.

Powder

Powder dulls shine. If applied over a creme base makeup, it sets the base to keep it from smearing while dulling the natural facial sheen. Males should leave a little sheen for a more natural look. Since cake makeups already have a matte finish, they don't need powder.

When powder is applied around your eyes, it should be done gently so that you don't squint. Squinting creates creases, which the powder may miss.

Other Details

Your nails should be cleaned and manicured if they will appear in close-ups.

Hair tends to get oily quickly under hot lights. If you perform often, you will need to shampoo often.

Receding hairlines can be filled in a little with the help of a sharp eyebrow pencil and short feather-like strokes.

Children generally look fine without makeup.

If shooting will continue over several days, you'll want to look the same each day. Take notes on what colors were used and where. Perhaps have someone take a Polaroid snapshot of you for reference.

THE INTERVIEW

The interview is a quick and inexpensive way to explain something without a disembodied narrator or a lecturer's stilted, talking face. The interview program is visually simple to do, though somewhat bland. The director may try to spice up the image by moving the interview to the expert's office, laboratory, workbench, or even outdoors—someplace associated with the expert's or the program's subject. Not only is this visually stimulating, but your guests are more at ease in familiar surroundings. The viewers may also get a better sense of your guests' personalities, associating them with their surroundings. And last, the surroundings offer the director the chance to shoot some good cutaways to be used to cover the host's flubbed questions or the guests rambling answers.

How to Interview Someone

Your object is to systematically extract information from someone while eliminating irrelevant information. Here are some methods for charming an interviewee into willing submission while getting your story. Some of these techniques seem to contradict each other. That's okay. Different situations call for different strokes.

1. *Lead with a question that the guest will enjoy answering.* Guests rarely walk out on an interview that's underway, so snag them first with a plum and then work up to the controversial or hard-to-answer questions.

2. *Listen intently and react to your question's answer.* Simply reading a list of prepared questions bores your guest and your viewers alike. To seem alive, the *interview should seem like a discussion.* That means listening, reflecting, restating, and reacting to the guest's response. Try to summarize key points to improve the audience's retention of the facts. Authenticate and substantiate points made by the guest. Illustrate your guest's ideas and include anecdotes; this not only shows interest in the subject but gives your guest a few seconds to think and relax. A relaxed guest with time to think will give you more reasonable and useful answers, making your interview more instructive.

But don't go too far with this process. You don't want to upstage guests by exhibiting superior knowledge of a subject or by performing verbal gymnastics around them. You simply want a stimulating discussion.

3. *Don't interrupt.* Ask only as many questions as are absolutely necessary to get the required information. Then shut up and let the guests talk. If they pause for a moment, don't jump in right away. Given a chance, they'll continue. *Nod your head,* maintain eye contact, and smile to show agreement, fascination, or surprise *in nonverbal ways.* This sort of reaction not only keeps guests talking but gives them confidence and works just as well as words at showing your interest. You won't believe the efficiency and effectiveness of this method until you've tried it.

4. *Set the tone of the interview.* Enthusiasm, like measles, is contagious. The interviewee often assumes the style of the interviewer during the course of questioning. If the interviewer is low-key and serious, the guest may gravitate to a somber, quiet monotone. If the interviewer is bright-eyed and bushy-tailed, the guest is likely to respond similarly with glint of eye and bush of tail.

5. *Be yourself.* If you try to sound like Walter Cronkite or Don Pardo, you're going to sound like a Walter Cronkite or Don Pardo imitation. Your audience will be distracted, if not entertained, by your attempted impersonation, and they won't focus on your guest as they should.

6. *Extinguish bad habits.* They quickly become tedious on TV and will drive your audience crazy. First to go should be the phrase "y'know." It not only sounds uneducated; it communicates no useful information. One way to unlearn this habit is to hold a conversation with a friend who's equipped with a dusty vacuum cleaner bag. Tell her to swat you in the chin with it every time you say "y'know." Works wonders. Next, get rid of "uh huh." Replace it with a nod. While you're at it, junk the "uhhh" you string between phrases and sentences. Also, don't end sentences with "and so on and so forth." And last, watch out for the "echo" syndrome, where you habitually repeat the guest's last phrase:

Guest: ". . . and the empty bottles make nice gifts."
Host: ". . . empties make nice gifts, huh?"

7. *Don't ask questions that require only a yes or no answer.* If you do, that's what you'll get. Then what do you say? Ask, instead, open-ended questions. Replace "Weren't you the first . . ." with "How did you become the first . . ." or "What got you interested in . . ." or "When did you first discover you could . . .?"

8. *Ask simple, not compound questions.* Compound questions are likely to have just the first or last part answered. Questions with double and triple negatives will simply boggle the mind. With long lead-ins, the audience is likely to forget the beginning of the question by the time they reach the end.

Reporter: "In the light of recent statistical reports indicating a rising trend in manufacturing-related unemployment and economic difficulties for American car dealers, do you oppose discouraging Congress from trying to stop the amendment to abolish the sanctions against foreign imports, and if so, why, and if not, what should be done?"

Congressman: "Yes, no, sometimes, and maybe."

9. *Do your homework.* Prepare for the interview by studying the guest's background and subject matter. Read his book; see her film. Not only will you be able to hold an intelligent conversation with guests in their areas of expertise, but you and your guests will probably enjoy each other more. And that enjoyment is what makes an interview come alive.

10. *If the guest's answer is unclear, rephrase the question and ask it again.* You must have asked the question for a purpose. What good is a nonanswer or circumlocution? Viewers dislike watching politicians slither out of direct answers to an interviewer's question. The interviewer, if given the opportunity, should restate the question, forcing an answer, or at least an ungraceful reslither.

11. *Save the guest who is in trouble.* The program is a teamwork affair. If the guest goes down the drain, so does the show. Try to present guests in their best light, whether they deserve it or not. For example, Simon Showoff, a self-proclaimed expert who obviously oversold himself and is now starting to look foolish, needs a bridge to another subject. One escape is to seek out some small thread of truth in Simon's dumb statements (there's usually a thread somewhere) and follow up on it:

Simon: " . . . and the kids today are all hoodlums."

Host: "Some kids seem to be. What do you think society is doing to change that?" Or . . . "Didn't Socrates say the same thing about youth in his generation?"

What do you do with Paralyzed Polly? She was a chatterbox before the cameras went on; now she's speechless. She's probably nervous. Try to lead with a simple question (but not a short-answer one) to make the guest experience some success. Try to center on the guest's pet peeve or some other favorite topic. As she begins to open up, encourage her with nods and smiles.

12. *Prep the interviewee.* In some cases, the director may want to edit together several testimonies, leaving out the interviewer's questions. One advantage to this format is that the interviewer, absent from the shot, isn't there to draw attention away from the response. Another advantage is that "stand-alone" responses can be PARALLEL-CUT or JUXTAPOSED (described further in Chapter 14) without the distractive repetition of the interviewer's questions. A possible side benefit is that anybody can ask the questions off-camera; it doesn't have to be the same interviewer throughout the shooting. And even the same interviewer doesn't have to dress exactly the same for each shoot.

 Mini Review

- To be a good interviewer, be a good listener.
- Ask questions that require full-sentence answers rather than simply a yes or a no.

Back to prepping. For the preceding format to work, the talent's answers must explain themselves, having the question built into the answer. The interviewees must be told to *load the first part of each answer with a strong topic sentence,* using basic subject-predicate syntax. Each sentence should contain useful information and be able to stand alone. Ideally, it should sound quotable.

Parallel cutting   Editing raw footage so that similar or parallel actions are seen one after another, making it look like "everybody's doing it."

Juxtaposition   Editing together opposites, such as opposing views or conflicting responses to a question.

For example, answers like "When I was about fifteen years old, in school," are useless. You want answers like "I first became aware of my ability to imitate gastrointestinal sounds when I was about fifteen years old, in school." Complete responses like this may now carry the show on their own.

Being Interviewed

There's a knock at the door. You answer it in your bathrobe and slippers with the heel that's split apart. Mike Wallace and the *60 Minutes* camera team blind you with photofloods, shove a mike up your nose, and ask, "When did you stop beating your wife?" You smile at their impossible-to-answer question and respond, "When she started taking bridge lessons. Now she beats me all the time." Chalk up five points for the interviewee. Other helpful hints:

1. *Make certain you understand the question.* It's easier to answer a question you understand, and your response is more credible when it answers the question directly. Have the interviewer rephrase the question if necessary.

2. *Keep one or two good lines in your pocket.* If you expect to be interviewed on the 6 o'clock news, chances are they're not going to show five minutes of you. More likely thirty seconds. Consider what a newsperson or interviewer is likely to ask. Then think up and memorize a witty, colorful, one-line statement that either deals directly with the subject or sidesteps it gracefully. The rest of the interview may end up in the editing raw footage pile, but your pithy one-liner will be too tempting for the director to pass up.

This, in fact, is a way to outmaneuver a manipulative or biased reporter. Despite the reporter's efforts to corner you into making *his* point, you can turn the tables by having a spicy, quotable statement, fact, or anecdote that makes *your* point. How can an editor discard the juicy nuggets while keeping in all the dull drivel that actually did tell the story? In fact, you might be able to gloss over the reporter's question with a plain vanilla answer and then launch into the point *you* want to make, using rum mocha chip language. Guess which will end up on the air? Politicians are famous for answering questions nobody ever asked.

3. *Be brief.* NBC News correspondent Michael Jensen once said, "TV news is to journalism what bumper stickers are to philosophy." There is generally no time for follow-ups to your answers, no amplification, no clarification. Whether it's panel discussions or news reporting, TV is hit-and-run. So make a positive point with a short declarative statement; then run.

4. *Don't fake an answer.* There's a saying, "If you can't dazzle them with brilliance, then baffle them with baloney." Well, phooey to that. If you don't know something, say so. No law says you have to know everything. Offer to find out the answer. Suggest someone else who does know the answer. And if you know the answer to a question but don't wish to divulge it, say, "I'm sorry, but that information is confidential right now," or something witty like "Would a gentleman kiss and tell?" Raise your own issues and answers with "I'm not ready to answer that question yet, but I can tell you this. . . ."

Another technique, useful in panel discussions, is to turn a difficult question over to a colleague. To give the colleague some time to think (a much-appreciated courtesy) and the director and cameraperson time to move to the other person, you might first announce, "I believe that's a question that Mr. Pevar can answer better than I can," turning toward him while finishing your sentence.

5. *Use "people talk," not industry jargon.* If your viewers are unfamiliar with your field, you won't gain credibility with long words and incomprehensible concepts. Use simple language, analogies, and concrete examples to illustrate your point. Don't call something a "tertiary propulsion module" if you can call it a backup rocket.

6. *Pay attention to the interviewer.* First, a discussion between two people is more interesting than a discussion between one-and-one-half people. Second, your wandering eyes will look shifty and evasive on camera.

7. *Avoid repeating negative words like "failed" or "couldn't" or "didn't."* It sounds too much like a lawyer's cross-examination.

8. *Remain cool when harangued.* Interviewers sometimes, and studio audiences often, can get pretty testy. They can ask venomous questions that are 99 percent complaint and 1 percent query. Now is the time to be cool, courteous, and superpleasant. You'll lose a lot of points (and surely your job as company spokesperson) by becoming hotheaded and responding in kind. A sense of humor helps immeasurably.

THE TALENT IS THE SHOW

Just a final note: The vitality and color *you* bring to the show will engage your audience. Take the time to think through your role in the show. What can you do to make your behavior fit the objectives of the show? Television tends to exaggerate, so if you're a dull character, you'll be even duller on the TV screen. If you're vivacious, you'll appear a bit manic on the screen. Be aware that whatever you *think* you're doing, that might not be how it's coming across on the screen. Keep an ear open for advice from the director, who, after all, is judging you only by what he or she hears and sees in the TV monitor.

 Mini Review

- If you're going to be interviewed, prepare in advance one or two succinct and colorful responses to anticipated questions.
- Be brief.
- Stay cool.
- Be interesting.

---

13 ON-LOCATION SHOOTING

Imagine yourself watching a typical interview show. Yadda, yadda, yadda, they drone. Not very exciting.

Okay, new scenario. Same talent, same drivel, but we add some shots taken outside the studio. Voilá, professional-looking drivel. The vast wasteland of talk television becomes punctuated with *movement*, *adventure*, and beseems a bit more informative.

On-location footage allows the director to take the audience places, not just describe them. It is the essence of TV news and documentaries. In fact, most professional television involves a *small* amount of studio production—usually introductions and segues—and a large amount of on-location footage.

USING ON-LOCATION FOOTAGE IN YOUR PRODUCTION

On-location footage can be used in three ways:

1. Silent images
2. Total cutaways with sound
3. Studio voice-over with background sound from the tape

Silent Images

In the first instance, the studio talent describes the scene: "Here is where the whoopie cushions are hermetically sealed and labeled for distribution. Next, they move down the assembly line. . . ."

For the preceding scene to occur on schedule, during the show the following events must happen like clockwork:

1. Someone on the production team (the videotape operator, probably) must load the pretaped sequence into a videocassette player and cue it up to the start of the scene.

2. Next, the operator backs up the tape to about five seconds *before* the start of the scene (so that the tape has a "running start" before the shots go "on the air"). He or she then STOPS the tape or leaves it in PAUSE, depending on how long it will be before it is used in the show (you can't leave the VCP in PAUSE longer than three minutes).

3. When the script gets near the spot where the tape will be introduced, the director calls "Ready to roll VT1" (or whatever), and the tape operator slips the machine into PAUSE. The TD finds the VT1 button on the switcher.

4. About five seconds before the tape will be used, the director calls "Roll tape," and the tape operator hits PLAY on VT1.

5. About three seconds after the tape operator starts the tape, the taped image stabilizes and the tape operator answers "Rolling."

6. About five seconds after the tape operator started the tape, assuming the tape image is stable on the VT1 monitor, the director calls "Take VT1," and the image shifts from the studio camera to the tape. Now the tape is being broadcast or recorded along with the studio sound, which may be the guest describing the scene.

7. The director must know when the scene ends, and when it approaches that point, he or she readies the TD and talent and cuts back to the studio camera.

8. The tape player is stopped.

And for any of the preceding events to transpire without a hitch,

1. The director (or someone) needs to know where the taped scene begins and ends.

2. The studio talent needs a TV monitor so that they can watch the scene to narrate it.

3. The whole tape playback system needs to be tried out before the show begins to make sure that the signals are passing correctly. (*One technical note*: Unless the switcher has built-in FRAME SYN-CRONIZERS, the VCP's signal must be sent through a TIME BASE CORRECTOR to synchronize the signal with the studio cameras.)

The point of this detailed explanation is that on-location shooting is just one step in a larger process, a complicated process in which many things can go askew. The final result, when it works right, is professional-looking TV, the seamless passage from one event or view to another. Since the playback process is complicated, it behooves the on-location shooter to "make the shots perfect," so that they play as expected. There may be no time during the studio production to make up for shots not included, shots taken poorly, shots that last too long or not long enough, shots that are too dark, or shots that have insufficient LEADER to allow the VTP to be backed up five seconds or so. The on-location shooter needs a clear understanding of what is wanted so that the footage comes back "perfect."

 Mini Review

- On-location footage can spice up studio interviews and talk shows.
- Weaving on-location footage into a live production requires significant advance preparation.
- The on-location shooter needs a clear understanding of how the director will use the footage so that the scene comes out the right length and covers the topic the right way.

Pretaped Segments with Sound

In this procedure, the scene cuts away from the studio entirely and the audience sees and hears the taped sequence. At the end of the sequence, we cut back to the studio.

Time base corrector   Electronic device to remove jitter and other timing abnormalities from a video signal, usually the signal from a VCP.

*Leader   Unrecorded space (from ten seconds to three minutes) at the beginning of a tape, often used to protect the actual program from threading damage. Also, unrecordable plastic tape attached to the beginnings of cassette rolls. In the case of on-location shots or shots that will be edited, leader also means five or more seconds of recorded video preceding and following the actual scene.

*Wild sound   Background sound without narration or performing going on. During editing, it can be mixed with the performers' sounds if they have to redo their lines in a quiet studio.

The taped sequence could have WILD SOUND—actual background sounds from the event—or it could have narration dubbed in, or it could be a combination of both.

The control room procedure is nearly the same as before except that the audio person turns up the sound from the tape and turns off the studio sound during the sequence. And since one more component (sound) is involved, there's one more thing to check and adjust before air time, and one more thing to go kaflooie during the show.

Studio Voice-over with Background Sound from the Tape

In this situation, the taped sequence plays with diminished sound while the talent discusses what's happening. The vestigial sound adds credibility and realism to the taped sequence:

"Here is where—BRRRT—whoopie cushions are—BRRRT—BRRRT—tested before being sent to—BRRRT—dealers throughout the country—BRRPSSSST—Oops, there's a bad one."

The studio procedure is the same as before except that the audio is more complicated: A proper mix of studio and taped sound must be found so that the taped sound doesn't upstage the live talent. And a mix of taped and live audio is one more component that can go amiss during the show.

Editing

All the aforementioned techniques apply to "live" TV production. TV news is produced this way. Even if the program is being taped, those techniques are quick and efficient; there's a lot of pressure to get everything right during the show, but when it's finished, *it's finished*. In the next chapter we'll explore editing a show in which all the taped segments are linked together, one at a time, to create the final tape.

 Mini Review

- On-location segments can be silent, or they can include sound that either takes the place of the studio sound or is mixed with the studio sound.
- Inserting pretaped sections into a live show may be difficult, but it is quick and efficient. The alternative is to edit the taped segments into the show.

SHOOTING ON LOCATION

Location shooting brings with it all the pleasures of camping out. You must remember to bring everything imaginable, or you'll end up with coffee but no coffeepot, a flashlight but no batteries, and perfume instead of insect repellent.

Preparations for a Local Shoot

The Northwest loggers had a saying: "Take time to sharpen your saw." If you ever expect to need your equipment in a hurry, take the time to pack it so that it is ready to go. Store things together, ready to carry away. Charge the batteries *first thing* after you return from an outing so that they will be ready if your next mission comes sooner than expected. Repair loose or broken parts or other equipment defects right away rather than "learning to live with them." Repair cables and plugs if they malfunction intermittently. In this way, you'll avoid having to run around wiggling and testing cables during a production. Keep the lenses and video heads clean. Leave a blank cassette in the camcorder at all times, ready to go. In short, be prepared.

Shooting on location.

What to Take with You

What you take is largely dictated by what you'll be doing. The watchword, nevertheless, is the same: Be prepared. For shooting about two hours of tape in the next town, one might bring the items listed in Table 13–1.

Some of these items may not apply to all productions and may be left behind. Location shooting just outside the studio may require bringing only a camcorder and tripod. The farther you stray from home base, however, the surer you must be that you have everything. If your shoot is part of a class exercise, your TV department may have a prepared kit of on-location video gear for you to sign out.

Before packing equipment for a journey of any importance, take this added precaution: *Connect all equipment together and make a one-minute sample tape. Next, play the tape to make sure everything works.* This is perhaps the most important step prior to going on location. This superfluous-sounding routine pays off in the long run! Most of the time, this testing procedure reveals no problems. About 20 percent of the time, it will. It's better to face your gremlins at the outset rather than getting bit by them on location. Also, when renting or borrowing equipment, it's smarter to discover missing or broken parts *before* you leave the premises—that is, before you accept total responsibility for them. You don't want to end up paying for parts *you* didn't lose or break.

 **Mini Review**

- Always keep your portable gear staged, batteries charged, and prepared for use at a moment's notice.
- Always test out your portable gear before taking it on location.

TABLE 13–1   What to Bring on Location

Items to Bring	Items to Bring as a Backup in Case Something Fails on Location
1 Camcorder, cassette, and carrying case.	1 additional camcorder if the shooting is very important. Shoot with both machines simultaneously, so that if the camera operator goofs up or the heads clog on one VCR during a shoot, the other will still catch the scene. Bring a complete set of accessories (batteries, tripod, tape) for the second machine. If the scenes aren't rare enough to require two-camera coverage but you're traveling a long way at some expense to do the shooting, bring a second camera anyway, and store it on the site. If the first machine fails, you'll have a backup with which to keep shooting.
1 3-hour battery.	1 additional 3-hour battery or 1 AC power supply. Either is needed in case the first battery dies prematurely or the shooting runs longer than expected.
6 half-hour cassettes in boxes.	4 extra half-hour cassettes in boxes. It doesn't cost anything to return with unused tape, but it is inexcusable to run out during a production. Having extra cassettes also makes it easier to categorize your shots during editing.
1 roll of masking tape and a *good* felt pen to label the tape boxes. Keeping track of (and not accidentally erasing) what you have is just as important as shooting it. The adhesive tape is also handy for unpredictable situations.	
1 portable tripod for each camcorder.	
1 lapel and 1 shotgun microphone with fifty feet of mike cable and an appropriate plug for the camcorder.	1 extra length of mike cable in case the first conks out.
1 pair of headphones with the proper plug for the camcorder. The headphones will permit you to accurately monitor audio during taping.	
1 thirty-foot headphone extension cord if the shotgun mike is to be aimed by a sound person who needs to hear what's being recorded.	1 spare earphone (a tiny one that fits in the camcorder carrying case).
2 portable lamps with tripods and barn doors.	2 spare bulbs for the lamps.
3 heavy-duty, grounded, multiple outlet extension cords. Two are for the lights; the third is for the camcorder if AC is used. The multiple outlets make it possible to power other accessories near the VCR (a TV monitor, a mixer, a lamp, or a battery charger).	2 extra extension cords. In case the first ones don't reach, these can be connected in series.
1 TV monitor/receiver with audio and video cables. This allows you to play back, with sound, the raw footage on site for you and others to evaluate.	RF generator and RF cable with a 75–300Ω adapter, in case you need to use someone else's TV set to view footage (i.e., the TV set in your motel room).
1 flashlight if auditorium-based shooting is necessary. The flashlight will help you see to find switches and sockets and to label the tape.	
1 set of close-up lens attachments, if appropriate.	
3 grounded AC plug adapters to allow you to use your three-prong AC plugs with wall sockets that have only two holes.	

TABLE 13–1 *Continued*

Items to Bring	Items to Bring as a Backup in Case Something Fails on Location
1 head-cleaning kit.	
1 audio kit, *if needed*. Kit includes a mixer, mixer batteries, mikes and cables, a cable going to the camcorder with the proper plug, assorted audio adapters, and an attenuator (in case you must record from someone's loudspeaker system).	
1 pad, pencil, and pen to take notes and sign forms.	
20 model release forms.	
1 copy of the script.	1 extra copy of the script.
1 enormous two-handled box to carry it all in.	Hernia insurance.

BASIC CAMCORDER OPERATION INSTRUCTIONS

If you (or your TV department) lost the instructions on how to operate the camcorder, here are the basics:

1. Assemble the parts if separated.
   a. Viewfinder (also plug it into the camcorder)
   b. Battery (also plug it into the camcorder)
   c. Microphone (also plug it into the camcorder)
   d. Tripod (if needed)
2. Press POWER (a light should go on).
3. Press EJECT (to open the cassette compartment).
4. Insert the cassette; close the compartment.
5. Remove the lens cap.
6. Look through the viewfinder. If you see an image, great. If not:
   a. Check for a CAMERA/VCR switch and turn it to CAMERA.
   b. Doublecheck that you have power. When in doubt about the battery, try plugging the AC power supply into a wall outlet and into the camcorder. If that brings the camcorder to life, perhaps your battery is dead and needs recharging.
7. If you have an earphone, plug it into the camcorder and then the other end in your ear (you can decide which end goes where) to check for sound.
8. Record a sample scene and play it back.
   a. Press and release the RECORD/PAUSE trigger to begin recording. Something in the viewfinder should light to verify you're recording.
   b. If your camcorder has automatic control of the iris and mike volume, you'll probably record satisfactory picture and sound. Sometimes you need to switch from AUTO to MAN to adjust these things manually for better results.
   c. Press and release the RECORD/PAUSE trigger to stop recording, then flip the CAMERA/VCR switch to VCR. Rewind the tape and play it. You'll see the picture in the viewfinder and hear the sound in the earphone—or—eject the tape and play it on another VCR.
9. If the tape plays okay, then rewind the tape and start over at step 3 and record for real.
10. If the camcorder is to be idle for 10 minutes or more, shut off its power to save-a-watt.
11. If the camcorder is to be idle for hours (like overnight), charge the batteries during this time. This assures they'll be "topped off" when you need them.
12. When done with the camcorder:
    a. Cap the lens.
    b. Remove your tape.
    c. Switch off the camcorder's power; remove the battery.
    d. Recharge the batteries.
    e. Disassemble (if necessary) the camcorder to repack it.

THE REMOTE SURVEY

Before trekking into the hinterlands with a crew and a ton of video gear, you may want to check out the site for suitability. The REMOTE SURVEY can save you a heap of headaches when it comes time to shoot. Here are some things to look for:

1. Where is the exact shooting location? Draw up precise directions to the site (to become the map for the crew to find the place).

2. Will there be any large distractions in the background (like a competing sponsor's billboard or ninety-nine kids screaming "hello" to Mommy)?

3. Is there a safe place to route your cables? Route them over doorways and tape them down on the floor to avoid trip-ups. Don't run your cables alongside electric power cables. The power may interfere with your signal. If you cross high-traffic points with your cables, put a carpet or mat over them.

4. Do you need to have parking reserved? Do you need admittance waivers (for sporting events, concerts, and the like)?

5. Are there machines nearby that generate audio and video interference, such as an x-ray machine, radar, ham radios, or high-tension power lines?

6. Do you need crowd control, "no parking" signs, areas roped off, traffic stopped?

7. Has anyone informed the company's or school's chief of security that you're coming? Do so personally. Perhaps the chief can arrange convenient parking spaces for you. Have security sign in your equipment if you want to avoid conflicts as you leave with it.

8. When do the employees change shifts? Will there be a giant turnover during your shoot?

Lighting

1. Where will the sun and shadows be during the shoot?

2. Do you have to shoot indoors with windows in the background? Can they be covered?

3. Where will the lighting instruments have to go? Is there power enough for them? Before you answer that question, consider the following: Who else, besides you, will be drawing power from those circuits at the same time?

Audio

1. Is there excessive ambient noise (machines, air conditioners, jet planes, typewriters, traffic)? Can any of this extraneous sound be silenced? Watch out for surprise sounds like intercom announcements or trash container pickups, especially those with trucks that go beep-beep-beep as they back up.

2. Can you get the mikes close enough to the talent? Lapel mikes are preferred in noisy environs.

3. If you are using a wireless microphone, is there interference from any electrical sources or competing transmitters? Try out the mike.

---

*Remote survey   Visit to a distant shooting location to determine production needs, strategy, and resources. Also, a written report of that survey.

*Release form   Legal document that someone signs, thereby granting you permission to videotape him or her and distribute the tape publicly.

Communications

The program usually falls apart when the director loses contact with the staff. Do you need an intercom, IFB, walkie-talkies, or cellular phones?

Release Forms

For classroom practice shoots, RELEASE FORMS aren't likely to be necessary. If your show is to be distributed, especially commercially, you had better get written permission from everyone involved before you take their pictures. Table 13–2 shows a sample RELEASE FORM. On the "in consideration for" line, you might put "one dollar," which legally indicates that the person was paid for his or her services.

Generally, you're free to shoot company employees in roles related to their jobs for in-house educational or corporate projects. Nevertheless, it's still wiser to have a signed release from everybody.

Public gatherings on the street don't require releases from the participants, but an individual interview with a "man-on-the-street" does.

If attending a sports event, you may wish to post a few notices warning that TV shooting is going on. Actually, the signs and cameras add an extra tinge of excitement to less popular contests, such as shuffleboard matches or poker competitions.

 Mini Review

- Before taking your equipment and crew on location, do a remote survey to check out lighting, parking, noise problems, etc.

PREPARATIONS FOR AN EXPENSIVE OR DISTANT SHOOT

If you're really going some distance or if the shoot is a substantial commercial venture, you may wish to bring the following items (in addition to those listed earlier):

TABLE 13–2   Model Release Form

In consideration for _____, receipt whereof is acknowledged, I hereby give _____ the absolute right and permission to copyright and/or publish, or use photographic portraits or pictures of me, or in which I may be included in whole or in part, or composite or distorted in character or form, in conjunction with my own or a fictitious name, or reproductions thereof in color or otherwise, for art, advertising, trade or any other lawful purpose whatsoever.

I hereby waive any right that I may have to inspect and/or approve the finished product or the advertising copy that may be used in connection therewith, or the use to which it may be applied.

I hereby release, discharge, and agree to save _____ from any liability by virtue of any blurring, distortion, alteration, optical illusion, or use in composite form, whether intentional or otherwise, that may occur or be produced in the taking of said pictures, or in any processing tending towards the completion of the finished product.

PRINT YOUR NAME _____   SIGN YOUR NAME _____

ADDRESS _____   _____

DATE _____   TELEPHONE _____

WITNESS _____

PARENT OR GUARDIAN SIGNATURE (If model is a minor) _____

The distant shoot.

1. The location owner's 24-hour phone number
2. Permits (parking, road closings—obtainable from police)
3. Location releases (owner's permission to shoot on his or her property)
4. Polarizing and graduated filters
5. Plywood (for bases, ramps)
6. Cue cards, magic markers
7. Rain tarp, raincoat, umbrella
8. Walkie-talkies
9. Garbage bags (also handy as raincoats for you or your gear—keep one in every coat pocket), broom, shovel (for cleaning up—before or after shooting)
10. Card table, folding chairs (for base of operations)
11. Clipboard, Post-it notes
12. First aid kit, sunscreen
13. Prop kit, makeup, small mirror (which is also handy for seeing behind your gear when making connections, and for positioning props and graphics perpendicular to the camera's line-of-sight)
14. Carpet (to lay over cables in high-traffic areas)
15. Repair kit
16. RELEASE FORMS
17. Moist towelettes (also handy for lunch cleanup)
18. AC outlet tester (to tell if there's juice before you tear your equipment all apart to fix it)
19. Black double-knit cloth (so it doesn't wrinkle) for
    a. Backgrounds
    b. To stop reflections
    c. To cover the gear in your van, thus making the van look empty from the outside.

 Mini Review

- The distant or expensive shoot requires additional preparations and attention to small details to ensure that the production goes smoothly.

SHOOTING FOR THE EDIT

Planning is the key to editing. It is a pleasure to start with a treasure chest of RAW FOOTAGE, molding it into a dazzling teleproduction. On the other hand, it is really the pits trying to change chicken feathers into chicken salad. By planning your shooting strategy before the edit, you can approach this ordeal with cassettes filled with the right shots, or you can approach it with an armful of chicken feathers.

1. *Provide sufficient material.* You can never have too much RAW FOOTAGE. If one scene doesn't work, it is always good to have another that you can use in its place. Here are some examples of what an ENG or EFP crew should bring back with them *besides* the footage they were told to get:

     a. CUTAWAYS, scenes of related or surrounding action that can be inserted to avoid a JUMP CUT. For example, after an interview, you would aim your camera at the interviewer reacting to the person's answers, perhaps nodding his or her head. It may also be helpful to have the interviewer ask the same questions a second time with the camera facing the interviewer (make sure that the questions are asked the same way as before so that the answers will be authentic).

     b. Hold your shots longer than normal. Doing this may be important only in one case out of ten, but that extra long-drawn-out shot may be just the thing for ending the newscast (while credits roll) or for showing something while the narrator catches up with his or her explanation.

     c. As you shoot and reshoot a scene, vary the pacing. Doing this is handy when shooting ads, as the editing for a thirty-second ad is quicker paced than the editing for a one-minute ad. The production will look best if the pacing of the performance matches the pacing of the editing. Furthermore, if the action happens quickly, it is easier for the editor to "get it all in" when editing a shorter version of the ad.

     d. Keep your OUTTAKES. The bleeps, blunders, and foul-ups that get recorded are called OUTTAKES. These are generally discarded (except when they are used on network TV programs). It is not expensive to keep them until the edit is completed, and you never know when an OUTTAKE may be useful. For instance, in a popular commercial, an actor's laugh was recorded between takes. The laugh looked so natural and spontaneous that it was inserted into the commercial.

     e. Shoot ESTABLISHING SHOTS to orient the viewer to locales and surroundings.

     f. Throw in an "arty" shot or two, such as a shot looking down on the action or up from the ground or through a leafy bush or through the reflection in a window. These unexpected gems help an editor spice up a bland but well-organized program.

     g. Shoot a few out-of-focus shots. These may later be used as backgrounds for titles.

     h. Record a few minutes of ambient sound. This may later become background sound in the final production or may fill in silent parts between narration or music.

---

*Cutaway   Act of "cutting away" (taking a shot of something else) from the main scene for a moment, possibly to hide jump cuts. Also, the name given to this backup shot, which is generally a long shot of a performer, a host, news reporters, or some other related scene.

*Outtake   Shot that for some reason (e.g., a flubbed line) you don't plan to use in the final production.

*Establishing shot   Introductory shot showing viewers where the scene takes place.

Pickup   Scene that "picks up" where another went askew, perhaps correcting a flubbed line, and continuing the scene to its conclusion.

*Jump cut   Edit from one scene to a very similar scene, causing the picture to "jump" from one position to another. Such edits should be hidden by video inserts (cutaways) of related scenes.

Editor controller   Remote control device that can backspace two or more editing decks, preroll them, and make them perform an edit.

*Backspace   Move a tape backward slightly and park it in preparation for an edit; give the tape space for the preroll.

Slate   Visible and/or audible cue recorded at the beginning (or end) of a take, identifying the take number for later reference.

2. *Reframe a shot when fixing an error.* Say that someone flubs a line. Instead of reshooting the entire scene, you might have the talent redo the scene, starting with the line *before* the flub. This is called a PICKUP because you are "picking up" just before where you left off. The problem is that when you edit these scenes together, you will have a JUMP CUT as the performer's head snaps from one position to another. To avoid this, reframe the shot (zooming in or out and arcing the camera to a different vantage point). If you do arc the camera to the side, have the talent commence speaking while looking forward as before, then turn toward you—*do not* start with his or her head in the new position.

3. *Check continuity.* Note the pacing of the scene so that it matches the next scene. Someone who just ran up a flight of stairs should be breathless in the next shot when he reaches the top. Also, try to duplicate facial expressions from shot to shot.

4. *Leave a ten-second preroll time before beginning the scene.* This leaves space for BACKSPACING during editing. Ten seconds of good stable video before the scene begins will ensure that the EDITOR CONTROLLER and TIME BASE CORRECTOR (if used) will be able to "lock onto" the signal for a reliable edit. If actors need to be cued, the camera/VCR operator can say to them, "Ready," start the VCR rolling, silently count off five seconds, then count backwards aloud . . . "five, four, three," then continue counting the last two seconds silently . . . and the scene begins.

And just to be safe, record some footage *after* the scene finishes, just in case the control room cuts away from your tape a moment late, or if the editor needs an extra moment before leaving your scene.

5. *Start each tape with one minute of color bars.* Doing this gets you past the dropouts that occur at the beginning of a tape because of threading, and it also allows the technicians to adjust playback levels when setting up the tapes later for an edit.

6. *Provide a SLATE, a handwritten note held in front of the camera telling what scene is being shot now.* Doing this will simplify locating particular shots for editing. The SLATE comes before the "five, four, three . . ." countdown and could be shown a few seconds after the camcorder starts rolling. The SLATE should contain the following information:
   a. Cassette or reel number
   b. Date
   c. Scene
   d. Take number

By holding the SLATE in front of the TV camera during the leader preceding each shot, you can clearly identify the scene and take. If a SLATE seems to be too much bother, then at least call out the take numbers so that they are recorded before each shot. Simultaneously, hold your hand in front of the camera with one or more fingers showing to indicate the take number. This technique is called a FINGER SLATE.

7. *Label your RAW FOOTAGE* so that it doesn't get lost. Mark it as CAMERA ORIGINAL or MASTER FOOTAGE or RAW FOOTAGE so that it doesn't get mixed up with copies that may look about the same.

8. *Remove the record lock buttons on your RAW FOOTAGE* after it is recorded. Doing this ensures that your precious shots won't get erased accidentally.

9. *Overlap lines between scenes.* Doing this will give your actors a "running start" as they say their lines and will make their voices sound more natural when the shots are edited together. This also allows for split audio and video edits during which you may edit from one picture to another, but the sound (the actor's lines) is still continuing from the first shot. Nine times out of ten this overlap is not needed, but occasionally it comes in handy during fancy edits.

10. *Use many short tapes for your RAW FOOTAGE.* While making your edit decisions and performing your edits, you'll be constantly going back and forth from one recorded scene to another. If the footage for scene 6 is at the beginning of a sixty-minute tape and the footage for scene 7 is at the end, you'll be twiddling your thumbs for about four minutes as the VCP shuttles from one scene to the other. A hundred edits like this can eat up a lot of time. If each cassette were only twenty minutes long, you would spend more time inserting and ejecting cassettes but much less time shuttling them.

Also, if your RAW FOOTAGE is to be cut into a "live" show, there may not be time for the VCR operator to locate the next scene during the show. In this case, it would be better to have each cut-in scene reside on a cassette of its own. In that way, each scene can be cued up on its own tape and ready to play during the show.

11. *Maintain similar light levels from scene to scene.* Unless you are switching scenes from night to day where scene brightness is *meant* to change, keep the light levels in your picture the same. Illuminate scenes to an equal brightness so that the edit doesn't call attention to itself.

 **Mini Review**

- Shoot for ten seconds before calling for action in order to ensure that your footage has a proper leader.
- Shoot cutaways on location.
- Label your tapes after you shoot them.
- Shoot many short cassettes of raw footage rather than a few long cassettes.

TRANSITIONS

Transitions are the methods we use to get from this shot to that shot. Sometimes you can't get there from here, and you need in-between shots to smooth the way.

Jump Cut

If you mounted your camera on a tripod and shot an interview and then edited together parts of the interview, you would see the person's head magically "snap" from position to position with each edited sequence. It would be very obvious that the tape had been edited. Such JUMP CUTS (or SNAP CUTS or CAMERA MAGIC, as they are also called) are obtrusive and disconcerting to the viewer.

When a shot changes, there should be a reason for the change, such as

1. A look at something new.
2. A look at the interviewer.
3. A look at the subject being talked about.
4. A different camera angle.
5. A closer or farther shot of the talent.

By showing something from a different perspective from shot to shot, you provide the viewer with a "reason" for the change in scene, making the edit less intrusive. You also make your program more enjoyable to watch.

To review, *change to a new kind of shot when you change shots.* Don't go from a long shot to another long shot or from a medium shot to another medium shot. Change from a close-up to a medium shot and then back to a close-up, or use some other varied combination of shots.

Besides changing shot size, also change the camera angle when cutting from shot to shot. Besides building a fuller perception of the subject, the change in angle smoothes the transition further. Figure 4–10 showed some examples of this concept.

If you have no other choices, you can cut between two similarly sized close-ups if people's heads are in different parts of the screen, but if they're not, the viewers will get the weird sensation that they saw one head transform into the other.

Situations do exist in which JUMP CUTS are desirable. Imagine a scene where the princess kisses her teddy bear and it suddenly changes into a prince. It's an easy feat to perform if you have a tripod. First, record your princess kissing the teddy bear. Have her freeze all action while you either PAUSE your VCR or leave the tape rolling, to be edited later. While she remains motionless, substitute the prince for the teddy bear. Call for "action" and then UNPAUSE (or continue rolling). When the tape is played back (or after it's been edited), the prince will suddenly appear in the bear's place. For this transformation to be convincing, you will need a steady tripod so that the camera doesn't move during the changeover and create a telltale "snap" in the background during the edit.

JUMP CUTS are employed (on purpose) in "hidden camera" commercials such as "taste tests." The SNAP CUTS make the editing obvious but add an air of authenticity and credibility to the scenes.

Cutaways and Cover Shots

When you know ahead of time where you are going to make an edit, you can purposely change the camera angle and shot size to avoid a JUMP CUT. If, however, you don't know where the edit will occur, you have no way of knowing whether the shots will butt together well. Usually they don't, and you'll have JUMP CUTS to hide. The trick here is to use our old friends CUTAWAYS, or COVER SHOTS.

The COVER SHOT might be a wide view of the talent speaking, one in which you can't see their lips moving, or it might be a shot of the audience, an interviewer, or an object being discussed. In this way, you switch from the close shot of the talent to a shot of something else, to another close shot of the talent. No one may realize that you edited out something but may think that you are trying to show *even more*.

Watch a newscast, and notice how the camera jumps from the reporter to the things that he or she is talking about. Observe how presidential press conferences are interspersed with shots of the reporters and photographers. Those folks aren't trying to show you their pretty lights and cameras; they're covering their edits. These press club shots, audience shots, and long shots, which are called COVER SHOTS or CUTAWAYS, are included as VIDEO INSERTS (explained in Chapter 14).

It may seem that I'm beating the subject of COVER SHOTS and CUTAWAYS to death here, but these shots are the essence of successful editing and on-location shooting. If you fail to get these shots, you'll indubitably be revisiting the location later to get them.

When an editor is putting together a series of shots, he or she wants to avoid JUMP CUTS that disturb the continuity of the scene. Wherever you are, whether CUTAWAYS are in the script or not, it is wise to shoot about one minute of CUTAWAYS, general scenes that can look appropriate when inserted into the story. Record audio, too, for WILD SOUND.

The CUTAWAY is used often in action sequences when action needs to be compressed. For example, if you were trying to show an exciting three-minute roller coaster ride in half a minute, the parts you edited out would create JUMP CUTS. The editing would become obtrusive. If you took the ride a second time and shot the faces of the participants, then took a few close-ups of the tracks zipping by, followed by an under-the-track shot of the roller coaster hurtling by, these shots could be interspersed throughout the segment to cover the JUMP CUTS. These shots would add drama and excitement to the scene and distract the viewer from the fact that the ride was shorter than a real one.

---

*Cover shot   Cutaway or a shot of a scene where you can't see the talents' lips moving.
Swish pan   Rapid, sideways movement of the camera as it goes from one scene to another, causing the image to streak.

Defocus-focus   Transition from one shot to another by defocusing the first shot, editing (or switching cameras), and following with another defocused shot that then comes into focus.

The WILD SOUND is used if new sound is to be dubbed in at any point later. Say your roller coaster rider was supposed to say "Let's go again!" as the ride came to an end, but he forgot, or maybe his speech was obscured by some other noise. Back at the studio, you could have him speak that line and edit his voice into the tape—but—you'd hear his words over a vacuous silence because the normal carnival background noise was missing. Such an edit would be jarringly obvious. *Solution*: Mix your WILD SOUND with the actor's new line during the editing process, and the new segment sounds smoother and more natural.

 Mini Review

- Change the kind of shot and camera angle when you change shots (i.e., close-up to medium shot, or front angle to side angle) to avoid jump cuts.
- Record a minute of natural background sound (wild sound) on location.

FANCIER TRANSITIONS

Walk-Past

Following people around as they walk from place to place is always hard to condense. One useful trick is to allow the performers to stride toward and past the camera (and out of the picture) and then to edit to another scene of them coming into view from alongside the camera. Also, performers may be allowed to turn corners or pass through doors, leaving the camera viewing an empty set. The next edit begins with another empty set with the performers entering a moment after the edit.

Condensing a long-distance drive into a few seconds is possible by having the vehicle start its journey in one location and drive into or over the viewer. If you survive, the next shot starts with the vehicle going away from (or out from over) the viewer into the new location.

Blank Surface

Here, the angry wife exits a room, slamming the door in the viewer's face, leaving the blank surface of the door filling the screen. The scene ends at this point, and you start the next sequence aimed at another blank surface, perhaps another door that later opens. Better yet, the second surface could be a sheet that disappears as the househusband pulls it from the line. Notice how this transition compresses time as it carries us from the scene when the wife leaves to the scene that reveals her husband's plight.

To travel from one place to another, one can tilt up past the treetops into the blue sky. In the next scene, starting with the blue sky, you can tilt down past the tops of city buildings to the new scene.

Similar to the walk-past is the walk-through, where the talent walks toward the camera and right into it, obliterating the picture. The next scene can begin with a camera close-up of the talent's back as it recedes.

Maintaining direction of motion is important. If you're cutting a shot that's moving, the shot that follows should be moving in the same direction. Say that the camera is panning across a toxic waste dump. If you cut to a close-up of glowing seagulls perched on a fifty-five-gallon drum, that shot should also be panning in the same direction, even if it's panning slowly and then comes to a stop. If you have a shot of a car speeding away to the left and then cut to a close-up of a tire kicking up gravel, the wheel should be moving to the left. If people are exiting the scene to the left, when you bring them into the next scene, they should enter on the right, still traveling to the left.

Swish Pan

To show a move from one location to another (as if to say, "Meanwhile, across town . . ."), pan the camera rapidly to a blur. The next scene starts with a fast pan that stops on the next subject that is to be viewed. The result looks like a hectic pan from one scene directly into another. SWISH PAN edits work beautifully only if they are planned. If the two adjoining scenes are not properly planned and the scene jumps from a pan or a zoom to a static shot, the result will look wretched. So if you can't plan your SWISH PAN edits to come together, avoid even the possibility of getting stuck in one by doing the following:

1. If panning or zooming a camera in a scene, come to a static shot before ending the scene.
2. Start scenes with a static shot before you pan or zoom.

In this way, all scenes begin or end with static shots and can be edited together in any order.

Defocus-Focus

One method of making a cut look smoother while adding variety to your edits is to defocus at the end of a scene, make your edit at another defocused shot, and then have the next shot refocus. For example, imagine a close-up of a guitar player's hand becoming fuzzy and then magically refocusing into a singer's face.

Or how about a zoom in and defocus on a burning candle, a calendar, a clock, or a baby's bottle? After the edit, zoom out and back into focus with the image of a burnt-out candle, an updated calendar, a reset clock, or an old man's wine bottle. Here, the defocus-focus implies the passage of time. It works a lot like the dissolve studied earlier.

Here are two things to keep in mind when you apply this method: First, it is far easier to get a close-up way out of focus than it is to get a medium or long shot out of focus. If you want to defocus easily, direct your attention to things you can get close-ups of. Second, use this method sparingly, or else the method won't add variety anymore.

Leading the Action

You are recording a child's birthday party including the usual bedlam. As you tape the proceedings, one child suddenly looks "stage right," and in a few moments all eyes are looking to the right. Now is the time to cut to Mom carrying the blazing birthday cake into the room. The children's looks made a perfect lead-in to your next shot. The viewer *expected* to see a new shot.

Seated performers shuffle, preparing to stand. There is your excuse to cut to a long shot of them as they get up and stroll off.

Somebody is holding a gem up to his eye. It's time for a close-up of the gem.

The runner lifts her hips in preparation for the gun. It's time for a long shot of the takeoff.

The switch from a medium shot to a long shot of a performer indicates that the performer is about to move or be joined by someone else. Cutting to a close-up of his face readies the audience to catch his expression. A gesture will be expected if you now switch to a medium shot. And a shot of the door prepares the viewers for an entry.

In each of these cases, the action prepares the viewer for a shot change. The transition from one shot to another becomes natural and comfortable to view. Making any of these shot changes without a specific purpose will not add variety to your show; it will only confuse your viewers. Therefore, change shots for a purpose, not for idle variety.

By building the preceding transitions into your editing strategy, your scenes will introduce each other and flow together. Notice also how transitions come in *pairs*. You left one scene and entered the next with a complementary shot. These shots don't mate together unless you *plan* to match the tail of one to the head of the next.

Mini Review

- Consider how shots are going to be joined together, and record the appropriate transitions at the beginning or ending of your scenes.

180° RULE

You almost never shoot any subject from opposite sides. The opposing shots can easily confuse the audience because what was moving left in one shot is suddenly moving right in the other.

Review the section on transitions in Chapter 11 and have another look at Figure 11–2. These remind us about the imaginary VECTOR LINE and how we can't cross it without disorienting our audience.

This mistake is very easy to do when you are shooting scenes that are hours, days, or weeks apart. If you forget how the flow of the action was moving, you have a fifty-fifty chance of starting your next scene with the flow going in the wrong direction. If you shot a patient in a hospital bed from one side that week and this week shot some more of him from the opposite side, you'll be unpleasantly surprised when you try to edit these scenes together. To avoid these problems, take notes and draw pictures showing your camera angles and setups. Doing this will ensure smooth continuity from scene to scene. And now, let's continue with more on continuity.

CONTINUITY

Al sits down at the table, picks up his knife and fork, and begins to cut his asparagus. "Cut," you call out, and he feverishly speeds up his sawing until he realizes that the scene is over. You continue the scene with the camera in another position for a close-up of his plate. "Okay, roll," you call out, and when Al realizes you are not calling for his buns, he again picks up his fork and dips into his mashed potatoes. Somebody is in for a surprise when editing time comes—somebody who didn't take notes or didn't examine the tail of the preceding scene to assure matched shots. How many viewers will you entertain with this little slipup?

One way to call the least attention to the exact position of something is to change shots while it is moving. CUTTING ON THE ACTION (as it is called) also makes the movement part of *both* shots, fusing the continuity between them.

For example, someone is about to walk out through the door. You shoot the scene first from the inside. The edit will occur *as the door begins to open*. Have the talent memorize which hand was on the knob and which foot was forward. Now run outside, prepare your door shot, and have the talent repeat the process of opening the door, hands and feet equivalently placed. The next edit begins as the door opens.

Changing shots the moment something happens immediately draws the audience into the action, their eyes naturally following the action. Cutting before or after the action is obtrusive, drawing attention away from the action and toward the edit itself.

CUTTING ON THE ACTION is a science. If you know you will have to edit scenes, contrive action to cut on. Have your actor turn to a blackboard, sit on the edge of the desk, or simply turn to address a new camera angle. When preparing RAW FOOTAGE, remember to repeat one scene's ending action at the beginning of the next scene, overlapping the action. Pay attention to detail—hand, foot, body, and face positions. Maintain screen direction; someone exiting the screen to the left should be moving to

---

Cutting on the action   Changing shots at the moment some action is taking place.

the left in the next shot. If you cut from a medium to a close shot while someone's head is turning, the head should be turning the same direction in both cases.

As mentioned earlier, each new shot should change *both* the closeness of the shot (image size) and the angle of the shot. This change in size and angle will help cover minor flaws in matching the action in the two sequences. And last, feel free to rehearse an action a few times before recording it. It will help everybody relax and perform smoothly.

 Mini Review

- Observe the imaginary vector line, and shoot the subject from one side only.
- Maintain continuity by having props and people in the same positions as you go from one shot to the next.
- Shot changes should occur during action in the scene.

SHOOTING STRATEGIES FOR ENG

No matter what kind of production you are doing—EFP, ENG, sports, or advertising—the basic laws still apply: Try to tell a story, and make the shots flow smoothly from one to another.

Television professionals come to each shooting situation with a bag of tricks up their sleeves (which must make it very hard to move). These are handy production strategies that work very well in certain situations. Before you add them to your own arsenal of strategies, it's a good idea to review the universal rules you've been bombarded with so far:

1. Shoot cutaways
2. Record a leader before the action starts
3. Preplan your transition shots

The Interview Shot

Used heavily in news and documentaries, the interview shot is a scene of a person talking. Here are some guidelines on how to shoot the scene.

1. If the scene is dramatic, use tight close-ups. You are searching for emotion in the face. Try to keep the eyes in the upper third of the picture and the lips in the lower third.

2. If the scene is not emotional, you can get by with medium shots and medium close-ups. In the medium close-ups, keep the eyes in the upper third of the screen. In the medium shots (waist shots), keep the face in the upper third of the screen.

3. Center the interviewee in your picture unless that person is speaking to someone off camera to the side. In this case, allow the interviewee to turn toward that person. Be sure to leave him or her a little extra space to "speak into."

4. Always be aware of the background—never forget that it is part of the picture. Make the interviewee's background work for you and not against you. If the background is distracting or runs contrary to the story (such as kids screaming, waving, laughing, and giving the finger to the camera in

---

*ENG   Electronic news gathering, portable video production for the news. Often, quick-and-dirty techniques are used with minimal equipment and crew.

*EFP   Electronic field production, producing TV shows outside the studio. Usually involves studio-quality equipment, techniques, and editing.

the midst of a tragic auto accident), arrange the camera and interviewee so that the background is a nearby bush (nobody can get in there to wave at you) or a busy street (nobody will stand in traffic to wave at you) or so far away that it can be put out of focus as you zoom in on the interviewee's face. Zooming in not only reduces the depth of field of your lens but will also leave less background to be seen.

5. Try to use the background if you can. If a woman's house just burned down, we should see the smoldering wreckage over her shoulder. If a man is inviting you to visit his new car dealership, then try to work it so that his sign is over his shoulder.

Stand-Up Reporter

A stand-up is an interview with the reporter or the interviewee standing, speaking directly to the camera.

1. To maintain good eye contact, shoot no tighter than a necktie shot and no looser than a waist shot.

2. If including an important background in the shot, frame the talent off center to leave more space for the background. Walking shots will add interest to the scene. Either move with the talent, or simply let the talent get bigger as he or she approaches you (remember to refocus as the talent approaches—not an easy task). If you attempt to zoom out as the talent approaches, the person's size will stay the same on the screen but the background will appear to "stretch" unnaturally behind him or her.

3. If the reporter is talking *to* the audience while walking, he or she should be walking generally toward the camera.

4. If the reporter is taking the viewer to another location or wants to show something behind him or her, then it's okay for the reporter to walk away from the camera.

5. Sometimes distractions come between your reporter and the camera. Typically, it's a bystander waving and trying to get his or her puss into your picture while you interview somebody. If you can't cordon off an area or get some other crew members to block for you, the next trick is to use a wide-angle lens and shoot very close to your subject. People are less likely to intrude when the camera and subject are only three feet apart. Be aware that when you do this, you may encounter special lighting problems. Be careful not to cast a shadow on your subject. On the other hand, if your camera has a light attached to it, either dim, diffuse, or bounce the light off something else so that you don't melt a hole in your poor subject from three feet away.

6. Want to save a ton of time editing? Have your reporter start each report with his own countdown, saying (after the camera rolls), "5, 4, 3, 2" (omitting 1, but pausing for it), then starting his or her on-camera report. If the reporter flubs a line, have him or her just count backward again (indicating a new start) and then begin the report again. Later, the editor can cue the tape to the "1" pause and hit edit-in to start the edit in one quick motion. If there's time in the field, recue the tape to erase the flub each time. If you can do that, the editor will see only "good" takes and won't have to sift through the bad ones. Yes, I know this conflicts with the "keep your OUTTAKES" rule listed earlier. We use different strategies for different situations.

 Mini Review

- The more emotional and dramatic the scene, the closer the shot should be.
- Stay aware of the background, making it add to rather than distract from your main character.

---

14 EDITING A VIDEOTAPE

Editing means different things to different people. In its broadest sense, editing is the organization and assembly of shots into a logical sequence.

Scripts, movie film, audiotape, and videotape can all be edited. The editing techniques are similar in that bad material is removed, good material is added, and segments may be moved from one place to another. The methods for editing each medium are different. Scripts may be changed with white-out liquid or a word processor. Movie film can be edited with scissors and glue or a professional MOVIEOLA and FILM SPLICER. Audiotape is similarly sliced up into wanted and unwanted segments and the pieces hitched together with SPLICING TAPE. Audiotape can also be edited by selectively copying desired portions of other audiotapes. Sound can also be edited with few mouse-clicks on digital audio workstations.

Years ago, videotape was edited by physically slicing it up and SPLICING the desired segments together. The process was tedious and often caused snowy patches in the picture. Nowadays, videotape is always edited electronically.

Some editing methods are quick and dirty. Others are planned and professional. Scenes can be recorded "live" as the camera sees them and assembled on the tape in chronological order. This process is called IN-CAMERA EDITING. In other cases, scenes may be shot and recorded on one tape and the best scenes selected and copied onto another tape, which becomes the final product. Those original scenes on the first tape are called RAW FOOTAGE, SOURCE TAPE, CAMERA ORIGINALS, or MASTER FOOTAGE. The scenes may be shot days apart, years apart, or miles apart and assembled in any order onto your final tape. The final version of the program, when all these parts are put together, is called the EDITED MASTER.

Movieola   Device for viewing and comparing several reels of film at a time while selecting segments to splice into an edited master film.

Film splicer   Mechanical device for clamping and neatly cutting and holding film steady for gluing.

Splicing tape   In audio, special adhesive tape used to attach the ends of audio tape together for continuous playback. To splice a tape is to cut it and attach it to another tape. A splice is also the point on a tape where two separate tapes were physically joined together.

*In-camera editing   Recording scenes chronologically, one after another, in the camcorder with the intention that all the shots will be used; a final tape emerges from the camcorder. To avoid glitches in the picture, an editing-capable camcorder must be used (it backspaces the tape to get a running start before editing-in the next scene).

*Raw footage   Recordings made directly from the camera, intended to be edited into a final program later.

Master tape   Original copy of the finished version of a tape. It could be the original footage of a "live" show or a program edited together from other tapes. The master is the best-quality copy of this program in existence.

*Edited master   Same as master tape, but created by the editing process.

*Insert edit   Recording of a new video segment amidst old, prerecorded video—unlike assemble edit, which places each new segment at the tail of the last segment.

Notice that in the case of movie film and audiotape, the program could be physically cut apart and physically reassembled from its pieces. In the end, if the edited program needed to be shortened or lengthened, parts could be removed or added. Videotape, on the other hand, is never physically cut (except to salvage a damaged tape). Unlike film and audiotape, once the edited version is finished, its length cannot be easily altered. A section may be erased with a new section recorded over it (called an INSERT EDIT), but doing that doesn't change the length of the whole show. If a show *had* to be lengthened, you would either have to reedit the tape from the beginning or go down one more generation and copy the part of the tape that came before the part you are adding, then add the new part, and then copy the rest of your old edited tape onto this new tape.

As you can see, it pays to make your editing decisions ahead of time. Once performed, some edits are hard to change. For this reason, there are computerized editing systems that allow you to make a list of what the edits should be, preview what the edits look like as listed, and then change the list to refine the program. Finally, the real edit is made from the list.

EDITING WITHOUT AN EDITING VIDEOTAPE RECORDER

Technically, it's simple to record something on videotape, stop the tape, start recording again, and so on until a show is completed. In fact, that's what your home VCR does when you program it to record several shows while you're away.

You may have noticed, however, when you played back the shows, there was a disruption in the picture and sound between shows (the highfalootin, professional term for this is GLITCH). If you try to edit by stopping your VCR (called a STOP EDIT), you'll get a GLITCH too. Very gauche.

Some VCRs and most camcorders will allow you to do PAUSE EDITS, which are the same as IN-CAMERA EDITS. PAUSE EDITS are neater than STOP EDITS and simple to do. Just start recording, then hit PAUSE when you don't want to record something. You then UNPAUSE (pressing PAUSE again) when you're ready to resume recording.

Once you've PAUSED, you can change camera angles or whatever, but you must UNPAUSE the VCR within three minutes or so or it will automatically switch to STOP. Camcorders may be more forgiving about this than VCRs, allowing you to PAUSE a shot and then, if the time runs out, powering down—*while staying in PAUSE mode.* When you again press the POWER button (maybe hours later), the camcorder springs to life, parked right where it left off in PAUSE.

PAUSE EDITS are fine for amateurs, but they cramp the styles of professionals. First, most VCRs and camcorders leave a tiny GLITCH at the PAUSE point. The GLITCH is hardly noticeable, but any GLITCH at all wreaks havoc for professional editors, professional signal processing equipment, and broadcast television. *No* GLITCHES are allowed. Second, PAUSE EDITS force the camcordist to shoot every shot in sequence. Most videographers would rather shoot a scene several times, then pick the best version.

Here's one more note about PAUSE EDITS: Pro camcorders have editing VCRs inside, and when they do what looks like PAUSE EDITS, they're not really PAUSE EDITS. They do the same things that editing VCRs do when you hit the EDIT button: They BACKSPACE the tape about five seconds, then play it for about five seconds (to get a running start), then switch to RECORD. This ensures a GLITCHLESS edit.

PAUSE edits, like buzzards, have their useful place on the planet. If your program doesn't have to be perfect (e.g., you're assembling the best shots of your vacation to inflict on your neighbors, or

---

*Glitch Disruption in the audio and video that causes the sound to warble and the picture to break up.
*Pause edit Editing of a videotape while recording, by pressing the pause button between takes.

Stop edit Technique of editing a videotape by stopping the VCR (pressing stop) at the end of one scene and then starting it recording again (pressing record/play) at the beginning of the next scene.

you're consolidating scenes from a school play for review by the cast), PAUSE edits are the way to go. They're quick, they're cheap (no special equipment is necessary), and anybody can learn how to do them.

The process of editing a live show goes as follows:

1. Hook up your VCR to a video and audio source (i.e., camera and microphone or switcher and mixer).
2. Make a short test recording to ensure that the picture and sound came out okay. If so, rewind the VCR, record ten seconds of nothing for a LEADER, then hit PAUSE.
3. Cue your talent, and then UNPAUSE the VCR.
4. At the end of the scene, hit PAUSE.
5. Repeat the process (starting with step 3) until your show is done.
6. At the end of the show, UNPAUSE to RECORD a minute of nothing for a tidy end LEADER.
7. To finish, hit STOP on the VCR.

If you are PAUSE EDITING from another videotape, the drill goes like this:

1. Hook up your VCR and VCP to copy a tape. (See Figure 14–1).
2. Make a sample recording to see if the signals are okay.
   a. Play the VCP.
   b. Switch the VCR to RECORD/PLAY and record for one minute.
   c. Stop the VCP and VCR. Rewind and play the VCR.
   d. If everything looks and sounds good, rewind the VCR and get ready to record for real.
3. Record ten seconds of nothing on the VCR for a LEADER, then hit PAUSE on the VCR.
4. Play the VCP to find the first scene. Get to know where the scene should start by playing that part over again. Then REVERSE SCAN to back up the player to *before* the scene.
5. Press PLAY on the VCP.
6. Poise your finger over PAUSE on the VCR, and when the scene comes along, UNPAUSE the VCR. (To UNPAUSE on some VCRs, you hit RECORD; on some, RECORD/PLAY; on some, PLAY. Refer to the VCR's instructions that you probably stuffed in your garage with last year's newspapers.)
7. At the end of the scene, hit PAUSE on your VCR.
8. Repeat the process until it's done or you're exhausted. End with a minute of black.

 Mini Review

- Once a videotape is edited, its length cannot be easily altered. Sections may be replaced with new sections, but that doesn't change the length of the whole show.
- Stopping a VCR or pausing it is a form of editing that may leave glitches in the picture.

Recording Something Over

You're recording the Memorial Day parade to send to Aunt Blanche. You've assembled fascinating shots of the flags and the bands; now, the horses are trotting majestically by . . . uh . . . whoop! You didn't really want to test Aunt Blanche's pacemaker with a giant, color, close-up of Dobbin doin' a dandy on the pavement! PAUSING at this point won't help; the toothpaste is already out of the tube, so to speak. The only choice is to REWIND a ways and replace the unsavory scene with something else, perhaps marching Girl Scout Troop 106.

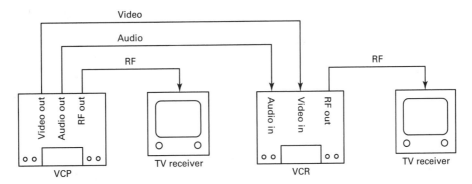

Notes:
1. The VCP's TV receiver is optional but handy for diagnosing problems.
2. The VCR's monitor could just as well receive direct audio and video from the VCR (rather than RF).
3. If the VCRs have Y/C connectors, use them to copy in preference to composite video.
4. If the VCRs have Y/R-Y/B-Y connectors, use them in preference to any of the above video cables.
5. If the VCRs have digital Firewire connectors, use those in preference to any audio/video cables.

FIGURE 14–1 Common setup for copying a videotape.

So you REWIND, PLAY, watch your viewfinder for a good breaking-off point, and then hit PAUSE. Next, hit RECORD/ PLAY. UNPAUSE when Troop 106 gets in range.

You may notice that such edits aren't as pretty as PAUSE edits (and it's not the fault of the girls in Troop 106). There may be a noticeable GLITCH. There may also be a rainbow or smear of colors lasting a few seconds.

This disruption is normal under the circumstances and is not your fault or a malfunction in your machine. If you must record over something, two things you can do to minimize the glitch are

1. Use the fastest tape speed for recording.

2. Make your edits on pauses in conversations or lapses in action. Then viewers don't feel as if they're missing something important. (*Note*: In Chapter 13 you learned to CUT ON THE ACTION, and now you're told to cut on PAUSES. These two strategies aren't contrary to each other: You CUT ON THE ACTION when you have an accurate editor making glichless edits. You cut on PAUSES if you're using amateurish GLITCHY gear that precludes your doing the job right).

EDITING WITH AN EDITING VCR

Common VCRs stop the tape from moving when you hit PAUSE and resume its motion when you hit UNPAUSE. They leave a GLITCH at the PAUSE point.

Professional editors need a running start and will switch from PLAY to RECORD the instant you tell them to EDIT. The switch is GLITCHLESS. Here's a typical scenario: You're recording a sewing lesson,

---

*Edit-in To begin recording new material; the beginning of an edit.

*Preroll To begin a tape playing so that it is up to speed and its signals are stable before an edit takes place.

*Editor controller Remote control device that can backspace two or more editing decks, preroll them, and make them perform an edit.

*Jump cut Edit from one scene to a very similar scene, causing the picture to "jump" from one position to another. Such edits should be hidden by video inserts of related scenes (cutaways).

and twenty minutes into the demonstration the instructor skewers her finger with a needle. You stop the tape, she washes off the blood, and now you're both ready to continue the exercise. Instead of starting from scratch, you could back up the tape to a scene where it would be easy to resume recording. You and the instructor study the scene to determine the best EDIT-IN point. You change the camera angle to avoid a JUMP CUT (in which the talent would suddenly snap to a new position). You back up the tape about fifteen seconds further, prepare the talent and cameras, hit PLAY, then watch the old scene approach the spot where you'll edit. You poise your finger over the EDIT button and give the talent her "ready" cue, then at the right moment hit EDIT and cue the talent. You're rolling again, just as before. You're erasing the bad stuff and recording good stuff. The edit point will look like a simple camera switch. Be aware of continuity; her finger shouldn't suddenly sprout a bandage.

Most other scenarios involve editing from another videotape. In this situation, *both* VCR and VCP have to be backed up (BACKSPACED) so that they can have a running start (called a PREROLL) before the EDIT-IN occurs. The process is complicated enough to require an EDITOR CONTROLLER to synchronize the machines and execute the EDIT-IN at precisely the chosen moment. You'll see more about this process shortly, but first let's cover the two *kinds* of edits a VCR can make.

 Mini Review

- When editing a scene with live actors, be sure to change the camera angle from its position before the edit in order to avoid a jump cut, a jarring transition where the talent snaps from one position to another before our eyes.
- Editing VCRs need to preroll the tape to give it a running start before they execute the edit. This process makes the edit glitchless.

ASSEMBLE EDITING

There are different strategies for piecing together the parts to a TV show. They go by these names:

ASSEMBLE EDIT

INSERT EDIT

AUDIO INSERT

VIDEO INSERT

---

*Assemble edit   Edit made on blank tape (or recorded over something to be discarded) whereby the first scene is recorded first, the second scene tacked onto the end of the first, the next scene onto the end of the previous scene, and so on, building chronologically to the end of the show.

*Insert edit   Recording of a new video segment amidst old, prerecorded video—unlike assemble edit, which places each new segment at the tail of the last segment.

*Audio insert   Audio dub performed in the midst of an already recorded tape.

*Video insert   Replacing a segment of old video with new video, in the midst of prerecorded tape. Audio is not affected (except for hi-fi audio imbedded in the video).

Punch-in assemble edit   Assemble edit that is executed manually, live, while the actors perform.

*Blacked tape   Video recording of black, used to prepare a tape for insert editing.

*Edit-out   To cease recording new material; the end of an edit.

Mode selector   Knob or button on an editing VCR that sets the VCR into the insert edit, assemble edit, video insert, or audio insert mode.

End insert   To stop insert editing; the button on a VCR that terminates an insert edit.

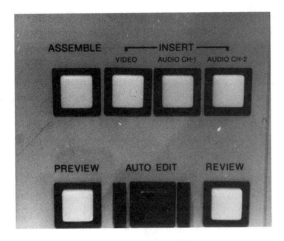

Edit buttons on an editing VCR.

ASSEMBLE EDITS are produced *in order* from the beginning of the program to the end. They may be performed on blank tape. You first set up the title and then record it. Next, you set up the first scene and record that. Next, you set up your second scene, then your third, then your fourth, until you're done.

The example of the seamstress given earlier was an ASSEMBLE EDIT done with a live actor. Some call this a PUNCH-IN edit because you punched the edit button as the tape played.

INSERT EDITING

INSERT edits are often made in the *middle* of a program. They are frequently used to correct an error or to change something after your program is finished. INSERT edits *do not* lengthen or shorten your program. They merely replace one part of your program with a new part. They are *always* made over previously recorded tape.

An entire program can be made out of INSERT edits. The INSERT edits may be recorded in sequence or out of sequence on a prerecorded or BLACKED tape. To edit a fifteen-minute tape using this mode, you would first record sixteen minutes of black using the ASSEMBLE EDIT mode; then you would rewind your tape and switch your VCR to the INSERT EDIT mode and record the beginning title, the first scene, the second scene, and so on in order; or if you wished, you could record the beginning title and skip ahead to the ending credits, then do scenes 3, 4, and 5, and then go back to insert scenes 1 and 2 later.

Notice that an INSERT edit is done over already-existing video (or black). The INSERT edit won't work if there isn't old video to come back to when you end the INSERT. If you expect your new material to run past the end of your old recording, then do an ASSEMBLE edit, not an INSERT.

To perform a manual INSERT edit of live action, here are the steps in detail:

1. See that your audio and video inputs are connected.

2. Check your audio and video levels by temporarily pressing RECORD/PAUSE (unless the VCR monitors them in the STOP mode). When finished, switch the RECORD button off.

3. Play the tape and learn the exact place where you want to EDIT-IN. Remember this spot and jot down the number on the tape's elapsed-time counter so that you can come back to the spot easily. You may also use the action in the scene as a guide to the EDIT-IN point.

4. Now, play ahead to find the appropriate place to EDIT-OUT—that is, to terminate the new recording and go back to the original presentation. Again, a pause in action and conversation is usu-

ally a good place to come back to the old material from your edit. Once you find the place, note the number on your index counter. If you wish, you may also use a stopwatch to accurately measure the length of time between the EDIT-IN and the EDIT-OUT points.

5. After learning the EDIT-IN and EDIT-OUT points, find the VCR's MODE SELECTOR and switch it to the INSERT EDIT mode. This prepares the electronics for what is about to happen.

6. Rewind the tape a ways so that when the edit is performed, the tape speed and motors have stabilized and are running smoothly.

7. Switch to PLAY.

8. When the edit point comes, push the EDIT button (or PLAY and RECORD buttons or whatever the manufacturer instructed), and cue the talent.

9. Pay close attention to your timing. Get ready to press END INSERT, EDIT, or whatever button stops the process. Unless the manufacturer says otherwise, switching to STOP is *not* the way to end an INSERT edit.

10. About half a second before the INSERT is destined to end, hit the proper button. Depending on the VCR, the EDIT-OUT may take up to half a second to actuate.

Essentially what you have done is to record a new passage starting with the first index number and ending with the second number. Doing this means that the performance must be timed to last *exactly* the length of tape you wish to delete. If the replacement scene is too short, you end up with a long, pregnant stare at someone's smiling face while you wait for the final index number to come up. You *must* wait for the number because if you terminate the edit too soon, you will end up not deleting the tail end of the segment you want removed. If the replacement scene is too long, you'll end up erasing your way into the following material, which you wanted to keep.

This process is not easy. Besides being mechanically difficult, it requires precision timing from the performers and the VCR operator alike.

The aspect of INSERT editing that makes it so difficult is the fact that once you've EDITED-IN, you're flying blind. You can't see what you are erasing; you see only what you are recording. You have no visual cue for when to stop, other than your counter or your timepiece. Add to this the fact that if you make a mistake and EDIT-IN too long a passage, you'll irrevocably erase the next scene as you record over it. For this reason, it is worthwhile to rehearse the edit several times in order to get the timing exact. You may wish to play the tape; *pretend* to edit (as it plays); have the performers dress-rehearse the scene; then *pretend* to stop the edit and, by looking at the screen at this point, determine how far off you were and what should be done about it.

An Important Technical Difference between Insert and Assemble Edits

When you ASSEMBLE-edit, the VCR records the picture, sound, sync, and CONTROL TRACK pulses. The VCR produces the CONTROL TRACK pulses in step with the incoming video. If you are ASSEMBLE editing, each edit point should have a perfect changeover from the old recorded CONTROL TRACK pulses to the

---

Control track pulses   Rhythmic signal recorded on a videotape's control track that guides the VCR during playback.

Color bars   Vertical bars of color used to test cameras and other video equipment.

*Master tape   The original copy of the finished version of a tape. This could be original footage of a "live" show, or it could be a program edited together from other tapes. The master is the best-quality copy of this program in existence.

Test signal   Video (or other) signal containing certain proper-

ties (like color bars) to show whether equipment is working as it should. Test signals meet certain technical specifications useful for calibrating other equipment.

SMPTE leader   Recording at the beginning of a tape that contains test signals (as specified by the organization SMPTE).

Slate   Visible and/or audible cue recorded at the beginning (or end) of a take, identifying the take number for later reference.

newly recorded CONTROL TRACK pulses. When edits are perfect, the old and new pulses line up perfectly. If, however, an imperfect edit is performed, there will be a GLITCH in this smooth train of pulses. This GLITCH will also appear in your picture.

INSERT editing, on the other hand, doesn't create CONTROL TRACK pulses. These pulses have to be laid down ahead of time (perhaps as you create your BLACKED tape). While INSERT editing, the VCR synchronizes the existing CONTROL TRACK pulses with the incoming video so that the picture is laid down in exactly the right place on the tape. During editing, the CONTROL TRACK is never touched. If it was laid down correctly at the beginning, it will remain good no matter what pictures you INSERT-EDIT on the tape. Bad edits won't hurt the CONTROL TRACK (they won't make good pictures, but at least they won't hurt the CONTROL TRACK). Figure 14–2 diagrams the differences between ASSEMBLE and INSERT edits.

You are more likely to get a *perfect* CONTROL TRACK throughout your tape if you've recorded it in your studio from beginning to end using your best equipment. Now you can trust your CONTROL TRACK. If instead you ASSEMBLE-EDIT your production, hungry gremlins may sneak up and bite you. If for any reason there is a deviation or corruption of the CONTROL TRACK, the videotape will not play correctly at this point. Your picture may roll, tear, break into snow or other garbage, depending on the circumstances.

Numerous electronic phenomena can wreck your CONTROL TRACK, but the most likely possibility, the one the pros all remember doing at least once, is errantly hitting the ASSEMBLE EDIT button when we

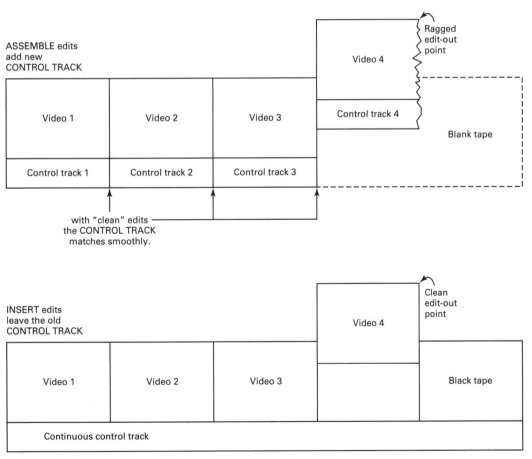

FIGURE 14–2 ASSEMBLE VS INSERT editing.

intended to do an INSERT on a completed—no doubt otherwise perfect—MASTER videotape. To err is inevitable. Machines don't forgive.

Now that you see the GLITCH, what can you do about it? The answer is nothing. You can't just redo that one edit on the tape, because the end of *that* edit will cause a new GLITCH at the end of the edit. If you try to fix *that* GLITCH with a new edit, the *new* ASSEMBLE edit will end in a GLITCH. You can't win.

In conclusion, it is best to first create a BLACKED tape in the studio and later INSERT EDIT your scenes onto it. You can still do the edits in order, as if you were ASSEMBLE EDITING.

Again, INSERT EDITING over BLACKED tape is strife insurance; you can have glitchy video or glitchy edits, but they can easily be replaced with clean ones—over the solid foundation of your stable CONTROL TRACK. I can't overemphasize the value of INSERT EDITING over ASSEMBLE EDITING.

The SMPTE Leader

While you're going to the trouble of BLACKING a tape, there's another step you can do: Add an SMPTE LEADER, a series of TEST signals useful to technicians who may need to adjust the videotape player when the program is played back or copied. SMPTE, the Society of Motion Picture and Television Engineers, has standardized this series of signals that can be recorded on the LEADER of your videotape and will be recognized (even expected) by others in the video industry. It is possible to create your SMPTE LEADER and a BLACKED master tape all at the same time. The accompanying boxes describe how.

Video	Black (for threading)	Color bars	Slate (visual ID)	Number countdown over black: 10, 9, 8, 7, 6, 5, 4, 3	Black	Program begins or continues with black if creating blacked tape for editing
Audio	Silence	1000-Hz tone at 0 VU	Reading of slate	8 audio beeps	Silence	Program or silence
	10 sec	10 sec	15 sec	8 sec	2 sec	

SMPTE VIDEO LEADER.

Mini Review

- The four kinds of edits are assemble edit, insert edit, audio insert, and video insert.
- Assemble edits are always performed in sequence, each new edit coming at the end of the work you have done so far.
- Insert edits must be made over prerecorded tape and do not have to be performed in order as do assemble edits.
- Assemble edits are risky; insert edits are much less likely to have glitches.
- Begin your edited masters with a SMPTE leader, which contains test signals and a countdown. This leader will help technicians prepare your tape for playback.

CREATING A BLACKED TAPE

INSERT edits can be made only over existing video and CONTROL TRACK. Although you could record your edits over old *Family Feud* reruns, it is generally neater to prepare (and stockpile) a number of BLACKED tapes.

A BLACKED tape is simply a tape recorded from beginning to end (or at least a little longer than your intended edited tape will be) with a stable, glitch-free CONTROL TRACK. You make such a CONTROL TRACK by feeding stable video (with sync) to your VCR, switching it to the ASSEMBLE or NORMAL mode, pressing record, and letting the machinery do the rest.

Where do you get a stable video signal? At Poverty Productions Inc., you would probably connect a camera to your VCR and let it record the image. It doesn't matter what the image is. In keeping with the concept of a BLACKED master, you could cap the lens. You may find it a little handier to aim the camera at a clock or stopwatch so that, while editing, you can tell at a glance how much time you have used.

If you have a switcher, you don't need to be bothered with the camera at all. Simply fade the switcher to *black* and record the black video. *Another option:* If you have a character generator, you can get BLACK out of that if you don't type in any words.

No law says that your tape has to be black. COLOR BARS are pretty. Many cameras make COLOR BARS as a handy reference signal. You can tape the COLOR BARS directly from the camera and feed the tape into the VCR. Here's one extra advantage of COLOR BARS: The beginning of every MASTER TAPE would have a stretch of COLOR BARS before the show starts as a reference signal that technicians may use to adjust the color signal as it comes from the VCR. If the VCR that plays the master tape is out of whack, the bars will be the wrong colors.

Video Insert Only

In the INSERT edit mode, you can replace the video and audio, or you can replace just the video or just the audio. For audio, you sometimes have the choice of replacing audio channel 1 or channel 2 or both.

VIDEO INSERT (or VIDEO INSERT ONLY) permits old video to be replaced with new video in the form of an INSERT edit without touching the existing sound portion of the program. *Exception:* Hi-fi audio is

CREATING AN SMPTE LEADER

Every important MASTER tape should have a LEADER, a length of tape that comes before the beginning of the program and takes all the threading abuse. Since your program is never manhandled, it is likely to have fewer dropouts, scratches, and stretches.

The LEADER can also contain SMPTE standardized test signals. Here is how to create your SMPTE LEADER and a BLACKED master tape all at the same time.

1. Record ten seconds of black (for threading).
2. Follow the black with ten seconds of COLOR BARS (most duplication houses prefer a full minute). During this time, record an audio tone of 1000Hz at a 0-VU volume level.
3. Follow this step with fifteen more seconds of black and silence. Later, you may go back and insert a visual ID (called a SLATE) while audibly reading the contents of the SLATE onto the sound track. The SLATE would immediately identify the name of the program, when it was produced, who produced it, where it was produced, what VTR was used to edit the program together (handy to know if the tape someday runs amuck and decides never to play correctly on any other machine but "mother"), and other trivia.
4. Follow step 3 with ten seconds of visible numbers that go 10, 9, 8, 7, 6, 5, 4, 3, at one-second intervals. This procedure should be accompanied by eight audio beeps at one-second intervals.
5. Following the eight beeps should be two seconds of black and silence. (In other words, the beeps for 2 and 1 in the countdown above are silent and invisible.)
6. At this point the program should start, but you could continue to record black and silence throughout the rest of your tape. You have just created a BLACKED tape.

As an extra step, you could also record SMPTE TIME CODE throughout the tape.

part of the video tracks. Replacing the picture replaces the hi-fi sound. The *linear* audio tracks (VHS and SVHS) or PCM tracks (8mm and Hi8) or digital audio tracks (DV) stay untouched.

Audio Insert Only

With AUDIO INSERT ONLY, you leave the video untouched and change only the audio. *Exception:* Hi-fi audio is part of the video tracks. You can change only the linear audio tracks (VHS and SVHS), PCM tracks (8mm and Hi8), or digital audio tracks (DV).

The process is much the same as we saw in Chapter 9 under AUDIO DUBBING.

Since the old material is erased as the new material is put on, a slip-up can be dangerous. It's wise to rehearse your AUDIO INSERT to make sure your timing is right.

If you can read lips or follow the action closely, you can use your picture as your guide to the EDIT-IN and the EDIT-OUT points. Otherwise, you may have to use your VCR's elapsed-time counter as a guide.

 Mini Review

- A video insert replaces the picture, leaving the sound behind (except for hi-fi sound, which is embedded in the picture).
- Audio inserts replace the non–hi-fi sound without affecting the picture.

EDITING FROM ANOTHER VIDEOTAPE

Advantages and Disadvantages

The problem with ASSEMBLE editing is that everything must be done in sequence. You progress through your shots in chronological order, unable to shoot the end scene first, then shoot all the airplane shots, and then go to all the bedroom scenes. If you could shoot all the similar scenes in one sitting, you could save a lot of running around locating your performers and setting up lights, audio, and so forth.

The problem with INSERT editing is that if you wish to *add* something to an existing tape, you have to *take something out* to make room for it. If you could alter the content of a show by simply removing scenes or putting in additional scenes, you could exercise uninhibited control over your production.

For these reasons, most professional teleproducers shoot RAW FOOTAGE or, as the film industry calls them, RUSHES. These are recordings made (on separate tapes, usually) at different locations, at different times, sometimes by different people. These tapes are brought back to the videotape editor,

---

*Raw footage   Recordings made directly from the camera, intended to be edited into a final program later.

*Time code   A way of measuring where (how far from the beginning of a tape) scenes are located. Usually refers to a magnetic pulse recorded on the tape that can be converted into a listing of hours, minutes, seconds, frames.

Jog   To move a videotape forward or back a very short distance (one or two frames) in search for the "perfect" place to edit.

Trim   Adding or subtracting numbers from the time code at the edit point to make the edit occur earlier or later than originally planned.

Shuttle speed control   Fast scan control allowing videotape to be played slower or faster than normal—useful when hunting for edit points on a tape.

who assembles the best scenes together to make a final tape. One nice thing about shooting RAW FOOTAGE rather than the real thing is that you can take chances shooting scenes that might not work out in the final production. If they don't work out, just don't use them; you're not stuck with them. Also, you can shoot the same scene over and over, perhaps from different angles, until you get it right. Afterwards, you can select the best of the RAW FOOTAGE to incorporate into your final production.

The disadvantage of editing from RAW FOOTAGE is that your final tape goes one generation down in quality. Every time you copy a tape (which you do whenever you edit from one tape to another), the signal degrades, making the picture fuzzier and the sound more muffled. (The exception to this rule is digital videotape.) The best you can do to mitigate against this degradation is to use the highest-quality video formats available (Betacam SP or DV if possible, never VHS or 8mm).

The mechanical process of editing from another videotape is the same as that for copying a tape, only you're doing little pieces at a time rather than a whole tape.

To make the pieces fit, you must always

1. Find the place on the VCR's tape where you want the edit to occur.
2. Find the segment in the RAW FOOTAGE that you wish to use.
3. Line both of them up so that when the VCP plays the desired segment, the VCR records it.

The preceding process is a bit difficult to do manually, so EDITOR CONTROLLERS were invented to keep track of things and guide the machines to accurate edits.

 **Mini Review**

- Editing parts of one tape into another tape allows you the flexibility of selecting and using your best shots in any order in your final production.
- One disadvantage of editing parts from another videotape is that the signal degrades in the tape-copying process.

EDITOR CONTROLLERS

An EDITOR CONTROLLER, or AUTOMATIC BACKSPACER, is an electronic device that is wired to the editing VCR and VCP and controls the two during an edit. Figure 14–3 shows how one may be connected.

Most industrial models have digital readouts for the VCP and VCR showing exactly where you are on the tape. They create this TIME CODE by electronically counting the CONTROL TRACK pulses on the tape as it plays.

When you load a tape into the VCP and start it playing from the beginning, the EDITOR CONTROLLER starts at 00:00:00:00 for the hours:minutes:seconds:frames.

Using this device, you can determine that a particular scene starts at 14 minutes, 32 seconds, and 12 frames from the very beginning of the tape.

These TIME CODE numbers are helpful for locating scenes or for logging events on a videotape for later editing. You could, for instance,

1. List the TIME CODE numbers of the various scenes on the tape.
2. Next, use those numbers to locate the first scene you wanted to edit.
3. Program the CONTROLLER to perform the edit, using those numbers.

Method 1:

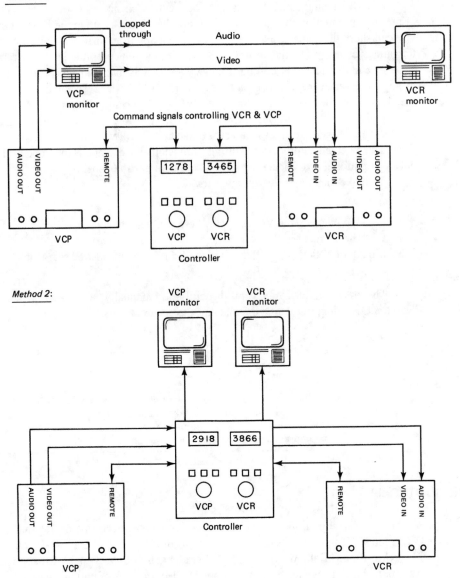

FIGURE 14-3 Connection of a professional EDITOR CONTROLLER.

On the other hand, it is also possible to edit tapes together without paying any attention to the TIME CODE numbers. The process might go like this:

1. Find the next desired edit-in point on the VCR "by eye." Then push an VCR EDIT-IN button to program the CONTROLLER (the CONTROLLER now automatically keeps track of the VCR's TIME CODE number).

2. Browse through your RAW FOOTAGE to find the scene you wish to take from the VCP. At the beginning of that scene, press the VCP EDIT-IN button to program the CONTROLLER (the CONTROLLER now keeps track of the VCP's TIME CODE).

EDITING CONTROLLER and professional editing VCRs.

3. Browse through the RAW FOOTAGE some more to find the end of the desired scene. Press the VCP EDIT-OUT button on the CONTROLLER. The CONTROLLER memorizes the VCP's TIME CODE.

4. Push the EXECUTE button, and the CONTROLLER will automatically BACKSPACE the two machines the proper amount. Next, both machines will start playing, and the VCR will be switched to the EDIT mode at the proper time.

5. When the VCP reaches the EDIT-OUT point, the CONTROLLER stops the edit, parking the VCR at the end of the scene, ready for the next edit.

Some EDITOR CONTROLLERS can perform an edit accurate to one-thirtieth of a second. That's a lot better than the one-second accuracy you might get from editing manually. With one-thirtieth-second accuracy, the user may PAUSE a tape, creep it forwards or backwards a hair (a technique called JOGGING), select precisely the point at which the edit must occur, and then, with a press of a button, have the machine execute the edit exactly as planned.

Some EDITOR CONTROLLERS allow you to rehearse an edit once the edit points are programmed. In this case, instead of pressing EXECUTE, you press PREVIEW, and the machines will go through the motions without actually performing the edit. You can see what the edit would look like by viewing a TV monitor connected to the CONTROLLER as shown in Figure 14–3, method 2. Once you've previewed how the edit looks on the monitor, you can decide whether to execute the edit or to reprogram the edit differently.

Most EDITOR CONTROLLERS have TRIM buttons that allow you to adjust an edit slightly. For instance, imagine you have just programmed the CONTROLLER to execute an edit when the VCR reaches 22:33:14 on its TIME CODE, while the VCP starts *its* scene at 38:49:20. When previewing the edit, you discover that the edit drags too long, and you wish to have it be more abrupt and faster paced. In other words, you wish to have the VCP start the scene just a little later, deeper into the action. You could do this by TRIMMING the number 38:49:20 up to 38:49:29 to cut one-third of a second off the beginning of the scene.

You could then rehearse the edit one more time to see if it looked better. If not, you could go back and add some more or TRIM back some of the time you added.

With TRIM you can add or subtract time to or from either end of the VCR's sequence *or* the VCP's sequence. *Everything* is adjustable.

EDITOR CONTROLLERS usually have a complete set of VCR controls, such as RECORD, PLAY, FAST FORWARD, REWIND, and PAUSE, on them for both the VCR and VCP. Many also have a SHUTTLE SPEED CONTROL that allows you to run the tape forward or backward at twice, three times, or maybe ten times the normal speed while you are viewing the picture on the TV screen. The SHUTTLE CONTROL may also allow you to play the tape at half-speed or slower. You may even be able to JOG the tape one frame at a time forward or backward while searching for the exact point you wish to edit. Cheaper CONTROLLERS have one set of tape transport buttons and a switch marked VCR/VCP. In the VCR position, the buttons apply to the VCR; in the VCP position, the buttons control the VCP.

Interesting note: You can tell the CONTROLLER what the VCR's EDIT-IN *and* EDIT-OUT points will be, and then tell the CONTROLLER what the VCP's EDIT-IN *or* EDIT-OUT point will be. Alternatively, you could tell the CONTROLLER the VCP's in *and* out points and the VCR's in *or* out point. The CONTROLLER doesn't want to hear in and out points for *both* machines because that information would be redundant; the length of the scene that's inserted from the VCP *has to match* the length of the scene that the VCR is recording. You wouldn't expect to record a two-minute scene from one minute of RAW FOOTAGE, would you? So the CONTROLLER calculates this last missing number for you.

 Mini Review

- Editor controllers use time code to keep track of the position of the tape on the VCR and VCP. With it you can select an edit point, preview the edit, change the edit if you don't like it, then execute the edit. The edit controller prerolls the tape machines to ensure a glitchless edit.

TYPES OF TIME CODE

VCRs and EDITOR CONTROLLERS find where they are on a tape by using TIME CODE. There are different flavors of TIME CODE having different accuracies and complexities. Some EDITOR CONTROLLERS can read/write several kinds of TIME CODE, but inexpensive consumer models work with only one.

For any device to know where it is on a tape, it needs a TIME CODE READER. This device could be built into a camcorder or VCR, be an optional circuit card that you add to a professional camcorder or VCR, or be a stand-alone device, like the professional model shown in Figure 14–4. Remember that for the READER to work, it has to be reading *its kind* of TIME CODE.

Here are two popular kinds of TIME CODE: the first is the simplest (and least accurate), and the second is the kind that the pros use.

Control Track Counters

When tapes are recorded, a CONTROL TRACK is also recorded. This series of pulses (30 per second) helps align the VCR during playback to make a smooth picture. Like sprocket holes in a film, each pulse looks the same. By RESETTING the VCR's counter to zero at the beginning of a tape, the VCR can pretty accurately tell where it is anytime thereafter. After 5 minutes of playing, for instance, the VCR will convert the 9,000 pulses that it sensed into the counter number 0:05:00 (0 hours, 5 minutes, 0 sec-

---

Time code generator   Electronic device that makes the time code signal, which may then be recorded on the tape.
Time code reader   Electronic device that decodes the time code from a tape on playback and converts it into recognizable numbers: hours, minutes, seconds, frames.
*SMPTE time code   Time code that is used to address every frame on a tape with a unique number to aid in logging and

editing. The time code format is standardized in the United States by the Society of Motion Picture and Television Engineers (SMPTE).
Vertical interval   The part of a video signal that doesn't show on the TV screen; the black bar (sync) at the bottom of the TV picture when it rolls.

FIGURE 14–4   SMPTE TIME CODE READER/GENERATOR does both jobs.

onds). Pro models may include frames in the counter display, such as 0:05:00:00 (0 hours, 5 minutes, 0 seconds, 0 frames).

If you insert a half-played tape, the numbers are meaningless; you have to rewind to the tape's beginning and hit RESET to start the count accurately.

Furthermore, most VCRs lose one or two pulses in PAUSE (they can't read the data slowly), and they lose track of dozens of pulses if you hit STOP and the tape unthreads completely.

When CONTROL TRACK counters come to blank tape, they stop counting (there are no control pulses to count). The numbers remain unchanged until the machine begins playing video again. For accurate counting, it is good to have continuous video from the beginning to the end of your tape.

Still, this is the most popular type of TIME CODE, used frequently with consumer and prosumer VCRs, and sometimes with professional gear. The pro gear, when it can't find accurate TIME CODE (i.e., SMPTE TIME CODE) will fall back on CONTROL TRACK. Any port in a storm.

CONTROL TRACK editing is fine when your RAW FOOTAGE is all on one cassette. If it's on many cassettes, it's a pain to rewind each and RESET the counter. For this reason, the pros use SMPTE TIME CODE.

SMPTE Time Code

The SMPTE (Society of Motion Picture and Television Engineers) TIME CODE is used by professionals everywhere and is very accurate. It gives a special number to every single frame (picture) on your videotape. Since the code is recorded on your tape, it can be read from the tape at any time, whether the tape has been half rewound or not.

SMPTE TIME CODE is created by a SMPTE TIME CODE GENERATOR like the one in Figure 14–4 (although some are small enough to fit inside a camcorder). This is an electronic box with a special clock in it that is able to create a digital code that is synchronized with the pictures on your video tape. Some VCRs can encode the SMPTE TIME CODE into the video signal; there it's called VERTICAL INTERVAL TIME CODE (it cannot be seen on the TV screen). Other VCRs record SMPTE TIME CODE on a spare audio channel.

SMPTE can be recorded on a tape while the tape is being recorded originally or can be DUBBED onto the tape later.

 **Mini Review**

- Two popular types of time code are control track and SMPTE.
- Control track time code is simple to use but is not 100 percent accurate.
- SMPTE time code must be specially recorded on the tape and played back through a time code reader. SMPTE time code, however, is very accurate, uniquely describing every frame of video.

To "read" the code off the tape, you need an SMPTE TIME CODE READER. The READER connects to the video output or the appropriate audio channel from the VCR or VCP and translates the code back into the readable numbers—hours:minutes:seconds:frames.

STEP-BY-STEP EDITING PROCEDURE

The mechanics of editing aren't too hard; it's mostly a matter of pushing buttons at the right time. The planning and decision making of editing is the hard part. The process will test your patience and your stomach lining. Planning, viewing the RAW FOOTAGE, logging the scenes, and charting the edits are all tedious, unglamorous ordeals. Perhaps that's why most folks skip these steps and end up making uninspiring productions.

Here's a general plan to follow:

1. Before you start, decide how your story will unfold and determine the scenes necessary to tell the story. Then shoot your RAW FOOTAGE.

2. View all your RAW FOOTAGE, and log each event with some sort of index number as shown in Table 14–1. For index numbers you could use

 a. The tape footage or time-elapsed counter on the VCR (but few counters are accurate).

 b. Control track pulses (you need an EDITOR CONTROLLER or a VCR with a control track counter; these have to be reset to 000 at the beginning of your tape and are accurate to within a few frames).

 c. SMPTE TIME CODE (this most accurate and convenient method requires an expensive reader/generator) or RC or other TIME CODE.

The SHOT SHEET or LOG/CUE SHEET (Table 14–1) makes it easy for you to find quickly the desired "take" on the tape when you get around to editing the scene into your final production. SHOT SHEETS are especially helpful when you record your scenes in January but don't edit them until August. In the SHOT SHEET shown, NG stands for "no good," CU for "close-up," and MS for "medium shot." You may wish to put a star next to the "take" that you like the most.

3. Plan your editing strategy by using an EDITING SHEET like the one shown in Table 14–2. First you lay out the sequence of scenes you wish to assemble, next you enter the counter numbers of these scenes from your SHOT SHEETS, and then you are ready to edit.

---

*Shot sheet   Index of all shots recorded on a tape. Includes time code numbers for each shot plus a commentary on the quality of each take.

Editing sheet   Plan that shows which shots will be used to create the edited master. Time code numbers and edit-in and edit-out points are generally listed.

Linear editing   Editing performed step-by-step directly with VCRs and on editing controller—no computers are involved.

*Nonlinear editor (NLE)   Computerized video editor that permits scenes to be selected and rearranged on the computer's screen before being assembled (by the NLE) on the master tape.

Video capture card   Circuit installed in a computer to change video signals into data that the computer can handle, and vice versa.

Digital/Analog converter   Computer circuit that changes computer data into video and/or audio signals.

Real time   Referring to something that plays, records, compresses, or decompresses as fast as it actually happened in real life.

*Edit decision list (EDL)   A refined editing sheet listing each shot to be recorded, the exact time code of edit-in and edit-out prints for each shot, any effects to be included, their duration, and other details. Often the EDL resides on a computer disk and is the script to drive the editing VCRs during the final edit.

RC Time Code or RCTC   Sony time code system for 8mm and Hi8 VCRs. Code identifies each separate frame and is recorded on a special track next to the video signal.

TABLE 14–1 SHOT SHEET for Logging "Takes"

SHOT SHEET
Project: Dining Out
Cassette #3
Date: 12/7/99

Take	Counter	Action	Comments
1	03:00:00–03:01:23	Leader	NG
2	03:01:24–03:01:44	Testing	NG
3	03:01:49–03:02:05	CU sandwich hits floor	Excellent
4	03:02:06–03:02:28	CU sandwich hits floor	Dark
5	03:02:31–03:02:55	CU sandwich hits floor	OK
6	03:03:00–03:03:26	MS sandwich hits floor	Fuzzy
7	03:03:28–03:03:56	Al sits at table	OK
8	03:04:01–03:04:20	Al sits at table	Glitch
•	•	•	•
•	•	•	•
•	•	•	•

Notice that the beginning and end titles can be shot "live" with a camera (as could other scenes) and be assembled along with taped scenes.

If your editing equipment is very simple or if your tape index is inaccurate, you may decide to play the edit sequence several times, rehearsing it, and then perform the edit manually, using the scene as a guide. If your equipment is advanced, you should be able to "edit by the numbers," selecting the scenes by their TIME CODE numbers and then having the machine execute the edits on the numbers you have selected. If you don't like the way that the edits are coming out, you can always pick new numbers and redo the edits.

TABLE 14–2 EDITING SHEET or EDIT DECISION LIST for Organizing a Sequence of Scenes

EDITING SHEET
Project: Dining Out
Cassette #27
Date: 12/15/99

Segment	Action	Cassette	Edit-in	Edit-out
1	Intro	Camera	—	—
2	Boy meets girl	5	05:15:13:02	05:15:15:21
3	Invites her to dinner	5	05:02:16:08	05:02:58:29
4	Takes her to restaurant	1	01:01:03:00	01:02:00:05
5	Sits at table	3	03:03:28:15	03:03:56:10
6	Orders jelly sandwich	2	02:41:20:16	02:41:23:20
7	Sandwich arrives	2	02:05:06:15	02:05:17:17
8	Boy spills sandwich	3	02:11:12:21	02:11:13:28
9	Sandwich hits floor	3	03:01:49:02	03:02:05:00
10	Girl leaves	1	01:06:02:03	01:06:04:11
11	Boy stunned	1	01:09:11:11	01:09:12:25
12	End	Camera	—	—

Mini Review

- Use a shot sheet to keep track of the scenes in your raw footage.
- Use an editing sheet to list the shots that you plan to use and the order in which you plan to use them.

NONLINEAR EDITORS

When you work with the VCRs directly, you're doing what is called LINEAR EDITING; you do one task, then another, in a straightforward pattern. Computers allow another kind of editing process, which is called NONLINEAR EDITING. Here, RAW FOOTAGE is played into a computer through a VIDEO CAPTURE CARD that digitizes the audio and video and stores the data on the computer's hard disk. Using specialized editing software, one can select scenes, arrange their order, add titles, change the sound, create transitions from scene to scene, and redo changes freely, just like editing text on a word processor. The program can be previewed on the computer. When the director (or editor) is satisfied with the show, it is played off the hard disk, back through a DIGITAL/ANALOG CONVERTER, to a VCR that records regular video and audio from the computer. The process is called NONLINEAR because segments of the show can be shifted and swapped easily, in any order inside the computer. Segments can be rearranged as often as desired without degrading the signals. Unlike LINEAR EDITING, NLEs allow you to lengthen or shorten your show by adding or removing scenes while the show is still inside the computer.

True digital NONLINEAR EDITORS (NLEs) capture video at a quality that is good enough for the final production. With the editor you can move icons representing the various scenes, add transitions (effects) between scenes, cut and paste parts of the program at will, and then play the final program back out to tape. Everything is done *inside* the computer: Titles, effects, and audio mixing all occur in one place, and the finished product is sent to tape.

Some NLEs (costing $40,000 and up) are faster than others, creating effects and transitions in REAL TIME. There is no waiting to see how something will look. Other top-of-the-line models have digital inputs/outputs to go directly to DVCRs. Moving signals digitally between machines avoids the signal degradation you suffer when copying analog signals. Some workstations permit many audio tracks to be manipulated. Lower-priced NLEs are unable to make high-quality signals; their images are good only for previewing what the final production may look like. Editing with these more primitive NLEs is a two-step process:

1. Copy your RAW FOOTAGE onto the computer and edit it as described earlier.
2. Using an EDIT DECISION LIST made by the computer in step 1, the computer acts as an EDIT CONTROLLER, BACKSPACING your VCP and VCR and RAW FOOTAGE tapes to make the final program. It's like having a robot sitting at the EDIT CONTROLLER carrying out all your previously made decisions. You just have to change tapes on the VCP when it calls for new RAW FOOTAGE.

Video can be stored and manipulated either uncompressed or compressed. To hold large amounts of uncompressed data, large, fast hard drives are used, or smaller, slower, cheaper *arrays* of drives are teamed up to work together. Here are other ways around the storage bottleneck: Review the RAW FOOTAGE first, then upload only the "good" shots. *Another shortcut:* Digitize the RAW FOOTAGE in a compressed format for a practical edit session with *all* your footage. Then once the desired shots have been selected, do the digitizing process *again*, only this time use no (or low) compression, but copy from tape only the scenes that will be used. The NLE will handle the details of finding and redigitizing the scenes; you just change the cassettes as needed.

Figure 14–5 shows the screen from a NONLINEAR EDITOR in the midst of editing.

PRINTOUT OF A PROFESSIONAL EDIT DECISION LIST

```
FINAL  CUT-VW
SMPTE  FRAME  CODE


RVTR=RVTR
```

EVENT	SOURCE	AUD/VID	CUT/DISSOLVE	DURATION	P-VTR IN	P-VTR OUT	R-VTR IN	R-VTR OUT	
0001	BLK	V	C		00:00:00:00	00:00:00:00	01:00:00:00	01:00:00:00	
0001	LOGO	V	D	010	01:00:00:01	01:00:03:28	01:00:00:00	01:00:03:27	
0002	LOGO	V	C		01:00:03:28	01:00:03:28	01:00:03:27	01:00:03:27	
0002	BLK	V	D	020	00:00:00:00	00:00:00:20	01:00:03:27	01:00:04:17	
0003	AUX	V	C		00:00:15:01	00:00:19:00	01:00:04:18	01:00:08:17	
0004	100	A12V	C		01:09:40:28	01:10:11:02	01:00:08:29	01:00:39:03	
0005	100	A12V	C		01:18:54:08	01:19:14:11	01:00:39:11	01:00:59:14	
0006	100	A12V	C		01:35:30:09	01:36:22:27	01:00:59:20	01:01:52:08	
0007	100	A12V	C		01:36:22:27	01:36:22:27	01:01:52:08	01:01:52:08	
0007	BLK	A12V	D	035	00:00:00:00	00:00:01:05	01:01:52:08	01:01:53:13	
0008	BLK	A12V	C		00:00:00:00	00:00:00:00	01:01:53:23	01:01:53:23	
0008	100	A12V	D	006	01:28:32:08	01:28:47:24	01:01:53:23	01:02:09:09	
0009	100	A12V	C		01:20:01:01	01:20:31:01	01:02:09:13	01:02:39:13	R
0010	100	A12V	C		01:30:14:27	01:30:48:23	01:02:39:19	01:03:13:15	R
0011	100	A12V	C		01:30:48:23	01:30:48:23	01:03:13:15	01:03:13:15	R
0011	BLK	A12V	D	035	00:00:00:00	00:00:01:05	01:03:13:15	01:03:14:20	R
0012	100	A12V	C		01:19:20:02	01:19:50:09	01:03:14:26	01:03:45:03	R
0013	100	A12V	C		01:11:04:27	01:11:34:20	01:03:45:09	01:04:15:02	
0014	100	A12V	C		01:11:34:20	01:11:34:20	01:04:15:02	01:04:15:02	

 Mini Review

- Nonlinear editors are computers that can accept video signals, digitize them, and allow you to arrange shots in any desired order.
- Higher-priced NLEs can handle high-quality signals that can be downloaded back to tape, thus making a finished product in one step. Lower-cost NLEs require two steps: First, you edit low-quality video on your computer screen to create an edit decision list (much like the editing sheet you made manually). Next, you load the raw footage into the VCP and the master tape into the VCR and let the NLE automatically carry out the editing process from tape to tape as it follows the edit decision list.
- The quality of the video signal through the NLE depends on how much compression you used. A lot of compression stores more video on your hard disk but at lower quality.

WHEN YOU'RE FINISHED EDITING

It's 4 A.M. Your masterpiece is finished. Amid a heap of candy wrappers and coffee cups, you stand up for the first time in twelve hours. It's time to call it a night, maybe have a martini, or maybe a nervous breakdown, right?

Oh, no, SMPTE breath!

Digitized video scenes (called CLIPS) are stored on the computer hard disk and are
represented here with a thumbnail icon.

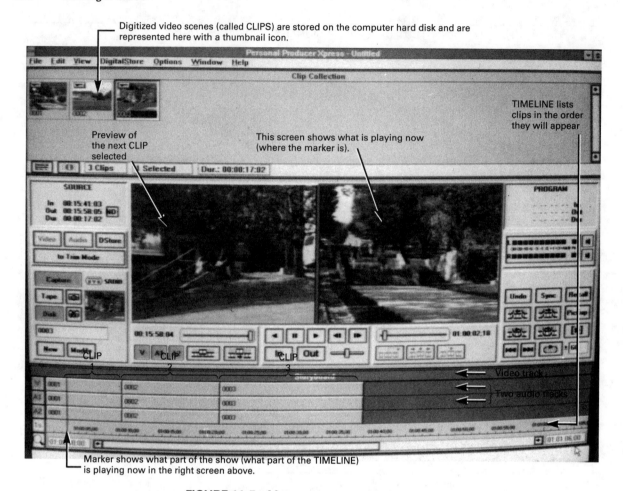

FIGURE 14–5   Matrox NON-LINEAR EDITOR screen.

Have you labeled your EDITED MASTER so that some joker doesn't come into the control room tomorrow morning and record a Bugs Bunny cartoon over your precious program? TV facilities are
filled with doodleheads who think that any program that isn't theirs is expendable. Label that tape!
Put it in a place safe from doodleheads. Pop out its erase-protect tab.

Is it possible that your editing VCR is sick but doesn't know it? It can be playing *your* tape back
okay tonight (tapes generally play well on "mother," even when she's crazy) but won't play it tomorrow
when the TV technician finishes "fixing" it. Copy your EDITED MASTER now, using the editing VCR to do
the *playing* and some other VCR to make the copy. This guarantees that one perfect playback of your
tape will occur before something happens to "mother," the VCR who can play your tape best. Besides,
even after all those hours, could you sleep knowing that there is only *one copy* of your masterpiece in existence? A second copy kept in another place is excellent insurance and aids sleep better than Sominex.

PRACTICES TO ENSURE A SUCCESSFUL EDIT

Many of the headaches faced in editing are the same ones found in simple tape copying, and they stem
not from muscle tension but from maintaining a stable, clean signal from the VCP. Every flaw in the

playback of the RAW FOOTAGE gets compounded in the copy. Here are some practices to help you avoid editing woes:

1. Don't edit near glitches, blips, video breakup, splices, or bad edits on the RAW FOOTAGE. These aberrations can foul up the speed of the editing VCR so that *its* edit comes out imperfect.

2. Don't change the TRACKING or SKEW controls on the editing VCR from edit to edit. Once these controls are set optimally, leave them throughout the editing session. On the VCP, just the opposite holds true. This machine should be optimized for each tape it plays in order to provide the best signal possible.

3. Keep your tapes clean. Leaving unboxed cassettes stacked in disarray around the editing console is not the way to keep dust out of your RAW FOOTAGE.

4. If you don't *need* a gadget (like an SEG or mixer) in the circuit between the VCP and VCR, take it out. The less you mess with a signal by passing it through other devices, the better.

Murphy's first law, "Anything that *can* go wrong, *will* go wrong . . . and at the worst possible time," applies exquisitely well to video editing. Murphy keeps an office of gremlins right next to every editing console. To keep Murphy from flushing your editing project down the tubes, take the following precautions:

1. Put adhesive tape (or a bandage, or something) over the RECORD button of your *playback* VCR. Pushing that button by mistake could wipe out your RAW FOOTAGE.

2. Double-check your mode. Don't get so wrapped up in what you're doing that you forget to *make sure that the editing VCR's MODE SELECTOR is in the proper position*. Untold numbers of tapes have been ruined by a selector in the ASSEMBLE position during the execution of an INSERT. Hours of audio tracks have been wiped out by an INSERT when a VIDEO INSERT ONLY was called for.

3. If you're now playing your MASTER tape on the VCR you used to edit with (i.e., you're making a safety copy from "mother" to another VCR), double check *all* the controls to make sure you don't accidentally record or erase your MASTER tape.

 Mini Review

- When you have finished editing, label the tape, remove its erase-protect tab, and make a backup copy of the tape.
- Don't edit near glitches in the raw footage.
- Don't adjust the editing VCR's tracking or skew controls during the edit. Do, however, adjust the VCP's tracking or skew controls to optimize the playback of the raw footage.
- Do something to make sure you don't mix up the VCR buttons with the VCP buttons and accidentally record over your raw footage.
- If insert-editing, double-check to make sure the VCR is not in the assemble edit mode.

---

*Tracking   Adjustment on VTRs so that they play the video tracks from the tape following exactly the path that the recorder took. Good tracking results in a clear, stable picture.
Skew   Control that adjusts the tape tension on a videotape machine to hold the picture steady during playback. When you have a skew error, the top of a TV picture flutters or pulls to the side.

15 HIGH-DEFINITION TELEVISION

HIGH-DEFINITION TELEVISION (HDTV), which was first demonstrated in 1973, promised to display wider, sharper TV pictures. Normal TV pictures are made of 525 horizontal scanning lines. The technique is sort of like painting a picture on a Venetian blind having 525 slats. Pictures could look sharper if we used more slats that were skinnier. HDTV proposed making the TV picture out of 1,125 scanning lines.

HDTV pictures are sharper not only in the vertical direction but also in the horizontal direction. Whereas normal TV pictures are composed of about 720 PIXELS (picture elements, or dots), HDTV will use 1,920 tinier, sharper PIXELS to make each scanning line.

Proposed HDTV pictures would be wider than today's TV screens. Today's TV screens are proportioned in a 4:3 ASPECT RATIO. HDTV is shaped 16:9, or one-third wider (see Figure 15–1).

When you see an HDTV demonstration, you are immediately impressed by how *smooth* the picture looks and how realistic the wide-screen image appears. After watching HDTV for a while, when you go back to normal NTSC, it feels as if you are going back to a manual typewriter after using a word processor.

Engineers, manufacturers, and even nations are having difficulty selecting one worldwide standard for HDTV. Many sources still disagree on the screen shape, number of PIXELS per line, number of lines per picture, and number of pictures per second, as well as more technical details about the color and contrast. In the United States, the FCC (Federal Communications Commission) must approve any system that is broadcast. TV equipment manufacturers don't want to start building new cameras and TVs until they know what the new standards will be.

One of the problems with HDTV is that there is so much detail in the picture that very high frequencies are required to transmit the information. In the analog world, two to five TV channels could be required to broadcast just one HDTV image. Fortunately, DIGITAL TELEVISION (DTV) has come to

---

*HDTV (High-definition television) Proposed method of displaying sharper, wider TV pictures than the present NTSC system. Pictures would be shaped into a 16:9 aspect ratio, composed of 1,125 scanning lines, each line having 1,920 pixels.
*Pixels Picture elements, tiny dots that make up the picture. In a camera, pixels describe the tiny light-sensitive transistors that sense the image.
*Aspect ratio Shape of a TV screen expressed in width com-

pared to height. Common TV screens have a 4:3 aspect ratio, meaning they are four units wide by three units tall.
FCC Federal Communications Commission, the regulatory body for broadcast television in the United States.
*DTV Digital television—TV that is broadcast, recorded, and processed digitally, possibly with extended definition like HDTV.

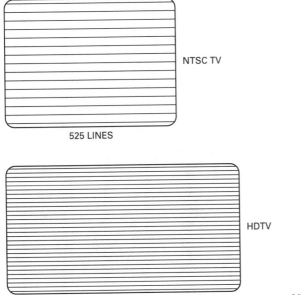

NTSC vs HDTV scanning lines.

the rescue with its mighty compression schemes that can fit six digitally compressed TV channels where one analog channel used to be or that can fit one digital HDTV channel where one analog channel used to be.

The metamorphosis of HDTV is as tangled as tax laws. The name HDTV, which meant one fairly specific kind of television, has been abandoned and replaced with the following:

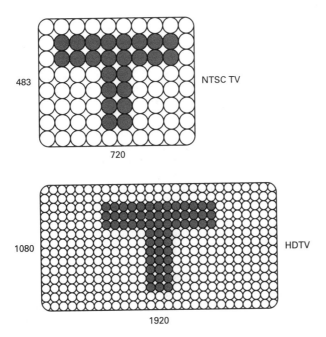

More pixels make HDTV sharper than NTSC.

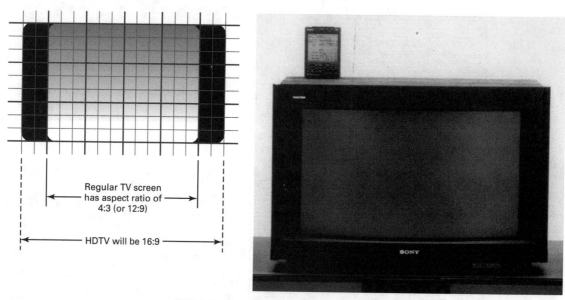

FIGURE 15–1   HDTV vs. regular NTSC.

- DTV: Digital television—TV that is handled digitally, whether or not it is high or low definition.
- SDTV: Standard definition television—DTV that is not high definition but that may have some improvements over NTSC.

 Mini Review

- High-definition television pictures differ from present television pictures in the following ways:
  1. HDTV is sharper than NTSC.
  2. The HDTV screen is wider than the NTSC screen.
  3. HDTV is digital; NTSC is analog.
- HDTV requires up to five times the bandwidth (channel space) of NTSC TV, but through digital compression, one HDTV channel or six SDTV channels can be squeezed into the space of one analog TV channel.
- SDTV will be digital television without the high-definition improvements.

ATSC   Advanced Television Systems Committee, a group formed to study DTV and make recommendations to the FCC.

Progressive scan   Method of making a computer picture by drawing all the scan lines sequentially from top to bottom.

Interlace scan   Method of making a TV picture by drawing the odd-numbered lines on the screen with one sweep, then filling in between them with the next sweep of even-numbered lines. The process is repeated approximately every 1/30 of a second.

NTSC   National Television Standards Committee, a U.S. organization that developed the NTSC video standards that ensure that all TV signals in the United States are compatible.

NTSC is also the name of the TV standard we use presently in the United States; DTV is the standard replacing it.

Bandwidth   Electromagnetic "room" for TV channels or computer data on a wire, cable, fiber, or airwave.

3/2 pulldown   Mechanism for showing movie film shot at 24 pictures per second over TV systems that make pictures 60 times per second.

SDTV   Standard definition television—digitally broadcast TV signals with about the same sharpness and screen shape as today's NTSC television.

Interpolator, or universal format converter   Device for changing one kind of DTV format into another.

DTV

Although the general population is used to the term HDTV, we, the cognoscenti, will use the term DTV from here on to describe this ever-evolving next generation of television. HDTV is a high-resolution subset of DTV.

What Is DTV?

DTV is a bunch of possible ways to do the same thing—transmit a digital TV signal. No one has yet agreed on the best way to do this. Even the FCC has not mandated a standard for TV screen shape or the number of scanning lines or PIXELS or sound channels the new TV system should have. It has merely mandated that DTV fit within the same channel space as the old system and that it doesn't interfere with other radio/TV transmissions, plus a few technical details important primarily to broadcasters.

There are thirty-six DTV formats being considered by the manufacturers. Why so many "standards"? Compatibility and compromise.

The Advanced Television Systems Committee (ATSC) has studied DTV since 1983. It first agreed that the new system should have twice the vertical and twice the horizontal sharpness of NTSC TV. Present NTSC TV has a horizontal resolution of 720 PIXELS and a vertical resolution of 525 lines (or PIXELS), of which 483 actually show (the remainder are just off the edge of your TV screen). Doubling both numbers gives us 1,440×1,050. Making the picture a third wider for the more pleasing 16:9 ASPECT RATIO increases the 1,440 horizontal PIXELS to 1,920. A ratio of 16:9 makes the vertical PIXELS nine-sixteenths of that, or 1,080. Thus, the ATSC has set a goal of 1,920 PIXELS by 1,080 PIXELS for DTV. A 1920×1080 PIXEL picture would indeed be beautiful, but it has been found to be too expensive to record and transmit using today's technology. Various organizations have proposed lesser resolutions of 1,280×720, or 704×480 PIXELS.

TV pictures can be scanned PROGRESSIVELY, all at once on the screen, or can be INTERLACED (odd lines make one picture, even lines the next). Computer monitors use PROGRESSIVE scanning. NTSC TV uses INTERLACE. PROGRESSIVE is better; images are sharper if you paint them all at once rather than filling in the gaps between lines in a later TV field. But PROGRESSIVE scanning uses twice as much BANDWIDTH as INTERLACE (important to broadcasters who have only so much to work with) because *all* the lines are being transmitted per TV picture rather than half the lines. So the war rages on between "better" (PROGRESSIVE scanning) and "economical" (INTERLACE scanning).

Another war rages between using NTSC's present scan rates (59.94 fields per second and 29.97 frames per second) and a simpler 60 or 30 rate. Since the NTSC numbers were invented years ago for technical reasons that no longer apply, 60 and 30 would be logical, except that converting old NTSC videos to DTV's 60 and 30 rates would be difficult; converting them to DTV at the 59.94 and 29.97 rates would be simple. Also, the professional VCRs such as D1, D5, DCT, Digital Beta, Digital S, DV, DVCAM and DVCPRO already use 59.94 fields per second.

The film people get involved with the 24 and 23.976 frame rates. Movie film is shot at 24 frames per second. Everything would be peachy if TV were 24 frames per second; DTV conversion would be easy. But showing a 24-picture-per-second movie at TV's 60-fields-per-second scanning rate is difficult and wasteful of bandwidth. You end up showing film frame *one* for 3 TV fields, then film frame *two* for 2 TV fields, then film frame *three* for 3 TV fields, then *four* for 2, and *five* for 3, and so on, using a film-to-video conversion technique called 3/2 PULLDOWN. Do the math, and you find that this is the simplest way to make 24 go into 60. *The point:* Many of the film pictures get repeated, resulting in wastefully redundant data that could be used for other things. The film people would have DTV run at 24 frames per second (or some even multiple) or 23.976 if the slightly-off NTSC scan rates are adopted.

The TV broadcasters see a market for plain vanilla SDTV, with the same resolution as today's NTSC. That arrangement works out to 704×480 PIXELS. They see profit in broadcasting six SDTV channels (with six times the advertising revenue) to you rather than one HDTV channel over their allotted bandwidth. The FCC mandates only that broadcasters provide one free digital TV channel to the public. It doesn't insist that the channel be high resolution. The other five channels could be other free TV shows, pay TV, or highly profitable Internet data. You see why the broadcasters would want SDTV. Also, by broadcasting 4:3 images, they avoid buying expensive 16:9 equipment and can reuse their old videotapes shot in 4:3.

The computer people are happy with VGA's 640×480 PIXELS in a 4:3 aspect ratio. That's what you need for word processing and other business applications. Computer manufacturers Compaq, Intel, and Microsoft are pushing for DTV to be introduced slowly as equipment gets better. They intend for you to be able to watch DTV on your computer screen. Because computers are capable of being upgraded quickly, they believe the first DTV audience will not be people with expensive new TVs, but people who souped up their computers to watch DTV on their computer screens.

Thus we get a hodgepodge of possible "standards" and no distinct standard. No wonder DTV is arriving at the pace of a geriatric snail.

Without a *single* format to hang your hat on, some TV stations will invest $30,000 or so in an INTERPOLATOR or UNIVERSAL FORMAT CONVERTER to change signals from one format to another. The device may upconvert NTSC videos to DTV (whatever variation of the format is desired) or downconvert a DTV signal to something recordable on existing VCRs. *Note:* Upconverting NTSC will not make the picture sharper; it will just make it compatible with DTV.

 Mini Review

- Manufacturers are having trouble agreeing on one DTV "standard."

DTV Audio

There are several "standards" for providing improved sound for DTV. The most popular is called Dolby AC-3. AC-3 provides 5.1 channels of sound, as diagrammed in Figure 15–2:

Channel	Position
1	Left
2	Right
3	Center
4	Left rear
5	Right rear
5.1	Subwoofer

Because the subwoofer channel has very limited frequency response (just low tones), it's not really a *whole* channel, so it gets the designation of .1 channel.

Unlike present TV stereo sound that offers mediocre fidelity and poor stereo separation, AC-3 yields excellent fidelity and separation, rivaling the best sound you hear at the movies.

A two-channel version of AC-3 would be used for SDTV.

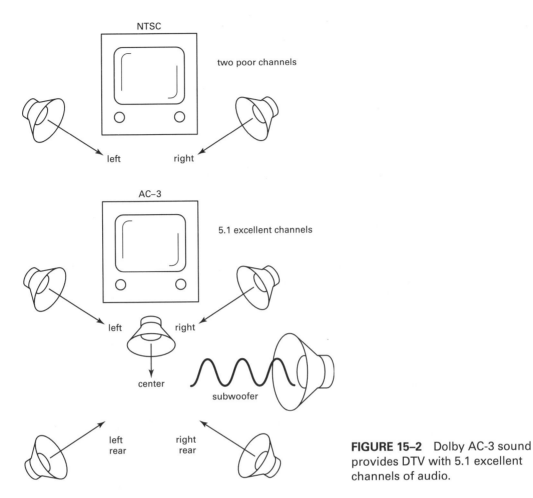

FIGURE 15–2 Dolby AC-3 sound provides DTV with 5.1 excellent channels of audio.

DTV'S ROLL-OUT SCHEDULE

On April 3, 1997, the FCC voted to lend all 1600 U.S. TV broadcast stations a second TV channel on which to transmit DTV versions of their analog TV fare. Each DTV channel would take up 6MHz of spectrum (as each NTSC channel does now). Broadcasters would be free to use it all for HDTV, SDTV, or SDTV plus some data services. In return, broadcasters in the top ten markets (biggest cities) must start DTV broadcasting in early 1999, with other stations following soon after. The FCC wants over 50 percent of the U.S. households to have access to three or more DTV stations by the end of 1999. All NTSC channels will be shut down by 2006.

The FCC will give every broadcaster a new extra TV channel to use during a nine-year transition period. The broadcaster's old channel, in most cases, will stay the same and will broadcast in analog NTSC. The new channel will be DTV. In 2006, the FCC will reclaim all the old NTSC channels and shut down NTSC broadcasting for good.

The new DTV channels will be 2 to 51, relinquishing channels 52 to 69 for non-TV uses.

WHAT DTV COSTS AND HOW IT WILL AFFECT YOU

HDTV sets cost about $6000 today. By 2001, when production models are rolling through the parking lots at Circuit City, the cost may slide to $2000. Regular DTV sets with low resolution but the ability to receive the DTV signals should appear at the same time at a lower cost. They are expected to have the 16:9 aspect ratio screens.

Before DTVs become affordable, Moe Mousepotato will probably be able to buy a computer monitor capable of DTV. It should cost only $100 extra to manufacture DTV-capable computer monitors.

To further satisfy Mousepotato's propensity for pointing and clicking, the broadcasters are likely to include a data channel along with the TV channel so that Moe can click an icon to download sports statistics while his favorite team gets clobbered or to download actors' backgrounds while Bruce Willis gets clobbered.

You'll have to buy a new TV, or at least a set-top box costing about $200, to convert DTV to NTSC for your old set.

All your other video equipment will slowly become obsolete. Converters will become available allowing you to play your heirloom tapes into a DTV set or make copies into the format du jour.

DV recorders are poised for an upgrade to DTV. In fact, the DV format was designed with DTV in mind, but the DVRs arrived before DTV did, and the manufacturers "dumbed down" the DV camcorders to NTSC quality.

If your school buys DTV equipment for its studio, it won't come cheap. Here are some sample prices:

VCR	$ 9,850
Camera	62,000
26-inch 16:9 monitor	7,700
	$79,550

 Mini Review

- DTV may offer 5.1 channels of high-fidelity sound.
- DTV broadcasts are scheduled to begin in 1999 and take over totally by 2006.
- The DTV channels will be different from the present ones.
- Converters will allow DTV broadcasts to be viewed on older TV sets.
- HDTV sets will cost $2000 to $6000. Studio cameras and VCRs will also be expensive.

SHOOTING IN HIGH DEFINITION

Will you have to relearn TV production for the digital era? No, thank goodness. Everything you've learned in this book will still apply. Lighting and sound still obey the same laws of physics as it makes shadows and echoes. The audience still needs to be told a story to keep their interest. Everything you do still requires scads of planning. It still behooves the director to delegate and communicate in order to pull his or her team together. Almost everything in the HDTV world stays the same as it was before the revolution.

Shooting in high definition will involve a few minor changes in TV production. For instance:

- You can hold shots longer—it will take time for the detail to sink in.
- You can use wider camera angles—the detail survives the long shot.
- You'll give up your cardboard sets—the all-seeing eye of the high-definition camera will spot any fakery. Set construction and painting will have to be more exacting.

EPILOGUE

Will reading this book or taking a TV course land you a job in broadcast TV? Probably not. There are very few jobs and many talented people in this field. The competition is fierce. Does this mean you'll never get to use what you've learned here? You're probably using your new skills already. Anyone who takes a TV production course never again watches TV the same way. Your new viewing skills make you a "gourmet" of lighting, sound, and camera angles. You see the flaws, you appreciate the effort, and you especially admire the triumphs that flicker across the phosphor screen.

The world of TV is more than broadcast TV, and you'll be pleasantly surprised at how many ways you can apply your TV skills in other arenas. Many businesses, institutions, and schools use TV for training and public relations purposes. In your capacity as an accountant, a math teacher, a firefighter, or a sports coach, you may find yourself producing videos for your organization. As a hobby or a side vocation, you may choose to shoot weddings, or town histories, or basketball games for cable TV. There are some who have made these hobbies into profitable careers.

And even if you never again pick up a camcorder or microphone, you will have learned lessons in leadership and teamwork that apply to life in general:

1. *Plan ahead:* Anything that *can* go wrong *will* go wrong unless you've worked out the details ahead of time.

2. *Keep it simple:* The more complex the plan, the more ways it can go awry.

3. *Delegate:* You can't do everything.

4. *Communicate:* Draw pictures, make lists, do whatever it takes to put the whole team on the same wavelength.

5. *Encourage, don't criticize:* Your crew/team/staff is composed of humans, all of whom have feelings that will make them either perform miracles for you or cause them to withdraw, underachieve, or even subvert your project. Morale counts.

6. *When done, thank the crew:* If you think this is unimportant, just wait until you knock yourself out for somebody and they fail to acknowledge it—how helpful will you be next time? Success visits the *appreciative* more often than it does the clever or the rich.

INDEX

(**Bold** numbers show page where word is defined)

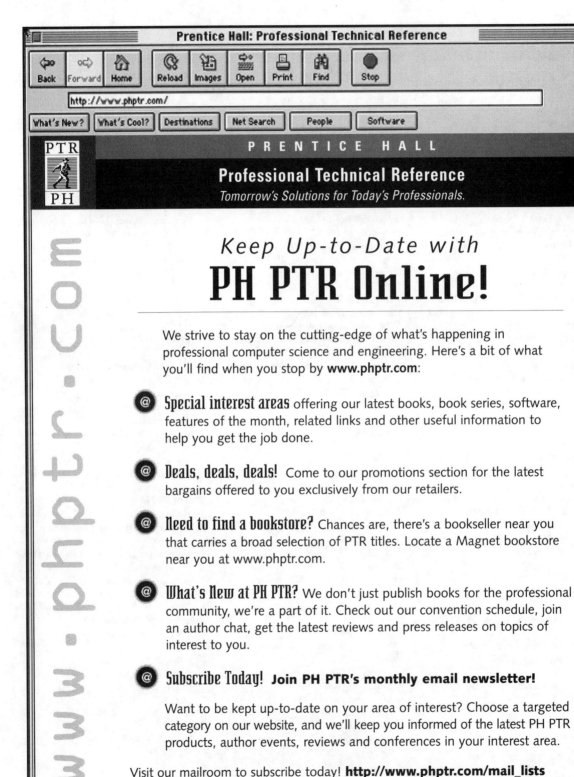